MISSIONS, MANTRAS, MIGRANTS *and* MICROCHIPS

MISSIONS, MANTRAS, MIGRANTS and MICROCHIPS

A History of the Indo–US Encounter, 1492 to the Present

LEONARD A. GORDON

PENGUIN
VIKING

An imprint of Penguin Random House

VIKING

Viking is an imprint of the Penguin Random House group of companies
whose addresses can be found at global.penguinrandomhouse.com

Published by Penguin Random House India Pvt. Ltd
4th Floor, Capital Tower 1, MG Road,
Gurugram 122 002, Haryana, India

Penguin
Random House
India

First published in Penguin Viking by Penguin Random House India 2025

Copyright © Leonard A. Gordon 2025

10 9 8 7 6 5 4 3 2 1

ISBN 9780670099993

Typeset in Adobe Caslon Pro by MAP Systems, Bengaluru, India
Printed at Thomson Press India Ltd, New Delhi

www.penguin.co.in

For my grandsons, Evan and Wyatt; my grand-nephews, Benjamin and Ezra; and my grand-niece, Simone: may they and their cohort help to make a better world than the one we, their elders, are turning over to them

Contents

Part III: New Nations in a Divided World, 1947 to the Present

Part IV: Cultural Explosion: South Asians in the Diaspora, 1947 to the Present

Preface

All of us are descended from migrants. Our species, Homo sapiens,
did not evolve in Lahore ... Nor did we evolve in Shanghai or
Topeka ... Even if you live today in the Rift Valley, in Africa ... your
ancestors too moved—they left, changed, and intermingled ... just
as I left Lahore, lived for decades in North America and Europe,
and returned to reside in the house where my grandparents and
parents once did ... utterly altered and remade by my travels.

None of us is a native of the place we call home. And none of us
is a native to this moment in time. We are not native to the instant,
already gone, when this sentence began to be written.

—Mohsin Hamid, 'We Are All Migrants',
National Geographic (August 2019)

How has it come about that Preet Bharara, Dinesh D'Souza,
Anand Giridharadas, Riz Ahmed, Priyanka Chopra, Zubin
Mehta, Satya Nadella, Mira Nair, Kumail Nanjiani, Indra Nooyi,
Kal Penn, Archie Panjabi, M. Night Shyamalan and many others
with South Asian names and backgrounds have become familiar in
the US over the past quarter century? Why did the Indian Prime
Minister Narendra Modi hold a gigantic rally in Houston, Texas,
in 2019, and why did it draw the American President there to stand
with him? Why is Tata Consultancy Services (TCS), a foreign-
based multinational company, the sponsor of the New York City
Marathon, the city's most important sporting event of the year?
How has it happened that many of our legal briefs and medical

records are farmed out overnight to India, and are presented the next day in America? Why do so many American cities now have an Indian restaurant and a yoga studio? Do we know that our Bose radios, and other acoustical devices produced by the Bose Corporation, were developed by the son of Indian immigrants? Are we aware that words and ideas such as mantra, karma, yoga, guru, bungalow, loot, Brahmin, nirvana, pariah, jungle, juggernaut, dungaree have travelled from South Asia to the West?

For close to two centuries, the British ruled a large part of India directly, and other parts indirectly. It was the age of empire and the Raj—as the British regime in India was known. The American colonies broke away from that same growing empire, and Americans, some free, some slaves, built a mighty nation. India was on the other side of the world and not intimately connected to the US. But there were relationships of various kinds from the 1780s onwards— significant to some, but not vital in large measure to either country— all mediated, until India achieved Independence in 1947 after the British Raj ended. The Raj, and later US–South Asian relations, was embedded in more global networks. The trickle of South Asians into the US was accompanied by much larger flows of South Asians into the Caribbean, South Africa, Southeast Asia and the UK. Although I mention these other connections, the focus of this volume is on American–South Asian interactions.

From the later twentieth century into the twenty-first, a new dawn has followed for these links between India and America, opening to a brightening day. There have also been some very dark shadows, such as the Bhopal gas disaster. But the scanty ties of the eighteenth and nineteenth centuries, followed by richer ones through three-quarters of the twentieth century, have been succeeded now by rapidly burgeoning relationships as India has sent large rivers of people and goods to America, and Americans have responded with growing interest and involvement in India.

In this account, I have tried to take a long view. I wanted, among several goals, to bring into focus some ignored and forgotten men and women, both American and South Asian, who connected the two countries. If they were not a Jawaharlal Nehru or a Mahatma Gandhi or a Martin Luther King, Jr, their names, work and achievements are scarcely remembered. Who, these days, has heard of Kumar Goshal, Ida Scudder, J. Krishnamurti, Charles Page Perin, John Bissell, or even Maharishi Mahesh Yogi?

Why should we study the connections of America and South Asia? Until recently these relations have not been as important as those between the US and China, or Japan, or the UK, or Mexico, but these exchanges are now gaining more prominence. This greater visibility is one effect of the increasing globalization of our world. India's increasingly rapid economic development over the last two decades and a half, her arming as a nuclear power, the visible intermingling of Indian culture with Western culture, and the extraordinary growth of the South Asian community in America have contributed to this new importance of India–US ties. India has been rising among the nations even as it still has vast numbers of poor citizens. The United Kingdom is a member of the Commonwealth of Nations but has faded as a great power.

I have chosen to pursue a few main strands of the story—first, missions, religious and secular; second, mantras, referring to Indian religions propagated and taught in the West; third, migrants, the flow of South Asians to America, at first slowly, then almost halted, followed by a great inflow. Then, the influx and opportunity for American citizenship, if not permanent residence, began again during and after the Second World War. But the great influx began in the late 1960s after the new immigration law was passed in 1965. This became nearly a cascade through the later decades of the twentieth century and the early twenty-first century. From a few tens of thousands, the South Asian American community has grown to almost four million in 2020. Although the primary objective of this volume is the US–South Asia connection, wider networks are also noted when appropriate.

This account is divided into four large sections:

- The Age of Empires: Columbus to 1919
- The Age of Gandhi: 1919 to 1948
- New Nations in a Divided World: 1947 to the Present
- The Cultural Explosion: South Asians in the Diaspora, 1947 to the Present

The themes are tracked through in each large section. These themes are:

1. **Missions:** In some cases, as in the case of Christian missions in India, and the history of Christianity in India, there is so much material and so many institutions created, that it was necessary to focus on a few. I chose to include the Vellore Mission, hospital and medical college in every chapter. I also chose to give a brief account of the two schools that the missionaries founded for their own children: Woodstock and Kodaikanal. Many writers and South Asians choose to forget, or greatly minimize, the roles the missionaries have played in South Asia, and may not like the pages and recognition given to the work of Christian missionaries, especially in the first few chapters of this work. I am not a Christian and do not share their beliefs, but as a student of India, I have come to believe that they made significant contributions to the growth of modern India, Pakistan and Bangladesh. They established schools, colleges and hospitals that offered good education and care. Most South Asians utilized these institutions for what they offered and did not accept the Christian teachings that came with it. Some of these missionaries—I am not sure what percentage— did not and could not understand much of Indian culture and religion because it conflicted with their strongly held beliefs. Nonetheless, missionaries such as Charles Foreman, Isabella Thoburn, Ida Scudder and others made positive inputs to the foreign society in which they became immersed. In the fullness of time, most of the foreign missionaries are long gone, but a

few of these institutions still live, though taken over by South Asians. They play a role here.

Under the rubric of missions are also placed the many Indian missions to the US and to the wider world. After attending the World Parliament of Religions in Chicago, 1893, Swami Vivekananda redefined the nature of his mission in America once he came to understand it more deeply. In an 1894 letter home to a fellow monk, he wrote: 'As our country is poor in social virtues, so this country is lacking in spirituality. I give them spirituality, and they give me money.

I do not know how long I shall take to realize my end...'[1] In the 1950s, India did seek out international roles which embodied its purpose of decreasing the possibility of continuing war. It mediated the end of the Korean War, and served as chair of the control commission for Indochina. India may possibly play this role again in trying to settle the war in Ukraine.

2. **Mantras:** Starting in the nineteenth century, Indian gurus, notably Swami Vivekananda, started to teach Indian religious philosophies and methodologies to Americans. More followed. Following the twentieth-century guides and organizations that first brought Indian spiritual wisdom to America—the Ramakrishna Mission, theosophists, the Self-Realization Society of Yogananda and Krishnamurti—as well as the more recent ones—the Hare Krishnas, Maharishi meditators and followers of Ram Dass—came a new generation in recent decades. Numerous temples have been erected as well.

    While gurus and a number of Indian religious temples and centres continue to thrive, yoga, in various forms, has spread even wider and deeper into American life. Almost every city and town has a yoga centre where one can learn exercises, breathing techniques and meditation. It appears that more than ten per cent of Americans are doing yoga. But it is not only the practice of yoga that is striking, whether for health or spiritual aid, but also the

---

[1] Vivekananda, Swami. 1962. *The Complete Works of Swami Vivekananda*. 8 vols. Calcutta: Advaita Ashram, p. 255.

widespread utilization of meditation techniques. These are viewed as measures to reduce stress and to increase business and personal efficiency in meeting daily challenges, while many teachers believe they also offer remarkable gains in health.

3. **Migrants**: Although small numbers of South Asians entered the United States from the late nineteenth century through the Second World War, and some stayed on indefinitely, racism remained a powerful idea. South Asians then were put on the Black section of the American binary of race. Some Indians insisted that they were 'Aryans', or 'Caucasians', meaning of the same race as white Americans, but the Supreme Court and the whites did not accept this argument. Almost every South Asian visitor commented on American racism, and on the restrictions on citizenship which were tightened with measures in 1917 (the barred zone) and the 1924 Act setting quotas for immigrants entering the US. All politically active South Asians in America, however categorized or labelled themselves racially, soon knew they had to fight the evil of racism. Yet, even as some spokesmen predicted the destruction of America that would occur if non-whites were allowed to enter, mix and possibly marry whites, the challenge to racial thinking and the practice of racial discrimination was slowly beginning.

4. **Microchips**: This refers to business relations. Along with a general account of economic connections, I have focused on the Tatas—present in each chapter—who have had a long and unique connection to the US and constituted a must among business links. Other important business links have been formed in the past few decades, but the Tatas have had links to the US for over a century.

5. **Mahatma**: A fifth 'M', the Mahatma, is also included in this discussion. With struggle for Indian political freedom developing even during the First World War, as that conflict neared its end, Mahatma Gandhi came to the fore to advocate for an Independent India. For Gandhi it was a quest for swaraj, or self-rule, that

always meant more than political or economic liberation. It also involved an inner transformation or liberation that resonated with ancient Indian ideals as well as modern Western ones. He argued that the means used were as important as the goals sought, an outlook that made him exceptional among modern political leaders. His comprehensive definition of swaraj, and his stress on the means utilized by those seeking change, helped to make him a guide to many outside India—among them American liberals, African Americans and others opposed to empire and oppression. Since Indians sought allies in their struggle for freedom against the British Empire, and since some Americans were attracted to Gandhi, ties developed between anti-imperialists in both countries. Gandhi's ideas simplified and stripped of some of their cultural content, have enriched American views of freedom, the good society and the means to achieve them.

At times the 'Ms'—missions, mantras, migrants, microchips and the Mahatma—have walked along separate paths, but they have also interacted and strengthened the two or more themes involved in such interplay. Gandhi's teaching, for example, impacted missions, mantras and migrants. His work in India involved business and he was a shrewd fundraiser as well, understanding that politics required monetary support. His supporters abroad, South Asian, American and Europeans, connected him to the Indian diaspora, and to reform movements around the world. As migrants—a few carrying Gandhi's message—others intent on education or business—moved to the US, at first in tiny numbers, later in considerable ones, they connected the two countries in business, missions and religion. But I have not found one cause, for example economic developments, shaping all of the others. These connections will be laid out as the narrative proceeds.

I have tried to go back, to the beginning of India–America connections in the eighteenth century, with some background on the West and India before that juncture, and then to the present. The themes are worked through each of the chosen historical blocks, demarcated by important events. I have, perforce, embedded my exploration of these themes in the developing political and economic contexts of each period.

I often use the term 'South Asia' and 'South Asians' because it is inclusive of India, Pakistan and Bangladesh, and Indians, Pakistanis and Bangladeshis. Although 'India', or British India, or the Raj works well enough up to 1947, from that point onwards we have two and then three nations, so 'South Asia' seems the necessary term. The British Library and even some scholars use the term 'East Indians', but this term had an imperial usage and should be retired.

Within the last half century, the term 'Asian Americans', has become common usage. This includes peoples from Pakistan and Afghanistan, east to Japan and Southeast Asia. When appropriate, this term is used which includes South Asians and many others.

Part I

The Age of Empires:
Columbus to Amritsar

Introduction

The British Empire and Anglo-America

'...then at last the Orient comes.

...The Originatress comes,

The nest of languages, the bequeather of poems, the race of eld, Florid with blood, pensive, rapt with musings, hot with passion, Sultry with perfume, with ample and flowing garments, With sunburnt visage, with intense soul and glittering eyes, The race of Brahma comes.

...Lithe and silent the Hindoo [sic] appears, the Asiatic continent itself appears, the past, the dead.'

—Walt Whitman, 'Broadway Pageant'

'[T]here is no country in the world where religion is such a power, such an element in the life of the people...Hindooism [sic] as a religion has nothing whatever to do with morality or virtue, but is only a means of propitiating angry deities. It is a religion of terror and fear... It is the worship of obscene gods by obscene rites. Its very gods and goddesses commit adultery and incest...There is another element which gives it a tremendous power for good or evil. It is Caste... Caste is a cold and cruel thing, which hardens the heart against natural compassion... Taking all these elements together, Hindooism [sic] must rank as the most despotic, the most cruel, and the vilest of all that is called religion among men...'

—Henry Field, American clergyman[1]

---

[1] Field, Henry M. 1877. *From Egypt to Japan*. NY: Scribner's, pp. 252–55.

'How much more admirable the Bhagvat-Geeta [sic] than all the ruins of the East!'

—Henry David Thoreau[2]

'Sisters and Brothers of America...'
—Swami Vivekananda at the World Parliament of Religions, Chicago, 1893

****

The story of the relations between India and America begins to take form as the American colonists were starting to struggle for Independence. Starting just after dusk on 16 December 1773, Bostonian George Hewes described his 'work' thus:

It was now evening, and I immediately dressed myself in the costume an Indian, equipped with a small hatchet, which I and my associates denominated the tomahawk, with which, and a club, after having painted my face and hands with coal dust in the shop of the blacksmith, I repaired to Griffin's wharf, where the ships lay that contained the tea ... I fell in with many who were dressed, equipped and painted as I was ... and marched in order to the place of our destination.

When we arrived at the wharf, there were three of our number who assumed an authority to direct our operation, to which we readily submitted...We were ordered ... to board all the ships at the same time ... In about three hours ... we had thus broken and thrown overboard every tea chest to be found in the ship ... We were surrounded by British armed ships, but no attempt was made to resist us.

We then quietly retired to our several places of residence...[3]

---

[2] Thoreau, Henry David. 2004. *Walden*. Ed. Jeffrey S. Cramer. New Haven: Yale U. Press, p. 55.
[3] Commager, Henry Steele and Richard B. Morris, eds. 1958, *The Spirit of Seventy-Six*. NY: Harper and Row, pp. 5–6.

Some residents tried to gather the tea—it was a prized beverage and not inexpensive—but all the floating tea was submerged by the next day. This largest of all tea parties was praised by many throughout the American colonies and reported to East India Company officials in London to whom the merchandise belonged.

Why had the colonists held such a tea party, consigning valued tea to the harbour waters? Why were indigenous Americans and the tea party participants called 'Indians' when India and the East Indies were around the far side of the globe? What was this East India Company whose treasured goods they had destroyed and how was it linked to the British government ruling the American colonies? What were the views of the colonists about the Company?

Colonists were sometimes said to disguise themselves as 'Indians' or 'Mohawks' when they were up to mischief. They knew that the British authorities would surely mete out some punishment for the tea dumping, so hiding their identities was appropriate. Although the colonists were ambivalent towards indigenous Americans, those Americans served as a symbol of America, put upon by rulers from across the sea. In the aftermath of the tea tax controversy, a cartoon appeared in a colonial newspaper of a nude indigenous American woman, prostrate, being assaulted by British men pouring tea down her throat. Americans identified the East India Company with the British government itself. The company, after all, was chartered by a government grant of a trade monopoly with India. They believed, not unfairly, that the government was attempting to solve the company's economic difficulties by shipping its tea to the American colonies with an import tax. They had contempt for the London government and the Company. 'Charles Thomson reported to Sam Adams and John Hancock that he had been circulating handbills "to kindle a flame of resentment against them (the East India Company) as ravagers of Asia, the corrupters of their country, the supporters of arbitrary power, and the patrons of monopoly".'[4] Abigail Adams, wife of a future president, called it 'that bainfull weed', but it had become

[4] Labaree, Benjamin Woods. 1979. *The Boston Tea Party*. Boston: Northeastern U. Press, p. 157

a popular drink.[5] The Company's tea imported into the colonies was to be taxed to help the British government pay its expenses for the late war against the French and was Britain's means to defend and govern the colonies. It would also assist the East India Company deal with its troubled finances. However, the colonists objected to 'taxation without representation' and the Boston Tea Party was their response to the preservation of the tea tax by the government even when other objectionable taxes had been dropped. The protests against tea importation were not confined to Boston: on 22 April 1774, Sons of Liberty in New York dumped crates of tea into their own harbour. The government in London responded with severe measures, the Coercive Acts—including closing Boston harbour— that led to the outbreak of the American Revolution.

Just as the British Empire, spearheaded by the East India Company in the east, was transforming itself from a commercial venture into dominion over a vast foreign territory, the American colonies were about to be lost from that empire. A new nation, the United States of America, grew ever larger, encompassing all the territories from the Atlantic coast to the Pacific. In making this new empire, the Americans ravaged and nearly destroyed all the earlier inhabitants or indigenous Americans in their path. They may have disguised themselves as those Americans, but they harboured little respect for them and assigned them to the bin of darker people, not on par with white, Christian Americans. As they were exterminating indigenous Americans, colonials were importing huge numbers of slaves from Africa. Later after grasping the whole continent south of Canada and north of those parts of Mexico not conquered, the United States made efforts beyond into far-flung territories. Were they 'settler-colonialists' as Dunbar-Ortiz, an historian of indigenous peoples, calls them? Like their fellow Europeans, were they simply another branch of the Westerners conquering and dividing the world, employing thousands, later millions of slave labourers on their

---

[5] Adams, John Quincy, 2017. *Diaries 1779–1821*. NY: Library of America, p. 603.

plantations? Or were they a special people, upon a hill, with a unique mission in the world and to the world? Or both?

The Boston Tea Party and the events that occurred on the American, European and Asian continents demonstrate how connected national, imperial, economic and political trends were becoming. Tea drinking had spread throughout the British Empire as the East India Company had the ability to import it from China directly and the taste for it grew apace among the colonists. The results of the American Revolution brought another potential player in the games of empire onto the stage, what some called 'the empire of liberty'. Eliminating the British intermediaries would permit the merchants and consumers of the new nation to import tea in their own ships and chart their own tastes through whatever connections in the wider world they might seek. These American leaders shared with Europeans conceptions of Asia including of India handed down over the centuries, slowly changing as direct contacts increased.

It is not possible to understand the United States' complicated relationship with India, without looking back at the complicated and nuanced history—that converged in the Boston Tea Party—not only of the two countries, but also the development of worldwide connections and empires. Shadowy conceptions of Asia gave way during the age of exploration to new perceptions and ambitions as European merchants, missionaries and administrators arrived in India from the sixteenth century, settling at first in small trading stations on the coast, and gradually pushing into the interior, where the British, outdoing their rivals—the French and the Portuguese— established an extensive territorial domain. Christian missionaries accompanied these early European adventurers, seeking to convert a huge 'heathen' population to what they saw as the one true faith. In Britain, continental Europe and America, Orientalist scholars learned South Asian languages and began to explore the complexities of Indian cultures, while Americans formulated new views of India, and occasional Indian visitors slowly informed American audiences about their homeland. British exploitation of resources in South

Asia, finally permitted the amassing of great wealth, and allowed the further subjugation of once free Indian communities.

From antiquity, Europeans propagated fantastic tales and rigid views of Asia well into the eighteenth century and some of these views still circulated. These European stereotypes descend at least from Aristotle in the fourth century BCE to Montesquieu in the first half of the eighteenth century. They referred to the territories from the Levant eastward as Asia, the East, the Orient, and, from the fifteenth century onwards, as 'the Indies', or 'East Indies' or even 'India', and lumped these diverse parts together as one.[6]

The late thirteenth-century account of the journeys of Marco Polo (1254–1324) from Venice to China by land and by sea, based on recollections told to the experienced author of romances, Rustichello of Pisa, describes the vast riches, great cities, and the active commerce of Asia. Although Polo dealt mainly with China, there is a section on India, in which he depicted several kingdoms in south and western India whose rulers sometimes possessed enormous wealth in jewels (pearls and precious stones), and the extensive trade carried on by Christians, Muslims (Saracens), 'idolators' (Hindus), and a few Jews with the Middle East and Europe to the west and with China to the east. Expensive commodities such as spices (pepper, cinnamon, ginger), textiles and gems attracted buyers at a time when the West was 'medieval' and the Mongols conquered vast territories in Asia and thrust into Europe. Polo also described yogis (sanyasins), the customs familiar to India-hands such as cremation, sati and decorous eating with the right hand. Columbus is said to have annotated his copy of Polo's narrative, struck by the tales of the riches of Asia or 'the Indies'.[7]

The story of Columbus's quest for the Indies remains the subject of controversy. Biographer Samuel Eliot Morison, who retraced the voyages at sea and by air about seventy-five years ago, maintained that Columbus was a skilled and resourceful sailor, truly 'an admiral of the Ocean Sea', however misguided he was about the size of the Earth and what part of the world he had reached. Others have

---

[6] Gordon 1997a, pp. 127–42.
[7] 1958, p. 260ff.

downplayed his skills and accomplishments, but none deny that he drew subsequent conquistadors and missionaries westward to the Americas and inaugurated a frenzied age of conquest. Following Columbus's belief that he had reached the 'Indies', the inhabitants of the Caribbean islands he did reach were called 'Indians', as were the native peoples of the continents of North and South America later occupied by Europeans.[8]

Not long after Columbus's first voyages on behalf of the Spanish crown, Vasco da Gama, sponsored by the Portuguese crown and building upon that nation's earlier efforts to round Africa, entered the Indian Ocean and made his way to India. Europeans called the native people of India 'Indians', designating them as 'East Indians', as they remained in the catalogue of the British Library until recently, in contrast to the inhabitants of the Caribbean islands who were called 'West Indians'. In the early twentieth century the inhabitants of India were also called 'Hindus' by some, and later, as they became ever more integrated into American society, as Asian Indians or South Asian Americans. Throughout there were complexities that made it difficult to herd South Asians into a rigid American schema of black and white.

> Noted historian of exploration Felipe Fernandez-Armesto has argued that the 1490s were a vital period of change, when Atlantic Europeans began reaching out to the world after centuries of chugging behind non-Europeans. The explorers cracked 'the Atlantic code', allowing them to sail both ways across the Atlantic, and gradually learned to navigate the Pacific as well. Through these new adventures in the Americas and Asia, Europeans, dependent on local guides and local knowledge, made much more accurate maps of the world and began to chart the interiors of continents.[9]

Alongside the explorers were missionaries seeking to spread the true faith, for e.g., Catholicism, and Columbus's missions included

---

[8] Morison, Samuel Eliot. 1942. *Admiral of the Ocean Sea. A Life of Christopher Columbus.* Boston: Little, Brown, pp. 131, 206.
[9] Fernandez-Amesto 2006, p. 182ff.

converting those not of the true faith. European understanding of Asia (in this context spanning present-day Pakistan to Japan) had a new beginning from the late 1400s. As Western explorers learned more about Asia, they slowly incorporated this new knowledge with old information and prejudices. The vision of the strange and fabulous East acquired from antiquity in the works of such writers as Herodotus, Hippocrates, Aristotle, Strabo and Arrian, and from the 'ridiculous' reports of the medieval traveller Marco Polo, were juxtaposed with more recent accounts from merchants, adventurers and missionaries. Enlightenment writers in the eighteenth century assigned to Asia and Asians a prominent role in comparative and historical schema for understanding cultures through time. By studying Asian languages, cultures and texts, scholars began more accurately to compare Asian traditions and cultural features to those of the West.

In the wake of Vasco da Gama, the Portuguese organized their Asian empire from Goa, on the coast of southwestern India. The Dutch and French soon developed trade in Asia, too. Finally, the British, eventually the most successful among them, set up small trading bases in western, southern and eastern India, governed by the British East India Company, whose first president, in 1684, of the commercial post at Fort St George, later the city of Madras, was the Boston-born Elihu Yale: the benefactor of the Collegiate School in Connecticut that is now Yale University. The Westerners who came to India sought primarily to trade, acquiring and controlling small trading stations. Only later did the trading stations, in times of political crisis in South Asia, afford Westerners bases from which to attempt not only to trade but to conquer, much of this transpiring before there was a United States of America.

With the loss of the thirteen American colonies, the British did not 'pivot to Asia', but had to realign their concerns. They retained their West Indian sugar islands and Canada, and now had to focus on what they would do vis-à-vis India. It was becoming a territorial colony and not simply a set of fortified, commercial bases. India was also becoming a focus of British colonial interest, and possible prosperity. How exploitative this might be was still an open issue.

With the merchants and soldiers and bureaucrats came the officials-cum-scholars, the Orientalists, who studied many aspects of India, usual from afar, especially the languages. Throughout his term as the first governor-general of Bengal, Warren Hastings, was an ardent patron of research into Indian civilization. While he saw the utility of learning about the native population by examining their culture, beliefs and texts, he also firmly backed those who were curious about strange religious texts in Persian and Sanskrit. Not all had a practical outlook on the usefulness of this 'orientalism'. Dictionaries of Sanskrit or Bengali might be useful in a revenue court, but their compilation might lead into hitherto unknown realms. Though at first for British use, these translations and commentaries spread far and wide, including into America.

The tradition of learning and cultural exploration started by Nathaniel Halhed, William Jones and other Orientalists, continued through the nineteenth century, though more vigorously taken up by continental European scholars and Americans as well. The British were even forced by their neglect of such learning by their own nationals to import men such as Max Müller (1823–1900) from Germany. In the US, this interest was embodied in the founding and continued existence of the American Oriental Society from the 1840s. In the second half of the nineteenth century, several American universities began the teaching of Sanskrit and the production of scholarly articles and books on Asian subjects.

The most eminent of the nineteenth-century American scholars of Sanskrit and linguistics was William Dwight Whitney (1827–1894), a graduate of Williams College, who was trained in Germany, and spent his teaching and scholarly career at Yale University.

Throughout his career he remained in lively contact with European scholars and spent great emotional and intellectual energy arguing with the German-born Oxford-based scholar, Max Müller. Whitney never ventured to Asia but, like other armchair orientalists, devoted days, weeks, months and decades to the study of

Asian languages and religions.
But it was all academic: they
probably had no direct contact
with Indians. Their Indias
were those of the imagination
and the text. Whitney
specialized in Vedic Sanskrit
and in the nascent field of
linguistics, or philology, as it
was called in the nineteenth
century. Though an agnostic,
if not an atheist, at Yale, then
a strongly Christian college,
Whitney was able to cope with
his doubts about Jesus Christ

William Dwight Whitney

as his colleagues had to deal with his 'materialism'.[10] He served as
corresponding secretary of the American Oriental Society (founded
in 1842), the main scholarly organization devoted to studying Asia
in the United States. Whitney was central to the spread of the
teaching of India's culture and languages, especially Sanskrit, in
leading American universities. On many occasions, he was asked to
recommend teachers and scholars for positions in language study.
Of these pupils, the most important was Charles Lanman, who
taught Sanskrit at Harvard from 1880 to his retirement in 1926.
Like Whitney, he taught the next generation of Sanskrit scholars
or interacted with them through participation in the American
Oriental Society. Lanman married Mary Hinckley in 1888, and
they spent their honeymoon in India. During that year, Lanman
purchased numerous Sanskrit manuscripts and books, as well as
other manuscripts that he bequeathed to Harvard. This was the
treasure trove from which emerged the Harvard Oriental Series
that was continued by scholars through the twentieth century.
Lanman was also the author of a Sanskrit reader that long remained

---

[10] Alter, Stephen G. 2005. *William Dwight Whitney and the Science of Language.*
Baltimore: Johns Hopkins U. Press, p. 31ff.

the basic text for students starting out in the language. As in India, a hands-on process from guru to student, and then from student-turned-guru to the next generation of students, continued through the following century.[11]

As East India Company servants and other Europeans explored Indian culture more searchingly and sympathetically, a counterview of Indian civilization formed, then flourished, in the nineteenth century. This counterview—hostile to Indian achievements, society, and religion—was propounded by enormously influential Europeans labelled evangelicals and utilitarians. Among these, Charles Grant (1746–1823) was a leading evangelist, and James Mill (1773–1836), a leading utilitarian.

However detached the new United States became from its 'mother country', relations with Great Britain and the British Empire remained important during the nineteenth century and thereafter. These relations, though culturally and economically salient for the Americans, were occasionally more heated politically. The biggest post-1812 crisis was during the Civil War. The Confederacy appealed throughout for recognition from the European powers. The British entertained the notion but whatever grievances it might harbour against the US, it would be difficult for a nation that had outlawed the slave trade to recognize a slave nation. The US did have to accept British neutrality in the war since the latter saw it as a conflict between belligerents. The war disrupted the supply of cotton for Britain's factories from the cotton producers of the south, but Britain increased cotton imports from India and Egypt. In September 1862, US President Abraham Lincoln issued the preliminary Emancipation Proclamation, freeing all slaves within the Confederate states. British sympathies for the Confederacy faded and the Union-British crisis passed.

During these events, the US was strongly represented in London (1861–1868) by Charles Francis Adams, Sr (1807–1886), son and grandson of presidents John and John Quincy Adams, with his son,

---

[11] 'Charles Rockwell Lanman', Wikipedia, https://en.wikipedia.org/wiki/Charles_Rockwell_Lanman; Alter 2005.

Henry Adams (1838–1918), serving as his secretary. The latter wrote, decades later, in *The Education of Henry Adams*,[12] that he started with the view of political leaders as honest and moral but learned that such men frequently lied when they believed they were telling the truth and could not be trusted. At first, he thought that Americans were inferior to the British, but came to believe that Americans were their equal, and, later, their superiors.

Henry Adams

Henry Adams taught history at Harvard and later moved to Washington DC, where he bought a home across from the White House, and became the intimate friend of John Hay (1838–1905). The latter served as secretary to Lincoln, and embarked on a long career of public service leading to posts as ambassador to Great Britain and foreign minister. These two men were the heart of an amorphous group of the Anglo–American elite that Adams called 'our gang'. The group included writers, professors, presidents and ambassadors who often shared their views and carried weight in the Anglo–American world up to the First World War; among them Henry Cabot Lodge (1850–1924), Charles Eliot Norton (1827–1908), Theodore Roosevelt (1858–1919) and a visiting Henry James (1843–1916).

Perhaps least known was Charles Eliot Norton, Harvard professor of art and archaeology and editor of the *North American Review*. Norton travelled back and forth to the continent, building friendships on both sides of the Atlantic. He had begun, however as a businessman working with an East Indian trading firm in Boston, for which he travelled to India in 1849. Norton brought writers on the two sides of the ocean in touch, including the Sanskritist William Dwight Whitney.[13] The members of

---

[12] Adams, Henry. 1973. *The Education of Henry Adams*. Ed. Ernest Samuels. Boston: Houghton Mifflin, p. 98ff.
[13] Alter 2005, p. 34.

Henry Adams's 'gang' rarely doubted that the Anglo–Americans were the drivers of the train of civilization as it chugged towards a resplendent future. The Americans in the gang admired the British Empire, and the British accepted that the United States was a rising power in the world.

The Anglo–American social and cultural world also included quite a few intermarriages, particularly of young, attractive, often moneyed American women with titled British men.

Among the most famous of these matches was the one in 1874 of Jennie Jerome (1854–1921), a stunning American heiress, to Lord Randolph Churchill (1849–1895), second son of the Duke of Marlborough. Lord Curzon, Viceroy of India (1898–1905), married Mary Leiter (1870–1906), a belle of Washington DC, and after her death in 1906, he married Grace Duggan (1885–1958), another American. Rudyard Kipling (1865–1936), the most famous British writer of the late nineteenth century, married Caroline Balestier (1862–1939) of Vermont, and settled in Great Britain after his youth in India. The number of these intermarriages was legion, spanning the 1870s to the early twentieth century, and helped integrate the Anglo–American elite. Consuelo Vanderbilt became the Duchess of Marlborough, May Goelet, the Duchess of Roxburghe, Flora Davis, the Marchioness of Dufferin and Nancy Langhorne married William Astor, an American who became British, and later 2nd Viscount Astor. Lady Astor became the first female member of the House of Commons, noted for her sharp tongue and as the hostess of the Cliveden set.[14] The match of Jennie Jerome to Randolph Churchill provided an offspring who did his best to tie the two countries together, preserve the British Empire and tie Great Britain to his mother's home country: Winston Churchill (1874–1965). As a young subaltern, a junior officer, and not one of the lower classes, Churchill served the Raj on the Indian frontier, began his journalistic career and developed his views on the British Empire.

---

[14] MacColl, Gail and Carol McD.Wallace, 2012. *To Marry an English Lord*, NY: Workman.

By the time of the Columbian Exposition,[15] America's ambitions were global, while the British Empire had reached the peak of its imperial project. In an address at the Columbian Exposition, historian Frederick Jackson Turner (1861–1932) declared the closing of the American frontier but the end of American expansion within continental limits did not mean the end of the 'manifest destiny' (the expansion across North America by settlers in the US). The exposition marked America's coming of age as a world power. Although the British Empire was still the first among empires, the US would challenge Britain's status, while in India, nationalism was awakening. This development, like the religious–cultural and the techno–economic ones, was to tie the US, a former colony, to India, in complicated and changing ways through the following decades.

The US began acquiring territories outside the continental US as the great powers divided up the world, but it was not yet a significant military power ready to compete with Britain or Germany. In 1890, President Grover Cleveland hesitated to annex Hawaii, but under President William McKinley, whose ambitions were greater, the US was shortly involved in the Spanish American War and the 'liberation' of Cuba, Puerto Rico and the Philippines—the last requiring a nasty but largely forgotten war against nationalist Filipinos. These actions were accompanied by the assertion of Anglo-Saxon superiority and its necessary role in transforming the world—attitudes countered at the same time by a reaffirmation of an American tradition of anti-imperialism. Prominent figures such as the philosopher William James (1842–1910), the industrialist Andrew Carnegie and the author Mark Twain joined the Anti-Imperialist League and opposed the Spanish–American War.[16]

With the assassination of President McKinley, Theodore Roosevelt, an admirer of the British Empire, succeeded him as

---

[15] The World's Columbian Exposition, also known as the Chicago World's Fair, was a fair held in Chicago from 5 May to 31 October 1893, to celebrate the 400th anniversary of Christopher Columbus's arrival in the New World in 1492.

[16] Beisner, Robert L. 1968. *Twelve against Empire. The Anti-Imperialists 1898–1900*. NY: McGraw-Hill, pp. 35ff, 165ff.

president. British officials, wary of a rising tide of Indian nationalism, encouraged him to speak out in support of British hegemony. In the late nineteenth century, the British Empire was at its zenith, having seized territory in Africa, acquired Hong Kong from China, colonized Singapore and conquered Burma. The sun never set on the British Empire, but shadows loomed. The Germans and Americans were rising economic powers surpassing Great Britain in iron and steel; even once-isolated Japan was becoming an economic and military rival. The Boer War (1899–1902) revealed the weakness of Britain's hold in South Africa. Although the British triumphed, they handed over control to European settlers.

It was during these years in the late nineteenth century fraught with nationalist longing and intermittent rebellion that Rudyard Kipling, an unapologetic imperialist, produced his famous corpus of stories, novels and poems. As a resident of India and Britain, and by his marriage to an American, Kipling is considered an 'Anglo-Indian-American' writer. Born in India, he was sent home for schooling

Theodore Roosevelt

in Great Britain, where he spent an anguished youth and some boisterous school days. In the 1880s he returned to India, where he became an accomplished journalist and then a writer of popular short stories. As Irving Howe suggests, although Kipling's work is clearly marked by imperialist and racist attitudes, he also depicted some very human characters in stories and poems that appealed to a vast readership, including some Indians, and entered popular culture through songs and films.[17]

At age twenty-four, Kipling left India, toured the United States, wrote about his travels, and settled in London. He befriended a young American, Wolcott Balestier, with whom he wrote a novel, *The Naulahka, A Story of West and East* (1892). After Balestier died suddenly

---

[17] Howe, Irving. ed. 1982. *The Portable Kipling*, NY: Penguin, p. xiiiff.

that same year, Kipling married Balestier's sister, Caroline, and lived for some time in Brattleboro, Vermont, before returning to live in southern England. Kipling travelled through the British Empire and wrote prolifically. Some of his stories and novels featured Western and American characters, as did the popular novel, *Captains Courageous* (1896), which featured diverse Americans. Many were set in India, including his most famous novel, *Kim* (1900).

Rudyard Kipling

In *Kim*, Kipling tracks the protagonist's journeys: into the intelligence service of the Raj, towards finding out his identity and heritage, as well as assisting and learning from a Tibetan Lama. Haunted by the image of a red bull on a green field, Kim learns he is Kimball O'Hara, though tanned by the sun and knowledgeable about the India of the Indians. Learning of his talents, he is trained by British officials and their Indian subordinates to work for the intelligence service to become a player in the 'Great Game'. He encounters Russians and their allies threatening British India, and he plays a role in defeating them. In Kipling's works, though Indians frequently lie, they can also be acculturated as Englishmen, make use of their native talents and become part of the apparatus of the Raj. Taught at St Xavier's and by Colonel Creighton, Lurgan Sahib, Mahbub Ali and Huree Babu, Kim becomes an invaluable asset of the Raj. Kipling is not unsympathetic to the Buddhist Lama, and several other Indian characters, but he is all in for the Raj and white dominance of the subcontinent. Who is Kim, the youngster who is a sahib, but knows India inside and out? He is akin to a young Kipling, in the spy service to defend the Raj, whereas in real life, Kipling chose journalism and literature. He is also a sympathetic character admired by generations of readers on both sides of the Atlantic who continues to entrance readers who may or may not share his values.

Although neither as polished nor as successful as Kim, the American characters of *The Naulahka*, an earlier work, were thrust into a complex Indian environment. Nicholas Tarvin pursues his lady love, Kate Sheriff, from the western United States to India, where she tries to help fallen women. The novel betrays racist attitudes throughout, contrasting the slackness of the Oriental with the vitality, good sense and selflessness of the Westerners. The Indians demonstrate a 'strange mingling of impassiveness and childishness' and 'primitive passions', while the white characters acquire humility and wisdom.

A similarly blatant racism characterizes one of Kipling's most famous poems, 'The White Man's Burden', which praised the American adventure in the Philippines:

> Take up the White Man's Burden—
> Send forth the best ye breed—
> Go bind your sons to exile
> To serve your captives' need;
> To wait in heavy harness
> On flutter folk and wild—
> Your new-caught, sullen peoples,
> Half devil and half child.[18]

Kipling here depicts the Filipino natives as 'wild' and 'sullen', demonic and childlike, unashamedly revealing the racist attitudes of even those Westerners who believed they were serving their 'captives' needs'.

As Harold Isaacs pointed out in *Scratches on Our Minds: American Views of China and India*, many of the 181 opinion-shapers whom he interviewed in the 1950s said that their image of India was derived in part from Kipling. Kipling's India was a vital part of what Bradford Perkins called 'the subculture of diplomacy' or what we might call political culture. For much of the twentieth century, his India—from Lahore, grimly portrayed in the short story 'The City of Dreadful Night' up to the frontier and beyond—resonated in the minds of his wide American readership. Allen Dulles, director

---

[18] Howe 1982, p. 602.

of the CIA (Central Intelligence Agency) in the 1950s and 1960s was a devoted fan of *Kim* as was Kermit ('Kim') Roosevelt, a CIA operative largely responsible for the coup in Iran in 1953 that placed the Shah back in control.[19]

After more than a century of revolution, war, rivalry and mutual suspicion, a new solidarity emerged between the US and Great Britain. The two decades before the outbreak of the First World War, as Bradford Perkins has argued, were the crucial period of 'the great rapprochement', a coming together of the two nations, which would be sustained over the next century through two world wars and episodic diplomatic tensions.[20]

At the end of the nineteenth century what Perkins calls 'the veteran (Britain) and the parvenu (the US)' conjoined, and political ties and personal connections grew stronger. The official connections frequently included matters of defence and intelligence. The unofficial connections, which might also overlap with the official, included such organizations as the Pilgrims Society; ecclesiastical contacts, especially between the Anglican Church and the Episcopal Church in the US; a great number of trans-Atlantic intermarriages and other personal contacts between reformers; and literary exchanges. Connecting links, such as those within the Churchill, Curzon and Kipling families, made the British feel at home in America, giving a warm, imperial glow to those relationships. At the same time, the American–South Asian ties that developed were triangular. Britain was always there mediating relationships. Sometimes the British receded into the background, but they were there, watching warily and in control.

These webs of connection included a not-so-subtle pro-empire, pro-British propaganda campaign that ran through the first half of the twentieth century. It included efforts to shape press coverage, and as the film industry developed, attempts to glorify the Raj and

---

[19] Issacs, Harold, 1980, *Scratches on Our Minds. American Views of China and India,* White Plains: M.E. Sharpe, 1980, p. 241ff.

[20] Perkins, Bradford, 1969, *The Great Rapprochement: England and the United States 1895-1914,* p. 15ff.

denigrate anti-British South Asians. Indian nationalists were slow off the mark, but later enlisted Americans critical of empire to help them show the deficiencies, if not the evils of empire. Eventually it became an all-out non-violent war of words and images.[21]

Intelligence operations constituted one crucial arena of Anglo–American interaction, which included spying on Indians and on Americans interested in India. British–Indian intelligence touched on American shores to keep an eye on their Indian subjects collaborating with Americans during the First World War, as part of their intelligence networks worldwide. Historian C.A. Bayly explored the development during an earlier period of British intelligence—gathering mechanisms within already conquered territory.[22]

The British were also concerned, beyond intelligence-gathering, with maintaining order. In the period after 1857, from 1874 to 1917, the Political and Secret Department of the India Office, London, was established to report directly to the Secretary of State for India. The Political Secretary received funds secretly from the Secretary of State's private checking account, and deposited it into his own, from which he paid agents working from London. Lord Morley's checkbook, now at the India Office Library, details such disbursements. This London-based department focused on Indian troublemakers anywhere, with links to the Calcutta government. This was a 'non-avowed and discreet affair'.

Meanwhile, in India in 1903, the Department of Criminal Intelligence (DCI) was established by the Home Department as the Raj's central domestic and foreign intelligence agency. It was concerned with revolutionary and 'anarchist' activity, watching students in the UK from about 1905. From 1905, the Home Department in India paid British intelligence to watch Indians in New York. By 1907, political groups were watched in London, Paris, North America, China and the Far East. Initially, Scotland Yard

---

[21] Hitchens, Christopher, 1991, *Blood, Class and Nostalgia, Anglo-American Ironies*, London: Vintage, pp. 82ff, 132, 313.
[22] Bayly, C.A. 1999, *Empire and Information. Intelligence Gathering and Social Communication in India, 1780-1870*, Cambridge U. Press.

(London's Metropolitan Police) was asked to watch Indians in the UK, but the police were ignorant of Indian nationalism; DCI wanted more savvy operatives. The solution was to dispatch, in 1909, two expert Indian policemen to the UK. One of them, John Wallinger (1869–1931), was put in charge of Indian Political Intelligence.[23]

Wallinger was based in London and had a field agent in Europe as nationalist plotting heated up there in the decade before and during the First World War. Though reports came from New York, much Indian activity had by then begun on the west coast of the US and Canada. The crucial agent there was Canadian native William Hopkinson (1880–1914), who had served in the Indian police and returned to Canada around 1910. Hopkinson knew several Indian languages and worked as an immigration officer for Canada, and as a translator for US immigration officials. In 1914, Hopkinson, then well-known despite frequently disguising as an Indian, was shot and killed by a Sikh. The British had lost their most knowledgeable agent in the US, but new agents were put in place and the flow of information about Indians in the US (as well as in Europe, Canada, East Asia and the Middle East) continued. Friendly or at least cooperative governments, including those of the US and France, contributed.[24]

During the First World War, British agents and their Indian sub-agents were linked into the headquarters for British intelligence for the US, based in New York City and was led by Sir William Wiseman (1885–1962). British intelligence in the US during the war, spied on Indian and Irish nationalists and political radicals. These observations continued until Irish independence and partition (1921) and Indian Independence (1947).[25] Wiseman formed a

[23] Popplewell, Richard J. 1995, *Intelligence and Imperial Defence, British Intelligence and the Defence of the Indian Empire 1904-1924*. London: Frank Cass, p. 57ff.
[24] Government of India, Home Department and External Department Files, 1905 to 1920.
[25] Jeffrey, p. 108ff.

remarkably close relationship with President Woodrow Wilson and his closest adviser, Colonel House.[26]

Around 1920, the British established the British Library of Information in New York City. It became a beehive of British propaganda efforts—it probably remains so—and one of its chiefs said that in the interwar period at least 30 per cent of its labour was concerned with India. In addition, of course, the British had their embassy and consulates throughout the US, reporting on Indians and Indian matters there. Working closely with the India Office on Indian matters, all of these agencies worked at information gathering and spreading propaganda in support of the British Raj. They linked to voluntary organizations like the Pilgrims Society and to Anglophiles eager to spread the gospel of the Raj.

In India, the government kept watch on American visitors, missionaries, journalists and others, restricting some from entering the subcontinent. The Home Department watched and controlled Indian 'troublemakers', a group thought to include nationalists, revolutionaries or 'anarchists', communists and socialists. Worldwide empires require worldwide intelligence networks. The British had constructed a gigantic octopus-like structure by the mid-1910s. It stretched from Hong Kong to Singapore to New Delhi to London to New York and California as well and supplied information to American officials for years to follow. The old imperialists and the rising imperialists were in the 'Great Game' together.

At the elite level was what Henry Adams calls 'our gang'. The descendant of two presidents, a noted historian and a Washington insider, Adams hosted important visitors from near and far across from the White House. Adams and his closest confidant, John Hay, had no great love for Roosevelt, but knew him well and participated in the building of an Anglo-American elite. Senator Henry Cabot Lodge was also an intimate of this group, and Roosevelt referred to the trio of Adams, Hay and Lodge as 'the three Musketeers of Culture'.[27] Adams noted at one point that Kipling when visiting

---

[26] Andrew 1996, p. 30ff.
[27] Hitchens, p. 163.

Washington has 'grown rather thick with our little Washington gang'.[28] But Kipling, though the leading literary exponent of the British Empire, was not a longtime Washington insider like Cecil Spring-Rice (1859–1918), or 'Springy' as his intimate friend Theodore Roosevelt called him.[29] Spring-Rice served in the British diplomatic service at the Washington embassy for many years and was Britain's US ambassador during the First World War. When Spring-Rice was serving in Europe and the Middle East, Theodore Roosevelt exchanged many letters with him and consulted him whenever he wanted background or inside news from Britain and other European powers.[30] Although Roosevelt never called himself an 'Anglo-Saxon'—the Roosevelts had Dutch origins—he stressed the superior qualities of white Americans.

There were also other intersecting relationships. William James greatly admired Kipling and thought he would get over his youthful attachment to imperialism and become a superior writer. Both Kipling and James were friendly with Harvard art professor Charles Eliot Norton, who had visited India in 1849; he was another member of the Anglo–American elite who crisscrossed the Atlantic while cheering the superiority of white men and their empires. When Winston Churchill lectured in New York City in 1900, he was amiably introduced by Mark Twain, the anti-imperialist known later for his devastating depiction of King Leopold's Congo, in his 1905 pamphlet 'King Leopold's Soliloquy', who observed that each side of the argument about imperialism had its point of view. This brief tour of the Anglo–American interface may conclude with some verses from a poem by Cecil Spring-Rice that mock the two stereotypical figures, the British John Bull and the American Uncle Sam, who personified their two nations:

---

[28] Adams, quoted in Lycett, Andrew. 1999. *Rudyard Kipling*. London: Phoenix, p. 369.
[29] Roosevelt, Theodore. 2004. *Letters and Speeches*. New York: Library of America, pp. 61, 89–90, 360.
[30] Hitchens, p. 162ff.

John Bull

I fear I do not like you, Sam, it's very, very sad
     But philosophic though I am, you make me very mad In
manners, courtesy and tact you do not much excel And, much as
I regret the fact, I wish you were in hell.

Uncle Sam

And now we're on the subject, John, I think it's time you knew
The sun has never shone upon a durnder cuss than you,
     And the world both friends and foes are filled with one desire
To punch the elevated nose of Mr. Bull, Esquire.[31]

British imperialism threaded through the nineteenth century with
the Raj established by 'aggressive men if not an aggressive nation'.[32]
(Although the US, as well, had from its origins fostered an imperialist
and expansive agenda, for many Americans, the concepts of 'empire'
and 'imperialism' had negative connotations; many wanted no part
of European conquest and exploitation. This anti-imperialist theme
runs through American history from the Revolutionary War, a revolt
against empire and for self-rule, into the present. The repertoire of
American rhetoric has always contained these possibilities: liberation,
self-determination and respect for the autonomy of the other. Some of
those whose right to autonomy was not envisioned by the American
Declaration of independence have used its rhetoric to justify their own
independence, including the writers of the Seneca Falls Declaration
of Sentiments (1848) in support of women's liberation, and Ho Chi
Minh, in writing the Declaration of Independence of the Democratic
Republic of Vietnam (1945).
     One of the staunch American anti-imperialists was the American
philosopher, William James. Theodore Roosevelt, an advocate of

---

[31] Phillips, William. 1953. *Ventures in Diplomacy*. Boston: Beacon Press, p. 71.
[32] Thompson, Edward J. and G.T. Garratt. 1934. *Rise and Fulfilment of British Rule in India*. London: Macmillan, p. 93ff.

imperialist ventures, had been James's student, and argued with his teacher incessantly. James would listen as Roosevelt went on, smiling but not replying. Had James replied, the dialogue would go on endlessly; young Roosevelt would not shut up, exasperating both teacher and fellow students. Later, teacher and student became opponents over imperialism and 'the fighting instinct'. Roosevelt was involved in war with Spain in Cuba as leader of the Rough Riders regiment. He was president when war between Americans and nationalistic Filipinos led to the slaughter of tens of thousands of Filipinos and the establishment of American rule there for almost half a century. Kipling cheered the Americans on, while James remained a critic. As the Spanish–American War neared, some citizens, including James, formed the Anti-Imperialist League, and James, whatever his reservations about joining, was for a time its vice president. He remained active until resigning in 1903, conceding that their cause had been defeated. But he did not give up his antagonism to foreign conquests, the domination of foreign peoples and what he saw as the desecration of American ideals. Through these years of war and conquest, he wrote powerfully and often, about these.

> We are now openly engaged in crushing out the sacredest thing in this great evils, [sic] injurious both to the conquered people and to the people at home who had been seized by 'war fever'.[33]
>
> ...
>
> Early on, James had written to a Boston newspaper:
> Human world—the attempt of a people long enslaved to attain to the possession of itself, to organize its laws and government, to be free to follow its internal destinies according to its own ideals... We are to be missionaries of civilization, and to bear the white man's burden, painful as it often is! ... The individual lives are nothing. Our duty and our destiny call, and civilization must go on! Could there as a more damning indictment of that whole bloated idol termed "modern civilization" than this amounts

---

[33] Perry 1935, II, pp. 310–11.

to? Civilization is…the big, hollow, resounding, corrupting, sophisticating, confusing torrent of mere brutal momentum and irrationality that bring forth fruits like this![34]

Mark Twain joined James opposing imperialist expansion. Twain had introduced and debated the young Winston Churchill in New York in 1900, and the businessman and philanthropist Andrew Carnegie.

Roosevelt—whom James thought had likely never emerged from 'early adolescence'—increasingly embraced British imperialism throughout his presidency, from 1901 to 1909. On 18 January 1909, Roosevelt gave a speech praising British efforts in India, which was widely quoted and reprinted by the British to show that support for the Raj extended even to the leader of the world's up-and-coming power. Roosevelt thought that the British in India were second only to the Americans in the Philippines in their wholehearted work to civilize native peoples. For Roosevelt, as for many Westerners of the period, on the continuum of civilization, tribal peoples of backward Africa and other areas were at one end, in the lowest position; Europeans generally were deemed the most civilized; but the Anglo-Saxons of Great Britain and the US were supreme. Below these hyper-civilized Anglo-Saxons were the less civilized, somewhat barbaric Russians, Germans and Japanese; and between these latter and tribal peoples were South Asians, Chinese, Filipinos and inhabitants of other European colonies, whose people were advancing under the astute tutelage of their rulers.[35]

In contrast to Roosevelt, who had travelled the world but had never been to India, William Jennings Bryan (1860–1925), a Democratic presidential candidate and later Secretary of State under President Woodrow Wilson (1856–1924; president 1913–1921), did go to India in 1906. After his extensive tour, Bryan wrote a damning attack on British rule that was circulated in the West by Indian nationalists and their allies. Drawing upon the writings of

---

[34] Ibid.
[35] Tilchin, William N. 1997. *Theodore Roosevelt and the British Empire. A Study in Presidential Statecraft*. NY: St. Martin's, pp. 19, 24, 57, 74.

Indian nationalist leader Dadabhai Naoroji (1825–1917) and Sir Henry Cotton's *New India, or India in Transition* (1885), Bryan concluded, 'British rule in India is far worse, far more burdensome to the people... than I had supposed.' He continued: 'The trouble is that England acquired India for England's advantage, not for India's, and that she holds India for England's benefit, not for India's. She administers India with an eye to England's interests, not India's...' Comparing the Raj unfavourably with the governance of the Czar in Russia, he condemned the exclusion of able Indians, like the reformer Gopal Krishna Gokhale, a leader of the Indian National Congress, from ruling their own country and hailed the growth of national spirit in India.[36]

In addition to missionaries, businessmen and the Tatas' American consultants, an increasing number of American travellers passed through India. Even before Indians visited American shores in significant number, travel books, lectures and the reports of returned missionaries informed Americans about India. A few travellers left detailed accounts, including America's most famous writer, Mark Twain. His income was generated from his travel books and lectures, which he squandered on rash investments. So he travelled again, writing well-paid letters to the press about his encounters, gathering the letters into books and garnering lecture fees. Twain's last travel book recounted his 1890s trip around the world, which included a few months in India.[37] He wrote, 'How I did loathe that journey round the world!—except the sea-part & India.'[38]

Although Twain wrote that 'India is a hard country to understand', he was entranced, appalled and captivated. He said he could watch the rich and colourful street life of Bombay

---

[36] Bryan, William Jennings. 1913. 'British Rule in India,' reprint of July 20, 1906 article in 'India,' as a pamphlet by the British Committee of the Indian National Congress.

[37] Ziff 2000, p. 171ff.

[38] Quoted in Ziff, Larzer. 2000. Return Passages. *Great American Travel Writing 1780-1910*. New Haven: Yale U. Press, p. 213.

forever. The trip down to the plains from Darjeeling via narrow-gauge railway was, he wrote, 'the most enjoyable day of my life'. However, he well understood the oppression of the masses by the British and higher-ranked Indians. As Ziff points out, India made Twain reconsider his white southerner's lifelong implicit support of slavery.

Twain was skeptical about Western missionaries: 'To speak plainly, we despise all reverences and all objects of reverence which are outside the pale of our own list of sacred things. And yet, with strange inconsistency, we are shocked when other people despise and defile the things which are holy to us.'[39] One of the interesting aspects of his Indian tour was his powerful and positive response to the variety of colours in the dress of Indians, but also their skin colour. He imagined an exhibition of the richness of Bombay dress with that of American and English costumes. Twain thought a white complexion 'a disadvantage'. He wrote, '...when it comes into competition with mass of brown and black the fact is betrayed that it is endurable only because we are used to it. Nearly all black and brown skins are beautiful, but a beautiful white skin is rare...'[40]

Although Twain enjoyed his India tour, he remained a Westerner in his admiration of the British Raj, and wrote of Warren Hastings, the first governor-general of Bengal, that 'he saved to England the Indian Empire, and that was the best service that was ever done to the Indians themselves, those wretched heirs of a hundred centuries of pitiless oppression and abuse'.[41] Twain assumed, as did many nineteenth-century British officials, that India was so divided—by caste, region, religion—that only the steel frame of the Raj had saved it from disintegration. He also presented a long account of British bravery in suppressing the Indian rebellion of 1857, ignoring Indian grievances.

---

[39] Twain, Mark. 1989 [1897]. *Following the Equator. A Journey around the World*. NY: Dover, p. 515.
[40] Ibid. p. 381.
[41] Ibid., p. 506.

Twain's accounts of India lacked the moral earnestness and Christian self-righteousness found elsewhere. With more than a hint of humour, for example, he writes of encountering Calcutta: 'It... (is) called the City of Palaces... And has a cloud-kissing monument to one Ochterlony. It is fluted candlestick 250-feet high. This lingam is the only large monument in Calcutta...'[42] An American visitor joking about the Raj raised the possibility of a new day in American–Calcutta relations, breaking the shroud of haughty Western superiority. Twain had recently been in Benares and was well acquainted with the significance of a lingam.

Twain suggested that India gave birth to many features of human culture, but mostly mocked Indian religion. Only the death rituals of the Parsis of Bombay earned some respect. Despite his tempered Western regard for the Raj, Twain evinced relativism, respect and an ability to watch, listen and learn in a very different world. In the decade-and-a-half after his 1890 world tour, Twain wrote among the sharpest criticisms of Western imperialism—European and American—that any American had written. Evidently, his days in India helped him understand man's brutality to man. In the 1901 essay, 'To the Person Sitting in Darkness', Twain observed: 'There must be two Americas: one that sets the captive free, and one that takes a once-captive's new freedom away from him...'[43] He did not disregard their depredations beyond India but reserved his harshest criticism for the Belgian King Leopold for his rape of the Congo in 'King Leopold's Soliloquy' (1905).[44]

William James, a contemporary of Twain's and his informal ally, numbers among the notable armchair visitors to India. He almost surely met Swami Vivekananda in Cambridge in the 1890s and reportedly debated Swami Abhedananda (1866–1939) of the Ramakrishna Mission, in which James's pluralism went to war against

---

[42] Ibid., 1989, p. 517.
[43] Twain, Mark. 1992. *Collected Tales, Sketches, Speeches, & Essays 1891-1910*. NY: Library of America, p. 467.
[44] Ibid., p. 661ff.

the swami's insistence on the unity of all things. In preparation for the lectures he delivered at the University of Edinburgh in 1901 and 1902, which resulted in the famous volume *The Varieties of Religious Experience: A Study in Human Nature* (1902), James studied the Vedantism of Swami Vivekananda and equated Indian and Western mysticism. Like Emerson and Thoreau, his Massachusetts intellectual forebearers, James was open to experiences and texts of many kinds from many cultures. He sought insight and spiritual guidance wherever he could find it and read the Upanishads and other Hindu and Buddhist texts, and listened to Edwin Arnold speak on the Mahabharata. Although James was a Protestant Christian, he wanted to understand the pathways of religious experience that flowed from the subconscious. He also recommended what he called 'relaxation', a kind of precursor of yoga, to his contemporaries. Both critical of imperialism and open to pluralism at the same time, James represented an important strand of American culture.

A new medium that would challenge the printed page and provide a different kind of portrayal of the civilization of India emerged during these years: that of cinema, all silent films at first. By 1912, the Edison company had produced newsreels including 'Hindu Fakir' (1902); 'Scenes in Delhi, India', 'Simla, India', and 'Views of Calcutta, India' (1912). By 1915, a feature film appeared, *The Bombay Buddha*, following upon a version of *Charge by the Bengal Lancers* (1902) from the America Mutoscope and Biograph Company. In *Soul of Buddha* (1918), a tragic tale of a Western lover and an Indian temple dancer, both lovers and their child were murdered by the priest of the temple.[45]

For the American intellectual W.E.B. Du Bois, British rule in India was simply part of a broader problem, one that he had identified as the key problem of the twentieth century: the colour line. Defying the Boston leaders of the Anti-Immigrant League,

---

[45] Jones, Dorothy B. 1955. *The Portrayal of China and India on the American Screen, 1896-1955.* Cambridge: Center for International Studies, MIT, pp. 51–52.

Du Bois questioned the achievements of 'Teutons' or white Anglo-Saxons in mankind's cultural and religious history. Du Bois noted the awakening of Asians and Africans who had long submitted to domination but were now seeking their equal place among the peoples of the Earth. Jim Crow laws, anti-Asian immigrant restrictions and imperialist expansionism prevailed, though it was challenged.

W.E.B. Du Bois

1

Missions

As Europeans began to think more deeply about Asia, they began to visit it, as well, not only to trade, but to pursue missions. Missions—derived from the Latin *missio*, meaning a 'sending forth'—are of two kinds. The first were missions seeking to convert peoples considered heathens to Christianity, the one true faith, as it was believed: initially Catholic Christianity, and, in time, a range of Protestant and post-Protestant creeds. Such missions go back to Christ, who was seen as the first missionary, and his apostles, including Thomas, who some Indian Christians and missionary historians believe brought Christianity to India, and especially Paul, who seeded early Christian churches in the eastern Mediterranean. Since then, for almost 2000 years, Christian preachers spread the word of God, sought to make converts and undertook good works, including teaching and healing. The second type of missions include political or diplomatic efforts by one or more persons sent abroad to conduct negotiations and watch over the interests of states or similar entities.

The great age of Christian expansion coincided with the age of explorations, when missionaries accompanied European soldiers, traders and administrators as they navigated around the globe, not only to India, but also to other parts of Asia, Africa, the Middle East and the Americas. Beginning in the sixteenth century, Catholic missionaries especially the Jesuit and Franciscan orders often accompanied the Portuguese and Spanish as they came ashore in the Americas, Asia and Africa. In the seventeenth and eighteenth centuries, mostly Protestant missions were sent to teach and organize early settlers to indigenous Americans in the North American colonies. As the British came to the fore amongst Europeans in India, they at first kept out missionaries whom they felt would interfere with their commerce and raise the opposition of Hindus and Muslims. Missionaries were confined within Portuguese and French territories or non-conquered areas until the early nineteenth century. Then evangelicals in Great Britain got the ban lifted on missionaries within the British dominion in India, known as the Raj. British and then American Protestant missionaries, as well as some Catholics, entered British India.

Often, the religious and the political intermingled in American expansionist ideology: God has chosen America, it was believed, to spread Christianity, rule and control, and teach democracy as well as market economics to the world.[1] The American missionary effort was invigorated by the Second Great Revival at the end of the eighteenth into the early nineteenth century. American Baptists, alerted to the plight of the world's heathens, contributed funds to the British Baptists at work in Serampore, years before American Baptist missionaries entered the fray.[2] These missions became associated, for many Indians, with the Raj that protected their Christian activists, although the relationship of the Raj and Christian missionaries was not always mutually supportive.

As the nineteenth century progressed, American Protestants came to recognize their minority position in a world full of what they called heathens and sent missions out to distant regions abroad and to indigenous Americans at home. Christian truth was offered to South Asians in the hope that many of them would choose the Christian path to spiritual freedom. It has also been argued by William Hutchison that Americans felt a call to missions abroad. Although America might be the 'City on a Hill', and so serve as an example to others, this metaphor soon supported a drive to assist

---

[1] Hutchison, William R. 1993. *Errand into the World. American Protestant Thought and Foreign Missions.* Chicago: U. of Chicago Press, pp. 40, 129, 131, 370, 38.

[2] Cox, *Imperial Fault Lines*, p. 29.

others in finding the true path. Deriving their beliefs from the Puritans, some nineteenth century Americans blended the mission of Christianity with the mission of America in a pressing forth to conquer the world for Christ and country.

Evangelicals seeking to spread the word, however, met with resistance in Hindu and Muslim India. Stephen Neill, former missionary and chronicler of the Christian efforts in South Asia noted, 'The Christian road in India has always been an uphill road.'[3] Some American and other Western missionaries focused on medical, educational and agricultural work rather than on conversion. By demonstrating to Indians the true path to freedom as they saw it, some remarkable work was done by Americans in India from the early nineteenth century to today. These contributions were made despite the ethnocentricity of most of the givers as well as of many American travellers to India.[4] Positive contributions were made in spite of the inability of some, perhaps many, missionaries to understand much about Indian religion, and in some cases, hostility to it. Although the Christian missions were officially neutral in the colonial period 1813–1947, their work was facilitated by and protected by the Raj.

A reported 1,800 American Protestant missionaries, from many denominations, were in India by 1910. Although those noted below are from the Methodists, Presbyterians, Reformed Church and Unitarians, the efforts of Baptists, Quakers, Congregationalists, American Catholics, Mennonites, touring preachers and those from other denominations, should not be belittled. Selection and brevity demand choice, but it is necessary to outline their work because before 1947, missionaries were the largest group of American residents in India.

The Scudders were one of the most remarkable American families devoted to missionary service, both evangelism and medical care. They showed that many good works could accompany conversions.

---

[3] Neill, Stephen. 1984, 1985. *A History of Christianity in India. I. The Beginnings to 1707. II. 1707–1858*. Cambridge: Cambridge U. Press, p. 309.

[4] Pathak, Sushil Madhava. 1967. *American Missionaries and Hinduism. A Study of Their Contacts from 1813-1910*. Delhi: Munshiram Manoharlal.

In 1819, John Scudder, trained in New York as a medical doctor, heard the call and went with his wife Harriet to Ceylon. Their legacy continued through their sons, grandsons and granddaughters well into the twentieth century. A member of the Reformed Church (then the Dutch Reformed Church), John Scudder was a man of almost fanatical devotion to the Christian cause. He and his wife endured decades of health and environmental difficulties that demanded near superhuman endurance, persistence and strength. He failed to understand that most Hindus were firm in their own beliefs and his admonitory lectures fell on deaf ears.

But his contributions to the medical care of south Indians in the first half of the nineteenth century deserve respect.

Of John and Harriet Scudder's nine sons, seven became missionaries. One son, Henry Martyn Scudder, had a troubled youth mostly in America, returned to India, secured some medical training, and also became fluent in Tamil. He gave his evangelical call to Tamilians in their own language and translated Biblical texts into Tamil. He wrote in the mid-nineteenth century: 'India's bright skies and sunny plains and luxuriant foliage have a charm for me... I love India, I love her soil, I love her people.'[5]

More than many nineteenth-century missionaries, Henry Scudder understood the difficulties involved in the conversion of Indians:

> I only wonder that they do not become more enraged. I think they often show great forbearance. The Christian missionary assails the Hindus at every point: his words are like fire upon their heads, and his thoughts shoot painfully through their bones. Yet they generally carry themselves toward the missionaries with much civility. The better class of them have a great deal of dignity.
>
> They are naturally of an inquisitive frame of mind. I must confess that since I have been here they have taught me a vast deal. They have set all my wits agog many a time. They are a loquacious

---

[5] Scudder, Dorothy Jealous. 1984. *A Thousand Years in Thy Sight. The Story of the Scudder Missionaries of India.* NY: Vantage Press, p. 83.

people, very fond of discussion… An oriental prefers simile to the close logical process. When I deliver the Message, it is assailed. Acute intellects press upon me their objections.

If I were asked to tell… what I thought the mightiest present obstacle to the onward course of the Gospel in India, I should unhesitatingly say "Caste." It is a monster that defies description… Its threads are woven into the very texture of his soul… No one can conceive of its universal power and malignancy until he comes in contact with it. It stands directly in the face of the Gospel which demands brotherly love and unity. The Gospel is unity. Caste is diversity. No two things can be more diametrically antagonistic.[6]

The caste issue notwithstanding, the numerous Scudders continued forward in Henry's wake and the following generations to preach, heal and build. Ida S. Scudder, daughter of John Scudder Jr, was born in Ranipet in 1870, and was left with Scudder's relatives in Chicago when her parents returned to India in 1883. Said to be a handful, she was sent off to the Northfield Seminary in Massachusetts, an institution founded by the renowned evangelist Dwight L. Moody (1837–1899).

Ida Scudder

Although she missed her family, she flourished. In 1890, her mother called her home for help. While assisting her parents, she is said to have learned of the deaths of three young Indian women in dire distress whose husbands would not allow a male physician to attend to them.

Although she had thought that she would live and work in the US, her life plans shifted. She resolved to return to America for medical training that would enable her to return to India and treat

---

[6] Ibid., p. 84.

such women in the future. She did that and more. Of her, more down the road.

Methodists were particularly active in north India. Among them was Bishop James Mills Thoburn (1836–1922), an Ohioan educated at Allegheny College who came to northern India in 1859 and served half a century as an evangelist and educator, rising to become a Missionary Bishop of India and Malaysia in 1888. As a young man of eighteen, teaching in a country school, he 'found Christ', felt the call to 'Go preach my Gospel', and then, learning that young men were urgently needed in India, committed himself to missionary work there. Throughout his account of his life, *My Missionary Apprenticeship*, Thoburn says that God guided his every decision through messages pressing him to pursue his life choices and work.[7]

In 1859, as a member of a Methodist party of nine reaching Calcutta after a four–month sea journey from Boston, Thoburn was appalled that other missionaries drank and partied; he resolved to stick to his own moralistic course of life. In Calcutta, Lucknow and at later postings, he learned that Christian efforts were 'little islands in a restless sea of humanity'.[8] When a small party of Methodist workers were assigned to Oudh and adjacent territories with a population of 17 million Indians, he started to grasp the enormity of their task. Not only was the cast of 'heathens' huge, he soon decided that they were weak in character, untruthful, 'given to all manner of subterfuges, ignorant and superstitious'. When buildings for church activities were erected with Indian workers, he thought they had 'little idea of hard, rugged labor'.[9] To bridge what he saw as a great gulf between advanced Westerners like himself and the native population, he underwent a new kind of education, vastly different from that provided by Allegheny College. He believed that life and work in India required him to be ready for the unexpected and the difficult.

---

[7] Thoburn, J.M. 1884. *My Missionary Apprenticeship*. NY: Phillip & Hart.
[8] Ibid., p. 52.
[9] Ibid., pp. 61–62.

Though preaching was his central commitment, Thoburn also tried to be a teacher of youth. He also preached to European communities in areas where he was assigned, at first reluctantly, but he learned that doing so was essential to reaching out to benighted Hindus and Muslims. Marrying the widow of another missionary, he learned that the education and care of Indian women was important, and the Methodists needed female aid.

As he spent further years in India, Thoburn saw that most converts came from the lower castes: untouchables and tribals. They frequently knew little or nothing of the new faith community they were joining and had decidedly mixed motives for doing so. Often there were non-violent wars within families and marriages over these conversions. Thoburn reported his Christian victories in his writings and downplayed the backsliding. Some of those who became Christians gained better employment and housing, but it was difficult to escape the clutches of the caste system. Many converts learned some English and Thoburn established schools and religious services both in English and in Indian languages. It is impossible to gauge what was gained and lost through these conversions and the limited but intense activity of missionaries.

Some Western education was provided in schools and, later, colleges that Thoburn and his colleagues founded amid their efforts at conversion. Thoburn's condescension towards Indian religions also must have had some impact on Indians he met. Although he harshly criticized Hinduism, he also followed Hindu pilgrims deep and high into the mountains and observed how they learned and taught their own religion so that he might be more effective.

His wife died within a few years, just after giving birth to a son, and Thoburn went home on furlough in 1863 in the midst of the American Civil War. He brought with him a young Hindu man, Harkua, to help care for his infant son. Most Americans had never seen an Asian Indian, and were befuddled by a man who was dark-skinned, but not African American. One stranger closely

examined Harkua, and declared, 'Well, he ain't a n****r anyhow.'[10]
Harkua heard many cruel and ignorant remarks about India, and
Thoburn said that in private, Harkua '...stoutly denied that India
was an inferior country and ... inclined to maintain... that there
were more bad people in America than India'.[11] Although Thoburn
was determinedly Eurocentric in his outlook, he respected Harkua's
patriotic outlook. Seeing widespread drunkenness and violence,
Harkua thought America was more heathen than India.

Returning to India, Thoburn was moved from one post to another,
rising rapidly in the Methodist missionary hierarchy. From a station
up in the lower Himalayas, he was sent to Moradabad, Lucknow and
Calcutta. Each posting required him to deal with different problems
and ethnic mixes. As a man of great energy, administrative talent and
adaptability, he coped with each challenge, supervising baptisms and
conversions, the building of schools, churches and parsonages, and
the acquisition of new languages.

Drawing upon his long experience, Thoburn wrote a handbook
in 1906 for prospective missionaries titled, *The Christian Conquest
of India*, which surveyed India's peoples, religions, history and
problems. Although he enumerated a few 'drawbacks' of the Raj,
he wrote, 'The verdict of the missionaries is that British control of
India is a marvellous example of efficiency, wisdom, progressiveness
and fairness to a subject race.'[12] When it came to the Indian people,
Thoburn was blunt:

> The Indians, while existing on scanty sustenance, have remarkable
> powers of endurance, but in physical strength and nervous energy
> one American is equal to about six of them... One element seems to
> be strangely wanting the mental equipment of the Indian people:
> they invent nothing... India may be said to be a rich country,
> inhabited by a very poor people.[13]

---

[10] Thoburn, 1884, p. 105.
[11] Ibid., p. 107.
[12] Thoburn, J.M. 1906. *The Christian Conquest of India*. NY: Eaton & Mains, p. 50.
[13] Ibid., pp. 50, 64–65, 70.

The faults for Indian deficiencies lay, Thoburn thought, in their religions, social customs and the caste system. Child marriage was a particular problem, and he borrowed the words of an American military gentleman in Calcutta to describe the caste system saying, it was 'a social ladder on which every man kisses the feet of the man above him, and kicks the face of the man below him'.[14] The evils of caste were compounded by the native religions. Of Islam he wrote that it was founded by a 'false prophet', and was 'the worst form of monotheism which has ever existed'.[15]

Thoburn found few saving graces in Islam and Buddhism, but virtually none in Hinduism. The notion that 'God is everywhere and everything,' he wrote, was one of its 'most pernicious beliefs, because it destroys all freedom and moral responsibility.'[16] Of the avatars of Vishnu, Krishna was the most 'debasing' and led him to his summary judgment:

Hinduism has robbed man of a personal God, and defaced the distinction between right and wrong. It has obliterated freedom of will through the fatalism that results from transmigration. The blighting effects of the caste system, the degradation and religious prostitution of womanhood, the corruption of the priesthood, the lust and immorality of the gods and goddesses, and its other vices, stamp Hinduism as one of the foulest, if not the foulest religion that the world has seen.[17]

Given the shortcomings of the people and the evils of their religions, the salvation of India could only come through continued British rule and increasing activity by Christian missionaries, Thoburn believed.

---

[14] Ibid., p. 79.

[15] Ibid., pp. 105, 106; Note: The author is merely reproducing the words of Thoburn in the manner that they were published and neither the author nor the publisher subscribes to or is adopting these words.

[16] Ibid., p. 112.

[17] Ibid., p. 118. The author is merely reproducing/quoting/reporting the words of Thoburn in the manner that they were published and neither the author nor the publisher subscribes to or is adopting these words.

Otherwise, India was damned. But he still said he had come to love India more than the homeland he had left behind.

Before about 1870, Methodists did not send single women to the field and married women were expected to play only a supporting role to their husbands. Thoburn was among the Methodist pioneers discovering that women missionaries were needed, indeed essential, to their efforts. After meeting with Thoburn on his furlough in the early 1860s, his own sister, Isabella, became one of the first Methodist women missionaries. In 1869, when the church formed a women's missionary arm, Isabella embarked for India in 1869, accompanied by another single missionary woman, Clara Swain, a trained medical doctor.

Women missionaries were one component of a general advance of women into roles previously reserved for men. That advance was marked publicly as the 1848 Seneca Falls convention approved a declaration of independence for women, calling for the vote, equal property rights, entry to all professions, and, later, equal pay for equal work. Thoburn wrote in his 1903 biography of his sister:

> The remarkable advent of Christian women into the great mission fields of the world some thirty or forty years ago, formed a part of a wider movement which affected the position of intelligent womanhood throughout the English-speaking world, and which to a less degree is making itself felt among all civilized nations at the present day... On every side we today see women employed in positions from which all women were rigidly excluded fifty years ago... a time had come when the laborers abroad could not afford to decline the help of lady missionaries who seemed to be prompted by the same motives, and to be called by the same Holy Spirit as their brethren... (I)t began to be perceived that some parts of the work in mission fields could only be performed properly by women.[18]

---

[18] Thoburn. *Life of Isabella Thoburn*, pp. 36–39.

Isabella Thoburn's companion Clara Swain, from Castile, New York, taught in a school for some years in her twenties, and aspired to be a 'Christian profession'. After training at the Castile Sanatorium and the Woman's Medical College of Pennsylvania, she and the Methodist Women's Missionary Society agreed to her assignment in Bareilly, northern India.

Isabella Thoburn

Before 1870, several missionary wives of Methodist missionaries worked as 'lay physicians', medical workers without medical school training, because Indian women refused care from male physicians. When traditional Indian medical help did not help, some women were willing to entertain Western treatments. A few American female lay physicians tried to train Indian girls in rudimentary medical work, and some Methodist missionaries, or their wives, wrote home asking that female doctors be sent. Not many were available; few American women were being admitted to medical schools, and fewer wanted to practice in India.

Soon engulfed with women patients, Dr Swain sought to open a hospital. Seeking a site, she and fellow missionaries journeyed to visit the Nawab of Rampur, who gave them a handsome gift of a property adjacent to their mission in Bareilly. Dr Swain gave basic medical education to young Indian Christian women who became 'fourth-grade doctors'. One missionary, Annie Ryder Gracey, wrote that an Indian told her, 'We need lady physicians very much… we did not know where to look for them, as our women are uneducated… Light has again dawned upon us from America.'[19] Medical care was not divorced from evangelism; dispensary cards in multiple Indian languages carried Bible verses. For missionaries and their home societies, Christ was the Great Healer, and the Great

[19] Gracey, (Mrs.) J.T. 1881. *Medical Work of the Woman's Foreign Missionary Society*. Methodist Episcopal Church. Dansville, NY: A.O. Bunnell, p. 43.

Teacher, too. The hope was that new orphanages, boarding schools, colleges, medical clinics and medical training facilities might enable missionaries to press their religious message. Some Indians became Christians; many did not. These boarding schools and orphanages were an integral part of the missionary effort.

Isabella Thoburn had taught at several institutions before going to India, where it was assumed that education would be her work. In 1870, she was sent to Lucknow, where her older brother was based. Although he moved on to Calcutta, she remained in Lucknow for the three decades of her service. Education was her focus, though evangelism was a key part—'teaching and preaching', she said. She founded a school for girls, and the church bought a large, handsome property in Lal Bagh where they erected additional school buildings and a hostel for the girls. Thanks to Thoburn's generosity and hospitality, it became a centre of Methodist life in northern India. Many of the girls were poor converts, aged six to twenty, but she demanded that all attendees pay minimal fees. Over the years the school became a college—the first women's Christian college in India. But Isabella Thoburn, principal when not on furlough for medical reasons, opened these institutions to those of every community, as Christian duty demanded.

When home in the US for health reasons between 1886 and 1890, Ms Thoburn was instrumental in establishing the role of a deaconess within the Methodist church. She worked in Chicago and Cincinnati, setting up headquarters for Methodist units that did medical and social work. On her final trip back to the United States in 1899, she was accompanied by one of her star pupils, Lilavati Singh, who spoke before Methodist audiences to demonstrate the effect of their educational mission in India. Singh was likely the first Indian woman many had seen in the United States—although she had been preceded by Pandita Ramabai in the 1880s. Bishop Thoburn said her command of English astounded Methodist preachers, and her knowledge of English literature surpassed that of many in the audience.[20]

---

[20] Thoburn. *Life of Isabella Thoburn*, p. 308ff.

Evaluators of the Thoburns' Christian crusade in India face a dilemma: on the one hand, the Thoburn siblings were generous and conscientious, evinced love for India and respect for the kindness of Indians, and improved the lives of their charges; on the other hand, they disliked and even hated the two major religions of India, Hinduism and Islam, and denigrated what they perceived to be characteristics of Indians and Indian society. Isabella Thoburn abhorred 'the malaria of heathenism'[21] and the 'spiritual degradation' she found in India, featuring the evils of caste, child marriage, polygamy and ignorance of the path to enlightenment, while Christianity, she felt, would give Indian women freedom for the first time. Looking back, the complex impact on India of the work of such Christians evangelists, whose self-righteous indignation and Eurocentrism were frequently displayed, is hard to judge for those with secular liberal values, whether Western or Indian. Should they be labelled 'cultural imperialists'? Should we dismiss their efforts to bring education as well as medical care to those from the lower strata of Indian society?

From the 1830s, American Presbyterians also established a strong presence in northern India (the Punjab and the United Provinces) with mission stations in Ludhiana in Punjab and in Lahore and then elsewhere. Charles W. Forman (1821–1894) from Kentucky, who attended Princeton Theological Seminary, was among the early Presbyterian missionaries to India. In Lahore, he founded a school that became the Lahore Mission College. His main object, Forman made clear, was trying to convert Indians, and the broader educational mission was subsidiary.[22] Forman suffered ill health and on several occasions returned to the United States, and the college was closed in 1869 following cholera epidemics in the Punjab. Forman reopened the college in 1886 and in 1888 turned over the principal's chair to J.C.R. Ewing (1854–1925), who for three decades, up to 1918, provided strong leadership. From a few dozen pupils in the

---

[21] Ibid., p. 129.
[22] Speer, Robert Elliott. 1928. *Sir James Ewing. 43 Years a Missionary in India*. NY: Fleming H. Revell, p. 65ff.

1880s, the school grew into the renowned Forman Christian or F.C. College, enrolling thousands in the twentieth century. Although a Christian college, with a daily one-hour religious class, it provided a largely secular education to many non-Christians and was known as one of India's finest colleges. Forman became one of the most important figures in the educational institutions of Punjab, sitting on every committee of consequence. Ewing also served a central role.

Historian John C.B. Webster has dissected the staffing, working and impact of many of these Presbyterian missions in north India, which conveyed what he calls the 'Princeton Theology':

> [T] his theology was derived from an infallible scripture...
> [I]t allowed only for one–way interaction. The missionaries who
> came to India as bearers of this truth had everything to teach
> and nothing of importance to learn; the Indians, as proponents
> of human systems, were expected only to accept the missionaries'
> truth with repentance...thanksgiving—or reject it to their
> eternal peril.[23]

These fiercely held beliefs did not accomplish the 'Christianization' of India, as only a very modest number were converted through the third quarter of the nineteenth century. The missionaries typically 'converted' or baptized groups of lower-caste and 'untouchable' Indians whose understanding of their new faith was questionable. There were, through it all, several notable high caste Presbyterian converts, the best-known being Kali Charan Chatterji,[24] who would play an important role in the Christian community not only in north India but worldwide.

Webster stressed that Indian converts had been neglected by mission historians. They were crucial in making Christianity an Indian religion, though hard for many Indians to accept. Close ties among Christian missionaries and Raj officials allowed Indians

---

[23] Webster, John C B. 1976. *The Christian Community and Change in 19th century North India*. Delhi: Macmillan, p. 34.
[24] Ibid., p. 48ff.

proud of their own faiths to portray Christianity as an alien religion that the rulers were imposing upon Indians. Only Indian Christians and the gradual formation of Indian churches largely independent of missionary control were palatable to many proud Indians. This independence was difficult so long as the purse strings were held by foreign missionary societies.

Missionaries and Indian converts founded schools, colleges, medical facilities and provided famine relief to demonstrate Christian values in action. The Presbyterians, particularly in Punjab, led in founding educational institutions, as did the Methodists in the United Provinces. Indian government and private schools caught up, but Christian facilities and programmes still had a wide influence. As the nineteenth century closed, missionaries had to reconsider the Princeton Theology and their intolerance of Indian faiths in order to maintain credibility. As Indian nationalism rose in the last quarter of the century, missionaries had to identify which aspects of Indian self-determination they could support.

For American missionaries, the benevolent British Raj was a necessary umbrella protecting their proselytizing. Even when slow conversion rates channelled more missionary energies into education and medical work, most missionaries maintained strong faith in Christianity and the Raj. They moderated their views of Hinduism as they came to understand it beyond platitudinous stereotypes. Some found bhakti, or devotion, as a path to realizing the divine that was parallel to their own. They began to talk of Jesus Christ as an avatar, differing from Hindu avatars, but as a God amid humanity with a special mission.

As the American economic penetration of India progressed, so did the missionary thrust. Like their nineteenth-century predecessors, ardent Christians in the early twentieth century sought to bring their message, generally an evangelical Protestant one, to inhabitants of other lands whom they considered heathens. In the last quarter of the nineteenth century, the preacher Dwight Moody inspired many young people to help those he viewed as an unenlightened folk abroad. Brought into the evangelical movement as a young man by Moody, John R. Mott (1865–1955) worked for the YMCA, which is an effort to unite all Christians in 'mind, body and spirit', and it spread widely in the British Empire. By the later nineteenth century, it was aiding young men and women in many parts of India, employing both American and British 'secretaries', who were organized by the Secretary for India, the American, Agnes Hill, who served from 1895–1906. By 1911, eleven American and twenty British secretaries were at work in India.[25]

Both Mott and Sherwood Eddy, also converted by Moody, were stalwarts of the evangelical inter-denominational movement, their aspirations captured in Mott's 1900 book, *The Evangelization of the World in this Generation*. Both lived to see Protestant churches amalgamated into the Church of south India, which was encouraged by the Edinburgh World Missionary Conference of 1910.[26]

Eddy came from a well-to-do family in Leavenworth, Kansas, attended Yale, and felt called to missionary work at the Northfield Student Conference in the 1880s. He had planned to go to China, but Mott convinced him to go to India as a lay evangelist, and secretary for students of the YMCA there. Although his main work was touring the country courting students, he undertook many different responsibilities during a decade-and-a-half working in south India. He learned Tamil, manned a missionary station at Batlagundu in the Madurai mission and worked at developing schools and famine relief in the 1890s. Considering what might be the best strategy for Christianizing India, he decided that the best course would be to train Indian Christian leaders who would in turn bring their countrymen to Christ. Like Bishop Thoburn and other earlier missionaries, however, he learned that converting those who had their own firmly held Hindu or Muslim beliefs and practices was no mean feat.

Although Eddy thought Indians 'more deeply religious than the Anglo-Saxons of North America', he also wrote that, 'the mass were

---

[25] Boyd, Nancy. 1986. *Emissaries. The Overseas Work of the American YWCA 1895–1970*. NY: Woman's Press, p. 33ff.
[26] Eddy, Sherwood. 1955. *Eighty Adventurous Years. An Autobiography*. NY: Harper, 1955, pp. 56–57.

sunk in illiteracy, idolatry, devil worship'.[27] Indians might be more spiritual than Westerners, but to be saved they needed to share his Christian beliefs and give up their own. Later in life, Eddy became an outspoken Christian socialist, but never gave up the liberal, but simple set of Christian beliefs that he and many other missionaries shared. Yet Eddy, like some of his missionary brethren, found in Mahatma Gandhi, a leader in the spiritualization and moral reformation of mankind and came to praise him above all other men—even though Gandhi was not a Christian.

Mott came from a more modest background and had to overcome his parents' desire that he enter the family lumber business. Moody and leaders of the YMCA saw a young man of drive and talent who might be a force in their efforts and did not let him get away. He was recruited to be one of two general secretaries of the YMCA for student organizing and recruitment when he was still a student at Cornell University. After weighing several choices before him, he agreed to join the YMCA for one year. He stayed for more than three decades becoming its general secretary and by his drive, organizing ability and determination, built the movement worldwide. His worldwide tours took him to India several times.

Mott and his colleagues aimed to unite Protestants, especially students, into a grand evangelizing effort. Robert Speer (1867–1925), head of the Presbyterian Mission Board, frequently joined him, as did Eddy. Once unchained from specific India assignments, Eddy and Mott went to China and found initial successes in gaining converts. Eddy wrote that it was easier to reach Chinese students with their Christian message than India's high-caste Hindus who impassively listened to pleas to stand up for Christ. With Eddy, Mott crossed the globe indefatigably, despite the difficulties of travel, helping to create the Worlds' Student Christian Federation to bring together young Christians across the globe. Later in life, he received the Nobel Peace Prize.

India became the adopted homeland of three other notable missionaries—William James Wanless (1865–1933), Ida S. Scudder (1870–1960) and Samuel ('Sam') Higginbottom

---

[27] Ibid., p. 32.

(1874–1958)—who worked with gritty determination to build, respectively, the Miraj medical complex and medical school, the Vellore Medical College and hospital and the Allahabad Agricultural Institute. The three brought Western medicine and agricultural science, benefitting many Indians, but it is uncertain whether they learned much about Indian culture and religion. Though their affection for individual Indians, especially converts, was not in doubt, they denigrated Hinduism and other Indian religions, adhering to a Christian ideology that hampered their efforts to relate to Indian outlooks.

Ida S. Scudder was an extraordinary doctor and institution builder. Her family had been missionaries in India for generations, but she hesitated for years before becoming a missionary doctor. She studied medicine at the Women's Medical College of Pennsylvania and at Cornell University Medical College in New York. While delivering a baby in 1898, she wrote:

> It was a long hard labor and I felt sorry for the poor little thing. The husband weep and wrang his hands in distress but we produced a fine baby for them in the end...[W]e certainly are learning lots...
>
> Oh! But the poverty is awful and often tears come into my eyes as I go from place to place and see the wretchedness of it all.[28]

Coming into her own as a doctor-in-training and a surgeon, Scudder worked hard and passed her final exams in 1899. Eyes on the future, she raised funds for a large hospital in Vellore in south India, where the Scudders had been missionaries and doctors for many years. She helped open the Mary Taber Schell Hospital in 1902. Shortly after her return to Vellore, her father died, but supported by her mother, Ida Scudder blossomed as an innovator in the delivery of medical services to rural Indians, and an institution-builder for Indian women physicians.

Once established in her own medical work, Scudder saw that India needed Indian women doctors. She established a nurses training

---

[28] Scudder Papers, F.46, Family Correspondence.

programme, and then a medical school for women, raising money and acquiring the land to do so. She raised more money for the women's facility from various denominations in the United States in 1907 and 1914 and received funding from the Madras government. In 1918, she opened a medical school, not a medical college, giving a lower degree, because it did not have all the required facilities. At the same time, she and other Scudder family members expanded the Vellore hospital into one of the foremost medical facilities on the subcontinent. Scudder also acquired one of the first automobiles in India, and starting around 1915, drove along rutted routes to set up roadside clinics. An earnest Christian who found intense satisfaction in her work and in close friendships, her remarkably long and fruitful career spanned the 1890s to the 1950s.

Sam Higginbottom was another young man touched by Dwight Moody in Great Britain and the United States. Born in Manchester, England, in 1874, he left school at age twelve and worked as a carriage driver and on his family's farms. He followed an older brother who had gone to the US and attended Moody's Mount Hermon School. Moody, he said, made each student feel 'wanted'.[29]

Higginbottom made it through Mount Hermon, two years at Amherst College, and then Princeton. Along the way he made contacts with officials of the YMCA, and with Robert Speer, head of the mission board of the Presbyterian Church, and Henry Forman, a Presbyterian missionary forced to leave India by family problems. Forman recruited Higginbottom to take his place for two years at Etah, India, a rural municipality in the United Provinces, and Speer arranged it so that the young man could go out without having attended seminary.

Although assigned originally to Etah, Higginbottom was redirected to Allahabad to teach economics and other subjects in a Christian college. He and his new bride, Ethelind Cody, took charge of a student hostel, teaching students to do chores and improve their

---

[29] Higginbottom, Sam. 1949. *Sam Higginbottom: Farmer*. An Autobiography. NY: Charles Scribner's; Hess, Gary R. 1971. *American Encounters India 1941-1947*. Baltimore: Johns Hopkins Press.

diet and general health. Through interactions with Indian farmers during field trips, Higginbottom saw that Indian agriculture was stalled: not only was agriculture less productive than in the West, but administrators, farmers and missionaries agreed that nothing could be done. Higginbottom disagreed.

On home leave in 1909, and recently married, Higginbottom threw caution to the wind and returned to college to learn all he could about agriculture. In two years, he gained an agriculture degree, raised money and returned to the fray. Surmounting many practical difficulties—beginning with dry and rutted land and insufficient funds—he established the Allahabad Agricultural Institute (AAI). He insisted on a hands-on approach: students learned the practical skills of farmers, the science of agriculture and the skills of raising livestock. Constant watch was necessary, he learned, to prod his students and farmer pupils to make crucial improvements. As his innovations produced greater yields in the fields and from the cows and other animals, visitors came from far and wide. He advised several of princes of Indian states and was hired on a part-time basis by the princely state of Gwalior. There he succeeded in boosting agricultural production until limited by what he believed was Brahmin resistance. Though his achievements were widely recognized, he believed that he could have had more influence if officials and missionaries had been more cooperative. The AAI gradually became a model for improving Indian agriculture.

Higginbottom's autobiography makes clear he had to overcome large obstacles right into the 1920s when he was falsely accused of mishandling funds. He was also called out for not emphasizing evangelism. Both Higginbottom and his wife were said to be hard driving, occasionally difficult, bosses. Colleagues said this exacerbated their problems.[30] The AAI was then detached from the North Indian Presbyterian Mission and placed under the control of the Presbyterian Foreign Mission Society at home. This slowed but did not stop Higginbottom. He continued for two more decades to

---

[30] Hess, Gary R. 1971. *American Encounters India 1941-1947*. Baltimore: Johns Hopkins Press, p. 44.

press his work and his vision of improving rural life on officials, the Congress party and anyone with the power to help.

Higginbottom was one of the first American missionaries to make a firm connection with Gandhi—possibly Gandhi's first good American friend. Higginbottom's 1916 speech at Benares, in northeastern India, caught the attention of Gandhi, recently returned from South Africa. The only missionary present at the inauguration ceremonies of the Benares Hindu University, Higginbottom argued that 'agricultural improvement through the education of the ryot was fundamental to economic progress'. Gandhi's spirited and positive response to Higginbottom's criticism of rich maharajas drove the assembled princes and other rich Indians to walk out of the future Mahatma's speech. But it led to a lifelong friendship. Gandhi continued to ask Higginbottom and the AAI for advice on cattle breeding and agriculture for forty years. Higginbottom gave Gandhi, sceptical of dehumanizing machinery that subtracted human beings from the equation of production, a positive view of the possibilities of American technology. Gandhi also appreciated Higginbottom's condescension-free advice.[31]

Out of his experience, Higginbottom summed up 'the mystery of a subcontinent':

If I were asked to put into one word the clue to the bewildering riddle I should say that the inner meaning of it is pride—a deep clinging to superiorities of race and caste and wealth and religion, with consequent forcing of inferiority on others, and bitter resentment when pride is wounded, as a way of life, even justified pride is found to be inadequate. The real and only serious cause of the resentment felt by Indian against the British is the assumption, largely instinctive, of superiority by the white race.[32]

Mincing no words, Higginbottom called out the upper castes of India, the British rulers and racist Americans. He had no doubt, that if free India followed some of his practical prescriptions learned over

[31] Ibid., p. 37.
[32] Higginbottom 1949, p. 191.

forty years as a student of agriculture, India would rise among the modern nations:

> The root cause of India's continuing poverty and low standard of living is her failure to use adequately the natural advantages and resources with which she is so richly endowed. Were she fully to use her soil, her water for irrigation and homes, her climate, her village wastes, her minerals and forests and above all, her people, her standard of living could be raised to compare favourably with any modern nation.[33]

Higginbottom initially struggled to keep the foreign staff he recruited. They found him too autocratic. But he shifted gears as he understood how he was creating difficulties for himself and the AAI.[34] Among the staff members who stayed for decades, was the engineer Mason Vaugh (1894–1978) who helped develop the 'Shabash plow', which became the standard model for north India.[35] The AAI was a pioneer in extension work and other agricultural projects in India over the succeeding decades. Its work connected Higginbottom and his institution to important players: William and Charlotte Wiser, Leonard and Dorothy Straight Elmhirst, and to John D. Rockefeller, Jr, and the Ford Foundation.[36]

In recent decades, the AAI has deteriorated, but Higginbottom deserves credit for triggering agricultural improvement in India. He was relentless in advocating the use of trenching (the use of waste to enrich soil) and improving livestock, seeds and farm implements. He convinced all concerned that India could feed itself, and that farmers could have better, more productive lives. He was a farmer-educator and was not ashamed to call himself one.

Among those who helped Higginbottom, especially through the first years in Allahabad, was Arthur Ewing (1864–1912), principal of

---

[33] Ibid., pp. 206–07.
[34] Hess, Gary R. 1971. *American Encounters India 1941-1947*. Baltimore: Johns Hopkins Press, p. 53.
[35] Ibid., p. 101.
[36] Ibid., p. 37ff.

Allahabad Christian College, the brother of James Ewing, principal
of Lahore, later Forman Christian College. These brothers aimed
to maintain educational standards for their colleges through several
decades of the British Raj. Of the two, James Ewing served much
longer and rose to more important posts. Even while continuing as
principal of Forman Christian College, James Ewing became vice-
chancellor of the Punjab University from 1910 to 1917. He was the
only American to become the vice-chancellor of an Indian university
during the Raj. Like Charles Forman, he made clear that his primary
objective was to convert young people to Christ; secular education
was helpful, but a secondary concern.[37]

Like Mott and Eddy, James Ewing worked for interdenominational
cooperation, in India and overseas. Different denominations, he thought,
should all call themselves 'evangelicals' and work together for a Protestant
world. The Presbyterian missions in India also had to face a concern that
troubled every foreign missionary enterprise: Indianization and creation
of an autonomous or independent Indian church. They wrestled with
this issue and related ones for decades. Foreign missionaries had to
decide to which church they belonged: the one at home or the one they
had taken the initiative in creating in India. There were complicated
issues of control and finances. Another issue raised by the Hunter
Commission on Education (1882), was the so-called 'conscience
clause'. Should attendance at Bible class and other religious functions
be compulsory at educational institutions founded by foreign missions?
Or could those of other faiths opt out? Ewing and many missionaries
saw Christian teaching as an integral part of the educational mission of
Forman Christian College and other church-run institutions.[38]

Another troubling trend for him was the rise of Indian
nationalism. A firm believer in the virtues and achievements of
the Raj, James Ewing saw radical nationalists as shortsighted and
dangerous. He worked closely at Forman Christian College with
a conservative nationalist, Kali Charan Chatterjee, and believed
moderate nationalism would not endanger missionaries. He lamented

---

[37] Speer 1928.
[38] Ibid., p. 195ff.

British hostility towards Americans during the initial years of the First World War. Why weren't Americans joining the fight, he asked, against the evil Central Powers?

In addition to the many schools and colleges they founded for Indians, missionaries started and supported two schools for their own children. The Woodstock School, in the mountains in Mussoorie in northeastern India, had a unique setting that looks out and up at Himalayan peaks and down to the plains. It was started in 1854 by British officers and American missionaries as the Protestant Girls School and later expanded. The other school to educate missionary children, Kodaikanal School, started in 1901 in a south Indian hill station. Sherwood Eddy's mother came out of retirement to serve as its first principal, raised funds to start the school and was instrumental in purchasing the Highclerc Hotel property where the school has since been based. From thirteen pupils, it has grown into the Kodaikanal International School, K–12, with alumni across the globe.

Today's thriving Vellore Medical College and Hospital, established in the early nineteenth century and funded by American and Indian (and some other) Christians, received in the years following the First World War new support from the Rockefeller Foundation. The first Rockefeller grant to Vellore, for one million dollars, was from the Laura Spellman Rockefeller Fund and went to the Jubilee Fund for 'Seven Women's Christian Colleges of the Orient': Isabella Thoburn College, Lucknow; Madras Women's Christian College; Christian Woman's Medical College, Ludhiana; and Kanigiri Boy's School. The Rockefeller grant to the women's colleges came with a condition: they had to raise $20,00,000 themselves; Ida Scudder led the drive and met the match. When John D. Rockefeller, Jr, called 'Junior', had taken over the Rockefeller Foundation in 1913, the Christian orientation of these schools was accepted;[39] by 1926, however, the Foundation encouraged Christian-only schools to broaden their recruiting.

---

[39] Woman's American Baptist Foreign Mission Society 1919–1929, Jubilee Fund, Folders 84–88, Box 7, Series 3, Lucy S. Rockefeller Collection, Rockefeller Archives.

2

Business
Trade and the Tatas

In 1784, having won independence from Britain, Americans began a growing trade with Asia, symbolized by dispatch of the refurbished privateer, the 'Empress of China' to the Chinese port of Canton. Throughout India's colonial period—that is, up to the end of the British Raj in 1947—the British mediated, sometimes restricted, American contacts and trade. During the Napoleonic wars (1803–1815), when the East India Company's business was gravely damaged, the US trade in imported textiles from India flourished, but after about 1820, it faded to insignificance until the period of the Civil War. Besides finished textiles, India supplied American traders with raw cotton, linseed oil, indigo and hides, as well as animals unknown in the US, including elephants. Although some British voices wanted to restrict American trade with India, others argued that it benefited all parties. Before long, the British became aware that a formidable competitor had arrived, and that American industry and methods rivalled their own and they were impressed by the American development of weapons with interchangeable parts.

Merchants from Salem and Boston, along with New York, Providence and Philadelphia, paid in silver for Indian goods. A few Americans settled briefly in Calcutta, Bombay and Madras, and a number of them contributed to the earliest American interest in and understanding of India. The Jay Treaty of 1794 complicated matters for American traders. It stipulated that goods from India had to be carried directly back to the US. However, in practice, such restrictions were largely ignored. Americans repatriated private gains of East India Company servants, carried trade along India's coasts and sold goods from India widely. The Isle de France (Mauritius) was a contact point for American traders who frequently acquired Indian goods there rather than docking in India proper.[1]

American merchant mariners had to cope with wars, British control of Indian markets and changing US administrations, which sometimes favoured overseas trade, and sometimes did not. American consuls in several cities, Bombay and Calcutta principally, were appointed irregularly from 1792 but were generally ineffectual.[2] Susan S. Bean tells how in the late eighteenth and very early nineteenth century, the India trade constituted about 5 per cent of America's foreign trade.[3] American trade with India was reportedly larger than that with China.[4] After the War of 1812, American trade with India fell, then revived in the 1840s and 1850s, but never again constituted a significant percentage of American overseas trade until the twentieth century.[5]

Among the American merchant sailors reaching India in the late eighteenth century, Amasa Delano (1763–1823) left a memoir describing Calcutta as two cities: the British 'city of palaces' and the crowded native areas. He wrote:

> The manner in which this town is built, furnishes a strong
> contrast between the English and the natives. The English dwell
> in houses which are extremely elegant, and resemble palaces...
> The apartments are spacious... Porticoes are made; flights of steps
> are before the houses; and colonnades give them a magnificent

---

[1] Gautam, Vinayshil. 1972. *Aspects of Indian Society and Economy*. Delhi: Motilal Baransidass, p. 143ff.

[2] Bhagat, G. 1970. *Americans in India 1784-1860*. NY: NYU Press, p. 85ff.

[3] Bean, Susan S. 2001. *Yankee India. American Commercial and Cultural Encounters with India in the Age of Sail 1784-1860*. Salem, MA: Peabody Essex Museum.

[4] Bhagat 1970, pp. 73–74.

[5] Islam, Sirajul. June 1994. 'The Cargo and Culture of the New Englanders' Voyages to Calcutta 1785-c. 1850,' V. 39, No. 1. *Journal of the Asiatic Society of Bangladesh*. Dhaka.

appearance. The part of the town, where the natives live, is directly the reverse of this [the British town]. The streets are narrow and crooked; the houses low, small, and ill contrived; they have commonly but one story; and many are built of bamboo, and covered with thatch.[6]

Among the salient themes in the early nineteenth century contacts with India was that of Christians confronting Hinduism. In extracts provided by Susan Bean, Rogers, a young trader, reacted enthusiastically to the colour and variety of Indian street life and proved a careful, amateur ethnographer of Bombay's many communities. Although antagonistic to the Hindu religion, he presents a nicely detailed word-picture of Elephanta Island (off Bombay), which he made a special effort to visit. Rogers was also extremely critical of the British, though he knew he needed their cooperation for trading.

Bean also presents extracts from the journal of Edwin Blood, a young man from Newburyport, who visited Calcutta as secretary to a supercargo in the 1850s. Blood provides a touching passage on the friendship of a *sircar*, or clerk, for a young American,

Such kindness as that of the old sircar for me is not soon forgotten: it sinks deep into the heart. And now, among the pleasantest recollections I have of my sojourn in the Far East is that, this poor old clerk, Hindoo [sic] and heathen that he was, of a different religion and race—[and I of] a race that despise and ill treat his countrymen, befriended me in a manner that would do infinite credit to the most exemplary professor of the Christian Faith![7]

Blood's tender and insightful tribute is an example of the close relationships between Americans and Indians that developed in

---

[6] Seagraves, Eleanor Roosevelt, ed. 1994. *Delano's Voyages of Commerce and Discovery. Amasa Delano in China, the Pacific Islands, Australia, and South America, 1789-1807*, pp. 239–40.
[7] Bean 2001, p. 245.

this period between mariners and their Indian agents.[8] With the Industrial Revolution, first in Great Britain and then in America in the first half of the nineteenth century, patterns of trade between Western countries and India shifted. The British began exporting cotton goods to India, and imports of Indian piece goods dropped precipitously. Needing Indian goods for export, the British began the export of Indian opium to China. Indigo was also an important export, though a mid-century rebellion of Indian growers hampered it. These crops were grown by Indian peasants, working under British planters to produce indigo, while opium was a government monopoly.

The India the Europeans entered in the sixteenth and seventeenth centuries had a thriving internal economy as well as considerable coastal and external trade. At first, Europeans paid in part with their own precious metals for Indian textiles and other goods, since the Indians, like the Chinese, did not need European products. With the break up of the Mughal Empire in the eighteenth century and as Europeans muscled further into internal and external trade, that pattern of exchange changed. With continuing conquests and the defeat of colonial rivals, especially the French, the British were better positioned to enter into trade with India.

During this period—the later eighteenth into the nineteenth century—the Industrial Revolution transformed first the textile, then the iron, coal and steel industries. Through the first half of the nineteenth century, transportation was shaped anew. Steam engines for industry and then transport on land and sea made Britain an economic powerhouse, for several decades the first among the Western powers. These developments impacted the Indian economy, as the British demand for Indian textiles declined and the demand for raw cotton rose. India became an importer of finished textiles instead of a major exporter. In addition, using Indian labour, the British constructed a system of Indian railroads which benefited their business interests while providing Indian travellers with a cheap means of transport.

---

[8] Bhagat 1970, pp. 63, 71.

Economic historians have outlined the great difficulties of developing large-scale industries in India.[9] As jute mills were built from the later part of the nineteenth century they were generally British-owned and run. By the 1880s, the British-owned jute industry was rivalling its progenitor in Dundee, Scotland; soon, Americans imported more jute products from India than from Great Britain.

Starting in the 1850s, Indians themselves began to build cotton mills, although they were not highly competitive at first. Initially, almost all the mills were in the Bombay area, built by entrepreneurs from diverse communities, and the mills soon spread to Ahmedabad and beyond. Some were built by Parsis, a small, well-educated and cosmopolitan minority community of Zoroastrians centred in the Bombay Presidency, who had emigrated from Persia centuries earlier and had long been involved in trade in western India. One family among them had been priests, but by the mid-nineteenth century, one of their number, Nusserwanji Tata (1822–1886), entered the general trading business and moved to Bombay. He formed partnerships that benefited briefly from the boom in cotton exports during the American Civil War. His son, Jamsetji (1839–1904), did their work in Hong Kong and Shanghai, and was in Britain when the sudden decline of the cotton market rocked the business. After four years in Britain broadening his outlook, having learned a lesson of caution in international business, Jamsetji helped his family recover and prosper in future enterprises.[10]

Against the advice of elders, Jamsetji Tata decided to build a better cotton mill, constructing it in Nagpur, not Bombay. The Empress Mills opened in the early 1870s and became one of the most successful Indian-owned cotton mills. It launched Jamsetji and Tata & Sons on a remarkable rise as an Indian and international conglomerate encompassing many different enterprises. Jamsetji lived

---

[9] Morris, Morris D. 1982. 'The Growth of Large-Scale Industry,' in Dharma Kumar, ed. The *Cambridge Economic History of India*. V. II, Cambridge: Cambridge U. Press, p. 555ff.

[10] Harris, Frank. 1958. *Jamsetji Nusserwanji Tata*. London: Blackie and Lala 2004a.

in Nagpur for several years and hired Indian and British managers, including foremen and machinists from the best mills in Lancashire, Britain's industrial centre. Gradually, the Indianization of the work force proceeded through apprenticeship programmes, and more generous provision was made than usual, towards the workers' housing and general welfare. The Tata companies became known for seeking the best help regardless of nationality and for taking care of workers. Machinery for the mill had to be purchased in Europe and Jamsetji Tata, an inveterate traveller, scoured the world for the best equipment, processes and personnel. Though a devoted Parsi, he understood the relativism of belief systems, writing in his diary in 1873 when on a trip through the Middle East: 'When arguing against the religious beliefs of a man why should you beg of him to have faith in all your absurdities while denying him the same privilege in regard to his own?'[11]

Once Jamsetji had his Empress Mills profitably underway and he had moved back to Bombay, he began to chart out the range of enterprises and activities that would involve him for his remaining decades. Although a supporter of the Indian National Congress, a confidant of nationalist leaders Dadabhai Naoroji (1825–1917) and Pherozeshah Mehta (1845–1915) and an important builder of India's economy, he avoided politics. However, when economic issues intersected with politics, such as on import–export issues and tariffs, Tata gathered data and allies, and made his views known. He began planning as early as the 1880s for an iron and steel mill, for a hydroelectric plant and for educational institutions and scholarships that might benefit India. Since all such enterprises would be enmeshed in the India of the British Raj, he felt a need for government help or to overcome obstacles. In the 1890s there was more openness to such initiatives by Indians—which the British did not block—as international competition increased and Indians demonstrated their competencies.

At the end of the nineteenth century, with the opening of the great age of American manufacturing and exporting, American

---

[11] Harris 1958, p. 297.

firms like the Singer Sewing Machine Company began to sell their goods in India. Following the traders of the earlier nineteenth century, a few American businessmen ventured to Bombay and Calcutta to hawk their wares.

Even as American intellectuals debated the legitimacy of Western imperial ventures, native entrepreneurs in India, participating in the industrial revolution that had begun in Europe but spread globally, launched dynamic and profitable business enterprises. While the British drove the development of railroads and the jute industry, Indians were heavily involved in the cotton industry and in trade, although industries like iron and steel at first, seemed out of reach. The Bengal Iron and Steel Corporation had gone through several incarnations and flopped, insufficiently capitalized, technically inadequate and poorly run.[12]

In 1882, Jamsetji Tata, the titan of the budding cotton industry who had attended the Chicago World Fair with a vision for the future, made preliminary investigations for an iron and steel plant in India. As he sought supplies of raw materials and possible sites for an iron and steel plant, Tata needed governmental cooperation—which the British, facing European and Japanese competitors, provided. Raj officials preferred an Indian producer to a foreign one.

Tata succeeded in his attempt to launch an iron and steel mill: TISCO, the Tata Iron and Steel Company. Based in Jamshedpur, part of the family of Tata companies, for more than a century it has been and still is today one of the great industrial enterprises of modern India. He had laid the groundwork for TISCO before he died in 1904, having twice visited the US to further his project: in 1893, when he sought advice in American steel mills; and in 1902, when he returned to hire American experts, meeting with executives mainly in Cleveland and Pittsburgh. Wealthy, highly intelligent and a well-informed world citizen, Tata was well received. He was directed to Julian Kennedy (1852–1932), whose firm Julian Kennedy, Sahlin and Company, would eventually build the great Indian iron and steel

---

[12] Morris 1982, pp. 588–89.

mill at what became Jamshedpur. Tata also hired Charles Page Perin (1862–1937) as his engineering consultant.

Tata met Perin on his 1902 trip, just before he died. Perin later recalled how Tata entered his office, stood and stared, then asked him to come to India and help him. Without hesitation, Perin agreed, and became a key aide to the Tatas.[13] As 'consulting engineer', Perin sent his associate geologist C.M. Weld to India to locate the best site for a mill. Based on a tip from an Indian geologist, P.N. Bose (1855–1934), a site was found near the village of Sakchi in eastern India. The Tatas poured their resources and American and other foreign expertise into building the mill.[14]

After Jamsetji Tata died, many doubted a steel mill would be built, but his son Dorabji Tata (1859–1932) took over his father's plans. Dorabji collaborated over the next two decades with several Indian directors; with Mr Padshah, chosen by Dorabji for an important role; with Perin's American team; with Indian labour; and with workers from Europe and the United States. The Tata name is still on the landmark mill, while Perin is almost forgotten, along with four other Americans who made untold contributions from the beginning. The Tatas owe much to Perin, whom they employed for some twenty years and who would serve as a director of the company. The correspondence between the Tatas and Perin attests that he was much more than an employee. They leaned upon his expertise and judgment; he often made key decisions. The phrase 'Ask Mr Perin' appears in many papers about crucial matters.[15]

The first matters involved financing and choosing the site. Dorabji Tata and his Bombay team reached out to British backers, but they seemed dubious about an Indian project, especially during the 1906–1907 downturn in the US. Instead, Dorabji sought and obtained Indian financial backing. It was the Swadeshi era when nationalist urgings mounted, and several Indians, including wealthy Indian princes, came forward. Then Perin sent out his associate

[13] Lala 2004, p. 21ff.
[14] Ibid., p. 22ff; Harris 1958, p. 146ff.
[15] Tata archives, Jamshedpur.

Charles Weld to tramp through the countryside and find the best site for the mill. After years of hard work and disappointment, at last, one site of large iron deposits was discovered, and then a second. Besides abundant iron ore, the site needed to be close to coal deposits, water and other materials used in fluxes, and had to have access to a rail line. When they identified the appropriate and chosen site, the Tatas purchased lands possessing the necessary natural resources, and Raj officials agreed to build a spur rail line. In his survey of 'The Growth of Large-Scale Industry' in India, Morris D. Morris recounts the Raj's encouragement:

> During the planning and construction phases, the Tatas received extensive official assistance—geological surveys, reduced transport costs, eased access to land and water rights, simplified import arrangements for construction materials, and an agreement that the state would buy 20,000 tons of steel raises annually for ten years at import prices.[16]

Julian Kennedy, Sahlin, and Company was hired to build the mill. The Swedish metallurgist Axel Sahlin (1855–1937) spent months in India, while Weld spent about four years. The Tatas were guided by Perin, who brought in Robert Wells, who had built comparable plants in Siberia and Turkey. One problem: Wells wanted the power to hire or fire while bringing the mill online. Tatas backed away, but Perin pushed for Wells, and he was hired, and did the job.

For more than two decades Perin undertook an amazing variety of tasks for TISCO: he hired and supervised the hiring of many personnel for the mill; he hawked TISCO iron and steel products in Europe, East Asia, especially Japan and China, and the US; he negotiated with government officials, particularly of the Raj, in India and London; near the end of the First World War, he pressed the Tatas to expand the mill; he trained Indian and American personnel to replace him and undertake some of his duties. It's difficult to overstate Perin's role at Jamshedpur, down to bookkeeping and

---

[16] Morris 1982, p. 589.

employee housing in the growing, unincorporated municipality. Throughout, Perin spoke of 'our' efforts, 'our' sales, 'our' necessary expansion. The Tatas rewarded Perin appropriately with large bonuses, and through the end of the First World War, he continued travelling the world for TISCO.

Perin bemoaned 'this terrible war' but saw both the positive and negative effects for TISCO. When a significant number of German workmen in the mill were interned by the Raj, Perin toured the UK and the US in search of replacements. He also continued to sell TISCO products where he could. At the end of the war, the US Peace Commission asked the Tatas to release Perin to assess war damage in Europe. But the Tatas, concerned with what was called 'the Great Expansion', would not release him from his contract. Perin was still the vital man, but from 1919 forward, he suffered occasional ill health and began to detach himself. Though he returned to India several times, once with his second wife in 1919, he never again played the same central role. But Perin's long connection to the Tatas ensured that they were on the path to developing a premier Asian manufacturing plant that has endured in the front rank of world steel producers.

Several other Indian business houses gained traction in the later part of the nineteenth and early twentieth century. The Marwaris (from the Marwar region in Rajasthan) actively expanded their economic activities in Bombay and Calcutta. Although there were many Marwari firms, one attained widespread attention not only for economic success and philanthropy, but also for political largess during the nationalist movement. Birla and Brothers, headed by G.D. Birla (1894–1983), started as a small family trading company but became a formidable business house.

The Birlas entered into the jute and opium trades in the late nineteenth century, and then into the stock market, precious metals, and industry, building a jute mill in Calcutta. They were also among the foremost Indian philanthropists of Calcutta, mostly through local charities. Although most Marwaris were engaged mainly in internal India trade and stocks, the Birlas also began supplying jute goods more widely during the First World War. G.D. Birla's skill in English and contacts with British businessmen in Calcutta enabled him to work between worlds, although the racism of Europeans in Calcutta, both personal and professional, rankled him.[17]

The Tatas were based in more cosmopolitan Bombay, and sought to employ the very best, regardless of nationality, for TISCO and their other companies. American executives at the top ranks of the TISCO management were part of a growing American economic involvement with India. Numerous American companies had opened offices in India and saw possibilities for sales. According to the list in *Thacker's India Directory 1921*, an annual business publication, more than 150 American companies, of great variety, had offices in India; among them such familiar firms as American Express (founded 1841), Cadillac, Chevrolet, DuPont, Ford Motors, General Electric, Goodrich Rubber, Hartford Fire Insurance, Heinz, Remington Typewriter, Singer Sewing Machines, Westinghouse Electric and US Steel.[18]

As early as 1895, word of horseless carriages reached India and a decade later the Ford Motor Company was selling cars far and wide. When the Raj held a reception in Delhi in 1911 celebrating the accession of Britain's King George V, A. Dodge, representing Ford in India, reported: 'The procession was magnificent. There were elephants, camels, Ford cars, and everything all mingled together...a beautiful showing.'[19]

Officials of the British Raj determined access to the Indian economy, and British interests, private and public, took precedence. In 1902, for instance, when the American giant Standard Oil wanted to explore oil in Burma, then still part of British India, the Raj denied

---

[17] Kudaisya, Medha M. 2003. *The Life and Times of G.D. Birla*. New Delhi: Oxford U. Press.

[18] Wilkins, Mira. 1970. *The Emergence of Multinational Enterprise: American Business Abroad from the Colonial Era to 1914*. Cambridge: Harvard U. Press, pp. 208–209.

[19] Wilkins and Hill 1964, p. 44.

permission.[20] Until 1947, the British decided who would go in and out, and which companies and interest groups, foreign or Indian, got preferential treatment. British journalist W.T. Stead argued early in the twentieth century that the world was threatened by Americanization. The British feared they might be displaced by America's rise.[21]

---

[20] Wilkins, Mira. 1974. *The Maturing of Multinational Enterprise: American Business Abroad from 1914 to 1970*. Cambridge: Harvard U. Press, p. 84
[21] Stead, William Thomas. 2009 [1902]. *The Americanization of the World*. Danvers, MA: General Books.

3

Mantras
Hindu Teachings and Texts

Rammohun Roy did not visit the United States, but his friend William Adam did and made contact with American Unitarians and with Ralph Waldo Emerson (1803–1882), a keen student of Oriental texts and teachings. Emerson and Henry David Thoreau (1817–1862), a naturalist and fellow transcendentalist, along with the contemporary writers Nathaniel Hawthorne (1804–1864), Herman Melville (1819–1891), and Walt Whitman (1819–1892), were testing, revising, and partially rejecting received Christianity in its nineteenth-century versions, and exploring the variety of the world's faiths. The attention these authors paid to Asian matters was one part of America's involvement in the age of exploration and the Enlightenment, and linked it to the activity of missionaries, explorers, and European intellectuals of the previous two centuries. While Hawthorne observed ships sailing to Calcutta from the docks of Salem, Massachusetts, Melville himself sailed to the South Seas on both military and whaling ships—alluding, for instance, in his novels *Redburn: His First Voyage* (1849) and *Moby-Dick, or The Whale* (1851) to the Indian and Burmese rivers—the Ganges and the Irrawaddy. Although neither writer visited India, the country figured in their imaginations and entered into American discourse. By about 1820, at Harvard as a student, Emerson was reading and commenting upon Indian texts and ideas, the intellectual legacy of his father, a Boston minister, who had read British translations of Indian texts. While Emerson shared the view that British rule was generally benevolent, he also found in ancient Indian texts increasing resonance with his own idiosyncratic religious views. He opened himself to diverse cultural influences from the Middle East, India and China, nonetheless retaining his Anglo-Saxon identification. Becoming uneasy with evangelical Christianity and even with the congealing Unitarianism of his earlier years, he came to a belief in a divine power present in each of us, though brought to full glory in few, an understanding that resonated with Hindu and Buddhist texts. For example, he composed several poems infused with Indian concepts ('Brahma', 'Maia', 'Hamitreya') and wrote in his journal in 1845 of the grandeur of Indian religion:

> The Indian teaching through its cloud of legends has yet a simple and grand religion like a queenly countenance seen through a rich veil. It teaches to speak the truth, love others as yourself and to despise trifles. The East is grand—and makes Europe appear the land of trifles. Identity, identity! Friend and foe are of one stuff, and the stuff is such and so much that the variations of surface are unimportant. All is for the soul, and the soul is Vishnu; and animals and stars are transient paintings; and light is whitewash, and durations are deceptive; and form is imprisonment and heaven itself a decoy. That which the soul seeks is resolution into Being above form, out of Tararus and out of Heaven; liberation from existence is its name. Cheerful and noble is the genius of this cosmogony. Hari is always gentle and serene; he translates to heaven the hunter who has accidentally shot in his human form; he pursues his sports with boors and milkmaids at the cow-pens; all his games are benevolent, and he enters into flesh to relieve the burdens of the world.[1]

Open to new perceptions of India, Emerson's attitudes towards slavery also evolved, becoming increasingly more critical. Once he met some African Americans who were clearly the equal of whites, he tempered his racism, while still adhering to the nineteenth-

---

[1] Emerson. Ralph Waldo. 2010. *Selected Journals 1841-1877*. Ed. Lawrence Rosenwald. NY: Library of America, p. 296.

century categorization of distinct races. He opposed brutal
American expansionism, hosted John Brown, hated the fugitive
slave law, and broke with a long-time acquaintance and hero, Daniel
Webster (1782–1852), over the latter's compromises with slavery.
Yet, Emerson never came to believe in the equality of indigenous
Americans with their conquerors.

Emerson befriended Henry David Thoreau, a younger Concord
man who had attended Harvard College, walked with him in the
woods, and come to live with his family. Like Emerson, he developed
an abiding interest in foreign religions, particularly Hinduism. He
was an inveterate hiker and explorer of nature and of the cosmos
within. When he sought a hermitage at Walden Pond, staying for two
years, two months, and two days, he continued his inner explorations,
and pondered how the winter's frozen pond contributed its ice to his
soulmates around the globe:

> Thus it appears that the sweltering inhabitants of Charleston and
> New Orleans, of Madras and Bombay and Calcutta, drink at my
> well. In the morning I bathe my intellect in the stupendous and
> cosmogonal philosophy of the Bhagvat-Geeta [sic], since whose
> composition years of the gods have elapsed, and in comparison
> with which our modern world and its literature seem puny and
> trivial; and I doubt if that philosophy is not to be referred to a
> previous state of existence, so remote is its sublimity from our
> conceptions. I lay down the book and go to my well for water,
> and lo! There I meet the servant of the Bramin, priest of Brahma
> and Vishnu and Indra, who still sits in his temple on the Ganges
> reading the Vedas, or dwells at the root of a tree with his crust and
> water jug. I meet his servant come to draw water for his master,
> and our buckets as it were grate together in the same well. The pure
> Walden water is mingled with the sacred water of the Ganges.[2]

Like Emerson, Thoreau left formal Christianity and his Western
outlook behind, as he explored other religious traditions and sacred

---

[2] Thoreau 2004, p. 288.

texts. The Vedas, the Upanishads, the Laws of Manu, the Puranas, the poems of Kabir were with him at the pond, as he wrote, 'I know of many systems of religion esteemed heathenish whose precepts fill the reader with shame, and provoke him to new endeavors, though it be to the performance of rites merely.'[3] As he wrote in another of his inner-outer travelogues, *A Week on the Concord* and *Merrimack Rivers* (1849), 'The Oriental philosophy approaches easily loftier themes than the modern aspires to; and no wonder if it sometimes prattle about them. It only assigns their due rank respectively to Action and Contemplation, or rather does full justice to the latter. Western philosophers have not conceived of the significance of Contemplation in their sense.'[4] Elsewhere, in a 1849 letter to a friend, H.G.O. Blake, Thoreau described himself as a yogi:

> Free in this world as the birds in the air, disengaged from every kind of chains, those who practice yoga gather in Brahma the certain fruits of their works. Depend upon it that, rude and careless as I am, I would fain practice the yoga faithfully. The yogi, absorbed in contemplation, contributes in his degree to creation; he breathes a divine perfume, he hears wonderful things. Divine forms traverse him without tearing him, and united to the nature which is proper to him, he goes, he acts as animating original matter. To some extent, and at rare intervals, even I am a yogi.[5]

Neither Emerson nor Thoreau, notable among their contemporaries, bowed before the unique and specialness of Christianity and Western learning. They sought many traditions in shaping their own beliefs and outlook, saying 'Yes' to the Bible, to Homer, Dante and Shakespeare, but 'Yes', too, to Indian texts. Though both were armchair investigators of India and the East, they did meet a few who had first-hand knowledge of India.

---

[3] Ibid., p. 212.
[4] Thoreau, Henry David. 1985. *A Week on the Concord and Merrimack Rivers; Walden; or Life in the Woods; The Maine Woods; Cape Cod.* NY: The Library of America, p. 111.
[5] 'Henry David Thoreau', Wikipedia.

Besides scholars and missionaries, they encountered several popularizers of Asian cultures, among them Edwin Arnold (1832–1904), the most widely known. Arnold had been principal of the Government Sanskrit College in Poona from 1856 to 1863. Returning home, he worked as a journalist, later turning to verse presentations of Asian texts and stories. Many American as well as British readers learned of India through Arnold's *Indian Song of Songs* (1875), and of Buddhism through his *The Light of Asia* (1879), which suggested parallels between the Buddha and Jesus Christ. Siddhartha, the prince of India, gave up a luxurious life to seek wisdom and, giving up his 'godly life', to serve others.[6]

Undeterred by critics, Arnold went on to publish *Pearls of Faith*, *The Song Celestial* and others. Although sympathetic to the cultures of Asia, even moving to Japan in his later years, Arnold was also a strong defender of the British Raj.[7]

Besides clear and understandable popularizers like Arnold, a handful of Western occultists and mystical religious seekers claimed they found truth by looking East. Among the best known were the Theosophists, a sect inaugurated in the 1870s by Madame Helena Blavatsky (1831–1891) and Henry Steel Olcott (1832–1907), which thrived among a dedicated coterie of followers well into the twentieth century. Though Blavatsky came from Imperial Russia and Olcott was an American, both believed that there were spiritual masters in the East, in Tibet and India. Madame Blavatsky said she formulated her doctrines during years in India and Tibet with Master Kuthumi, and had learned of the Lord Maitreya, the highest of the high. With Olcott, she formed the Theosophical Society and established its base at Adyar, near Madras, India. Surviving scandals and infighting, in time, they attracted Annie Besant (1847–1933), a former atheist, and Charles Webster Leadbeater (1854–1934), a lapsed Anglican priest and accused child molester, who headed the Society when the original founders were gone. They preached that a world master would come

---

[6] Arnold, Edwin. 1890. *The Light of Asia*. Boston: Roberts Brothers, p. 94ff.
[7] Schramm, Richard H. 1964. 'The Image of India in Selected American Literary Periodicals: 1870-1900,' Ph.D. thesis, Duke University.

forth and embody Lord Maitreya on Earth, and would be a saviour
of the world. He had not yet appeared in the late nineteenth century,
but they were determined to find him.[8]

At the World Parliament of Religions at the Columbian
Exposition, or Chicago's World's Fair of 1893, a young Hindu holy
man wearing a bright orange turban rose to speak. In impeccable
English, he began, 'Sisters and brothers and of America...' Thus
Swami Vivekananda of Calcutta introduced himself to those of many
faiths, some who travelled to Chicago to learn from others, and some
intent on pressing their beliefs on the less enlightened. The response
to his unusual opening was '...a peal of applause that lasted for
several minutes'.[9]

The Parliament of Religions was organized to demonstrate
the superiority of Protestant Christianity. Organizers invited
representatives of other religions including representatives of the
religions of India, plus Christian missionaries serving there. A special
reception was held for delegates from India, China and Japan.[10] How
would Americans respond to the messages and attendees from Asia?
Would Americans start to form different relations to South Asia
than their British cousins who presided over the Raj?

Despite the temporary economic setback of the Depression of
1893, on the eve of the American Century—as the twentieth has
been called—the US was enjoying a long period of growth. The
Parliament of Religions was one of numerous conclaves, lectures
and exhibitions at the Columbian Exposition, where a White City
was constructed with lighting by Westinghouse, apart from a giant
Ferris Wheel. Buffalo Bill's Wild West show entertained 27 million
attendees.

---

[8] Jayakar, Pupul. 1986. *J. Krishnamurti*. New Delhi: Penguin, p. 21ff; Washington,
Peter. 1993. *Madame Blavatsky's Baboon*. NY: Schocken, p. 68ff; Vernon, Roland.
2002. *Star of the East. Krishnamurti the Invention of a Messiah*. Boulder: Sentient,
p. 11ff.
[9] Barrows, John Henry. Ed. 1893. *The World's Parliament of Religions. The
Columbian Exposition of 1893*. 2v. Chicago: Parliament Publishing, p. 101.
[10] Barrows, I and II, 1893.

Notables attending included the President Grover Cleveland, Theodore Roosevelt, the authors Henry Adams and Mark Twain (1835–1910), and Jagatjit Singh Sahib Bahadur, the

Maharaja of Kapurthala. A common theme was America's thrust into the world to take its place among the powers, shown, for instance, by Theodore Roosevelt's recent account of the triumph of English-speaking civilization over the savage peoples of the Earth, and Americans' advance across North America.[11] Henry Adams wrote: 'Chicago asked in 1893 for the first time the question whether the American people knew where they were driving.' Adams answered that he did not know, but would try to find out.[12]

Robert Rydell, a scholar writing about American fairs, has argued that the 1893 Fair was imperial and racist, confirming the hegemony of mainly upper- and middle-class white Americans as it mocked China and was condescending towards a rising Japan. Its anthropology exhibits showcased stereotypical primitives from around the world, whose 'backwardness' highlighted the superiority of white Anglo-Saxons.[13]

The renowned south Indian artist Raja Ravi Varma (1848–1906) provided ten paintings of 'The Native Peoples of India' that were displayed in the fair's ethnographic sections—not exhibited in the arts pavilion as representing the art of India.[14] To Westerners, non-Western art was not 'art'." It would be more than a century before Indian art emerged on international markets to be judged alongside Western art.

In many ways, the twentieth-century links between America and India began with the World Fair of 1893, and the associated World Parliament of Religions, which drew Indians and Americans

---

[11] Morris, Edmund. 2001. *The Rise of Theodore Roosevelt.* NY: Modern Library, p. 470ff.
[12] Adams, Henry. 1973. *The Education of Henry Adams.* Ed. Ernest Samuels. Boston: Houghton Mifflin, p. 343.
[13] Rydell, Robert W. 1984. *All the World's a Fair. Visions of Empire at American International Expositions, 1876-1916.* Chicago: University of Chicago Press, p. 38ff.
[14] Bald, Vivek, Miabi Chatterji, Sujani Reddy, Manu Vimalassery, eds. 2013. *The Sun Never Sets.* NY: NYU Press, pp. 283–97,

who would help build those links. Among the Indians there was a spectrum of religious spokesmen, including Swami Vivekananda, then on his first visit to the West, and P.C. Mazumdar of the Brahmo Samaj, on his second. During his stay, Swami Vivekananda acquainted thousands of Americans with Indian religious truths and methodologies. Mazumdar represented one branch of a significant Hindu reform movement that already had ties to America. They would present to Americans two versions of Hinduism.[15]

Another Indian visitor was more interested in commerce. Jamsetji Tata, the Parsi businessman from Bombay, encountered previously, came to the Fair to see and explore the possibility of building a steel mill in India. He and Swami Vivekananda had met on their voyage from Japan, and shared a desire to revivify India. Tata had already built a successful textile enterprise, but he wanted much more. During this American visit, he made contacts that he would expand over the next decade, enabling his sons to realize his dreams of steel, power and science. On 23 November 1898, Tata wrote to Vivekananda:

> I very much recall at this moment your views on the growth of the ascetic spirit in India, and the duty, not of destroying but of diverting it into useful channel. I recall these ideas in connection with my scheme of a research institute of science for India... It seems to me that no better use can be made of the ascetic spirit than the establishment of monasteries or residential halls for men dominated by the spirit, where they should live with ordinary decency and devote their lives to the cultivation of sciences— natural and humanistic.[16]

Both Vivekananda and Tata were highly intelligent, ardent Indians, distressed that India was ruled by a foreign power. They contributed

---

[15] Doniger, Wendy. 2009. *The Hindus. An Alternative History*. NY: Penguin, p. 636ff; Eck, Diana L. 2001. *A New Religious America*. How a 'Christian Country' Has Become the World's Most Religously Diverse Nation. NY: HarperCollins, p.1ff.
[16] Quoted in Sen 1975, from <u>Marg</u>, XVI, March 1963.

to the nationalist movement in different ways, and reached out to America for very different purposes. Finding America to be a spiritual desert, Vivekananda decided to water it, expanding from his primary mission to raise funds for his religious organization in India. Tata, seeking technical expertise, returned nearly a decade later, when he located the key person needed to assist the Tatas in starting their iron and steel mill. India–United States trade had waxed and waned from the later eighteenth century, but Tata's prospective endeavour was a new and important step forward for India.

While Ida S. Scudder and other Christian missionaries attempted to convert those they viewed as heathens, Swami Vivekananda, who made such an impression at the World Parliament of Religions in Chicago, was spreading the teachings of his own Hinduism in the rising but temporarily depressed America of the 1890s. Vivekananda stayed in the US for several years, teaching Americans about Hinduism, yoga and meditation, while raising funds for his Indian work. He also made later visits through 1899. Whether or not he had a decisive impact, he was easily the earliest successful Indian religious teacher in America.[17]

Responding to the America he encountered, however, Vivekananda shifted his mission. The Swami found that 'America is now the chief home of Kubera, the god of wealth'.[18] He also put it this way: 'As our country is poor in social virtues, so this country is lacking in spirituality. I give them spirituality, and they give me money.'[19]

Along with the materialism, Vivekananda found what he called spiritual hunger. It was his new responsibility to satisfy America's spiritual needs with his teachings and establishment of centres of the Vedanta Society. Believing that his version of Vedanta was more religiously valuable and tolerant than the Protestantism he

[17] Burke, Marie Louise. 1966. *Swami Vivekananda in America New Discoveries.* Calcutta: Advaita Ashrama, rev. ed.
[18] Vivekananda, Swami. 1975. *The East and the West.* Calcutta: Advaita Ashrama, p. 65.
[19] Vivekananda, Swami. 1962. *The Complete Works of Swami Vivekananda.* 8 vols. Calcutta: Advaita Ashram, p. 255.

encountered, sometimes in nasty confrontations with ministers and missionaries, Swami Vivekananda held classes, organized religious conferences and lectured throughout the United States for several years.

Vivekananda found the United States had many positive qualities, including great energy, organizational skills, warm hospitality, little poverty, and a high status accorded to women. He made many friends in America, mostly women. In an 1894 letter he wrote:

> Last year I came to this country in summer, a wandering preacher of a far distant country... and American women befriended me, gave me shelter and food, took me to their homes and treated me as their own son, their own brother. They stood my friends even when their own priests were trying to persuade them to give up the 'dangerous heathen'—even when day after day their best friends had told them not to stand by this 'unknown foreigner, may be of dangerous character'. But they are better judges of character and soul—for it is the pure mirror that catches the reflection.[20]

Elsewhere he wrote, 'It is the women who are the life and soul of this country. All learning and culture are centred in them.'[21]

Along with the warm welcome came acrimonious exchanges with Protestant ministers and returned missionaries. Protestant criticism of India led Vivekananda to present a defence of many Indian institutions and practices. He denounced Christian attempts at conversion and any need for Western missionaries in India. One of his famous speeches was called, 'Religion Not the Crying Need of India'. His India needed to acquire new strength and skills, and perhaps independence from foreign rule, but not new, foreign, and often hostile religious teachings and teachers. He found resonance for his belief in divine love in the teachings of Christ but viewed missionaries in India not as true spokesmen for Christ but as aggressive Westerners striving in another way to control India. His retorts to Protestant

---

[20] Ibid., p. 248.
[21] Ibid., p. 252.

critics and his defence of caste, image worship, the doctrine of rebirth, and Hindu treatment of widows drew rancorous responses, including very personal attacks.

Although Vivekananda recognized that India required guidance in a number of areas touching on national strength, organization and health, he was at the same time compelled to inform Protestants that America needed lessons he and other Indians could offer, in selflessness, spiritual values, religious toleration and wisdom. In speeches in Chicago and numerous talks touring the US, Vivekananda touted the tolerance of his Vedantic Hinduism. Never, he said, would a Hindu bother a Muslim, Christian, or Parsi in India. Insisting that the divine was dwelling within each of us, he attacked repeatedly the Christian idea of original sin. In his major address in Chicago, he said: 'Allow me to call you, brethren, by that sweet name—heirs of immortal bliss—yea, the Hindu refuses to call you sinners. Ye are the Children of God, the sharers of immortal bliss, holy and perfect beings. Ye divinities on earth—sinners! It is a sin to call a man so; it is standing libel on human nature.'[22]

Each of us, Vivekananda said, should stay throughout life with that religion whose seed was planted in us at or near birth. He said that Christian missionaries, if they insisted on coming to India, should feed people and not preach. He also skilfully answered the Protestant charges of image worship and polytheism that were used as cudgels to malign Hinduism. Vivekananda insisted that anyone could become one with the divine; therefore attacks on the caste system, as linked to religion, were irrelevant. Caste was a social matter and had no connection to religion. Further, he maintained that Hindu teachings were consistent with modern science, and had interesting ideas on the relation of Judaism to Christianity and Buddhism and Jainism to Hinduism. He implied that Judaism, in not recognizing the Messiah, had devolved into the faith of a small minority, while Hinduism, by absorbing other faiths, had advanced. But he also criticized Hindus for not learning from Buddhism a more profound compassion.[23]

---

[22] Ibid., I, p. 11.
[23] Ibid., p. 21.

Between his several visits to the US, Swami Vivekananda returned to India and Calcutta. He was visited in India during 1898 by Sara Chapman Bull (1850–1911) and Josephine MacLeod (1858–1949), accompanied on their long trip by Swami Saradananda, one of Vivekananda's emissaries to the US. They settled briefly in a house near Belur Math and together with an Irish disciple, later named Sister Nivedita (and initiated into the Ramakrishna Order), they discussed and learned from Vivekananda. Subjected to criticism as 'unclean women', and seemingly unmoved by the plight of poor Indians suffering from famine, they travelled to Srinagar and Almora to see the natural glories of India. Mrs Bull had been and continued to be an important financial backer of the activities of Swami Vivekananda and the Ramakrishna Order. Josephine Macleod, later called 'Tantine', was a lifelong supporter.[24]

Vivekananda was the first high-profile Hindu guru in America, but many others followed. In 1897, Swami Abhedananda, also of the Ramakrishna Order, came to New York and continued the work of Vivekananda for over two decades. Accompanying Swami Saradananda to Boston, he debated William James, as he claimed, set up the Vedanta Society in New York City, taught regular classes, and gave public lectures. Some American disciples, who were recognized as swamis were given Indian names. He formed a circle of connections to Sanskrit Professor Charles Rockwell Lanman at Harvard and Professor A.V. Williams Jackson at Columbia. In the course of his work for the Mission, he also made numerous trips to Europe before retiring to India in 1921. But his tour of duty was marked by crisis as well. The New York centre split between followers of Abhedananda and Paramananda (1884–1940), a younger monk who had been assisting him. Although a vote favoured the older monk and he remained in charge, he kept taking long breaks in Europe.

Paramananda moved to Boston and established a new centre, then established another in Los Angeles. He travelled, usually by train, between the two centres, stopping in the Louisville-Cincinnati

---

[24] Syman, Stefanie. 2010. *The Subtle Body, The Story of Yoga in America*. NY: Farrar, Straus and Giroux, pp. 62–67.

area to establish another smaller centre.
More personable than Abhedananda,
Paramananda flourished until he died an
early death in 1915.

Other monks of the order continued
the mission of ministering to Americans.
Centres of the Vedanta Society were
set up in California, first in northern
California, and several continue today,
long supported by local members. No
funds from India flowed for this work,
but Americans raised the necessary
finances for buildings and activities.[25]

Swami Abhedananda

These centres have been headed, almost always, by swamis of the
Ramakrishna Order trained in India. They have needed a variety of
skills in the US, including the ability to speak English well and explain
Hindu concepts clearly. Although Swami Trigunatita (1865–1915),
the founder of the San Francisco centre, did not speak English well,
he brought music to the meetings. Historian Carl Jackson has also
noted that Trigunatita openly expressed political opinions including
socialistic views, although swamis had been told not to so indulge
themselves.[26]

The popularity of yoga in America starts with Swami
Vivekananda teaching what he called Raja Yoga, and with a strange
American who assumed the name of Pierre Bernard (1875–1955).
Vivekananda did not teach asanas, or yogic physical exercises, but
Bernard did.[27] Bernard started in his birthplace, Lincoln, Nebraska,
training in the 1880s with Silvais Hamati, an Anglo-Indian perhaps
from Calcutta. In 1889 they moved to San Francisco, and then

---

[25] Jackson, Carl T. 1994. *Vedanta for the West. The Ramakrishna Movement in the
United States.* Bloomington: Indiana U. Press, p. 52ff.
[26] Ibid., pp. 58–59.
[27] Love, Robert. 2010. *The Great OOM, The Improbable Birth Yoga in America.* NY:
Viking; Syman, Stefanie. 2010. *The Subtle Body, The Story of Yoga in America.* NY:
Farrar, Straus and Giroux.

in the late nineteenth century to New York City. Bernard taught yoga from apartments and town houses in Manhattan and gained notoriety when charged with kidnapping amid exaggerated press accusations of lewdness and sexual encounters. Bernard was released but continued to hire showgirls trained as instructors by Blanche De Vries (1891–1984), his consort, then wife. He taught hatha yoga, as opposed to Swami Vivekananda's Raja Yoga, which was taught in the several US centres of the Vedanta Society in existence by the First World War and continues even now.

Bernard based his enterprise in a Rockland County estate in New York with the help of a member of the Vanderbilt family and other wealthy backers. He did teach yoga there but it was de-emphasized as he stressed other health-related activities. In the later 1920s, he went bankrupt and faded away with a mixed legacy. He was widely read in Indian philosophy and yoga texts and left a great library. He did some real teaching and brought yoga into

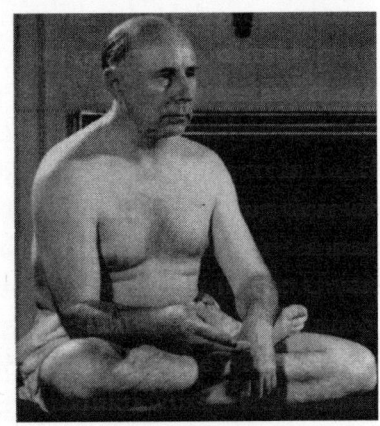

Pierre Bernard

the public eye, and associated it with health. But he was controversial, and led some to see yoga as dangerous to public morals. In the 1920s, Paramahansa Yogananda (1893–1952), about whom more later, founded the Self-Realization Fellowship, which helped keep yoga in the public eye.

The Theosophists, for their part, fastened on a young Indian, Jiddu Krishnamurti (1895–1986), whom British author Charles Leadbeater, a member of the Theosophical Society, saw with an 'aura' on an Adyar beach in 1909 when Krishnamurti was fourteen years old. The young man was initiated by Leadbeater and accepted by Theosophy president Annie Besant as the chosen one—a new saviour, a fusion of a Hindu avatar and a Christian messiah. The Society set up the Order of the Star of the East, a cadre of would-be spiritual masters with Krishnamurti, first among them. In 1912 he and his brother Nitya were sent to Great Britain for further education.

They were dressed elegantly, tutored, and rotated through the homes of wealthy British Theosophists for almost a decade. Though Krishnamurti later emerged as a popular spiritual teacher, he did so by departing from the path his guides had plotted.[28]

Indian nationalists began to visit America, too. Although Vivekananda and Jamshetji Tata should surely be counted among workers for the rebirth of the Indian nation, they avoided the explicitly political. Others, more political, were soon to arrive on American shores.

---

[28] Jayakar, Pupul. 1986. *J. Krishnamurti.* New Delhi: Penguin, p. 21ff; Washington, Peter. 1993. *Madame Blavatsky's Baboon.* NY: Schocken, p. 68ff; Vernon, Roland. 2002. *Star of the East.* Krishnamurti the Invention of a Messiah. Boulder: Sentient, p. 11ff.

4

Immigrants, Nationalists and Transients

Although many Japanese and Chinese, both students and workers, visited the United States before the 1890s, few Indian merchant sailors did, and even fewer students and intellectuals. Ishuree Dass, one of these few, a young Indian who journeyed to the US in 1846 and briefly attended Lafayette College and Princeton Seminary, deplored American ignorance of his homeland and in his *A Brief Account of a Voyage to England and America* (1851), writes:

> [T]he Americans have a very poor and ridiculous idea of India... [T]he ignorance which reaches even the educated and the learned is most strange.... Their ideas of the Hindoos [sic] are most certainly derived from their own Indians; and when they speak of savage and uncultivated life they almost always allude to the 'red man of the West', and whenever they think of India they very probably picture to their minds a country covered with jungle or... waste and barren, miserable huts, natives dressed in bear and lion skins, and adorned with ornaments of bone and beset with large herds of wild horses and ferocious animals.[1]

They did not know, he said, that India had had a 'long continued civilization and extensive manufactures . . .'[2]

---

[1] Dass, Ishuree. 1851. *A Brief Account of a Voyage to England and America*. Allahabad: Presbyterian Mission Press, pp. 72–73.
[2] Ibid.

Also among the few visitors in the 1880s were Anandibai Joshee (1865–1887) and Pandita Ramabai (1858–1922), who came separately and for different reasons, but met briefly in Philadelphia in 1886 when Ramabai travelled there to attend Joshee's graduation from the Woman's Medical College of Philadelphia. Joshee had made the remarkable journey from India to study medicine in an era when there were no Indian female physicians and Indian women declined to be examined by men. Shortly after her return to India, however, she died of tuberculosis, depriving her countrymen of the benefits of her training.

Ramabai's book, one of the earliest attempts by an Indian to explain Indian society and religion to Americans, was focused on the hard life of India's women. She detailed the restricted childhoods, the lack of education, and the harsh self-images inculcated into Indian girls, who were generally consigned to an arranged marriage at a tender age, and transferred as a piece of property to her husband's family, where as a lowly subordinate, she was allowed no freedom of movement or thought. Ramabai used her own observations plus many quotations from Hindu texts. After delineating the plight of widows, many of them still children, she asked for help from her 'Western sisters', American women she had come to admire. She said Indian women—her focus was on high-caste women—needed education and freedom, and she believed they ultimately needed Indian rather than foreign teachers to guide them.

Pandita Ramabai

Ramabai also published in the Marathi language *The Peoples of the United States* (1889), an account of America based on observations and information collected during 1886–1888.[3] She idealized some aspects of American life but emphasized American ideals of equality

---

[3] Kosambi, Meera, ed. 2003. *Pandita Ramabai's American Encounter.* Bloomington, Indiana: Indiana U. Press.

and liberty and strong local institutions to push her compatriots, male and female, to improve their society. Addressing racism, she pointed to prejudices against the Chinese, and 'red Indians', as well as against African Americans.[4] But she felt that caste prejudice in India was much worse.[5] She overplayed the local knowledge and cultural level of Americans, portraying them as studying Latin and reading poetry in their spare time, imbued with civic consciousness and tolerance. But she also criticized 'national egotism': the belief that America was better than any other country. She spoke at local meetings and at universities, and John R. Mott (1865–1955), coming to his life's vocation of recruiting and organizing Christian students and workers, listened to her at Cornell University.[6] In the following decades she met and interacted with American missionaries including Sherwood Eddy (1871–1963).[7]

Ramabai said that she extended her stay from what began as a brief visit to more than two years because she was so impressed with American education and especially the rapid rise in education for women at every level, including the professions. It was her belief—upheld by many recent researchers worldwide—that women's education was crucial for societal advancement. She detailed how women's education had vastly improved over the past two generations:

> The learned American woman Frances Willard has said that this glorious nineteenth century has seen many wonderful scientific discoveries; but the most wonderful of them is Woman's discovery of herself. This is borne out by considering the history of women's collective effort during the past forty years...[8]

---

[4] Ibid., pp. 114ff, 157, 168.

[5] Ibid, p. 118.

[6] Mathews, Basil. 1934. *John R. Mott. World Citizen*. NY: Harper, pp. 63–64.

[7] Eddy, Sherwood. 1955. *Eighty Adventurous Years. An Autobiography*. NY: Harper, 1955, p. 34.

[8] Kosambi 2003, p. 190.

Finding American women actively working in voluntary associations and committed to a variety of reforms, Ramabai hoped that Indians, male as well as female, would work to create a better India. Temperance organizations were a model. Although she contrasted the position of women in America with their low status in India, she saw the need for advancement in America as well, especially the granting of political rights. She also admired the industriousness of Americans and the separation of church and state. This inspired her to work for reform in India. Like some of her Western predecessors who gained insight from real or imaginary journeys to distant places—Montesquieu, Voltaire and Alexis de Tocqueville among them—she used her views of a foreign land to highlight weaknesses of her home society and press for improvement.

Returning to India, Ramabai became a social worker and social reformer, helping degraded and abandoned women and working in famine relief, for temperance, and against smoking. The Ramabai Association in the United States provided help with funding. She established the Sharada Sadan in Bombay, then shifted to Pune and founded the Mukti Sadan, enlarged later into the overtly Christian, Mukti Mission. She expanded, from working with high caste women only, to include lower castes, losing some of her support.

Although American visitors to India were few, many Indians learned of the United States through the press and writings of Americans. Jyotirao Phule (1827–1890), a lower caste reformer from Maharashtra (in western India), was influenced by missionary views but also by the radical Deism of Thomas Paine as expressed in *The Age of Reason* (1794). Phule became an educator and with his wife opened a school for girls from the lowest groups in society. His father turned him out, finding his programme too radical. Phule continued to advocate and work for education of women and of the lowest castes including untouchables, whom he called *shudratishudras*, throughout his life. He founded several more schools in the 1850s, including a night school for working people. In the 1860s, he established a house for illegitimate children and their mothers and challenged the caste order by opening the household water tank to untouchables. In the next decade he helped found the Satyashodhak Samaj ('Truth-Seeking Society'), a radical reform organization, and became a member of the Pune Municipal Council actively seeking changes in society. Phule was one of the first to see parallels between the plight of slaves in the United States and the lowest castes in India.[9] In *Slavery* (1873) he wrote: 'Dedicated to the good people of the United States as a token of admiration for their sublime disinterested and self-sacrificing devotion in the cause of Negro Slavery; and with an earnest desire, that my countrymen may take their noble example as their guide in the emancipation of their Sudra Brethren from the trammels of Brahmin thraldom.'

Indian nationalists began to visit America, too. Although Vivekananda and Jamshetji Tata should surely be counted among workers for the rebirth of the Indian nation, they avoided the explicitly political. Among the earliest nationalist of a more political bent to arrive was Bipin Chandra Pal (1858–1932); yet his four-month speaking tour in 1900 focused less on Indian nationalism and more on the cause of temperance. Pal identified with one branch of the Brahmo Samaj, but was also devoted to the Vaishnava teacher Bijay Krishna Goswami (1841–1899). Some Brahmos were comfortable with Christianity, but Pal was a critic. Though he had attended mission schools in his native Bengal, he—like Vivekananda—had scant patience with the West's despatch of missionaries to India.

In 1898, Pal was awarded a two-year grant to study theology in Great Britain. Based in Oxford, he spent a year listening, learning and speaking for temperance in England and Scotland. He received a rousing welcome in Glasgow until it was learned that he was not a Christian. Finding that the grant was too restrictive, hampering him from expressing his political views, Pal resigned from it. Invited to New York by temperance organizers, he advocated temperance and edged into politics. Based there, he spoke widely, and learned that Americans were freer, less condescending, and more open than the British. Like Vivekananda and other Indian visitors, Pal came

---

[9] McDermott 2013, pp. 160–61.

to admire the education, progress, and outspokenness of American women. But he was affronted by American racism. He was allowed to identify with and travel with whites, but he saw how Blacks were systematically excluded from public institutions and travel facilities. He compared the plight of Blacks to untouchables in India. From the age of fourteen, he had disowned and attacked India's caste system; here was another version of it.

In a New York hotel lobby, an American greeted Pal bluntly: 'You have come from a country [which is] ... destined to be the teachers of the world. But you cannot fulfil this destiny until you are able to look at the world horizontally into the face.'[10] Pal immediately knew what he meant: for India to be able to teach, it must acquire equality with other nations. Pal was headed in that direction and took the message to heart. He returned to India, and within a few years became a leader of the Swadeshi movement, and a prominent journalist. Like many nationalists under the Raj, he was soon imprisoned for his refusal to testify in court against another Indian leader.[11] Pal proved to be a passionate Indian nationalist who over decades of struggle, pressed for self-rule.

During the Swadeshi years in the first decade of the twentieth century, several Indian nationalist leaders visited the UK to speak there for Indian self-government. Dadabhai Naoroji had been elected to Parliament, but around 1905, G.K. Gokhale and Lala Lajpat Rai both addressed workers as well as Parliamentarians there, pressing their cause. In mid-1905, Rai interrupted his UK work to journey to the US for a month to speak to American audiences about British exploitation of India, and the need for Indians to run their own country.[12]

Asian immigrants to the US were few until the late nineteenth century. Chinese and Japanese labourers came for the Gold Rush and

---

[10] Chatterjee, Saral Kumar. 1984. *Bipin Chandra Pal*. New Delhi: Publications Division, Government of India, p. 76.
[11] Ibid., p. 73ff; Sen, Dictionary of National Biography III, pp. 284–87.
[12] Nagar, Purushottam. 1977. *Lala Lajpat Rai. The Man and His Ideas*. New Delhi: Manohar, pp. 18–21.

stayed to help build the continental railway, although the former were soon barred by the Chinese Immigration Act of 1882, and the latter by a 'gentleman's agreement' that restricted Japanese immigration. Students from both countries came in modest numbers, and traders and merchants' representatives came from India. Drawing on census reports, demographers S. Chandrasekhar and Haridas Muzumdar report that only 676 South Asians arrived in the period 1820 and 1900, but 4713 came between 1901 and 1910; and in the next two decades, 2082 and 1886 respectively. The numbers remained small until significant changes in American immigration law in the third quarter of the twentieth century. Between 1908 and 1923, only sixty-seven Indians became naturalized American citizens.[13]

The first South Asian immigrants were mainly Sikh peasant farmers who were pushed out of Canada and ended up in California in the early 1900s. They struggled to survive in an increasingly anti-Asian America where white supremacists aroused fears of the 'tide of turbans' that could engulf America. Many of those early Sikhs immigrants initially hoped to return home with the wealth they earned in America. Some did, but most remained. Some became landowners, and a Sikh community grew around Stockton, where the first Sikh gurdwara was built in 1915.[14]

Looking back from almost a century later, Indian-American author Chitra Banerjee Divakaruni wrote painful, powerful poems about those Sikh settlers, their customs, and their matches.[15] As bringing wives and potential brides from India was difficult, and then became impossible, Indians began marrying Mexican women. These marriages were made for all the usual reasons: love, companionship, desire for a family, and control of property.[16]

---

[13] Chandrasekhar, S., ed. 1984. *From India to America. A Brief History of Immigration*. La Jolla, California, Population Review Books.

[14] La Brack, Bruce. 1988. *The Sikhs of Northern California 1904–1975*. NY: AMS Press, p. 127ff.

[15] Divakaruni, Chitra Banerjee. 1997. *Leaving Yuba City*. NY: Anchor Books, p. 95ff.

[16] Leonard, Karen Isaksen. 1992. *Making Ethnic Choices. California's Punjabi Mexican Americans*. Philadelphia: Temple U. Press.

Our view of Indian immigrants has been expanded by Vivek Bald's research into subaltern peddlers, seaman and workers who made it into the US in the first half of the twentieth century—mostly in New York and New Orleans. Working at a variety of jobs, they married the women they found, including Blacks and Hispanics, and made lives for their mixed families. Bald is vague about actual numbers. Hundreds? Thousands? A modest number of South Asians stayed and became Americans, with American descendants.[17]

Meanwhile, on the subcontinent, as Britain strengthened its hold, it attempted to mould India in its own image. In 1857, pockets of resistance had swelled into a large but uncoordinated revolt against the British, known as the Indian Mutiny or, as V.D. Savarkar called it, the First Great War of Indian Independence. The British prevailed, supported by Indian loyalists, and aided by the absence of a single concerted strategy on the part of the rebels. The tide of Indian nationalism rose in the late nineteenth century, and resistance slowly grew as well among the general Indian population. An Indian elite emerged, educated in Western-style schools, fluent English-speakers, even as they continued to use their own languages and practice their own religions. They wanted greater self-rule. They created the British Indian Association, and then the Indian Association; these were succeeded by the Indian National Congress, formed in 1885 by Indians leaders from the Western-educated population of the three major presidencies: Bombay, Madras and Bengal. Although these men—at first there were just men—advocated peaceful petitioning, by the end of the century, a few ardent nationalists wanted violent resistance. Nationalists of both varieties sent emissaries and workers abroad, and fashioned extensive networks that were rarely well-organized or capable of effective communication. These efforts will be discussed later in this chapter.

The British responded by offering India reforms, both locally and nationally in 1909 and 1919, which offered limited opportunities for Indians to participate in self-rule. Moderate nationalist leaders

---

[17] Bald, Vivek. 2013. *Bengali Harlem and the Lost Histories of South Asian America.* Cambridge: Harvard U. Press.

accepted the terms offered and took appointments or stood for election, while the more radical and alienated, who demanded independence, derided the reforms.

In the US, the race, colour and citizenship status of Asian Indians were problematic. Some Indians were determined to be 'Aryans and therefore white', and thus eligible for naturalization. But were they Black, brown, white, mixed, or something else? Some claimed that they were white whatever the colour of their skin. Until 1917, American judges had some discretion in deciding whether a South Asian before them was eligible for citizenship as 'white'. Entry was always allowed to 'students, businessmen, and visitors', but after 1917, India was considered part of the 'barred zone' covering most of Asia, from where immigration was restricted. The immigrant Taraknath Das (1884–1958) claimed to be Aryan and white; although he was brown-skinned and a member of the Shudra caste (the lowest above the Untouchables), an American judge granted his citizenship in 1913, although other American officials were opposed.[18]

In October 1916, a San Francisco newspaper reported that Superior Judge Franklin Cole of El Centro, Imperial County, 'declares that if the Hindu applicant for citizenship can prove that he belongs to a certain caste recognized as "white" he is eligible to become an American'. The decision was based on previous federal court rulings that 'both held that a Hindu of the best class who can prove that he is a member of the Aryan race, is eligible to American citizenship', the newspaper reported. The story quoted Ram Chandra, a 'prominent San Francisco Hindu': 'Ethnologically, all the upper classes of India are Aryan and therefore eligible to American citizenship. All the Hindus who are now here are Aryan. They are white people in the same sense as are the Greeks, Italians, and Spaniards . . .'[19] But in 1923, the US Supreme Court ruled Indians 'obviously not of the white race' (*sic*). They could no longer

---

[18] Mukherjee, Tapan K. 1998. *Taraknath Das. Life and Letters of a Revolutionary in Exile.* Calcutta: National Council of Education, Bengal.
[19] Sareen, T.R. ed. 1994. *Selected Documents on the Ghadr Party.* New Delhi: Mounto, pp. 165–66.

become citizens. The Immigration Act of 1924 set strict quotas, and the course was determined for two decades. No South Asian could become naturalized except for the few who served in the American military during the First World War.[20] But the effort to equate an upper-caste Aryan Indian with American Caucasians, and therefore to consider them white, did not die. The issues of skin colour and race have resonated through the history of South Asians in the US. Besides the problems that arose in the US, lay the issue of colour in South Asia. From ancient times to the present, fairness has been prized over dark skin colour. In arranged marriages from those days into recent times, skin colour is an attribute at play.

Amid the new restrictions, the US government moved to strip some naturalized Indians of their citizenship. The majority were denaturalized. A few, perhaps with greater resources and better contacts, receiving assistance from public figures and Congressmen, fought tenaciously to retain their citizenship. They had renounced citizenship of British India upon becoming naturalized as Americans, so if stripped of their American citizenship, they would become stateless, along with their American wives.[21] After complicated legal wrangling, William Howard Taft, the former president and then chief justice of the Supreme Court, ruled that res judicata, or legal precedent, made them citizens. Those already de-naturalized lost out.

Americans struggled in their communities, too, over how to think about Indians. At first the blanket term 'Hindus' was applied to Indians, although most in California were Sikhs and most of the peddlers and seamen were Muslims. To distinguish South Asians from native Americans, the term East Asian Indians was used. Even in the twenty-first century, a number of terms are used: Asian Indians, South Asian Americans, Asian Americans, or just Americans. South Asians, like other Americans, can choose how to identify themselves, or use more than one identifying term depending on the context.

---

[20] Varma, Premdatta. 1995. *Indian Immigrants in USA. Struggle for Equality.* New Delhi: Heritage, pp. 114, 130.
[21] Ibid., p. 233ff.

Despite the legal obstacles, Indians continued to come to the US, especially students, businessmen and religious teachers. Among the students and potential agitators, Taraknath Das came in 1906—fearing arrest if he returned to India—and attended the University of California and University of Washington, and subsequently Norwich Academy, a military college, to train so he could help drive the British from India. Dhan Gopal Mukerji (1890–1936), younger brother of Jadu Gopal Mukherjee (1886–1976), a well-known revolutionary in India, came around the same time to study, work and agitate. Others, like Prafulla Mukherji, a politically involved engineer, came to study, stayed on, worked, and associated himself with the Independence movement. A peace activist, he lived into his mid-nineties, devoted to his causes to the end.[22]

One of the most extraordinary students was B.R. Ambedkar (1891–1956). Although an untouchable from the lowest rung of India's social hierarchy, Ambedkar showed such great promise that the Gaekwad of Baroda awarded him a scholarship to study at Columbia University from 1913 to 1916. He settled into Livingston Hall and roomed with a Parsi, Naval Bhathena, who became a lifelong friend. His course load in three years was astounding: twenty-nine in economics, eleven in history, six in sociology, five in philosophy, four in anthropology, and three in politics, among other classes. In later days he praised his teachers, especially John Dewey, Edwin Seligman and James Harvey Robinson. Ambedkar wrote two MA theses, one on the National Dividend of India, another on ancient Indian commerce. His seminar paper on castes in India provided the springboard for several later, major publications. In 1916, Ambedkar moved on to the London School of Economics, and within a decade completed PhD dissertations there and at Columbia. He was also called to the bar. His remarkable academic accomplishments were but an early chapter in his career, which culminated in his leadership of millions of untouchables in India. He served as the nation's first law minister and was a major author of the Indian Constitution. But he left no footprint in the US other

---

[22] Mukherji Papers.

than his academic work. He was one of first to profit greatly from his education in the US.[23]

The South Asian agitators in the US during these years had some devoted American helpers. Hardly anyone today in India has heard of Jabez T. Sunderland (1842–1936), a Unitarian minister of British birth who lived and worked most of his life in the US, pouring out a stream of books and articles, many on religion, but also about India, where he visited in 1895 and 1913. On his first visit to India he helped establish the Unitarian Union in the Khasi Hills; on the second he worked to bring all theists together, as participants in a 'universal religion'. To tribal people in the hills, he made a connection that lasted for decades, though mainly through encouraging letters he sent from America.

For more than four decades, Sunderland worked tirelessly to drum up support from America for Indian Independence. Many organizations were formed in the US to help India, and to understand India, from the 1900s to the mid-1930s; he was a pillar of support for almost everyone. As each organization folded or blended with another, never discouraged, he moved on and helped new organizations grow. In the 1890s he had contacted Ramananda Chatterjee (1865–1943), a Brahmo, who was in Allahabad working for the Samaj, while Sunderland, following the example of Rammohun Roy, was trying to bring together the Unitarians of the US and Britain and the Brahmo Samaj. Sunderland came to India in 1913 with plans to unite Christian denominations but was stymied by the outbreak of the First World War. He never returned to India but became America's fiercest critic of the British Raj.[24]

Another American who briefly tried to help the Indian cause in the early twentieth century was a wealthy New York lawyer of Irish descent, Myron Phelps (1856–1916), 'who had written a series of "Letters to the Indian people", printed in *The Hindu* of Madras. In 1907, he started an Indo-American National Association followed in 1908 by an India House, intended as a lodging house and a meeting

---

[23] Keer, Dhananjay. 1954. *Dr. Ambedkar. Life and Mission.* Bombay: Popular Prakashan, p. 31ff.

[24] Sunderland Papers; Bose 1974, p. 81ff.

place for Indian students in New York.'[25] (Some Indian students and would-be revolutionaries from London emigrated to New York from India House in London and circulated a harshly anti-British publication, *The Indian Sociologist*. Relations between Phelps and the students broke down and New York's India House was closed in February 1909. Phelps had just received an extraordinary letter from Rabindranath Tagore (1861–1941) in answer to his questions about India Society and decided to depart for India. Tagore succinctly analysed the pluses and minuses of Indian society and put forth what he believed was India's message for the world. Phelps reached India in 1910, wandering the sub-continent and visiting Tagore at Shantiniketan, where they discussed the Brahmo philosophy and Theosophy. Phelps made no further contributions to the Indian cause.

Along with those who became permanent residents, quite a few transients from India came to America before Independence in 1947. One was Rabindranath Tagore, the country's foremost man of letters and winner of the Nobel Prize for Literature in 1913. Ananda Lal, a scholar of the theatre and Tagore, has searched out the response of the *New York Times*, to Tagore's prize, which it announced in its issue of 14 November 1913, commenting: 'It is the first time that this prize has been given to anybody but a white person.' The next day the paper editorialized: 'Some of us feel a surprise more than faintly tinged with resentment at an award of the Nobel Prize for Literature that passes over all Occidental writers of prose and poetry and falls on a Hindu bard with a name hard to pronounce and harder to remember.' The writer argued that the award went against the principle that money and glory should be kept in the family, but derived consolation from the fact that 'Babindranath (*sic*) Tagore, if not exactly one us, is, as an Aryan, a distant relation of all white folk. Moreover, though of Eastern birth, he is of Western education, and though he is said to write his verses first in Sanskrit—which seems queer, that being a language now spoken by nobody—he

---

[25] Dutta, Krishna and Andrew Robinson, eds. 1997. *Selected Letters of Rabindranath Tagore*. Cambridge: Cambridge U. Press, p. 73.

translates them into good, sound English before submitting them to the large public.'[26]

Whether or not Tagore was aware of the supercilious and racist responses to his Nobel Prize, he continued to travel to the West, visited America, and had his son Rathindranath study agriculture at the University of Illinois. As was the case for other South Asians applying for citizenship, Tagore's 'Aryan-ness' calmed fears that non-Aryans were insinuating themselves with Europeans and Americans.

Although Tagore wrote no lengthy description or assessment of the US, we have a few snippets. One of Tagore's earliest biographers, Basanta Kumar Roy, asked Tagore in 1912 what he thought of America. Krishna Kripalani, a biographer, writes that:

Tagore praised the country and its climate—he had enough of both space and sunshine which he missed in England—and expressed his admiration of the people's drive and efficiency, 'unrivalled businessmen, splendid organizers and agriculturalists, and matchless engineers', adding that he, however, wished he saw more evidence of people's interest in culture, 'even though agriculture suffered a little'. Roy reminded him that staying in that small provincial town he hardly had any opportunities of meeting many cultured people who in any case were scattered all over that vast continent . . .[27]

On later trips, Tagore met with insensitive customs officials and was uneasy with the bustle of America. Still, during a 1916 visit, he composed an essay, 'Nationalism in India', including general remarks about America as an offshoot of Europe, but growing, and unfinished:

If it is given at all to the West to struggle out of these tangles of the lower slopes to the spiritual summit of humanity, then

---

[26] Tagore, Rabindranath. 2001. *Three Plays*. New Delhi: Oxford U. Press. Translated by Ananda Lal. (quoting November 1913.'Topics of the Times: Our Case Isn't Desperate.' *New York Times*. p. 10), introduction.

[27] Kripalani, Krishna. 1962. *Rabindranath Tagore. A Biography*. NY: Grove, p. 225.

I cannot but think that it is the special mission of America to fulfil this hope of God and man. You are the country of expectation, desiring something else than what is . . . I realize how much America is untrammeled by the traditions of the past, and I can appreciate that experimentalism is a sign of America's youth. The foundation of her glory is in the future, rather than in the past; and if one is gifted with the power of clairvoyance, one will be able to love the America that is to be.[28]

Tagore described the sickness of a Europe that was much more tied to the past and tradition than America, and which had been 'tempted out of her path by her pride of power and greed of possession'.[29] He then went on to compare America and India:

A parallelism exists between America and India—the parallelism of welding together into one body various races. In my country, we have been seeking to find out something common to all races, which will prove their real unity. Her problem was the problem of the world in miniature. India is too vast in its area and too diverse in its races. It is many countries packed in one geographical receptacle. It is just the opposite of what Europe truly is, namely one country made into many. India being naturally many, yet adventitiously one, has all along suffered from the looseness of its diversity and the feebleness of its unity. Be it said to the credit of India that this diversity was not her own creation; she has had to accept it as a fact from the beginning of her history. In America and Australia, Europe has simplified her problem by almost exterminating the original population. Even in the present age this spirit of extermination is making itself manifest, by inhospitably shutting out aliens, through those who themselves were aliens in the lands they now occupy. But India tolerated difference of races from the first, and that spirit of toleration has acted all through her history.[30]

---

[28] Tagore, Rabindranath. 1917. *Nationalism*. New York: Macmillan, p. 123.
[29] Ibid., p. 125.
[30] Ibid., pp. 127–37.

Tagore found an interesting parallel between his own country and the country he was visiting. To Americans, he was more acute in criticizing America than his remarkably idealized India. His hope for toleration in India between all castes and communities led him in this direction.

Some Indian nationalists came to the US early in the twentieth century specifically to support resistance to the British Raj, and worked actively for Indian Independence until it was achieved in 1947. Much of the work of Taraknath Das and others was propaganda, courting American officials and public opinion; Das was dismissed from the Norwich Academy for being anti-British. He was a founder of the paper, *Free Hindustan*, and an ally of Har Dayal (1884–1939) and others on the West Coast who formed the Ghadar Party in 1913. Between 1907 and 1910, Das moved between the West Coast and New York, trying to mobilize South Asians in the US to drive out the British and claim their rights in Canada and the US. In New York, he was aided by George Freeman, the Irish editor of the *Gaelic American*. Das was employed by the US Immigration Service as a translator and was involved with Indian students in San Francisco. His paper was proscribed and then closed, possibly under British diplomatic pressure.

Around 1910, Har Dayal came to the US and established himself in California. Beyond teaching Indian philosophy in California, he formed a worldwide propaganda organization to inspire expatriate Indians to go home and drive the British out. Starting in 1913 and continuing into the 1920s, then intermittently, some of those connected to the Ghadar ('mutiny') movement lived in a house in San Francisco and put out a nationalist paper in several Indian languages. In the Bay Area there were conflicts between loyalist Indian students with the local swami of the Ramakrishna Mission, against more radical students and Sikh workers, mobilized by Das and Har Dayal. Under threat of arrest, his influence fading, Har Dayal fled from the US in 1914 and went to Europe. He participated in Indian efforts to fight the British Empire during the First World War in the Middle East, but later became a less fiery nationalist, re-entered the US, and died there in 1939.[31]

---

[31] Brown, Emily C. 1975. *Har Dayal. Hindu Revolutionary and Rationalist.* Tucson: U. of Arizona Press, p. 85ff.

The Ghadar party was taken over mainly by Sikhs whose paper spouted extreme language about the Raj. The British tried to muzzle the paper, but were frustrated by the First Amendment. In early 1914, more than 200 Sikhs aboard the *Komagata Maru* were prevented from landing, and remained aboard ship in Canada's Vancouver harbour for weeks. They were then shipped back to India by the Canadian authorities. Outrage over the incident led other newly radicalized Sikhs to leave the West Coast and return to India. There, many battled police, were arrested, while others scattered to preach revolt.[32]

Many historical accounts of the *Komagata Maru* voyage and restraint in Canada, and then its return to India have a narrow focus. More recent analyses by Seema Sohi and Renisa Mawani have widened the prisms through which to look at this event. Sohi has connected some passengers and leaders abroad to the more global intents of the Ghadar Party. Renisa Mawani comes to the story of the voyage with her 'oceans as method' approach widening the view to all the Earth's connected waters, and focusing on the legal complications of maritime law, overlapping and unclear land laws, and hostility of the Canadian authorities and their allies. Her approach is quite unique in linking the waters of the Earth to developments on land. She shows how those on board the ship felt that through freedom of the sea, and as citizens of the empire, they were entitled to land as British citizens anywhere in that empire. They had cruel lessons to learn. Gurdit Singh, the organizer and financier of the voyage was hamstrung as officials of the empire tried to prevent it, and then prevent the passengers from landing in Canada.

Although the migrants, mostly Sikhs from the Punjab, thought they were British citizens, upon arrival they were labelled as British subjects, with limited rights within Canadian jurisdiction. Mawani shows how imperial, dominion and provincial laws were contradictory, but nevertheless, the Canadian courts ruled that the passengers could not

---

[32] Sohi, Seema. 2014. *Echoes of Mutiny. Race, Surveillance & Indian Anti-colonialism in North America*. NY: Oxford U. Press, p. 92ff; Singh, Khushwant and Satindra Singh. 1966. *Ghadar 1915*. R & K Publishing; Josh, Sohan Singh. 1977. *Hindustan Gadar Party. A Short History*. New Delhi: People's Publishing House, p. 59ff; Sawhney, Savitri. 2008. *I Shall Never Ask for Pardon. A Memoir of Pandurang Khankhoje*. New Delhi: Penguin, p. 107ff.

enter. A small number who had been previously domiciled in Canada were allowed to enter. Both Mawani and Sohi show Indian migrants connecting to the long colonial history of the exploitation of indigenous people, those trapped into slavery as well as indentured servitude. The cooperation of the American, British and Canadian authorities is exemplified by the career of William Hopkinson, once of the Indian police, then employed by the American and British authorities to report on the actions of South Asians along the west coast of North America. Though way down in the human hierarchy by Canada's white rulers, the Indians did not deplore the even more desperate plight of the indigenous peoples of Canada. The analyses of Sohi and Mawani have enriched our view and brought the voyage of the *Komagata Maru* into world history.

There were repercussions for what was seen as extreme political activity in Canada and the US as well. Das and several Sikhs bought handguns and ammunition and were arrested by the authorities. W.C. Hopkinson, the most important British/Canadian/American agent observing Indian nationalists, was attending the trial of a nationalist, Mewa Singh, when Singh pulled a handgun in the courtroom and killed him—and was hanged, in consequence, in January 1915.[33] That same month, Swami Trigunatita, head of the Ramakrishna Mission in San Francisco, was murdered in his temple by Louis Vavra, a Hungarian immigrant and one-time disciple who nursed a grievance against all preachers—yet another example of smaller acts of violence not confined to the battlefields of Europe.[34]

Taraknath Das participated in many kinds of actions, but in the long run did not approve of individual acts of violence, but favoured education, discipline and preparations for a larger, revolutionary rising against the Raj. He lost favour with the Ghadarites in San Francisco, led by Ram Chandra after the departure of Har Dayal. While Indians were urged to return to their native land to make trouble for the Raj, Das separated from his former Ghadar colleagues and left for Europe in November 1914.[35]

---

[33] Sohi 2014, p. 147.

[34] Mukherjee 1998, p. 61.

[35] Ibid., p. 64ff.

5

The First World War

The guns of August not only signalled the beginning of what was then called the Great War in Europe but also led Indians and other politically active and informed colonial peoples to make choices. Many Indians in this war and in the Second World War fought with Great Britain, the Raj, and the US. A minority—few in this war, more in the next—sat out the war or identified with and even fought on the other side. Colonial people, subjects of the British, the French and the Dutch, had to determine how to shape their efforts for self-rule and freedom during these wars.

In the First World War, Indian princes, upper class Indians, and Indian Liberals or Moderates chose the side of the rulers. Hundreds of thousands of ordinary Indians fought in the Middle East and Europe for the British Empire. A few even joined the American army[1] and some supporters contributed monetarily. The Tata Iron and Steel Company actively worked for the war effort, lowering prices for some products and was praised by Raj officials.

But some Indian nationalists inside, and outside India, saw the war as an opportunity to weaken the Raj. Some, like Mohandas Gandhi, returned to India from South Africa in 1915, advocating non-violent means to greater self-rule. Back in India, Gandhi first toured and listened. He made contacts and joined local struggles while finding his way into nationalist organizing.

---

[1] Mozumder, Suman Guha. March 16, 2018. 'Band of Brothers,' *India Abroad*. XLVII, No. 24.

The British had extensive international intelligence operations watching Indians abroad, including in the US, where the Ghadar group and some other revolutionaries advocated violent means, sought German help, and plotted to end the Raj. The British were concerned with hostile South Asians, but even more with Irish nationalists, some who carried out the short-lived but violent 1916 Easter Rising in Dublin. Before and during the war, Irish and the South Asian nationalists supported each other, mainly by words, not deeds. The British were wary of Irish-American clout in the US. At the same time, British propagandists encouraged American entry into the war. Cecil Spring-Rice became for a time their ambassador in Washington, while Colonel William Wiseman headed British intelligence in New York.

In 1914, Lala Lajpat Rai (1865–1928), a leading nationalist in India, was in Great Britain and was prevented by the British from returning to India. After spending a few months in Japan in 1915, he settled in New York City, doing nationalist propaganda, while working to undermine British rule without violence. Rai had earlier visited the US briefly in 1905. Hampered by lack of finances, Lajpat Rai on this visit was aided by funds sent by Bal Gangadhar Tilak (1856–1920), another nationalist leader, and from the success of his books. He produced a stream of books and pamphlets and *Young India*, a paper calling for Indian self-rule on behalf of his small organization, the Home Rule League of America. Blunt and gregarious with a keen intelligence, Lajpat Rai proved one of the most adept of Indian nationalists abroad.[2]

Rai spoke widely, made friends with Irish nationalists and Black Americans, and testified before a Senate committee on Indian Independence. He noted the similarities between the plight of African Americans and the lowest castes and Untouchables in India. He was particularly interested in questions of race and power and visited Black colleges in Atlanta and Tuskegee Institute. He also

[2] Chand, Feroz. 1978. *Lajpat Rai*. Life and Work. New Delhi: Publications Division, Government of India, p. 285ff; Nanda, B.R., ed. 2005-2006. *The Collected Works of Lala Lajpat Rai*. Vols. 6, 7, 8. New Delhi: Manohar. Vols. 6-8.

suffered from American racism. To fill out his American education, Rai toured the US in 1914, studied its history, and wrote *The United States of America* (1916), the fullest treatment of American society written by a South Asian during the Raj.

Lajpat Rai welcomed American allies against the British Raj but freely criticized American life. In his account of American society, he was assisted by an American writer offering a short version of American history and a description of women's groups, but the rest was Rai's. Just as he was appalled by Untouchability in India, he was repelled by white Americans' prejudice against its Black citizens. He thought that most Americans were driven by the desire for power and pleasure, to the detriment of inner and more tempered concerns. He noted that Americans contributed money to convert the heathens, thinking they had provided for their own souls—while church attendance was dropping. Lajpat Rai observed the appeal of mysticism to Americans:

> America is the land of fads... Anyone can set up a school of thought of his own... He is sure to find some followers and some admirers... Mysticism particularly appeals to the occident most intensely... Hence the great charm that oriental systems of thought have for the people of America. The oriental religious thought has deeply affected the thought of the West and many a modern religious sect could be traced to some idea borrowed from Buddhism or Vedanta. Even the new schools of Christianity bear the marks of contact with the East... many a fraud is being practised in the name of the Orient by unscrupulous persons... Sometimes he [the American] gets hold of a needy Oriental, a Hindu, a Muslim, or a Chinaman, makes a tool of him, uses his name, keeps him in the background, credits him with occult powers, advertises his holiness and achievements and carries on a rousing trade.[3]

Rai sharply criticized phony swamis, and even the Ramakrishna Mission, for not sending its 'best men' to America. Although he

---

[3] Lajpat Rai, Lala. 1916. *The United States of America*. A Hindu's Impressions and a Study. Calcutta: R. Chatterjee, pp. 189–90.

offered sharp criticism of Christian organizations and missionaries, he had kind words for Unitarians for their link to the Brahmo Samaj and also their kindness to him while he was in the United States.

Near the end of his book on America, Rai surveyed Indians or Hindus, as they were commonly called, in their adopted home. He wrote of South Asian labourers on the West Coast who were subject to prejudice:

> The real objection lies in a prejudice which has been accentuated by economic considerations. The Hindu is a formidable rival in the field of labor as well as trade. So is the Jew. The Jew, however, has a white skin and has adopted the habits and manners of the Europeans... The Hindu is also Caucasian by race, it is true, but then his color and his habits and his manners are so different that the Europeans are not prepared to acknowledge that his racial origin is the same as theirs... More or less all Asiatics share the same prejudice which is shown against the Hindu, but the political status of the Japanese and the Chinese being high at home gives them advantage over the Hindu. The Japanese has to be tolerated because he is a citizen of a country which recently whipped one of the great powers... Against the Chinese Americans do not feel the same bitterness as they display against the Jap or the Hindu. The former they hate; the latter they hold in scorn; but the Chinese they pity.[4]

Like other South Asians, Lajpat Rai believed South Asians were 'Aryans' and members of the large racial category of Indo-Europeans, the dominant race worldwide. This view was rare among white Westerners. His pain for those suffering from race prejudice in the US and from caste prejudice in India was acute. Rai wanted to fight prejudice worldwide, to reform the caste system, and to eliminate hierarchy through non-violent means.

Lajpat Rai met the journalist Agnes Smedley (1892–1950) and taught her about India. He supported non-violent protest, mocked by Ghadarites and others advocating Independence by any means

---

[4] Ibid., pp. 411–12.

necessary. Smedley worked for India's cause for several years and then moved to Berlin, where she formed an intimate tie to the Indian nationalist Virendranath Chattopadhyaya (1880–1937), brother of poet and nationalist Sarojini Naidu. This tempestuous relationship broke down and Smedley headed to China, where she advocated the Chinese communist cause. Her powerful novel, *Daughter of Earth*[5] portrays an Indian character based on Lajpat Rai that draws upon her period of learning from and helping him.

Refusing repeated offers to join groups and individuals plotting against the Raj with or without German help, Lajpat Rai continued along the mainstream, non-violent Congress path. On the American conquest and rule of the Philippines, he displayed ambivalence. His first response was that it was a menace to liberty and a betrayal of 'the spirit of the Republic'. But convinced by US government statistics and handouts that a great deal, particularly in education, was being done for the Filipinos, he moderated his view. Convinced that the Americans had a timetable for improvement of local conditions, he dropped his condemnation.[6]

Launching his periodical *Young India* as a voice for the Home Rule League, Lajpat Rai put his aims as such:

> Our work is open and perfectly constitutional and legitimate. We have no pro-German sympathies and we do not intend to meddle with American politics. Our work is for India and for humanity... The time is opportune... for the people of India to lay their case before the civilized world. So far they have neglected their opportunities and let the judgment go in default against them... The League aims at Home Rule within the British Empire... Its work in this country is purely educational. It doesn't contemplate any kind of action either open or secret... It hopes to be of use to American statesmen in arriving at a correct knowledge of Indian affairs as preliminaries to a durable world-peace.[7]

---

[5] Price, Ruth. 2005. *The Lives of Agnes Smedley*. Oxford: Oxford U. Press, p. 59ff.
[6] Lajpat Rai, 1916, pp. 296–325.
[7] V. I, No. 1, January 1918.

Lajpat Rai puts the goals of the movement more modestly than his colleagues in the extremist wing of the Congress, Tilak and Aurobindo Ghose (1872–1950). They demanded swaraj or self-rule with no foreign control; Rai and many mainstream Congressmen, including Gandhi, still talked of self-government within the British Empire.

In contrast, the Ghadar members and others called for violent revolt in India. An Indian using the name 'M.N. Roy', (Narendranath Bhattacharya) was involved in a failed plot to smuggle arms from the Dutch East Indies to Bengal. He went to California, then to New York, was arrested, and fled while out on bail to Mexico. He eventually went to Moscow, joined the Third Communist International and became a founder of the Communist Party of India. Roy proved a difficult associate. German entreaties to join their efforts during the war floundered, and later Roy opposed other Indians in Berlin vying for Moscow's favours.[8] As in the US, extremist Indian nationalists were suppressed in Britain, particularly after the assassination of an official in 1909. Some moved to Paris or Berlin or the US, some earning degrees in the US, and some joining in anti-British activities in the US before or during the First World War.[9]

The US entry into the First World War was marked by powerful repressive measures by the American government. The Committee of Public Information spread anti-German, pro-Allied propaganda. The Espionage Act was passed and German–Americans, already suspect, were subject to more severe treatment. There was also a crackdown from 1917 to 1920 on left wing Americans and foreigners which culminated in the so-called 'Red Summer' of 1919.

Taraknath Das and other nationalists in the United States plotted to smuggle German arms into India. This was part of Germany's war efforts to undermine the British Empire. The Berlin India Committee, founded as part of the Indian–German efforts to undermine the British Empire, was led by Virendranath

---

[8] Roy, M.N. 1964. *M.N. Roy's Memoirs*. Bombay: Allied, p. 14ff.
[9] Overstreet Gene D. and Marshall Windmiller. 1959. *Communism in India*. Berkeley: U. of California Press, p. 19ff.

Chattopadhyaya. The committee worked with German officials to send missions to the Middle East, Afghanistan and the United States.

Das went to Berlin, the Middle East, then back to Europe. After difficulty renewing his American passport, in 1917, Das went to the US and then Japan. Upon returning to the US and just after the US entered the war on the side of the British, Das and 104 others—Indians and Germans, were indicted; thirty-seven were tried in what is called the Hindu Conspiracy or Ghadar Case, in 1917–1918. The background of the case makes it clear that before US entry into the war, British and American officials were cooperating, exchanging information and watching Indians and Germans. But with the US entry into the war, this cooperation went into high gear with intelligence officers William Wiseman and Robert Nathan (1868–1921) supplying the appropriate questions. The British, headed by Ambassador Spring-Rice, and Wiseman and Nathan, representing Indian Political Intelligence, pressed their objectives and gained full American cooperation.[10]

British intelligence foiled almost every German–Indian plot: in the Middle East, East Asia, South Asia and the United States. They turned Indians against other Indians, and Americans against Indian friends. They broke German secret codes and cracked German spy rings before they became active, and rooted out conspiracies by pressuring, perhaps torturing or threatening suspects, often with the support of Indians loyal to the Raj. C.R. Cleveland, Director of Indian Criminal Intelligence, wrote in the confidential report, 'Political Trouble in India':

> The British Government has been fortunate, I think, in having in its service, or at its disposal, a number of devoted and loyal Indians who have shown as little inclination to fraternize with the seditionist as a fox-terrier with a rat. There have also been a number of British officers who have looked upon the tracking of dangerous sedition as the big game of their life.[11]

---

[10] Jeffrey, Keith. 2010. *The Secret History of MI6*. New York: Penguin Press, p. 110–20.
[11] Ker, James Campbell. 1973. [1917]. *Political Trouble in India 1907-1917*. Delhi: Oriental, p. vi.

German officials and their Indian contacts were tried in San Francisco. Most were found guilty. The British supplied the evidence and sent numerous intelligence agents and police, some from India to the US, to prepare the prosecution. These included Sir George Denham and Robert Nathan. The US attorney trying the case said of Das, 'I believe he is the most pronounced figure of the war for infamy and treachery . . . is one of the most dangerous characters that could be abroad in any country at any time.'[12] On the last day of the trial, one Ghadar defendant, Ram Chandra, smuggled a gun into the courtroom, perhaps in his turban, and shot and killed another defendant, an opponent within the movement. A court security officer then killed Chandra. The violence may have influenced the jury. Das and some others were sentenced to prison, Das for two years. Some were deported.[13] All the German arms smuggling plots failed, but efforts to undermine the Raj from abroad continued after the war.

While Das was in prison in Fort Leavenworth, he and New York associates Agnes Smedley and Sailendranath Ghose were charged with violating the Espionage Act. Smedley and Ghose were arrested, but the case was weak and eventually dropped. Ghose, a science graduate from Calcutta and a protégé of Das, became friendly with Smedley, and in 1919, formed with her the Friends of Freedom for India (FFI). Its goals were to secure Indian independence from the British and to protect the civil rights of Indians in the US. Smedley, a tireless worker for the Indian cause, secured the support of some American liberals and socialists;[14] all of the first officers of the organization were Americans. In late October 1920, Das emerged from Fort Leavenworth and was hustled to New York where he became executive secretary of the FFI. After gaining citizenship in 1913, Das almost lost it because of his involvement in the Hindu Conspiracy Case of 1917. Although convicted, Das had American friends who fought for him. He kept his citizenship, stayed out

---

[12] Mukherjee 1998, 126; P.R.O., Foreign Office files 371, 372
[13] Hindu Conspiracy Trial Record, 1917.
[14] Price, Ruth. 2005. *The Lives of Agnes Smedley.* Oxford: Oxford U. Press, p. 47ff.

of jail, and wrote frequently for the Indian press, particularly *The Modern Review* published in Calcutta, about events in the US and throughout the world. In 1924, Das married Mary Keatinge, a divorcee considerably older than himself. He and his wife temporarily fled to Europe as a means of preserving his US citizenship. They later founded the Taraknath Das Foundation to help Indian students abroad, long an interest of Das.

Das, Smedley, and some other Indians in the FFI had support from Irish independence workers. When Eamon De Valera came to New York, a joint dinner was held for him at which Indian and Irishmen spoke. The legatees of Lajpat Rai's group were opposed to the more far-reaching ends sought by the FFI.[15]

---

[15] Mukherjee 1998, p. 167ff.

6

Conclusion

By the early 1890s, compared to Chinese–American and Japanese–American relations, Indian–American connections were sparse, but growing. Hundreds of American missionaries were in India running hospitals, clinics, schools and colleges, supported by funding from their churches back home. Some American businesses opened offices and American consuls were established in major cities—but not usually welcomed by British economic rivals.

British efforts to restrain American entry into their empire signalled that America and others had become powerful rivals in the quest for markets, raw materials, and all other gifts of empire, formal or informal. By century's end, the British-led Confederation of Canada was clearly demarcated from the United States. The British continued to have interests in the Caribbean and South America, but the sun shining on the British Empire was no longer at high noon. The British and Americans were joined, however, in their belief in the superiority of Anglo-Saxons. The domestic counterpoint to spreading the Christian gospel to the 'heathens' of Asia and Africa was American racism at home. Although the Civil War and the 13th, 14th and 15th Amendments had formally freed African Americans, the second half of the nineteenth century was marked by increasing racism. From the mid-nineteenth century, the Gold Rush brought the Chinese. Tens of thousands of labourers came and stayed to help build the railroads, and to find niches in American society in which they could work and live. Antipathy to them developed rapidly, especially on the West Coast, and this antagonism culminated in the Chinese

Exclusion Act of 1882 and vicious race riots targeting Chinese workers. The Exclusion Act was renewed and led to the demarcation of a barred zone from the Middle East to Japan in the first decades of the twentieth century which, of course, included South Asia, given the prevailing anti-Asian sentiment. The unwillingness to concede equal status to African Americans and indigenous peoples extended to Asians who had found their way to America, ostensibly the land of freedom and equality.

The American Oriental Society was supportive of research on Indian religion, and armchair scholars of Sanskrit, following the lead of William Whitney and John Avery, delved into the subtleties of Indian texts. However, successors to Emerson and Thoreau, public intellectuals who championed Asian wisdom and countered Western ethnocentrism, were rare. But American Protestant leaders made an opening to Asia by calling for a World Parliament of Religions to be held in conjunction with the great Chicago World's Fair of 1893. Their aim was to show the superiority of their faith. Many of their missionaries to Asia thought they were bringing truth and light to the heathens of India and China. The door to India was to open a little wider through unforeseen events at the fair.

Ezra Manela has called 1919 as 'The Wilsonian Moment' in his 2007 book of that title, and the year began hopefully for non-Europeans. Woodrow Wilson, who had outlined his Fourteen Points proposing national self-determination in 1918, just after the US entered the First World War, believed that his plan would bring lasting peace to the world. Called the 'greatest man in the world', he headed to the Versailles peace conference brimming with confidence, only to encounter disillusionment. Wilson's programme for self-determination was accorded to white Europeans only—not surprising given the Southerner Wilson's racist outlook. The British and other victorious imperialist powers wanted hands off their empires. The Versailles treaties awarded mandates to the Great Powers, while Asian and African nationalists left empty-handed, their hopes belied. The Russian Revolution, Russia's early exit from the war and peace with Germany led to Russia's exclusion from the conference. The Germans had little choice but to sign a treaty imposing an extraordinary burden of reparations. Although Manela may overestimate the impact of this moment, nationalist movements were surging in the non-Western world, and the seeds of future political action, within and without Europe, were planted.

It is important to note that extremist Indian nationalists, with considerable following, had been advocating self-determination and Independence for India for a generation. Tilak announced in the 1890s that 'Swaraj (self-rule) is my birthright, and I shall have it.' In the intense Swadeshi years of 1905–1908, Aurobindo Ghose, the best writer among the Swadeshi leaders, wrote:

> Organized resistance in subject nations which mean to live and not to die, can have no less an object than an entire and radical change of the system of Government; only by becoming responsible to the people and drawn from the people can the Government be turned into a protector instead of an oppressor. But if the subject nation desires not a provincial existence and a maimed development but the full, vigorous and noble realization of its national existence, even a change in the system of Government will not be enough; it must aim not only at a national Government responsible to the people but a free national government unhampered even in the least degree by foreign control.[1]

Indian nationalists who had worked through the First World War, agitated against but could not block the Rowlatt bill. Their hopes were raised in the 'Wilsonian moment' but were curtailed by the limited scope of the Montagu-Chelmsford reforms (Government of India Act, 1919). Lajpat Rai, throughout the First World War, had called for Indian self-rule before Wilson's Fourteen Points were formulated. The mass demonstrations of the Swadeshi period prepared the way for the larger ones led by Gandhi from 1918 onwards. Indian nationalism was for greater mass mobilization with the goal of complete self-rule and a few, then more, adopted

---

[1] McDermott, Rachel F., Leonard A. Gordon, et al, eds. 2013. *Sources of Indian Tradition*. Vol. II, New York: Columbia U. Press, p. 274.

Aurobindo's call for Independence. The issue of self-determination for all peoples—colonized, fragmented and dispersed as they might be—was more salient in the public arena, with a new, wider legitimacy for claims to self-determination.

Some of Lajpat Rai's American supporters remained loyal even after he left America in 1919. Jabez T. Sunderland was the most devoted. But the main agitation for Indian self-rule remained in India, led by Gandhi. The Mahatma argued that Indians had to improve their own society whether or not there was a British Raj. Tagore delivered a similar message in 1905 in an essay, 'Our Swadeshi Samaj', namely, we have to rebuild our society, whether foreigners help us or not.

The two-and-a-half decades between the World's Fair of 1893 and the Versailles Peace Conference of 1919 saw enormous changes in the relations and interactions between the US and South Asia. Thousands of Indians, or Hindus as they were then called, entered the United States to farm, do business, study, or agitate against the British Raj. Some nationalists gained support from Americans, some prominent, to counteract propaganda put out by the British Office of Information.

Swami Vivekananda taught yoga and meditation for parts of three years. Other teachers of these disciplines from the Ramakrishna Mission and other organizations, as well as freelancers, followed. Although it is difficult to say whether that knowledge of India changed appreciably, at least a few South Asians spoke of their own traditions and society, alongside the voices of American missionaries.

The missionaries themselves changed their game slightly. Although most still aimed at 'the conquest of India' for Christ, they went further than before in providing medical services and education. They saw that competition between denominations was harmful to their cause; John R. Mott, Sherwood Eddy, and others, organized cooperation among denominations.

Although American economic involvement in India was still small, an increasing number of American companies began setting up offices in India, and one great American–Indian enterprise came to fruition. This was the Tata iron and steel plant in Jamshedpur, with Charles Page Perin's crucial assistance in bringing the mill into operation. It was India's, and perhaps Asia's, largest iron and steel mill for years. American involvement continued for decades, even as Indianization of the work force and management continued. However, American involvement in the Indian economy was restricted as long as the British ruled India and determined who could do what and where.

Indians were divided on the First World War. Conservative or liberal nationalists supported the British; several million Indian troops were involved in the Allied war effort and 74,000 died in the Allied cause.[2] Tata Steel contributed to the 'arsenal of democracy', though India had foreign rulers. A small number of Indians volunteered for the American army, while others plotted with Germans to smuggle arms into India and overthrow the Raj.

Until America entered the war, Indian nationalists of different persuasions went in and out of the US organizing, plotting and propagandizing. The US government, allied to Great Britain, swept up plotters, German and Indian, advocating and working for violence in the Hindu Conspiracy Case. In India, however, Mahatma Gandhi was coming to the fore in the nationalist movement. Lajpat Rai, a prominent nationalist, against the use of violence, laboured in the US from 1914 to 1919, to gain support for Indian self-rule. Some activists in the US formed the Fellowship for Reconciliation in 1915 and the American Friends Service Committee in 1917, which grew out of British and American traditions of non-violence, both religious and secular.[3] These organizations, and others formed in the following decades, drew upon Western traditions, and later on Gandhi's teachings.

The ties between the British Empire and a rising America involved intelligence and surveillance, friendship, marriage, commerce and emigration creating many cross-Atlantic connections. There were marriages as well, especially between moneyed Americans and impoverished British aristocrats. The Anglo-American world was about to be more seriously challenged by rising nationalism in Asia.

---

[2] Berg, A. Scott, ed. 2017. *World War I and America*. NY: Library of America, p. 848.
[3] Lynd, Staughton, ed. 1966. *Nonviolence in America: A Documentary History*. Indianapolis: BobbsMerrill, p. xxxiv.

Part II

Age of Gandhi, 1919 to 1948

Mr. M. K. Gandhi of India is 'the greatest man in the world'.

—John Haynes Holmes, Community Church, New York, 1921[1]

Gandhi-ism and all it stands for will, sooner or later, have to be grappled with and finally crushed. It is no use trying to satisfy a tiger by feeding it on cat's meat.'

—Winston Churchill[2]

You're Mahatma Gandhi. You're the top! You're Napoleon brandy.

—Cole Porter, 'You're the Top!' (popular song, 1934)

The President of the United States of America and the Prime Minister, Mr. Churchill... respect the right of all peoples to choose the form of government under which they will live; and they wish to see sovereign rights and self-government restored to those who have been forcibly deprived of them.

—The Atlantic Charter, 12 August 1941[3]

---

[1] Holmes, John Haynes. 1954. *My Gandhi*. London: Allen & Unwin, p. 9.
[2] Churchill, Winston. 1968. *Churchill: Four Faces and the Man*. Baltimore: Penguin, p. 97.
[3] Hofstadter, Richard. 1982. *Great Issues in American History*. V. III. From Reconstruction to the Present Day, 1864-1981. NY: Vintage, pp. 399–400.

[T]he problem of the twentieth century is the problem of the color line.'

—W.E.B. Du Bois[4]

---
[4] Berg 2017, p. 46.

1

Mahatma Gandhi and America

When John Haynes Holmes, a noted downtown New York City preacher, based at the Community Church, announced in 1921 that he would identify 'the greatest man in the world' the following Sunday, speculation was rife. Former President Woodrow Wilson, once given this appellation, was no longer on the scene and the failure of his crusade for the League of Nations had stripped him of his lustre. Lenin? Hardly, in an America of 'the Red Scare', terrified of potential violent revolutionaries. Theodore Roosevelt, a possible candidate, was dead. Upon whom would Holmes place the crown?[1]

He announced that the greatest man was Mr M.K. Gandhi of India, but few had heard of this opponent of the British Raj. Gandhi had grown up in India, passed the bar in London, and moved to South Africa. There he had become a champion of the rights of the Indian minority community and devised a unique form of protest against what Indians felt were unjust regulations. Gandhi called the method of opposing such laws and regulations as satyagraha

John Haynes Holmes
Source: Wikimedia Commons

---

[1] Holmes 1954, p. 9.

or non-violent resistance. It was not passive, but active resistance, that demanded of its opponents some response or effort at change and compromise. Mahatma Gandhi (1869–1948) returned to India from South Africa in 1915. After a year of watching and learning, he involved himself in local struggles of peasants and mill workers and challenged the leadership of the Indian National Congress to adopt his programme. By 1918, Gandhi—a skilled organizer and astute judge of those who would help him—came to the fore in the Congress to lead the struggle to improve the lives of the masses and gain national autonomy for India.[2]

Then came Amritsar. In 1919, officials in Amritsar, Punjab, had banned public meetings but Indians had joined one at a city park (Jallianwala Bagh). The military fired on the large crowd, killing several hundred and wounding many. This act of the Raj turned Gandhi, a critical and sometime supporter of the government, both in South Africa and in India, into a determined opponent.

In response to Amritsar, Gandhi and his supporters launched the Non-Cooperation Movement in protest against the Raj. As part of that protest, he called all Congressmen to work at the charka, or spinning wheel, to produce Indian cloth and enable a boycott of British imported cloth. It also included the boycott of government schools and colleges and law courts. It was sporadic but it still went forward until a local act of violence by some members of the Non-cooperation Movement led Gandhi to halt it in 1922. After his imprisonment from 1922 to 1924 on the charge of sedition, he continued to press his handloom (khadi) programme, and supported the reform, but not the elimination of India's caste system, as yet. He began calling those who were unluckily consigned to the bottom rung and lifelong subservience as 'Harijans', or children of God.

The British government enacted the Government of India Act of 1919 also called the Montagu-Chelmsford reforms, which

---

[2] Guha, Ramchandra. 2018. *Gandhi*. The Years that Changed the World 1914-1948. NY: Vintage; Cortright, David. 2006. *Gandhi and Beyond*. Nonviolence for an Age of Terrorism. Boulder: Paradigm; Dalton, Dennis. 1993. *Mahatma Gandhi*. Nonviolent Power in Action. NY: Columbia U. Press.

called for a dual government, or 'dyarchy' where some departments of provincial governments would be run by Indian ministers. The limited nature of the steps, along with the Amritsar massacre, blemished the Act for most, but not all nationalists. Those willing to work for the implementation of the Act, now called 'Liberals', were conservative nationalists. Some nationalists, called Swarajists, tried to block these reforms from within the legislative councils, while Gandhians continued to work his constructive programme outside these bodies.

Smaller nationalist organizations committed acts of violence, and the few that were caught by Raj officials were summarily tried and executed. The case of Bhagat Singh in Punjab attracted the most attention when he was convicted of setting off a bomb in the legislative assembly and sentenced to death. There were widespread protests in India, but he was executed in 1931. Congressmen who failed to halt his execution voted, over Gandhi's hesitancy, for dominion status in 1928, and for Independence in 1929, if progress towards dominion status was not made.

With Gandhi at the reins in 1930, the Congress undertook a new mass campaign of resistance against the government production of and tax on salt—centred on the famous Salt March. To dramatize the resistance to the salt tax, Gandhi organized a march of some 200 miles to the sea, where demonstrators picked up salt deposited on the shore without paying the required tax. The protesters were assaulted by Raj forces, scandalizing the world. Press articles appeared in the US and throughout Europe. In response, Viceroy Lord Irwin, initiated talks with Gandhi, who was invited to London to participate in the Second Round Table Conference in late 1931.

The Conference ended with no agreement amongst Indian representatives on the proposed expansion of electorates and move towards self-government. Gandhi returned home, revived Civil Disobedience and Congress leaders found themselves imprisoned shortly after. Meanwhile, the British issued the Communal Award, giving reserved seats and separate electorates to Untouchables, those whom Gandhi called 'Harijans'.

This proposal was anathema to Gandhi who undertook a fast unto death to prevent its implementation. Dr B.R. Ambedkar, the Untouchable leader and Columbia University graduate, was prevailed upon to make some alternative arrangement with Gandhi and the Congress. Gandhi and Ambedkar agreed to a scheme whereby the Untouchables would gain seats in provincial assemblies but give up separate electorates. Although Ambedkar later said he regretted his agreement, this scheme was written into the Government of India Act of 1935 passed by the British parliament. Diehards, those most opposed to reform, led by Winston Churchill, voiced reservations. Churchill called attention to what he called 'three hundred primitive people placed in our care'. It was not clear where Gandhi, Jawaharlal Nehru and Ambedkar fit among those 'primitive people'.

Between the world wars, British intelligence, home (MI5) and abroad (MI6), kept its eyes on Indian nationalists including the US-based Ghadar which was fading rapidly. At first the main focus was international communism organized by the Communist International (Comintern) which included a number of Indian and American communists. In India the trials of extremist nationalists and communists had drawn attention, and M.N. Roy, a founder of the CPI, had been apprehended by the Raj in 1931, and was serving a jail term in the 1930s. With the exception of the Chittagong Armory Raid in 1931, Indian and American communists and other leftists were less interested in violent revolution and more on labour and mass organizing. They still talked of violent overthrow of capitalist and colonial governments, but Comintern agents from abroad and Indian communists plus renegade followers of Roy, struggled to organize workers and peasants.[3] Through the 1930s, the focus of British intelligence shifted to the dangers from German and Italian fascism and Japanese right-wing extremism. After 1934, the communist line shifted to the United Front, with communists joining socialist and nationalist organizations, and making their influence felt. Indian nationalists abroad might be socialists or non-socialists, but their

---

[3] Williamson, Horace. 1976 (reprint of 1935 edition). *India and Communism*. Calcutta: Editions Indian, p. 107ff.

goal was Indian Independence by peaceful means, and they wanted Americans and Britons of every political persuasion to accept this as a legitimate goal.[4]

Among Congress leaders through the inter-war period, Nehru was the most internationalist and linked Indian nationalism into wider causes and issues. He joined the League against imperialism and visited the Soviet Union in the late 1920s. After release from prison in the 1930s he went to Europe where his wife Kamala died in 1936. After visiting Great Britain, he also showed support for the Republican side in the Spanish Civil War. Although never a communist, and later its critic, Nehru became a socialist and supported anti-racism, anti-fascism, and anti-imperialism also advocated by those who were communists. Although most of his education was in the UK, Nehru did not form closer links there again until he met V.K. Krishna Menon and many others there in the 1930s. Menon was from Kerala, a graduate of the London School of Economics, Labour member of the St Pancras borough council for fourteen years, leader of the India League and a strong voice for Indian Independence. He presented the Congress case in Great Britain. In 1932, he had reorganized an earlier organization into the more active India League and met Nehru in 1935. In 1938, Nehru had the Congress recognize the India League as its official link in Great Britain.

With the publication of his autobiography, *Toward Freedom* (in India, it is known as *An Autobiography)*, he became more widely known outside India. He befriended American singer, actor and activist Paul Robeson, and met Shapurji Shaklatvala, a member of the Tata family, who had spent his life in the UK, had become a communist and was elected to the British Parliament.

Although Nehru did not visit the US until 1949, his writings, and then Madame Pandit's (his sister, Vijaya Lakshmi) years in the US

---

[4] Jeffrey,. 2010. 172ff; Andrew, Christopher. 2009. *Defend the Realm*. The Authorized History of MI5. NY: Vintage, p.139ff; Brecher, Michael. 1959. *Nehru. A Political Biography*. London: Oxford U. Press, p. 104ff; Gopal, Sarvepalli. 1976. *Jawaharlal Nehru. A Biography*. V. One 1889-1947. Cambridge: Harvard U. Press, p. 97ff; Overstreet, p. 59ff.

contributed to his growing reputation as an anti-imperialist as well as an Indian nationalist leader. His younger colleague, Subhas Chandra Bose, also spent part of the 1930s in Europe, and more pragmatic than Nehru, voiced his anti-fascism and anti-racism ideals to friends, but did not broadcast them loudly for fear of alienating potential allies against the British Empire. Both met with Palme Dutt, theoretician of the Communist Party in the UK, and other top leaders of the Labour Party. Dutt, part-Indian, whose book *India Today* gained almost Biblical status among Indian communists pushed Bose to retract the positive words he had penned about blending fascism and communism in his book, *The Indian Struggle*. Gandhi's international stature grew and his campaigns of non-violent resistance attracted supporters in many countries, while Nehru and Bose were tuned into vital international issues of this desperate decade. Important international connections across continents were forged in the 1930s with Nehru, Menon, Gandhi, Bose, Dutt, Saklatvala and Robeson, as well as West Indian George Padmore, and W.E.B. Du Bois playing key roles. As Susan Pennybacker has argued, the Scottsboro Case in the US, the Meerut Trial in India, the Moscow trials, and other issues helped forge such webs of contact.[5]

The British Empire became the British Commonwealth of Nations, and then later the Commonwealth, as the British gradually came to terms with rising nationalism in India. A provision of the 1935 Act was provincial autonomy: for the first time Indians would compose the cabinets of the provinces, but with safeguards reserved for the Raj. Elections for the expanded provincial assemblies with larger electorates were held in the winter of 1936–1937 to choose the members of these bodies. Gandhi, though usually unhappy with electoral politics, reluctantly agreed when many other Congress leaders wanted to participate. The Congress put forth candidates to see, if it gained a majority in the provinces, whether it could govern. The Muslim League put up candidates as did some regional parties, and many independents ran as well. The Congress gained a majority

---

[5] Pennybacker, Susan D. *From Scottsboro to Munich.* Race and Political Culture in 1930s Britain. 2009. Princeton: Princeton University Press, p. 16ff.

in seven of eleven provinces, and coalition ministries were formed in provinces where the Congress did not win a majority. In the latter category were Bengal and Punjab, two of India's most important provinces where the population included a Muslim majority and significant Hindu or Sikh minorities. Along with the formation of Indian cabinets in the provinces, a new viceroy, Lord Linlithgow, took charge. With the opening of the European war in 1939, and the Raj's declaration of war on behalf of India, Congressmen resigned, and a new phase of political life began as the world entered another shattering conflict.

Meanwhile, all through the late 1920s and the 1930s, a propaganda campaign was undertaken on behalf of Gandhi's programme and Indian self-government. The propaganda war was waged in a world of improved technology and communications. Millions now had radios and watched movies which by the end of the 1920s had sound. Air transport was becoming commercialized. Messages via telephone and telegraph connected London and Delhi, New York and Calcutta. These new means of communication were utilized by political advocates, though experienced governments had an advantage. Before long, Gandhi could talk to Americans who listened on their radios.

Among Gandhi's supporters abroad were British and American Quakers, and others such as Roger Baldwin (1884–1981), Pearl Buck (1892–1973), John Haynes Holmes (1879–1964), A.J. Muste (1885–1967), and Jabez T. Sunderland (1842–1936). The British had the upper hand in the United States because of their official establishment, extensive funds, and the general goodwill Americans felt for Britain. They were aided by American ignorance of India and of Gandhi's methods. When Gandhi was asked if he had a message for America, he began by saying that Americans should discard British propaganda and start to learn about what was really going on in India—his truth while speaking to the British and the British exploitation of India. Friends of Freedom, spearheaded by Taraknath Das and a few other Indian Americans in the early 1920s, disintegrated and disappeared. Although there were other small and ineffectual groups, there was no active or successful organization until the India League of America was revitalized by J.J. Singh, an Indian–American activist and businessman who lived in New York, in the later 1930s.[6]

Gandhi had numerous interactions with Americans, which involved a range of important subjects. These included the universal viability of non-violent resistance; religion and conversion; the use of modern technology in India; the nature of the relations between India and the West; fascism; birth control, prohibition; and comparisons between the plight of African Americans in the United States and the oppression of the Untouchables in India. Indeed, he was disturbed by the racial discrimination against African Americans that characterized American society. He listened to reports of ill treatment and lynchings and developed a special solicitude for African American correspondents and visitors including Edward Carroll (1910–2000), Benjamin Mays (1894–1994), Howard Thurman (1899–1981) and Channing H. Tobias (1882–1961). Gandhi was also disturbed to learn that South Asians, along with other Asians, were barred from naturalization as American citizens, an indicator of American racism. He maintained his contacts over the years with a few of the South Asians who emigrated to the US, or were long-term visitors, and learned from them how Asian Indians were treated in America.

Although Gandhi recognized America as a dynamic Western nation, it was for him infected with some of its distasteful diseases: materialism, racial prejudice, religious arrogance and an imperialist drive for conquest and exploitation of less developed peoples. At the same time, it had a tradition of anti-imperialism, equality and non-violent resistance. Though American advocacy of Indian Independence would be of value to his cause, Gandhi never felt that India was inferior to America or any Western country. India might be able to learn some things from America, if such lessons were offered without condescension; but at the same time, India had much to teach—if America was willing to learn.

---

[6] Mukherjee 1998, p. 190ff.

Among the Americans whom Gandhi most trusted were missionaries, or former missionaries, and ministers, including Frederick B. Fisher (1882–1938), Sam Higginbottom, E. Stanley Jones (1884–1973) and Satyanand Stokes (1882–1946). They all sympathized with the Indian struggle in their different ways and each formed a relationship—some only at a distance—to Gandhi. Several grasped the significance of his non-violent resistance and linked it to their backgrounds in Biblical teachings.

Higginbottom's close relationship to Gandhi has already been outlined. Samuel Evans Stokes, renamed Satyananda Stokes, contacted Gandhi in 1920 and identifying with nationalist India, became an adopted Indian. He joined the Congress and served a term of imprisonment for his participation in the Non-cooperation Movement. He had come to India in 1904 from a Quaker family and had done social service, become an educator, an apple breeder, an Indian citizen married to an Indian Christian, and in 1932, a Hindu.[7]

An earnest Christian and a lifelong seeker, the Methodist bishop Frederick Bohn Fisher also contributed to India's cause. He was an omnivorous reader who investigated Hinduism as he continued to study his own religious tradition. Bishop of Calcutta from 1920 to 1930, Fisher had come to India as a missionary in 1904, and met Gandhi in 1917, just as the latter was becoming a leader on the national scene. Fisher described him as a fighting pacifist, a canny idealist and the positive embodiment of a new man in a new age. He wrote, 'Why not accept today in the bonds of the Universal Church of Christ such men as Gandhi and Tagore and Natarajan … others … following the Christ although they never had a Christian put water on their heads? The very power Gandhi wields is living proof of a … Christian experience.'[8]

As catholic as he was in his outlook, even Fisher could not see that Gandhi might not want to be labelled a Christian. However,

---

[7] Stokes, Satyanand. 1977. *National Self-Realisation*. Delhi: Rubicon, p. 5ff.

[8] Fisher, Frederick B. 1932. *That Strange Little Brown Man Gandhi*. NY: Ray Long & Richard R. Smith, p. 109ff.

Fisher presented, as had Sunderland, a well-argued case for Indian Independence and condemnation of the continuation of the Raj. He also did his best to see parallels between Hinduism and Christianity, narrowing the gap between the religious traditions. By so doing, he felt that he shared a religious outlook with Gandhi and Tagore that transcended specific faiths. That Gandhi embodied the spirit of Christ better than most living Christians, or possibly any, heightened the need for self-evaluation.[9]

In 1932, Fisher published a book about the Indian he so greatly admired: *That Strange Little Brown Man, Gandhi*.[10] In her biography of Fisher, his wife Welthy devoted a section to a weekend that he and C.F. Andrews (1871–1940), spent with Gandhi and Tagore. In this moment friendship and common values overrode particular cultures and religions.

E. Stanley Jones, another Methodist missionary, similarly portrayed Gandhi as the embodiment of the spirit of Jesus Christ in his 1925 book, *The Christ of the Indian Road*. Noting the rising interest in Jesus in India, Jones maintained that though Gandhi called himself a Hindu and not a Christian, 'by his life and outlook and methods he has been the medium through which a great deal of this interest in Christ has come'.[11] More concerned with converts than Fisher, Jones believed the future of India was and had to be in Christ. He saw Gandhi as a vehicle for Christian teaching, which was a great benefit to the missionary effort.

Although Jones hoped for the conversion of Indians, Gandhi on numerous occasions expressed his antipathy to religious conversions. Like Vivekananda he thought most men and women should stick to the faiths they were raised in. Since some of the missionaries were focused on the number of converts as a marker of their success, Gandhi questioned their religiosity. Were they

[9] Fisher, Welthy Honsinger. 1944. *Frederick Bohn Fisher*. World Citizen. NY: Macmillan, pp. 65–68, pp. 125–34.
[10] Fisher 1932, p. 109.
[11] Jones, E. Stanley. 1925. *The Christ of the Indian Road*. London: Hodder and Stoughton, p. 86.

being paid or judged and rewarded per convert? What did this have to do with service or truth? He did not call for all Christian missionaries to leave India, but rather for their devotion to service. If they were willing to work and serve regardless of the number of conversions that were achieved, then they would be welcome in India. India needed selfless workers for the poor and for public health and such like, but it did not need more religious choices. When visitors such as the famous mentor of missionaries and Chairman of the International Missionary Council, John R. Mott, questioned Gandhi on the shortcomings of missionaries, Gandhi told them what he thought.[12]

Gandhi's most dedicated advocates based in America were the Unitarian minister John Haynes Holmes, a lifelong pacifist and co-founder of the NAACP and the ACLU, and Jabez Sunderland. Holmes—one of the foremost speakers from the pulpit at New York's Community Church. In 1918, he had first learned of Gandhi, and in 1921, Holmes named Gandhi the 'greatest man in the world'. For the more than forty remaining years of his life, he was a champion of Gandhi in America—Gandhi himself called Holmes 'my advertising agent'. By leading a great people to freedom through non-violent resistance, as Holmes viewed it, Gandhi followed in the footsteps of the Buddha and Christ. Holmes wrote in 1949:

> In my extremity I turned to Gandhi, and he took me in his arms, and never let me go. Away across the globe he cared for me, and taught me, and reassured me. In London, in 1931, I met him and found him indeed my saint and seer... He gave me a peace of mind and a serenity of soul which will be with me to the last.[13]

As editor of *Unity*, starting in 1926, Holmes published Gandhi's autobiography serially, and joined almost every organization that was formed in America to support India's freedom struggle.

---

[12] Gandhi, Mohandas K. 1958-1995. *Collected Works*. 100v. Delhi: Government of India, Publications Division, V. 40, pp. 57–61; V. 64, pp. 33–41.
[13] Holmes 1954, p. 9.

When in 1931, Holmes finally met Gandhi in England, he was not disappointed; he continued his advocacy of Gandhi and India's cause through his visit to India in late 1947.

Like Holmes both a Unitarian and a supporter of Indian freedom, Jabez T. Sunderland had visited India between 1895–1896 and 1913–1914, but brought to India's cause mainly by Lala Lajpat Rai, he never met Gandhi. While remaining a devout Christian, he became an ardent exponent of the great achievements of Indian civilization, and of the necessity of the country's Independence.

Expanding and deepening an earlier book on India, in 1926 Sunderland completed *India in Bondage*. It is a powerful anti-British diatribe, skilfully argued and backed by facts and figures. He said that Indians were perfectly capable of ruling themselves and dismissed imperial ideologies that asserted their racial, political and cultural inferiority. The Raj should depart immediately, abandoning their claims that no such thing as India existed, or that India, whatever it was, would fall apart when they left.[14]

Once the book came out, copies disappeared rapidly. British officials declared it 'seditious' and moved to halt its distribution. After that, copies were scarcely obtainable. Sunderland's book was published in Great Britain and in the US. Indians and foreigners alike pronounced it the most powerful statement yet produced, to call for the end of the Raj. Gandhi appreciated Sunderland's persuasive power as a great asset in the propaganda war.

Less concerned with the fate of Christianity than with the fate of India and Indians, British and American Quakers played an important role as social service workers and as connectors between the British Raj and Indian nationalists. This latter activity was principally undertaken by British Quakers, many of

---

[14] Sunderland, Jabeez T. 1929. *India in Bondage*. Calcutta: R. Chatterjee, 1929, p. 10f.

whom had American connections and were members of the India Conciliation Group.[15]

Several American writers in the pre-Independence period played a crucial role in presenting the philosophy and methods of non-violent resistance that Gandhi had developed. Of these, the most important was the social philosopher Richard Gregg (1885–1974), who although a Christian, presents a secular and humanistic case for the efficacy and universal value of non-violent resistance. Trained at Harvard as a corporate lawyer, Gregg went to India in 1925 and stayed about four years, part of it at Gandhi's ashram and part of it with Satyanand Stokes in Kotgarh in northern India. Gandhi grew fond of Gregg—whom he called 'Govind', linking Gregg to his favourite animal, the cow, and his favourite deity, Krishna—and recommended Gregg's writings to those seeking to understand his methods. In 1927, in introducing Gregg's comments *in Young India*, Gandhi wrote:

> The readers of Young India are familiar with Mr. Gregg's name. He is studying in a very concrete manner and with a passion worthy of a patriotic son of the soil the many questions affecting this land. His studies and experiments in hand-spinning continue unabated. He is experimenting in education of the backward classes. He is interested in the welfare of these classes. And in that connection, he is studying the question of agriculture.[16]

In 1934, after this close contact with Gandhi, Gregg published *The Power of Non-Violence*, which drew upon the social sciences, legal

---

[15] Tinker, Hugh. 1976. *Separate and Unequal*. India and the Indians in the British Commonwealth 1920-1950. Vancouver: U. of British Columbia Press, pp. 224–41; Rufus Jones, 'Mahatma Gandhi and Soul Force', Radhakrishnan, Sarvepalli, ed. 1956. *Mahatma Gandhi*. Bombay: Jaico, pp. 124–29; Sykes, Marjorie. 1980. *Quakers in India*. A Forgotten Century. London: George Allen & Unwin; Reynolds, Reginald. 1952. *A Quest for Gandhi*. Garden City, N.Y.: Doubleday; Chakravarty, Subash. 1991. *The Raj Syndrome*. New Delhi: Penguin, p. 165ff.

[16] Gandhi, Mohandas K. 1958-1995. *Collected Works*. 100v. Delhi: Government of India, Publications Division, V. 33, pp. 461–62.

studies, military theory, biology, philosophy, and especially modern psychology, Freudian and non-Freudian, to make the case for non-violent resistance. His penetrating use of this literature helped make Gandhian methods more accessible to Westerners and he argued that non-violent resistance is a universally useful method within and between nations.

Gregg maintained that Gandhian training involved many of the same virtues as military training, yet was part of much more humane and psychologically healthy means of solving conflicts. He used the striking image near the opening of his work of 'moral jiu-jitsu':

> Non-violent resistance acts as a sort of moral jiu-jitsu. The non-violence and good will of the victim act like the lack of physical opposition by the use of physical jiu-jitsu, to cause the attacker to lose his moral balance. He suddenly and unexpectedly loses the moral support which the usual violent resistance of most victims would render him. He plunges forward . . . into a new world of values . . . He loses his poise and self-confidence . . . The user of non-violent resistance, knowing what he is doing and having a more creative purpose and perhaps a clearer sense of ultimate values than the other, retains his moral balance. He uses the leverage of a superior wisdom to subdue the rough direct force or physical strength of his opponent.[17]

Non-violent methods of conflict resolution, Gregg argued, dissipate fear, anger and hatred, save energy and harness positivity, especially love; in contrast, violence generates more hatred. Non-violent methods, said Gregg, had the capacity to remould the world—and he and Gandhi were aiming for nothing less than that eventual goal.

Krishnalal Shridharani (1915–1960), born in Gujarat, a precocious and successful poet in his native language, joined Gandhi's Salt March in 1930. In 1934, he came to the US to pursue graduate courses in journalism and sociology at NYU and Columbia University.

---

[17] Gregg, Richard B. 1959. *The Power of Nonviolence*. Nyack, N.Y.: Fellowship Publications, p. 43.

In his PhD thesis on Gandhian methods, published in 1939 as *War without Violence*, Shridharani stressed the vital relationship between means and ends, and indeed, their interchangeability.[18] During the twelve years that he remained in the US, he also lectured and wrote on Indian affairs, and met some of Gandhi's American friends, who worked with expatriate Indians to influence public opinion for Indian freedom. His book became a key text for CORE, a leading civil rights organization.[19]

Even as they sympathized with his struggles, two American religious writers were more critical of Gandhi: the Christian theologian Reinhold Niebuhr (1892–1971) and the Zionist spokesman Hayim Greenberg (1889–1953). Having inclined to pacifism and socialism, Niebuhr sought, though unsuccessfully, to meet Gandhi in London in 1931, and in that year wrote an article favourably appraising Gandhi's methods.[20] In 1932, he published his major work, *Moral Man and Immoral Society*, which argued that social and political conflict often necessitated the use of coercion and even violent means for good ends. Those ends included those that Gandhi pursued: equality for the oppressed within nations, and the liberation of colonies from the grip of imperialism.

Niebuhr harshly criticized Christian pacifism, insisting that even Gandhi's non-violent resistance might involve coercion and could lead to violence and destruction. He blurred the line between violent and non-violent methods, preferring the latter where possible. He also differentiated Gandhi's methods from Christian pacifism in the West by arguing that Gandhi's approach factored in political concerns: 'in him political realism qualified religious idealism...'[21] Niebuhr tried to synthesize his Marxist, Christian, and philosophical

---

[18] Shridharani, Krishnalal. 1939. *War without Violence. A Study of Gandhi's Method and Its Accomplishments*. NY: Harcourt, Brace.

[19] Kapur, Sudarshan. 1992. *Raising Up a Prophet. The African American Encounter with Gandhi*. Boston: Beacon Press, pp. 121–22.

[20] Seshachari, C. 1969. *Gandhi and the American Scene. An Intellectual History and Inquiry*. Bombay: Nachiketa Publicatons, p. 125ff.

[21] Niebuhr, Reinhold. 1960. *Moral Man and Immoral Society*. NY: Scribners, p. 244.

backgrounds into what he believed were a more 'realistic' approach to a conflict solution. His analysis remains one of the major American critiques of pacifism and of Gandhi. It is one that advocates of non-violence, both Christian and secular have tried to rebut.

The New York-based Zionist Hayim Greenberg participated in a larger international dialogue between Gandhi and spokesmen for the Jewish people in Europe, Palestine, and the US.[22]

In 1937 and 1939, he published letters he had addressed to Gandhi.[23] After praising Gandhi for his work for the Untouchables of India, Greenberg asked Gandhi to understand the plight of other 'Untouchable' groups in many parts of the world, such as African Americans and Jews. He thought that Gandhi had fallen prey to Muslim propaganda in India about Zionists emigrating to Palestine. He defended those Zionists in 'An Answer to Gandhi' and explained the difficulties Jews in Nazi Germany faced in committing themselves to non-violent resistance. He asked Gandhi to consider the differences between the merely oppressive British rulers of India and the utter brutality of the Nazis: 'A Jewish Gandhi in Germany, should one arise, could "function" for about five minutes—until the first Gestapo agent would lead him, not to a concentration camp, but directly to the gallows.'

Almost a decade later, when Greenberg was memorializing Gandhi after the latter's assassination, he remembered Gandhi's 'loving kindness', a quality he possessed at the same time that he was a 'social crusader'. Rather than to Buddha, Greenberg compared Gandhi to the ancient Indian Emperor Asoka, who had brought compassion to political activism. Greenberg also saw parallels between Jewish traditions of non-violent activism and Indian ones, which allowed him to feel closer to the fallen Mahatma.

---

[22] Shimoni, Gideon. 1977. *Gandhi, Satyagraha and the Jews: A Formative Factor in India's Policy towards Israel.* Jerusalem: The Hebrew University; Gordon, Leonard A. Summer-Fall 1975. 'Indian Nationalist Ideas about Palestine and Israel,' *Jewish Social Studies*, XXXVII, Nos. 3–4, pp. 221–34.

[23] Greenberg, Hayim. 1953. *The Inner Eye.* V. I. NY: Jewish Frontier Association. Vol. I, pp. 157–61, pp. 219–38.

As Gandhi emerged in the years following the First World War as the foremost political leader of India, American journalists interviewed him frequently and wrote about him often. The most successful of the American writers—in copies sold, and in notoriety—was Katherine Mayo (1867–1940), a freelancer with a project pleasing to officials of the Raj. Her book, *Mother India* (1927), by far the most widely read American work on the subject, cheered the British and infuriated Indian nationalists.[24]

It began, not surprisingly, with an account of a visit to the Kali Temple in Calcutta, told to arouse fear of and antipathy towards those involved in blood sacrifice, idol worship, and discomfiting hygienic practices. Passing semi-naked sadhus as she toured the temple, Mayo recounted: 'One, a madman, flings himself at us, badly scaring a little girl who is being towed past by a young man whose wrist is tied to her tiny one by the two ends of a scarf. "Husband and wife," says [her guide] Mr. Haldar. "They come to pray for a son."'[25]

Mayo linked Hindu customs such as child marriage which she considered degrading and reprehensible to the Kali Temple. These customs, she believed, only the British Raj had the power and vision to change. When a Theosophist told Mayo that the Kali Temple did not represent all of India, she repeated his words to a learned Bengali Brahmin. He replied:

> Your English friend is wrong. It is true that in the lower castes the percentage of worshipers of Kali is larger... But hundreds of thousands of Brahmans, everywhere, worship Kali, and the devotees at Kali Ghat will include Hindus of all castes and conditions, among whom are found some of the most highly educated and important personages of this town and of India.[26]

---

[24] Jha, Manoranjan. 1971. *Katherine Mayo and India*. New Delhi: People's Publishing House, p. 9ff.

[25] Mayo, Katherine. 1927. *Mother India*. NY: Harcourt, Brace, p. 7.

[26] Ibid., p. 10.

But to Mayo, the degrading and immoral practices associated with Hinduism as exemplified at the Kali Temple, and evident throughout India, required a direct and forceful response. She was well launched on her diatribe against Hinduism, Indian society and Indian nationalists.

Her sweeping critique of Indian civilization, although Mayo had met Gandhi, did not focus on him. Her book, because of its crucial place in the propaganda war concerning India, entered into his concerns and provoked his ire. Seeing the sexual depravity of Indians as the root of that civilization's manifold evils, she tried to use both Gandhi's own arranged marriage at an early age and an essay by Tagore on Indian marriage to show that they, the most eminent of Indians, approved of child marriage. Further, while appropriately quoting Gandhi's remarks on poor sanitary practices, she also quoted his words out of context to demonstrate his opposition to Western medicine—while at the same time, by agreeing to an appendectomy by a Western surgeon, he showed himself to be a hypocrite. She condemned Gandhi's programme of non-violent resistance, as in the following passage that is clearly about his movement:

> The doctrine of non-cooperation with the established Power led nowhere, as all now see. The mystic doctrine of spiritual war, a war of 'soul-force', that uses the language of hate while protesting theories of love, had logically and insistently projected itself upon the material plane in the form of the slaughter of men. The inability of individuals to subordinate personal, family or clan interests and to hold together for teamwork had been demonstrated. And the fact had been driven home to the hilt that neither Hindu nor Muhammadan could think in terms of the whole people.[27]

Mayo was not incorrect that some campaigns of non-violent resistance led to sporadic violence, but her dismissal of his method was surely precipitate. Her eagerness to show that only the British could lead India forward led her to dismiss Gandhi and satyagraha.

---

[27] Ibid., pp. 353–54.

Mayo's *Mother India* sold so many copies in the West and was so positively reviewed that it evoked many responses. Of these, one of the most acute was by Gandhi himself, entitled, 'Drain Inspector's Report', published in *Young India*, 15 September 1927. In the best-known section of Gandhi's response, he wrote:

> The book is cleverly and powerfully written. The carefully chosen quotations give it the appearance of a truth book. But the impression it leaves on my mind is, that it is the report of a drain inspector sent out for the one purpose of opening and examining the drains of the country to be reported upon, or to give a graphic description of the stench exuded by the opened drains. If Miss Mayo had confessed that she had gone to India merely to open out and examine the drains of India, there would perhaps be little to complain about her compilation. But she says in effect with a certain amount of triumph, 'The drains are India'... The book is without doubt untruthful, be the facts stated ever so truthful.[28]

Gandhi went on to show how Mayo had 'taken liberty with my writings',[29] specifically on Gandhi's supposed antipathy to Western medicine and Tagore's implicit approval of 'child marriage'.[30] Hurt by what he saw as the untruthfulness of Mayo's enterprise, Gandhi nonetheless believed that her book was still a work for Indians—not foreigners—to read. Indians needed criticism and self-reformation, and even if Mayo distorted and exaggerated, she called attention to issues, such as sanitation and public health, or the condition of women, that needed attention.

Some Indians visiting America, or even at home, felt that they had to formulate an answer to Mayo's diatribe, which had become a bestseller in America, a country usually uninterested in India. More than a decade later, when Tagore was in the US, he commented on *Mother India*:

---

[28] Gandhi 1995, V. 34, pp. 539–40.
[29] Ibid., p. 541ff.
[30] Tagore letter, 4 January 1928, reprinted in Mukerji, *Son Answers*, pp. 105–108.

I do not feel any enthusiasm in contradicting this book, knowing that most of her readers are not interested in truth but a piece of sensationalism that has the savour of rotten flesh. Now that this woman has discovered a mine of wealth in an unholy business of killing reputation, no appeal to truth will prevent her plying a practised hand in wielding her assassin's knife, carefully choosing for her victims those who are already down.[31]

Among other respondents to Mayo was the Bengali writer Dhan Gopal Mukerji (1890–1936), who had settled in the US and assumed the task of faithfully and artistically portraying the land of his birth for the benefit of American readers. He had had considerable success with his books for children including *Gay-Neck, The Story of a Pigeon*, which won the Newbery Prize for children's literature. Enraged by Mayo, he challenged her to provide sound documentation for the sexual depravity she identified as the root of the degradation she saw everywhere in India. He gathered testimony from missionaries and moderate Indians who had come to the defence of India but had not gotten a fair hearing in the Western press. In the course of his defence, Mukerji rushed to the rescue of defamed Bengal:

'Bengal,' she says, 'is the seat of bitterest political unrest—the producer of India's main crop of anarchists, bomb-throwers, and assassins. Bengal is also among the most sexually exaggerated regions of India and medical and police authorities in any country observe the link between that quality and queer criminal minds.' Which police, and what medical authorities we are not told... like modern literature modern nationalists are pornerastic... what Miss Mayo says against the Bengalis without any validity is this, 'many little bookstalls where narrow-chested, anaemic, young Indians students, in native dress, brood over piles of fly-blown Russian pamphlets.' The words 'Russian pamphlets' bristle with fierce red possibilities. But there is no chance of such an occurrence, because

---

[31] Kripalani, Krishna. 1962. *Rabindranath Tagore. A Biography*. NY: Grove, p. 343.

according to the Post Office and Sea Customs Acts the police not
only proscribe but confiscate any such literature.[32]

The comments of Tagore, Mukerji, and others, show how wounded
Indian readers were by Mayo. She had effectively contributed to
arousing a 'hate America and hate the West' campaign in her efforts
to condemn Indians and defend the Raj. Mukerji did note all the
Western voices, such as that of American missionary E. Stanley
Jones, who had come to India's defence. Mukerji remained stunned
by the success of Mayo's work. He could only go on with his own
writing and translations to present to America what he thought was
a truer picture of his native land.[33]

    In Mayo's wake, another talented and ambitious woman
writer followed. Patricia Kendall (1901–1973), an elegant New
York socialite of old Virginia origins and an Anglophile like her
predecessor and hostile to India, wrote a polished account of India
based on four visits, entitled *Come with Me to India*.[34] Her book sold
thousands of copies in the Depression and her version of Gandhi is
of interest, since she had a greater interest in his politics than did
Mayo. Kendall had some help from British officials during her 1930
visit to India, and when in the next few years she demanded more aid,
it was grudgingly given. The British recognized her contribution to
their cause in America but also saw some negative qualities. Angus
Fletcher of the British Library of Information, New York—the
main British propaganda unit in the United States—wrote to R.A.
Leeper of the News Department of the British Foreign Office, on 29
January 1932:

> Mrs. Patricia Kendall... has consulted the Library very frequently
> in the last year... she consumes a great deal of our time... She
> apparently intends to do Mr Gandhi's cause as much harm as
> possible, and she seems anxious to collect spicy gossip... She is

[32] Mukerji, Dhan Gopal. 1928. *Ghond the Hunter*. NY: Dutton, pp.105–108.
[33] Mukerji, Dhan Gopal. 1930. *Disillusioned India*. NY: Dutton.
[34] Kendall, Patricia. 1940. *Come with Me to India*. NY: Charles Scribner's.

to publish an article on 'The Economic Consequences of Mr Gandhi'... she seems to expect us to cook the facts and figures to suit her case. The lady's eyelashes are as false as the vermillion of her lips, but the words of her lips and the meditations of her heart are inspired with the truth according to the Government of India.[35]

Drawing on her own interview with Gandhi in March 1930, as well as works by British authors, mostly officials, and a few conservative Indians, Kendall asked, 'Who is this man whom asceticism has induced willingly to relinquish a life of ease and whom worldliness impelled determinedly to grasp a position of power, who lives like a monk and rules like a monarch?'[36] Her answer was that he was a man of 'fanatical' ideas whose Indian campaigns 'have invariably led to violence' which 'he has always regretted—but never remedied'. He was a 'political opportunist' with the 'habit of idle promises', who had written an autobiography full of 'puerile discussions'. With lengthy extracts from British memoirs such as Michael O'Dwyer's, *India as I Knew It*,[37] Kendall made every effort to show that the Punjab violence of 1919 was incited by Gandhi and that he was responsible for the Amritsar massacre.[38]

Although Kendall wrote articles in periodicals and broadcast her views on radio, she never made the formidable impact that Katherine Mayo had. Meanwhile, Gandhi's focus was elsewhere. The Salt March of 1930 and then the Second Round Table Conference of 1931 drew outstanding American reporters to India and to Britain, among them the experienced foreign correspondents Webb Miller (1891–1940) and William Shirer (1904–1993). Miller was based in London, but was sent off to India to cover the Salt March—but having been prevented by Raj officials, never met Gandhi during his few months in India. He was the only foreign correspondent who

---

[35] Govt of India, Info Dept, L/I/1/1424
[36] Kendall 1940, p. 334.
[37] O'Dwyer, Michael. 1925. *India as I Knew It*. London: Constable.
[38] Kendall 1940, p. 369ff.

covered the Gandhian demonstration at the Dharasana salt works about 150 miles north of Bombay. As more than two thousand khadi-clad demonstrators advanced towards the salt deposits, in Miller's account:

> Suddenly . . . scores of native police rushed upon the advancing marchers and rained blows on their heads with their steel-shod lathis. Not one of the marchers even raised an arm to fend off the blows. They went down like tenpins. From where I stood I heard the sickening whacks of the clubs on unprotected skulls . . . Those struck down fell sprawling, unconscious or writhing in pain with fractured skulls or broken shoulders. In two or three minutes the ground was quilted with bodies.[39]

The Government of India tried to stop his dispatches, but some got through, for Miller had 'discovered a hole in the censorship'.[40] He continued: 'My story of the beatings at Dharasana caused a sensation when it appeared in the 1,350 newspapers served by the United Press throughout the world.'[41] Then it was read into the Congressional Record in Washington and printed as a pamphlet by Gandhi backers in the US. This story of brutality by officers of the Raj against unarmed and fearless demonstrators struck a counterblow to the negative views about India of the likes of Mayo and Kendall and called into question their portrayal of a benevolent Raj.

Miller sympathized with Gandhi and other anti-imperialist movements. His accurate and moving reporting in India gained him interviews with Gandhi in London during the Mahatma's 1931 visit. Miller was a devoted fan of Henry David Thoreau and happened to ask Gandhi if he had heard of the American writer. Gandhi's 'eyes brightened and he chuckled'.[42] Then Gandhi recounted how he

---

[39] Miller, Webb. 1936. *I Found No Peace*. NY: Simon and Schuster, p. 342.
[40] Ibid., p. 199.
[41] Ibid., p. 198.
[42] Ibid., p. 238.

had read Thoreau in South Africa and how it had been a formative
influence for him. Miller describes Gandhi's response:

> From long reading of Thoreau I am convinced that his philosophical
> conceptions emanated largely from Indian literature. In *Walden*
> he repeatedly mentions the Vedas and other Hindu literature
> and once says: 'I... who loved so well the philosophy of India...'
> It would seem that Gandhi received back from America what was
> fundamentally the philosophy of India after it had been distilled
> and crystallized in the mind of Thoreau. This perhaps explains
> why the Hindu mentality so readily accepted his ideas.[43]

Miller had met all the leaders of Europe and America but found
Gandhi 'the most fascinating and inscrutable' of all the notable
figures he had met.[44] The news from Dharasana made Miller's
words and the path of non-violent resistance world-famous. In
1931, Gandhi, almost unknown outside India, was *Time* magazine's
'Man of the Year'.

William Shirer, famous for his works on the Third Reich and the
fall of the French Third Republic in 1940, was a twenty-seven-year-
old correspondent for the *Chicago Tribune* when he was assigned
to India in 1930 and met Gandhi on 22 February 1931. Shirer
reported from India on Gandhi, and then from England, but waited
nearly half a century to write in his *Gandhi: A Memoir* (1979) a full
account of his interaction with Gandhi and the importance of the
Mahatma in his life.[45] Shirer, like Miller, was more sympathetic to
the nationalists led by Gandhi than to the Raj. Of the British, he
wrote, 'Ruling India brought out the worst in them.' After time in
India, he returned to Europe to pick up the Gandhi story when the
Mahatma arrived in Europe in 1931. Gandhi was pleased to see him
because Shirer had, Gandhi said, reported his words 'truthfully' even

---

[43] Ibid., pp. 239–40.
[44] Ibid., p. 40.
[45] Shirer, William L. 1979. *Gandhi*. A Memoir. NY: Simon & Schuster
Touchstone.

when he did not understand them.[46] Shirer considered Gandhi's opening speech to the Round Table Conference one of the greatest he had heard. For Shirer, Gandhi was the most remarkable man he had met.[47] He wrote:

> Gandhi was my greatest teacher, not only by what he said and wrote and did, but by the example he set... what did he teach me? I suppose the greatest single thing was to seek the Truth, to shun hypocrisy and falseness and glibness, to try to be truthful to oneself as well as to others, to be skeptical of the value of most of life's prizes, especially the material ones, to cultivate an inner strength, to be tolerant of others, of their acts and beliefs, however much they jarred you, but not tolerant of your own faults.[48]

Shirer also wrote: 'I count the days with Gandhi the most fruitful of my life. No other experience was as inspiring and as meaningful and as lasting... What I had got from Gandhi helped me to survive.'[49]

Like Shirer, John Gunther (1901–1970), formerly a correspondent for the *Chicago Daily News* came to India and met with Gandhi. He devoted nearly a quarter of his *Inside Asia* to India.[50]

Inside Asia roughly alternates portraits of important leaders with chapters giving general information on the geography, social groups and recent politics of the different areas of Asia from Japan to Iran. Each chapter has precise information gathered from background works, current reports, interviews and observations. The writing is crisp and efficient, but is also pungent and strikingly astute, as can be seen in the opening of Gunther's portrait of Gandhi:

> Mr. Gandhi, who is an incredible combination of Jesus Christ, Tammany Hall, and your father, is the greatest Indian since

---

[46] Ibid., p. 158.
[47] Ibid., pp. 242–44.
[48] Ibid., p. 239.
[49] Ibid., p. 244.
[50] Gunther, John. 1939. *Inside Asia*. NY: Harper, p. 242ff.

Buddha. Like Buddha, he will be worshipped as a god when he dies... No more difficult or enigmatic character can easily be conceived. He is a slippery fellow. I mean no disrespect. But consider some of the contradictions, some of the puzzling points of contrast in his career and character. This man who is at once a saint and a politician, a prophet and a superb opportunist, defies ordinary categories.[51]

Gunther explores some of the contradictions, for example, Gandhi's attitude towards the Untouchables. 'Mr. Gandhi devotes the largest share of his energy nowadays to uplifting the Untouchables, but he resisted with his life an attempt to remove Untouchability from Hinduism... He adores the Untouchables and would do anything for them—except remove them from Hinduism, which makes them what they are.'[52]

Drawing mostly on Gandhi's autobiography, Gunther sympathetically recounts Gandhi's life history, his years in South Africa, his growing political interest and influence, and his return to India. He underscores the 'sexual motif' in Gandhi's life and called him a 'supreme egotist' which Gunther related to Gandhi's attitude to God.[53] Gunther cites as examples of the Indian's 'astute political sense' Gandhi's use of khadi and his 'invention' of Satyagraha.[54]

After describing the Salt March as one of the remarkable events in modern history, Gunther proceeds to explain why at present (1937–1938), Gandhi and the Congress were largely cooperating with the Government of India, probably drawing upon a visit to his ashram. Gunther considers the Gandhi of early 1939 a 'force for moderation in Indian politics',[55] quite unlike the extremist and instigator of violence that British officials and American Anglophiles perceived. Gunther had no axe to grind, and unlike Miller and Shirer, he had no

---

[51] Ibid., p. 344.
[52] Ibid., p. 345.
[53] Ibid., p. 344, 351.
[54] Ibid., p. 1939, 354.
[55] Ibid., p. 369.

event—witnessed at first-hand—to describe. His balanced account of Gandhi and India was a significant part of Gunther's bestselling book, read by many Americans.[56]

On 13 September 1931, Gandhi made a radio broadcast, arranged by the Columbia Broadcasting System, to the American people. It was Gandhi's first radio address, and he spoke lucidly, although without great preparation, keeping his foreign audience in mind. He said:

> If India is to revive the glory of her ancient past, she can only do so when she attains her freedom. The reason for the struggle having drawn the attention of the world... (lies) in the fact that the means adopted by us... are unique... they are purely and simply truth and non-violence... We feel that the law that governs brute creation is not the law that should guide the human race... (T)he world is sick unto death of blood-spilling. The world is seeking a way out, and I flatter myself with the belief that perhaps it will be the privilege of the ancient land of India to show the way out to the hungering world.[57]

Even before his 1931 broadcast, although Gandhi never went to America himself, he sent his confidants Sarojini Naidu (1879–1949) and then C.F. Andrews to the US to do positive publicity work for India. Following Naidu's mission to America of a few months in 1928–1929, and that of Andrews in 1929 and 1930, Vithalbhai Patel (1873–1933), a senior Congress leader from the Bombay Presidency, also visited during 1932–1933.

Sarojini Naidu toured up and down the states speaking in schools, colleges, churches and huge halls. The encomiums rolled in, for Naidu was a fine speaker with a rich, resonant voice, a passionate nature, and spoke the words of a poet nationalist. Miss Dorothy Waldo, principal of the Dana Hall School in Wellesley, Massachusetts, wrote to Gandhi what a great impact Naidu had

---

[56] Ramsdell, Daniel B. 1983. 'Asia Askew: US Best-Sellers on Asia, 1931-1980,' *Bulletin of Concerned Asian Scholars*. Boulder, Colorado. V.15, No. 4, pp. 2–25.
[57] Muzumdar, Haridas T. 1932. *Gandhi versus the Empire*. NY: Universal, p. 166.

made on her students: '[T]hey responded universally to the magnetic inspiration of the Presence...' Gandhi had been a 'storybook figure' to them, but now, as one said, 'Gandhi seems real to me now and I know what he is trying to do.'[58]

In a letter to Gandhi, published in *Young India* in January 1929, after speaking in Cincinnati, Naidu wrote that her last weeks had been a period of 'veritable delight and revelation':

> This young country and this young nation have made a profound and intimate appeal to my heart, my imagination, my vision, understanding and faith... and through all the incredible tumult and turmoil of daily existence, I find the spirit of a valiant and vital Seeking, seeking, seeking for some truth, some realization, finer and higher than the Old World has yet conceived or expressed... And though today stone and steel and gold be their only symbols, they express the challenge and dream of youth in all its unspent and invincible courage, ambition, power and insolent pride... a challenge to the old. It is to me moving and so inspiring and I watch with a prescient tenderness and trust... through what anguish and sacrifice and renunciation must this new young world find fulfillment of its Vision of Beauty, Truth and Victory....[59]

Like Lajpat Rai some fifteen years earlier, she visited Black colleges and neighbourhoods, and wrote, 'It breaks my heart to see the helpless, hopeless, silent and patient, bitterness and mental suffering of the educated Negroes... They are the socially and spiritually outcast children of America...'[60]

In another letter to Gandhi, published in *Young India* on 30 May 1929 after visiting a Hopi reservation, Naidu wrote, 'There is a freemasonry that binds all primitive world races in a common bond, for the folk spirit, whether in India, Roumania, Zululand or the

---

[58] Grover, Verinder and Ranjana Arora, eds. 1993. *Sarojini Naidu*. Great Women of Modern India. Vol. 2. New Delhi: Deep and Deep, p. 238.
[59] Ibid., p. 244.
[60] Ibid.

Arizona Desert, expresses itself very much in the same symbols...'[61] After watching a dance of the Buffalo Hunt and Victory dance, an educated Hopi said to her: 'This country once belonged to me and my people. We are dying out, but they may kill us, they can never conquer us.' His words expressed the same yearning for national identity felt by Asian Indians in her homeland. Later, witnessing the struggles of Sikh labourers in California, she wrote, 'I have come to the conclusion after my visits to Africa and America that the status of Indian settlers can never be satisfactory anywhere till the status of India is definitely assured among the free nations of the world.'[62]

Among the many high points of her visit, Naidu spoke at New York's Town Hall on 'Will India Be Free?' to a banquet given by the Indian community at Columbia University's International House, and as arranged by Holmes, at a national Thanksgiving service arranged by religious organizations at Carnegie Hall.[63] In tribute to her successful tour, C.F. Andrews commented that, '... she has won the heart of the West, and they will never forget her'.[64]

Naidu's tour overlapped with that of former Anglican clergyman and peripatetic world missionary C.F. Andrews, who travelled widely on assignments given to him by Gandhi, and also accompanied Tagore on some trips. He advised on labour disputes, explained Gandhi to foreigners, corresponded with the highest British officials, reported on race relations and Indian minorities in diverse parts of the world, and wrote unceasingly about Gandhi.

Andrews was to have accompanied Tagore on an American tour in 1929, but Tagore called off his visit and Andrews continued alone to the US, Canada and British Guiana, to raise funds for Tagore's school at Shantiniketan and to explain India and Gandhi to Americans.[65] Since part of Andrews' charge was to counter the

---

[61] Ibid., p. 247.
[62] Ibid., p. 248.
[63] Ibid., p. 245.
[64] Ibid., p. 250.
[65] Tinker, Hugh. 1979. *The Ordeal of Love*. C.F. Andrews and India. Delhi: Oxford U. Press, p. 234ff.

views of Katherine Mayo, he met with her in early 1929 to try to understand her point of view. The outcome was that he withdrew his charge that she had a political motive. He wrote to Tagore, 'She clearly has political bias...'[66] (He was criticized for whitewashing Mayo, a British lackey and an enemy of India, but Andrews sloughed this off).

Through his acquaintance Leonard Elmhirst (1893–1974), who had worked at Shantiniketan for several years, Andrews was invited to make the New York apartment of Elmhirst's wife, Dorothy (1887–1968), a Whitney heiress, his home base. He travelled, lectured, preached widely, and went south to the Tuskegee Institute. Andrews wrote to Gandhi on 18 March 1929, that it was 'quite wonderful... The hearts of those Negroes there in Tuskagee are with you in every way that is indescribably real and deep.... It is a real asram, both of prayer and work'.[67] *The Tuskegee Messenger* reported:

> Tuskegee has had a messenger from the East. His spirit was a spirit of simplicity, of repose, of reflection and peace. He had a message, a plain unadorned story of the two greatest spirit in the world today, Tagore and Gandhi. Always there was the note of India's aspiration, of the self-denial of its leaders, and of the unity of their cause with the upward striving of all suppressed groups. He desired to establish bonds between Tuskegee in America and Santiniketan in India, which are dedicated in the same spirit to the same cause of emancipation.[68]

Andrews also met with Black leader W.E.B. Du Bois (1868–1963) who had long supported the Indian freedom struggle.

While in America, Andrews was drawn into the controversy over the barring of Indian naturalization as American citizens. He had complained in November 1929 that, 'The racially insulting

---

[66] Chaturvedi, Benarsidas and Marjorie Sykes. 1971. *Charles Freer Andrews*. New Delhi: Publications Division, Government of India, 1971, pp. 237–38.

[67] Tinker 1979, p. 234.

[68] Chaturvedi 1971, p. 238.

Asiatic Prohibition Law of 1924 still remains on the Statute Book of the United States...'[69] (But when a proposal was put forth that those Indians who were Aryans should be allowed naturalization, he opposed the measure writing, 'It is racial in principle, and it would not help [the] non-Aryan Southern India. I am trying instead for a quota system into which racial distinctions do not enter'.[70] Some north Indians may have agreed with his distinction between Aryans of the north and non-Aryans of the south, but most Westerners rejected it, as they would not accept any Indians as Aryans.

While in the United States, Andrews crossed paths with Edward J. Thompson (1886–1946), a former Wesleyan minister and educator, writer and teacher of Bengali whom he had known from Shantiniketan. Although they exchanged pleasantries, they shortly found themselves on opposite missions in the United States. While Andrews was a defender of Gandhi and an apostle of Indian nationalism as well as his Christian faith, he was also in contact with the highest officials of the Raj, and often a go-between linking official India and Gandhi. Thompson found himself, almost unwillingly, a strong defender of his own government because criticism of the British in America seemed to him harsh, one-sided, and unfair.

Thompson, another important connect of nationalists and the Raj had written an unsparing critique of the British for their cruel response to the rebellion of 1857 in his *The Other Side of the Medal*. After his death in 1946, Jawaharlal Nehru, shortly to be the prime minister of India, wrote to Thompson's son, E.P. Thompson, on 10 April 1946, that his father 'has been a real peacemaker between nations and peoples' and 'a link between England and India'.[71] Like Andrews, Thompson was respected and heard by all parties, contributing his bit to mutual understanding and communication. In this situation, they found themselves taking opposing stances and

---

[69] Ibid., 1971, p. 246.
[70] Ibid., p. 245.
[71] Edward J. Thompson Papers, Bodleian Library, Oxford University.

Thompson told his friend Peter Lyon on 9 February 1930, that, 'C.F. Andrews is in America and talking a lot of bosh.'[72]

On a teaching assignment at Vassar College from August 1929 through July 1930 Thompson felt he had to defend Great Britain and its rule in India against criticism by Indians, Americans and uninformed British as well. He felt that pro-nationalist charges against the Raj went largely unanswered and this allowed anti-British sentiment to fester and grow. Thompson joined in the efforts of the British Information Services to defend the Raj and was part of the British government's American propaganda wing. Thompson wrote feverishly and debated mainly Indian opponents at forums organized by the Foreign Policy Association which were broadcast over the radio. In Baltimore and New York, he debated S.N. Ghose, who presented the Congress point of view, while Thompson spoke for the British government and the Raj. Thompson wrote to Peter Lyon on 27 June 1930, that, 'I am very sick of controversy. You have no idea how unfair and lying a propaganda goes on here.'[73]

He maintained that most writing and speaking on India was filled by the pro-nationalist advocates with false and misleading figures that he could only correct after the fact. One of his targets was J.T. Sunderland's *India in Bondage* of which he wrote to the *London Times* on 21 July 1930, that, 'He is a generous and enthusiastic man, but everything he writes is crowded with false assumptions...All the harm in the world is the work of the British... His reckless partiality and sweeping style need no comment...'[74]

The support system in the United States in speaking for Britain included the British Library of Information, the British Embassy in Washington, D.C. with its information section, the Information Department of the Government of India, London, and unofficial organizations such as the Pilgrims Society. The latter was founded in 1902, 'to promote good-will, good-fellowship, and everlasting peace between the United States and Great Britain', according to its

---

[72] Ibid.
[73] Ibid.
[74] Govt of India, London, L/I/1/1534.

website. The British government sent articulate spokesmen to the United States to plead its cause to oppose complete Independence for India, suggesting that a slow pace to self-government would suffice.

In November 1932, Vithalbhai Patel, former president of the Bombay Municipal Corporation and former president of the Indian Legislative Assembly, undertook a five-month tour of the US. Having trained as a barrister and lobbied for Indian political advancement in London, Patel was an experienced visitor to the West. Despite his poor health, he lectured and debated representatives of the British government in many corners of the US during his stay. His gruelling tour led to his death at the age of sixty within a few months after his return to Europe.

As the former chief executive of Bombay, a major Indian city, Patel was welcomed, officially and non-officially, in many American cities. His biographer noted that Americans were 'touched by this feeble old man with his Whitmanesque beard, with his wonderful Gandhi cap, and with his body swathed in the symbolic white of khaddar...'[75] In the approximately eighty-five speeches and debates he gave, the 'feeble old man' was quite forceful in his focus on imperialism as the root of the world crisis unfolding in the 1930s. He often began his speeches in this way:

> I am now speaking to my American sisters and brothers... who stand in the vanguard of present-day progress. I am in the land of liberty... I know that you are bound closely to Britain by the ties of blood and relationship. Imperialism has been typical of the old country, Britain, but it has always been against the free will of the people of America, and your national existence commenced with your War of Independence against Britain. Your love of liberty is thus greater than any sentimental allegiance you may owe to the past. Therefore, I may speak my mind freely to you on the curses of Imperialism.[76]

---

[75] Patel, Gordhanbhai I. 1950. *Vithalbhai Patel*. Life and Times. 2v. Bombay: Sree Laxmi Narayan Press, V.1, p. 1193.
[76] Ibid., pp. 1194–95.

Patel then detailed Britain's economic exploitation of India which had contributed mightily to its own enrichment and development. Next, he explored Britain's disarming of India and denial of political rights. Differentiating India from the white, self-governing colonies of Australia and Canada, he insisted India and Britain were totally alien 'with nothing in common'. Consequently, India would never become a member of the British Commonwealth and would prosper only if it achieved complete Independence. In a speech to Irish Americans in Chicago, Patel likened the British domination of India to its exploitation and control of Ireland—but Ireland, unlike India, would soon be completely free. He recognized in Irish-Americans a strong potential ally in rallying American support for Indian freedom.

In New York, Patel debated former Secretary of State for India, Wedgewood Benn, at a meeting convened by the Foreign Policy Association at the Hotel Astor. Patel again outlined his case against imperialism and for worldwide disarmament. He maintained that the British were the world's foremost imperialist power and were opposed to the disarming of nations. Although Britain sent Indian representatives to international bodies and conferences, Patel said that no Indians believed these nominees of the Raj actually represented them.

Pressed by Benn, Patel downplayed the enmity between Indian Hindus and Muslims, arguing that some Muslims were allied with the Congress, and that if granted Independence, Indians would work together, regardless of religious fissures. Jabez T. Sunderland considered Patel the most effective spokesmen for Indian national freedom and attended his address at Vassar College and noted the applause he received.[77]

Sudarshan Kapur has skilfully investigated one important, but heretofore neglected chapter of the story of Gandhi and America: the connections between Gandhi and African Americans in the decades before the Civil Rights movement of the late 1950s. After

---

[77] Ibid., V. 2, pp. 1204–05.

the First World War, when Gandhi came to the fore in India, African American leaders Marcus Garvey (1887–1940) and W.E.B. Du Bois began to call attention to links between freedom struggles in India, Africa and the US, emphasizing the common colour of the exploited, and the whiteness of Western exploiters. Thus began a feeling of solidarity between those social and politically conscious African Americans struggling for equality and justice in the United States and Indian nationalists led by Gandhi.[78] Dubois appealed to Gandhi for a message for African Americans in 1929, and Gandhi responded with heartfelt and supportive words. Though Dubois wondered about the efficacy of non-violent resistance, he wrote positively about Gandhi for decades thereafter.[79]

Numerous press reports and visits between India and America built webs of influence and mutual learning that connected activists in both areas. Not only did African Americans want to learn about Gandhi's methods and successes, but Gandhi was curious to understand the American race situation better. In 1914, even before Gandhi had returned to India from South Africa, the Indian nationalist Lala Lajpat Rai had toured the United States, visiting Black institutions and meeting Black leaders. Once Lajpat Rai had returned to India, African Americans learned of Gandhi's work from extensive coverage in the Black press and from members of the South Asian community in America, particularly Taraknath Das, Dhan Gopal Mukerji and Haridas Muzumdar.

In 1936, small groups of Black American leaders made two visits to India which enabled them to see Gandhi, exchange views, and on their return to the US, spread the word about Gandhi. In early 1936, the first group, including Howard and Sue Thurman and Edward and Phenola Carroll, met with Gandhi. As the Americans interrogated Gandhi about South Africa and India and his philosophy of non-violent resistance, Gandhi, in turn, asked them searching and serious questions about America. Gandhi tried to clarify that 'non-violence',

---

[78] Sudarshan 1992.
[79] Lewis 1995, 90, pp. 358, 409.

even spelled out as the negation of violence in English, was a positive force. And Gandhi is said to have suggested that it would be through African Americans that the world learned his message. At the end of 1936, Benjamin Mays, dean of the School of Religion at Howard University, and Channing Tobias, a senior official of the YMCA, also met Gandhi.[80] Upon their return, all of these visitors, particularly Howard Thurman and Mays, spoke extensively about the Indian leader.[81] Thurman had attended college with Rev. Martin Luther King, Sr, and had conversations with King's son, Martin Luther King, Jr (1929–1968), which helped point that young man towards the message and methods of Gandhi. He would be the leader of the American Civil Rights movement, but then he was a minister-in-training studying the Bible. King numbered Mays, principal of Morehouse College, as one of his mentors and later friends.

Through the interwar period and during the Second World War, a number of organizations sprouted which would contribute to a later mass movement for civil rights. These included the Fellowship of Reconciliation (FOR), the Congress of Racial Equality (CORE) and the March on Washington Movement (MOWM). Crucial figures in these organizations were connected to Gandhi, Gandhians and to each other. The Fellowship of Reconciliation was an international organization of British and (soon) American members who were interested in conflict resolution.

A.J. Muste, a leader of the FOR steeped in Western pacifist traditions, learned of Gandhi after the First World War, and added Gandhian ideas to his arsenal of conciliatory techniques. James Farmer (1920–1999) and Bayard Rustin (1912–1987) were both schooled in the FOR and Farmer, in 1942, was the most important founder of CORE. A. Philip Randolph (1889–1979), a trade unionist and African American activist, organized the MOWM which hoped to carry out direct non-violent action during the Second World War, but it had to be de-mobilized; the idea later took shape as the 1963 March on Washington. Farmer, Rustin, Randolph, Muste among

---

[80] Gandhi 1995, V. 64, pp. 221–25, 397–402.
[81] Kapur, Prophet, p. 81ff.

others, were links from the inter-war period to the great age of the Civil Rights Movement of the 1950s and 1960s.

Besides those who found inspiration in Gandhi's work and method, there were also those who admired him but found his approach inappropriate for American Blacks. W.E.B. Du Bois, a fabled elder by 1943, but still a strong voice in the Black community, cautioned that Gandhi's method might work for a large majority opposing a foreign government, but would not work for a small minority opposing a powerful majority resistant to change.[82]

Although Du Bois never visited India, he did write a novel revolving around America and India in 1928, *Dark Princess*. A gifted essayist and historian/sociologist, this venture into fiction by Du Bois seems to me an embarrassing failure as a novel. An Afro-American boy from a small town by chance joins a colloquy of leaders of the so-called dark races of Asia and Africa meeting in Berlin, and is enchanted by an Indian princess, the Maharani of Bwodpur. Du Bois tracks their adventures and misadventures through the US in the 1920s. Quite ludicrously her princely state is a stand-in for India, India's religions are jumbled together, and their love flourishes as they each sample the work life of the American labour classes. In conclusion Du Bois calls for the talented tenth of the darker world in Asia, Africa, and the Americas to gather and struggle against the evil power of the white world in Europe and America.

Similarly—although the Black press was mostly favourable to Gandhi, and indeed, idealized him—the columnist George Schuyler argued in the prominent Black paper, the *Pittsburgh Courier*, that Gandhi's methods would not work for blacks in America. He said that force had to be met with force and was dubious that a relatively small minority by non-violent resistance could overturn the racist policies of the majority.

As Gandhi learned more about America and was asked to compare the plight of the Untouchables with that of Blacks in the United States, he said slightly different things at different times. At one point, he insisted that the Untouchables were better off because

---

[82] Lewis, David Levering, ed. 1995. *W.E.B. Du Bois. A Reader*. NY: Henry Holt, pp. 409–10.

there were no Indian legal bars against them whereas there were Jim Crow laws in the United States. When Gandhi heard of lynchings and race riots, he maintained that nothing like that occurred in India by caste Hindus against Untouchables.

One other prominent American activist in a different line who visited Gandhi in the mid-1930s was Margaret Sanger (1879–1966). This was, however, not the beginning of Sanger's interest in Gandhi and India.[83] Indian birth control organizations started work seriously in the 1920s and in 1925, Gandhi reaffirmed his opposition to the movement. The editorial pages of *The Birth Control Review*, in New York, presumably written by the editor, Sanger herself, responded to him bluntly:

> Mahatma Gandhi, the great leader of India, has recently given public utterance, in the columns of Young India, to his opinion concerning 'artificial' methods of Birth Control. 'There can be no two opinions about the necessity for Birth Control,' writes Mahatmaji, 'but the only method handed down from ages past is self-control or "Brahmacharya". It is an infallible sovereign remedy doing good to those who practise it. And medical men will earn the gratitude of mankind, if instead of advising artificial means of Birth Control they will find out the means of self-control. The union is not meant for pleasure but for bringing forth progeny.
>
> And union is a crime when the desire for progeny is absent.' Self-control, austere unrelenting asceticism, is in brief, in the ethics of Mahatma Gandhi, 'the only noble and straight method of Birth Control'.[84]

From the opening salvos of this non-violent, but rather testy and even nasty set of exchanges that extended over more than a decade,

---

[83] Chesler, Ellen. 1993. *Woman of Valor*. Margaret Sanger and the Birth Control Movement in America. NY: Anchor Books Doubleday; Ramusack, Barbara N. Fall 1989. 'Embattled Advocates: The Debate over Birth Control in India, 1920-40,' *Journal of Women's History*. V. 1, No. 2, p. 34ff.

[84] Birth Control Review, Sept. 1925, IX, No. 9

it is clear that both sides fired from almost immovable positions. The editorialist for the *Birth Control Review* went on to attack Gandhi fiercely and to make more explicit the values for which Sanger and her supporters stood:

> This thoughtless utterance—profoundly thoughtless, we are sorry to say—of India's great leader places him in the category of those traditional dogmatists and reactionary moralists for whom this world is irremediably a vale of tears and whose irresponsible 'idealism' has indeed made it one... We are happy that our friends in India are so vigorously combating it. Life, we challenge these opponents, is neither an evil, a malady, nor a disease to be avoided. Life is the supreme experience, into which we must unreservedly and joyfully plunge. Sexual expression is one of the most profoundly spiritual of all the avenues of human experience, and Birth Control the supreme moral instrument by which, without injury to others nor to the future destinies of mankind on this earth, each individual is enabled to progress on the road of self-development and self-realization. Human salvation is not to be attained by a steady diet of the bitter fruit of renunciation.[85]

In the positive vision of human life presented here, sexual experience is 'profoundly spiritual' and a part of human self-realization. For Sanger and her supporters, birth control by women was a royal road to emancipation and freedom. It would offer them control over their own bodies, allow them to choose to have children, when to have children, and the opportunity to enjoy sexual experience without the possibly unwanted consequence of pregnancy.

By 1925, Sanger was gathering allies in India, particularly since she had a formidable opponent, a 'reactionary moralist', who was the acknowledged leader of nationalist Indians. Among the allies she gained was India's most famous writer, Rabindranath Tagore, a critical nationalist who did not share all of Gandhi's moral views. Tagore wrote Sanger a supportive letter that was published in the

---

[85] Ibid., editorial.

December 1925 issue of *The Birth Control Review*. In the editor's response, she gladly shook the hand Tagore offered to her and praised his values and vision and that of her other allies in India. She wrote, in part:

> The struggle is thus beginning between humanitarians and ascetics in India. It is beginning without the funds and friends of India are encouraged to aid financially through the *Birth Control Review*. With Tagore as leader and such lieutenants (Prof. R.D. Karve and Prof. N.S. Phadke—L.G.) as these to teach India that the real issue is not between Birth Control and self-control, but between Birth Control and starvation, abortion and infanticide, there is no doubt about the outcome.[86]

Tagore did not assume practical leadership of the birth control fight in India and for political reasons the Government of India underplayed any interest in population control. The issue was debated, however, by the All-India's Women's Conference, among whose members there were many Sanger supporters and some opponents. In late 1935 and early 1936, preceded by her British ally Edith How-Martyn, Sanger visited India and attended a session of the AIWC.[87]

Sanger's main purpose in visiting India was publicity work and practical demonstrations for birth control. She brought supplies, demonstration models and films, and toured India in her cause. In December 1935, she travelled to Wardha, Gandhi's ashram in central India, to take a crack at gaining some support for her efforts. Arriving on his weekly silent day, she had to wait for her conversation with the Mahatma until the following day.

They began by agreeing that they both were for the emancipation of women and for birth control. As they discussed the means to these goals, their differing values came into play. In presenting a version of this meeting in *Harijan*, Mahadev Desai (1892–1942), Gandhi's long-standing secretary, said that Gandhi's philosophy sought

---

[86] Ibid, V. IX, No. 12.
[87] Ramusack 1989, p. 47ff.

'self-realisation through self-control'. Gandhi insisted that love was spiritual while sexual activity except for reproductive purposes was pure animal lust. He said:

> When both (i.e., husband and wife—L.G.) want to satisfy animal passion without having to suffer the consequences of their act it is not love, it is lust. But if love is pure, it will transcend animal passion and will regulate itself. We have not had enough education of the passions. When a husband says, 'Let us not have children, but let us have relations,' what is that but animal passion? If they do not want to have more children they should simply refuse to unite.[88]

Gandhi argued that if people were properly educated and disciplined—part of his vision of true swaraj or self-rule—then they should be satisfied to have sexual relations three or four times in their lifetimes for the purpose of procreation and should otherwise abstain. Of course, Sanger had a completely different view of the place of sexual activity in human experience and she tried to argue with Gandhi that his way could only be for the few ascetics, not for the common man. Gandhi responded that he had learned from his wife and some other women who had been in his ashrams and believed that abstinence would work for all. There could be no meeting of minds, and the testiness on Gandhi's side crept into the final paragraph of Desai's version of the interview:

> And yet as Mrs. Sanger was so dreadfully in earnest Gandhiji did mention a remedy which would conceivably appeal to him. That method was the avoidance of sexual union during unsafe periods confining it to the 'safe' period of about ten days during the month. That had at least an element of self-control which had to be exercised during the unsafe period. Whether this appealed to Mrs. Sanger or not I do not know. But therein spoke Gandhiji the truth-seeker. Mrs. Sanger has not referred to it anywhere in her interviews or her *Illustrated Weekly* article. Perhaps if

---

[88] Gandhi 1995, V. 62, pp. 157–58.

birth-controllers were to be satisfied with this simple method, the birth-control clinics and propagandists would find their trade gone...[89]

Sanger wrote a letter responding to Desai's article which he printed in the 22 February 1936 issue of *Harijan*. It was followed by further nasty and condescending comments by Gandhi's spokesman in which he referred to Gandhi's somewhat positive remarks about what is now called 'the rhythm method'. Desai said that as a truth-seeker, Gandhi was trying to find common ground with Sanger. He concluded, 'Whereas Mrs. Sanger's method leaves one free to indulge oneself all the days of the month, this particular one seemed to have the credit of imposing on one certain measure of self-control.'[90] Desai himself could not exercise much self-control as he went on to assail 'unseemly propaganda' for birth control.

The opposing views of Margaret Sanger and Gandhi embodied very different visions of human life and freedom. For Sanger, freedom meant self-fulfillment, self-realization and a range of choice for the world's women (and indirectly for men as well) which many did not have, especially the poor. It involved the end of the subjugation of women to their husbands' desires. For Gandhi, also concerned with freedom, it also meant self-realization but this required discipline and strict control of all the passions whether for sex, food, or one too many experiences. It was a quest for God and truth and his God demanded control—what Sanger called warped 'idealistic asceticism'. To her, sexual experience was or certainly could be 'profoundly spiritual'; to Gandhi it always involved lust. He had fought with his inner demon of lust for many decades and he was not about to compromise his views to conciliate Margaret Sanger, though his views on the rhythm method were less negative. The testiness of the exchange—on both sides— betokens that each realized that the other was a person of standing in the world's moral community, but that neither could sway the other, since their worldviews were so far apart and held so passionately.

---

[89] Ibid., p. 160.
[90] *Harijan*, Feb. 22, 1936.

2

Missions East
Religious and Secular

Although religious missions continued after the First World War—and continue today—secular missions to India began to expand. At first, benefactions of the Rockefeller Foundation went to support institutions of a religious nature, perhaps due to the Baptist background of Founder John D. Rockefeller, Jr (1874–1960). But soon other grants were made that did not favour religious institutions at all—among them one establishing a chair in tropical medicine at Calcutta University in 1916.[1]

The Rockefeller staff looked at the public health situation worldwide. They worked through national governments and particularly liked working within the British Empire. Dr Victor Heiser (1873–1972), a Rockefeller public health specialist, visited India in 1915 and 1921, while in 1926, Dr William S. Carter (1869–1944), a Rockefeller doctor and Director of Medical Education for the foundation, evaluated all the medical colleges in India. He recommended that, above all, India needed a school of hygiene and public health. After some discussions in New York, the Rockefeller Foundation offered to provide India with such a school, offering a minimum of property, physical plant, and equipment, although their long-range plan was more expansive.[2]

---

[1] Fosdick, Raymond B. 1952. *The Story of the Rockefeller Foundation*. NY: Harper, p. 44ff.
[2] Gordon, James S. 1987. *The Golden Guru*. The Strange Journey of Bhagwan Shree Rajneesh. Lexington: Stephen Greene Press.

Over the next seven years, they worked to establish the All-India School of Hygiene and Public Health that opened in 1932, and was able to appoint the Raj official, Lieutenant-Colonel A.D. Stewart to be its first director. After Stewart left in 1935 and when difficulties arose under an Indian acting-director in the 1930s, the Rockefeller Foundation pulled one of the ablest men out of its China programme, Dr John B. Grant (1890–1962), to take up the directorship of the School from 1939 to 1945. After 1945, they left the School to find its own way,[3] as is the general practice of both the Rockefeller and Ford Foundations: they help start institutions or programmes, then leave them to be supported by government or private sources.

The Rockefeller Foundation also targeted certain diseases that it hoped to help eliminate worldwide, among them malaria, endemic in India. In 1934, the foundation sent Dr Paul Russell (1894–1983), a leading malaria expert, to India, where he did research for about eight years, producing a series of reports on the different ecological settings in which malaria mosquitoes bred in the various regions of India. It was hoped that this would be a step towards its eradication, but not much action followed upon his research.[4] In independent India, a serious run at cutting malaria was made in the 1960s and 1970s, but a relapse has ensued.

In addition to its work in the health field, the Rockefeller Foundation extended its hand to Higginbottom's Allahabad Agricultural Institute, discussed earlier. In 1921, it gave a grant of $50,000 allowing the AAI to purchase land, and later in the 1920s, funded its programmes. Prakash Kumar has recently explored the complexities involved in the foundation's pattern of giving, but also denying aid, at different moments.[5] This early link to Indian agriculture is a foretaste of its later support of the research that led, in the 1960s, to what was called the 'Green Revolution'. In 1935, the Rockefeller Foundation set up an office in New Delhi to oversee

---

[3] Carter Survey of Medical Education, Boxes 7–10, Series 464, Record Group 1.1, RFA.

[4] Russell Reports 1934-41, Box 11, Series 464, Record Group 1.1, RFA, RAC.

[5] Kumar, Amitava. 2019. *Immigrant, Montana*. NY: Vintage, p. 8.

all of its activities in India. Remaining in operation for thirty years, it was the headquarters from which the foundation implemented its expanded activities in medicine, agriculture, and the humanities during the 1950s and 1960s, the golden age of American involvement.

Another smaller but important secular mission involved unique relationships forged between the US, India and Great Britain by Leonard Elmhirst, with associated grants from the Elmgrant Trust. Elmhirst was a young Englishman who, found unfit for military service in the First World War, went to India for a year with the YMCA. Through Lionel Curtis (1872–1955), editor of the *Round Table* and shaper of reforms for India, Elmhirst was sent to Sam Higginbottom at the Allahabad Agricultural Institute. There he worked for some time as Higginbottom's secretary and learned about the problems of Indian agriculture. Higginbottom strongly recommended that Elmhirst study agriculture in the US, believing that in America, Elmhirst would get more practical training that would prove more useful on his return to India. After much soul-searching, in 1919, with a borrowed fifty pounds plus a ticket to sail across the Atlantic, Elmhirst made his way to Cornell University and received his degree in agriculture.

While there, in connection with fund raising for the Cosmopolitan Club, he met Dorothy Payne Whitney Straight, a young widow with a large fortune.[6]

Dorothy's first husband, Willard Straight, a graduate of Cornell, had been a diplomat, financial expert and soldier, who by intellect and charm had risen from modest beginnings to executive positions.[7] The Straights started *The New Republic*, a liberal political weekly with Herbert Croly as editor, and purchased *Asia*, an elegant publication stressing commerce and tourism. The Straights, like Dorothy's parents, mixed with the Astors, Vanderbilts, Roosevelts, Harrimans and Morgans in elite New York and Washington society.

---

[6] Swanberg, W.A. 1980. *Whitney Father, Whitney Heiress.* NY: Scribner's, pp. 460–62; Elmhirst 1975.
[7] Swanberg 1980, p. 278ff.

After Straight's death in 1918 in the worldwide flu epidemic, as heiress to part of the fortune of William C. Whitney and his wife Flora Payne Whitney, Dorothy supported Elmhirst's request for financial help for his club at Cornell and planned a new student union building with his aid. A personal relationship began.[8]

While in the US, Elmhirst met Rabindranath Tagore, who wanted to start an agricultural reclamation project on an estate he had bought near his school, Shantiniketan, outside Bolpur, Bengal. With financial aid from Dorothy Straight, Elmhirst made his way there in 1921, and by the following year, he had organized an agricultural development scheme to reinvigorate rural life. Working successfully there for a year, Elmhirst then travelled with Tagore as his secretary to Latin America and other places for two more years. Then he had to decide upon his future.

Elmhirst overcame his doubts about marriage to a woman of wealth, and proposed to Dorothy, who eventually accepted. When they married in 1925, they decided to start an experimental school and a cultural centre near the town of Totnes, Devon, rebuilding Dartington Hall, a run-down former manor house and estate. They used some funds for their work there and to support industrial and agricultural projects in Great Britain, but also, beginning in the early 1930s, to support international projects through what they called the Elmgrant Trust. Although many of their projects were down-to-earth, their range of connections—Leonard Elmhirst to Tagore, Dorothy Elmhirst to the Roosevelts and wealthy Americans—made them highfliers in the world of philanthropy. In touch with members of India's political and cultural elite including Gandhi, Jawaharlal Nehru, and the dancer Uday Shankar (1900–1977), they supported valuable projects, quite a few of them in India, within their means.[9] Although there were numerous international grants, the Elmhirsts' main work was the reconstruction and revitalization of Dartington Hall, and the founding of the experimental, coeducational school there that opened in 1926. With many possible models in mind and

---

[8] Ibid., p. 460ff.
[9] Elmhirsts' Papers, Dartington Hall.

having visited schools in Great Britain and the US, they drew upon
a proposal drawn up by Tagore and Elmhirst called 'sikhsa-satra', or
'planning for a village school', which read in part:

> Freedom for growth, experiment, enterprise and adventure, all
> are dependent upon Imagination, that greatest of gifts… to 'open
> wide the mind's caged door', this is the most vital service that it is
> in the power of one human being to render to another… like the
> lamp of Aladdin endows him with the power to create a new work
> for himself… Life, to be life at all, has to be lived…[10]

There were striking similarities as well as some differences between
Tagore's school at Shantiniketan and the Elmhirsts' at Dartington.
In both schools, there was to be an informal interaction between
pupils and adults or seniors, with a minimum of rules. Both schools
valued bringing the pupils closer to nature and encouraging the arts,
and stressed learning by doing rather than by rigid book-learning.[11]

Among those whom the Elmhirsts supported was Uday Shankar.
While Dhan Gopal Mukerji was writing and Kumar Goshal acting,
Uday Shankar was dancing. Though never trained as a classical Indian
dancer, he created a modern style of dance infusing his dance troupe's
presentations with Indian stories and elements. He embodied great
vitality and physical beauty as well as facial expressions (abhinaya)
that were a part of more traditional Indian dance. Shankar borrowed
from pathbreakers like Vaslav Nijinsky and Isadora Duncan, but
also drew on Indian arts, costumes and mythology. He danced with
Anna Pavlova, who had previously toured the United States, and the
impresario Sol Hurok arranged for Pavlova and Shankar to tour the
West in 1931. On a tour of India in 1929, Shankar had seen Indian
classical dance, but realized that he could not be and would not be
such a dancer. His path was different and more appealing to Western
audiences, who while they may not have understood some of the

---

[10] Young, Michael. 1982. *The Elmhirsts of Dartington*. The Creation of an Utopian
Community, p. 83.
[11] Ibid., p. 153.

Indian symbolism enacted, responded to his unique creations in the 1930s. His younger brother Ravi Shankar (1920–2012) danced with the troupe in his early years and then trained as a classical Indian musician, gaining worldwide fame as India's best-known musician.

After the Dartington Hall reclamation and school were well under way, the Elmhirsts turned some attention to *Asia* and hired Richard J. Walsh (1886–1960), head of John Day publishers, as editor. Walsh shifted gears at the magazine, deciding to focus on international affairs and the cultures and literatures of Asian countries.[12] Gertrude Emerson (1890–1982), was an associate editor with *Asia* in the 1920s, and its resident India expert. Eager to understand Indian life from the viewpoint of its peasants, she spent a year living in a village and published *Voiceless India* in 1930. Her book was well-reviewed and a foreign edition had an appreciation by Tagore.[13]

By 1923, even before he had been introduced to Gertrude Emerson, the agriculturist Boshi (Basiswar) Sen (1887–1971) had met Leonard Elmhirst. Seeing value in Sen's research in plant physiology, Elmhirst provided support to Sen from the mid-1920s. Sen felt he was carrying forth the work and message of Swami Vivekananda, as a disciple, and yet as a trained and practising scientist he would revive India and connect it to the physical world. He started his own laboratory in Calcutta after he was unable to work out a satisfactory relationship with the renowned scientist Jagadish Chandra Bose (1858–1937), who had been his guide. A few years later, with the support of the Elmhirsts, Sen was able to set up his laboratory in Almora, in the Himalayas.

Boshi Sen had met Gertrude Emerson in Calcutta in 1927. They renewed their relationship during the year she was living in northern India doing the research that would result in Village India. They met again in New York where he had accompanied an elderly, Western female disciple of Vivekananda, Sister Christine, whom he helped to place in a nursing home. In November 1932 after her death,

---

[12] Conn, Peter. 1996. *Pearl S. Buck*. A Cultural Biography. Cambridge: Cambridge U. Press, p. 82ff.

[13] Emerson, Gertrude. 1930. *Voiceless India*. Garden City: Doubleday.

Sen and Gertrude Emerson married. The Sens had a double tie to the Elmhirsts, who continued as owners of *Asia*: she as a corresponding editor of the magazine, based in India, and Boshi Sen as a prominent recipient of Elmgrants and friend of the Elmhirsts. As Sen put it, 'Dorothy and Leonard gave me my freedom.'[14]

The tie to Richard Walsh and *Asia* shortly involved another powerful link to Asia, for in 1935, he married Pearl Buck, America's most prominent author of fiction about China. Born Pearl Sydenstricker, she was the daughter of American Presbyterian missionaries and had lived in China for most of her life. Although she married another missionary and remained on missionary service for some years through the 1920s, she embarked on a new career as a writer. John Day published her first novel and subsequent ones, including *The Good Earth* (1931), which depicted Chinese peasant life and became a bestseller. She divorced her missionary husband and in 1935, she married Walsh, and they shaped *Asia* into a critical voice against Western imperialism in Asia. Pearl Buck was castigated by her own church for speaking out against the value of Western missionaries in China. She also wrote the novel *Mandala: A Novel of India* (1970), which did not display the same fine touch as had her novels about China. With the funds from her book sales, Buck was able to start several new and different philanthropic organizations, including one that was the first to help with the adoption of Asian children. In 1941, she and Walsh purchased *Asia* from Dorothy Elmhirst and continued to publish it for some years.[15]

The Institute for Pacific Relations (IPR), established to better inform Americans about Asia, was another kind of secular mission. Organized in 1926 by Edward C. Carter (1878–1954), a former YMCA worker and involved in *The Inquiry*, a Protestant magazine about public issues, it was supported by the Rockefeller and Carnegie Foundations as well as private contributors.

---

[14] Mehra, Girish N. 2007. *Nearer Heaven than Earth*. The Life and Times of Boshi Sen and Gertrude Emerson Sen. New Delhi: Rupa, p. 237.
[15] Conn 1996, p. 244ff.

Relocating in 1930 from Hawaii to New York, it held a series of international conferences devoted to the discussion of contemporary issues,[16] and published a journal, *Pacific Affairs*, which has continued into the present, decades after the IPR was shut down in 1961. It also supported research projects and published many reports, books and essays.

In 1929, Carter chose a young scion of the wealthy Vanderbilt family, Frederick Vanderbilt Field (1905–2000), to be his secretary, who would later rise to become, until 1940, an important leader of the group. Owen Lattimore (1900–1989), a director on the IPR board and a leading scholar of China and inner Asia, became editor of *Pacific Affairs* in 1933.[17] In the 1930s, Field and a wealthy friend, Philip Jaffe (1895–1980), founded *Amerasia*, a magazine more explicitly political than the other publications of the IPR. It was supportive of the Soviet Union. Both Field and Jaffe were members of the Communist Party USA, and Carter a fellow-traveller. After the Second World War, in a climate cool to Soviet influence, these connections brought the IPR and *Amerasia* under severe scrutiny and criticism.[18]

During these years as well, scholarly interest in India deepened, leading to the establishment in 1934 of an American School of Indo-Iranian Research, spurred by W. Norman Brown (1892–1975), a classicist who had earned his PhD at Johns Hopkins University under the renowned Sanskrit scholar Maurice Bloomfield (1855–1928). For decades afterward, Brown guided the organization of American studies on India with

---

[16] Field, Frederick Vanderbilt. 1983. *From Right to Left*. An Autobiography. Westport: Lawrence Hill, p. 82ff.

[17] Field 1983, p. 82ff; Lattimore, Owen. 1950. *Ordeal by Slander*. Boston: Little, Brown, p. 163ff.

[18] Caute, David. 1979. *The Great Fear*. The Anti-Commuist Purge under Truman and Eisenhower. NY: Touchstone, p. 310ff; Lattimore 1950, p. 73ff; Newman, Robert P. 1992. Owen Lattimore and 'Loss' of China. Berkeley: U. of California Press, p. 22ff; Klehr, Harvey and Ronald Radosh. 1996. The Amerasia Spy Case. Chapel Hill: U. of North Carolina Press, p. 38ff.

energy, intelligence and verve.[19] He also played an important
role in the American Oriental Society and in obtaining funds
for archaeological research in India. Although some leading
American universities had had professors of Sanskrit since the
later nineteenth century, there was no organization in the US
focused on the totality of studies of India, ancient and modern,
until Brown took the helm. Brown himself had taught in India
during the 1920s. In 1926, he was appointed professor of Sanskrit
at the University of Pennsylvania. During the Second World War,
his scholarly efforts were put on hold when he became head of
the India section of the Office of Strategic Studies (OSS), an arm
of the American war effort.

While secular missions to support and study India took flight
in the inter-war period, the promotion of Christian missions also
continued without interruption. The Vellore Medical School and
Hospital continued to expand, and as funds permitted, acquired more
land and built additional buildings. Joined by other dominations, the
Reformed Church backed their activities and began to nominate
candidates for the medical school. In 1922, fourteen young women
graduated from the school and, out of 140 applicants, approximately
thirty candidates were accepted for the next year. In 1922, Ida Scudder
was awarded the Kaiser-i-Hind medal by the Raj, a recognition
she accepted although she never sought honours. In 1927, Vellore
received a different kind of recognition: Mahatma Gandhi, who
generally disapproved of Christian missions, accepted an invitation
and visited.[20] While he objected to the efforts by missionaries to gain
conversions, the Mahatma blessed the positive work accomplished by
Ida Scudder and Sam Higginbottom.

With help from the Rockefeller Foundation and government
aid, Vellore acquired a GE X-ray machine, for the use of which they

---

[19] Elder, Joseph W. and Maureen L.P. Patterson. 1998. *History of the American
Institute of Indian Studies*. Printed Manuscript, Madison: University of Wisconsin,
p. 50ff.
[20] Wilson, Dorothy Clarke. 1959. *Dr. Ida*. The Story of Dr. Ida Scudder of Vellore.
NY: McGraw-Hill, p. 182ff.

instituted a training course in 1933. In 1931, following her medical training, Ida B. Scudder, a member of the fourth generation of the family to work in India, went to Kodaikanal for Tamil language study and then joined the staff. She had attended Northfield Seminary like her aunt Ida S. Scudder, Vellore's founder; then she went in turn to Mt Holyoke College and from 1925 to 1929, the Women's Medical College of Philadelphia. From 1936 to 1939, she trained as a radiologist in the US and Great Britain and headed the radiology section of the hospital.[21] Hesitant at first, she threw herself into it and thrived for decades, making important contributions to the medical programme.[22]

One significant change in the twentieth-century operation of Vellore is that although doctors and evangelists worked together, medical and missionary functions were carried out by different persons.[23] The Vellore Medical School was not yet a medical college as Ida S. Scudder had hoped it would be one day. In the late 1930s, as the Government of Madras outlined the additions and improvements necessary for Vellore to upgrade to a medical college, Ida B. Scudder came to believe that the upgrade could only be carried out if the school were made co-educational. A controversy ensued among its backers as the change was instituted.

William H. Wiser (1890–1961) and his wife Charlotte Viall (1892–1981) stand out among the unusual and pathbreaking missionaries who came to India in the early twentieth century. After they graduated from the University of Chicago, Wiser went out first, in 1915, as a rural missionary of the Presbyterian Church; Charlotte came a year later, and they were married in Allahabad. Wiser taught at the Allahabad Agricultural Institute and they both did social work and helped at industrial cooperatives in Kanpur and Allahabad. In 1925, they moved to the village of Karimpur, befriended the villagers, and stayed for five years. They wanted to better understand

---

[21] Georgia, Jennifer. 1994. *Legacy and Challenge*. The Story of Dr. Ida B. Scudder. Saline, Michigan: McNaughton & Gunn, p. 83ff.
[22] Ibid., p. 48ff.
[23] Scudder 1984, p. 313.

the lives of the students at the agricultural institute and have a framework for grasping the problems facing ordinary people. In Karimpur, they not only carried out their village survey, but acted as pioneer anthropologists, paving the way for many foreign and Indian anthropologists and other social scientists who would follow. The fruits of their village stay are documented in their books *Behind Mud Walls, 1930–1960*[24] and *The Hindu Jajmani System: A Socio-Economic System Interrelating Members of a Hindu Village Community in Services*,[25] now considered classic texts on village life.

The Wisers settled into their long stay as they befriended the villagers, offered them medical help, kept an open house, and provided transport to the town of Mainpuri in their Ford Touring Car to anyone game enough to come along. Their acute and unsentimental account of village life, written with verve and compassion, explores leadership patterns, the social hierarchy, and the lives of women and young people. The Wisers' commitment to spreading the message of Christ through teaching and lived example is evident in their approach to the Untouchables, noted in *Behind Mud Walls* in a chapter, 'The Untouchables', dedicated to that issue. A conflict arose between the Wisers and village leaders over just this issue when a nine-year-old Christian Untouchable boy, Muni—the same age as their own son Arthur—began to attend the village school. All the village children boycotted the school once Muni attended. Numerous compromises were suggested to help resolve the disagreement, but none worked. Though the son of the village headman attended a town school that enrolled Untouchable children, the men of Karimpur would not permit this intermingling in their village. The relationship of the Wisers to the village *bhangis*, or Untouchables, converted to Christianity, taught them lessons about what Christianity meant at the grassroots level.

---

[24] Wiser, William H. and Charlotte Viall Wiser. 1989. *Behind Mud Walls 1930-1960*. With sequel by Susan S. Wadley: The Village in 1984. Berkeley: U. of California Press.

[25] Wiser, William H. and Charlotte Viall Wiser. 1936. *The Hindu Jajmani System: A SocioEconomic System Interrelating Members of a Hindu Village Community in Services*. Lucknow: Lucknow Publishing House.

However much they integrated into village life, the Wisers remained committed Christians whose idea was to serve and through service bring others to their Christian understanding of the world. Later, they authored a Christian primer for missionaries endeavouring to work in rural areas, *For All of Life*. In the early 1930s, the Wisers returned to the US and were based at Cornell University, William earning a PhD in rural sociology and Charlotte a degree in nutrition. Returning to India, they taught until 1941 at the North India Theological College in Saharanpur. Back again in the US during the Second World War, they organized appropriate committees in America and India, gained backing from the Presbyterian and Methodist churches and returned to India in late 1945, and established the India Village Service which grew out of their understanding of local life and the message of Christ. In 1945, they issued a brochure which reads in part: 'It purposes to develop, under the direction of a committee in America and a committee in India, an intensive non-institutional programme of village improvement through agricultural extension, rural industry, co-operative organization, and other aspects of improved rural living in a few contiguous areas…to serve as a model for the regeneration of rural India (where 90 per cent of Indian people live).'[26]

William Wiser was to be director of the project and they immediately set to work. The Wisers explained that they drew upon the work of the Allahabad Agricultural Institute, the extension service of the US Department of Agriculture, and the Near East Foundation in Macedonia, Greece. They said that though the project would enlist a majority of Christian workers, it would serve all villagers regardless of caste, community or religion and they wanted to work in concert with government efforts to improve rural life.

By late 1945, the Wisers set up shop in Etah District, in United Provinces (UP). The Development Commissioner of UP helped them to find a home for their work in the Marehra Seed Store area and they utilized houses vacated by Muslims who had left for

---

[26] Wiser, William H. 1949. *India Village Service After Four Years*. Lucknow: Lucknow Publishing House, pp. 12–45

Pakistan after 1947. Although at first they recruited educated and committed Christians for crucial roles, they aimed to have villagers take over as soon as capable men and women were identified. Wiser wrote in his assessment after four years of work that they developed a mutually helpful relationship with government officials. Indian Village Service helped train government village level workers just after the war, while the government paid salaries for some workers on their side of the work and gave valuable advice.[27] Their work grew out of a Christian vision, but it linked up to more secular projects they conducted later often with government help.

Meanwhile, in Vellore down south, there were several changes in the offing. With the implementation of provincial autonomy and the elections in 1936–1937, the Madras Legislative Assembly gained a Congress majority. Among the steps taken by the assembly in 1938 was the abolition of the LMP medical degree and the decision to recognize only the MB and MS degrees. Its abolition had an immediate and strong impact on the Vellore Medical School for Women: Vellore would have to be upgraded to a college with expanded facilities and classes, or close. It would not close, but would need to chart a new path, about which there were intense disagreements.

After discussions in India, the UK and the US amongst the relevant bodies, Ida S. Scudder and her allies decided that they would make Vellore a co-educational medical college on the model of the medical school for men at another Christian institution in Miraj, western India. They would do everything necessary to satisfy the requirements of Madras University for a full-fledged medical college, and worked vigorously to raise the needed funds, hire the additional staff, and build the larger clinical and other facilities required. The opposing faction, led by Ida S. Scudder's long-time supporter, the missionary Lucy Peabody (1861–1949), argued that the funds had been raised for a women's institution and now this unique institution, when incorporated into a new co-educational college, would vanish.

---

[27] Wiser, William H. and Charlotte Viall Wiser. 1943. *For All of Life*. NY: Friendship Press, 1943; Wiser 1949, pp. 11–49.

Ida S. Scudder responded that turning co-educational was the only way to save and improve the institution.

The Vellore school was also faced with time limits. The medical school, under the new dispensation, was not allowed to admit new students in 1938 and 1939. In 1941, Ida S. Scudder returned to the US to raise the funds, an extremely difficult journey in wartime, but she persevered. She had help from Dr F.M. Potter of the Reformed Church, and they enlisted help from twenty mission boards as well as doctors and educators in the US. In 1945, the Vellore Medical College gained temporary affiliation with Madras University. Unqualified affiliation was granted in 1950, around the time that Ida celebrated her eightieth birthday, and Dr Hilda Lazarus (1890–1978) became the first principal.[28] Ida retired but continued for another decade to join in the work of the institution she had founded. In May 1960, she died at her home in Kodaikanal at age ninety and after some sixty years of work in India. Her niece, Ida B. Scudder (1900–1995), and many old and new staff continued to work at making Vellore Medical College and Hospital one of the premier medical facilities in India. At the memorial for their founder, they read from her favourite Biblical passage, 1 Corinthians 13:4–13: 'Love is patient; love is kind… It bears all things, hopes all things, endures all things… faith, hope, and love abide, these three; and the greatest of these is love.'[29]

The work of Leonard and Dorothy Elmhirst in creating Dartington Hall and setting up the Elmgrant Trust has been described earlier. Leonard Elmhirst was especially skilled in the field of agricultural development. His efforts in this field continued from his work in Bengal in the 1920s to his activities with the estates in Devon that the Elmhirsts had purchased. He helped organize a society of agricultural economists and also continued his lively interest in helping Indian agriculture. An opportunity arose during the war when in 1943, Richard G. Casey (1890–1976), an Australian diplomat, was appointed governor of Bengal.

---

[28] Scudder 1984; Georgia 1994, pp. 117ff.
[29] NRSV Bible with the Apocrypha, The. Compact Edition. Oxford University. Press, Oxford, 1995, p. 71.

Elmhirst had previously worked with Casey in Egypt in 1942, and in 1944, Casey made Elmhirst his honorary agricultural adviser in Bengal. The worst of the Bengal famine was over, but Bengal badly needed to secure the future of its peasants. Elmhirst connected with the economist Sudhir Sen (1907–1989), a specialist in agricultural development, and agricultural engineer, William L. Voorduin (1897–1977), whom Casey had had brought from the Tennessee Valley Authority project in the US for advice on the rivers of Bengal. The connections of Elmhirst and Casey to top officials in the US, India and the UK were used whenever necessary, as they cut red tape to manoeuvre around bureaucratic obstacles.

Together, they focused on the Suhrawardy River which, if properly dammed, would provide a regulated source of water and electricity. Their plans were eventually embodied in the Damodar River Valley project. Although not carried out precisely in the way that they planned, in the decades after Indian Independence, dams were built and water and electricity supplied.[30]

---

[30] Leonard Elmhirst, Oral History, Elmhirst Papers.

3

Mantras

Following upon Swami Vivekananda, who in 1893 had impressed an American audience by his electrifying appearance at the Chicago World's Fair, the figure most responsible for bringing Indian religious teachings and yoga to the US is the guru Yogananda, as Diana Eck argues in *A New Religious America*.[31] Given her claim, and a similar one made by the 2014 documentary film, *Awake: The Life of Yogananda*, he deserves some attention.

Yogananda had grown up in Ranchi and encountered and trained with his guru Lahiri in Benares and in the Himalayas. Assigned by Lahiri to preach to America, Yogananda travelled westward, landing in Boston in 1920. He preached in Boston until 1925, then found more fertile ground for his teachings in Los Angeles. With the help of a wealthy American backer, he purchased a mansion on Mt Washington which became his headquarters. He founded the Self-Realization Society and initiated many Americans as well as Indians to his chosen path, that of *kriya* yoga. His book, *Autobiography of a Yogi*, written in the 1940s, revised before his death in 1952, and frequently reprinted, has had a wide distribution.[32]

Like his predecessor, the philosopher and reformer Keshub Chandra Sen, who had attempted to integrate Christian theology with Hinduism, Yogananda had ingested Christianity and placed

---

[31] Eck, Diana L. 2001. *A New Religious America. How a 'Christian Country: Has Become the World's Most Religously Diverse Nation*. NY: HarperCollins.
[32] Yogananda, Paramahansa. 1979. *Autobiography of a Yogi*. Los Angeles: Self-Realization Fellowship.

Jesus Christ in the pantheon with a
line of prophets and spiritually fulfilled
men and women, giving him his due
as an avatar. For Yogananda, however,
Jesus Christ is one avatar among many,
while for believing Christians, Christ
is the one son of God bringing truth
to Earth and taking all men's sins
upon himself in his great sacrifice.
What Yogananda does is to place
Jesus Christ among many healers,
miracle-doers, truth-bringers, avatars,
including his guru, his guru's guru, and
himself. What Western readers made

Yogananda

of the obscure discussions of seemingly dead gurus is unclear, but
Yogananda attracted large audiences in the US. Thereby he attracted
the attention of Indian political intelligence in the mid-1920s, and
met with President Calvin Coolidge in the late 1920s.

Yogananda's effort met with some scepticism. An official of the
Britain's New York Consulate suggested that Yogananda 'deals in the
usual type of psychological platitudes that emanate from the Hindu
apostles of new religions who derive lucrative incomes by imposing
upon certain elements of the American public. He is usually careful
to avoid reference to political questions...' An official of the Los
Angeles consulate said that a man and woman who had worked for
Yogananda had come to see him. 'They regarded him as more or
less of a swindler and as misleading women...'[33] When Yogananda
went to lecture in Miami in 1928, he was hounded from the city
because local men considered him 'a coloured man' and thought it
inappropriate for a man of colour to lecture white women. Yogananda
was physically threatened, but sought an injunction against police
interference with his lectures. Eventually, he withdrew and agreed
not to lecture because he was a 'loyal British subject'.

---

[33] Govt of India, file L/P&J/12/358.

Nonetheless, Yogananda persevered, spent most of his last thirty-two years in the United States, which he had come to admire greatly, and gained disciples, including many Americans, some of whom he initiated into his order and gave leadership positions within the Self-Realization Fellowship. Yogananda did not rely upon Indian disciples from his school in Ranchi or Calcutta, but placed his faith in Westerners whom he said could learn his yogic discipline of the will as well as any Indian. The Self-Realization Society spread far and wide in the US and abroad.[34] Yogananda was attuned to the American style of publicity, enabling him to draw large crowds to his lectures and attract followers. A host of Westerners and Indians lavished praise upon him in the documentary 'Awake', including well-known figures, George Harrison (1943–2001), the Beatles guitarist, and alternative-medicine advocate Dr Deepak Chopra (1946–).

Besides Yogananda, the Indian religious teacher Jiddu Krishnamurti, gained attention and fame from the inter-war period onwards. Son of a lower government officer from Andhra, he and his brother Nitya had been brought to the grounds of the Theosophists in Adyar. At first they were given a filthy and broken-down hut and ignored. But the British author Charles Leadbeater discovered Krishnamurti and persuaded his associates that this young man could be a kind of messiah and the vehicle for Theosophical truths and revelations. Krishnamurti and his brother were then educated and groomed by the Theosophists in Adyar and in Great Britain. Prompted by messages from Leadbeater who claimed he daily received messages from astral deities, Krishnamurti was made into an international spiritual leader, and he began to give talks and make brief presentations during his largely European years—1912 to 1921. A book, *At the Feet of the Master*,[35] was put out in his name, though it appeared to be a collection of Leadbeater's messages to him, and was widely distributed in Europe and the United States. Hints of scandal and doubts about Krishnamurti's impending divinity led to the breakaway of a section of the American Theosophists, whose

---

[34] Govt of India, L/P&J/12/358.
[35] Krishnamurti, Jiddu. 1910. *At the Feet of the Master.* Adyar: Theosophical Society.

concoction of tantric beliefs and symbolism drawn from Hinduism and Buddhism, together with Christian elements, provided what some Westerners then were seeking. From 1922 onwards, Krishnamurti had a series of personal revelations and experiences that he later called 'the process'. He felt the divine come in and through him and suffered intense physical and mental pain through it all. What might it mean? Was it the fulfillment of the beliefs of the Theosophists as formulated by Besant and Leadbeater? At first it seemed so to Krishnamurti, but gradually he broke with the Theosophists and their beliefs.

In the late 1920s, Krishnamurti dropped Theosophical dogmas and insisted that no one should follow any religious guru or sect but simply seek the divine truth within. Although he said he was no messiah, he donned the mantle of 'World Teacher', telling his followers that he had connected to the 'Beloved', which seemed to mean the divine power, and that he was on Earth simply to help them get there themselves. When the boy Leadbeater had chosen became a man, he found a truth and inner power without the symbols and paraphernalia of Theosophism, thereby humiliating and enraging that movement's devout believers and leaders.

Krishnamurti moved to Ojai, California in the 1920s, though he lectured throughout the world, collaborating with scientists and meeting with other religious teachers, political leaders, and seekers, among them the author Aldous Huxley, to be discussed below, directing them to find their own truth within.[36] He later made peace with the Theosophists and occasionally lectured on their grounds, where this writer listened to him in 1964. When I professed ignorance of who he was, a true believer told me that thousands of people worldwide would give up their right arm just for the opportunity to hear him. I went.

In 1930, Wendell Thomas, a scholar who had closely studied Hinduism and read his Freud, published his book, *Hinduism Invades America*. Thomas and Harry Emerson Fosdick, introducer of the book, noted that missions by then were going both ways: American Christian

---

[36] Jayakar 1986; Vernon 2002.

missionaries to India, and Indian Hindu missionaries to the US. Thomas argued that the Vedanta Society and Yogananda's followers were spreading Hinduism through the land. Although his choices were appropriate, he exaggerated their influence on American society, even as he himself noted the declining membership in the Vedanta Society. Founded by Vivekananda, it set up centres in major American cities staffed by Ramakrishna Mission monks brought from India.

One of Thomas' many insightful comments is that in India, learning from Christian missionaries the importance of social service, the Mission made this a major focus, while in the US, the Vedanta Society kept to its work of propagating Hinduism. Writing in the late 1920s, Thomas did fieldwork at the Society and at Yogananda's lectures. In his analysis, his pointed out the differences in approach: the Society did not adapt its message to its American audience, while Yogananda learned American marketing techniques and incorporated elements of American culture into his teaching. His careful research, gathering information on almost every Hindu speaker or teacher in the US, plus on Sikhs and Buddhists as well, would make any social scientist proud. In summary, he wrote,

> ...Hinduism has impressed itself on American life: on miracle-loving people through Hindu 'fakes' and 'fakirs', on individual religious truth-seekers through the Vedanta movement, the Yogoda Society, and other Hindu and Hindu-like cults, on cultural liberals through the Threefold Movement, and on students, teachers and scholars through International School, learned lecturers, cultural organizations and certain Western philosophers and poets.[37]

Thomas insisted that Hindu teachings were a dogma, not science or the one Truth, like the teachings of other religions, no better, no worse. Just more sweeping in the assertion that Hinduism offered the highest, most all-encompassing truth. He also argued that Hindu ideas infiltrated Greek and Christian thought from antiquity, and into the nineteenth and twentieth centuries.

---

[37] Thomas 1930, 242.

4

Immigrants, Nationalists and Culture

By 1923, due to the Thind decision of the US Supreme Court, Indians were deemed to be 'obviously not of the white race', and after the passage of the Immigration Act of 1924, they could no longer become citizens. Yet, a trickle continued of businessmen, students, and Indian nationalists and their supporters, of whom some were only passing through, while others stayed for a longer period. Demographer S. Chandrasekhar and Haridas Muzumdar have estimated that there were 1,886 immigrants from South Asia in the 1920s and 496 in the 1930s. As Vivek Bald has suggested, more may have come informally and stayed, but there are no hard numbers. None could become citizens as some earlier immigrants had, so that the number of South Asians who were citizens and immigrants was very small, even compared to the number of those from Japan and China. Among the South Asians who came to the US and remained permanently or for some protracted time are those noted here: the religious leaders Paramahansa Yogananda and Jiddu Krishnamurti; the scholar Taraknath Das; the mathematician, farmer, and politician Dalip Singh Saund (1899–1973); the writer Dhan Gopal Mukerji; the actor and producer Kumar Goshal (1899–1971); and the art collector and theorist Ananda K. Coomaraswamy (1877–1947).

The impact of the 'barred zone', (which included Asia), the Thind decision, and then the Immigration Act of 1924, was to crush some hopes of American citizenship, and endanger the naturalized citizenship of South Asians already citizens. The US government moved to strip those naturalized during the first two decades of the twentieth century of their citizenship, and most lost it, including A.Z. Mozumdar, a religious teacher.[1] Taraknath Das, who had married an American woman, Mary Keatinge Morse, twenty years his senior, fought together with her to preserve his citizenship as well as hers. They went off to Europe and spent the better part of a decade, coming and going, until Das' friends and contacts persuaded the US government to allow Das and his wife to retain their American citizenship. Never denaturalized, they received new passports in 1927.[2] But they were the exceptions.

Taraknath Das served a prison sentence in Fort Leavenworth. But he had made friends in the US who defended his citizenship at a time when some naturalized Indians lost theirs. Das fought denaturalization proceedings for years and by the mid-1920s, he emerged with his citizenship intact. From about 1913, he wrote frequently for the Indian press, particularly *The Modern Review* of Calcutta, informing his countrymen at home of events in the US and throughout the world. At the same time, he wrote for Western audiences about developments in India. Earning a PhD in international relations at Georgetown University, he sought to teach and write, rather than agitate. With his wife's help, he established the Taraknath Das Foundation in Germany and the United States, to help Indian students abroad. Das continued teaching, writing articles, and giving out these grants until his death in 1958.[3]

The talented writer Dhan Gopal Mukerji, met earlier as one of the respondents to Katherine Mayo's hostile *Mother India*, was one of the most effective presenters of that region's civilization to American readers. Around 1909, the nineteen-year-old Mukerji made his way to Japan, then to the US, where he encountered International Workers of the World, usually called Wobblies, spiritualists, anarchists, Indian farm workers, and other Americans. He also studied, enrolling first at the University of California, Berkeley, and then at Stanford, where

---

[1] Lal 2008, p. 39.
[2] Mukherjee 1998, pp. 184-191.
[3] Mukherjee 1998.

in June 1918, he met and married the American graduate student Ethel Ray Dugan, called 'Patty'. To avoid California's miscegenation statute, Mukerji identified himself as a 'Caucasian', though his skin was deep brown. They moved east and a son, Dhan Gopal Mukerji, Jr, was born in New Bedford, Massachusetts, in 1919. Then they moved to New York, and Mukerji published his first books of poetry, translations, and a play. He was the best-selling author among South Asians in America, with only Tagore and Kipling better known as writers about India.

In 1923, Mukerji published *Caste and Outcaste*, an autobiographical work where, under the topic of 'caste', he reflected on growing up in India as an 'outcaste' and about coping with America.[4] Labelling himself 'an unquiet spirit',[5] he detailed how he learned from his parents about Indian traditions and the duties of a Brahmin priestly family going back hundreds of years. He told of encounters with animals—his family lived on the edge of a forest—and how he imbibed the rich story lore of India. At fifteen, he left home on a pilgrimage to the northern mountains and to Benares. He was searching for some 'supreme experience', his way to the infinite silence towards which he was moving.

Besides succumbing to the charm of his stories in *Caste and Outcaste*, one must ask: what India does Mukerji present to Americans? It is a romanticized, spiritualized, Brahmin India, a version of the India of his childhood that he chose to put before foreigners who had scarcely any previous understanding of India. Through his account, Mukerji says, 'Hindus do such-and-such', 'Indian mothers act like this', 'Indian weddings are like this', but the Indian culture he presents is that of upper caste, fairly well-to-do Indians who do not have to struggle for their next meal. It is not the India of the great majority in the early twentieth century who lived below the poverty line; of the Untouchables, there is hardly a mention. How would Mukerji answer such a crass, materialist's critique of his India? He might have said that ancient, spiritual

---

[4] Mukerji 2002.
[5] Mukerji 2002, p. 117.

India lived on into the present, not only in the traditions of Brahmin families such as his own, but in the lives of ordinary people, in their songs, in their rituals, in their beliefs.

As for America, Mukerji depicts a world of poor strugglers, dreaming anarchists and Indians plotting revolution in their homeland from afar. In the epilogue to *Caste and Outcaste*, Mukerji offers some comments on America. In part, he writes:

> So a Hindu, who wants to find a complete antithesis to his race and culture, had better avoid Europe and come straight to America. The future of this country is more staggering than the past of India. A supreme desolation is America's, and this desolation is as alluring as that of the Himalayas. I found in America's air the sharp taste of freedom, not freedom from politicians, not freedom from economic conditions, but freedom from the dead. No dead generations rock the cradle of the new-born here….
>
> America is a seed continent. All the world and all the nations are planting their best and their worst seed in this spring-smitten island. Asia has planted her mysticism, Europe has sown her seeds of diverse intellectual culture, and Africa has offered her innocence.
>
> America is victorious, India is conquered. America is carefree. India is careworn. America lynches Negroes, India illtreats her untouchables. America believes in herself. India is too old to believe in herself. India has caste. America aims at equality… The differences are so extreme that the extremes must meet. Both India and America are mad. India has been mad with peace and America mad with restlessness. It is this madness that has drawn me to them both.[6]

In California, and then on visits to India, Mukerji made contact with the Ramakrishna Mission and the Vedanta Society, its branch in the West. Even with his move to the West, Dhan Gopal strengthened his own ties to it. As a disciple of Ramakrishna Paramahansa (1836–

---

[6] Mukerji 2002, pp. 222–23.

1886), he wrote *The Face of Silence*, about the spiritual founder of the Mission. During his 1922 visit to India, he stayed for some time at the home base of the Ramakrishna Mission, the Dakshineswar temple complex, north of Calcutta on the banks of the Ganges. He talked with those who had known Ramakrishna to gather material for his own account of a spiritual guide he may well have believed was an avatar, an incarnation of the divine, and the members of whose order were his gurus through his life in the United States and India. The most important of them was Turyananda who was personally trained by Ramakrishna. Mukerji visited him in Benares just before his death. Thus he pursued his quest for the ultimate silence wherever he might be on planet Earth.[7]

Mukerji's books for teenagers make maximum use of his heritage. Animals become characters with a special and conscious life, as a pigeon, an elephant, or others who come alive in these animal tales.

Twenty-six years ago, I emigrated from a Brahmin home and a temple in India. In that time I have revisited my country twice… Yet the core of my consciousness is Hindu. I know nothing of the so-called changes over quarter of a century. When I think of India it is sadhus and gods that come to my mind. In a sense you are an Indian Sadhu. I left as a boy of 19; now I am aging. Yet I am unaltered. What a crystallization! If this is not soul or God what is it? You who live in India do not live so incisively as I do in my inner Temple—the temple of childhood days there in Bengal… Many incarnations have I spent in India; if the Lord wishes me to come there again I will obey him… There is nothing finer than the Hindu spiritual thought. From the Upanishads to Shri Rama Krishna the depth is limpid but superior to the depths of other forms of inner life… All my books and lectures are loved because they seek to imprison a single bubble of that mighty stream of inner consciousness… India has a spiritual message for the world, that our efforts can hardly do no more than hint of it is clear.[8]

---

[7] Mukerji 1926.
[8] Jawaharlal Nehru Papers, Dhan Mukerji File.

Mukerji's powerful attachment to the Brahmin life and learning of his youth persisted. Though he spent most of the last twenty-seven years in the West, in his mind, he still lived mostly in India, allowing that India to filter through his writing to Americans. Compared to the beautiful and poetic life of the India he imagined, he found the West materialistic and humdrum. Following the founder of the Ramakrishna Order, Swami Vivekananda, Mukerji thought that America needed an infusion of Indian spirituality. But when faced by sharp criticism of America in India by students, he became a defender if not of the US, at least of some of its ways.[9] India could learn from America, he proposed, about how to deal with children's health, hygiene and the vocational training of women.[10]

Mukerji's January 1935 letter to Nehru was frank and upbeat compared to what followed. Manuscripts were rejected. His difficulties hit him, his wife and son hard. Searching for peace and silence, a theme for years, Mukerji committed suicide in 1936. Just before his death, he was in contact with swamis of the Ramakrishna Mission in New York as well as in India. They had recognized his spiritual quest by sending him an ochre robe, usually reserved for initiates of the Ramakrishna order. His passing was lamented through the world of letters in the United States and among educated Indians at home. His wife wrote to Roger Baldwin, a mutual friend of Dhan Gopal and Nehru on 5 September 1936:

> Don't worry about Dhan. He is happy at last. Life had lost its flavor and meaning to him. He could take no real satisfaction in friends, work or new experience. He longed for only one thing— 'to be united with the Lord'. He tried in every way possible to gain that complete identity he wanted.
>
> Finally the longing was too great. He 'threw himself into the arms of the Lord'.[11]

---

[9] Mukerji 1930, pp. 30, 48.
[10] Mukerji 1930, p. 30.
[11] Jawaharlal Nehru Papers, V. 51.

After Mukerji grasped the silence of death, other spokesmen had to carry on for India.

Among them was yet another talented Bengali immigrant, Kumar Goshal (earlier Prafulla Kumar Ghoshal), the eldest son (of ten children) of a medical doctor Jatindranath Ghosal, who had been involved in the early revolutionary movement against the Raj. After graduating from the Basirhat School, Kumar left for Calcutta, attended City College and then the Scottish Church College. He wanted to study dramatics, but conservative family friends of the Ghosals criticized the plays put on by his dramatics club; Kumar said, 'I will go to such a far place that the friends of my father won't be able to touch me.'

In 1920, just as Mahatma Gandhi was reviving the nationalist movement, Kumar left for Europe. He told a journalist in 1944 that he had headed for America because even then, to young people in Calcutta it was the promised land. Arriving in New York in October 1920, he worked at numerous odd jobs from New York to Detroit to Hollywood. He put on an Indian play, probably D.L. Roy's 'Chandragupta', which he is said to have translated and written down from memory.[12]

Kumar remained on the fringe of the film industry and then returned to New York and his first love: the theatre. In New York for about the next fifteen years, Kumar worked in theatre, dancing, acting, and later directing. He played a Greek in Brock Pemberton's production of 'The Marionette Man', and in November 1927, played an African in Oscar Hammerstein's operetta 'Golden Dawn', which opened the New Hammerstein Theater. On Broadway and off, Kumar played a great variety of 'ethnic' parts, among them a Mexican, a Chinese, a Russian, a Latin in the Valentino mould, and an American-Indian, perhaps an Inca. Never once did he play a Hindu; following the line of the old joke, Kumar said, 'They tell me I'm not the type.' He was brown-skinned and a foreigner. There was little cross-casting in those days, so the closest he could come to playing a Westerner was to play an Italian hoodlum.[13]

---

[12] Interviews with family of Kumar Goshal, Calcutta, January 25, 1985.
[13] Braggiotti, 1944.

With the Depression, however, at least part of the American theatre moved in a political direction. Like several of his colleagues in the theatre, Kumar put on theatrical productions that would arouse social and political consciousness as well as provide an aesthetic experience. As economic catastrophe struck, Kumar's political awareness matured. He participated in the Workers Laboratory Theater and worked with the Friends of the Shock Troop, then began teaching and directing at the New Theater League's St Felix School in Brooklyn. In June 1936, Kumar directed the Siftons' play 'Blood on the Moon', a drama about Nazi Germany, which a reviewer found 'a powerful exposition of the realities of fascism'. In the fall of the same year, Kumar acted in a main part in the Brooklyn Progressive Players' production of Albert Maltz and George Sklar's well-known play, 'Merry Go Round', an exposé of corrupt municipal politics.[14] Looking for new avenues of employment, Kumar did weekly radio broadcasts for the League for Industrial Democracy, but could not accept a position offered to him in the Federal Theater Project because he was not and could not become an American citizen. Although he acted on Broadway in Marc Connelly's 'The Flowers of Virtue', a play set in rural Mexico that, again, warned against fascism, Kumar's acting days were done.

In the US during the war, the South Asian actor Kumar Goshal became an author. In 1944, Kumar told a journalist that in 1941 he had dropped into the office of the magazine *Amerasia* and said that someone ought to write an article on the Hindu-Muslim problem in India. Shortly afterwards, he was home writing his first article, 'India—A Key to Victory', published in March 1942.[15] It argued that India was important to the present war efforts of the Allies and that the US was crucial to the future freedom of India. Calling for a flow of American technicians to India, 'to build a giant arsenal of the East', he said that full and speedy mobilization of the resources of India would greatly assist the Allied war effort. Pointing to the Atlantic Charter of 1941, he wanted Americans to raise their voice on

---

[14] Review, *Brooklyn Daily Eagle*, November 1, 1936.
[15] Amerasia 1942, VI: 1, 36-41.

behalf of the peoples of India. In his view of Indian internal politics, Kumar praised the Congress. He called it 'the truly representative organization of the Indian people', 'a genuine people's movement' and credited it with an international outlook.

During the following years, Kumar kept writing and lecturing about India. He was a fine and talented speaker, able to command the attention of his audience with his storytelling gifts, his beautiful voice and passionate concerns. In 1944, Kumar published his first full-length book, *The People of India*. He told the author Mary Braggiotti:

> I do not look on India as India against Britain, or vice versa. I look on India in the world-wide scene... I try always to think of how India's problems can be solved in terms of winning the war and then preserving a lasting peace... There's one thing about which I'm almost fanatical. It's the fact that Americans feel that since the beginning of time India has been traveling one direction, America in the opposite direction... I try to destroy that myth. India is behind rather than dissimilar from Europe. For instance, in Europe, too, there is a form of caste system almost identical to India's...
>
> India can't be unfrozen until it is industrialized and its economic system changed. But a country can't change its economy until it has political power. That's why the American Revolution was fought.[16]

Kumar saw economic factors as crucial and intimately linked to political factors.

Moreover, he did not see India as exceptional or unique, particularly in its socioeconomic or political structures. It was like the West of a previous era, part feudal and part capitalist, and as soon as its people gained political power, they would undergo the

---

[16] Braggiotti March 1, 1944.

necessary economic transformation that would make India a modern, industrial nation.

He realized that Gandhi had played a crucial role in mobilizing nationalist India, but he saw Gandhi as a bundle of contradictions. It was necessary, he argued, to think of Gandhi in terms of India, not India in terms of Gandhi. Kumar maintained that the Indian people were not non-violent. He expected in time that the progressive forces in India—such as peasant organizations and trade unions, as in other countries—would triumph over reactionary Western capitalism and imperialism. Kumar hoped that a modernizing Indian economy would destroy the caste system, including untouchability, and defuse the Hindu–Muslim conflict.

In the post-war period, Kumar also began to make new American friends, including the African American luminaries W.E.B. Dubois (1868–1963) and Paul Robeson (1898–1976), as well as new Indian friends including Enuga Reddy, Asok Dutt and K.P. Dalal. Kumar wrote his second popular book, writing in the introduction to *People in Colonies* (1948), that 'the colonial problem, and its solution must be an integral part of any plan for world peace'.[17] Another was to tell the story of colonial conquest and rule and the struggle for freedom in clear, direct language. He moved from region to region: from Africa, to China, to India, to Southeast Asia, to the Caribbean, etc., maintaining throughout that, 'the motive power behind the conquest of colonies, then, has been economic'. Through it all the colonies fared badly. Their peoples were ruthlessly exploited under alien rule, while their conquerors told the exploited the benefits they had brought in their wake. Kumar argued that, 'empires were maintained the way they were acquired: by trickery and violence'.[18] Their economies remained primarily extractive and agricultural.

In 1917, the Ceylonese-Tamil-British immigrant Ananda K. Coomaraswamy took up residence in Boston. He had been raised in Britain by his widowed British mother, but returned when in his twenties to Ceylon (later Sri Lanka) and then to India, where while

---

[17] Goshal 1948, 14.
[18] Goshal 1948, p. 14.

identifying as an Indian nationalist and opponent of imperialism, capitalism and industrialization, he dedicated himself not to politics but to the revival of India's great traditions in art and religion. Gathering a collection of art and craft products and documents through travels up and down the subcontinent, he hoped to start a museum and art centre in India but received little encouragement. Then he met a wealthy American, Denman Ross (1853–1935), a collector of Indian art, and a trustee of the Museum of Fine Arts in Boston. Ross offered to buy Coomaraswamy's collection, merge it with his own, and donate the pieces or the articles to the Boston Museum; at the same time, he arranged to have Coomaraswamy appointed the Boston Museum's Keeper of Indian and Muhammadan Art. Coomaraswamy accepted and moved to Boston for the last three decades of his life. From that time, the museum housed one of the most important collections of Indian art outside of India, and Coomaraswamy authored catalogues for the collection and produced a stream of articles and books unmatched during those years by any other scholar of Indian art in the world.[19]

Coomaraswamy argued that the most spiritual and aesthetic art was to be found in India, especially during its golden age from the fourth to eighth centuries, and in the medieval West from its origins to about 1400 CE. His writings and lectures on this theme constituted a riposte to the conventional Western assessment of Hindu art as grotesque and unaesthetic which, as Partha Mitter shows in *Much Maligned Monsters*,[20] prevailed from the Renaissance through the nineteenth century. Giving short shrift to modern art and to any products tainted by industrial production, Coomaraswamy championed Indian painting, sculpture and temples as well as Indian crafts. But he went further: he thought that Indian religion and

---

[19] Mohan, Jag. 1979. *Ananda K. Coomaraswamy*. New Delhi: Publications Division, Government of India p. 47ff; Lipsey, Roger, ed. 1977. *Coomarawamy, Selected Papers*. 2v. Princeton: Princeton U. Press. Vol. I, xxixff; Brown, Rebecca M. 2009. *Art for a Modern India, 1947-1980*. Durham: Duke U. Press, pp. 41–43.
[20] Mitter, Partha. 1992. *Much Maligned Monsters*. A History of European Reactions to Indian Art. Chicago: University of Chicago Press.

social organization before a decline under foreign rule, to be clearly superior to that of the West. In an essay in *The Dance of Shiva*, for example, he employs a Marxist dictum to portray the caste system as egalitarian:

> ['T']he Hindus grasped more firmly than others the fundamental meaning and purpose of life, and more deliberately than others organized society with a view to the attainment of the fruit of life; and this organization was designed, not for the advantage of a single class, but, to use a modern formula, to take from each according to his capacity, and to give to each according to his needs... even with all its imperfection Hindu society as it survives will appear to many to be superior to any form of social organization attained on a large scale anywhere else, and infinitely superior to the social order which we know as 'modern civilization'.[21]

Coomaraswamy had the good fortune, since he was the fair-skinned interracial child of an upper-caste Tamil and a British woman, to be accepted into Western society. In Boston he mingled with the so-called Boston Brahmins, the first families, and escaped the insults, indignities, and exploitation experienced by those in the lower reaches of India's caste society. Thus unburdened, he could praise the caste system of his imagination—which he deemed to be the world's finest social system—in which the different castes were all equal, each having its own function.

In his theory of art, Cooomaraswamy maintained that the finest art was produced from deep within the artist by a process like yoga. This art was not the self-expression of an ego hungry for fame and fortune, but as self-realization merging the higher self with the Divine. He linked art to religion through yoga, in a spiritual bonding; by this kind of mystical process, the highest art was produced. But how could such art be produced in this modern, decadent age? He identified some educational institutions where at least an approximation was

---

[21] Coomaraswamy, Ananda K. 1957. *The Dance of Shiva*. Revised ed. NY: Noonday, p. 4.

possible. He recommended Tagore's school at Bolpur, Bengal, but above all the Gurukula school of the Arya Samaj at Hardwar, which, he wrote, 'The most conspicuous feature of the system is its return to the impersonal and philosophic concepts of culture which have always been characteristic of the East, and the combination of this ancient wisdom with modern and practical knowledge.'[22]

During his nearly half-century of writing, Coomaraswamy made lasting contributions to the understanding of Indian art history.[23] Yet at the same time, he idealized key features of Indian society that had attracted criticism: the caste system, the marriage system, the subordination of women and the rule of the elite. This bicultural gentleman who benefited so fully from Western education, philanthropy, and the relative openness of America to talented foreigners, systematically denigrated the modern West. For all his idealization of the Indian custom of arranged marriages, he himself was married four times to talented Western women.

Just as South Asians who came to America transmitted their vision of India, some Americans ventured into Indian territory, interpreting that civilization in fiction and in film for the benefit of their compatriots. The popular writer Louis Bromfield (1896–1956) did so in several of his novels which helped shape American views of India, most successfully in *The Rains Came* (1937), a bestseller based on his experience in two trips to Baroda, India, in the 1930s. Although in comparison to two great works on India by the British authors E.M. Forster and Paul Scott, it lacks the symbolic complexity of the former's *A Passage to India* (1952) or the epic scope of the latter's *The Raj Quartet* (1973 and 1977), Bromfield's book is a sensitive narrative set in a Gujarati-speaking princely state named Ranchipur that resembles Baroda. What is unusual is the blending in of American identities with the British and Indian elements. A central figure, Tom Ransom, for instance, is a British-American with roots on both sides of the Atlantic who finds a home, and fulfilment, in India.

---

[22] Ibid., p. 164.
[23] Mitter 1992, p. 277ff.

In portraying the interplay of American and British elements, Bromfield details the West's declining vitality seen in the dissipation of the American mid-west and far-west, the Western world's best hope. Yet several of the novel's strongest characters are American missionaries, the Smileys and Aunt Phoebe, and the British—Miss Hodge, Miss Kirk and Miss MacDaid. Although the West has 'declined', it has sent some of its last strong and fiercely dedicated members to Ranchipur. They are its last gasp. In India, in contrast, the novel shows how a new vitality was welling up, displayed in such figures as the Maharaja (modelled on the Gaekwad of Baroda, Sayajirao III, ruled 1875–1939); Jobnekar, an Untouchable leader (possibly modelled on Dr Ambedkar); and nationalist activists. India is awakening: it has its problems of caste and community, but is moving forward.

Bromfield's novel was transformed into an Oscar-winning film in 1939: *The Rains Came*, with Tyrone Power and Myrna Loy. All the main characters were played by Westerners, as Twentieth Century Fox, which spent $2.5 million on the film, was apparently unable to find South Asians for important roles. In 1955, in a remake entitled, *The Rains of Ranchipur*, the main characters were again played by Westerners, Richard Burton among them. Although the number of South Asians living in Great Britain and the US increased rapidly through the second half of the twentieth century, Westerners continued to play South Asian characters into the 1980s, as they did in the film version of *A Passage to India* (1984) directed by David Lean. Despite this inauthentic casting, both the films based on Bromfield's *Rains* celebrate the India that is rising. In the first, one character is told by a female admirer: 'You are India, the new India ...' In the second, he is called 'a man of destiny'.

From the 1920s onwards, American films were widely circulated and popular in India. Although the Indian film industry was well underway, many felt that the Americans, and perhaps Europeans, were ahead in the film game and went out to see these foreign films. The Indian Cinematograph Committee of the Government of India issued five volumes of evidence of that attitude, which included this statement of the manager of a Lucknow cinema: 'I will tell you the class of pictures that draw—anything big that Charlie Chaplin does, anything big that Douglas Fairbanks does, which means every picture of his. Mary Pickford has a good audience, Jackie Coogan is a universal favourite. Rudolf Valentino also draws.'[24] The audiences were likely a mixture of Europeans and well-to-do Indians. The day of mass Indian movie attendance and the phenomenon of Bollywood, the Indian film industry based in Bombay (now Mumbai), was still in the making, but there were a host of studios in Bombay and able actors that Western producers might have made use of but did not.[25]

Americans, for their part, made some films set in India, though often made in a Western studio. Many of these films, especially the 'epics' of the 1930s, drew on Rudyard Kipling stories or similar tales. Officials of the Raj made every effort give these films a pro-empire direction.[26] The British Raj is threatened, either by hordes from across the Afghan frontier or from one princely state or another, or by the thugs, an early-nineteenth-century robber cult—worshippers, it was said, of the goddess Kali—that preyed on travellers. The film *Gunga Din* (1939), based on Kipling's 1890 poem of that name, depicts noble British soldiers (Cary Grant, Douglas Fairbanks, Jr and Victor McLaglen) who help to subdue wicked Kali cultists on the frontier. One of the film's heroes, unusually, is an Indian soldier, played by Sam Jaffe; Kipling's poem is recited as he dies saving the Raj.

Wee Willie Winkie (1937), directed by John Ford, is notable for featuring Shirley Temple, America's favourite little girl movie star, who is somehow in India with her American mother, and related to a British officer. Our little heroine confronts the wicked Khoda Khan, who is threatening India with his savage hordes from just across the

---

[24] Cinematograph Committee, *Evidence*, V.2, p. 487.

[25] Mukherjee, Debashree. *Bombay Hustle. Making Movies in a Colonial City.* NY: Columbia U. Press, 2020.

[26] Hitchens, p. 82ff.

frontier; somehow she tames him, and so brings peace to an India seen as quaint and potentially violent.

Another Hollywood star, Errol Flynn, the dashing hero of many a swashbuckler, had his Indian day starring in *The Charge of the Light Brigade* (1936) which took remarkable plot turns connecting India's northwest frontier with the Crimean War. Flynn saves the life of a frontier chief Surat Khan, but then witnesses the slaughter by Khan's men of British and Indian men, women and children at a frontier fort in India. Khan has now joined his Russian allies at the Crimean front, while Flynn and his regiment are sent from India to Turkey where they carry out the famous charge, memorialized six weeks after the event by Alfred Lord Tennyson's 1854 poem, of 600 British cavalrymen riding into the valley of death. By their sacrifice, they win the day for the British, and Flynn's character dies killing Surat Khan.

The Lives of a Bengal Lancer (1935), another story of imperial triumph over a native uprising, was a big hit and commercial success that was nominated for eight Oscars including best picture. Purportedly based on Francis Yeats-Brown's autobiography of the same title (1930), it had little to do with that book or with Bengal. It presents an uprising on the northwest frontier led by Mohammed Khan (Douglass Dumbrille), supported by the beautiful seductress of innocent British officers, Tania Volkanskyaya (Kathleen Burke). Native Americans played the South Asians in the film, continuing the familiar pattern of rarely employing South Asian Indians to play themselves. The trio of lancers are Lieutenants McGregor (Gary Cooper), Forsythe (Franchot Tone), and Stone (Richard Cromwell), son of the regiment's colonel—of whom his assistant remarks that 'men of his breed have made British India'.

Captured trying to frustrate Khan's plot to grab a huge cache of ammunition, the lancers are tortured, yet finally foil Khan's plot and kill him—so all is saved, and Paramount Pictures, the film's producer, has awarded another American tribute to the British Empire. Not only was it a smash hit in the United States and Great Britain, but Adolf Hitler declared that it was one of his favourite films and commented, 'I like this film because it depicted a handful of Britons holding a continent in thrall. That is how a superior race must behave and the film is a compulsory viewing for the SS.'[27]

Son of India (1931) raises the issue of what was long called 'miscegenation', or interracial marriage. At the time of its release, many states in America had laws against such marriages, although interracial children had been born in the US since the seventeenth century. The marriage in question in the film is between an Indian, Karim, played by Ramon Novarro—as usual the South Asians in this film were played by non-Indians—and an American woman, Jennie Darsey, played by Madge Evans. Jennie's brother Will Darsey had years earlier saved Karim's life and career, and Karim had pledged undying gratitude to him. When the question of marriage arises, Will exerts every pressure to prevent it; Karim remains true to his vow of gratitude, and the match is off. An Indian holy man had explained to Karim that the highest value is renunciation: by calling off the marriage, he could transform this Earthly love into something higher, abandoning its early fulfilment and treasuring it within himself.

Around the time that MGM released this film in 1931, portrayals of miscegenation were banned from the American movie industry, a prejudice affecting South Asians who had been deemed not to be members of the 'white race' by the 1923 Thind decision of the Supreme Court. Several prominent South Asians—Taraknath Das, Kumar Goshal, Dhan Gopal Mukerji and M.N. Roy—married white American women, but lived in states that did not ban miscegenation. Other South Asians in America married African Americans and Mexicans.

In an earlier film, *The Black Watch* (1929), the issue of miscegenation is implicit in the romance between a British officer, Captain King (played by Victor McLaglen), and the frontier woman, Yasmini (Myrna Loy), who is the leader of a rebellion it is his secret duty to foil. Yasmini falls in love with him, telling him she is an Aryan descendant of the Greek conqueror Alexander the Great.

---

[27] Wikipedia article on the film: https://en.wikipedia.org/wiki/The_Lives_of_a_Bengal_Lancer_(film).

He persuades her to call off the rebellion, but when her followers do not accept her pleas to disband, she is killed in the ensuing battle. The racial logic here seems to be that even if Yasmini and King had married it would not have been miscegenation because she was an Aryan, a descendant of Alexander.

Many of the Indian lead roles in Western films set in India, even into the 1980s, were played by Western actors. One exception was Sabu (1924–1963), believed to be Sabu Dastagir, an Indian from the princely state of Mysore, who played both lead and secondary parts in British and American films from 1938 to his early death. After the British films *Elephant Boy* (1937), *The Drum* (1938) and *The Thief of Baghdad* (1940), he starred in *The Jungle Book* (1942), and several American films. Becoming an American citizen in 1944, he served in the American Army Air force in the Second World War. After the war, he played an important role as the young general in *Black Narcissus* (1947) which won several Oscars.[28]

Hidden from sight over many decades was the true story of Merle Oberon's background. She passed as white, presented a false background story, and did not want the general public to know that she was what was called an 'Anglo-Indian', i.e., someone of mixed South Asian and Western birth. This was revealed in a biography published after her death, *Princess Merle*, and is now leading to further explorations of her life.

In addition to these feature films, James A. Fitzpatrick made a series of short documentaries for MGM about India, which were often shown along with the main event. Among these were *Ancient India* (1937), *Bombay* (1936) and *India on Parade* (1937). These films stressed that even though one might find a veneer of modernization or wealth in parts of India, behind it, under it and around it lay an unchanging India dominated by caste and tradition that had not changed for hundreds of years.

While American writers and filmmakers depicted India for an American audience, a small and gifted group of Americans journeyed

---

[28] 'Sabu', Wikipedia, https://en.wikipedia.org/wiki/Sabu_(actor).

to India, bringing distinctively Western music to the East. These were jazz musicians including Leon Abbey and his seven-piece band, Teddy Weatherford, and others, who played for weeks, months, and even years, in Calcutta and Bombay from the mid-1930s onwards.[29] Some American musical groups including the Fisk Singers had visited India much earlier, in the 1890s, but these new arrivals were different.

Labelled jazz musicians, but blending swing and Latin American music with jazz, they played to enthusiastic throngs at hotels such as the Taj Mahal in Bombay. A native Indian inspired by this music, slightly changing his Goan name 'Fernandes' to Frank Fernand, began a long and successful career in Bombay. An historian of this era recounts:

> The thick shellac records that set him off on his journey of discovery bore the names of Ellington, Armstrong and Cab Calloway, and Fernandes grew addicted to hot music. Jazz, he said, gave him 'freedom of expression'. He still looked at the sheet music, of course, but he knew that it could take him only so far. 'Like Indian music, jazz can't be written,' he said. 'You have to feel it. There are 12 bars, but each musician plays it differently. You play as you feel—morning you play different, evening you play different.'[30]

The rich connections between American jazz musicians, as well as the development of very talented Indian jazz musicians, linked the two countries in unique ways for the next few decades.

As the Second World War and the propaganda war continued, film studios continued to turn out their products for the public. Some films were overtly political, featuring heroic and patriotic Americans and British versus swarthy, ruthless Japanese. Among them were *They Met in Bombay* (1941), starring Clark Gable as a jewel thief turned British war hero who courted Rosalind Russell;

---

[29] Fernandes, Naresh. 2016. *Taj Mahal Foxtrot*. The Story of Bombay's Jazz Age. New Delhi: Roli, p. 13ff.
[30] Ibid.

So Thee I Hail (1943), set in Bataan and Corregidor; *The Story of Dr. Wassell* (1944), with Gary Cooper as a heroic American doctor on a mission to China with Lorraine Day as his nurse; and *Behind the Rising Sun* (1943), which depicts the outbreak of the Second Sino-Japanese war in 1937 and the consequent Rape of Nanjing, featuring the conflict between a single heroic Japanese with the baleful majority of Japanese participants. India is only a distant backdrop in most of these war movies centred in East Asia.

Two notable writers, one American and one British, offered paeans to Indian spirituality in late wartime novels, the second of which was made into an American film. The first, written earlier but published in 1945, is Theodore Dreiser's *The Stoic*, the third volume of a trilogy about a sleazy but successful American businessman. After making a fortune by any and all means, he drops out of the commercial world, and as his life winds down, finds solace in Indian religious teachings.

The second novel, Somerset Maugham's *The Razor's Edge* (1944), inspired a 1946 film starring Tyrone Power, a top Hollywood leading man. Again, like Dreiser's businessman, the central character is dissatisfied with his life in the West, goes off to India, and finds a guru in the Himalayas who guides him to a truer path. He came to feel released from his body, and says, 'I felt I was free... one with God.' He returns to the world and the West happy, yet aloof from the passions and drives that had sent him to the East. The Indian guru is played by a Westerner, as had been the pattern in earlier Hollywood depictions of Asian guides.

Another film, *Black Narcissus* (1947), a British production with American participation, also features a holy man: a silent member of a Himalayan royal family. He has turned to meditation and seems to preside quietly over the lively, even deadly events around him.

Although it is said that he is revered, nothing is presented of his beliefs. A group of Western nuns, led by Deborah Kerr as the Sister Superior, tries to establish a clinic and school near Darjeeling in the mountains amongst Asians repeatedly described as 'children' who know nothing of education or medicine. A young prince seeking education, who flits in and out of the action, joins the young girls at their school. He is played by Sabu, a South Asian actor, exceptional at a time when Asian characters are generally played by Westerners— including this one, which has Jean Simmons, suitably darkened, portraying a lower-caste dancing girl, who seduces the young prince. The condescension of Westerners towards the mountain folk characterizes this film that won Oscars for art direction and cinematography and was a hit in Britain and America.

During the war years, as in the 1930s, American jazz reached parts of urban India.[31] The presence of hundreds of thousands of American troops and other personnel in India, with their musical attachments, and the broadcasting of jazz over Radio SEAC, fostered wider and deeper relations to this music. Indian bands and audiences had a mixture of foreign and Indian musicians, who experimented with blending of Indian and Western music. Frank Fernand (1919– 2007), for one, composed a piece called 'Probhat' (Dawn) with a trumpet solo and orchestral accompaniment based, he said, on an Indian theme.[32]

---

[31] Ibid., p. 79ff.
[32] Ibid., p. 104.

5

Business

By the 1920s, American multinationals expanded modestly into international markets, including India.[1] These worldwide enterprises included banking, extracting raw materials, oil refining, sales branches, and investments in manufacturing. The Ford Motor Company established an assembly plant in India and invested in jute mills and power companies, while RCA, Kodak and Westinghouse set up offices in India.[2] As in many parts of the world, American efforts rivalled those of the British and they succeeded in replacing them in some markets even within the British Empire.[3] Through the late nineteenth century and first decades of the twentieth, America rose gradually to become India's second largest trading partner after Great Britain, with Japan in third place. In 1920–1921, the US garnered 7.5 per cent in total value of India's foreign trade; in 1930–1931, 9.2 per cent; and in 1940–1941, 17.2 per cent.[4]

Even as the US was becoming an international economic powerhouse, India was continuing, although slowly, to industrialize. From its early days, Tata Steel, or TISCO, continued to contribute

[1] Wilkins, Mira. 1974. The Maturing of Multinational Enterprise: American Business Abroad from 1914 to 1970. Cambridge: Harvard U. Press, pp. 153–55.
[2] Wilkins, Mira and Frank Ernest Hill. 1964. American Business Abroad. Ford on Six Continents. Detroit: Wayne State U. Press, p. 129, 191, 299.
[3] Wilkins 1974, p. 155ff.
[4] Chaudhuri, K.N. 1982. 'Foreign Trade and Balance of Payments,' in Kumar, Dharma Kumar, ed. The Cambridge Economic History of India. Vol. 2: c. 1757-1970. Cambridge, p. 865; Bagchi, Amiya Kumar. 1972. Private Investment in India 1900-1939. Cambridge: Cambridge U. Press, p. 87.

mightily to the Indian economy, giving essential assistance to government efforts during the First World War and building from there. Of the hundreds of American employees of TISCO, one stands out: John L. Keenan (1889–1944), general manager from 1930–1937, and author of the notable memoir, *A Steel Man in India* (1943). After graduating from Yale in classics, Keenan went, inexplicably, to work at a steel mill in Gary, Indiana, then in 1913, followed his former boss there, T.W. Tutweiler (1879–1950), to India. Louis Bromfield described Keenan succinctly: 'Lustiest of all the engineers was Keenan. A big Irishman, he liked people and whiskey and horse-racing, and most important of all he liked Indians, all kinds of Indians . . . never . . . have I encountered anywhere such vitality.'[5] Tutwiler himself was said to be a gruff, able man who knew how to produce steel.

Keenan was able to see things from an American, rather than British perspective. Coming out by sea to India the first time, he was told by British India hands that Indians were usually unintelligent and incompetent, and making steel was way beyond them. Once on the job and working with Indians, he found them just as able as Westerners and just as capable of making steel as the British who derided them. What Indians had not had before was the opportunity to work in a world-class steel mill, to live in a modern company town with many amenities, and, if given the training, to take over every job in the mill. Keenan soon learned that if he gained some competence in Hindi and Urdu and spoken Hindustani, he would be able to get more done with his Indian colleagues. Working at this goal with several Indians at the mill, he became fluent—a fluency that made his twenty-five years in India more successful and pleasurable. Observing Indians of different backgrounds working well together, however, he was optimistic, writing in 1943 about the possibility of a harmonious future for India.

Coming on board at TISCO as early as 1913, Keenan considered himself one of the old hands. He got to know Charles Page Perin well and understood his vital role in TISCO's operations. In 1916,

---

[5] Keenan 1943, p. xi.

in a discussion with Perin about expanding the mill's capacity, the geologist, looking ahead, wanted significant enlargement. Keenan explained:

> That was like Perin. As soon as one goal was achieved, he urged for a higher one.
>
> He was always seeking, never satisfied or complacent. While he was visualizing such tonnages in 1916, you could count on your fingers the blast furnaces in America which could average 500 tons a day for any length of time. Perin lived to see a furnace produce 36,000 in one month.[6]

Jack Keenan

Although there was some resistance, Perin's plans went through in the end. But when by 1923, the expansion had been completed, a serious danger arose: several foreign steel firms, with the help of their respective governments, started dumping steel into India at below cost. Tata almost went under and Tata officers besieged the government for help. John Peterson, a former ICS officer who had quit government service and joined Tata's as director-in-charge of the steel plant operating from Bombay, wrote a recommendation to the government to protect the steel industry. In response, the Central Legislative Assembly passed the Steel Industry (Protection) Act. The State Bank of India provided a loan to the company to bridge the financial crisis, and with new tariffs on foreign steel,[7] TISCO began to thrive again. Economic historian and analyst Amiya Bagchi

---

[6] Keenan, John L. 1943. *A Steel Man in India*. NY: Duell, Sloan and Pearce, pp. 95–96.
[7] Lala, R.M. 2003. *Beyond the Blue Mountain*. A Life of J.R.D. Tata (1904-1993). New Delhi: Penguin, p. 39.

attributes their success—exceeding that of other Indian enterprises—to their 'versatility and flexibility'.[8]

TISCO also thrived because of its willingness to hire skilled personnel regardless of nationality. For a quarter century, the general managers of the steel mill were always American: in succession, Robert Wells, 1912–1913; Barton Shover, 1913–1916; T.W. Tutwiler, 1916–1925; Charles Alexander, 1925–1930; and John L. Keenan, 1930–1937. Many of the engineers, who served for shorter periods, were Americans, as were some of the ordinary steelworkers, while other steelworkers came from Wales and Germany. The First World War created a serious problem because Germans, as enemy nationals, had to be interned and others had to be brought to fill in. Some Britishers also held management positions, but decisions were usually made jointly by Charles Perin in the US, the top brass in Jamshedpur, and the owners and trustees of Tata and Sons in Bombay.

Tata also made a vital connection to the American firm, General Electric, a relationship that began in the late nineteenth century when Jamsetji Tata met George Westinghouse in the US, and it continued for decades. From early on, GE provided turbine motors, support services and other machinery for TISCO. Keenan wrote:

> A large part of the tremendous debt to American firms which Tata's had contracted in building the greater extensions was owed to the General Electric Company... We seldom had a complaint on a piece of General Electric equipment, but whenever we did, the machinery was replaced promptly and without question... GE not only supplied excellent equipment, they went out of their way to train Indians in their American plants so that the men could go back to India and operate machinery expertly, perhaps for a competitor. The company maintained a staff of engineers in Calcutta who were always ready to come out to Jamshedpur... The present Tata chief electrical engineer [1943—L.G.] is a former General Electric man.[9]

---

[8] Bagchi 1972, p. 291.
[9] Keenan 1943, pp. 108–09.

Keenan also remarked on the social tensions he observed between Indians and their self-styled British superiors which struck him occasionally, but many Indians every day. He observed that young Indians, some of whom had been educated in England and had made British friends, were snubbed by British people in India. Also, such Indians were often passed over for employment, a situation that engendered bitterness, hostility to the foreigner rulers, and in a few cases, recruitment to militant nationalism, including revolutionary terrorism. Keenan understood that people in his position, even when he became general manager at TISCO, were there to train Indians to take their place. He accepted this situation and saw it as natural and inevitable.

The quarter century of Keenan's years at TISCO saw the building of the unincorporated company town, Jamshedpur. The workers, foreign and Indian, were given good housing, medical care, and below-cost prices for food. What Keenan noted, as he moved up the management ladder, was that the Indian workers did not notice these benefits and only judged their welfare by the size of their pay packets. In the 1920s, there were several serious strikes and political figures came to Jamshedpur to help settle them. Keenan noted the role played by Gandhi's friend C.F. Andrews, who made a special contribution to industrial peace there. R.M. Lala (1928–2012), house historian for the Tatas, and others, identified Bengali leader Subhas Chandra Bose (1897–1945) as a crucial peacemaker.[10] It was the time of significant unionization in India and with different political organizations trying to help as well as benefit from this trend. As part of the management team, Keenan was highly critical of some of the union organizers for cleverly and unfairly disrupting production and dishonesty in the collection and use of union funds. Employees and union organizers had different views. Peaceful labour relations resumed thereafter and labour and management were able to confront problems without any serious strikes for a half-century thereafter.

---

[10] Lala 2004a, pp. 126–28; Gordon 1990, pp. 103, 173–74, 247, 300.

Besides building a company town with amenities for its staff that were superior to almost any other firm in India, Tata and Sons looked ahead to other projects. One was the creation, at the behest of Dorabji Tata, of the Institute of Metallurgical Technology in Jamshedpur. This institute trained the personnel needed for the coming decades. Many of its graduates joined the firm and rose up the ladder to department heads. Another project went way beyond TISCO. The Indian Institute of Science in Bangalore, an institution that had been the dream of Jamsetji Tata, who sought to make India world-class in science, was funded by Tata and by the government.

These educational institutions were elements in a significant Tata training project that widened from the 1920s and continues. The notion that India needed the best-trained personnel it could provide, started from Jamsetji Tata, who had instituted the Tata Scholars programme and given young Indians grants to study abroad. It continued with the management training programmes for several Tata businesses and the launching of the Tata Institute of Social Sciences in 1936, the Tata Centre for Cancer Research, 1941, and the Tata Institute of Fundamental Research in 1945.

Besides a steel plant and a science college, the third of Jamsetji Tata's dreams was hydroelectric power. He wanted to provide sufficient power for Bombay's people and its growing industries. The Tata Hydro-Electric Power Supply Company was established in 1910, and gradually became the chief supplier of power to the Greater Bombay region.[11] It later formed power companies in other areas of India.

A project that Jamsetji Tata set in motion during his lifetime was the building of the Taj Mahal Hotel on the Bombay waterfront. It was one of the earliest such enterprises by an Indian and ensured that Indian visitors would not be denied accommodation during the Raj.

Subsequently many other hotels—more than sixty—were built and acquired as Indian Hotels Company became a vast and international group, including hotels in New York City and Boston.

---

[11] Lala 2004, p. 47ff.

In 2007, when I visited the Taj Mahal Hotel, the managing director of the hotel group was Raymond Bickson, a large, friendly man from Hawaii whose father had run a motel there. It was a mark of Tata's cosmopolitanism in personnel that they had reached out to hire an experienced American who had worked in Europe and New York to head their operations.

During the inter-war period, Tata Sons and Tata Industries reached out like a giant octopus into diverse businesses producing a range of industrial and consumer products. Among the areas they entered were the production of vehicles and chemicals, which in time became two of their largest and most successful enterprises. Having started with locomotives, they invited German and later Japanese truck and vehicle makers to produce these in India. Ford and General Motors promoted and sold their products without any challenger for some time, but then had to face stiff competition. The intense interest in aviation of J.R.D. Tata (1904–1993), who had become chairman of Tata Sons in 1930, also spurred their entry into this field.

While Tata Sons and later Tata Industries are mainly a business group of remarkable spread, Tata enterprises were also active in welfare and philanthropy. Among their most notable projects is the Tata Memorial Hospital in Bombay, and welfare programmes in areas surrounding Jamshedpur, and in south India as well, connected to their tea plantations. Starting from Jamsetji Tata, many members of the Tata family have established trusts to provide for beneficiaries outside their family and the Parsi community. That they have had a vision for a better India has helped them not only to do business but also to assist the poor, the sick and the promising.[12] Looking over his long career and the rise of the Tata Group as a giant and successful business group, Keenan knew how wrong officials had been in arguing that Indians could not gain proficiency in science and industry. Jamsetji Tata, the founder of Tata Sons, served as chairman from 1887 to 1904. Dorabji Tata succeeded his father as chairman

---

[12] Ibid., p. 253ff.

of Tata Sons, serving from 1904 to 1932, followed by a relative, Sir Nowroji Saklatvala, 1932–1938, and then J.R.D. Tata, 1938 to 1991. J.R.D. was succeeded by Ratan N. Tata, 1991 to 2012, and as interim chairman in 2016. The remarkable longevity and continuity of the firm has been a plus through a century-and-a-half of expansion, success, failure and strife.

Among the other Indian business houses that were thriving and expanding in the inter-war period was Birla Brothers, involved in the jute and cotton trade and manufacture, but did not develop significant international ties or employ many non-Indians. During the early 1920s, G.D. Birla, leader of this family business for a half a century, had moved from the politics of his community, the Marwaris, into Indian politics, and had ties with Lala Lajpat Rai and M.M. Malaviya (1861–1946). He had made the acquaintance of Mahatma Gandhi and began giving funds to political projects. Birla joined the Congress Party and in 1926 was elected to the Central Legislative Assembly. Although the government was wary of his connection to Gandhi, Birla increasingly became a voice speaking to the Raj on behalf of Indian big business and supported the pro-tariff proposal of the Tatas that was essential to the survival of TISCO. Feeling that their Hindu nationalism was too narrow, Birla moved away from Malaviya and Lajpat Rai and edged closer to Gandhi and to Motilal Nehru, father of Jawaharlal Nehru, the future first prime minister of India. After the death of his second wife in 1926, Birla often visited Great Britain to keep abreast of business, and national as well as international issues. When the US emerged during the Second World War as a critical player for India and in the international economy, Birla began travelling there as well.[13]

As the most important leader of the Federation of Indian Chambers of Commerce (FICCI), Birla was belatedly invited to the Second Round Table Conference in London in 1931. He accompanied Gandhi to London and gradually became a nationalist spokesman on economic affairs, which Gandhi admitted he had

---

[13] Kudaisya, Medha M. 2003. *The Life and Times of G.D. Birla*. New Delhi: Oxford U. Press, p. 58ff.

trouble understanding. The issues at stake included currency, banking, and tariff questions. The conference itself floundered on the communal question and the Indian delegates returned home empty-handed. Though Birla continued to support Gandhi, he became more detached from the Congress, asserting the positions of the Indian business community that did not always coincide with those of the Congress. Nonetheless, he had Gandhi's ear while also speaking to the government, and thus was a valuable intermediary for both sides. Unlike the Tatas, Birla played an open and important role in Indian politics.

6

The Second World War

On 1 September 1939, when German tanks rolled across the Polish frontier and the nations of Europe, the Second World War—the first war in human history of truly worldwide scope—had begun. Once the British government declared war on Germany, it also brought the British Commonwealth into the war. But was this India's war? Great Britain, through Viceroy Lord Linlithgow (originally Victor Hope; 1887–1952) declared war on Germany on behalf of India. Most Indian nationalists resisted calls to join the war effort. What has been called 'the hollow alliance' of the three Axis Powers—Germany, Italy, and Japan—was now aligned against the Allies, principally Britain and France, and their empires from 1939 to 1941. The US offered aid, but was not yet directly involved. For some Indian nationalists, however, they could not join the anti-Axis struggle without gaining a roadmap for India's advance to self-government.

To the British, the Second World War was a war of survival, triggering change at home and within their once-great empire. Though a prescient Winston Churchill had been calling for rearmament through the 1930s, the appeasers were not listening. With the defeat of France in 1940, the British saw the dangers and called Churchill to the prime ministership. With Churchill at the helm, with Leopold Amery (1873–1955) as Secretary of State for India and Lord Linlithgow as Viceroy, this team did all in its power to keep the hands off Axis foes or off American friends of the empire. Churchill's words still echo: 'I have not become the

King's First Minister in order to preside over the liquidation of the British Empire.'[1] Churchill was pressured to advance towards Indian self-government, even though he believed that inappropriate for 'backward' peoples.

Once Britain declared war on Germany, the viceroy followed, declaring war on behalf of India, having consulted no nationalist opinion; alienated by this action, the Congress ministries in seven provinces resigned, and Gandhi and his Congress colleagues moved towards confrontation with the Raj. They abhorred fascism—but once it was known that, by 1940, London was being bombed, they hesitated to launch an attack on the British in their hour of desperate danger. Congress members undertook individual satyagraha in 1940; a few were arrested, but this disruption did not greatly challenge the Raj. President Roosevelt helped the Chinese resist the Japanese, and in March 1941, the Lend Lease Act allowed the US to lend or lease war supplies to the Allied powers. Principally, these were Britain, China, the Free French, the Soviet Union and India, as a British colony. The US endorsed the Atlantic Charter of August 1941, which outlined 'four freedoms', picking up the theme of the right of a people to self-determination. It read, in part:

> The President of the United States of America and the Prime Minister, Mr. Churchill... respect the right of all peoples to choose the form of government under which they will live; and they wish to see sovereign rights and self-government restored to those who have been forcibly deprived of them.

The Charter did not call for the freedom for peoples in colonial empires, as Churchill insisted that it should not. Through the war, Churchill for the British, and Charles de Gaulle (1890–1970) for the free French, envisioned revived empires once the fascist challenge was beaten. Indian nationalists, however, reading the Atlantic

---

[1] Gilbert, Martin. 1991. *Churchill.* A Life. NY: Henry Holt, speech, Nov. 10, 1942, p. 734.

Charter, wanted to know what self-determination they were to have
as a result of this war for freedom. They did not accept Churchill's
reservations about its inapplicability to European empires.[2]

On 7 December 1941, the Japanese attacked Pearl Harbor,
leading the US to declare war first on Japan and then on Germany,
and to join the Allied effort. These events not only brought the US
into the war, but eventually brought tens of thousands of American
troops to India, which served as a base camp for the India-China-
Burma and Southeast Asia theatres of war. To this great conflagration
of the Second World War, Americans, Britons, Indian nationalists
and separatist Indian Muslims, brought different agendas.

As the war broke out in September 1939, Kamaladevi
Chattopadhyay (1903–1988), feminist and nationalist, was visiting
Great Britain. When young she had met Pandita Ramabai and
Annie Besant, and following the dissolution of her marriage to
Harindranath Chattopadhayay, a younger brother of Sarojini Naidu,
she became active in the Congress and social movements. At every
step she encountered Western racism: in Britain, on the Dutch
vessel, and later in the US when she went there sometime in 1940.
Though she planned to return to India, Eleanor Roosevelt (1884–
1962), President Roosevelt's wife, encouraged her to stay and learn
about America. She stayed eighteen months, touring up and down
the country.[3]

Kamaladevi met members of the South Asian community and
spoke to women's groups. In the Deep South, she was exposed to
crude racism; when she protested, she was excused, since she was an
Indian, not an African American. She learned from South Asians of
their resentment at being denied American citizenship. The anger
of South Asians and African Americans was balanced against the
warm reception she received from women's groups.

Kamaladevi's tour overlapped with that of British aristocrat
and politician, Duff Cooper (1890–1954), one of the emissaries of

---

[2] Pandit, Vijaya Lakshmi. 1979. *The Scope of Happiness*. NY: Crown, p. 167.
[3] Chattopadhyay, Kamaladevi. 1986. *Inner Recess, Outer Spaces. Memoirs.* New
Delhi: Navrang, p. 235ff; Oral History, NMML.

the British government sent to sway American opinion during the war. His talks were guided by the British ambassador, Lord Lothian (originally Philip Kerr; 1882–1940), and on Lothian's death, by former viceroy, Lord Halifax (originally Edward Wood; 1881–1959). As a member of the Anglo–American elite, Cooper met President Roosevelt, publishers of leading magazines, and Hollywood stars. He debated Kamaladevi. She challenged his assertions about British rule in India, insisting that it was based on force. The American audience, she said, supported her and cheered.[4]

Lord Halifax
Source: Wikimedia Commons

Before the war broke out, the Indian army had fewer than 2,00,000 troops and had little equipment appropriate for mobile and mechanized warfare. Over the next five years, it grew rapidly to more than 20,00,000. At first, Indian troops were sent to defend the British Empire in North and East Africa,[5] little thought given to the need to defend the Indian homeland and British interests to the east of India. That reality came to be understood when the Japanese assault on Pearl Harbor in December 1941 was accompanied by a Japanese offensive through Southeast Asia. Already occupying French Indochina, the Japanese attacked Hong Kong, Malaya and Singapore. By 15 February 1942, Malaya and Singapore fell and the Japanese pressed westward through neutral Thailand into Burma,

---

[4] Kamaladevi, Oral History, NMML; Cooper, Diana. 1985. *Autobiography*. NY: Carroll and Graf, p. 500ff.
[5] Raghavan, Srinath. 2016. *India's War*. World War II and the Making of Modern South Asia. NY: Basic Books, p. 64ff.

where the British were routed and fell back into India. The Japanese wrought havoc not only with the British Empire, but also those of the Dutch and the French. The Japanese victories signalled dramatically the end of the white man's reign in Asia, though signs of decline had been increasing over the years. The Japanese proclaimed, 'Asia for the Asians', but nationalist India wanted no foreigners, Asian or otherwise, to make decisions for them.

From 1941, two more world powers, the Soviet Union and the US, were engaged, and there ensued an unprecedented mobilization of manpower and resources by all involved in the conflict. Germany and Japan had been building for war through the 1930s, but those powers that had sought to avoid war—Great Britain, France and the US—needed to expand their forces and armaments to face the enemy. The entry of the Soviet Union into the war on the side of the Allies prompted a reconfiguration of allegiances and priorities. The Comintern and communist parties around the world had opposed the Allies, who they said were fighting an 'imperialist war' that pitted one group of exploiting nations against another. Once the Soviets became allied with Britain and the US it became a 'people's war', and communist parties in Britain, the US and India joined the war effort. The Government of India legalized the Communist Party of India, long an anathema.

Pressed to produce goods necessary for the war effort, Indian industry contributed significantly, although hampered by British fears of India's industrial development.[6] One Indian businessman, for instance, who wanted to produce trucks and planes in India, was prevented from doing so. For the most part, India was called on only to do repairs and provide spare parts for essential vehicles. In his 1943 memoir, the Irish American John L. Keenan, the former General Manager of TISCO, claimed that India had also become, like the US, an 'arsenal of democracy' in support of the Allied war effort, although this enhanced production was mainly in areas like textiles and jute where India had developed capacities. From 1942, however, once Americans needed to supply their own forces in India

---

[6] Voigt, Johannes H. 1987. *India in the Second World War*. New Delhi: Arnold-Heinemann, p. 72ff.

and Chinese troops in Burma, they pushed for as much help as possible from Indian industry.

According to the report of the Grady Technical Mission sent from the US in March 1942 to assess India's economic capacities for the war effort, India was in sorry shape. It lacked sufficient power, railway traffic was disorganized, and many industrial plants were dysfunctional. Recommendations followed. To realize its industrial potential, India under the Raj, had to press forward in every major industry including transport, petroleum, and iron and steel production to produce machine tools and vehicles necessary for the war. Once there was an American influx, American engineers building airfields and docks and working on the Burma Road connecting the subcontinent with China, India became a war machine.[7] The Raj pressured by the Americans, also spurred industrial production.

By the opening of the war, India's trade with the US had increased considerably since early in the century. In 1910–1911, Indian exports to America were 6.4 per cent of total exports, but by 1940–1941, they had risen to 13.9 per cent, while exports to China and Japan decreased and those to the UK fluctuated. In 1910–1911, imports to India from the US were 2.6 per cent of total imports, whereas in 1940–1941, they rose to 17.2 per cent, indicating much expansion.[8] Though trade with India was but a small part of American foreign trade, the war connection stimulated economic relations and prepared the way for a more prosperous future.

Although Indian industry was not encouraged, or even allowed, to produce airplanes, in the late 1930s J.R.D. Tata, Director of Tata Sons from 1926, and group Chairman from 1938, started Tata Air Lines, mainly for mail delivery. In 1942, Tata floated a plan to produce Mosquito fighters, but British officials refused. The British wanted no future competition from an Indian aircraft industry.

The war effort spurred slow growth in steel production at TISCO, and a significant transition began in 1943. After three decades of

---

[7] Raghavan 2016, p. 325ff.

[8] Roy, Tirthankar. 2002. *The Economic History of India 1857-1947*. New Delhi: Oxford U. Press, p. 226.

American managers, Feroze Jehangir Ghandy became the first Indian general manager of the steel mill, and the entire workforce was moving ahead with Indianization. Syed Habib Ahmed (1915–2000), an assistant in the budget department, testified to the mixture of Indian, American and British employees, the productive activity of highly skilled managers, and the upgrading of health benefits for employees. Ghandy took it upon himself to raise money to buy expensive Spitfire aircraft for the British and was congratulated for his efforts by Lord Beaverbrook,[9] who wrote to him, 'Heartfelt thanks for a gift that brings to all of us in Britain encouragement and inspiration for the stern task that lies ahead.'[10]

Although India did not produce tanks and planes during the war, a writer about their war efforts notes that the Tatas were forging bulletproof plates and rivets to be mounted on war vehicles nicknamed 'Tatanagar'. The Tatas were proud about the first report from the 8th Army in the Western Desert that when a 75 mm shell had burst against a 'Tatanagar', the metal plates had buckled but had not been holed and all of its occupants had escaped uninjured.[11] The Tatas also developed special alloys products useful to the war effort.[12] During the war, Tata Chemicals also began producing caustic soda, liquid chlorine, bleaching power, and other chemicals of industrial use. After the war, it produced sodium bicarbonate and then other items of industrial and consumer value.[13]

Not only did Tata and Sons branch out into the chemical field, but it increased production at India's greatest steel plant, and provided some important personnel for the wartime government. Homi Modi (1881–1969), a Tata Director, became a member of the viceroy's Executive Council in charge of supplies. Later in the war, Ardeshir Dalal (1884–1949), another director, joined the government of Lord

[9] Max Aitken; 1879–1964.
[10] Lala 2003, p. 215; Ahmed, Syed Habib. 2001. From South Asia to North America. An Autobiography 1915-2000. Oxford: Oxford U. Press, p. 196ff.
[11] Lala 2003, p. 215.
[12] Raghavan 2016, pp. 327–28.
[13] Tata Chemicals website; Lala 2004, 85ff.

Wavell (Archibald Wavell; 1883–1950). From the production for the war effort by Indian businesses, to the huge numbers of Indian troops fighting for the Raj, to the few select Indians serving in high positions of government, it was clear that much of India supported the Allies against the Axis.

With the entry of the US into the war in December 1941, and the shift of its powerful industrial might to war production,[14] American goods were shipped to India and utilized mainly for the fight against Japan. Whereas the war boosted the American economy, it marked the economic decline of Great Britain, which was forced to borrow heavily from the US and even from India to support its war effort. As Soviet premier Joseph Stalin (1878–1953) is said to have remarked at the Teheran Conference in 1943, 'The most important things in this war are machines... The United States... is a country of machines.'[15] The war marks a high point for American industry and productivity as the war effort required enormous output of vehicles, weapons, ammunition as well as all kinds of materiel, to support not only American, but Chinese, Russian and other forces around the world. The biggest American corporations including DuPont, Ford, General Electric and US Steel shifted from peacetime production to wartime output. And ten million new workers, women and men, Black and white, were sucked into the expanding workforce. Historian David M. Kennedy gives a summary:

> The engines of the military economy roared on, pounding out by the war's end a fantastic statistical litany: 5,777 merchant ships, 1,556 naval vessel, 299,293 aircraft, 634,569 jeeps, 88,410 tanks, 11,000 chain saws, 2,383,311 trucks, 6.5 million rifles, 40 billion bullets. By comparison, Germany made 44,857 tanks and 111,767 aircraft; Japan a handful of tanks and 69,910 planes; Britain, over the much longer period of 1934 to 1945, just 123,819 military aircraft.[16]

---

[14] Kennedy, David M. 1999. *Freedom from Fear.* The American People in Depression and War, 19291945. NY: Oxford U. Press, p. 363ff.
[15] Ibid., p. 615.
[16] Kennedy, David M. 1999. *Freedom from Fear.* The American People in Depression and War, 19291945. NY: Oxford U. Press, p. 655.

The Allies of late 1941 started on the defensive, but within a year they geared up and took the offensive, and the greater weight of their economies and manpower resources began to tell.

Even before the US entered the war, anticipating the need to expand the armed forces, Roosevelt had pressed Congress to enact the Selective Service Act, which in 1940, passed on one vote in the House of Representatives.[17] From a small and ill-prepared army, the US rapidly built up the armed forces needed to fight on multiple continents against formidable opponents. By their performance in battles in North Africa, Europe, Asia and the Pacific, US forces gained the respect of their enemies. At a meeting in Tokyo in August 1979, in which I participated, retired Japanese military officers from the Second World War admitted they had underestimated the Americans capacity to fight. General Seizo Arisue (1895–1992), head of Japanese intelligence from 1943–1945, said that previously he had thought American soldiers only good 'for screwing French girls'.[18]

Mobilization for war meant intelligence gathering along with industrial development and troop expansion. An important aspect of the Anglo–American relationship in the First World War, when British intelligence had an office in New York City headed by Colonel William Wiseman, was that cooperation in intelligence was more elevated during the Second World War. William Stephenson, a Canadian, had set up a private intelligence operation in Scandinavia in the 1930s, and he was chosen by Stewart Menzies, the head of MI6 to head operations in the US. Based in New York through 1945, Stephenson organized intelligence and propaganda efforts for the British. At first he wanted the US in the war against fascism, and then he wanted to connect to the American efforts in building a formidable, joint intelligence operation. Making contact with the Anglophile, Colonel William Donovan (1883–1959), Stephenson recommended him as Roosevelt's envoy to London in 1940 to connect with British intelligence services and politicians and shape a new American intelligence agency. The British had broken the

---

[17] Ibid., pp. 495–96.
[18] Interview with General Seiko Arise, Tokyo, 4 August 1979.

code of the German Enigma machines and once the American and British intelligence services were cooperating, they fed the Americans selective results of their findings, especially on German U-boats in the Atlantic. The Americans had cracked Japanese codes—an effort they called 'Magic'—and so they too had some special intelligence to barter with their allies.

These allies also kept their eyes on each other for each had national interests that did not coincide with the other.[19] The British were intent on preserving their Empire, while the Americans, at least under President Roosevelt, did not want to become the defenders of European empires unless it was necessary to do so to preserve alliances.[20] In Britain, Churchill had MI6 and his personal agents, watching the Americans as well as the Axis. MI6 focused on intelligence gathering, and counter-intelligence outside the UK; MI5 on internal work, and the Special Operations Executive [SOE], later combined with MI6, developing missions against the enemy. Manpower for both MI5 and MI6 was recruited from the British establishment—the upper and upper-middle classes, Oxford and Cambridge—and the Indian police and intelligence services. The head of MI5 from 1941 to 1946 was David Petrie, a former top Indian intelligence officer.[21] The British wanted to continue watching Indian nationalists in the US, while Americans, jockeying between imperialist aims of their own, and anti-imperialist traditions, wished to terminate such activity. In the US, the creation of the Office of Strategic Services (OSS), then its link to the development of the CIA after the war, was a step for the United States towards a worldwide intelligence operation. The OSS had its eyes in every direction. In this sphere as in others, America followed in the steps of imperial Britain, undertaking what Christopher Hitchens called 'receivership'. Hardly had the Americans stopped their wartime

---

[19] Stafford, David. 1999. Roosevelt and Churchill. Men of Secrets. NY: Overlook.
[20] Smith, Joseph B. 1976. Portrait of a Cold Warrior, NY: Ballantine Books, p. 242ff.
[21] Page, Bruce, David Leitch, Phillip Knightley. 1981. The Philby Conspiracy. NY: Ballantine Books, p. 109ff.

cooperation with the Viet Minh in Vietnam, they helped the French regain control of their colony. In the next generation they replaced the French completely with disastrous consequences.

The Cripps Mission

Because of the surprising, even shocking advance in 1942 of the Japanese military machine through Burma, the British wartime national cabinet sent a special mission to India. Headed by Sir Stafford Cripps (1883–1959), a minister of Labour Party background with sympathies for Indian Independence, it arrived in spring 1942. Its goal was to try to negotiate an agreement with the major Indian parties, so that Indian nationalists would rally to the Allied side.

The prize held out to the Congress was dominion status after the war—implying full Independence—with the power to shape an Indian Constitution. During the war, the Congress would enter the viceroy's executive and be given considerable, but limited, responsibility. R.J. Moore has summarized some further provisions of the offer which was designed to bring on board not only the Congress but also the Muslim League and the princely states: 'Provinces dissenting from the constitution might achieve their freedom separately. The need for such a settlement was indicated by discussions with the Muslim leaders in December 1939, and the August 1940 offer had assured the Muslims that they would not be coerced into a Hindu-dominated dominion. The right of the princes to stand out of the post-war Union of India was a further break with the no-freedom-without-unity policy.'[22]

Cripps' negotiations were likely doomed from the start. Churchill had excluded India from the Atlantic Charter, convinced that it needed another generation, or more, of British tutelage; he had only begrudgingly sent Cripps on his mission. Viceroy Linlithgow proved to be a staunch ally of Churchill, informing the prime minister secretly when he felt that Cripps was going beyond his brief.

---

[22] Moore, R.J. 1979. *Churchill, Cripps, and India 1939-1945*. Oxford: Clarendon Press, p. 75.

Cripps blamed the Congress leaders for his failure and seemed to shift to the right, closer to Churchill, after the debacle of his mission. The plan offered that the viceroy and the military would remain in charge; in the future, the Muslim League and the princes were to be given leave to divide the subcontinent into a multiplicity of states. A few Congressmen, particularly the south Indian leader C. Rajagopalachari (Rajaji, 1878–1972), argued that Muslim sub-nationalism had to be allowed but delimited as strictly as possible. Rajaji wanted to accept the Cripps offer, but he was overridden and temporarily left the Congress.[23]

In March 1942, Roosevelt sent Colonel Louis Johnson (1891–1966), a former War Department official to New Delhi, as his personal representative. He supported the offer of dominion status after the war, and some role in the present government under the viceroy. The Congress wanted an Indian defence member of the viceroy's council, to cooperate with the British commander-in-chief and the Allied war effort. Johnson, an unlikely candidate for such a go-between role, thrust himself actively into the discussions as an intermediary between Cripps, Congress leaders, the military leader Wavell and Linlithgow. He and Cripps wanted the defence member to be an Indian with some real responsibilities. What Churchill, Amery and Linlithgow would agree to was something quite different: a defence member in charge of stationery, barracks and fuel. At one point, Johnson and Cripps seemed to have brought Wavell over to their side, and Cripps thanked him.[24]

Once Churchill got wind of this, he clamped down firmly on Cripps, and the proposed solution was taken off the table, the original feeble offer brought back, and the negotiations collapsed. Roosevelt tried, too late and in vain, to reignite the talks, but was informed that the Cripps Mission was over. The prime minister wanted no American intervention.[25] Churchill was said to have danced in

---

[23] Ibid., p. 107.
[24] Mansergh, Nicholas, ed. 1970, I, *The Transfer of Power 1942-7*. 12 vols. London: HMSO, 1970-1983, p. 556.
[25] Ibid., pp. 564, 614.

delight when this was clear. There would be no important step towards Indian self-government, at least while he was in charge.[26] Viceroy Linlithgow, as well, wanted no American interference in their sphere, and decried their 'meddling'. Nehru and Gandhi reached out to Roosevelt to ask him to interfere for the sake of India and Allied victory, but the President would go further and endanger the British alliance for the sake of India. Christopher Hitchens showed in tracking Roosevelt–Churchill relations through a close reading of their extensive wartime correspondence, not only Roosevelt, but other American officials and senators had pressed forward both American expansionism and anti-imperialism. Churchill in his fierce defensive moves dodged and weaved trying to protect what he variously called the British Empire or British Commonwealth from US inroads. He was only successful in the short run. In the long run, the days of the British Empire were waning.[27]

From 1939 onwards, the British sent their representatives to the US to gain American support for the war effort. But Indians in the US and their American allies condemned the imprisonment of Congress leaders, including Nehru, in 1941. Even Edward J. Thompson (1886–1946), a former Wesleyan minister and educator who had toured the US years earlier defending the British Empire, was exasperated by the imprisonment of his friend Nehru and argued with A.H. Joyce of the India Office that he could no longer speak positively for the empire he had defended from 'Calcutta to Chicago'.[28] Pearl Buck, co-owner of *Asia* magazine with her husband Richard Walsh, wrote to Churchill about how much damage the incarceration of Nehru had harmed Britain in America.[29]

---

[26] Venkataramani, M.S. and B.K. Shrivastava. 1979. *Quit India*. The American Response to the 1942 Struggle. Delhi: Vikas, p. 96ff.

[27] Hitchens, Christopher. 1991. *Blood, Class and Nostalgia*. Anglo-American Ironies. London: Vintage, p. 200ff.

[28] Lago, Mary. 2001. *'India's Prisoner'*. A Biography of Edward John Thompson 1886-1946. Columbia: University of Missouri Press, p. 290.

[29] Conn, Peter. 1996. *Pearl S. Buck*. A Cultural Biography. Cambridge: Cambridge U. Press, p. 241ff.

Amid the jockeying of American, British and Indian interests in the early war years, journalists followed the very different views. Louis Fischer (1896–1970) and Edgar Snow (1895–1972) had contrasting views of Gandhi. Louis Fischer had spent many years in Europe, including fourteen years in the Soviet Union, as a correspondent. At first enamoured, then disillusioned with the Soviet Union, Fischer came to Gandhi recommended by Jawaharlal Nehru, whom he had met some years before in Europe. Fischer spent a week, 3 to 10 June 1942, at Gandhi's ashram and wrote *A Week with Gandhi*.[30]

Fischer's visit to Gandhi in June 1942 came at a crucial moment: it was just after the failure of the Cripps Mission and just before the August uprising. Following in the footsteps of Gandhi's Boswell, the activist Mahadev Desai (1892–1942), Fischer tried to record the entire dialogue of every conversation he had with Gandhi, even their bantering at mealtime. At the end of his week's diary, Fischer gave an overall impression of Gandhi:

> Part of the pleasure of intimate intellectual contact with Gandhi is that he really opens his mind and allows the interviewer to see how the machine inside works...He gives immediate expression to each step in his thinking...He did not talk at me; he talked to me... when I asked Gandhi something I felt that I had started a creative process...If you strike right with Gandhi you open a new pocket of thought. An interview with him is a voyage of discovery, and he himself is sometime surprised at the things he says...That is why I learned so much from Gandhi and so much about Gandhi. Gandhi sometimes takes delight in expounding ideas which are impractical anachronisms. He is aware that he cannot turn back the clock. He cannot abolish the automobile. But he can make fun of it.[31]

Overcoming the physical discomforts of Gandhi's ashram, Fischer expressed the pleasure and liveliness he found in and with Gandhi.

---

[30] Fischer, Louis. 1942. *A Week with Gandhi*. NY: Duell, Sloan, and Pearce.
[31] Ibid., pp. 116–18.

Gandhi, in turn, treated him as an equal and asked for his opinions on Hitler, Stalin, Eleanor Roosevelt and America.

The most important matter to Gandhi at the time of Fischer's visit was the immediate exit of the British. Like Shirer, Gunther and Snow, Fischer was primarily concerned about Allied victory in the war against the Axis powers. Shirer and Snow both wrote that Gandhi had no accurate idea of the evils of fascism. The exchanges with Fischer showed that though Gandhi hated war, he certainly wanted the Allies to win. But like most Americans of the Second World War period, Fischer's dialogue with Gandhi was both an effort to understand the Mahatma and an exercise in persuasion. These Americans wanted Gandhi, the Congress, and nationalist India to stand with the Allies against what the latter thought was the threat of worldwide barbarity and darkness, if the Axis won. Nehru, who joined Fischer at Gandhi's ashram during that June 1942 week, felt this Allied concern more strongly than did Gandhi.

Nehru, like Gandhi, wanted India's freedom as part of any wartime participation in the struggle against fascism. For many Indians, British rule was as bad as the fascism they learned about from the press. Few Indians knew of Nazi or Japanese cruelties at first-hand, but they did know by direct experience about the Amritsar massacre and British sins. Gandhi said to Fischer, 'I do not wish to humiliate the British. But the British must go. I do not say that the British are worse than the Japanese... But I do not wish to exchange one master for another.'[32] Fischer pushed Gandhi to explain what he meant by his statement that the British should depart and leave India to God. Did Gandhi want the Japanese to walk in and take over India? Gandhi said, 'No, Britain and America, and other countries too, can keep their armies here and use Indian territory as a base for military operations. I do not wish Japan to win the war. I do not want the Axis to win. But I am sure that Britain cannot win unless the Indian people become free.'[33]

---

[32] Ibid., p. 25.
[33] Ibid., p. 32.

Fischer was not done. He wanted an even more clear-cut statement of support for the Allied cause. 'I think,' said Fischer, 'the war has to be fought and won. I see complete darkness for the world if the Axis wins. I think we have a chance for a better world if we win.'[34] Gandhi did not come around. Indian freedom was his priority. Fischer talked to Gandhi and Nehru about an impending civil disobedience movement and wondered how it would affect the war effort of the Allies. They made it clear to him that Britain had to make serious concessions to Indian nationalism, or, war or no war, they would foment trouble.

Before he left the ashram, Fischer had become an envoy to the viceroy and to President Roosevelt. A few weeks later, Gandhi sent Fischer a letter to deliver to the American President. Dated 1 July 1942, and addressed 'Dear Friend', Gandhi told Roosevelt of his ties to America and what he had learned from Thoreau. Then he wrote:

> Of Great Britain I need say nothing beyond mentioning that in spite of my intense dislike of British rule, I have numerous friends in England whom I love as dearly as I love my own people... I have nothing but good wishes for your country and Great Britain. You will therefore accept my word that my present proposal, that the British should unreservedly and without reference to the wishes of the people of India immediately withdraw their rule, is prompted by the friendliest intention. I would like to turn into good will the ill will... and thus enable the millions of India to play their part in the present war... I venture to think that the Allied declaration that the Allies are fighting to make the world safe for the freedom of the individual and for democracy sounds hollow, so long as India for that matter Africa are exploited by Great Britain, and America has the Negro problem in her own home.[35]

By his end-run around the British Indian postal service and for his sympathies with nationalist India, as well as for anti-imperialist

---

[34] Ibid., p. 33.
[35] Fischer, Louis. 1962. *The Life of Mahatma Gandhi*. NY: Collier, pp. 526–27.

speeches which he made upon return to the United States, Fischer earned the ire of the Raj, of the British government in London, and of its embassy in Washington. He came close to Gandhi and was rewarded with Gandhi's confidence in him. Edgar Snow visited India several times and met Gandhi in 1930 and 1942. He was in India in January 1948 and wrote a moving account of Gandhi's assassination. But Snow was a China man: he liked and respected the Chinese and he brought the Chinese communist movement to the attention of the world in Red Star over China (1937). Then he became a regular correspondent for the Saturday Evening Post with a large readership. India and Indians, however, did not inspire the same respect in him, and he found Gandhi a cranky and boring old man. The fluidity of mind that Fischer admired, Snow found ridiculous. Only in Nehru and a few other cosmopolitan leaders of the Congress did Snow find admirable qualities.

As Fischer had come to India in the critical period just before the August Resolution of 1942, which would lead to the imprisonment of leading Congress members, Snow too, was there and even closer to the culminating moment. Snow lived near the top Congress leaders at the time of an important working committee meeting in July 1942, and spent evenings arguing with Nehru, Maulana Azad, Sarojini Naidu and Asaf Ali.[36]

Snow interviewed many Indians and was able to describe even the rigid and reactionary viceroy, Lord Linlithgow, with some compassion. However, Gandhi was his bête noire. Although he knew many thought Gandhi a great man, he had difficulty finding positive things to say about Gandhi. He wrote in People on Our Side (1944):

> No political party carrying such enormous national responsibility was ever afflicted with a spokesman given to utterances so likely to bewilder and antagonize the world as was Congress under Gandhi the Mahatma... Gandhi exhibited the vagaries his own efforts to make up his mind as candidly as a housewife hangs out her weekly wash... yet... Gandhi still personified and articulated... the leadership

---

[36] Snow, Edgar. 1944. *People on Our Side*. NY: Random House, p. 46.

of India to the masses. His contradictions did not bother them. A lot of the incomprehensible things he said were addressed to the mystical Indian soul which intuitively understood him. And when he spoke 'logically' he was talking for the Indian bourgeoisie, which supported him both morally and financially. Nobody else in India could play this dual role of saint for the masses and champion of big business, which was the secret of Gandhi's power. With all his vacillation he never deviated from his fundamental objective, which was to keep Indian attention focussed on the British as their main enemy. He did not want the movement to be side-tracked by the red herring of fascism versus democracy.[37]

Snow was more a man of the international Left, at least in his sympathies, than most of the American correspondents, and a simple Marxist analysis was part of his repertoire. Gandhi was linked to his big business patrons and 'disciples' more directly, in Snow's view, than those of Miller, Shirer, or Fischer. And Gandhi's contradictory statements from day-today bothered him as they had not bothered Fischer. Indeed, Fischer found Gandhi's fluidity of mind, his openness to show himself in the process of making up his mind, wholly admirable. To Snow, Gandhi's thought processes on display were a disaster and his account is intercut with some ridicule of 'the old man' whose day, he thought, had passed.

As an American completely devoted to the anti-fascist crusade, he also thought Gandhi naive about fascism and destructive of the Allied struggle with the Japanese and Germans. This led him to walk out on Gandhi in 1942 when the Mahatma had asked him to stay for a few moments of private conversation after a joint interview with several correspondents. Snow did respect Nehru and learned of the intra-Congress arguments about the proposed civil disobedience movement in the summer of 1942. Snow believed that Nehru was stalling, hoping for American intervention and British concessions that would allow the Congress to rejoin the government and to support the Allies in the war. When such developments did not materialize, Nehru agreed to

---

[37] Ibid., pp. 44–45.

the August Resolution that led to the prompt imprisonment of all top Congress leaders including Gandhi and himself. Calling Gandhi 'the little Generalissimo', Snow wrote an account of Congress failures and the Raj's repression for his American readers.[38]

With the Congress now out of commission, Snow saw the Communist Party of India gathering strength and thought that Indian communists would play a major role in India in the near future. His antipathy to Gandhi led him to underestimate the power and tenaciousness of the Mahatma, but Snow did correctly surmise that the British had to go and soon.[39]

Quit India

With the failure of the Cripps' mission, the British propaganda forces in the United States—including the British Office of Information, the Embassy led by Lord Halifax, assisted by Indian agent-general Girija Shankar Bajpai (1891–1954), and visiting helpers from the UK and India—pressed ahead with the message that the Congress was responsible for its collapse. The British government sent the Canadian businessman Graham Spry (1900–1983) to the US. He had accompanied Cripps to India and he was to brief Roosevelt and other Americans about the Congress' role in the failure of the negotiations,[40] suggesting that the Congress and Gandhi might have pro-Japanese sympathies and were hampering the war effort.

The British effort overwhelmed the vocal counter-effort of South Asians in the United States and their allies. Most Americans believed the British version of what had transpired and its implications for the war effort. Gandhi was no longer a heroic figure but a stumbling block to an all-out effort to defeat Germany and Japan. Norman Thomas (1884–1968) and his Socialist Party and a few other Americans still

---

[38] Ibid., pp. 47–54.
[39] Ibid., p. 50ff.
[40] Venkataramani, M.S. and B.K. Shrivastava. 1983. *Roosevelt Gandhi Churchill. America and the Last Phase of India's Freedom Struggle.* New Delhi: Radiant, p. 42.

supported Gandhi's demand for an immediate advance towards self-government in exchange for whole-hearted support for the Allies.[41]

The propaganda war was on in Great Britain as well as in America and India. One of the notable British interlocutors in this complicated public discourse was the author George Orwell (1903–1950) who was a commentator on the BBC about Indian affairs even as he pursued his own writing, and wrote a monthly letter to an American magazine, thus spanning three continents. In his broadcasts for the BBC, he hailed Cripps and the mission and was hopeful of its success.[42] When it failed, he did not blame any single party more than the other but rebutted fascist commentaries about the debacle. In private, in his wartime diaries, he was blunt. He wrote, in part:

> It has flopped after all... in his speeches Cripps seems to have caught certain inflexions of voice from Churchill... No question that Cripps' speeches etc. have caused a lot of offence, i.e. in India. Outside India I doubt whether many people blame the British Government for the breakdown. One trouble at the moment is the tactless utterances of Americans who for years have been blahing about 'Indian freedom' and British imperialism, and have suddenly had their eyes opened to the fact that the Indian intelligentsia don't want independence, i.e. responsibility... I think on balance the Cripps mission has done good, because without discrediting Cripps in this country... it has clarified the issue. Whatever is said officially, the inference the whole world will draw is that (a) the British ruling class doesn't intend to abdicate and (b) India doesn't want independence and therefore won't get it, whatever the outcome of the war.[43]

---

[41] Venkataramani and Shrivastava 1979, pp. 190, 263; Swanberg, W.A. 1980. *Whitney Father, Whitney Heiress*. NY: Scribner's, pp. 268, 330.

[42] Orwell, George. 1985. *The War Commentaries*. Ed. W.J. West. NY: Pantheon, p. 60ff.

[43] Orwell, George. 1970. *The Collected Essays, Journalism and Letters of George Orwell*. Ed. Sonia Orwell and Ian Angus. 4v. London: Penguin, 1970, V. 2, pp. 473–74.

In effect, Orwell blamed Indian nationalists for the 'flop', insisting that they only wanted to oppose and never wanted political responsibility. Further, he wrote that the majority of Indians 'are inferior to Europeans'.[44] Although he considered himself a man of the left, and close to Indian novelist Mulk Raj Anand (1905–2004), a nationalist resident in London, Orwell, like Cripps, in the exigencies of war, had moved closer in outlook to the British establishment headed by Churchill, Amery and company. Although Orwell had written an insightful novel in the 1920s, *Burmese Days* (1934), about the days when he served in the Indian police in Burma, and a splendid essay, 'Shooting an Elephant' (1936), he was out of touch with the aims of Indian nationalists eager to take the reins of power and end British rule and racism.

Through the 1930s and 1940s, Krishna Menon continued to lead efforts for Indian freedom in the UK. Said to have been charming, brilliant and abrasive, Menon came to know important members of the Labour Party, made contacts throughout the British Isles, knew the Mountbattens as well as Britain's communist leaders. Having a dedicated, smart and connected person like him at the heart of empire, was a boon for the Congress. Nehru, close to him for a quarter century, knew his shortcomings, but felt that the positive heavily outweighed the negative. Menon defended the Congress position on the Cripps offer as too little and too late.[45]

Among the small number of South Asians temporarily or permanently resident in the US, most outspoken was Krishnalal Shridharani, whose book about Gandhi's methods, *War without Violence* (1939), was analysed earlier. During the war years, he published *Warning to the West* (1942), which explained the views of Indians in America and in India towards the war, and brought Japan and China

---

[44] Ibid., p. 474.
[45] Kutty, V.K. Madhavan. 1988. *V.K. Krishna Menon*. New Delhi: Publications Division, Government of India, p. 33ff; Gupta, Partha Sarathi. 1975. *Imperialism and the British Labour Movement, 1914-1964*. London: Macmillan, pp. 255, 258; Ramesh, Jairam. 2019. *A Chequered Brillance. The Many Lives of V.K. Krishna Menon*. Gurugram: Penguin India, 80ff, pp. 229–31.

into his account of Asian responses to Western imperialism, arrogance and racism. Shridharani insisted that he shared the Allies' antipathy to the Germans and Japanesewar-makers, but the Anglo-Saxons had to be more understanding and make some changes if they wanted the people of India on their side. Here is his case:

> To the Indian people, the Anglo-Saxon self-confidence, its quiet assumption of superiority, was far more unpalatable than any economic exploitation or military defeat... His preposterous arrogance was born of his unthinking assumption that a culture superior in some ways was bound to be superior in all ways. He gave evidence of his native provincialism when he passed judgment upon the rightness of one civilization in comparison to another... But the self-sufficiency of the West has prevented a parallel recognition of the universal of some of the finest achievements of the East. The East is the richer for its knowledge of the West; it now has its own heritage as well as the best of Europe and America. The West is poorer; it has refused to learn.[46]

However, Shridharani, though intensely hostile to Western imperialism and all its ramifications, also opposed the Axis powers. So he continued his case:

> It never occurs to the typical Anglo-Saxon that he should seek out the causes which turns the rest of the human race against him, despite the knowledge of the revealed and far more sinister depravity of the other side—the Axis partners. He fails for example to realize that in racial pride and discrimination, the Nazis are merely imitating the Anglo-Saxon.[47]

What did Shridharani want? He wanted those he called 'the Anglo-Saxons' (the British, French, Dutch and less so, Americans) to

---

[46] Shridharani, Krishnalal. 1942. *Warning to the West*. NY: Duell, Sloan and Pearce, pp. 44–45.
[47] Ibid., p. 187.

become aware of their racism and recognize the case against their continued imperial rule. He drew upon anthropological studies of race, passages in autobiographical writings of Gandhi and Nehru, and possibly, painful personal experiences to build his case. He advocated an immediate grant of further self-government for India that would bring Indians wholeheartedly into the war effort. In one shrewd chapter of his treatise against the West, he quoted the liberal Labourite Cripps of 1939 against the Conservative Cripps of 1942. He wanted a halt to the British propaganda effort in America that had tilted Americans against Gandhi and Nehru. Looking forward to a post-war era, he envisioned an alliance of both India and China with Russia at the heartland of Eurasia as the most important bloc of nations. Like Nehru, he did not see the grave shortcomings of Chiang Kai-shek (Chiang Chiehshih, Jiang Jieshi; 1887–1975) as the leader of China and he saw Chiang and Nehru hand-in-hand leading Asia forward. Yet he, like others, saw the coming end of Europe's Asian colonies and a new day after the war.

Shridharani's account paid some attention to left-wing Congress leader Subhas Chandra Bose who left India in early 1941 and reached Berlin. Bose worked alongside the Axis powers because he feared that the British would never leave India unless driven out by force of arms. He recruited Indians trapped in mainland Europe by the war to join him in organizing a propaganda centre in Germany, broadcasting anti-Allied programmes to India in several Indian languages. Then he cooperated with the Germans in forming the Indian Legion composed of Indian soldiers captured by the Italians in North Africa. They were retrained by the Germans to fight against the British, but never saw action.

Once the British capitulated at Singapore in February 1942, the Japanese victors captured many British and Indian troops there. Colonel Fujiwara Iwaichi (1908–1986), the leader of a cell of Japanese intelligence, organized some of these Indians into an anti-British force, the Indian National Army. The Indians in Southeast Asia, both in the community and in the INA, had heard that Subhas

Bose was in Berlin and requested that he be brought to lead their efforts against the British. Bose made the long voyage first in a German submarine, then in a Japanese one, arriving in Southeast Asia by the spring of 1943. With the support of Prime Minister Hideki Tojo (1884–1948), Bose reorganized and revivified the INA, while establishing a provisional government of free India, the Azad Hind, which declared war not only on Great Britain but also on the US. The small INA force Bose led, joined with the Japanese in the invasion of India through Burma that began the following year. Thus Indian troops fought both with and against the British and Americans in the Asian–Pacific war.[48]

The Phillips Mission

In late 1942, President Roosevelt sent the second of his two personal representatives to India: William Phillips (1878–1968), holding ambassadorial rank, arrived in January 1943 and stayed into May. Although it was supposed that he, like Johnson, would be firmly supportive of British views, instead, upon on-site investigation, he became a critic of empire, and wanted self-government for India to advance much more rapidly than Churchill, Amery or Linlithgow envisioned. Sharp criticisms of first Johnson's, then Phillips' views were conveyed to the British Embassy in Washington. These were passed on by the ambassador, Lord Halifax, a former viceroy, to American officials, and through informal channels by Churchill to Harry Hopkins (1890–1946), Roosevelt's closest adviser.

Of the two American representatives, William Phillips was the more dangerous to the British because he had held several important ambassadorial posts, had served as undersecretary of state on several occasions, and as a member of the American old-boy East Coast elite, was an intimate of Presidents from Theodore to Franklin Roosevelt. As Phillips had had diplomatic postings to London since shortly after the turn of the century and loved

---

[48] Gordon, Leonard A. 1990. Brothers against the Raj. A Biography of Indian Nationalists Sarat and Subhas Bose. NY: Columbia U. Press, p. 491ff.

London, the British at first heartily approved his appointment. But once he, like Johnson, began to explore Indian issues from within and to shift his views, and even sought an interview with the imprisoned Mahatma Gandhi, every effort was made by the powerful trio of Churchill, Amery and Linlithgow to expel him from India. Summoned home in May 1943, Phillips expected to return to India in a month or two, but he never returned, although he retained the title of the President's personal representative to India for almost two more years. His expulsion was a mark of Roosevelt's acquiescence to Churchill on Indian issues.

When his tour in India ended, Phillips reported to Roosevelt, who talked his way through their face-to-face meeting, while Phillips wrote his summary statement. He wrote on 14 May 1943, in part:

> Indians feel that they have no voice in the government and therefore no responsibility in the conduct of the war. They feel that they have nothing to fight for as they are convinced that the professed war aims of the United Nations do not apply to them. The British Prime Minister, in fact, has stated that the provisions of the Atlantic Charter are not applicable to India, and it is not unnatural therefore that the Indian leaders are beginning to wonder whether the Charter is only for the benefit of the white races... The attitude of the general public toward the war is even worse... There would seem to be only one remedy... and that is to change the attitude of the people of India towards the war... Words are of no avail... It is time for the British to act. This they can do by a solemn declaration... that India will achieve her independence at a specified date after the war... and... a provisional representative government will be established... [W]e should have a voice in these matters. It is not right for the British to say 'this is none of your business' when we alone presumably will have the major part to play in the future struggle with Japan.[49]

---

[49] Phillips, William. 1953. *Ventures in Diplomacy*. Boston: Beacon Press, pp. 388–89.

Although Roosevelt dealt with lower British officials about ways the US might assist their war effort, he never spoke directly to Churchill about such matters. Accordingly, around the time that Phillips wrote the above letter, Churchill was in Washington, and not wanting to confront the prime minister himself, Roosevelt sent Phillips to see him. Churchill dismissed Phillips' views and waved him aside. After this meeting, Phillips wrote, 'It was only too clear that he (Churchill) had a complex about India from which he would not and could not be shaken.'[50] Phillips' words leaked to a journalist, infuriated the British.[51]

The American Influx

In 1942, as first Colonel Johnson and then William Phillips were sent to India as President Roosevelt's personal representatives, American army and air force personnel flooded India in unprecedented numbers. The subcontinent became the back office supporting the war in China that Chinese forces fought with American aid; and at the same time, it was the provider of men and supplies for the war in Europe and for the massive British and Indian resistance being readied to confront the Japanese.

General Joseph Warren Stilwell (1883–1946), chief of staff to the Chinese general Chiang-Kai-shek, was also based in India, making forays to Chungking (southwestern China) as necessary. A dynamic and outspoken officer, Stilwell was caught between a stubborn and corrupt Chiang-Kai-shek, reluctant to commit his troops to combat, a cautious British command in Delhi and Kandy, and higher-ups in London and Washington—where British politicians and military men thought the China theatre peripheral to the war effort. Stilwell believed US President Roosevelt idealized the Chinese and Chiang Kai-shek, never realizing his grave shortcomings.[52]

---

[50] Ibid., p. 390.
[51] India Office records, L/I/1/812.
[52] Stilwell, Joseph W. 1948. *The Stilwell Papers*. NY: William Sloane, p. 21ff; Tuchman, Barbara. 1971. *Stilwell and the American Experience in China, 1911-45*. NY: Bantam, p. 293ff.

Stilwell wanted to train Chinese troops in Ramgarh (north-eastern India), use them for the eventual attack on Burma, and then move them into China via the Burma Road to face the Japanese. American SOS officers and Indian labour helped construct a forty-seven-mile road from Ledo in Assam into Burma in mid-1943 but was stalled by the threat of Japanese attack and overextended supply lines. The efforts in India and into Burma under Stilwell were moving ever more slowly. He hoped to attack into Japanese-held Burma in mid-1943; Wavell thought it too early and put it off.[53] Eventually, a small US combat force was brought in for special operations similar to those carried out behind Japanese lines by the British. The American support effort of trainers and supply personnel amounted to more than 10,000, not counting the air forces.

Almost all the air supply transports available were being used to ferry supplies to China alongside Chinese planes, while Claire Lee Chennault (1893–1958), the American military aviator who led the 'Flying Tigers' and the Republic of China Air Force, persuaded higher-ups that he could do serious damage to the Japanese in China from the air.

While in 1942, Stilwell leaned on Chiang-Kai-shek to get his troops into battle, John Paton Davies, Jr (1908–1999), the American general's liaison officer to the civil authorities, was sent to India to report to Stilwell on conditions and personalities there. Davies roamed far and wide in India, meeting Gandhi, Muhammad Ali Jinnah (1876–1948), Nehru, Ambedkar and Rajagopalachari among others, and he was struck by the complexity of India. When he met Gandhi at Wardha, he said that he had come to learn from the Mahatma. Gandhi replied, 'Most Americans come to tell us what to do.'[54] Davies learned that Americans were viewed differently from the British: they were seen as friends of freedom for India who could and should pressure the British to leave India. He believed that while the British might preserve the empire through the war period, once

---

[53] Tuchman 1971, p. 583ff.
[54] Davies, John Paton, Jr. 2012. *China Hand*. An Autobiography. Philadelphia: U. of Pennsylvania Press, p. 66.

the war was over, they could do so no longer; the empire had had its day. Davies later wrote an autobiography, published posthumously, including many of his notes and observations on his Second World War experiences.

The British were not happy with the influx of Americans but viewed their help as necessary and set up a propaganda office in India to instruct Americans about India and the Raj. It was to supplement America's own efforts to educate their armed forces about the strange new society in which they were living, working and playing. The American Office of War Information came to India in 1942, often clashing with British entities. It was tasked to educate Indians about the US, and to educate Americans about the war and India, but not to comment on politics except indirectly in a discussion of the post-war world.

The US Army issued guides to India, among them 'A Pocket Guide to India' which quoted a Department of State bulletin saying, 'American forces in India will exercise scrupulous care to avoid the slightest participation in India's political problems, or even the appearance of doing so…' As the army's main aim was to aid China, if any personnel were involved in disturbances, they were to take only 'defensive measures'. Some brief facts about Hindus, Muslims and Sikhs were presented and soldiers were warned against harming any animals. Of the British, the guide continued, 'remember they are naturally reserved' and don't like showing off, and Americans should not brag about making more money than them. Of Indian women, the guide suggested that soldiers should not stare at them or address them and that, 'many will run at the approach of a white man'.

Another army pamphlet said that soldiers were to drink only boiled water. Then it delved into another matter: dealing with prostitutes. It would be best to avoid them, but if you do not, it continued:

As in any port city in the Orient, Calcutta is riddled with venereal disease. Studies show that professional prostitutes are 150% infected (half have one and the other half have two). That good-looking amateur whom you think you convinced by your personal charm may be just the baby to hand you a gift package unwrapped.[55]

The guide then listed a list of prophylactic stations throughout Calcutta. These warnings notwithstanding, venereal disease spread rapidly among American troops in the Calcutta area.

Although the army warned against any involvement in Indian politics, some politically conscious soldiers still sought to learn what was happening to the Raj and Indian nationalists during the war. One of them, Harold Leventhal (1919–2005), later a well-known New York concert producer, and Sipra Sarkar (1931–2008), daughter of Indian historian and communist Professor Susobhan Sarkar, described to me the operation of study circles for Western leftists in Calcutta during 1944 and 1945, one for British leftists, the other for Americans, which met in the Sarkars' Elgin Road house. The American novelist Howard Fast (1914–2003), a communist from 1943–1953, also referred to these groups, describing Leventhal's organizing talents in his memoir, *Being Red*,[56] and later dramatized his visit to Calcutta in a novel, *The Pledge*.[57]

Leventhal's service included time in the signal corps working in a pigeon training unit, and then with a service unit based in Tollygunge, south Calcutta. Appalled by the racism of white American soldiers, Leventhal reached out to the Indian communists, and also met Nehru and Gandhi when the war ended, and the Congress Working Committee held a meeting in Calcutta. He found the Indians friendly, some because they thought the Americans had money and they needed to earn some. In 1946, once the war was over and the Americans were leaving and destroying much of their equipment, he succeeded in distributing American typewriters to Indian friends.[58]

---

[55] 'The Calcutta Key,' 1945. Information and Education Branch United States Army Forces in India-Burma, p. 75.
[56] Fast, Howard. 1998. The Pledge. NY: Dell, p. 121ff.
[57] Fast, Howard. 1998. *The Pledge*. NY: Dell.
[58] Leventhal, Harold, NY, 1997.

In her *India at War: The Subcontinent and the Second World War*,[59] Yasmin Khan tells us that of the approximately 150,000 American military personnel who were based in India during the war (but not at the same time), about 22,000 were African Americans. Their interactions with white troops and officers, and with Indians and the British and Chinese in India, had complex consequences, including insults to the African Americans were insulted and discriminated against and made them aware of their place in an evolving world. Khan quotes a passage from an American military questionnaire filled in by a staff sergeant:

> I am a Negro soldier. Whether the Army wants to believe this or not, morale among Negro soldiers is deplorably low and it will continue to be so long as negroes are delegated a second class position in the army... The effect has been to make America lose her number one position among ideologically respected nations. The writer has made numerous contacts with intelligent, educated Chinese and Indians and he is convinced that a deep mistrust and even an actual dislike of America now exists among these peoples. The Indians... are powerless. The list of insults and discriminations ... is too long for detailed discussion... There are barber shops and hospitals at this base which will serve Chinese and Indians, but refuse to serve us. My own Army tells me in no uncertain terms that it prefers to cater to alien peoples than to me—and I am expected to be proud of my unit and Army?[60]

OSS in India

In 1941–1942, William Donovan's intelligence organization became the Office of Strategic Services, or OSS. Once General Stilwell was working from India and China, and US Army and Air Force personnel were heading to South Asia, the OSS placed a team of observers in New Delhi, which in time, became a team of hundreds

---

[59] Khan, Yasmin. 2015. *India at War*. New York: Oxford U. Press, p. 269ff.
[60] Ibid., pp. 269–70.

pursuing diverse objectives. One of its departments was Research and Analysis, or R&A, with groups in Delhi and Ceylon, where Lord Louis Mountbatten (1900–1979), Supreme Commander of Allied forces in Southeast Asia, had his headquarters.[61]

The OSS in India was subject to British direction and was instructed not to delve into Indian politics. From among its operatives, who included formidable women as well as men, came a number of important American experts on South Asia of the next generation. Those experts included David G. Mandelbaum (1911–1987), later an anthropologist; Joan Bondurant (1918–2006), later a political scientist and the author of Conquest of Violence: The Gandhian Philosophy of Conflict (1958), a fine book about Gandhi's methods; Maureen L.P. Patterson (1923–2012), the long-time South Asian librarian at the University of Chicago and, years later, my tennis partner; Cora Dubois (1903–2001), famous anthropologist, and my guide into Indian studies at Harvard in the 1960s; Olive Reddick (1896–1970), long-time head of the United States Educational Foundation in India (USEFI) in Delhi; and Robert Crane, book buyer for the OSS, later a historian. The India Section was headed by Sanskrit scholar W. Norman Brown. Reddick, a graduate of Hood College, had been a teacher in India and she initiated Patterson and Bondurant into the complexities of British–Indian politics. These men and women, like many in the OSS, sympathized with the goal of Indian nationalists—the rapid advancement of India to complete self-rule.[62]

According to the OSS operative Elizabeth McIntosh, later author of Sisterhood of Spies: The Women of the OSS (1998), Patterson and Bondurant in violation of British stipulations, began to gather information about Indian politics and to contact Indians of all shades of political opinion. They provided many reports on political issues and personalities deemed of great value by OSS headquarters

[61] Smith, R. Harris. 1992. OSS. The Secret History of America's First Central Intelligence Agency. Berkeley: U. of California Press, p. 242ff.
[62] McIntosh, Elizabeth P. 1998. Sisterhood of Spies: The Women of the OSS. Annapolis: Naval Institute Press, p. 189ff.

in Washington. The contribution to the war effort by these women and others has been largely under-reported.

The Bengal Famine

The tragic Bengal famine of 1943 took two to three million lives in a population of some sixty million. It has often been called 'man-made'. After centuries as a rice exporter, Bengal had become a rice-importing area, leaving large numbers of landless workers behind. The war exacerbated the problem of importing rice from outside, for previously much had been obtained from Burma, but Burma, beginning in 1942, sent only Indian refugees and defeated British and Indian troops. In preparation for a possible invasion, intending to deprive Japanese invaders of transport and food, the government began a boat-denial policy—which was in effect a rice-denial policy—as it interrupted the usual flow of foodstuff in the Bengal countryside. Further hindering that flow, a severe cyclone hit some of the districts bordering on the Bay of Bengal, particularly Midnapore.

From late 1942, cultivators began holding back grain supplies and prices began to rise.

The Government of Bengal intervened in the market process, trying price controls, threats against hoarding, and then allowing the market process free rein. The government was also determined to see that Calcutta, centre of the Raj in eastern India, did not experience a significant shortfall. Some traders were allowed to buy up what they could in the countryside to ensure that Calcutta did not starve. These traders were not closely supervised and seem to have played a negative role.[63]

In late 1942, Bengal Prime Minister A.K. Fazlul Huq (1873–1962) issued some warnings, but he and his coalition were out of office before the full force of the famine hit in summer and fall 1943. The Muslim League-dominated coalition headed by Khwaja Nazimuddin (1894–1964) took office in April 1943, although the

---

[63] Greenough, Paul R. 1982. *Prosperity and Misery in Modern Bengal: The Famine of 1943-44*. NY: Oxford U. Press; Gordon 1990, p. 504ff.

British governor, Sir John Herbert (1895–1943), had promised an all-party national coalition. H.S. Suhrawardy (1892–1963) had become minister for civil supplies and received criticism for the inept handling of the deteriorating situation. The grave situation was mishandled at every level of government from the viceroy, Lord Linlithgow, who refused to visit Bengal in 1943 as the famine struck, to Herbert, the governor, widely renowned as inept, to ICS officers who may have meant well but were out of their depth. This was admitted quite frankly by one of the most important of these ICS officers, Leonard Pinnell, when I interviewed him in 1971.[64]

Some analysts have argued that there was not in fact a serious shortfall in grain production, but that responsibility lies with two of the factors mentioned above: the breakdown of the grain-marketing system and the failure of the usual distribution system. Janam Mukherjee has argued persuasively that millions of rural Bengalis had been living in a near famine state for more than a decade before 1943, and for years afterward. When the other factors came into play, many of them, whatever resistance they offered, died.[65]

Relief efforts were also inadequate and neighbouring provinces refused to rush to Bengal's aid. The new viceroy, Lord Wavell, who assumed office in mid-October 1943, immediately visited Bengal and did his best to improve the situation and prevent a recurrence the following year. But near-famine conditions continued for another three years.

Since news about the famine spread among South Asians in the US, the call for food relief went forth. Several funds were set up to buy supplies, and American Quakers were among those who assisted the relief effort. Churchill and officials in London and Delhi responded totally inadequately. Though Linlithgow, his replacement Wavell, and secretary of state for India, Amery, tried to get more food for Bengal, Churchill's attitude was: they're just

---

[64] Mukherjee 2010, passim; Mukherjee 2015, passim; interview with Leonard Pinnell, ICS, Woking, 1971.

[65] Mukherjee, Janam. 2015. *Hungry Bengal: War, Famine, and Riots at the End of Empire*. Gurugram: HarperCollins.

Indians, let them die. The United Nations Relief and Rehabilitation Administration (UNRAA), a relief agency set up by the Allied powers organized to help those in need in countries decimated by the war, was unable to act. Following the guidelines literally, Herbert Lehman (1878–1963), director-general of the UNRAA and other officials, maintained that India had not been hit by the war and therefore deserved no relief. Some outsiders, struck by this callous response as about 1,00,000 Indians starved to death each month, tried to change the guidelines to include India. As the scope of the disaster became clear to all, even Churchill requested that grain be sent to Bengal by the Allies, but American officials said that they lacked the needed shipping facilities. The failure of officials of the Allied powers to respond to the Bengal tragedy was an unforeseen blow to India in crisis.[66] In explaining the famine to Americans in 1944, senior Raj official Frederick Puckle said that the famine just happened, and that the British tried to help but bore no responsibility for it,[67] an evasion decried by many Indian writers and scholars. The consequences of the boat denial policy, the decision to feed the army and neglect civilians, the indifference and incompetence of officials from the viceroy-down, were never acknowledged. Madhusree Mukerjee, a scholar who has recently investigated the matter, heaps the blame on Churchill, but arguably it should be spread more widely amongst officials and politicians. Janam Mukherjee in *Hungry Bengal* has analysed the famine from the ground-up and spreads the blame more widely.

To Partition

While writers and truth-seekers were developing their religious views in wartime America, decisive battles were raging in Europe and Asia. The Second World War would end in Europe in May

---

[66] Venkataramani, M.S. 1973. *Bengal Famine of 1943*. The American Response. Delhi: Vikas; Mukerjee, Madhusree. 2010. *Churchill's Secret War. The British Empire and the Ravaging of India during World War II*. NY: Basic Books.
[67] India Office records, L/I/1/812, report of April 14, 1944.

1945 with the surrender of Germany; in Asia it ended in August 1945 with the surrender of Japan. The struggle in Asia especially involved India.

In 1944, the Japanese invaded India from Burma, which they had successfully occupied, forcing British and Indian combatants to retreat. They had been spurred by the zealous claims of Subhas Chandra Bose that the Indian Army and the Indian population would turn against the Raj when he and the Indian National Army appeared on the Indian frontier. But this time the fight for Burma was very different from 1942. Now the Japanese faced an Indian Army retrained by British Field Marshal William Slim and his efforts succeeded and the Japanese were compelled to retreat, as detailed in Slim's memoir of the struggle of 1942–1945, *Defeat into Victory*.[68] Bose's Indian National Army, which constituted a modest component of the attacking Japanese forces, was also badly beaten.[69]

Meanwhile, the main American thrust against the Japanese was in the Pacific, where the US air, naval and amphibious forces pressed towards the Japanese home islands. Although the British and the Americans differed greatly on the strategy for defeating the Japanese in Asia, their campaigns, in the end, complemented each other. As they advanced, their scientists were at work in the deserts of the American southwest working on the atomic bomb. The atomic bomb project on the scientific and practical side was led and organized by J. Robert Oppenheimer. Although a theoretical physicist, he was a polymath and a gifted linguist whose studies had included learning Sanskrit. He referred to the Bhagavad Gita often, most notably after observing the first atomic explosion when he quoted the line, 'Now I am become death, the destroyer of worlds.'[70] The efforts of Oppenheimer's team bore fruit in mid-1945 when two bombs were ready to be used to deliver a crushing blow on key Japanese locations. The first was dropped on Hiroshima on 6 August 1945, and a second on Nagasaki on August 9. Overcoming the desires of some Japanese

---

[68] Slim, Viscount William. 1971. *Defeat into Victory*. London: Corgi.
[69] Gordon 1990, p. 518ff.
[70] Bird, 309.

military men to keep on fighting, the Japanese emperor called at last for surrender. It took place on 15 August 1945, and the Second World War was over.

The fighting was over, but a host of questions now had to be answered. Were the former colonial rulers to return and again take control of their domains in Southeast Asia? Like Churchill, they could not visualize a world without their colonies. Charles de Gaulle wrote in his memoirs, that the empire was essential to France. He was determined to grasp back 'French' Indochina. There was a problem, however. The Viet Minh, led by Ho Chi Minh, who had been waiting for the opportunity that the war offered to get the French out, led a struggle against the Japanese—a struggle that was aided by the US. In September 1945, before a huge crowd of his countrymen, he declared the independence of Vietnam in a statement that echoed the American Declaration of Independence.

But the foreign powers were not done with Vietnam. The nationalist Chinese and the Americans occupied the north of the country, and the British entered in the south to disarm the Japanese. British Major-General Douglas Gracey (1894–1964) with the forces of the Indian army under his command, did his best to crack down on the Viet Minh and other Vietnamese political groups in the south, preparatory to the return of French troops.

Jawaharlal Nehru, then head of India's interim government, learned about the use of the Indian army in Vietnam and told the press on 1 January 1946: 'We have watched British intervention there [in Indonesia and Indochina] with growing anger, shame and helplessness that Indian troops should thus be used for doing Britain's dirty work against our friends who are fighting the same fight as we.'[71]

In 1945, the French returned to Vietnam where they would fight the Viet Minh until the peace settlement of 1954. The Americans allied with the French, fearing the rise of communism in France itself, if they did not. The British and the Americans, whatever their

---

[71] Hammer, Ellen J. 1966. *The Struggle for Indochina 1940-1955*. Stanford: Stanford U. Press, pp. 121–22.

reservations about French rule, enabled the French reconquest.[72] At Nehru's urging, the Indian troops were withdrawn by the end of 1945. But neither the Indians nor the Americans were done with Vietnam.[73]

Another issue that remained at war's end was the prosecution of those of the vanquished enemy for actions deemed too horrible to be dismissed as the unavoidable consequences of armed conflict. Turning their attention to those who had betrayed British interests during the conflict, the British sought out those who had fought for the Indian National Army and so faced British forces and the Indian army in the field. They targeted three officers for trial, who were charged not only with treason against the King-Emperor, but also murder or accessory to murder for involvement in the execution of deserters from the INA. The three—Captain Shah Nawaz Khan (1914–1983), Captain P.K. Sahgal (1917–1992), and Lieutenant G.S. Dhillon (1914–2006), the first a Muslim, the second a Hindu, and the third a Sikh—were educated, articulate and committed to Bose and the INA mission. They had been actively involved in the military actions on the Burmese–Indian frontier in 1944–1945, and in the recruitment of Indian troops to the INA.[74]

Meanwhile, the Indian public was learning about the Indian National Army. During the war, the Raj had skilfully blacked out news of the INA from both the army and the Indian public. But once the war was over, and restrictions on the media lifted, and as news arrived from Indians in Southeast Asia and from returning INA soldiers, the story of the INA spread far and wide. Rather than condemning the INA for betraying the Indian Government and its British masters, the Indian public made the army and its commander into heroes: it was an Indian Army, after all, that had fought for Indian freedom. Political organizations throughout

---

[72] Buttinger, Joseph. 1968. *Vietnam: A Political History*. NY: Praeger, p. 215ff.
[73] Bayly, Christopher and Tim Harper. 2007. *Forgotten Wars*. The End of Britain's Asian Empire. London: Allen Lane, p. 138ff; Voigt 1987, p. 276ff.
[74] Gordon, Leonard A. Summer 2017. 'The Red Fort Trial: Justice by a Dying Colonialism,' *IIC Quarterly*, pp. 1–30.

India as well as, belatedly, the Hindu nationalist movement and the Muslim League, supported the three defendants and called for the trial to be halted. In response, Raj officials dropped the number of defendants and suggested milder sentences. Many in the Indian Army were angry about 'this hero worship of traitors'[75]—but not as many as previously, as Indian troops and officers, too, had been touched by nationalist fervour.[76] The trial went forward, and a panel of army judges convicted the three officers, but in the end they were released in response to widespread demonstrations. Some American troops in the process of withdrawing from India were caught up in the upheaval, but most Americans were just spectators in these post-war years of the events leading up to the British withdrawal.

The longest of the post-war trials were held from April 1946 to November 1948—the international Tokyo War Crimes Tribunal. It prosecuted Japanese military officers and civilian leaders charged with crimes against peace, including conspiracy to wage aggressive war and conducting such a war; with crimes against humanity involving the treatment of prisoners of war and civilian populations; and with conventional war crimes.

The Tokyo Trial touches India more directly than other major post-war prosecutions—the Nuremberg (1945–1946) or Eichmann Trials (1961) of German officials and officers—because India was vitally involved in the Pacific and Asian theatres of war and because an Indian judge played an important and controversial role. There were eleven judges, of whom the last two, from India and the Philippines, were added as the trial was about to begin almost as an afterthought. Radhabinod Pal (1886–1967), the Indian judge, who had not been the first choice of Raj officials, arrived late—a non-critical delay, since judgments of the court only required a majority vote. Following Nuremberg guidelines, the prosecutors laid out

---

[75] Mansergh 1976, VI, *The Transfer of Power 1942-7*. 12 vols. London: HMSO, 1970-1983, p. 246.
[76] Ibid., p. 252.

evidence for a conspiracy to undertake aggressive war, pursued in a series of decisions through the period 1928–1945.[77]

There were many critics of the charges concerning aggressive war. The defence insisted that all of Japan's moves from 1928 to 1945 were dictated by self-defence, and argued as well that the judges were using ex post facto law on crimes against peace and humanity. In his lone dissent, which extended to more than 1000 pages, Judge Pal argued that the evidence presented about aggressive war was weak, as no clear line could be drawn between a nation's self-defence and aggressive action. He further argued that one should not hold individual government officials responsible for actions of the state, thus rejecting the prosecution's argument of so-called 'command responsibility'. Pal brushed off alleged Japanese war crimes in China, portraying China as a failed state into which the Japanese were justified to enter. He did admit that there were some ordinary war crimes by Japanese soldiers in Nanjing and elsewhere, but he excused officials at the top for these crimes. He seemed to identify with Japanese Pan-Asianism as a cause worth supporting against Western imperialism.[78]

The majority of the judges convicted almost all the defendants; seven were sentenced to death, and sixteen to imprisonment. Pal found all the defendants innocent on all charges. The court did as little as possible to make his findings and judgment see the light of day. American officials rued the day they decided to include an Indian judge in 'their' trial of Japanese officials and military officers.[79]

Although the US had withdrawn its military forces from India by mid-1946, it remained involved with Indian affairs. In 1946, concerned with the food situation, Viceroy Wavell worried that the US, which had supplied wheat and flour during the wartime crisis, was cutting back too drastically in exports to India, and asked the

---

[77] Bass, Gary J. 2002. *Stay the Hand of Vengeance*. The Politics of War Crimes Tribunals. Princeton: Princeton University Press, p. 171ff.

[78] Minear, Richard H. 2001. *Victors' Justice*. The Tokyo War Crimes Trial. Ann Arbor: University of Michigan, p. 45ff.

[79] Ibid., p. 32.

India Office to express his views to the Americans.[80] Another issue was that of possible American bases in India as it moved to dominion status. In 1946, the Americans were pressing to negotiate directly with Indian officials, while the British maintained that any such efforts should be done through them.

The India Office consulted the British Chiefs of Staff who responded, 'The Americans have raised the question of air bases for their use in India... we should prefer to undertake ourselves any negotiations for these bases with the Indian Government...'[81] During the war and post-war period, the British were coping with their decline as a world power and the rise of the upstart Americans. They resisted where they could, and sought to preserve a place among the pre-eminent powers.

Meanwhile, in India, planning for a post-war world had begun even in the last years of the war, and in particular, for a renewed Indian economy once Independence was achieved. The more advanced thinkers of the Raj formulated the Damodar Valley project, while in the private sector, the Wisers began the Indian Village Service. The Indian business sector announced their design for a future Indian economy in the Bombay Plan of 1944. Historian Rajat Ray has given a list of the plan's authors:

> The eight signatories of the Bombay Plan were representative of a wide crosssection of India's business world... [T]hese... were Sir Purshotamdas Thakurdas, 'King Cotton' of Bombay; J. R. D. Tata... G. D. Birla, representing the second biggest business house... Sir Ardeshir Dalal, a Parsi stockbroker... Sir Sri Ram, of the DCM complex of north India; Kasturbhai Lalbhai, the leading mill-owner of Ahmedabad; A. D. Shroff, a stockbroker of Bombay; and John Matthai, an economist and a Tata director... The Bombay Plan was a demonstration of the solidarity of the

---

[80] Mansergh 1976, VI, pp. 390, 510.
[81] Ibid., p. 521.

Indian business class in favour of a structural transformation of India's colonized economy.[82]

The business leaders listed an ambitious set of goals of doubling per capita income in fifteen years, doubling agricultural output, and multiplying industry five times. India would have to focus on power and capital goods development. Long dependent on foreign sources for machinery, chemicals, railway engines and vehicles for land, sea and air, India now needed to produce these elements of a modern economy. Big business asked for a lead role in moving India rapidly forward once the foreign ruler exited the scene.

The foreign ruler would soon depart. At war's end, the project of Indian Independence got underway. In Britain, the Labour Party came to power led by Prime Minister Clement Attlee, and released Indian Congress leaders. In India, an interim government for an Independent India was formed and its representatives elected, but immediately faced widespread unrest arising from competing Hindu and Muslim interests. Despite Gandhi's attempts at negotiation, and the earnest leadership of the last two Indian viceroys—Wavell through 1946—and Mountbatten from 1947, the conflict could not be assuaged. In the end, India was Partitioned into Muslim-majority and Hindu-majority territories, which would be recognized as the two separate nations of Pakistan and India.

American journalists were spectators of these tumultuous events, and of the assassination of Gandhi, India's spiritual leader and peacemaker, in January 1948.

From 1944, British officials encouraged negotiation between the Congress and Muslim League, which led to the Cabinet Mission plan of 1946. This plan provided for an interim government of Indians, but still under the Raj. The British believed that this plan offered the possibility for a united, federal and free India. They enlisted the aid of the US to contact some of the essential Indian negotiators, Nehru

---

[82] Ray, Rajat K. 1979. *Industrialization in India*. Growth and Conflict in the Private Corporate Sector 1914-47. Delhi: Oxford U. Press, pp. 334–35.

first, to accept and pursue this plan.[83] Nehru listened, and when he and the Congress seemed to agree to it with reservations, Viceroy Wavell allowed the Congress to form this government. The Muslim League, angered by this action, held a Direct Action Day, which led to violent clashes between Hindus and Muslims, particularly in Calcutta in August 1946.

Thousands died in the 'Great Calcutta Killing', and Gandhi came to Calcutta to try to end the violence. He worked with the Chief Minister H.S. Suhrawardy even though Suhrawardy was blamed by many for allowing the violence to break out in the first place.[84] Subsequently, Gandhi went to the district of Noakhali in east Bengal in an effort to stem the tide of Muslim attacks there on the minority Hindu community. He was visited during his mission there by British Quaker Horace Alexander (1889–1989) and a prominent African -American Christian, William Stuart Nelson (1895–1977), dean of the Howard University School of Religion. At one point, Gandhi asked Nelson to lead the group gathered there in a Christian hymn. Nelson later wrote, 'The impression which I bore away... derived from the extraordinary spiritual and intellectual qualities which he revealed in even in so short a time . . .'[85] This effort by Gandhi in Noakhali as well as his work in Calcutta achieved some gratifying success at limiting the violence.

On the national stage, the Muslim League, reluctantly agreed to join the interim government, but in practice blocked many of its actions. During the period of the interim government, with Nehru at its head, the US moved to upgrade its diplomatic relations with India,[86] planning to establish embassies and ambassadors in Washington and New Delhi. Frederick Pethick-Lawrence (1871–1961), Secretary of State for India in the Attlee government, accepted this arrangement

---

[83] Mansergh 1980, IX, *The Transfer of Power 1942-7*. 12 vols. London: HMSO, 1970-1983, p. 120.
[84] Gordon 1990, pp. 566–68.
[85] Gandhi, Rajmohan. 2006. *Mohandas*. New Delhi: Penguin, p. 577.
[86] *Mansergh 1979, The Transfer of Power 1942-7*. 12 vols. London: HMSO, 1970-1983, pp. 302, 346.

despite the reluctance of some British officials, suggesting that it would counterbalance the Russophile views of some of the Congress leaders.[87] The Congress-dominated interim government, while the Raj was still in place, was taking control of its foreign relations as best as it could.[88] Not only was there an interim government in New Delhi, but a shift had occurred from a Government of India controlled by the Raj to a new world of independent nations, not only in South Asia, but throughout Asia, and, in time, in Africa.

In early December 1946, having been asked to take a more active role in pressing Indian leaders to agree to the Cabinet Mission formulation, the US government, through Acting Secretary of State Dean Acheson (1893–1971), issued a statement about the Indian situation calling for Indian leaders 'to grasp this opportunity to establish a stable and peaceful India'.[89] Acheson went on to declare that the US 'has long taken a sympathetic interest in the progress realization of India's political destiny'. He lauded recent plans for economic advancement and pointed with pride to the establishment of full diplomatic relations. As he had been asked to do by the British, he said that a settlement in India was vital for the world and not just the British and the Indians.[90]

Both the Congress and the Muslim League presented their respective cases to the American public through unofficial and official representatives. M.A.H. Isphahani (1902–1981) and Begum Shah Nawaz (1896–1979) spoke for the Muslim League and for Pakistan and met with Undersecretary of State Dean Acheson.[91] As Isphahani explained, 'He [Jinnah] sent me to the *Herald Tribune* Forum in October 1946 to present the case of Muslim India and there ordered me to tour the USA and the continent explaining the Muslim demand for Pakistan.'[92] In contrast to Isphahani's position,

---

[87] Ibid., p. 346.

[88] Ibid., VIII, p. 228.

[89] Mansergh 1980, IX, p. 149.

[90] Ibid.

[91] Kux 2001, 10.

[92] Isphahani, M.A.H. 1967. *Qaid-e-Azam Jinnah As I Knew Him*. Karachi: Forward, p. 104.

the India League and Madame Pandit continued to advocate a free and united India. The Americans, like the British, believed that a divided India would be weaker and fall prey to outsiders. Officials of the Raj and the US were dubious and fretful that an independent state of Pakistan would be created.

At the end of 1946, with the Congress and Muslim League at loggerheads in the interim government amid a deteriorating law and order situation, Wavell packed off the leaders of both groups to London for a conference. The pleas of the British and Americans were not answered. The meeting failed to produce the necessary signs of cooperation. Facing what looked like a dead end, and committed to Independence for India, Attlee decided in January 1947 to strike out on new ground. Wavell was terminated as viceroy and the new and last viceroy, Lord Louis Mountbatten, was chosen. Mountbatten's charge was to transfer power no later than August 1948 to one or more new states. He arrived in March and set to his task with his usual energy.

After meeting all the principals, listening to their views, and getting a sense of their personalities, Mountbatten decided that the gap between the Congress and the League was too deep to bridge. Although he maintained that he had always wanted to transfer power to one India, within a few weeks he committed himself and his government to dividing India—an outcome for which he blamed Jinnah's rigidity.

Not only did Mountbatten have to persuade all the parties to a particular plan for division, but he had to set a calendar for the steps forward. He worked on Congress leaders Sardar Patel and Nehru and got them to agree to Partition, but only after specifying that independent India was the main legatee of the Raj and Pakistan the seceder. Mountbatten did not satisfy the Bengalis, the Sikhs, or the Muslims, including Congress leader Maulana Azad and the Pathan followers of Abdul Ghaffar Khan (1890–1988) in the Northwest Frontier Province. According to Azad, Patel was the first to come around to accepting Partition, and he pressed Nehru and then Gandhi to do likewise. The latter two were more opposed than Patel to the division of India on the basis of religion, but eventually both were pragmatic enough to recognize that many were coming to accept it. Partition could only be opposed, Gandhi said, if public opinion were against it. As he explained to Sarat Chandra Bose (1889–1950), who had been working for an undivided, independent Bengal, this public opposition to Partition was not there. He could do nothing. On Partition day, Sarat Bose and Gandhi sat in silence.[93]

Jinnah certainly was unhappy with the 'maimed, mutilated and moth-eaten' Pakistan that would result from the plan—a Pakistan lacking East Punjab, West Bengal and Calcutta—that Mountbatten offered him in May 1947. Mountbatten was following the logic of the Rajaji (C. Rajagopalachari) formula: you must divide India so that the maximum number of Hindus (and others) who want to remain in India are on one side, and the maximum Muslims who want to leave are on the other. This principle necessitated the division of the two large and important provinces of the Punjab and Bengal. Unwillingly, Jinnah accepted the deal, as did the Congress.

Although the US was in the background during the negotiations for Partition, it was prominent in the minds of many. It was the focus of future trade relations, a possible source of arms, and a close ally of the British in an emerging bipolar world. Many of these issues were raised in talks that a range of Indian leaders had with Mountbatten. The viceroy usually made only brief references to these conversations, but he reported on the views of Krishna Menon more fully in his account of their meeting on 22 April 1947:

> He expressed his fear to me of American absorption from every point of view. He thought that Mr. Grady had been shooting off his mouth in a manner which revealed only too well and clearly what the Americans' object in India was: they wished to capture all the markets, to step in and take the place of the British, and finally he did not exclude the possibility that their aim might even be to get bases in India for ultimate use against Russia.[94]

---

[93] Gordon 1990, p. 588.
[94] Mansergh 1981, X, p. 200.

Whether Nehru also harboured these fears at the time is not known. But since Menon represented India at the United Nations in future years, his view in 1947, and subsequently of the US as a grasping, expanding world power, and his frequent conversations with Mountbatten, must be noted.[95]

With the main lines of division set, with riots continuing, with the loyalty of Indian police and armed forces uncertain, Mountbatten set the date of 15 August 1947 for a forced march to a British exit, a year earlier than originally planned by Attlee. Attaching his countdown calendars on the walls of relevant offices, instructing his staff and political leaders, on 3 June 1947, just over two months after the formal agreement to the Partition plan that had been reached, Mountbatten pressed for a British withdrawal from the Raj that had been their empire's crown jewel. Everything had to be divided, and the boundary commission had to set to work. Lord Radcliffe (Cyril John Radcliffe; 1899–1977) was appointed to head this body, but its findings were not to be announced until after August 15. A procedure for dealing with the 500-odd princely states also had to be laid out and implemented. As the British wanted, the US did its best to stay out of the question of the accession or non-accession of the Indian princely states and even urged the Arab nations to do the same.[96] Very concerned with this issue, Mountbatten urged the states to accede, most of them to India. Mountbatten moved ahead on the schedule set by his countdown calendar, for he feared even greater violence if he did not. Whether Mountbatten moved too fast or acted appropriately to fulfil his mission to South Asia will be debated forever.

As the Partition plan was implemented, millions of Indians—Hindu, Muslim and Sikh—tried to move, Hindus and Sikhs to India, Muslims to Pakistan. Estimates are that approximately 2,00,000 Indians were killed by other Indians as they endeavoured to migrate. It is one of the great tragedies of the twentieth century.

---

[95] Ramesh 2019, pp. 233, 264–301.
[96] Mansergh 1983, XII, *The Transfer of Power 1942-7*. 12 vols. London: HMSO, 1970-1983, pp. 231, 380.

Also involved was the division of the assets of British India between the two new nations. When in the late months of 1947, the new Congress government refused to transfer promised assets to Pakistan, Gandhi undertook a fast to force the transfer. His fast worked and the process went forward, but it gravely angered some Indians who felt it was too favourable to the Muslims and their new nation. A few of these Indians plotted the assassination of Gandhi, and succeeded in achieving it, at the end of January 1948.

During these immediate post-war years, while Americans were interested in the great drama being played out in India, several American journalists had front-row seats and wrote movingly about it. One of these was Margaret Bourke-White (1904–1971), an incomparable photographer, searching interviewer and sensitive writer.

Bourke-White was an admirer of Gandhi's whom Gandhi liked and jokingly called 'my torturer'.[97] In her book, *Interview with India* (1950), Bourke-White wanted to show that the great man whom she admired was also a human being. She thought that the West knew only a distant, saintly Mahatma. Where Edgar Snow had ridiculed Gandhi, Bourke-White was always gentle and respectful, while at the same time she carefully delineated what she saw as Gandhi's talents and his major failings.

Bourke-White's most vivid chapters on Gandhi are about his final fast in January 1948, and then an interview on the day of his assassination. She learned that, like herself, Gandhi was a multi-talented communicator. Gandhi, she wrote, 'in spite of his prejudices against the machine age, was as quick as any other political leader to take advantage of modern methods of communication. Shortly after Independence Day he began the practice of having his nightly prayer speech broadcast to the nation... over All-India Radio'.[98] She had cultivated numerous contacts and friendships including Nehru and

---

[97] Bourke-White, Margaret. 1963. *Portrait of Myself*. NY: Simon and Schuster, p. 272ff.

[98] Bourke-White, Margaret. 1950. Interview with India. London: Phoenix House, p. 38.

several of those closest to Gandhi were in her circle. She had their perspectives on Gandhi's fast, along with her own. She broadcast them for Americans and took her photographs. She wrote, 'I saw the power and courage with which he led the way in the midst of chaos... Gandhi risked his life to stem the destructive fury of religious hatreds...'[99]

In addition to exercising her journalistic skills to show the greatness of Gandhi near the end of his life, she also relentlessly explored some of his shortcomings. Two topics especially gnawed at her: Gandhi's idea of trusteeship, particularly with reference to some of India's wealthiest men, like Gandhi's New Delhi host, G.D. Birla; and the plight of the Untouchables. She believed that Gandhi preached the idea of trusteeship, but did not closely observe how it worked in practice. And while Gandhi talked of his love of the Untouchables, he did not really see how they lived and how some of these rich trustees treated them. She questioned both Gandhi and Birla about their thirty-two-year-long friendship and about trusteeship. She toured factories, workplaces, and the living quarters of the Untouchables. Then she wrote:

> It would have been easy at some time during those thirty-two years for Gandhi to walk a short way, just a few miles, and see for himself whether the fulfilment of the trust measured up to his faith in the trustee—or, what was more important, to his faith in the trusteeship principle. That he did not look, or if he looked that he did not correlate what he saw with the principle, was an attitude which one of my Indian friends referred to as 'the blind eye'. This outlook was not peculiar to Gandhi... It is only that it was more startling to meet it in Gandhi because of the down-to-earth quality of his leadership and because of his love of truth... The 'blind eye' failed to flash that image of conditions in the trustees, where his beloved harijans and other working-men lived in squalor... because of a deeply rooted and instinctive attitude. It was not merely to protect his friend Birla... and owners

---

[99] Ibid., p. 184.

of wealth. It was to protect the old order: a simple, pre-machine age order whose passing he would not admit....Gandhi had no ambition to reshape the structure of society. He wanted to reshape the individual human heart. He cared very deeply about bringing out the best in every man.[100]

As she pressed Gandhi about trusteeship and how well Mr Birla had fulfilled this ideal, she found that at a certain point Gandhi drew the curtain. He did not want to talk about it any longer.

Bourke-White went on to another subject that bothered her and about which she wanted Gandhi's views: the atomic bomb. He said that he believed that America should stop making the bomb. She went on:

> I began speaking of the weight with our new and terrible atomic knowledge hangs over us... Holding in our uncertain hands the key to the ultimate in violence, we might draw some guidance, I hoped, from the apostle of non-violence... I became aware of a change in my attitude toward Gandhi... felt in the presence of a new and greater Gandhi.
>
> It took me the greater part of two years to respond to the undeniable greatness of this man whom millions of devoted Indians accepted as <u>bapu</u>—father. Perhaps it was harder for me, an American, to hurdle his antiquated ideas on the machine age... because to me the machine has always been a glorious thing... On our own side of the globe, our world seemed in danger of dissolving, and I felt this steady voice might have something to say to us.[101]

She asked how Gandhi would meet the atomic bomb; 'by prayerful action,' he answered. They said their goodbyes. Scarcely was Bourke-White down the street a few blocks from Birla House when she learned that Gandhi had been shot. She hurriedly returned

---

[100] Bourke-White 1950, pp. 181–82.
[101] Ibid., pp. 183–85.

and witnessed the aftermath of the assassination and Gandhi's funeral. She probably conducted the last interview with Mahatma Gandhi before the light went out. Edgar Snow was also there and he reconsidered his harsh view of Gandhi. In the *Saturday Evening Post*, 27 March 1948, Snow wrote, in part: 'This small man, so full of a large love of men, extended beyond India and beyond time... There was a mirror in the Mahatma in which everyone could see the best in himself, and when the mirror broke, it seemed that the thing in oneself might be fled forever.'[102]

In the last months of Gandhi's life another famed American correspondent, Vincent Sheean (1899–1975), had a premonition of Gandhi's death. Sheean said to his friend William Shirer, 'I've got to go out to India and see him before he is gone. There is something he alone can teach me about the meaning, purpose and significance of life.'[103] Shirer had been telling Sheean of how important Gandhi was in his own life for many years, but Sheean resisted. The latter said, 'I wasn't ready. Now I think I am. But I have to get it from Gandhi himself.'[104] Sheean took his time but came to India and had two meetings with Gandhi. The third was scheduled for the hour after Gandhi's prayer meeting on 30 January 1948.

Drawing on his two meetings with Gandhi, his extraordinary experiences at the funeral ceremony in Delhi and the immersion of ashes at Allahabad, Sheean began to dig more deeply into Indian culture and Gandhi's life. In 1949, he published *Lead, Kindly Light*, a searching inquiry into Gandhi's life and religious understanding, Sheean's interviews with Gandhi, and his effort to come to terms with and use Gandhi's truth for himself. It is sympathetic to Indian cultural traditions and more adulatory towards Gandhi.

Sheean recounts his conversations with Gandhi and their impact upon him, but also the central teachings of Hinduism and Indian culture, of Gandhi's life, and of the modern precursors of Gandhi.

---

[102] Shirer, William L. 1979. *Gandhi*. A Memoir. NY: Simon & Schuster Touchstone, p. 227.
[103] Ibid., p. 226.
[104] Ibid.

Whereas Louis Fischer wrote a fine biography of Gandhi, and Shirer a moving memoir, Sheean wanted more from Indian culture for himself than either of these two. He was a spiritual seeker and a student. Although he was a first-rate journalist, at that time on assignment for *Holiday* magazine, what he wanted was a truth or truths to live by. Western materialism, industrialism, violence (even in a good cause), and positivism had become almost meaningless to him. At his Vermont retreat in 1947, he consulted those he called his 'three Jewish doctors'—Marx, Freud and Einstein—but believed only Gandhi could help him.[105]

In India, he combined the reporter, the serious student and the truth-seeker. He found correspondences between ancient Greek and Indian thought which provided some meaningful guidance. Gandhi, however, was the guru he had sought and they communicated with few words, Sheean believed. In the moments he had spent with Sheean, Gandhi had brought him to a realization of God that Sheean had resisted all his life. Further,

> The principal things he communicated to me was the necessity of the renunciation of the world. He was at great pains to show that the fruits of action are not forbidden and that the world could be enjoyed, providing it is first renounced. This means, of course, that a man must at all times be ready to give his life for the truth. It involves a great decision, which, once made, can never be retracted... [W]hat he had communicated to me— renounce the world and receive it back again as the gift of God— was not Christian, but Hindu... [T]he litany of Gandhi's truth, as it had occurred to me innumerable times beside his cremation platform, came back with the force of prayer: 'Kurukshetra is in the heart of man.'
>
> And there let it remain. And there let it remain.[106]

---

[105] Sheean, Vincent. 1949. *Lead, Kindly Light*. NY: Random House, p. 232.
[106] Ibid., pp. 232–35.

Anticipating Gandhi's death for months beforehand and then standing nearby as it happened—soon after his intense and powerful spiritual meetings with Gandhi—sent Sheean into shock. He became dizzy and developed blisters and wandered around the garden of Birla House for hours after the event. Days later he was unsure of his bearings. He obtained a ticket on the special train carrying Gandhi's ashes to Allahabad and was present at the immersion with others on the shore and in the river at the sacred confluence. He had what he called *darshan*, made a visit to Benares, and went to stay with Gertrude Emerson and Boshi Sen, in Almora.

Recovering from the shock, he tried to understand what he had learned and where he was to go. Besides those spiritual truths just mentioned, he reviewed Gandhi's life as that of a *karmayogin*—as prescribed in the Bhagavad Gita—and came to the conclusion that Gandhi's main contribution to the world was the idea and example of satyagraha. He wondered whether it was a universally applicable concept as Richard Gregg argued. Sheean had his doubts. He thought individuals might follow it, but not as a concerted movement.[107]

In 1948, Gandhi's own *Autobiography: The Story of My Experiments with Truth* was published in book form in the US and was a bestseller. In 1949, Sheean published his book on Gandhi and his experiences. In 1950, Fischer's fine biography of Gandhi was published along with Margaret Bourke-White's superb portrait of India and Gandhi. No one expected that experiments in satyagraha in America—guided by Gandhi's teachings—were soon to follow.

Sir Frederick Puckle, in 1947, still instructing and guiding Americans, wrote to A.H. Joyce just after Partition that he had had a conversation with Walter Lippmann, who then wrote a column proclaiming that the Partition carried out by Attlee and Mountbatten was 'a work of genius'. Puckle was pleased and wrote how well he thought his team had played its last innings.

---

[107] Ibid., p. 212ff.

7

Conclusion

Through the 1920s and 1930s, in the wake of the Great War and the Versailles Peace Conference, Mahatma Gandhi strode centre stage in India and made an impress upon the West as well. Though Edwin Montagu (1879–1924), Secretary of State for India, on tour in the late 1910s met Gandhi and said he saw an ascetic who lived on 'air', many Indians spied a new leader who resonated with them. Gandhi continued to lead the quest for swaraj, meaning self-development and self-rule. His campaigns in the early 1920s and early 1930s did not succeed in reaching the goals of Indian nationalists, but they brought the involvement of greater numbers in India. American journalists and writers came to watch, meet him, report, hail and criticize.

Indian nationalists and the Raj sent representatives to the United States to fight the propaganda war for the conquest of the American mind. Though there seemed to be a warm reception for speakers of both sides, at least by these men and women themselves, America was held back from engagement with India by its isolationism, the continued control of access to India by the British, and by the setback of the Great Depression from 1929 onwards.

Although small numbers of South Asians continued to enter the United States through these decades, and some stayed on indefinitely, racism remained powerful. The main thrust of this racism was against African Americans, but other groups considered non-white were touched as well. Jews, mostly eastern European, and southern Europeans were in the 'almost white' category, and were effectively restricted as well. New immigrants were to be like the earliest ones: northern Europeans. Gradually what was meant by 'white' changed. The Irish made it in, and then later the eastern and southern Europeans. Jews and Italians 'became' white.[1] From decade to decade, census and racial categories loosened. But in the pre-Second World War period they were hardened. They loosened during and after that war, and as there are more and more mixes, new categories will likely emerge.

Almost every South Asian visitor commented on American racism and on the restrictions on citizenship which were tightened with measures in 1917 (the barred zone) and the 1924 Act setting quotas for immigrants to the US. Although some Indians insisted that they were 'Aryans', or 'Caucasians', meaning of the same race as white Americans, whites did not accept this argument. All politically active South Asians in America, however they labelled themselves racially, soon knew they had to fight the evil of racism. Some predicted the destruction of America would occur if non-whites were allowed to enter, mix and marry whites. The challenge to racial thinking and the practice of racial discrimination was slowly beginning.

Although such racism against African Americans and Asians persisted, America's links to Asia including India grew during the inter-war period. In addition to Asia magazine, a popular, illustrated production for the general public, the Institute of Pacific Relations and the Indo–Iranian section of the American Council of Learned Societies offered more serious inquiries into both contemporary affairs and the long history of Asia. The Japanese invasion of China starting from 1932 gave the US good reason to want to understand Asia better as it was in flames.

In the context of the worldwide Depression, new leaders emerged who offered solutions to the problems it created, including Franklin Delano Roosevelt (1882–1945) and Adolf Hitler (1889–1945). Great Britain, its vast empire, renamed 'Commonwealth', was

---

[1] Ignatiev, Noel. 1995. *How the Irish Became White*. Cambridge: Harvard U. Press; Brodkin, Karen. 1994. *How Jews Became White Folks and What that Says about Race in America*. New Brunswick: Rutgers U. Press, p. 138ff.

falling back from the front rank of world economic powers. Its navy was considerable, its armed forces spread over several continents, but in basic industries it was now behind the United States, Japan and Germany. India was building its own industries and British leaders of the Raj began to argue for Indian economic rights in trade, rather than one-sided trade terms to only satisfy British interests.

As the international scene darkened with the Japanese invasion of China and the German takeover of Austria and then Czechoslovakia, it showed that efforts at appeasement were a failure. Roosevelt said that the aggressors needed to be quarantined, while rearming the US. The steps to war in Europe culminated in the German invasion of Poland on 1 September 1939. What this new conflict would hold for every nation, every colony, every person, no one knew. Gandhi's message reverberated, but the guns of war were blazing.

With war and Partition, resonances remained amid the establishment of new ties and shifting power relations. Free India and Pakistan began to establish their own relations with the US, no longer mediated by Great Britain. The war contributed to the Independence of India, Pakistan and Burma, later Malaysia and Singapore, as well as other countries in Southeast Asia. The Japanese failed at conquest but dealt a deathblow to the white man's empires.

The US was entering into a greater role than ever before in its relations to all parts of Asia and had an opportunity to make its own mistakes and blunders. At the beginning of the twentieth century, the US had connections with Japan, China and the Philippines, but scant interest in South and Southeast Asia. However, a bevy of powers including Great Britain and the US helped the French return to Indochina, and the Dutch to Indonesia. The cynosure of the American eye was on Europe, and this was the case until the Second World War. But the war started a big refocus. The Pacific was not yet an American lake, but it had become almost as important as Europe.

Both world wars marked the gradual decline of British political and economic power, and the British Empire or Commonwealth dominated by the United Kingdom. As it slid down, the US was rising, a process Christopher Hitchens and others have called 'receivership'.[2] The US was to 'receive' the former colonies, mostly indirectly, and try to use them in ways similar to their former rulers. Churchill and the Conservative Party, of course, tried to block, or at least slow this process. Deborah Baker in *The Last Englishmen* has given a detailed account of how some of the UK elite climbed Himalayan peaks, mapped northern Indian areas and helped as well as subverted the Raj.[3] They did not slow the British departure. Behind the scenes at Yalta, the British and the Russians were dividing up Europe, but also warily moving away from the alliance that had won the war. With a new President in the US not as firmly committed to making the relationship to the Soviet Union as positive as possible, and with hostility to communism returning, new configurations in world politics were shaped. There is no certain date for the commencement of the Cold War. Western countries opposed the Russian Revolution from its beginning in 1917, and 1919 saw the first Red Scare in the US. It took until 1933 for the US to recognize the Soviet Union, and troubled relations continued into 1941. Once the Germans invaded the Soviet Union, Great Britain allied with the Soviet Union, as did the US. Once the Axis surrendered, relations between the Allies became testy and, in 1946, often hostile.[4] In March 1946, Churchill, a world figure although no longer prime minister, gave his famous 'iron curtain' speech warning of a Soviet threat.[5] What part the new nations of India and Pakistan were to play in these new arrangements was now up to their leaders. They had grasped the reins of sovereignty and now had to adjust them for the ride ahead.

---

[2] Hitchens 1991, p. 252ff.

[3] Baker, Deborah. 2018. *The Last Englishmen*. Love, War, and the End of Empire. Minneapolis: Greywolf Press.

[4] LaFeber, Walter. 1972. America, Russia, and the Cold War, 1945-1971. NY: John Wiley, p. 21ff; Patterson, James T. 1996. Grand Expectations. The United States, 1945-1971. NY: Oxford U. Press, p. 112ff.

[5] LeFeber 1972, p. 30; Toye, Richard. 2011. Churchill's Empire: The World that Made Him and the World He Made. NY: St. Martin's, p. 267ff.

Part III

New Nations in a Divided World, 1947 to the Present

1

Introduction
New Nations and the US

Millions of souls Nineteen seventy one
    Homeless on Jessore road under gray sun
    A million are dead, the millions who can Walk toward
Calcutta from East Pakistan . . .
    September Jessore Road rickshaw 50,000 souls in one
camp I saw
    Rows of bamboo huts in the flood Open drains, & wet families
waiting for food . . .
    Where are the helicopters of US AID?
    Smuggling dope in Bangkok's green shade.
    Where is America's Air Force of Light?
    Bombing North Laos all day and all night?

—Allen Ginsberg, 'September on Jessore Road'

'At my core, I am a fighter. It comes from being an immigrant, born in India, raised in the States, living an Indian life at home and an American one outside while growing up. Assimilation was part of the fight, and fighting for certain rights and responsibilities was also part of the struggle.'

—Indira Ganesan, Key Reporter (Spring 2019)

As the midnight hour tolled on 15 August 1947, Jawaharlal Nehru, now the prime minister of independent India, spoke to his new nation from the legislative assembly chamber. Earlier the same day in Karachi, Governor-General Muhammad Ali Jinnah assumed the reins of the other new nation emerging from the British Raj: Pakistan. India and Pakistan, while they remained in the Commonwealth of Nations, were now free to form their own ties to the US and to other nations of the world. But the guiding lights of the struggles for an independent India and a separate nation of Pakistan—Gandhi for India, Jinnah for Pakistan—were soon gone, both in 1948: Gandhi to an assassin's bullet, Jinnah to failing health.

India forged ahead led by Gandhi's chosen heir, Jawaharlal Nehru, who was determined that India take an active role in world affairs. With the Cold War rapidly engulfing and dividing the world, he believed that India by not joining either side might play a positive role in lessening hostilities between the two emerging blocs of nations led by the US and the Soviet Union. Nehru was attacked by some American politicians for failing decisively to take the side of the West. American Secretary of State, John Foster Dulles, attacked neutralism in the Cold War as evil.[1] Although India needed American aid, its leaders were not intimidated. Dorothy Norman, a Nehru friend, deplored what she felt were Nehru's close associate, Krishna Menon's '...distorted, inaccurate, and mischievous' statements about the US as untrustworthy and imperialistic.[2]

Pakistan, a much smaller and weaker nation split into two wings, which were thousand miles apart, faced problems more pressing than settling world conflicts. Both new nations were in turmoil in the immediate aftermath of Partition coping with the departure and arrival of hordes of desperate people from the other nation.[3]

---

[1] Kinzer, Stephen. 2013. *The Brothers. John Foster Dulles, Allen Dulles, and Their Secret World War*. NY: St. Martin's, p. 199ff.

[2] Norman, Dorothy. 1987. *Encounters. A Memoir*. NY: Harcourt Brace Jovanovich, p. 274.

[3] Khan, Yasmin. 2015. *India at War*. New York: Oxford U. Press, p. 128ff; Ahmed, Syed Habib. 2001. *From South Asia to North America. An Autobiography 1915-2000*. Oxford: Oxford U. Press, p. 215ff.

Great Britain retained links to its former colonies through intelligence connections. MI5 continued station security liaison officers (SLOs) in India for years. The British limited the revelations they passed to the Government of India because of Menon's antipathy to the UK and the US.[4] The CIA expanded its networks across the globe through these post-war decades, sometimes sharing, sometimes hiding its work from MI6, which did the same. The 'special relationship' was not always frank and was often competitive. Through these same years, the US including its international intelligence arm was competing with the Soviet Union and its intelligence organ, the KGB, for influence through the Third World including South Asia.[5] This economic, political and cultural competition has continued into the present in a variety of shapes and guises.[6] The Soviets gave financial support to the Communist Party of India as well as distributing free books to prospective Indian readers as parts of their political and propaganda efforts.[7] According to files from the Mitrokhin haul (smuggled out of Russia), the KGB went much further: they concocted false documents about evil deeds of the CIA which they passed on to Indira Gandhi, Indian prime minister from 1966–1977 and then again from 1980–1984. These included threats to assassinate her, and US support for Sikh separatists. She believed that these documents were accurate, and this fuelled her anti-Americanism.[8] The combination of actual CIA machinations worldwide plus KGB misinformation spurred anti-American feeling in India for the nearly half century of the Cold War. Although a very small minority of American scholars, Peace Corps volunteers,

---

[4] Andrew, Christopher. 2009. *Defend the Realm. The Authorized History of MI5*. NY: Vintage, p. 442; Aldrich, Richard J. 2002. *The Hidden Hand. Britain, America, and Cold War Secret Intelligence*. NY; Overlook Press, p. 114.

[5] Andrew, Christopher and Vasili Mitrokhin. *The World was Going Our Way. The KGB and the Battle for the Third World*. 2005. NY: Basic Books, p. 312ff.

[6] Wested, Odd Arne. 2005. *The Global Cold War*. Cambridge: Cambridge U. Press, p. 73ff.

[7] Sager, Peter. 1967. *Moscow's Hand in India. An Analysis of Soviet Propaganda*. Bombay: Lalvani, p. 27ff.

[8] Andrew 2005, pp. 312–40.

and staff of foreign NGOs were CIA collaborators, many were tainted with this label. For example, in a CPI pamphlet of 1968 we learn that the 'Peace Corps is essentially a spying organization working to undermine Indian democracy.'[9]

In an interview with the Indian Home Secretary in 1972, he read out a false police report about me suggesting a connection to the CIA because I made two copies of my notes in the National Archives of India. He cleared me; I was soon allowed to continue research in India.

An uproar occurred in 1967 when *Ramparts* magazine revealed secret CIA support for a range of activities including for an American student association and for the Congress for Cultural Freedom, an international cultural organization, that, inter alia, produced the magazines *Encounter* in the UK and Quest in India.[10] In Calcutta, Abu Sayeed Ayyub, co-editor of Quest, upon being informed of this funding, promptly resigned, saying that he did not know of this. Whatever hostility to the US was generated, however, there was a flow, growing slowly larger, of South Asians to the US, which remained attractive. US government information reading rooms in Indian cities provided the latest newspapers and periodicals from the US and were packed with Indian readers.

Another aspect of the intelligence war plus other interactions during the Cold War led to what some perceived as 'a special relationship' between India and the Soviet Union, which has continued, sometimes strongly, sometimes weakly, into the present day. Even while Prime Minister Modi cautioned President Putin of Russia about war-making in 2022, he has supported an effort to keep the Russian economy afloat by buying Russian oil and arms.

After the first American ambassador had completed his term in India, in 1951 Chester Bowles (1901–1986) a successful businessman, government official and former governor of Connecticut asked

---

[9] Observer. 1968. 'Truth about the Peace Corps'. New Delhi: People's Publishing House.
[10] Weiner, Tim. *Legacy of Ashes. The History of the CIA.* 2008. NY: Anchor Books, p. 41.

President Truman for the India post and served as ambassador between 1951 and 1953 and 1963 and 1969.[11] Bowles invited the Indian employees of the embassy to share its amenities as the equals of the Americans. His children attended an Indian school, and he reached out to Indians and to Prime Minister Nehru. Bowles explained American antipathy to communism and sought to understand why Nehru, though opposed to Indian communists, seemed to underestimate the worldwide threat of communism. They agreed, however, on India's development priorities and India's need for aid.

Bowles called for Americans to pay more attention to Asia and welcomed American visitors to India, among them Eleanor Roosevelt, widow of the late President Roosevelt, and the prominent African American writer J. Saunders Redding (1906–1988). Mrs Roosevelt was widely admired and welcomed for her leadership of the UN Human Rights Commission and her role in drawing up the Universal Declaration of Human Rights. Although Mrs

Chester Bowles
Source: Wikimedia Commons

Roosevelt had put forward the words 'all men are created equal' in the Declaration, she accepted a change to 'all human beings are created equal', suggested by the Indian delegate, Hansa Jivraj Mehta (1897–1995).[12] Devoted to the advancement of women, Mrs Roosevelt understood the importance of the change in wording.

---

[11] Bowles, Chester. 1955. *Ambassador's Report*. London: Victor Gollancz; Bowles, Chester. 1971. *Promises to Keep. My Years in Public Life 1941–1969*. NY: Harper & Row, pp. 244–57, pp. 457–584.
[12] Cook, Blanche Wiesen. 2016. *Eleanor Roosevelt*. V.3. NY: Viking, V.3, p. 558.

During her visit, Mrs Roosevelt sought to understand India's problems and what was being done about them. At Indian universities, she was confronted by hostile, communist-inspired students, with whom she attempted to converse. Although she admired Nehru, she found his sympathies for communism difficult to understand. In defending America—its freedom, democracy and capitalism—she argued that the drive for material success shared by Americans was

Eleanor Roosevelt

inspired by spiritual aims not unlike Indian spirituality. She believed it essential to support India as a counterweight to China. She wanted aid from UN agencies to be combined with the US Point Four aid and grants from the Ford and Rockefeller Foundations.[13]

In 1952, the US State Department sent Saunders Redding on an extensive tour of India to speak for and about the US.[14] Since America's troubled racial history was familiar to educated Indians, American propaganda operators chose a moderate Black writer like Redding, committed to integration, opposed to Black nationalism and firmly committed to democracy, capitalism and freedom, to represent the US in India. Firmly anti-communist, Redding confronted views of the communist world in India more sympathetic than those in America. On his tour, he encountered journalists, college students and intellectuals who pressed him hard, about American racism, anti-unionism and imperial ambitions. Many Indians he faced adhered to an idealist view of communism and a negative view of the US and could not understand how a Black man could defend America. They believed that Blacks and Jews were discriminated against, that

---

[13] Roosevelt, Eleanor. 1953. *India and the Awakening East*. NY: Harper.
[14] Bowles, Chester. 1955. *Ambassador's Report*. London: Victor Gollancz, p. 316.

Blacks were lynched and denied education, and that there was no freedom of the press or speech in America. Redding wrote:

> The Indian people believe that . . . American designs in India are imperialistic. They believe that the various American organizations— Ford Foundation, Rockefeller Foundation, the Fulbright program— are tools of imperialism. The Indian people believe that American policy is opposed to the 'liberation and rise' of the colored peoples of the world . . . [T]hey charge both democracy and capitalism with delays, cynicism and exploitation. The Indians believe that they can take the best from communism, the best from socialism, and the best from democracy and create something better for themselves . . . There is a hard, solid core of communism in India... professors, writers, journalists, politicians, and students . . . Until I came out to India, I had no idea that there was in me so great an urge to defend America or that there were so many dangerous untruths to defend her against . . .[15]

Redding visited India as the early Cold War was at fever pitch, when US House and Senate committees demanded to know whether this actor, or army officer, or public official was a communist. Leftists like Paul Robeson and W.E.B. Du Bois were watched by government agencies and denied passports, as the blacklist also enveloped Hollywood.

Communism in India had gained adherents during the pre-Independence period, though it had lost ground by supporting the Allies including Great Britain in the Second World War, from 1941 to 1945. From 1948 to 1951, the Communist Party of India (CPI) went through an ultra-left period. In 1951, the CPI moved away from violent tactics and entered Parliamentary politics. Some Indian observers of events in China hoped for a communist

---

[15] Redding, Saunders. 1954. *An American in India*. Indianapolis: Bobbs-Merrill, pp. 275–76.

revolution in India to overthrow its capitalists and bypass the bourgeois Congress.[16]

In the same way that the US government sent Redding to India to combat anti-Americanism, in the late 1950s and early 1960s it sent American jazz musicians, including Dizzy Gillespie, Duke Ellington and the Dave Brubeck Quartet to attract jazz-intoxicated South Asians to America's cultural achievements. These tours were interwoven with Cold War events and the American government's objectives. They met with Indian musicians and fans—although Brubeck later rued being used for this government effort—and Indians, especially in Bombay, were happy to have had the opportunity to interact with these musicians.[17] Writing of his visit to Bombay, Brubeck said that he had 'tried to play piano behind Abdul Jaffar Khan', a renowned sitar player.

> His influence made me play in a different way. Although Hindu scales, melodies, and harmonies are so different, we understood each other. I feel that a few more meetings we would have been playing jazz together. The folk origins of music aren't too far apart anywhere in the world.[18]

Gillespie visited East Pakistan but skipped India because of official US antipathy to non-alignment. Brubeck did tour India with great success in 1958. It helped a recrudescence of jazz in Bombay where it had flourished in the 1930s. It had lost ground when many jazz musicians had shifted to composing and playing for the films produced in India's Bollywood.[19] After the Brubeck group's visit, Duke Ellington and his orchestra came to India in 1960, Sonny Rollins in 1969 and Mahalia Jackson sang in 1971. These visits were followed by the participation of American musicians in the Bombay

---

[16] Meisner, Maurice. 1999. *Mao's China and After*. NY: Free Press, 1999, p. 228ff.
[17] Fernandes 2016, pp. 137ff; 159; Von Eschen 2004, pp. 33, 47–53, 123, 152, 223, 247–49.
[18] quoted in Von Eschen 2004, p. 52.
[19] Fernandes 2016, p. 158ff.

Jazz Yatra in 1978. Besides the performances and interactions of jazz musicians with Indian musicians and fans, one of America's foremost folk singers, Pete Seeger, made several visits. I attended a concert at Kolkata's Maidan in the mid-1960s. He came again in subsequent decades and teamed up with local singers to rouse and involve the audience. Seeger never came under US government sponsorship since the latter viewed him as a crypto-communist. Seeger, like many of the jazz musicians, was critical of American foreign involvements, particularly in Vietnam. However, since the jazz tours were such a positive for the US, government officials chose to ignore the antipathy many musicians had to American adventures abroad.

Besides the visit of Redding, then African American diplomats, and musicians, the US State Department was ever so slowly opening its doors to African Americans. Carl Rowan lectured in India during 1954, and in 1961 became the director of the United States Information Agency. These efforts were an effort to neutralize worldwide criticism of American racism.

Pete Seeger
Source: Wikimedia Commons

Unlike Mrs Roosevelt and Saunders Redding, who were first-time visitors to India, Olive Reddick was an old India hand when in 1951 she became the director of the US Educational Foundation in India (USEFI). The USEFI, which she led until 1965, had been instituted by the US Congress in support of the 1945 initiative of Senator William Fulbright (1905–1995) of Arkansas who stressed the importance of mutual understanding between the US and other countries in the aftermath of the Second World War. With degrees from Ohio Wesleyan University, Columbia University and Radcliffe College, Reddick taught at Isabella Thoburn College, Lucknow, and Hood College, Baltimore, participated in the Women's International League for Peace and Freedom, and from 1944–1946 had worked in

India for the OSS. The USEFI programme she led provided avenues by which Indians could go to America and brought American scholars to India. It was the fulcrum of an international exchange hub. Reddick also helped promote American studies in India. An American Studies Research Centre was set up in Hyderabad, and she helped plan Indo–American History meetings.[20]

The heart of India's posture of positive neutrality was to minimize world conflicts. India put itself forward in the Korean and Indochina conflicts as a peacemaker. In 1950, India voted for the UN motion to oppose North Korean aggression, yet as head of the Neutral Nations Repatriation Commission it played a vital role in working out the settlement that brought the fighting to a halt and facilitated the exchange of prisoners.[21] India played a crucial role as chair of the group of three nations charged with carrying out the Geneva Accords of 1954 on Indochina, including an election. The US, believing that the Vietnamese communists would win the election, prevented it. As chair of the Control Commission trying to carry out the vote, India was frustrated, but unable to change the course of events. A civil war ensued, and India and the Control Commission were pushed aside.[22]

Smaller and more vulnerable than India, Pakistan officials made clear that they were anti-communist and open to an alliance with the Western countries. In 1954–1955, Pakistan became a partner of the US in SEATO (Southeast Asia Treaty Organization), an alliance of non-communist states, and a recipient of US arms as well as economic aid.[23] Nehru and his foreign policy advisers, as well as the Indian public, disapproved of American military aid to Pakistan. As Nehru wrote to business leader G.D. Birla, this assistance '... has completely changed the position of India vis-à-vis Pakistan ... and ... cast an enormous burden on us, which affects all our development

---

[20] Note from Mary Atwell, archivist, Hood College, 28 November 2017.
[21] Heimsath, Charles H. and Surjit Mansingh. 1971. *A Diplomatic History of Modern India*. Bombay: Allied, pp. 66–74.
[22] Buttinger 1968, p. 475ff.
[23] Kux, Dennis. 2001. *The United States and Pakistan 1947-2000*. Disenchanted Allies. Washington: Woodrow Wilson Center, p. 51ff.

schemes. This is the . . . result of American aid to Pakistan'.[24] In India and Pakistan, public opinion was hostile to US involvement in the Indo-chinese conflict, during the French period up to mid-1954, and then during the period of growing American involvement.

Prime Minister Nehru made three trips to the US, in 1949, 1959 and 1961. The first and third were official visits during which he conferred with the American President. The second was to attend a session of the UN. Nehru's interchanges with American Presidents and top officials were strained. His sister, Madame Pandit, put a positive gloss on the 1949 visit,[25] but he seemed to be constricted by his long-held view of the US as the key member of the Western, capitalist, imperialist group that opposed the socialist group. He seems to have inherited British condescension towards America from his student days in Great Britain. When American businessmen during his first visit told him how much they were worth, as a mark of their superiority to others, he winced and long remembered it. This response was tempered by his warm relations with Chester Bowles, Douglas Ensminger (1910–1989), John Kenneth Galbraith (1908–2006), Albert Mayer (1897–1981) and other American visitors, officials and personal friends. By the time of his 1961 visit, Nehru was ill and aging, and failed repeatedly to connect positively to American leaders.[26] Nehru's cousin, B.K. Nehru (1909–2001), the Indian ambassador then, wrote that although the prime minister admitted that he had long disliked Americans, whom he found brash and boorish, the reason for

B.K. Nehru with John F. Kennedy
Source: Wikimedia Commons

[24] Nehru to Birla, 2 April 1957, Birla-Nehru Correspondence, NMML.
[25] Pandit 1979, pp. 251–54.
[26] Kux 1993, p. 193ff.

the failure to connect to Kennedy and his circle was that his health was failing.[27]

Nehru's sister, Mrs Pandit, had spent quite a few years in the US, where she toured widely, made friends and met people from every part of American society. She had a more positive view of Americans and of the possibilities that a regenerated US could play in the world. She noted that there was anti-Indian feeling in America, which she tried her best to counteract. What annoyed her was that American officials and politicians treated her as a woman, rarely as a diplomat representing India. An exception was Dean Acheson, Secretary of State in the later years of the Truman administration, who found Nehru difficult, but was charmed by Madame Pandit and recognized that she represented India.[28] Mrs Pandit, who came to America in 1944, was the most widely known, admired Indian in the US.[29]

Madame Pandit was, however, although sometimes assisted, often disturbed during her American years by the arrogance of V.K. Krishna Menon, who succeeded her as head of the Indian delegation to the UN, serving in that role from 1953 to 1962. Menon was implacable towards the US.[30] However, he could make friends and contacts, for example, with Henry Cabot Lodge, that evinced his complexities. Madame Pandit disapproved of Menon's hostilities and coped with Americans like Acheson and Dulles. The Canadian political scientist, Michael Brecher, who interviewed Menon commented:

> The tone and sweep of Menon's derisive comments on 'American Imperialism' suggest an intense emotional antipathy, as well as intellectual disdain. Typical of the far Left is his distinction between the 'American people,' for whom he shows friendliness, if

[27] Nehru, B.K. 1997. *Nice Guys Finish Second*. Memoirs. New Delhi: Penguin, pp. 324, 405ff.
[28] Acheson, Dean. 1969. *Present at the Creation*. My Years in the State Department. NY: Norton, p. 419.
[29] Brittain, Vera. 1965. *Envoy Extraordinary*. A Study of Vijaya Lakshmi Pandit and Her Contribution to Modern India. London: George Allen & Unwin, p. 64ff.
[30] Ramesh 2019, p. 397ff.

not affection, and the 'state of mind' of the United States political elite which expresses itself in a foreign policy of intervention wherever possible on the assumption of a 'God-given right to police the world.' Towards the latter he shows relentless hostility.[31]

At the UN, speaking on Kashmir, Menon argued India's case cogently, but there was no advance towards resolution. With no settlement on the Kashmir situation, Pakistani officials turned to the US for aid, especially military aid. Secretary of State John Foster Dulles visited South Asia twice in 1953 and was received warmly in Pakistan. In that year and later, Pakistani officials, including Mohammad Ayub Khan (later General; 1907–1974), head of the Pakistani army, who was also rising in the political hierarchy, came to the United States to court Americans and petition for aid and did in time win American commitments. The Americans welcomed Pakistan to their side in the Cold War, gave aid in increasing amounts and had Pakistan join SEATO and CENTO (Central Treaty Organization).[32]

By stressing military aid, it became apparent, the military and even civilian leaders of Pakistan were avoiding the necessity of building the domestic economy and raising the masses of Pakistanis out of poverty.[33] The Americans also realized that there was a trade-off: any Pakistani help they received was countered by Indian antagonism. American leaders downplayed the anti-Indian element in the agreements with Pakistan. Dulles responded more positively to Muslim leaders than to Hindu ones. Vice-President Richard Nixon (1913–1994; vice-president 1953–1961) was also a champion of Pakistan. Through the Eisenhower–Dulles years, India–US ties did not significantly warm, although modest American economic aid was provided. With the election of President John F. Kennedy (1917–63; president 1960–63) in 1960, however, a new day was

---

[31] Brecher, Michael. 1968. *India and World Politics*. Krishna Menon's View of the World. NY: Praeger, p. 301.
[32] Harrison, Selig. 1978. *The Widening Gulf*. Asian Nationalism and American Policy. NY: Free Press, p. 260ff.
[33] Haqqani, Husain. 2013. *Magnificent Delusions*. NY: Public Affairs, p. 56ff.

expected. Those whom David Halberstam collectively portrayed and ironically labelled *The Best and the Brightest*[34] took over in Washington, D.C., among them McGeorge Bundy (1919–1996), John Kenneth Galbraith and Dean Rusk (1909–1994). The Kennedy team included those who believed that force would win through in certain situations (including Bundy and Rusk), and those who were dubious (including Bowles and Galbraith). Anti-communism was tempered by a more subtle understanding of the value of positive neutrality. Most of the 'best and the brightest' saw Vietnam solely in American and Cold War contexts, having no understanding of Asian nationalism nor a care for the fate of the Vietnamese people.[35] As the second Vietnam war expanded in the 1960s and half a million US military personnel fought against the NLF (National Liberation Front) and the DRV (Democratic Republic of Vietnam), people around the world saw it as the conflict between a Western military giant and an Asian midget.[36]

India was represented in the US by many able ambassadors following Madame Pandit, who was succeeded in turn by B.R. Sen (1898–1993) in 1951–1952; G. L. Mehta (1900–1974) between 1952 and1958; M.C. Chagla (1900–1981) between 1958 and 1961; and B.K. Nehru, between 1961 and 1968. There were numerous ties between these and other members of the relatively small Indian elite: Sen and Chagla had been at Cambridge together, along with K.P.S. Menon, an important member of India's foreign service. The US ambassadorship in New Delhi, 1961–1963, of the Harvard economist Galbraith, was a boon for India. He had visited India starting in the 1950s, formed a relation to P.C. Mahalanobis (1893–1972), an adviser of the government, and was respected by Nehru and other government officials for his sound economic advice.[37]

---

[34] Halberstam, David. 1972. *The Best and the Brightest*. NY: Random House.

[35] Halberstam 1972, p. 41ff; Bird, Kai. 2000. *The Color of Truth*. McGeorge Bundy and William Bundy: Brothers in Arms. NY: Touchstone, p. 177ff.

[36] Harrison, Selig. 1978. *The Widening Gulf*. Asian Nationalism and American Policy. NY: Free Press, p. 159ff.

[37] Galbraith, John K. 1969. *Ambassador's Journal*. NY: NAL. 1994.

During Galbraith's tenure in New Delhi, Nehru agreed to the Peace Corps coming to India, and the provision of American economic aid. This peaceful scene of 1961–1962 exploded with the Cuban missile crisis, and the Indo-China border conflict.[38]

The India–China border dispute between the Raj and Imperial China dated back to the late nineteenth century. With India and China concerned with freedom and Independence through the first half of the twentieth century, the border dispute lapsed. With Indian Independence, and the victory of the Chinese communists in 1949, the nations had a renewed interest in their boundaries. The US was drawn in as a secondary party and took India's side. The steps towards the conflict unfolded through the 1950s with misunderstandings and deliberate obfuscations. The Chinese pushed into India's north-eastern frontier region in the Himalayas with forces equipped for war in the mountains. The Indians lacked good intelligence, properly trained troops, adequate materiel, reliable communications between civilians and the military, and a robust presence in the contested areas. Prime Minister Nehru trusted in China's goodwill and the judgment of his defence minister, Krishna Menon. Stories of Indian ineptitude have filled volumes of memoirs.

The Chinese, spurred by the determination of Chairman Mao Zedong (1893–1976), claimed that India had attacked in force and counter-attacked powerfully, displaying their overwhelming superiority.[39] They halted near their claim lines and proclaimed a unilateral ceasefire. Indian and Chinese forces have roughly observed those ceasefire lines for more than half a century, with neither side daring to provoke the other to change them. Galbraith noted in his journal entry for 28 October 1962, 'Our military relations with the Indians, always rather distant, have become extremely intimate these last days.' (Galbraith 1969, 388) Once Nehru and his military and civilian officials recognized that a Chinese challenge at the border was imminent they appealed for military aid to the UK, the US and

[38] Galbraith 1969, p. 18ff. Fischer 1998, 16970; Pope 1972.
[39] Raghavan, Srinath. 2010. *War and Peace in Modern India*. New Delhi: Permanent Black, p. 298ff.

the Soviet Union. Soviet leader Khrushchev stalled because he did not want to damage relations with the Chinese. Only the Americans had equipment and supplies that could have made a difference. Since Galbraith was close to President Kennedy, his pleas for this aid were expedited. Galbraith maintained that the Americans never asked the Indians to give up positive neutrality; after all, the US had benefited from Indian peace-making efforts in Korea and Indochina; successful only because India was non-aligned and acceptable to both sides. Galbraith noted that the India–China border conflict dealt a blow to the aging Nehru. He died in 1964.

Pakistan had closely observed the conflict and listened to the pleas of outside powers—British, American and Russian—not to get involved. But Indian military weakness was noted. In 1965, Pakistan provoked a border clash which turned into a war, in which India's superior capacity was evident. The USSR brokered a ceasefire signed in Tashkent as 1965 turned into 1966. The ink was hardly dry when Indian prime minister, Lal Bahadur Shastri (1904–1966), who had replaced Nehru as prime minister after the latter's death in 1964, suddenly died. Congress chiefs replaced Shastri with Indira Gandhi (1917–1984), Nehru's daughter.

Although Indira Gandhi had long been close to her father and served in a number of political posts, her own outlook and talents were not well known. Overcoming her father's hesitancy, she married Feroze Gandhi (no relation of the Mahatma), a Parsi, by whom she had two children, Rajiv and Sanjay. By 1948, she joined her father at Teen Murti House, separated from her husband. Indira Gandhi turned into a strong prime minister and a patriot, more intent on maintaining her political strength than any ideology.[40] She relied on her sons and coterie and split the Congress party when she could not get her way. She served from 1966–1977 and from 1980–1984, until she was assassinated.[41]

---

[40] Guha, Ramchandra. 2007. *India after Gandhi*. NY: HarperCollins, p. 434ff.
[41] Ali, Tariq. 1985. *The Nehrus and the Gandhis*. An Indian Dynasty. London: Picador, p. 13ff.

The US had given arms to both sides in the 1965 conflict. When India and Pakistan used these arms against each other, in violation of the conditions of the grants, the Americans cut off arms aid to both parties. Deprived of F-104 fighters they were seeking from the US, India turned to the Soviets, who provided them with MiG fighters and allowed for them to be made in India. The Pakistanis turned to the Chinese, with whom they were forming close relations.

To India's annoyance, they arrived at a border settlement. The US continued to give economic aid to India and Pakistan, and eventually resumed military aid to Pakistan.

There was another serious disparity that American aid and advice did little to remedy: that between the two wings of the country. The military, civil servants, big landowners and industrialists in the west, dominated the distribution of aid funds and ignored complaints from the Bengalis in the east. A majority of the population lived in East Pakistan and earned a good deal of the country's foreign exchange, but the region lagged behind in economic growth. A cultural divide between the country's two wings was apparent at the outset, and it was exacerbated by economic policies through Pakistan's early decades. Swadesh Bose, an economist, commented:

> East Pakistan was squeezed in this industrialization process, and resources from there were transferred to West Pakistan through a triangular pattern of trade. East Pakistan's trade surplus with foreign countries was absorbed in West Pakistan through exchange and import control measures and only a part of it was offset by East Pakistan's trade deficit with West Pakistan which largely supplied excessively high-priced manufactured goods to East Pakistan. According to one estimate, during the period 1948 to 1961 the total transfer of resources from East to West Pakistan through the triangular trade was worth about Rs. 2,500 million.[42]

This process of squeezing the East and helping the West through policies, licensing procedures and the allocation of foreign aid

---

[42] Bose in Kumar 1982, V.2, p. 1022.

continued through the 1960s. Although the original Pakistan resolution called for two Islamic nations, with Partition, the nation of Pakistan was uncomfortably constituted of two distinct regions: West Pakistan and East Bengal. The roots of Bengali separatism within Pakistan can be traced through the tangled course of twentieth century South Asian politics. The fragile tie between the two wings of the eventual Pakistan was, first, a common Islamic identity and, second, opposition to rule by a powerful central government. For Bengalis the language issue was crucial from the beginning of Pakistan as a nation. Jinnah announced in 1948 that Urdu would be the language of Pakistan. The Bengalis, powerfully attached to their language as much as to their religion, were incensed from then onwards. They felt that their language, their culture and their role in their new nation was being slighted and minimized from the outset. A language movement was launched to gain parity for Bengali as an official language of Pakistan. This movement grew and, in 1952, was watered by the blood of martyrs. This spurred Bengalis to organize a movement in opposition to the ruling elites, West Pakistani civil servants, businessmen and the military. To West Pakistanis, on the other hand, the Bengali Muslims and their large Hindu minority— there had not been the almost total departure of non-Muslims as in West Pakistan—were not trusted. Although H.S. Suhrawardy was briefly a leader of Pakistan, the military led by General Ayub Khan seized control of the nation-state from the politicians in 1958 and held power until 1968. After the fall of Ayub Khan, General Yahya Khan (1917–1980) became leader, and in 1969 agreed to hold national elections based on universal suffrage. The Awami League, led by Sheikh Mujibur Rahman (1920–1975), advocated a six-point programme featuring strong regional autonomy and won almost all the seats in East Pakistan. Since the allotment of seats was by population, his party gained a majority in the national assembly and he should have become prime minister. Yahya Khan, however, moved in a different direction. After flying in troops from West Pakistan, he arrested Mujib and other Awami League leaders and cracked down on any opposition. This action set off a civil war in which the Bengalis, poorly armed for such a struggle, formed a resistance front.

The US, meanwhile, supported Pakistan. Through his years as vice-president and then as private citizen and President, Richard Nixon had leaned to Pakistan over India. In 1969, making an exception to the arms embargo to the two countries, the US agreed to send an arms package to Pakistan. With this move, Indo–Soviet ties strengthened. As refugees from Bengal flowed into India, Indian diplomats called for a halt to the repression and civil war. No negotiations were possible by that time. The US, going against the warnings of several diplomats, 'tilted' as President Nixon demanded, in favour of the Pakistani government and sailed the Seventh Fleet into the Bay of Bengal. In turn, India signed a friendship pact with the Soviet Union that had been agreed to earlier. China, aligned with Pakistan, remained quiet throughout.[43]

Henry Kissinger (1923–2023), Secretary of State during the Nixon administration, recounted developments in the Pakistan crisis in his memoirs, and the blame, he says, lay with Indira Gandhi. In his view, she was a cold-blooded politician aiming at Indian regional dominance and could only attain it by war with Pakistan. Although there was some provocation, she was the war-maker, he wrote; Pakistan, an American client state, was innocent. Kissinger did admit that foreign service officers within the State Department were opposed to their government's backing of the Pakistani government which they viewed as ruthless, and were sympathetic to India's plight. After the secret documents known as the Anderson Tapes were made public, Kissinger and Nixon admitted that they had lied. (Kissinger 1979, 848ff)

In December 1971, after millions more Bengali refugees descended into India, and no solution appeared in sight, the Indian army invaded East Pakistan and soon defeated the Pakistan army, capturing some 90,000 Pakistani troops. In the negotiations that followed, Mujib was released from prison in West Pakistan, Pakistani captives were released, and a new independent nation of Bangladesh was created. Nixon and Kissinger, dismayed by

---

[43] Bass, Gary J. 2013. *The Blood Telegram. Nixon, Kissinger, and a Forgotten Genocide*. NY: Vintage, p. 3ff.

the results—a weakened Pakistan and a stronger India—blamed India for the crisis.[44]

In the aftermath of the conflict, in late 1972, Nixon sent scholar and public intellectual Daniel Patrick Moynihan (1927–2003) to India as the new US ambassador. He had opposed the Nixon-Kissinger policy during the crisis. Moynihan negotiated a settlement of the huge cache—some $4 billion in rupees—that were owed by India to the US under the PL 480 agreement. India had agreed to pay for the food aid, given it in rupees, and with interest, these had accumulated to this considerable sum. Eventually the US wrote off more than half of the amount, though some US Congressmen took issue with the write-off. Nixon wanted to get past this issue, promoted a bipartisan agreement to do so and witnessed from afar Moynihan presenting a check for more than $2 billion in rupees to the Government of India.[45]

During 1971, the Bangladesh crisis drew international attention and aroused sympathy for the plight of the East Bengalis. Two great musicians responded to the crisis, Ravi Shankar suggesting, and George Harrison organizing, a concert at Madison Square Garden in New York City that took place on 1 August 1971. It brought together a range of South Asian and Western musicians, performing without pay for a significant cause and voicing a fervent cry against the American government's tilt towards Pakistan.

The concert for Bangladesh was also a demonstration of the syncretism, of the array of fusions of Western and Indian music that had been developing for more than a decade. It joined culture and politics and social concerns in a unique and memorable way. It was also a conspicuous sign of the connection of the Beatles—and other musicians and artists—to South Asia and its culture. After the Indian opening number played by Ravi Shankar, Ali Akbar Khan and Ustad Alla Rakha, George Harrison invoked 'Hare Krishna', as he began to sing 'My Sweet Lord', which seemed addressed to his chosen deity.

---

[44] Kissinger, Henry. 1979. *White House Years*. Boston: Little, Brown, p. 968ff.
[45] Kux, Dennis. 1993. *Estranged Democracies*. India and the United States 1941–1991. New Delhi: Sage, p. 309ff.

Though there were other spiritually inclined numbers, the effort was a practical one: to raise money for UNICEF. The considerable funds raised were used to benefit suffering children on both sides of the India–Bangladesh border. Guitarist Eric Clapton said, 'This will always be remembered as a time that we could be proud of being musicians. We just weren't thinking of ourselves for five minutes.' (Notes to CDs of 'The Concert for Bangladesh') Ravi Shankar was pleased that his initiative and Harrison's organizing skills had attracted so many to their effort and that two concerts had to be held on the same day. He said, 'Overnight the word "Bangladesh", the name of the country was all over the world. It created such a good wave of publicity for the newborn country.'[46] He was also happy that they raised some $14 million for suffering children. As a son of Jessore district, Bangladesh, he felt at home and was feted when he visited his homeland.

While South Asians were moving into mainstream America in every sphere, relations between the US, India, Pakistan and Bangladesh were changing. In the 1970s, after its triumph in the Bangladesh War, India went through its own period of political trauma, the Emergency. In 1975, a court in Allahabad ruled that Mrs Gandhi had violated election law. Mrs Gandhi moved to declare a national state of emergency, signed by India's President. What followed was a two-year period of autocratic rule. Mrs Gandhi called for a Parliamentary election in 1977, and in a fair election, Mrs Gandhi's Congress party was defeated by a coalition led by the Janata party. This coalition ruled, ineffectively, into 1980. Then another election brought Mrs Gandhi back to power. Although there was pointed criticism of the imposition of the Emergency in the US, and quietly in India, there was not much attention to South Asia, until the Soviet Union, India's strongest ally, invaded Afghanistan, bringing South Asia back into the American gaze.

US relations with Pakistan have been troubled since the inclusion of Pakistan into the circle of American 'allies'. Military and

---

[46] Shankar, Ravi. 1999. *Raga Mala*. An Autobiography. NY: Welcome Rain, p. 220.

economic aid have dipped and grown and then been drastically cut again. The antipathy of Pakistanis to America has been used by the Pakistani military and intelligent services for their own purposes, mainly to deflect attention from their deficiencies. Husain Haqqani has detailed how successive regimes have ramped up anti-American sentiment, presenting false evidence of American perfidy.[47] After 1971, with the break up of Pakistan and the establishment of Bangladesh, official American interest in South Asia abated. The Pakistani President who then became prime minister under a new Constitution in 1973, Zulfikar Ali Bhutto, appealed for renewed US military aid, offering the Americans bases on the Arabian Sea, but to no avail. The Americans gave non-military aid but did not want to become Pakistan's main arms supplier again. Bhutto was overtaken by a military coup in 1977, tried for election crimes and then executed in 1977. Once again Pakistan was under military rule.[48]

Interest in Pakistan awakened only with the Soviet invasion of Afghanistan in 1979. The Pakistanis had played an active role prior to the Soviet direct involvement by backing Islamists opposed to the leftist Afghan government. With the Soviet military supporting the leftists in Afghanistan, the war was on between this government and the Islamists backed by Pakistan. Suddenly Pakistan was a frontline nation in a newly animated arena for the Cold War. American leaders hoped that this might be the Soviets' 'Vietnam', a catastrophic and draining involvement. The American government stepped in to help the Afghan rebels, even as the Pakistani ISI (Inter-Services Intelligence) insisted that the aid be channelled through them. Americans supplied extensive military aid that funded Islamists from around the world to flood Afghanistan in a fight they perceived as their enemy, the godless communists.

The American aid mission had unforeseen consequences for Afghanistan and the US. American aid to Pakistan greatly increased. Ronald Reagan offered a much more substantial package than President Carter's 'peanuts'. For the next generation, the Pakistanis

---

[47] Haqqani 2013, pp. 115–17.
[48] Ibid., p. 170ff.

were delighted to get this American aid, which they used for their own purposes. Pakistan wanted American support against what it saw as imperialist India but was willing to talk of backing American anti-communist aims in order to get the desired aid.[49] Through the 1980s, the Americans had no qualms about what the consequences of the aid to the mujahedeen, or Islamic guerilla forces, might lead to. Some coalesced into the Taliban, a political and religious organization, backed by the Pakistani ISI. With the Russian decision to withdraw in 1989, American interest waned. Soon the Taliban controlled Afghanistan, although they faced regional opposition, and at the same time allowed al-Qaeda, a small militant Islamic group under Osama bin Laden, to find a home.

During this period, India underwent a series of traumatic events. Mrs Gandhi had returned to power in 1980 and under her gaze a separatist movement grew in the Punjab demanding the creation of Khalistan ('Land of the Khalsa') as a separate Sikh homeland. Those Sikhs gathered arms in the Golden Temple, the most important Sikh shrine in Amritsar. The Government of India perceived a threat to the Indian state, and under Operation Blue Star, Indian military forces moved into the temple in 1983. In response, Mrs Gandhi was assassinated by her Sikh bodyguards. Congress leaders decided that her apolitical son, Rajiv, should be her successor. Rajiv took a different approach in some matters than his mother. Advised by Sam Pitroda, he undertook several initiatives, one of them a new path in telecommunications that boosted economic advancement,[50] a move e to liberalize the economy which economic advisers had suggested.

During these same years, the US was concerned about the spread of nuclear weapons in South Asia and was disappointed that India and Pakistan refused to sign the nuclear non-proliferation (NPT) treaty. The government of India argued that the NPT was hypocritical: the original nuclear powers sought to deny the weapons they already possessed to others seeking to have them. First India, and then Pakistan, developed nuclear weapons, although for years

---

[49] Ibid., p. 271ff.
[50] Panagariya, Arvind. 2008. *India: Emerging Giant*. NY: Oxford, p. 370ff.

Pakistan denied it was doing so. President Zia lied repeatedly to the US, as heads of state often do, pledging on his 'honour' that his country was not doing so. Worried about neighbour China as a nuclear power, India had its own reasons for going nuclear, and Pakistan, in turn, wanted to keep up with its larger neighbour, and so busily pursued the 'Islamic bomb': the first nuclear weapon to be made by an Islamic nation.[51] American Congressional amendments required that the President sign off each year that Pakistan had not risen above a certain level of development for nuclear weapons. President Reagan and then George H.W. Bush signed off as required, while continuing aid to Pakistan. But Pakistan did have nuclear weapons and in 1990 a rise in tensions between India and Pakistan came close to nuclear confrontation.[52] In 1992, Bush refused to sign off on Pakistani non-nuclear weapons presence. Aid was briefly cut. But then under President Bill Clinton, with Islamists in Afghanistan perceived as a potential danger to the United States, it was resumed. This Islamist danger was manifested in the first attack on the World Trade Center in New York in 1993. Americans seemed to deny— although it was evident to some—that the Taliban and, indirectly, al-Qaeda were linked to the Pakistani ISI. Hassan Haqqani implies that American officials did not recognize that the Pakistanis were deceiving them.[53]

Further attacks in 1998 on American embassies in East Africa, and in 2000 on the naval vessel USS Cole moved President Clinton to order missile strikes against al-Qaeda in Afghanistan. In this raid some Pakistanis were killed, but not bin Laden. He and his organization were perceived as a threat to the US, but it was not understood how great a danger they posed. Then came the attacks of 11 September 2001, the infamous 9/11. Al-Qaeda operatives

---

[51] Gould, Harold and Sumit Ganguly, ed. 1992. *The Hope and the Reality*. US-Indian Relations from Roosevelt to Reagan. Boulder: Westview, p. 111ff; Kux 1993, p. 314ff; Haqqani 2013, p. 206ff

[52] Andrew, Christopher. 1995. *For the President's Eyes Only*. Secret Intelligence and the American Presidency from Washington to Bush. NY: HarperPerennial, pp. 516–17.

[53] Haqqani 2013, p. 170ff; Coll, Steve. 2004. *Ghost Wars*. NY: Penguin, p. 121.

hijacked four American commercial airliners and crashed two into the World Trade Center in New York, downed a third near Shanksville, Pennsylvania; the fourth crashed into the Pentagon in Washington, D.C. American officials had gravely underestimated the skill of the al-Qaeda plotters, overlooking signals that Middle Easterners were taking flight training in the US, while the FBI and CIA had failed to share intelligence. (Coll 2004, 371ff; Coll 2018, 11ff) On the morning of 9/11, people 'dropp[ed] like flies' from the enormous heights of the World Trade Center, preferring to die by jumping than by another kind of painful death. Later, as could be viewed live on television, the towers fell. Among the nearly 3,000 who died were people from many nations, including more than sixty South Asians from diverse communities. (India Abroad, Sept 21, 2018)

The American invasion of Afghanistan followed when the Taliban would not surrender bin Laden and the members of al-Qaeda. The US moved directly into combat without having a clear vision of what a long-term arrangement for that country might be. Civil strife had overtaken Afghanistan once the Soviets exited in 1989, when the US largely withdrew from the area. The Taliban suppressed rival mujahedeen groups in 1996, but would not surrender al-Qaeda, to which it had given a safe haven. The US invasion ensued, and the Taliban were seemingly defeated and gone. However, according to the account by Anand Gopal, one of America's most astute investigators of the Afghan wars, the US failed to manage the next stage: the creation of a stable government for the country.[54] Some clever and ruthless men, among them tribal leaders, won contracts from the US at exorbitant rates and then moved with American aid to eliminate rivals.

The story of Akbar Gul, or Mullah Cable, runs through Gopal's fine book. Although a member of the Taliban in the 1990s, he had forsaken them and supported Karzai and his American supporters in late 2001. However, he was ground down by those newly in-charge, so that he felt almost coerced to return to his Taliban comrades,

---

[54] Gopal, Anand. 2014. *No Good Men among the Living*. NY: Picador, p. 80ff.

and take up the fight anew. Put in charge of Chak district, Gul proved a skilled opponent of foreigners with much more fearsome firepower at their command.[55] The war against the Taliban waged by the US and the Afghan government flared up again and in 2021 ended with the triumph of the Taliban and the exit of Americans from Afghanistan. By their ruthlessness and cruelty, the Taliban, like the forces on the government side, have earned the enmity of many ordinary Afghans, but the support of others. According to the Pashtun proverb used by Gopal for his title: 'There are no good men among the living, and no bad ones only among the dead.'[56]

The involvement in Afghanistan from the 1980s to the present has also complicated the US relationship to Pakistan. American arms for the mujahedeen in the 1980s were linked to aid to Pakistan. Pakistani leaders and their intelligence service, the ISI, pursued their own agenda. Arguing that the army and the ISI have dominated the country since the 1950s, Christine Fair, an American analyst of Pakistan and American foreign relations, calls Pakistan 'an army with a country'.[57]

As US relations with Pakistan shifted course, so did American aid to Pakistan. Eugene Staples, a US government official who headed the aid mission in the 1980s, was blunt in his assessment. Pakistan, he says, has been rife with corruption, paid little attention to education and public health, and has benefited little from billions of dollars in aid. Usually, half of the aid was for the military, while the other half went to large and generally unproductive projects. Drawing on his experience as director of the Ford Foundation in India during the 1970s, Staples pressed the shapers of aid to Pakistan to give more generously to more modest, but more effective, non-government organizations (NGOs).[58] During the Soviet involvement

---

[55] Ibid., p. 8ff, 183ff.

[56] Ibid., p. 2.

[57] Fair, C. Christine. 2014. *Fighting to the End: The Pakistan Army's Way of War.* NY: Oxford U. Press; Fair, lecture, Columbia University, April 11, 2019; Coll 2018.

[58] Staples, Eugene. 2007. *Old Gods New Nations.* NY: Universe., p. 154ff.

in Afghanistan, from 1979 to 1989 or so, American aid rose. With the Soviet departure, it was cut almost entirely. Then after 9/11, it was offered and accepted again. But as the ties between the ISI and the Taliban were revealed, the US pressed Pakistan to cut this link, or have the aid cut again. Under the Trump administration, aid was in fact cut, as American officials saw negligible gains from it.

The Pakistanis have chosen to support some groups Americans have called 'terrorists' when it suited what they believed were their national interests. Occasionally they have cracked down on those called the Pakistani Taliban, but allowed first al-Qaeda, and then the Afghan Taliban, to gain havens on the Pakistani side of the porous Pakistan–Afghanistan border. By some accounts they did more than allow havens to the Taliban: the ISI helped and directed the Afghan Taliban and its leaders. The US, an international intruder, was exploited by those it thought it was controlling, and even helping, by its lack of understanding of the forces at play on the ground. [59]This is not an unfamiliar pattern in the history of Western imperialism.

American forces in 2003 carried out an invasion of Iraq leading to inattention to Afghanistan, allowing the Taliban to rise again. The Pakistanis allowed the Taliban to reorganize on their side of the Afghan frontier, where Mullah Omar, their leader, as well as some other commanders took up residence. Al-Qaeda was set back in 2011 when bin Laden was tracked down and killed by American Special Forces in Pakistan. This event inflamed anti-American sentiment in Pakistan, since the Pakistanis, who had been sheltering him, were not forewarned by the US of the Special Forces operation. [60]

As relations with Pakistan deteriorated, the US did extricate its military and aid mission from Afghanistan in 2021, though not all of its citizens and helpers. The US continues its troubled relationship with Pakistan, which helped the Taliban's return to power. Though relations with Pakistan have been frayed to breaking point, and aid to

---

[59] Fair, lecture, 11 April 2019.
[60] Chomsky, Noam. 2008. *The Essential Chomsky*. Ed. Anthony Arnove. NY: New Press; Johnson, Chalmers. 2004. *The Sorrows of Empire*. NY: Metropolitan Books; Roy, Arundhati. 2019. *My Seditious Heart*. Chicago: Haymarket.

Pakistan has been cut back, ties to India have improved, leading to a boom in trade between the two nations. Meanwhile China, bordering Pakistan on the north, and observing the deterioration of relations between the US and Pakistan, has expanded its already considerable relationship to Pakistan.[61] The Chinese have been advancing with their ambitious Belt and Road project across Central Asia, expanded ties to Sri Lanka and Pakistan. These Chinese ventures have pushed India and the US closer together as they see China's emblematic red star rising ever higher over Asia and beyond.

US–India relations were already improving during President Clinton's administration and his visit to India in 2000 helped. Under George W. Bush, the US ceased pressuring India to forsake its nuclear programme, as a recent analysis by Blackwill and Tellis summarizes:

> During… Bush's presidency, US officials gave up their longstanding insistence that India relinquish its nuclear weapons, allowing Washington and New Delhi to sign a landmark nuclear accord and opening the way to heavy US investments—diplomatic, economic, and military—to facilitate India's rise. Successive US administrations provided liberal access to military technologies and promoted India's role in international institutions, culminating in President Barack Obama's endorsement of Indian aspirations to permanent membership in the UN Security Council.[62]

The authors further point out the shared opposition of India and the US to Chinese expansion. This upward trend of US–India joint efforts was set back by the Trump administration's use of tariffs as an instrument of its foreign policy, aiming to restrict Iranian oil sales and limit arms sales to American products. Although still a much weaker country than the US, India has its own view of its national interests, and how these are to be achieved. Each nation wants the maximum level of trade and cooperation that its interests will allow.

---

[61] 'US-Pakistan Ties', *New York Times*, 18 December 2018.
[62] Blackwill Robert D. and Ashley J. Tellis, Sept–Oct. 2019. 'The India Dividend,' *Foreign Affairs*, p. 173.

The appointment of Richard Verma as US ambassador to India in 2014 may be seen as a mark of the growing closeness between the two nations, as well as of the rise of South Asian Americans into public service positions. Born in 1968 to Indian immigrant parents, Verma grew up in Johnstown, Pennsylvania, earned a BS degree at Lehigh University, and law degrees at American University and Georgetown University. When Donald Trump assumed the presidency, he stepped down from that post, became vice chairman of the Asia Group, an advisory firm to businesses seeking to thrive in Asia, and began serving as a commentator on international issues.[63]

In India in recent years, the Bharatiya Janata Party, or BJP, has gradually risen to power. In 2014, gaining a majority in the Lok Sabha, the Indian Parliament, and no longer needing other parties in order to rule, it formed a government led by Narendra Modi. A skilled politician from Gujarat, Modi had been in the RSS, a social and cultural organization with deep links to the BJP, a Hindu nationalist party whose principal goal (when its nationalist programme is tempered) is robust economic development for India.

Although Modi himself had been banned from the United States for what was believed to be his role in a pogrom of Muslims in Gujarat in 2002, once he became prime minister, this ban was cancelled. Modi rose on the global stage, commanded a huge rally in New York's Madison Square Garden, and seemed for the moment, India's only national leader. The BJP and its American affiliates had long been courting the support of NRIs.[64] Modi reached out to other national leaders across the globe and welcomed more foreign investment. Modi was elected to his post with the support of many of the young as well as powerful business groups. Although economic growth seemed on track through his first term, job growth, vital for young Indians, was insufficient. Continuing to present himself effectively as a powerful

---

[63] *New York Times*, 'Lawyer Nominated as Ambassador to India,' 19 September 2014; 'Richard Verma', Wikipedia.
[64] Rajagopal, Arvind. 2001. *Politics after Television*. Hindu Nationalism and the Reshaping of the Public in India. Cambridge: Cambridge U. Press, p. 237ff.

leader, willing to stand up to Pakistan when necessary, Modi and the BJP were again victorious in the 2019 Lok Sabha elections.

On 22 September 2019, Modi appeared at a huge rally at NRG Stadium in Houston, Texas: the 'Howdy, Modi' gathering, which brought US President Trump onstage with him. The hero of white nationalists in America and the hero of the Hindu right in India happily praised each other's leadership. Modi had not forgotten the NRIs; although most of the growing minority of South Asian background has usually favoured the Democrats, Trump used the occasion to praise this particular minority, and implicitly to appeal for their votes.[65] Some lonely protesters paraded outside the Houston football stadium as Modi spoke. Indian Prime Minister Modi returned to the US in June 2023, and was feted by President Biden and spoke to the US Congress. With the US in search of stronger alliances with non-Chinese rising powers, Modi has been courted by US officials including President Biden, but has not condemned the Russian invasion of Ukraine since it has enabled India to buy Russian oil more cheaply. While moving to silence some of his domestic critics, and allowing Indian Muslims to suffer, Modi has made every effort to realize the Indian dream of becoming a power among the powerful. Increasingly present on international stages, he hosted the meeting of the G20 in New Delhi in 2023, and brokered its non-condemnatory language on the Russian invasion of Ukraine.

Modi's visit in June 2023 connected with an organizing and fundraising effort by the Hindu right in the US: the VHP (Vishwa Hindu Parishad, or World Hindu Council), first registered in this country in 1970. Arvind Rajagopal has profiled its work:

Its growth during the 1990s has been rapid. Over half their work is in Bal Vihars or Children's Education Programs and in youth camps. The VHP also publishes literature on the 'Hindu way of life', arranges seminars and lecture tours for visiting spiritual figures, provides family counseling 'with a Hindu outlook on life', and operates social service projects... [T]he VHP promotes a

---

65 'Howdy, Modi', *New York Times* report, 23 September 2019.

network of contacts and affiliations with other Indian religious and social organizations in the US, and often their own members may occupy prominent positions in these other organizations.[66]

Through his research and by participating in one of the summer camps, Rajagopal noted that the VHP modified their Indian approach to such activities for the US context, changing their message to adjust to American cultural pluralism. The BJP and VHP in America have also been engaged in fundraising for their work in India. The reciprocity between these organizations in India and in America have benefited their expansion on both continents.[67] Beyond their goals of cultural education and fundraising, they have worked to shape world history textbooks in the US to present their views of Hinduism and Indian history.

Reciprocating Trump's Houston event, Modi invited Trump to India in February 2020. Now we had 'Namaste Trump', with the American President proclaiming his love of India in a huge rally in Ahmedabad.[68] Whatever personal chemistry there was between the two, they shared their antipathy to Muslims, whom they often characterized as terrorists, their attraction to authoritarian rule, their love of huge spectator events and their celebration of the significant economic advances achieved by their administrations. Although Modi pulled out all stops for Trump, the latter was burned in effigy in Kolkata, and riots against the BJP's new citizenship policies flared in New Delhi during his few days in India.

---

[66] Rajagopal 2001, pp. 239–40.

[67] Ibid., p. 239ff; Kamat, Sangeeta and Biju Mathew. 2003. 'Mapping Political Violence in a Globalized World: The Case of Hindu Nationalism,' *Social Justice*. Vol. 30, No. 3, pp. 4-16, 4ff.

[68] *New York Times* reports, 22, 23, 24, February 2020

2

Two Cold War Stories
Daniel Thorner and Kumar Goshal

As a casualty of the Cold War and the McCarthyite persecutions of the early 1950s, the American economic historian Daniel Thorner (1915–1974) lost his teaching position at the University of Pennsylvania, and with his wife and three young children, moved to India and stayed for eight years. Having written his PhD on the beginning of Indian railroads under the Raj, he was equipped to deal with contemporary economic matters in India, and soon became an integral member of the Indian intelligentsia with special expertise on the history of agriculture, land reform and tenancy. In 1960, he was invited to the Sorbonne in Paris, where he remained, with his family, for the rest of his life. He and his wife, the noted scholar Alice Thorner, visited India frequently. In 1971, they were in Dhaka when the Pakistani army cracked down on the Awami League and helped Bengali economists escape the brutal murders of the cultural elite of East Pakistan. Daniel Thorner and Alice were among the non-official Americans who made important contributions to India in the decades just after its birth as a new nation.

Just before his death in 1974, Thorner wrote an overview of Indian development in the quarter century after Independence. He noted significant industrial development:

> The score of years since India became independent in 1947 have witnessed a veritable industrial revolution. India has equipped herself with the basic facilities required for practically every branch

of modern manufacture. An impressive corps of Indian engineers, scientists, and technicians has been brought into being... Advanced techniques have also been introduced in a segment of Indian agriculture. In sharp contrast to the relative stagnation in the decades before independence, foodgrains output since 1947 has nearly doubled.

India's decision to industrialize was embodied in the series of Five Year Plans... Steel mills, machine-building works, newsprint, pharmaceutical, heavy electrical, and other factories owned and operated by government corporations accounted for about half of industrial investment during the first three Plans. The other half of the new industrial plant is in the hands of private enterprises: domestic, foreign, or a combination of the two... [T]he fact that several of the large public enterprises have a poor performance records leaves the Government vulnerable to criticism.[1]

While he was positive about most of the above, he was critical of the considerable foreign debt incurred, and even more unhappy about the course of land reform, noting that 'the former landlords did what they could to evade the new laws... [and] the large public expenditure on rural improvement served to put money into the pockets of a minority of landholders and cultivators in each village'.[2] Writing just as the Green Revolution was underway he saw that certain areas in specified districts were given considerable aid allowing them to double their output. This unequal development contradicted the hope of Nehru and many Congressmen that the path forward would be 'egalitarian, cooperative and socialist'.[3] He worried about the poor, tens of millions left behind, as a minority thrust ahead.

While Daniel Thorner moved from the US to India, Kumar Goshal had come to the US in 1920. In 1947, while visiting India, Kumar Goshal received a letter from Cedric Belfrage about contributing lively pieces about India for the *opening issues of the*

---

[1] Thorner, Daniel. 1980. *The Shaping of Modern India*. Delhi: Allied, p. 136.
[2] Ibid., pp. 245, 247.
[3] Ibid., p. 247.

National Guardian. In his first article for the *Guardian*, 'India: The Pot Boils Over', published on 20 December 1948, Kumar noted that India's basic economic problems remained unsolved and that popular discontent was rising in West Bengal and the Telangana region. He was harsh in his criticism of officials who did not face up to the real problems necessitating fundamental change in Indian society.

In 1949, on his return to the US, Kumar was blacklisted, as were many people in the arts, education and public life, during the McCarthy era. Almost overnight, Kumar could no longer get lecture bookings, and found it difficult to pay rent. His wife Judy Goshal became the main breadwinner often typing for law firms that needed work done overnight. Kumar searched for other work and contributed articles to the *Guardian*. He was listed as a contributor from the *Guardian*'s inception in 1948 until November 1952, when he became a regular staff member, serving as an expert on the new nations of Asia and Africa. He remained on the staff through 1963, writing almost weekly and contributing hundreds of articles. Belfrage said of Kumar:

> Kumar was a good journalist and a conscientious person... In my day as editor he was one of our best people, and with his experience and knowledge did much to make the then un-christened 'Third World' come alive for us. Also he had more understanding than most of the others of the appalling financial problems of the paper and made solid contributions to fund-raising as a speaker.

> —Cedric Belfrage, letter to this writer, 2 August 1985.

In addition to his writing, Kumar often made coast-to-coast lecture tours to speak on foreign affairs for the benefit of the *Guardian*. Using his earlier career in the theatre to good advantage, he became their most popular speaker and expert fundraiser. Although not a trained scholar or experienced journalist, he could present vital issues of foreign affairs vividly. One theme he addressed was the extension of American power abroad, followed by private investment, as the

US replaced the European imperialist powers in Africa, the Middle East and Asia. He also believed, perhaps foolishly in hindsight, that the socialist societies were outpacing capitalist societies and minimized, at least through 1962, any internal problems within socialist countries and any conflict between them. At the same time, he identified the internal struggles within capitalist societies and within such Third World nations as India and Nigeria and pointed to capitalist rivalries. Consequently, he ended up with an idealized picture of the socialist world and a realistic one of the capitalist world. (Goshal articles in the *Guardian*, 1952–1963)

In the summer of 1961, Kumar made a three-month trip to Africa and India, visiting Guinea, Ghana, Nigeria, Tanganyika, India, Israel and eight other nations. Although he had had contact with the African scene through the Council on African Affairs, this journey gave him first-hand knowledge necessary for a writer and speaker on contemporary international affairs. During these years, he also wrote many articles about South Africa that he saw as an imperialist bastion that was tottering even in 1961 and would eventually fall to African majority rule. On his way back from India in 1961, Kumar stopped to visit Israel, a country he had admired greatly in certain aspects from afar. Although he made some good friends, especially among the communists in Israel, and described the 'incredible achievements of the Israelis', he saw the many problems there as well. In a deeply moving article, he reported on a long interview with an Israeli Arab leader who told of the increasing bitterness of the Arab minority and the necessity for Israel to confront the dilemma of its Arab population. In 1950, he began writing about Vietnam, viewing Ho Chi Minh (1890–1969, President of North Vietnam 1945–1969) and the Democratic Republic of Vietnam as the 'right' side and the French and subsequent American-backed regime in the south as the 'wrong' side, predicting that the escalation of American troops in that conflict was bound to fail. As for the land of his birth, he praised India's international role as peacemaker between the two polarized camps and championed her advocacy of positive neutrality. But he was critical of India's internal development since

Independence, believing that reactionary forces blocked Nehru from realizing his goals.[4]

Kumar was proud of India's effort to bring China into the UN community of nations, but he was troubled by the developing border crisis between India and China. His view conflicted with the analysis of several other *Guardian* writers, who placed the blame for the conflict on India. Kumar responded in time, on 17 January 1963, in the article 'Political Aspects of the India–China Dispute', which placed the India–China dispute in wider contexts including its connection to the Sino–Soviet split. Kumar wrote, 'The Chinese were bent on destroying the underpinnings of Soviet influence in India... but Soviet–Indian friendship persists. If China expected their pressure to result in the fall of the Nehru government, it was mistaken... India today is more united than it has been since the period of Gandhi's peak popularity.' A few weeks later, Kumar wrote an article on the ramifications of the dispute, 'India–China Dispute a Test for Neutral Nations'. This article was more even-handed than his earlier one blaming China, but it was clear that the whole conflict disturbed him.[5]

He had become unhappy at the *Guardian* and its editor was unhappy with him. After an exchange of charges, Kumar was fired in May 1963, ending his fifteen-year involvement with the *Guardian*. Kumar's last years were difficult, as he was in ill-health and remote from the vital life of New York in which he had so long been involved. From 1963–1966, Kumar wrote articles and reviews—none about India though—for the *New World Review*. He also completed a short book with Victor Perlo, *Bitter End in S.E. Asia* (1964), one of the early critical views of America in Indochina. Kumar's last piece, 'Books as Anti-War Weapons', a review of books on the Vietnam War, appeared in the *New World Review* in October 1966. Kumar lamented that the American public was still apathetic about the war and hoped that these books and pamphlets 'will give more people the

---

[4] *Guardian*, July 25, August 1, 15, 22, September 12, November 7, 21, December 5, 19, 1960; February 6, March 13, May 1, May 22 to October 30, 1961.
[5] *Guardian*, January 17 and February 28, 1963.

courage to protest'. He died in 1971, having spent his adulthood in the US but still linked to his Indian origins, hopeful of a progressive future for both nations.

Like others on the left in the US, Kumar had been caught up in the maelstrom of the second great Red Scare, when anti-communism was whipped up to fever pitch, its heat searing many. The anti-communist fervour led to international involvements in Latin America, Iran, but especially in Indochina—which, by its bitter end, brought death and suffering to millions.

3

A Personal Interlude
In Search of an Indian Visa

In the spring of 1971 while assistant professor of history at Columbia University, I was awarded a senior Fulbright grant to do research in India on the history of twentieth-century Bengal. Having done research in India from 1963 to the spring of 1965, and having completed my PhD, I was looking forward to the publication of a revised version of my thesis, and I was confident of a productive time in India. Appropriately, I took a year's leave from my academic position and prepared for my work abroad. What I needed first was a research visa from the Government of India. Every time I checked on the status of my application, I was told, 'It is pending.'

Although I knew that I could not enter India without such a visa, nor get my funds and a ticket to India from the Fulbright programme, nevertheless, I left for Great Britain to start the part of my research that I would do there. I anticipated no long-term serious problem. Settling in London, a favourite city, was no problem, and though I had a small summer grant from my university, I became anxious as weeks and then months passed and no visa was forthcoming. I contacted every conceivable person I thought could help: the Indian Ambassador in Washington; my Columbia colleague and the former undersecretary general of the UN, Arthur Lall; the senator from the state where I had been awarded my PhD, Edward Kennedy of Massachusetts; and the Indian High Commissioner in London, as well as friends in India. Nothing, nothing, nothing. The appeals seemed to do no good. I could not understand whether I was at fault or whether Americans were being blamed and penalized for actions of their government on the India-Pakistan-Bangladesh crisis, or whether there was some other cause. The not-knowing made me more unsettled and apprehensive. With my money running out near the end of the year, I was told at the Indian High Commission that I had been refused a visa. A foreign government need give no reason for such a refusal. You are out.

It was a bad time for Indo–American relations: the crisis between the two wings of Pakistan had precipitated repression, large-scale violence, the movement of millions of refugees to India and then the invasion of East Pakistan by the Indian army. The United States government of Richard Nixon, for reasons of realpolitik, had sided with the Pakistani military regime. The American Seventh Fleet had sailed into the Bay of Bengal as a warning to India. Americans were no longer very welcome in India. Did the general political situation have anything to do with my refusal? Since other American scholars did get visa clearance, I doubted that this had anything to do with the matter. Did my concentration on Bengal, divided between West Bengal (part of India) and East Bengal (part of Pakistan), and now in the midst of a conflict between the two wings of Pakistan, with India involved as well, cause concern? I didn't know.

On the advice of a friend, Professor Wayne Wilcox of Columbia University, serving as Cultural Officer of the US Embassy, London, I decided to go to Bangladesh via India. He helped me to get a new passport without the Indian stamp, 'visa applied for' in it. He said: try to work on at least part of Bengal while you have your leave from Columbia. I purchased a ticket to Dhaka that necessitated a brief stop in India. When I landed in New Delhi, I saw that there were eight hours before my connecting flight to Dhaka. I asked whether I could visit friends in the city. Opening my new passport, the immigration official stamped, 'Good for three weeks in India'. I changed my reservation to three weeks hence and decided to try to find out about my visa denial.

I contacted my best-informed Indian friend, the journalist, Nikhil Chakravartty. He investigated and learned that unless a cabinet minister intervened, I would never do research in India again. But he could not find out the reason. He contacted Professor Hiren Mukherjee, Communist Party of India (CPI) MP from Calcutta, a mutual friend and leader of the Opposition in the Indian Parliament. Professor Mukherjee made an anti-American speech on Public Law 480 expenditures and then crossed the floor and asked Mr K.C. Pant, Minister of State for Home Affairs, to reconsider the matter. Mr Pant agreed to reopen the case and summoned me to the Home Ministry. A burly, friendly man, son of one of the Gandhian leaders of India's freedom struggle, he said, 'While we are reconsidering the matter, you may stay in India.'

Nikhil urged that I get a group of my Bengali friends to write a joint letter to Mrs Gandhi, prime minister and also home minister, appealing for my visa. So I went to Calcutta. Once there, I contacted Professor Sushoban Sarkar, a senior and respected teacher of history at Presidency College, to write the letter. I had met him through his pupil, later a well-known writer and teacher, Ranajit Guha. Sarkar had guided me through some of the shoals of Bengali historical waters as I moved ahead with my research. He said, all too modestly, 'How can I write to the prime minister?' In Calcutta, I sat down with him, and we composed a brief letter extolling the virtues of my research and praising my character.

Shameless, but then a crisis is a crisis. Then I went from friend to friend asking them to sign this letter. I recruited Dr Sisir Bose, Director of the Netaji Research Bureau and a leading paediatrician; poet and critic Bishnu Dey; and my close friends, Professor P. Lal, director of the Writers' Workshop, and Jyoti Datta, a poet and journalist. I did not know Abu Sayeed Ayyub, literary critic and former editor of *Quest*, as well as I knew the others, but he agreed to sign.

Finally, I went to film director Satyajit Ray. He was happy to sign and had some suggestions. First, he said, 'Put my name on the outside of the envelope. Mrs Gandhi does not like me, but she must open a letter from me.' Sarker, Ray and Dey were either communists in the

CPI or fellow-travellers, the others opposed the communists, then strong in West Bengal. Ray said that I should get a recommendation from his cousin, the Chief Minister of West Bengal, Siddhartha Shankar Ray, a Congressman close to Mrs Indira Gandhi. I had trouble getting an appointment. Satyajit Ray got on the telephone and arranged it himself. I had a brief *darshan* with the chief minister and he said, 'We like you in West Bengal and I will send Mrs Gandhi a message.'

I had met most of these friends through my teacher, Edward Dimock, and then through a new friend, David McCutchion, who taught comparative literature at Jadavpur University. He took me to meet Professor P. Lal, founder and impresario of the Writers' Workshop, a kind of collective for Indians writing in English, which they all considered to have become an Indian language. Lal was an intelligent, shrewd, talented writer and publishing entrepreneur, had brought together like-minded writers starting the late 1950s and published their works in beautifully bound and edited volumes from his own home.

David also brought me to meet Bishnu Dey, considered Bengal's foremost poet and an excellent translator of English poetry into Bengali. Dey was a striking looking man with high cheekbones, a triangular face with penetrating eyes. He encouraged me in my research and introduced me to his close friend, Professor Hiren Mukherjee.

Through Dimock, I had met Jyoti Datta during my first week in Calcutta. Jyoti was a short, wiry man with a sharp intellect who wrote movie reviews for the leading English-language daily, *The Statesman*, and poetry in Bengali. He, in turn, introduced me to his friend, Abu Sayyid Ayyub, an editor of *Quest* and a literary critic.

My doctoral research had led me to Dr Sisir Bose. Netaji was Subhas Chandra Bose, his uncle and the most popular Bengali political leader of the Independence struggle. I introduced myself and Dr Bose was ever helpful, and I became friendly with his whole family, his wife Krishna and children Sugata, Sarmila and Sumantra. Dr Bose, in turn, asked my help with the editing of the collected works of his uncle and this led to a long, mutually beneficial relationship.

While the matter was pending, I made a trip to Bangladesh, but had trouble returning to India. I was able to arrange an interview with Subimal Dutt, ICS, the Indian High Commissioner there, and we had a long, friendly talk about the Bengal cadre in the ICS, many of whom I had interviewed while marooned in Great Britain. He personally signed for my visa so I could return to India.

Upon returning to Calcutta, I heard that someone had been spreading a rumour that I had stolen documents and that was the root of my visa problem. I went to the head of the intelligence branch of the police in Calcutta, Bikash Kali Basu, and said I had learned of this rumour. 'If I have stolen documents, please arrest me.' He replied, 'No, no, we have no problem with you here. Your problem is in Delhi. Please return to Delhi.'

I headed for New Delhi. Before long I was summoned to an interview with Mr Govind Narain, ICS, Home Secretary of the Government of India, the highest official in charge of internal security. I, an assistant professor of history at Columbia University, was being scrutinized by him and a large file—it looked to be a foot tall—sat on his desk. How likely would it be for the attorney general of the US to give a hearing to a junior Indian academic who had been refused a visa for the US? Mr Narain, along with Subimal Dutt, was among the few surviving ICS cadre, senior civil servants, from the British Raj period, as opposed to those recruited to the Government of India after 1947. Most of these ICS men still in government were elderly and highly respected and in vital positions.

The Home Secretary, a friendly but direct, elderly man with thin greying hair, asked, 'How do you know Satyajit Ray?' I explained that I had met him through a mutual friend, an Englishman, who did the English subtitles for his films. After the Englishman suddenly died, we became closer friends, mourning the death of a beloved man. How did I know these other leaders of the cultural elite of Calcutta? The Home Department had made a brief report on each person who had signed the letter to the prime minister.

I recalled the circumstances in which I had met all of these eminent persons and satisfied the Home Secretary that I knew all the signatories. There were also letters from Hiren Mukherjee and my teacher Michael Brecher in the file. And a letter of recommendation for a Columbia University student. Why had I written a letter for someone who wanted to study birth control? Did I not know that this would not sit well with the Government of India? No, I did not. And I knew that Siddhartha Shankar Ray had written a positive note on my behalf at the urging of his more famous cousin.

Then to the heart of the matter: he said to me, I have a report made in the National Archives of India. I will read it out and you may answer. 'Mr. Gordon is making copies of files in the National Archives to send to centers of international affairs at Harvard and M.I.T.' I had been a graduate student at Harvard while doing my research so there was a connection to Harvard and Cambridge, Massachusetts. But I had had no connection to any centre of international affairs, CIAs, for short. I persuaded him. He said he would check further, but he would recommend my research visa. We shook hands on it.

I waited expectantly. After his recommendation, the matter was sent one rung up the ladder to Mr K.C. Pant and then to the top: Mrs Gandhi, the prime minister. It sat in her office or on her desk for several months. Finally, I went to see another Bengali friend, Mr Surendra Mohan Ghosh, a revolutionary in pre-Independence days from Mymensingh, an important informant for my history of Bengal politics, and lately, the leader of the Congress party in the Rajya Sabha. I said, 'Mr Ghosh, I have waited and waited and have spent all my money.' I asked if he could help. Sympathetic and greatly irritated at the delay, he called Mrs Gandhi.

I had a research visa the next day. But later on, a joint secretary in the Home Ministry, whose decision had been overridden, succeeded in blocking me from getting any of the funds from my Fulbright grant. He had sent the Fulbright office a message: 'This is to inform you that Dr. Gordon's research must be paid for in dollars.' The Fulbright programme was using counterpart rupee or Public Law 480 funds and had no dollars. I went to the head of the Fulbright program, an American, who was having trouble renewing his visa. He said, 'I am more interested in getting my visa renewed than in helping you.' I never got the Fulbright grant nor the accompanying ticket. Fortunately, I did persevere and was able to get some funds from Columbia University, the American Philosophical Society and the American Council of Learned Societies. This scant funding enabled me to spend six months in India doing my research. I worked in Delhi and I worked in Calcutta. I did the best I could.

I later learned that the matter had come to Mrs Gandhi's attention. She said to the American Ambassador, Kenneth Keating, that she was annoyed with a person named Gordon who had organized all the Bengalis in India on his behalf. Professor Ainslie Embree, serving as Cultural Officer of the US Embassy, reported this to me. He knew of the notorious fractiousness of Bengali political life. Upon hearing of Mrs Gandhi's remark, he said to Keating, 'Mrs. Gandhi should hire Gordon. Who else can organize all the Bengalis in India?' I told Embree, my senior colleague at Columbia University, that the campaign had been orchestrated by Nikhil Chakravarty who understood how the system worked. I did have friends, but Nikhil knew how to get things done.

Another report had it that Mrs Indira Gandhi said to someone, 'If the communists want him (i.e., me), they can have him.' This was interpreted to mean that if the CPI wanted me to have a visa (Bishnu Dey, Professor Hiren Mukherjee, Satyajit Ray, Sushoban Sarkar), it was not worth the trouble to let this matter fester. I certainly had friends in the CPI, but I had carefully chosen the signatories and included four people who were decidedly unfriendly to the communists. Nikhil specified 'friends who can vouch for you', and had not suggested that political affiliation had anything to do with it. But it is also true that Professor Hiren Mukherjee had opened the door for my quest.

I was told, however, that I had to be based in New Delhi, not Calcutta, and that I had to focus on Indian nationalism and not study Bengali or any matters specific to Bengal. It was a difficult time, the time of the Naxalites and the crisis between East and West Pakistan, and it would not do to have a troublesome foreigner in a troubled part of India. Since I had to spend a lot of unexpected time in New Delhi, I joined the American Club, for which I was eligible because I was, nominally at least, the holder of a US government grant. I ate in the American restaurant: all food except the buffalo steaks guaranteed to be flown in from the US. I swam in the American pool, attended American movies in the embassy building. India was, I was told, a 'hardship posting', and all these officials had an extra 30 per cent or so added to their salaries for suffering through their Indian days.

Since I had always loved playing softball, I joined a team to play in the league that held its games in a large baseball stadium built behind the American Embassy. There was a press box, a large scoreboard, hot dogs and American beer, direct from home. I had been directed to the communications director of the embassy who was the coach of the Union Carbide team and was allowed to join. I was amazed at how softball was the centre of the community life of the Americans official in New Delhi. There was a women's league and a children's league, as well as the one I played in. The wife of our slugging third baseman told me: 'It's very dull in India when it's not the softball season.' I played a little, but was annoyed at not being used more and eventually quit the team which went on to win the league championship.

While living in New Delhi, I contacted old friends. One of these, an American anthropologist married to a Sikh, was teaching American history at the American International School. There was, she told me, no work on India in the curriculum. Would I give a lecture on Indian history? I did. But parents and children back then were determined to have the same courses as a school, say, in Kansas or Oregon. No strange courses about, or exploratory excursions into, India. That was then. A few years later, the talented Sharon Lowen, an American expatriate who has become accepted as an Indian classical dancer, ran the arts programme and organized Indian field trips.

It was 1972, and it was also the time just after the Bangladesh crisis and the division of Pakistan. As I shopped in Connaught

Place, I was frequently assailed by Indians—suspecting that I was an American—as retribution for Nixon's sins. The tilt towards Pakistan with the Seventh Fleet sailing into the Bay of Bengal was a crime for which all Americans were responsible. How could they know that, raised by leftist parents, I had been taught to hate Nixon since I was ten. I did not realize that those years were the end of a certain era—that of a big AID (American government aid programme) and the Ford Foundation's dominating presence among NGOs in India. Those days were also the opening of another era: a much larger emigration from India to the US.

What is there to learn from these personal anecdotes of the 1970s? Americans, many up to the present, are quite insular: we don't learn much about foreign cultures, nor study their languages except in small numbers. It is no surprise that we were short of Arabic translators in Iraq. Next, Americans abroad are suspect, sometimes with good reason, because the government has used ordinary Americans abroad as sources of information. The CIA connection to the Congress for Cultural Freedom—revealed just a few years before my hearing—was just one of these secret and damaging ties. My friend Abu Said Ayyub was the editor of its magazine in India, *Quest*, but said he never knew of this support.

I also learned the power of friendship: Indians came to my rescue when Americans could not or would not. Friendship can cross all boundaries. I learned that the Indian elite is relatively small for such a populous country. And that it helped to have friends in this elite. But what of Americans unjustly accused and without Indian friends? Might such people—and also American graduate students—think twice about investing in an Indian specialization? Might the Government of India have been cutting off careers for potential experts who might also be friends of India in a variety of ways? And, of course, without more Americans learning about India, the insularity would continue. I understood a little of the asymmetry between a Westerner in trouble in India and what might happen to an Indian in trouble in the US.

But these experiences also led me to ask: what is America doing abroad? Why are we, I have to say 'we', so timid and insular as well as so arrogant? What had been the impact of American institution building and efforts in India over the years? What relation did Americans have to the British Raj? And what about all the asymmetries? I knew there were only a modest number of Indians resident in the US in those days. What role, if any, had Indians had in America's development? What were the roots of the American–Indian connections and how had they worked out over time? This was the start of my interest in exploring the themes discussed in this book.

The first version, not very different, of this story, was written about forty years ago, although it remains vivid in my mind. For the following decades, until the early 1990s, I remained on a 'grey list'. Every time I wanted to go to India, to do research or give a lecture, my visa application had to be forwarded from the Indian Consulate in New York City to the home ministry in New Delhi for clearance. There were often long delays that caused havoc. The visa might be given the day I was supposed to leave or was delayed even longer. Finally, I asked Nikhil Chakravartty if he could have my name removed from the grey list. He succeeded. Since then, I have had a ten-year, multiple-entry visa and no further problems. I have visited India many times over the years and have maintained many of the warm ties with Indian friends. By now most of those who helped me in 1972 are no more. I have lamented the passing of each of them.

For many years since the Bhopal tragedy of 1984 (when the Union Carbide fertilizer plant there exploded) I was embarrassed by my connection to a rapacious multinational corporation and I had hidden away my made-to-measure uniform. Recently, I have taken it out as an artefact of the early 1970s in India. As a critical American, I thought we had to face up to our actions. So the Union Carbide story as well as much more positive American connections, like that of the Ford Foundation, are presented and analysed in what follows.

4

Business, Trade, Aid and Development

The government of Pakistan, with fewer trained civil servants, administrators and economists than India, reached out to America in the early 1950s. An important fruit of this quest for aid was the Harvard Advisory Group (HAG) that was formed to help assist Pakistan on economic plans. It began work with a Ford Foundation grant in the early 1950s and flourished through the mid-1960s. The Harvard advisers formulated economic plans, collected better data and prepared budgets,[1] while they pressed Pakistani leaders to focus some attention on economic development. Initially frustrated by political instability, that effort advanced in 1958 with General Ayub's successful coup and the general decided that economic development was crucial for Pakistan. Agriculture production expanded under his tenure.

The Englishman Adam Curle (1916–2006), a member of the Harvard group who lived in Pakistan from 1956–1959, was sent out again in 1963 and 1964 as an adviser to the Planning Board on education. In a report on his experience, he recounted the dismal state of the schools at the lower levels and the appallingly low pay and preparation of the teachers.[2] Education under the Raj and in early free Pakistan, he noted, was not linked to development and the expenditures on it were infinitesimal. The political instability in

---

[1] Rosen, George. 1985. *Western Economists and Eastern Societies*. Agents of Change in South Asia, 1950-1970. Baltimore: Johns Hopkins U. Press, p. 158ff.
[2] Curle, Adam. 1966. *Planning for Education in Pakistan*. Cambridge, MA: Harvard U. Press, p. 45ff.

Pakistan during the 1950s caused further harm. Offering a small sliver of hope, he foresaw at least the possibility that under the Basic Democracies system instituted by President (earlier General) Ayub, there was a path for more local involvement in development, including in education.

Curle noted that Pakistan development plans contained wholly unrealistic goals for moving swiftly towards universal literacy—and indeed, almost half a century later, those goals still have not been reached. Curle also spoke of the dilemmas faced by foreign advisers who could only provide limited help. A foreigner might offer modest guidance, but the energy needed for implementation must come from the locals.[3] What an adviser needed, Curle insisted, was a local collaborator, as he discovered himself when, in 1964, in what Curle called 'an intensely satisfying collaboration',[4] he worked closely with Namdar Khan in drawing up the education section of Pakistan's Third Plan. It was up to the Namdar Khans and their fellows to whom they would pass the baton to lead Pakistan's development hopes. In addition to the Harvard advisors, the Ford Foundation, in part, funded the Pakistan Institute of Development Studies. By the late 1960s, it finally had a Pakistani director, Nurul Islam, from East Pakistan, and was publishing a first-class journal of research findings.[5]

During its early years of virtual stagnancy, the Pakistani economy was beset with political turmoil and lack of a firm hand at the top. Although from 1958, General Ayub supplied this stronger hand, he also presided over government support for industrial development that favoured urban entrepreneurs at the expense of peasant farmers. Although the focus shifted slightly to agriculture in the 1960s, still there was, as Swadesh Bose observed,

...[A]n increasing concentration of income and wealth in the hands of relatively few who owned and controlled many industrial

---

[3] Ibid., pp. 1–17, 141, 165, 173, 185, 191–92.
[4] Ibid., p. 173.
[5] Rosen 1985, pp. 181–82.

and financial enterprises. In 1969 it was claimed, in a much-publicized statement, that about twenty families controlled 66 per cent of Pakistan's industrial assets, 70 per cent of insurance funds and 80 per cent of bank assets... 'The 'trickle down' effects in the urban areas are very slight.'[6]

With the advent of Independence, the Indian economy was moving ahead on several fronts. Consequently, most of the old British managing agency groups in India closed, no longer adequately equipped to compete in a very different economic environment. A student of empire and its aftermath, Michael Kidron, has analysed their rapid closure as the Indian business community came to the fore. Kidron writes:

> [W]ith independence the balance of advantage for the Indian investor swung decisively towards 'national' capital: it was the leaders of the Indian business community who now possessed detailed knowledge of government intentions... [P]urely Indian business enjoyed a freedom from scrutiny and criticism in politically sensitive areas such as tax avoidance and evasion, relations with licensing and enforcement authorities...[7]

For several decades, Independent India would have a 'mixed economy', consisting of a public sector of important industries, including iron and steel, aviation and atomic energy, alongside private capitalist enterprise. The practitioners of private capitalism often claimed they were hamstrung by a 'license Raj' compelling them to obtain a government license or approval for many of their moves. Although the Nehru era of the 1950s to mid-1960s, as Arvind Panagariya has argued persuasively, was relatively liberal, over nearly the next two decades, there were increasing restrictions on

---

[6] Kumar, Dharma, ed. 1982. *The Cambridge Economic History of India*. Vol. 2: c. 1757–1970. Cambridge: Cambridge U. Press, V.2, p. 1025.
[7] Kidron, Michael. 1965. *Foreign Investments in India*. London: Oxford U. Press, p. 43.

imports, foreign exchange and investment, as well as rising licensing demands. This was the Indira Gandhi era, during which there were two wars with Pakistan, the oil crisis of 1973, the Emergency and the nationalization of most banks.[8]

Although the government of Independent India reserved new developments in certain industries for public ownership, the private sector of the mixed economy still managed to grow, if not thrive. Already in the 1930s and 1940s, British capital had started to withdraw, and the large Indian firms, particularly the Tatas and the Birlas, were on the move.[9]

Tata and Sons, the largest private conglomerate of companies, was expanding and changing. In 1951 it had sixty-eight public companies ranged over twenty industries.[10] In 1938, succeeding his cousin, J.R.D. Tata was elected chairman of Tata Sons, at age thirty-four the youngest ever to succeed to this position, and served for five decades in this demanding role. A French citizen until 1929 (his mother was a Frenchwoman), Tata returned to India after being educated in France, England and India, and having served in the French armed forces.

After Independence, Tata Steel (formerly TISCO) expanded its steel-making capacity and resisted nationalization. In order to expand, Tata Steel obtained the necessary influx of capital through a loan from the World Bank, with which Tatas had a productive relationship for decades to come.[11] Enjoying good relations with the Government of India, Tata Steel managed to avoid nationalization; even its work force, enjoying benefits that they wanted to preserve, joining in the resistance to a government takeover. At the same time, other Indian steel mills were developed in the public sector. A major disagreement between India and the US took place over possible

---

[8] Panagariya 2008, p. 22ff.

[9] Kidron 1965, pp. 22–23.

[10] Ibid., p. 23.

[11] Kust, Matthew J. 1964. *Foreign Enterprise in India*. Laws and Policies. Chapel Hill: U. of North Carolina Press, p. 66; Boquérat, Gilles. 2003. *No Strings Attached?* India's Policies and Foreign Aid 1947-1966. New Delhi: Manohar, p. 187.

American aid for the Bokaro steel mill, a public sector project. In the end, the US awkwardly backed out of its promised support, and the Soviet Union, seeing a tempting opening, stepped in and gave the needed support. The Birlas tried to set up a steel mill in Durgapur, but were eventually stopped by the government.

In 1945, Tata moved to build locomotives and TELCO (Tata Engineering and Locomotive Company) was established, the first element of a giant enterprise. From locomotives and railway wagons, they moved into the production of trucks, and Tata Motors, as it was renamed, became the largest producer of trucks in India. Collaboration with an American firm was not available, so an agreement was made with the German company Daimler-Benz which lasted through the 1960s. Expanding remarkably from headquarters at Jamshedpur, to Pune, to Lucknow, TELCO became the producer of 70 per cent of the medium and heavy commercial vehicles plying the roads of India.[12]

Some other Tata enterprises that had been started earlier continued to thrive. Tata Chemicals thrived as its production of soda ash and other items of industrial and consumer value expanded, becoming in time a highly successful integrated inorganic chemical complex, the largest of its kind in India.[13] Tata Electric, providing hydroelectric power to the large state of Maharashtra, grew as the need for its products expanded.

Along with their industrial concerns, Tata has also provided training facilities, including the Tata Management Training Centre at Pune and the Tata Steel Technical Training School in Jamshedpur. More than almost any other industrial group, Tata provided medical care facilities for its workers throughout its numerous industrial and agricultural plants in India. In addition to medical provision for its own workers, Tata Trust funds were utilized to help establish the Tata Memorial Hospital, the Tata Institute of Fundamental Research and the Tata Institute of Social Sciences.[14] Although Tata

---

[12] Lala 2004a, p. 91ff.
[13] Lala, Wealth, p. 90.
[14] Lala 2004a, p. 62.

has been involved in a number of industrial disputes and has acted opportunistically upon occasion, it is credited for providing good benefits to its workers and helping to build research and medical facilities of inestimable value to India.

A pilot himself, J.R.D. Tata, together with a friend, the aviator, Nevill Vintcent (1902–1942), founded Tata Airlines in 1932, and just before the Second World War, he initiated Tata's entry into the delivery of mail by air. In 1948, after the war, Tata formed Air-India to be an international airline, but it had hardly gotten off the ground when the government moved to nationalize airlines. Acrimonious meetings followed, disputing whether there should be one corporation for international service and one for domestic. Air-India, the international service, became a government corporation from 1953, but asked J.R.D. Tata to stay on as its chairman. He did, once it was agreed that the international and domestic services would be separated. He became a director of Indian Airlines, the domestic service. Though Tata was shut out of private enterprise in aviation, he was confident that on his watch, Air-India met high international standards.[15] In 2021, with Air India in dire straits, Tata purchased the airline from the Government of India, outbidding other interested parties. Certain restrictions were imposed on a possible later transfer. Tata leaders must have smiled at how the flight to nationalization had turned around, landed and took a return flight to Tata Sons.[16]

A new entry into the post-war world was the computer, spurring efforts to speed up data collection, organization and analysis. Tata and Sons set up a new unit to do such work for all its companies, but many were resistant and did not want outsiders to infringe on their work. Those in the new unit persevered, rented out time on IBM mainframe computers, and in the 1960s and early 1970s sought contracts wherever they could. When IBM exited from India in the early 1970s, an agreement was made with Burroughs, another American mainframe manufacturer, enabling the unit now named

---

[15] Lala 2003, p. 132ff.
[16] Television report on NDTV, 8 October 2021.

Tata Consulting Services (TCS) to get contracts and send personnel abroad for training as well as jobs.[17]

The close links developing between India and the US in the computing field are apparent in a cursory account of the career of Subramaniam Ramadorai (1945–), who aside from his role as a valued government adviser, would become CEO and managing director of TCS from 1996–2009 and vice-chairman of TCS until 2014. After his education in India, he studied and worked in the US from 1969 to 1972, when he returned to India and joined TCS at its inceptions. He then went back to the US for advanced studies in 1979 and 1993.[18] This back-and-forth may have been slightly unusual, but after Independence, the flow of Indian students, from a trickle, became a steadily growing stream. What was perhaps also unusual for Ramadorai was that he left a well-paid job in the US for a much lower beginning one with a start-up firm—albeit a Tata one—in India. He joined a highly educated, talented and energetic team at TCS and worked there for forty-two years, rising to become CEO of an Indian company with a worldwide reach, one of the world's powerhouse business consulting firms.

Although somewhat tethered by the license Raj, the Tata conglomerate of companies, now more than 100, continued to expand and innovate from the 1970s to the present. As noted above, they even regained ownership of Air India, which they began as Indian Airlines in the 1930s. It was nationalized in the 1950s, did well, then poorly, and the Government of India decided to sell it off in 2021. Tata won the bidding war. Their development is in line with significant growth by several Indian conglomerates in this era. Since Tata companies are so many, so diverse and global, its development over the past half-century is complex. First, the Tata Group had to deal with the abolition of the managing agency system. Thereafter, each Tata company had 'to become an independent entity with its own board of directors. The writ of Tata Sons was no longer implementable on them; its role was limited to advice and

---

[17] Ramadorai, S. 2013. *The TCS Story and Beyond*. Gurgaon: Penguin, p. 30ff.
[18] Ramadorai 2013, p. 13.

persuasion'. Directors were changed, companies were eliminated, but amid these shifts, according to a Tata historian, 'the cohesion of the group was maintained purely by the power of J.R.D.'s charismatic personality'.[19]

J.R.D. Tata, who had served as chairman of Tata and Sons since the mid-1930s, continued in his stewardship into the 1980s, but individual company heads within the Tata Group gained considerable power. In 1991, just as India was entering an era of economic liberalization, guided by Dr Manmohan Singh, the chairman's torch was passed to J.R.D.'s nephew, Ratan Tata. Born in 1937 and schooled in India, he gained a degree in architecture from Cornell University in the US and studied at Harvard Business School. In 1961, the younger Tata joined Tata Steel at the lowest level, working in the blast furnace, then worked with several of the other Tata companies until, in 1991, J.R.D. selected him as his successor. According to one biographical account:

> When he settled down into the new role, he faced stiff resistance from many company heads some of whom had spent decades in their respective companies and rose to become very powerful and influential due to the freedom to operate under JRD Tata. He began replacing them by setting a retirement age, and made individual companies report operationally to the group office and made each contribute some of their profit to build and use the Tata group brand. Innovation was given priority and younger talent was infused and given responsibilities. Under his stewardship, overlapping operations in group companies were streamlined into a synergised whole... During the 21 years he led the Tata Group, revenues grew over 40 times, and profit over 50 times...He boldly got Tata Tea to acquire Tetley, Tata Motors to acquire Jaguar Land Rover and Tata Steel to acquire Corus. All this turned Tata from a largely India-centric group into a global business, with over 65% revenues coming from operations and sales in over 100 countries.[20]

---

[19] Shah, Shashank. 2018. *The Tata Group*. Gurgaon: Penguin, p. 31.
[20] 'Ratan Tata', Wikipedia.

Not only did some of Tata's older businesses such as TISCO and TESCO and Tata Beverages continue to flourish, change and expand, but altogether new companies were organized and began to flourish. The most remarkable of these is TCS, which emerged into the business services industry in the 1970s.

Over the following three decades, TCS became one of the most important members of the Tata family of companies, rivalling the other top Tata enterprises, which include Tata Steel (previously TISCO), Tata Motors (previously TELCO), Tata Power, Tata Chemicals, Tata Global Beverages (previously Tata Tea), Tata Teleservices, Titan Industries, Tata Communications and Taj Hotels. TCS's role internationally has been particularly notable. From the start, most of its work was carried out overseas and strong connections were forged between India and other nations, notably the US. By the beginning of the twenty-first century, Tata was doing several billion dollars' worth of business consulting in the US and had more than fifty offices nationwide. By 2020, Tata was a multinational conglomerate, receiving more than 50 per cent of its revenue from outside India, a major contender in global commerce in a diverse range of fields. Not only does it have a significant presence in the US and the UK, but in Southeast Asia and Africa as well. It is even edging into China.

Tata Steel, as it is now known, was at the outset the first successful steel mill that was Indian-owned. Although, as noted in earlier chapters, Americans had helped develop the company and served as managers for almost thirty years, the top direction came from Tata Steel directors and the chairman of Tata and Sons. It has faced difficulties along the way, but has continually produced high quality products for more than a century. On a tour of the steel mill at Jamshedpur in 2008, I noted the advances in computerization of the processes involved and the paucity of a numerous and visible workforce. At that time, the mill employed 16,000 workers at the Jamshedpur mill, and Tata Steel a total of 35,000 nationwide. It once had 75,000 employees, but decade by decade, as it became more automated, it shrank. With the acquisition of Corus Steel in Europe and other small mills and the opening of a new steel mill in

India, despite suffering setbacks resulting from the lowered prices set by Chinese firms, and the need to shed some of its European acquisitions, Tata Steel remains one of the larger steel producers in the world.[21]

An unincorporated municipal area with a population of more than one million, Jamshedpur is relatively clean as befits a newer city and has no old monuments to the Raj; it has, however, memorials to Jamsetji Tata, as the founder. Tata Steel provides healthcare and other services to its employees, a program that started in Jamshedpur and has spread to some other Tata sites and businesses, which demonstrate more responsibility for employee welfare than do many other enterprises.

Other executives of Tata companies in India included, as of 2007 and 2008, the Americans Darryl Green, CEO of Tata Telecommunications, and Raymond Bickson, the managing director of Taj hotels. Green, with deep Mormon roots and affiliation, attended the Tuck Business School at Dartmouth and had a long career in AT&T, eventually working for them in Japan. He met Ratan Tata in 2005 and joined Tata to help them build their presence in the Indian telecom market. Bickson came from Hawaii, where his father had managed a motel, and Bickson had always wanted a career in hotels. After he had worked in the hotel business in Europe and New York, Tata hired him to help run and expand their hotel enterprises.

Within a little more than a decade, Taj Hotels has acquired properties in the Middle East, the Indian Ocean area and the US. It created a splash with the purchase of the Pierre Hotel in New York City, a famed and elegant hotel on Fifth Avenue, and the Ritz Carlton Hotel in Boston. They have now acquired a number of other chains of hotels in different price ranges, becoming a leading participant in the global hotel accommodations enterprise.[22] Employing able Americans like Green and Bickson, as Tata and Sons has done for over a 100 years, shows its willingness to reach out beyond India

[21] Bhat, Harish. 2012. *Tata Log*. Gurgaon: Penguin, p. 174ff.

[22] Witzel, Morgen. 2010. *Tata*. The Evolution of a Corporate Brand. New Delhi: Penguin, p. 5ff; Lala 2004, p. 54ff.

and the Parsi community to find the most skilled executives and managers available.[23]

Another of the core companies of Tata is TELCO which became Tata Motors in 2003. From its beginnings as a manufacturer of locomotives, it has looked for other avenues of production. So it began to produce large trucks, then smaller ones and then edged into automobiles. Its mini-truck, Ace, proved quite successful; its Indica consumer automobile somewhat successful, and its Nano automobile very problematic, both for the company and for consumers. Ratan Tata invested considerable personal attention in the development of the Nano, but its production was marred by a serious controversy: some West Bengal farmers and politicians objected to Tata's takeover of the site for its manufacture in Singur. Tata Motors decided to move production to Sanand in Gujarat, a more favourable political environment. Narendra Modi, then chief minister of Gujarat, quickly made Tata Motors at home, regardless of the local impact.[24]

Jamsetji Tata's vision included making steel in India, developing a world class institution in science education and research, and providing power for the Bombay area. All his dreams had to be carried out by his successors. What started as Tata Electric Companies became Tata Power. Its creation and growth has helped to assure power supply sufficient for the Bombay Presidency, which has become the states of Gujarat and Maharashtra.[25] While curtailing manufacturing in some directions, Tata has branched out into others, and among the most successful of these have been the beverage, watch and jewellery businesses. In January 2000, a deal was consummated merging Tetley and Tata Tea. Since then, Tata Tea has become Tata Beverages and is an international firm of consequence.[26]

Beyond the Tata commercial brand—a kind of mission one analyst summarizes as trust, reliability and commitment to the nation—

---

[23] Lala 2003, pp. 38, 60–62.

[24] Shah 2018, p. 112ff; Rosling, Alan. 2018. *BOOM Country?* The New Wave of Indian Enterprise. Gurugram: Hachette, p. 23; Witzel 2010, p. 145.

[25] Shah 2018, p. 302ff; Rosling 2018, p. 111; Lala 2004, p. 47ff

[26] Bhat 2012, p. 150ff; Shah 2018, p. 152ff.

another aspect of the workings of Tata and Sons over its long history has been its involvement in research, education and health services,[27] an effort that has been, if not unique, certainly praiseworthy. This work began from the vision of Jamsetji Tata, discussed earlier, to found the Indian Institute of Science in Bangalore. He also started a programme for Tata scholars, designed to enable young Indian women and men to advance their education.[28] This programme has been followed in the Tata Institute of Social Sciences in 1936, the Tata Memorial Centre for Cancer Research and Treatment in Mumbai in 1941, the Tata Institute of Fundamental Research in 1945, the National Centre for the Performing Arts, the Centre for Advancement of Philanthropy in Mumbai in the 1980s, and recently, a cancer hospital in Kolkata.[29] In addition, Tata Trusts and individual Tata family members have set up programmes in the US at the Harvard Business School and the University of California, San Diego. These serve the public good and exemplify what the founder believed was part of the mission of those successful in business: to build a better India and a better world through thoughtful use of profits. Whatever charges may be made against some of its business dealings—and some are credible—Tata has also used a handsome share of its vast earnings for the wider good. In worldwide perspective, it is certainly in the company of the Ford, Rockefeller and Carnegie Foundations. In fact, it may have done more for its workers and the surrounding communities than these did for their workers.

In sum, Tata and Sons has become over the past two generations a multinational grouping of companies with global clout. Despite this notable success, Tata and Sons has also had to overcome some serious setbacks over its long history. Empress Mills in Nagpur, an innovative and highly successful enterprise, went downhill in the latter part of the twentieth century and was turned over to the government. Efforts to set up an auto manufacturing plant in West Bengal were met with strong opposition and the plan was abandoned.

---

[27] Witzel 2010, p. 129.
[28] Lala 2004a, p. 138ff.
[29] Shah 2018, p. 333ff; Lala 2004, p. 17–18, p. 38ff; Lala 2003, p. 388.

Some international acquisitions proved more problematic than profitable. Outside financial analysts have argued that the acquisitions of Corus Steel and Land Rover-Jaguar (from Ford) were costly mistakes, which Tata sought to rectify.[30] Tata Finance collapsed in 2003, and had to compensate investors as well as possible.[31]

Even the handover of the chairmanship of the Tata Group went aground after Ratan Tata gave the chairmanship to Cyrus Mistry in 2012. Mistry's family had acquired a share in Tata and Sons in the 1930s, and that stake grew to 18.5 per cent, the largest bloc held by any party outside the Tata family, which controls a 66 per cent stake held by a set of charitable trusts. Mistry and his family are Parsis, like the Tatas, but took Irish citizenship. Mistry attended school in Mumbai, took a BS degree in civil engineering at Imperial College, London, and then an MSc in management from the London Business School. He became managing director of Shapoorji Pallonji and Company, succeeding his father, and joined the board of Tata and Sons in 2006. However, Ratan Tata was reported to be unhappy with the direction taken by the new chairman and succeeded in unseating him in 2017.[32] Ratan Tata briefly reoccupied the chairman's seat, and then N. Chandrasekaran was appointed the new chairman in February 2017. Mistry did not leave quietly, and legal challenges to his removal were filed.[33] He was replaced by Ratan Tata on an interim basis. Then Mistry was killed in a road accident. Two years later, in 2024, Ratan Tata died in October 2024 after more than two decades at the helm. He helped to make Tata and Sons the global conglomerate it is making mistakes but forging ahead.

Though beset with some serious problems in recent decades, Tata and Sons continues as a highly respected brand, and has continued to push forward internationally into new areas. A recent

---

[30] C.P. Chandrasekhar, 'Tata Rides the Recession, *Frontline*, July 3, 2009
[31] Witzel 2010, pp. 17–18.
[32] Prosenjit Datta, 'Why Tata Sons removed Cyrus Mistry as Group Chairman,' *Business Today*, 23 January 2017; 'Cyrus Mistry,' Wikipedia
[33] Rosling 2018, p. 2.

assessment by the *Economist*, however, has pointed out extremely serious problems facing the Tata and Sons group.[34] Noting that the individual firms are not closely or sufficiently integrated to help each other, they said that financial woes are now besetting some of these companies. Never static, as international linkages have become more problematic, Tata has opened more factories in India.

The Tata Group companies and Tata philanthropies have been subjected to withering criticism, however, by one of India's best-known public intellectuals, Arundhati Roy. Placing Tatas with Reliance, Infosys, and the other big business groups of India, she has attempted to demonstrate in *Capitalism: A Ghost Story* (2014) that they have ruthlessly despoiled the earth, uprooted local peoples, and pressed forward to dominate the economy, the society, the culture, and with others, the politics of India.

> The Tatas… run more than one hundred companies in eighty countries… They own mines, gas fields, steel plants, telephone, and cable TV and broadband networks, and run whole townships. They manufacture cars and trucks and own the Taj Hotel chain… [and] a chain of bookstores… Their advertising tagline could easily be You Can't Live Without Us… India's new megacorporations… are those that have managed to muscle their way to the head of the spigot that is spewing money extracted from inside the earth. It's a dream come true for businessmen—to be able to sell what they don't have to buy.[35]

She charts how they have expanded into rural India, taking ground from which to extract minerals, or on which to build factories. Insisting that Tatas have cared little for those displaced by its greed for growth, she almost mocks their philanthropic work, while also praising its excellent achievements in education and health care. Appropriately, she links Tata's good works to those of the Carnegie and Rockefeller

---

[34] 'Crisis for Tata and Sons', 23 October 2020.
[35] Roy, Arundhati. 2014. *Capitalism: A Ghost Story*. Chicago: Haymarket, p. 9.

Foundations.[36] The ill-gotten gains of these huge business groups may have done some good, she suggests, en route to conquering and running the world. She also notes how Narendra Modi, first as the chief minister of Gujarat, and later as prime minister of India, has helped and had the help of, business groups like the Tatas.

Although the Indian business community strongly criticised the Congress government for impeding their growth during the post-Independence decades, many businesses grew nonetheless. Among them was Birla Brothers, whose leader, G.D. Birla, continued to communicate privately with Nehru through the last two decades of the latter's life about business and political matters. One of the key organizers of the business lobby, Birla helped to reorganize FICCI, the Federation of Indian Chambers of Commerce and Industry, as well as a smaller Industry Council, set on influencing friendly cabinet ministers and other officials. They worked after Independence to grow and protect private sector enterprise. Learning how democracy worked in Nehru's India, Birla saw that first pronouncements or five-year plans or restrictive bills could be significantly modified by lobbying efforts.

Birla did not confine his lobbying efforts only to India, but also pursued them energetically in Washington, D.C., with the US government, the World Bank and the International Monetary Fund. He sought increased aid and more foreign investment for India, while exploring how India might adapt to gain additional aid, both from the Americans and from international institutions. Birla was in close touch with George David Woods (1901–1982), president of the World Bank, who provided links to the American business world. In the mid-1960s he almost wore out the trail from India to Washington D.C., so frequent were his visits.

The Birla group expanded and diversified significantly in the post-Independence decades. Birla's excellent biographer, Medha Kudaisya, summarizes its achievement:

> [I]n the first decade of independence... Birla's business empire expanded vigorously. At the time of independence the traditional

---

[36] Ibid., pp. 20–21.

business strength had been in jute, textiles, banking and publishing. Recent diversifications had been in insurance, textile machinery, automobiles, bicycles and plastics. The decade following... was marked by expansion into several key sectors of the economy such as engineering, tea, chemicals, non-ferrous metals, glass, aluminium, shipping and aviation... Together with the Tatas, the Birla group accounted for approximately one-fifth of the physical assets of the corporate sector by 1958.[37]

With the collaboration of the Kaiser Corporation, USA, the Birlas set up the Hindustan Aluminium Corporation (HINDALCO). In addition, they produced rayon pulp, planned their fertilizer enterprise, Zuari Agro Chemicals, and began producing Ambassador cars.[38] Under the loosely expansive roof of a society that looked to be socialist, the Birlas were thriving. In 1951, they controlled 245 companies with interests in eleven more.[39] Although concerned with production, not with greater equality, the Birlas, like the Tatas, set up large charitable enterprises, centred on education, but also in temple-building.

In the succession struggle after the unexpected death of Prime Minister Lal Bahadur Shastri in early 1966, Birla pressed for the election of Indira Gandhi over Morarji Desai (1896–1995; prime minister 1977–1979). Birla hoped that the relaxation of restrictions on the private sector that he saw under Shastri would continue and that he would be a political insider as, to a great extent, he had been for decades. However, once in power, after Indira's visit to Washington in 1966 and the revaluation of the Indian rupee, Indira Gandhi took a turn to the left, supported by many Congressmen, the CPI and independents. She instituted renewed and stricter licensing requirements on big business, then turned to bank nationalization—a move that hit the Birla group hard since their United Commercial

---

[37] Kudaisya 2003, p. 331, 336.
[38] Ibid., pp. 330ff.
[39] Kidron, Michael. 1965. *Foreign Investments in India*. London: Oxford U. Press, p. 22.

Bank was a keystone in their vast operations. G.D. Birla, who had been an insider during the nationalist era and even under Nehru, was now excluded, and the Birla group was portrayed as the most corrupt of the large business groups. Although G.D. Birla would not forsake the Congress, younger Birlas entered politics as independents or supporters of the pro-business Swatantra Party. The elder Birla went into semi-retirement, and undertook pilgrimages. The Birlas were still the second largest business grouping after the Tatas, but they could not proceed with the same swagger as before. They began to set up new enterprises in Southeast Asia rather than India.

While some American economists advised on economic development plans for India, the American businessman John Bissell (1931–1998) also became involved in India's growth. A Yale graduate and navy veteran with a background in marketing, Bissell came to New Delhi in 1958 under a grant from the Ford Foundation to see how Indian handicrafts and their sales might be improved. He had worked for Macy's and Far Eastern Fabrics, and was enticed by the prospect of India. Working under the Handicrafts Board, Bissell toured India, meeting craftsmen, and searching for ways to improve their products and facilitate their sales. After a one-year renewal of the Ford grant, he continued to tour the countryside, and, unimpressed with many aspects of the handicraft production and sales operations, he decided to form his own company.

He envisioned an export business with worldwide sales, with these starting from his mother's retail store in Canton, Connecticut. After drawing up a prospectus, he returned home, gathered family and friends at a September 1960 meeting, and asked for investors to come forward. Fabindia was first incorporated in the US. Bissell put together samples of fabrics, clothing, and home furnishings and hired an agent in America to sell the goods. The first year or two proved very difficult, but Bissell persevered, and within a few years Fabindia was making a profit and grew into a successful export business with modest sales within India.

Demanding that craftsmen do their best to create new lines, patterns, and colour combinations, and meet deadlines, Fabindia moved forward and began to expand. As sales passed the $1,00,000-mark and continued to rise, Bissell did significant reorganizing. In the 1970s, the company became an Indian export firm, Fabindia Overseas Ltd, and opened its first retail store in Greater Kailash, a neighbourhood of south Delhi. As its product line expanded, Fabindia sold ever more cotton and woollen goods, and also moved into silk.[40]

In September 1963, Bissell married Bimla Nanda—intelligent, effervescent and a remarkable networker—who worked for the American Embassy and ran a nursery school. Listed first on the foreigner registration list in Delhi, he devoted his life to India, which became his adopted country. The Bissells elder son, William, born in 1966, later joined the business, and the company pressed forward in the next stage of its growth. Fabindia had to make a major organizational change in the mid-1970s. The Government of India demanded that foreign companies own no more than 40 per cent of a business operating mainly in India. Alive to the challenge, Bissell established Fabindia, Inc., an Indian company, linked to, but separate from the American company, Fabindia USA. He became the managing director of the new entity.

As it was gaining exposure and very positive reviews, Fabindia made a strong connection to Habitat, run by Conrans, a British company that became their biggest overseas buyer and operated in France as well. Fabindia, though, was destined for more: it gradually became the centre of a successful worldwide business enterprise, thriving domestically, as well as exporting to Asia, Europe and the US. It took over more and more sections of Greater Kailash market, which became their Indian headquarters. Before long, the company became extremely popular sellers of reasonable clothing and house-ware especially to the expanding middle class.

Extracts from John Bissell's letters to his parents, utilized in Radhika Singh's acute account of the company, attest to his unhappiness during the 1970s and 1980s with political events in

---

[40] Singh 2010, p. 18ff.

India, as well as with the high taxes on business.[41] As a foreigner married to an Indian woman and committed to a life in India, he had no intention of involving himself in politics. However, he was related to CIA operative Richard Bissell, his uncle, and this caused him some discomfort because he was not happy being linked to a senior American intelligence operative. However, Richard Bissell was his uncle and nothing could change that.[42]

Although Fabindia continued to grow through the last quarter of the twentieth century, it also had to face difficult times. The link to the Conrans was almost completely severed when the company was sold to IKEA, which had a completely different business model and no personal tie to the Bissells. So, new markets had to be located. William returned from the US after college, and attempted a related but distinct business venture of his own with craftspeople in Rajasthan. A failure at first, it was reorganized and was incorporated, then became more securely linked to Fabindia as a supplier. As the business expanded, it began to use mill-produced goods, crowding out its earlier preference for handicrafts, a direction that frustrated Meena Chowdhury, assistant to John Bissell, who resigned in anger at this shift. In 1993, John Bissell had a severe stroke while in America. He moved back to New Delhi. Embodying values some have called those of a Connecticut Yankee: humility, honesty (no bribes to be given), generosity, hard work, he sought to help the community as well as to make a profit. He died in 1998.

After his stroke, Meena Chowdhury returned to the company and effectively managed it for another decade. William joined and took a leading role. During the later twentieth century, Fabindia fostered what came to be called 'the Fabindia look', a distinctive style in home furnishings, garments and then organic food and health products.[43] As this look grew in popularity, William pressed for domestic expansion and what occurred in these years and into

---

[41] Singh, Radika. 2010. *The Fabric of Our Lives*. The Story of Fabindia. New Delhi: Penguin, p. 85ff.
[42] Obituary for John Bissell, *New York Times*, 3 March 1998.
[43] Singh 2010, p. 97ff.

the new century was more an explosion than a modest expansion. Fabindia set up more than 100 stores throughout India.[44] It clearly benefited from the liberalization that resulted from Manmohan Singh's economic reforms, and from the rapid growth of India's middle class.

As domestic sales skyrocketed, foreign sales, for some time, diminished. But in time, Fabindia found new ways to sell its goods abroad, opening some foreign stores and also selling its goods online—a move requiring the computerization of the company's operation——and in stores not its own. From the start, John Bissell had had a vision of social and cultural progress for India's craftspeople, a vision pursued also by William Bissell once he took on a leadership role. He initiated the idea of artisan, or Supplier Regional Companies, in which the artisans gained shares in their production units. Much earlier, Fabindia had helped set up a school in Rajasthan; now William wanted Fabindia to more vigorously pursue the betterment of life for its suppliers. He, like his father, knew that to further these aims you also had to run a successful business. He brought in a skilled business consultant, Sunil Chainani, who helped formulate their plans for expansion. They brought in more professionally trained staff, and reached out for additional capital to WCP Mauritius Holdings, a company 'promoted by Wolfensohn & Company LLC', the latter a private investment firm set up by James Wolfensohn, former president of the World Bank.[45]

An unusual feature of Fabindia, started by John and continued by William Bissell, is its allowing women to play an important role, as Radhika Singh writes in her history of the company:

John Bissell had always maintained that women made the most committed and loyal workers. 'The best managers in this country are women,' he had once said to Monsoon. In fact John had many theories about why women worked better than men, but essentially

---

[44] Ibid., p. 203ff.
[45] Ibid., p. 272.

he respected them for their management skills, juggling different personalities and budgets in a household.[46]

Fabindia has faced some problems over the past several decades. One has been the decreasing part that the 'handicraft' element has in the goods it sells. A second was the dissatisfaction of employees with wage increases. Another was a dispute with the central Khadi board over the use of a Khadi mark on its goods. Fabindia agreed to remove the mark.

Moving to a broader view, India engaged in foreign trade as it had for centuries, but now trade with the US grew, supplanting Great Britain as India's main trading partner: 'In 1963–64, Britain supplied 15 per cent of imports and took 21 per cent of exports, compared with 34 and 17 per cent for the United States, 12 and 7 per cent for the Common Market countries, 11 and 13 per cent for Eastern Bloc countries, and 8 and 13 per cent for Japan.'[47] But India's trade with the US was still, during the first half-century of Indian Independence, a small percentage of total US trade. Significant change took place in the 1980s, when more American companies began to take root in India.

It is necessary to underscore the vibrancy of the private sector of the Indian economy in the decades after Independence. Yes, it was the 'Licence Raj', and there were limitations on business operations. But it would be inaccurate to characterize India's economy as socialist, with Russians standing by to impose the Soviet model. India had to find its own path; its large public sector enterprises were established but did not do well. Over time there was loosening, even under Nehru, then tightening under his daughter Indira Gandhi. What India did not overcome during the 1950s and 1960s was its inability to provide on a regular basis sufficient food for its population. It was inhibited by limited foreign exchange, as well as foreign trade and foreign investment inadequate for a nation of its size. Galbraith has argued, drawing on investigations in the development field and his

---

[46] Ibid., p. 210.
[47] Kidron 1965, p. 34.

experience of India, that an essential prerequisite for India or other developing countries to advance into the rank of developed countries was '... an educated and, in consequence, a competent and social and economically motivated population'.[48] In this regard, India is still catching up. Entrepreneurs in the private sector grumbled that they were too restricted to move ahead as they wanted and as India needed them to. That may well have been the case. But on other fronts, including education and infrastructure, India also needed to move forward, and did not do so expeditiously.

For the half-century after India and Pakistan gained the status of independent states, they remained minor economic players in the world economy and vis-à-vis the United States. Both South Asian nations were recipients of aid, but they were not significant trading partners. American companies were content to sell goods to these new nations at a modest level, but not to make any important investment in South Asian economies, an investment further discouraged by the forced exit from India of IBM and Coca Cola in the 1970s. From Independence into the 1980s, successive Indian governments expected public sector enterprises to rapidly develop the economy, gradually eliminate poverty and reduce inequality. Private sector businesses, large and small, existed the whole time, but were not favoured or helped. Under the Licence Raj, corruption flourished, as some businesses advanced. But India is a vast country, and as Harish Damodaran has amply documented, many of these private sector companies forged ahead, despite the shackles placed upon them. Some lobbied against possible nationalization (TISCO), and some expanded their enterprises into Southeast Asia and other foreign climes. By various means, this huge, though hampered, private sector was finally unleashed.[49]

Tethered to a slow rate of growth in the first decades after Independence, India began to change economic direction from

---

[48] Galbraith, John K. 1994. *A Journey Through Economic Time*. Boston: Houghton Mifflin, p. 162.
[49] Damodaran, Harish. 2008. *India's New Capitalists*. Ranikhet: Permanent Black, p. 23ff.

the 1980s, then more rapidly from 1991, when it entered the world economy more significantly. As unexpected as the brash and powerful entry of China from the early 1980s, India's rise was a surprise to most outside observers. They had already witnessed the economic resurgence of Japan and the so-called 'Four Asian Tigers' of South Korea, Taiwan, Singapore and Hong Kong, but China and India were potentially much bigger players on the world stage. Now reduced to only the west wing of its former territory, Bangladesh having been severed and become a separate nation, Pakistan had to come to terms with its diminished stature. Bangladesh, a small new nation burdened with an immense population density, had to emerge from its condition as a 'basket case', as American strategist Henry Kissinger had characterized it.

Economist Arvind Panagariya has argued that the economic crisis of 1991 triggered wholesale and significant changes in the Licence Raj that had hindered Indian economic development. Faced with an acute shortage of foreign exchange, the Government of India under Prime Minister Narasimha Rao and Finance Minister Manmohan Singh made an agreement with the IMF and the World Bank for loans that were conditioned on extensive liberalization—a liberalization that some in government and many in business had long wanted. Restrictions on both imports and exports were significantly relaxed, the rupee was devalued, and the growth rate in industry, agriculture and services began to climb to levels unknown in free India's history.[50] While many will agree with Panagariya's account of the shift in economic policy, other related matters are in dispute, among them the rate of poverty, the question of inequality, and the cause of farmer suicides. Thomas Piketty has argued, for instance, backed by a mountain of data that inequality increased in India from the 1980s onward, as it did in the US, the UK, and many other countries.[51] Many agree that India lags behind in many social services, especially public health and education.[52]

---

[50] Panagariya 2008, p. 78ff.
[51] Piketty 2020, p. 20ff.
[52] Drèze and Sen 2013, p. 107ff.

One consequence of the economic transformation of the 1990s was the displacement of many older business houses by newcomers. Harish Damodaran has detailed how these new entrepreneurs, mostly from south and western India, forged ahead, while only a modest number of older houses, among them the Birlas and Tata and Sons, managed to thrive in the new economic environment. Alongside these two business conglomerates, a number of other enterprises such as those led by the Mittals and Hindujas have emerged as worldwide businesses.[53] Alan Rosling, an able and experienced business executive turned entrepreneur and investor, has been investigating the entrepreneurs who have generated the recent business surge, focusing in the passage below on a group of ninety-two:

> The... stronger, common theme is the importance of exposure to the US, either for education or for employment. Forty-two per cent of the 92 had spent time in the US, and this was slightly higher among the New Generation (44 per cent) than among Manmohan's Children (38 per cent). Further, a number of the entrepreneurs who had not lived in the US had been exposed to American business thinking by working for multinational companies (MNCs) in India, and of course all have been immersed in American culture through the media and the Internet. Hence my contention that the story of the rise of entrepreneurship in India is in good part the story of the opening up of—or, in the most positive sense, the 'Americanization of'—the Indian mind.[54]

Woven into Rosling's analysis of interviews with Indian entrepreneurs, financial backers, and top businessmen, are details of their education and employment in America and with American businesses. What is important, beyond that the US is the most salient foreign destination for education and work, is that some of those who might have stayed on in America for the rest of their careers, are, in the second decade of the twenty-first century, returning to India to try their hand at entrepreneurship.

---

[53] Damodaran 2008, p. 13ff.
[54] Rosling 2018, p. xxvii.

That trend is a mark that India has moved up the economic ladder to become a destination as desirable as any other for successful work and life.[55] For decades, the complaint was heard of a 'brain drain' that picked India dry of its best young women and men. But in this new scenario, America provides education, experience, even funding, and India increasingly reaps the benefit as more and more young men and women who have gone to the US return to India. At the same time, some of the venture capital needed and supplied to prospective Indian entrepreneurs comes from organizations run by South Asians based in America. This interaction constitutes another important bridge between the two nations, over which flow people, capital, goods and—who knows to what extent—a common mindset.

The links between India and the US since 1991 are unlike those that characterized the first four and half decades post-1947. Then, the interest in India was merely casual, while the principal export to that nation was food. But now Americans and their leaders have come to see India as an economic and political player of world significance, and no longer a backwater. In 2016, according to US government figures, India was the ninth largest trading partner of the US, with $67.7 billion in total (two-way) trade in goods, constituted by US exports totalling $21.7 billion, and imports $46 billion; at the same time, exports in services were $20.3 billion, and in imports $26.8 billion. What were the main goods and services exchanged? The US exported precious metals and diamonds, machinery, optical and medical instruments, mineral fuels, and electrical machinery, while it imported diamonds, pharmaceuticals, mineral fuels, textiles and machinery, and in foodstuff—spices, rice, tree nuts, essential oils, and processed fruit and vegetables. US imports from India in services included those in telecommunications, computer and information services, travel, and research and development. Recently the US became India's largest trading partner, while India moved up to a higher rank on America's list of partners.

---

[55] Rosling 2018.

Although the US had a trade deficit of $24.3 billion in 2016, an increase of 4.2 per cent over the previous year, it has considerable direct investment in India, including investment in scientific and technical services, banking and manufacturing. Although the sum invested is much lower than that for equivalent investments in China, still India has become a significant trading and investment partner of the US in this century.[56] Like China, India is seen as a vast potential market with its growing middle class, significant numbers of educated workers, especially in technical fields, and a possibly expanding manufacturing sector. In a setback, India fell victim in June 2019 to President Trump's tariff policies, which stripped away the special status India had enjoyed and exempted billions of dollars of Indian goods from American tariffs.[57] Under Trump, as well, the US has applied tariffs to steel and aluminium, adversely affecting India. In response, in June 2019, India put high tariffs on a range of American goods, including agricultural and electronic products. In addition, the US has also tried to prevent India and China from importing oil from Iran.

American companies, however, now see India as a gigantic potential market and want in. Some have a considerable presence such as Microsoft, GE, Texas Instruments, and others. The *New York Times* noted recently in an article about Hyderabad, an important city in south-central India: 'Apple. Google. Facebook. Uber. All have big offices in Hyderabad. So does Amazon, which this year opened its largest office building in the world right here, a futuristic campus with 15,000 employees.'[58] Although many have entered, the Indian government, lobbied by smaller firms and retailers, has moved to put some restrictions on just how widely or easily retailing multinationals can move into the Indian market.[59] It is also putting '... new rules

---

[56] US government trade report, updated, March 22, 2017.

[57] 'US Removes Special Status Used by India to Skip Tariffs', *The New York Times*, 1 June 2019.

[58] Jeffrey Gettleman, 'In an Indian City...' 21 December 2019, The *New York Times*.

[59] 'India Limits Web Sales by US Retail Giants', 27 December 2018, The *New York Times*.

on e-commerce that restrict the way Amazon.com Inc. and Walmart Inc.-backed Flipkart do business'.[60] India has become a sufficiently important and confident participant in the world economic scene that it will fight for its own interests, and not fold before US pressure.

In the post-1965 era, South Asians entered the US to study and do business, at first a trickle, then a goodly flow, then followed by a torrent, not only have many of these men and women made their mark in the American economy, but some have served to connect the American and Indian economies in ever new ways. One vital area of connection in computer-related industries and Internet services holds the promise of tying the two countries together in dense webs of connectedness and profitability—at least for some. NRIs and overseas Chinese have been instrumental in building up Silicon Valley, the California home of many American global technology companies. These relations mark a new era of linkage, a new phase of the Industrial Revolution in which India and Indians are in on the ground floor. This makes Indians, players for high stakes among other high-stake players, and accepted as such both in Silicon Valley and on Wall Street, as well as in Bangalore and Bombay. Starting as experts trained at Indian Institutes of Technology and at a few other top Indian institutions and American universities, South Asians have become managers and leaders of big firms. Among the important linkers are Vinod Khosla, the founder of Sun Microsystems, based in Menlo Park, California, and subsequently a venture capitalist as well; Sunil Paul, founder of Brightmail.com; Srivats Sampath, CEO of McAfee.com; Gururaj 'Desh' Deshpande, chairman of Sycamore Networks, based in the Boston area; N.R. Narayana Murthy, founder of Infosystems Technology, Bangalore, the first Indian company listed on an American stock exchange, the Nasdaq; and Vivek Wadha, founder of Relativity Technologies, based in North Carolina. Along with Amar Bose, these men and others, have made millions of dollars, in some cases, billions. The firms to which they are connected or which they lead employ thousands.

---

[60] 'Donald Trump plans to end preferential trade terms for India', 5 March 2019, *The Hindu*.

The Silicon Valley pioneer Vinod Khosla, for example, was born in 1955, grew up in New Delhi, attended the IIT in Delhi, and then moved to the US for further education; there he received a master's degree from Carnegie Mellon University, and an MBA from the Stanford Graduate School of Business. After founding Sun Microsystems with Stanford classmates, he moved on to make his mark as a venture capitalist, interested in a diverse set of issues including clean technology and education. One of the founders of The Indus Entrepreneurs (TiE), which supports startups with funding, in 2004 he formed his own venture capital firm, Khosla Ventures. He also, perhaps foolishly, carried on a long-term effort to prevent public access to Martins Beach across his property. His efforts to make ethanol an alternative, cleaner fuel, and his wife's work in education, were more worthy of his time and skills.

South Asian Americans have also gained leadership roles in top US firms and financial institutions outside of Silicon Valley: firms such as Pepsi-Cola, Microsoft and Google. The very successful Microsoft CEO Satya Nadella may serve as one example for many. Born in 1967 to Telugu-speaking parents in Hyderabad, his father an IAS officer, Nadella's earlier education was in India. Then he moved to the US, gaining an MS in computer science and an MBA at the Booth School of Business, University of Chicago, which prepared him for his first position at Sun Microsystems, from where, in 1992, he soon moved to Microsoft. Working his way up, he held posts in research and development and its business division, and led the way for the company to embrace cloud computing.

In 2014, Nadella became the third CEO of Microsoft. Once in charge, he formed more positive relationships to competitors like Apple, thereby pulling down the barrier between Microsoft and the Linux operating system. In an interview on *Bloomberg News*, he said he had made every effort to change the culture of Microsoft, to search for a positive purpose for the firm. This is embodied in its revised mission statement: 'empower every person and every organization on the planet to achieve more'. Nadella's commitment to continued learning and growth hit a temporary snag shortly after he became

CEO when he made what many saw as an insensitive statement about women employees. He quickly realized that he was 'completely wrong'. Subsequently, he has made an effort to understand the role, possibilities, and position of women in Microsoft. In 2017, he published *Hit Refresh*, his account of his life and his views of technology's role in the future growth of humankind.[61]

The multinational company that Nadella heads has a presence in India as well as around the globe, as do those led by other exemplary South Asians. Among these, mention should be made of Pichai Sundarajan, anglicized to Sundar Pichai, who became CEO of Google in 2015 and, in December 2019, CEO of Alphabet, the holding company for the Google group of companies;[62] Indra Nooyi, who served as Pepsico's CEO for twelve years and lately joined Amazon's board;[63] Ajay Banga at Mastercard, now at World Bank; and Arvind Krishna at IBM.[64]

Aside from the leading roles played by these and other South Asians in American enterprises, and along with the significant entry of American multinationals into India, a number of Indian multinationals have taken root in the US. One of these is Tata Consultancy Services (TCS) to be discussed below. But others have had and have a growing presence including Infosys and Wipro, among world-class business consulting firms burgeoning from India. Wipro can serve as an example.

Azim Premji, the founder of Wipro, obtained a BS degree from Stanford University in the mid-1960s, but upon the death of his father, returned to India to take charge of the family's firm, Western Indian Vegetable Products. In the 1980s, he expanded this business from cooking oil and laundry soap into the IT area, shortening the

---

[61] Interview with David Rubenstein on *Bloomberg News and Finance*, October 25, 2017; 'After the Reboot', *The Economist*, October 24, 2020; 'Satya Nadella', Wikipedia.

[62] 'End of Era for Google as Founders step aside,' The *New York Times*, December 4, 2019; 'High Stakes for Low-Key Google Chief', *New York Times*, October 22, 2020; 'Sundar Pichai', Wikipedia.

[63] 'Indra Nooyi Retiring', profile in *New York Times*, March 24, 2019.

[64] 'The Leader Who Promised No Layoffs', *New York Times*, November 8, 2020.

name to Wipro. It collaborated with Sentinel Computer Corporation in making minicomputers. Moving into a great variety of business fields, it now operates in six continents and has forty facilities in twenty-three US states. Its promotional literature depicts its expanse:

> This includes Wipro's four large-scale delivery centers in Dallas, Tampa, Indianapolis and Atlanta, along with an innovation center in the heart of Silicon Valley to display Wipro's state-of-the-art solutions and engage with leading technology companies. Features at these centers include digital pods and rapid prototyping labs to increase collaboration and realize speed for our customers... Wipro Ventures is a strategic investment arm that focuses on investing in early-to-mid-stage startups... We place a high value on everyone having access to a quality education, and our charitable endeavors reflect this value. One such instance is Wipro's creation of a partnership with the University of Massachusetts and the University of North Texas to educate teachers in STEM fields to become the leaders in these topics.[65]

Wipro has launched an innovation centre in Silicon Valley. Like Infosys and TCS, Wipro has a multinational employee force numbering many more than 1,00,000. The development of these companies over the past four decades bespeaks India's emergence as a full participant in the world economic system. In the nineteenth and twentieth centuries, India accepted American missionaries who helped educate India's youth; now, in contrast, Indian multinationals are developing facilities that assist in educating the youth of America. The arc of empire has been repositioned and is shifting direction decade after decade.

As South Asians in prominent business positions in America, economists with a South Asian background entered into academia, public life and forums. Although some have focused more on the American economy, others have helped shape discussions of the Indian economy, problems of inequality, and world economic

---

[65] Wipro website.

trends. Among them is Amartya Sen, winner of the Nobel Prize in economics in 1998. One of the world's foremost public intellectuals as well as a giant in the field of economics, Sen has continued to explore his Indian roots, and looked critically at its economy even as he has taught for years in the West. Whereas many economists have been sceptical about democracy in India, arguing that a more authoritarian government would work better for an industrial society, Sen has eloquently argued the reverse: that democracy is best both for India's economic development and for human rights.

Born in 1933, and raised in Dhaka and at Shantiniketan, Rabindranath Tagore's school in West Bengal, Sen attended Presidency College, Calcutta, and later received his PhD in economics from Cambridge University. He has taught at the Delhi School of Economics, the London School of Economics, Oxford and Cambridge Universities, and is presently Thomas W. Lamont University Professor at Harvard University. A pioneer in social choice theory and a leader in the study of welfare economics and famines, and in bringing together economics and philosophy, he has helped establish the United Nations Human Development Report as an annual snapshot of the progress of the world's nations in advancing the welfare of their citizens. In 2022, in his late eighties, Sen has written a memoir, *Home in the World*. It is both a personal memoir and an investigation of the social and cultural worlds that have shaped his life.

While Sen has attended to the role of government in development, he has stressed the importance of public education, especially of women, health care and the alleviation of poverty. In a recent assessment, Sen and his co-author Jean Drèze have criticized the neglect of the real interests of the downtrodden:

> The 'relatively privileged'... who may be no more than a fourth or fifth of the total population, comprise different strata—varying from tycoons... to educated ordinary people... who are not particularly rich but enjoy level of living that separate them from the masses of the underdogs of society... [M]any of the

demands that are often called 'populist,' such as higher pay scales for public sector employees or low fuel prices, are in fact primarily demands of the relatively affluent, with limited benefits—if any—for the underprivileged…These demands… actually deflect public resources that could be used to reduce the astonishing deprivation of the really deprived. The biggest gainers… come often form the most prosperous and affluent—the rich who drive around in luxury cars and SUVs that consume state-subsidized diesel, the large landowners who use free electricity to tap free groundwater, and the fertilizer companies that have been raking huge subsidies for many years in the name of food security for the common people.[66]

Economist Jagdish Bhagwati, University Professor at Columbia University, a Gujarati who had been a fellow student with Amartya Sen in Calcutta and Great Britain, has a decidedly different view of socialism and the free market. While many Indian intellectuals supported Nehruvian economic and social policies, he became a trenchant critic of the first Indian prime minister's programme. Bhagwati argued that socialism, as exemplified by the Five Year Plans, limited foreign investment and prevented competition, while free trade would enhance growth and reduce poverty. He writes as an insider, having been involved in research for the First Five Year Plan and then later, after 1991, as an adviser to the Government of India, in urging the liberalization of trade and the freeing of the economy from controls. Based in New York, Bhagwati played an important role in pressing Indian leaders to take a different policy course.

Raghuram Rajan, another economist from India mainly based in the United States, has played a significant role in shaping the Indian economy. Chief Economist at the International Monetary Fund from 2003 to 2006, and currently the Katherine Dusak Miller Distinguished Service Professor of Finance at the Chicago Booth School of Business, he served as the governor of the Reserve Bank

---

[66] Drèze, Jean and Amartya Sen. 2013. *An Uncertain Glory*. India and Its Contradictions. Princeton: Princeton U. Press, pp. 268–69.

of India from 2013 to 2016, returning to Chicago after his tour of official duty in India. Co-author with Luigi Zingales of *Saving Capitalism from the Capitalists* (2004), and author of *Fault Lines: How Hidden Fractures Still Threaten the World Economy* (2010), he also published *The Third Pillar: How Market and the State Leave the Community Behind* (2019). Rajan's writings demonstrate his ability to put economic issues into clear English and present them to laymen. In *Fault Lines*, he presents a penetrating explanation of the economic crisis of 2008, though he might be seen to pull his punches against greedy American bankers and short-sighted regulators.[67] With Sen and Bhagwati, Rajan exemplifies the significant role that South Asians abroad have in shaping the Indian economy.

Ruchir Sharma, neither an academic nor in a public administrative role, is head of Emerging Markets and Global Macro at Morgan Stanley Investment Management, and writes frequently for major news media about national economies around the globe. In his incisive *Breakout Nations* (2012), he decries those who believe they can understand a nation's progress from an armchair at home, so he spends a week each month in some foreign country checking in. He addresses similar themes in *The Rise and Fall of Nations: Forces of Change in a Post-Crisis World* (2016) and *The 10 Rules of Successful Nations* (2020), while as a close observer of the Indian political scene, in his *Democracy on the Road: A 25-Year Journey through India,* (2019), he takes a close look at its changes over time. His clear and incisive presentations are invaluable to a general audience.

These economists of South Asian background often address the issues of inequality and poverty, which are important worldwide, but especially for India. Those named here, like several of their American brethren such as Paul Krugman and Joseph Stiglitz, have noted increasing inequality in many nations. Bhagwati would like the market to solve the problem. For others, interventions by governmental bodies, NGOs, and social movements are vital.

---

[67] Rajan, Raghuram G. 2010. *Fault Lines*. Princeton: Princeton U. Press, p. 18.

Although the career paths of the economists discussed to this point have been upward, one of the highest fliers fell precipitously. Rajat Gupta, born in Kolkata in 1948, was educated at IIT Delhi, and the Harvard Business School. He then joined McKinsey and Company, one of America's most prestigious financial advisory firms, rising to become its leader in 1994. During his thirty-seven years there, he also joined the boards of major corporations, served as adviser to the UN and to the Rockefeller Foundation, chaired the Bill and Melinda Gates Foundation, and played a founding role at both the Indian School of Business and the American India Foundation.

In 2011, Gupta was linked to hedge fund manager, Raj Rajaratnam and the Galleon firm he founded, and charged with insider trading. Although Gupta vigorously denied the charges, he was convicted in 2012 and sentenced to two years in prison, which he served from 2014 to 2016 at Federal Medical Center Devens in Ayer, Massachusetts. This has been skilfully detailed by Anita Raghavan in *The Billionaire's Apprentice*. Upon his release, Gupta again pleaded his innocence, and published his memoir *Mind Without Fear* (2019) to present his side of the affair. Andrew Ross Sorkin procured the first interview with Gupta just as the latter's book was published. Sorkin recounts, in part:

> He is aggressively unrepentant. He maintains he is innocent despite the jury verdict against him on three counts of securities fraud and one charge of conspiracy... he notes that he shouldn't have trusted Mr. Rajaratnam and that he spoke a little too loosely when he discussed Goldman's corporate secrets on a phone call that the FBI secretly recorded... Mr. [Preet] Bharara was the crusading United States attorney for the Southern District of New York who prosecuted both Mr. Rajaratnam and Mr. Gupta... Mr. Gupta is mad at Mr. Bharara... 'That I, like many of those guys he targeted, was a fellow Indian only burnished his tough-guy aura.' ... the case against Mr. Gupta revolved around the day in the fall of 2008 when Warren Buffett agreed to make a crucial investment in Goldman Sachs... Sixteen seconds after Goldman's

board finished discussing Mr. Buffett's soon-to-be-announced investment, Mr. Gupta called Mr. Rajaratnam. Mr. Rajaratnam then started buying Goldman shares.[68]

Bharara wrote in his memoir, *Doing Justice: A Prosecutor's Thoughts on Crime, Punishment, and the Rule of Law* (2019), 'that accusations about hostility towards a fellow Indian were "comical" and "absurd"'.[69] Goldman Sachs' former chairman Lloyd Blankfein, attacked by Gupta for testifying in the trial, responded that Gupta should own up to his own actions.[70]

Economic relations between India and America have also been characterized by a flood of American companies establishing themselves in India. A few like General Electric, Citibank and several automobile companies have long histories in India, while others entered during the pre-liberalization era, and still others have arrived in the past twenty to thirty years as the business climate and rules changed. These 'invaders', as they have been called, smelling India's huge market, have included tech giants, large wholesalers, a growing number of American fast-food businesses, and retailer Walmart.

Some of these companies came and operated without incident. Others did not. Three cases warrant a close look. The first is Union Carbide, which precipitated one of the biggest industrial disasters in world history. The second is Enron, whose Dabhol energy plant debacle caused huge financial losses. The third is Monsanto that tried to monopolize the sale of its seeds for certain valuable Indian crops.

Union Carbide was founded in 1898 and gradually acquired other chemical companies. From 1927 to 1932, during the construction of a West Virginia tunnel project led by the company, unprotected workers were asked to mine silica and many died from exposure to silica dust. But its biggest disaster was yet to come.

---

[68] Andrew Ross Sorkin, 'Rajat Gupta is Unrepentant for His Crimes,' *New York Times*, 22 March 2019.
[69] Bharara, Preet. 2019. *Doing Justice*. NY: Knopf, p. 203.
[70] Sujeet Indap, 'Goldman disturbs Rajat Gupta's post-prison calm', *Financial Times*, 24 March 2019.

At a Union Carbide India pesticide plant in Bhopal, Madhya Pradesh, on 3 December 1984, methyl isocyanate (MIC) gas was accidentally released, exposing the crowded local population to the gas and other chemicals. This is part of the account given by twelve-year-old Ramesh, a tailor's apprentice:

> I must have gone to sleep around 9 p.m... in the middle of the might I heard a lot of noise... People were shouting 'Get up!' 'Run, run!' 'Gas has leaked!'... [T]he room was full of white smoke... [M]y eyes started stinging as if someone was burning a lot of dried chilies and every breath was burning my insides... The gas was getting in through my mouth. Through my nose... My father refused to leave... I did not know that the gas could kill people but while running away I had seen a little child crying beside his mother who was lying beside the road... Early in the morning we set out for home. My eyes were swollen and my chest was aching... we saw a lot of dead cattle lying around and a lot of people too... I saw a lot of dead bodies of men, women and children lying in front of the Union Carbide factory gate... Two of my friends Santosh and Rajesh had also died.[71]

The state government confirmed almost 4000 deaths, some 40,000 permanently disabled, and several hundred thousand more suffering from a variety of ailments. Unofficial figures were much higher. Investigations showed that almost all the safety features of the plant had been turned off for economic and other reasons. Even a warning siren intended to protect the local population had been turned off and only alerted plant workers. As the gas spewed out it affected almost the whole population of 8,00,000 in Bhopal.[72]

The Government of India sued Union Carbide and the company settled out-of-court for $470 million in 1989. Efforts to extradite

---

[71] Hanna, Bridget, Ward Morehouse, Satinath Sarangi. eds. 2004. *The Bhopal Reader*. NY: Apex Press., pp. 4–5.
[72] Hanna 2004, p. xxivff; Lapierre, Dominique and Javier Moro. 2002. *Five Past Midnight in Bhopal*. NY: Warner Books, p. 97ff.

the CEO of the company at that time, Warren Anderson, failed, and the company did not adequately clean up the plant site in the aftermath. The families of those killed and injured received little or no compensation, due both to the insufficiency of the funds provided by the company and to Indian government corruption. A few years later, Union Carbide was acquired by Dow Chemical, which asserted that it had no responsibility for the earlier disaster. Stock in Union Carbide Ltd, India was later sold and the funds partially used to build a hospital for the victims. The many journalists and scientists who studied the event found that when the plant was constructed, the safety measures that had been planned were not implemented. A few Indian employees of the plant were eventually convicted of negligence, and Anderson disappeared from sight. The catastrophe, which testifies to the greed and carelessness of the responsible parties, stands as a permanent black mark against Union Carbide, an American company that tried to shift all blame to its Indian subsidiary. The enduring effects of the contamination of Bhopal's ground water as well as other environmental risks are documented.

Now, Enron. It was a Houston-based energy conglomerate, which grew from a deliverer of natural gas into a multi-faceted company that traded in gas futures, built energy plants in places distant from its home in Texas, and had executives deeply involved in convoluted accounting schemes that led to criminal prosecution and eventually destroyed it.[73] After an initial success building the Teeside plant in the UK, it entered into many deals to build energy plants in developing countries. The biggest of these arrangements was made in 1994 with the government of the state of Maharashtra, India, to build a huge energy facility at Dabhol. Although promising competitive prices, it turned out that once the plant was built, the prices offered were exorbitant. The Government of Maharashtra declined to pay these prices. The deal collapsed and the plant was temporarily shut down. Enron lost almost a billion dollars, and the Dabhol failure

---

[73] McLean, Bethany and Peter Elkind. 2004. *The Smartest Guys in the Room*. The Amazing Rise and Scandalous Fall of Enron. NY: Penguin; Prashad, Vijay. 2003. *Fat Cats and Running Dogs*. Monroe, Maine: Common Courage Press, pp. 100–13.

contributed to its decline. Enron continued to operate worldwide until 2001, when its inflated stock price and financial shenanigans were revealed, as were those of its auditor, the firm, Arthur Andersen. Both Enron and Andersen failed. The top leaders of the firm, Ken Lay and Jeffrey Skilling, were convicted of their crimes. But Rebecca Mark, who was not among the employees charged with financial fraud and insider trading, escaped to flourish in other ventures. It was she who had consummated the Dabhol contract as head of Enron Development, its third-world investment wing, and extracted extraordinary conditions from the Maharashtra government. She left Enron in 2000, cashing out her stock for $82 million.

Vijay Prashad evinces (2003) that the India involvement of Enron was only one of its many foreign ventures that displayed a similar pattern of extracting extraordinary terms from foreign countries, sometimes with the help of US government agencies and officials. Thus the 'fat cats', or capitalists, worked hand-in-hand with the 'running dogs', pliable government officials, to wrangle the deals they arranged. Like Union Carbide, Enron is a name that arouses deep anger when it is mentioned in India. But India needs and wants foreign investment, and the door to such investment remains mostly open regardless of those failures.

Monsanto, the third American company causing serious problems for India, was responsible, like Union Carbide, for many deaths. Founded in 1901 in St Louis as a chemical company, Monsanto became one of the world's leading insecticide and pesticide producers, which brought it into India. Then the company moved into the food and seed businesses as well. First it tried to manipulate genes to increase milk production in cows, which had, as a positive effect, the production of more milk, but as a negative effect, injury to the cows—an effect Monsanto hid as best it could. Then it moved into seed production, developing genetically modified seeds for what was known as 'Bt cotton'. These seeds purportedly had insect-fighting properties, but they were also produced to be sterile, meaning that new seeds had to be purchased annually, and were, in addition, more expensive than the seeds traditionally used by

Indian cotton farmers. A Monsanto subsidiary pushed them into the market without adequate trials and demonstrations, but successfully lobbied the government nonetheless, and so cornered a large part of the Indian market for cotton seeds. The seeds briefly repelled certain insects, but then the plants succumbed to other insects, and did not yield the promised results. Raj Patel, an analyst of the world food scene wrote:

> In India in 2005, the Indian state of Andhra Pradesh… banned Monsanto from licensing its genetically modified cotton seed on the grounds that they had been ineffective. Yields were lower, and more prone to disease, than non-genetically modified crops. The experiment had a terrible human cost: 90 per cent of farmers who had committed suicide in Andhra Pradesh and Vidarbha had been growing genetically modified cotton.[74]

In addition to farmer suicides, the Monsanto misadventure prompted unrest. In 1998, in the nearby state of Karnataka, the Karnataka State Farmers' Association fought against Monsanto and their seeds by burning the sites of field trials and raiding their offices in Bangalore and tearing up their files.[75]

The Monsanto deceptions continued for years in India, as well as in other countries.[76] Social scientists have investigated the issues of genetically modified (GMO) seeds and farmer suicides, and some have presented data to show that the Bt cotton seeds were more effective than ordinary seeds. Further, they insisted that farmer suicides have been taking place for generations, and that although there have been increased numbers in recent decades, Monsanto's seeds cannot be identified as the principal cause. Several documentary films, focusing on the Vidarbha area in Maharashtra, have pointed

---

[74] Patel, Raj. 2007. *Stuffed and Starved*. The Hidden Battle for the World Food System. Brooklyn: Melville House, p. 138.

[75] Ibid., p.140; Saini, Angela. 2012. *Geek Nation*. How Indian Science is Taking over the World. London: Hodder & Stoughton, p. 90ff.

[76] Robin, Marie-Monique. 2010. *The World According to Monsanto*. NY: New Press, p. 291ff.

to Bt cotton seeds as leading to crop failure, indebtedness, and suicide. From the 1990s onwards, there have been more than 60,000 reported suicides in Maharashtra, with an average of ten every day. The Indian government, concerned with farmer suicides across the country, has offered cash payments to families of suicide farmers. But this has not reversed the trend lines, and both indebtedness and suicides continue to be crucial issues in rural India.[77]

Monsanto has marketed GMOs for corn and soybeans worldwide, as well as those for cotton. At every stealthy move, it successfully lobbied the governments concerned so as to avoid the normal testing of its products before they were released on a grand scale. These resulting problems have affected not only India and Indian farmers, but also, as Raj Patel has persuasively argued in *Stuffed and Starved: The Hidden Battle for the World Food System* (2007), small farmers in all corners of the globe. In the last decade to the present, Monsanto has continued to face lawsuits for the disastrous consequences of the application of its products in France and the US.[78]

---

[77] 'Farmers' suicides in India', Wikipedia, presents the arguments and data on suicide numbers.
[78] *New York Times*, 12 April 2019

5

Missions Revised

With Indian (and Pakistani) Independence on 15 August 1947, American organizations no longer had to work under the umbrella of the British Raj, but could operate more directly with Indians on projects of common interest. In the decade after Independence, consulting with the Government of India, the Rockefeller Foundation greatly expanded the range of its activities in India. In 1958, Morarji Desai, the Finance Minister of India, met with Dean Rusk, the president of the foundation from 1951–1961. The foundation and the Indian government—or at least Desai—were not in accord. Desai defended the role taken by the government: 'It is a necessary policy, he says, in order to insure that the RF and other agencies make the best possible use of their funds…and to enable the government of India to take appropriate account of outside grants when making its decisions about allocation of government funds... the Indians are in a far better position to know the best opportunities and greatest needs in India than RF officers can be'. Desai added:

> [T]here is also risk of undue pride on the side of donors and loss of self-respect on the side of recipients, which damage the character of both. Operating with government aid and advice will help to avoid these evils. If donors are unwilling to extend their aid in due humility and through procedures which protect the self-respect of the recipients, India will gladly do without their gifts.[1]

---

[1] Memo of Interview, Dean Rusk with Mr. Desai, Indian Minister of Finance, September 12, 1958, Folder 2 , Box 1, Series 460, Record Group 1.2, RFA, RAC.

As the conversation proceeded, Desai and Rusk disagreed further. When Rusk insisted that the foundation could better choose Indian recipients for grants in science, Desai replied that even in science, the Government of India had superior wisdom as to which candidate should be chosen. When Rusk asked if India wanted to create institutions on the order of Cambridge or Oxford, world-class institutions, that is to say, Desai said that the time for India to pursue that goal had not yet come. India's need was to bring up the least within their own country to closer equality with the best. The meeting between Rusk and Desai points to the principal issue at stake. Rusk wanted foundation funds to be used to bring Indian institutions up to a world-class standard, while Desai, looking at India's many poor, wanted to spread donated funds to lesser institutions that served those other than an elite few.

Although Rockefeller was foiled in obtaining control of the choice of individual and institutional beneficiaries without finance ministry intervention, the foundation had no intention of stopping its programmes in India. In his memo on the meeting with Desai, Rusk said that India, after the US, was the biggest recipient of Rockefeller funds and had great needs and potential. He would soon go to India himself to talk to other Indian officials and had no intention of acceding to Desai. Yet since the 1950s, it had been Rockefeller's pattern to work through national governments and get their approval. Eventually, the Rockefeller Foundation and the Government of India worked out mutually satisfactory guidelines.

From 1948–1973, the golden age of its work in India, the Rockefeller Foundation greatly expanded its operations. By 1966, it had fifteen of its personnel in India helping to oversee numerous proposals and grants in medicine, agriculture, the social sciences and the humanities. The medical program was extensive and had the deepest roots. The foundation continued to work with institutions like the Vellore Medical College and Hospital,[2] imposing the condition that its places be open to Christians and non-Christians alike.

---

[2] Vellore-RF correspondence 1955, Folder 468, Boxes 51, 52, 53, Series 464, Record Group 1.2, RFA, RAC.

A crucial member of the Rockefeller team overseeing India grants was Chadbourne Gilpatric (1914–1989). A Harvard graduate and Rhodes scholar at Oxford who had worked at the CIA before joining the foundation in 1949, in 1956 he rose to be associate director dealing with grants for urban design and the humanities. Gilpatric was instrumental in setting up programmes in linguistics that had a wide impact on language study and learning in India and the US. He also helped support a number of smaller but valuable projects such as V.K. Menon's books on the transfer of power and Khushwant Singh's history of the Sikhs.[3] In 1967, Gilpatric turned his attention to agricultural education and directed a study to document 'changing agricultural conditions on small farmers in Uttar Pradesh'.[4] Following its successful efforts at improving agricultural productivity in Mexico, the Rockefeller Foundation, in combination with USAID and the Ford Foundation, helped India greatly expand agricultural productivity—that step forward called the Green Revolution.

Alongside the Rockefeller Foundation's expanding operations in India in the post-Independence period in 1951, the enhanced and restructured Ford Foundation, the largest private American foundation then, came onto the stage—'the fat boy in the canoe', as Rockefeller President Dean Rusk described it. Paul G. Hoffman (1891–1974), first president of this new Ford Foundation, decided that India—one of the two Asian giants along with China, but the only one that was non-communist—was to be a focus of serious investment by the foundation. Assistance to India would demonstrate what a free people equipped with wealth and wisdom could do to help others attain equal success. If poverty were alleviated in India, Hoffman seemed to think, India would be won for the West and for democracy. In 1951, Hoffman visited India, and Prime Minister Nehru encouraged the foundation to invest in projects sanctioned by India.

---

[3] Rockefeller Foundation archives, files on Gilpatric's work in India, Folders 713–79, Boxes 73–80, Record Group 464, Series 1.2, RFA, RAC.
[4] Biographical sketch in Rockefeller Foundation Archives.

Hoffman recruited as the foundation's representative in India, the agricultural sociologist Douglas Ensminger, who had received BA and MA degrees from the University of Missouri and a PhD from Cornell and later worked from 1939–1950 for the US Department of Agriculture's land-grant college programme. Ensminger visited India in 1951 and took up his job in 1952, becoming in time, the most powerful representative of the Foundation abroad. Ensminger worked closely with the Government of India through Nehru and other top officials, but also with the trustees of the Foundation in the US. In his lengthy memoir of his India days, Ensminger described himself as a 'change agent' loosed in a society pinioned by tradition and in desperate need of change.[5]

During the 1950s and 1960s, providing American technical assistance to developing or Third World areas was a prominent goal for Ensminger and the Ford Foundation. In the case of India, technical assistance consisted largely of bringing foreign experts—most often Americans, but also Europeans, Canadians, etc., to offer guidance. Although Ford provided elaborate orientation programmes for these visiting foreigners, it underestimated the difficulties they would face of living and working in a distant culture and making substantial contributions. In this heyday of American overseas institution building, however, confidence started high—both in the capacity of the foreigners to assist and in the rate at which India and Pakistan could progress.

In the period 1951 to 1995, the Ford Foundation made about 2,500 grants to India, expending $128 million by one account, and $275 million by another—in either case, the sums expended were staggering, as were the number of projects supported. Much early attention was given to the area of community development. The effort had modest results, but prepared the way for more attention to the needs of village India and the Indian masses. Ensminger stressed the need for technical aid to agriculture more than holistic community development.[6] Even while focused on rural society,

---

[5] Ensminger. Oral history. Ford Foundation Archives.
[6] Staples, Eugene. 1992. *Forty Years of the Ford Foundation in India*. NY: Ford Foundation, p. 23ff.

Ensminger helped develop institutes of public administration and management and technology and programmes to assist Indian universities, consistent with Ford's frequent inclusion in its projects of some kind of education or training component. To further this interest in education, Ensminger recruited F. Champion Ward (1910–2007) from the University of Chicago to serve as educational specialist for the foundation.

Among other goals, Ward hoped that by giving grants for general education to a number of Indian universities, he would help them provide the breadth of knowledge that he thought students at America's best universities were getting. The results were modest at best.[7] A pamphlet by a Delhi University leftist group in 1968 maintained that Ford's efforts in aiding the university were aimed at corrupting and controlling it for US foreign policy aims.[8]

Under Ensminger, the foundation also became involved in urban planning in India, first in Delhi, but soon in a big way in Calcutta. In that city, the Calcutta Metropolitan Planning Organization, consisting of international experts, mostly American and Indian colleagues, put together a Master Plan—which, despite some achievements, met with numerous unforeseen problems in implementation.[9] When Ensminger finally stepped down in 1970 after an unusually long tenure, the foundation entered a new mode of operation in India, more modest financially, and shrank the number of Americans it employed in India from over a hundred in 1968 to a dozen in 1973.

An issue that bedevilled both the Ford and Rockefeller Foundations in the early post-Independence period was their connection to the CIA. In 1960, Dean Rusk wrote to American Ambassador Ellsworth Bunker (1894–1984) that he had heard

---

[7] TFF Grant Files 58–58, University of Delhi; 59–05, University of Baroda; 59–16, Aligarh Muslim University. Also see F. Champion Ward, *Oral History*.

[8] Chakravarty, Subhash, convener. 1968. 'US Facts Speak about Aid & Education'. Delhi: Front against US Imperialist Penetration, p. 31ff.

[9] FF Grant File on the CMPO is 61–217; interviews with S. K. Roy, Calcutta, 21 January 1997, and Nirmala Banerjee, Calcutta, 19 January 1995, participants in the project.

that Indian Defence Minister Krishna Menon had said that the Rockefeller Foundation 'had some connection with the CIA'. Rusk was incensed particularly since the remark had come from one 'who is presumed to know something about such things...' Rusk insisted that the foundation, in order to work in more than sixty countries stayed clear of intelligence activities, and promised to pull out of India completely if Government of India officials continued to spread such a story.[10]

The study of available Rockefeller Foundation files yields no evidence of a relationship between the foundation and the CIA in the early post-war period, although in 1949, Chad Gilpatric had moved directly from the CIA to the foundation. In the case of the Ford Foundation, however, there is some evidence of a CIA connection. The Ford Foundation made grants to organizations which were also supported by the CIA, including the Congress for Cultural Freedom (CCF), an international cultural and intellectual organization that in the 1950s and 1960s attracted leading intellectuals worldwide to its programmes. Kai Bird reports in his biography of John J. McCloy (1992) that McCloy (1895–1989) as the chairman of the Ford Foundation Board of Trustees, and other Ford officers, made an agreement with the CIA: the foundation would occasionally support organizations in which the CIA was interested; the CIA agreed not to recruit foreign area trainees of the Ford Foundation until after their training.[11]

From its inception, the CCF received operating funds from the CIA that were channelled through a foundation in New York City. The CIA gave the CCF about $10,00,000 annually, and the Ford Foundation, which from 1957 on, openly funded the organization's conferences and publications, gave about $5,00,000. In 1967, the

---

[10] Rusk to Ellsworth Bunker, 22 July 1960, Folder 3, Box 1, Series 460, Record Group 1.2, RFA, RAC.

[11] Bird, Kai. 1992. *The Chairman.* John J. McCloy, The Making of the American Establishment. New York: Simon & Schuster, p. 357ff; Coleman, Peter. 1989. *The Liberal Conspiracy.* The Congress for Cultural Freedom and the Struggle for the Mind of Postwar Europe. New York: The Free Press, p. 220ff.

leftist American magazine *Ramparts*_published details of CIA backing for many organizations including the CCF.[12] The CCF at first denied, then admitted the support. The director of the CCF resigned and CIA funding was apparently halted. The CCF was slightly reformed as the International Association for Cultural Freedom, and the new director, Shepard Stone, a former high official of the Ford Foundation, was a close associate of McCloy's. The Ford Foundation, then headed by McGeorge Bundy, funded a number of what they called 'CIA orphans', which included the reformed CCF and the Asia Foundation. With several former high officials of the Ford Foundation admitting to knowledge of the CIA involvement,[13] clearly it was no secret within the organization's higher reaches.[14] Chadbourne Gilpatric of the Rockefeller Foundation was also well acquainted with the CCF, but on one occasion at least declined to support a prospective periodical from Asia that would be under its auspices. Remarkably, these revelations and the virulent attacks on the CCF in the Indian press and throughout the Third World did not seriously harm the Ford Foundation in India. It had gained sufficient goodwill to ride out all these storms.

As American confidence waned, the activity of the Rockefeller and Ford Foundations in India diminished. The Rockefeller Foundation pulled out of India in 1973, choosing to emphasize international programmes rather than national ones, and the Ford Foundation decided to greatly cut back on the number of Americans working for it in the subcontinent. Ford not only needed to cut expenditures because of financial losses, but also decided that it would be a grant-making organization rather than a supplier of technical experts from abroad. For a variety of reasons, a new day had dawned. Thereafter, more reliance would be placed upon Indian experts and institutions,

---

[12] Saunders, Frances Stonor. 2000. *The Cultural Cold War.* NY: The New Press, p. 63ff.

[13] Francis X. Sutton, Dobbs Ferry, August 15, 1996, and Eugene Staples, Washington, D.C., 8 August 1996.

[14] FF Grant File for CCF is 57–395; Ensminger, Oral History, Box 1 I, A. 17. 9 May 1972.

and on working through NGOs rather than through the national government. It is clear that the high hopes for the easy alleviation of poverty and transformation of India, Pakistan and Bangladesh had been an overreach. There had been progress, and the foundations had assisted, but wealth thenceforth would be apportioned more sparingly.

Furthermore, the work of the foundations, including the Rockefeller and Ford Foundations, met with biting criticism, as in, for example, Joan Roelofs' *Foundations and Public Policy: The Mask of Pluralism.*[15] Taking a Marxist perspective, Roelofs argues that the large liberal foundations, including Carnegie, Rockefeller and Ford, play a 'hegemonic' role in shaping public opinion and diverting potential attacks on the neo-liberal order, and so effectively support the aims of Western governments. Working through the media, think-tanks, and other institutions, they co-opt those who might oppose them by helping targeted beneficiaries move towards modest goals rather than more disruptive radical change, and so serve as 'sources of deradicalization'.[16] Offering a contrary case, Roelofs does note Ford's support for 'Books for India', which allowed Indians to purchase selected American publications for greatly reduced prices. However, she makes little further reference to specific grants, and gives no evidence of having delved into grant files in the Ford Foundation archives.

What have these foundations learned from India? They have learned humility, as the centralized system of funnelling grants in the early period has been replaced by more diverse paths to supporting development. There has been progress, and the foundations have played and continue to play a role, but the wealth is now apportioned more sparingly as it has been seen that the improvement of the world does not depend merely on the wisdom, or choices of a few Americans. Lessons must be learned from

---

[15] Roelofs, Joan. 2003. *Foundations and Public Policy*. The Mask of Pluralism. Albany: State University of New York.
[16] Ibid., p. 57.

Indians, Japanese and Chinese as well as Americans, from villagers as well as economists, environmentalists and sociologists.

In the early 1970s, after the departure of the Ford Foundation's Douglas Ensminger, those who followed him as the representative in New Delhi drastically cut back foreign staff from more than 100 to scarcely more than a dozen. The foundation became a grant-giving organization and most of these grants went to Indian NGOs. As Eugene Staples has written, summarizing this work: 'Grants to NGOs address a variety of problems—the economic production activities of poor people, both rural and urban; land, water and forestry conservation and management, employment—particularly as it involves women; education; reproductive health; child welfare; legal rights and cultural identity.'[17] Citing some of the earlier grants to NGOs, Staples writes:

> One of the early small grants, in 1979, went to the now world-renowned Self Employed Women's Association (SEWA) in Ahmedabad. SEWA used Ford Foundation funds to help organize and train female street vendors and artisans... Another early grant went to a group of voluntary agencies in Ranchi in South Bihar to organize and evaluate village-level community forestry projects... Under a Foundation grant for field research, the Central Soil and Water Conservation Research and Training Institute at Dehra Dun worked with the Haryana State Forestry Department. They discovered that small check dams built at the top of watersheds at very low cost—usually for about $10,000—produced astonishing results in controlling erosion.[18]

Yet even as it encourages Indian philanthropy, the Ford Foundation continues to work in India, especially in the areas of water and forestry resources, women's health, education, employment and cultural endeavours. In recent decades, the foundation's leadership has become more diverse, with a woman and members of minorities,

---

[17] Staples 1992, p. 27.
[18] Ibid., pp. 27–28.

serving as its president since 1979: Franklin Thomas, 1979–1996; Susan Berresford, 1996–2007; Luis A. Ubiñas, 2008–2013 and Darren Walker, 2008–present. Most of its funds and grants are expended in the US, but more than a third of grants are given for work abroad with India always among the leading recipients.

The tale of the Rockefeller Foundation and India differs. It had begun its grants to India during and just after the First World War and opened its New Delhi office in 1935; there was also a smaller office in Hyderabad. In 1956, it made an agreement covering agricultural programmes and assistance. In the early 1970s, this agreement was ended, when the Government of India informed the foundation that the goals of its grants to India had been achieved. The Rockefeller Foundation then moved to close its operations in India, although a representative of the agriculture programme remained in New Delhi for some time thereafter. It is not clear why the office and most India grants were terminated. The foundation shifted its attention to other countries, including Indonesia and African countries.

The Rockefeller Foundation has not written off India as a recent joint announcement by the Rockefeller Foundation and Tata Power makes clear. With Rockefeller support, Tata Power launched TP Renewable Microgrid Ltd, an effort to supply power at a very modest cost to '10,000 microgrids across rural India, providing clean power to nearly 5 million households and businesses, directly impacting the lives of 25 million people over the next decade'. With input from researchers at IITs in India and MIT, this initiative will use all kinds of biomass to help run these microgrids and empower millions who have been without a reliable and cost-effective source of power for home and work.[19]

The election in 2017 of Rajiv Shah as president of the Rockefeller Foundation is yet another turn in the foundation's link to India. From a Gujarati background, Shah grew up in Pennsylvania and was educated in medicine and administration in the US and the UK. Rising in federal government service during the Obama

---

[19] Rockefeller Foundation, Monthly Report, November 2019.

years to become director of USAID from 2009 to 2015, Shah is one of the able South Asian Americans to reach impressive heights in American public service and management.

With a population of about 350 million at the beginning of the twentieth century, but 1.4 billion by 2020, India is now the world's most populous nation. Should foreign organizations and governments and international bodies be involved in trying to control the population growth? India in the 1950s, under Prime Minister Nehru, reached out for international help and the Ford Foundation stepped forward with aid in the 1950s. An agreement in 1959 stated that the foundation would 'assist in the development of research on the problem of educating people to accept family planning practice'.[20] By the late 1960s, however, as US government aid entered the field, the Ford Foundation decreased its aid to population-related projects.

In 1952, at about the same time that the Ford Foundation turned to population questions, John D. Rockefeller III, also concerned with population, participated in the founding of the Population Council and became the chairman of its board of trustees for the next quarter century. The Population Council gave grants to Indian institutions and to South Asians for training in relevant disciplines. In the 1950s and 1960s, the Ford Foundation supplied half of the funds for the work of the Population Council. At first India welcomed such aid, but soon the presence in India of Westerners doing this work triggered a reaction. Nehru was one of those who welcomed Ford aid at first, and a few years later railed against foreigners employed in the enterprise of population control. Led by its own personnel, India assumed the task of addressing the population problem, an effort that culminated in the campaign to check population growth by Indira Gandhi's son, Sanjay Gandhi, who in the mid-1970s, notoriously, oversaw the eradication of slums and the forced sterilization of untold numbers of poor men. In 1977, with the end of Mrs Gandhi's Emergency and her election defeat, this campaign ended. In 1980, the death of Sanjay Gandhi put an end to his gruesome work which,

---

[20] Caldwell, Jon and Pat Caldwell. 1986. *Limiting Population Growth and the Ford Foundation Contribution*. London: Frances Pinter, p. 42–3.

as the world learned about it, helped spur a reaction against the reliance on sterilization as the way to control population growth. India continued to encourage family planning as part of a more integrated local and national development. Although Indian leaders saw foreign aid provided towards this effort as tainted by the hand of the giver, a neo-imperialist 'gift', they did accept funds from the Population Council and other foreign donors.

In her *Capitalism: A Ghost Story*, a critique based largely on that of Joan Roelofs' in *Foundations and Public Policy* (2003), Arundhati Roy lists the kind of programmes she opposes but that she believes are supported by the foundations and governments of both the US and India. She is against community development schemes and microfinancing for the poor to start businesses. She is against aid to feminist causes, or those promoting Dalits, because these endeavours split the united front needed to oppose international capitalism. She believes that giving grants to students to study in the US tames them and 'buys them off', so that they fail to become the fierce critics of American and Indian capitalism that they are needed to be. She also believes that the Ford Foundation works, essentially, as a tool of the American government, as do most foundations and many NGOs. Indeed, the only exit from the 'Philanthropoid' mess Roy depicts, constituted by the interplay between these philanthropic entities and the state, even though she occasionally concedes some benefits, is to close them.[21]

Inderjeet Parmar, a scholar of South Asian background based in the UK, writes in the same vein in his *Foundations of the American Century* (2012). He views the Ford, Carnegie and Rockefeller Foundations mainly as extensions and tools of American foreign policy. In posing this argument, he deals with Indonesia, Nigeria and Chile, mentioning neither India or China—a surprising omission given that in the first half of the twentieth century, China was a main Rockefeller focus, and that in the second, India was perhaps the foremost recipient of grants from the Ford Foundation. Moreover, although the foundations and their staff members undoubtedly shared values with Americans in government and with AID,

---

[21] Roy 2019, p. 632ff.

they carried out hundreds of projects beneficial to the host country. Sometimes, they made mistakes; but when such foundations and other NGOs were determined to be working in some way not in the interests of the host country, they were terminated.

Training Experts on the Third World

Within the context of the international Cold War and the growing involvement in Indochina, both the US government and the Ford Foundation became concerned with the paucity of American expertise on both the Soviet Union and the non-Western world. In 1958, the National Defense Education Act was passed 'to strengthen the national defense and to encourage and assist in the expansion and improvement of educational programs to meet critical national needs...'[22] Title VI of this Act provided funding for language and area studies, which still continues with a slightly changed title some sixty years later. Foreign languages were ranked according to their importance for national defence: Russian and Chinese had the highest priority, or four stars, while Bengali followed close behind with three. Because the Communist Party of India was strong in West Bengal, Bengali had high priority. In 1951, the Ford Foundation had initiated its Foreign Area Fellowship Program 'in response to a deepening concern that the United States educationally ill-equipped for its role in the post-war world.'[23]. The Ford programme including the nations of the Asia, Africa and Latin America, the Soviet Union and Eastern Europe, and later included Western Europe as well.[24] Some 2,000 scholars were granted fellowships under the programme from 1952–1972, and of these 185 were focused on South Asia. During the first

---

[22] 'NDEA', in Wikipedia.
[23] Soderlund, Dorothy, ed.1973. *Directory, Foreign Area Fellows 1952-1972*. NY: Social Science Research Council, 1973, Introduction.
[24] McCaughey, Robert A. 1984. *International Studies and Academic Enterprise*. NY: Columbia U. Press, p. 154ff.

two decades, the programmes of the federal government and the Ford Foundation between them trained many of America's experts on South Asia, and centres were established at leading universities to implement training programmes. For South Asia, the scholars trained did not have an initial South Asia connection, except for a few who came from missionary families.

Once the Immigration Act of 1965, which formally removed *de facto* discrimination against Southern and Eastern Europeans as well as Asians, was implemented, tens of thousands of South Asians came to the United States, in time affecting the profile of many South Asian experts. Not only did some of these immigrants themselves offer expertise, but their children had connections to South Asia, and often, language skills that earlier trainees under the NDEA and Ford programmes spent years trying to acquire. The population of experts on South Asia grew apace.

The establishment of the American Institute of Indian Studies (AIIS) was yet another important development connecting America to India. Professor W. Norman Brown, Sanskritist, and organizer of the South Asia programme at the University of Pennsylvania, was the driving force and first president. Brown was successful as an organizer and academic entrepreneur as well as scholar and writer for a wider public as Maureen L.P. Patterson wrote in her history of the AIIS.[25] Brown helped put together the best South Asia centre at the University of Pennsylvania, bringing scholars from a range of disciplines together. Gradually other centres also came up, notably at the University of California, Berkeley, the University of Chicago, the University of Wisconsin and Columbia University. Aided by government funds for language and area centres, these centres like the one at Penn, were interdisciplinary. Under the library programme of Public Law 480, these and other universities were given copies of books published in India, invaluably improving their collections.

---

[25] Elder, Joseph W., Edward C. Dimock, Jr., Ainslie T. Embree, eds. 1998. *India's Worlds and US Scholars 1947-1997*. New Delhi: Manohar, p. 35ff; McCaughey 1984, p. 102, 185.

Enlisting other notable scholar-administrators as successors in his efforts, Brown enlisted Ainslie T. Embree from Columbia University (president of AIIS, 1971–1973), Edward C. Dimock, Jr, from the University of Chicago (president of the AIIS, 1973–1986), and Joseph W. Elder from the University of Wisconsin (president of the AIIS, 1986–1994). At headquarters in India, the AIIS brought in Pradeep Mehendiratta, first as office secretary, then successively as administrative assistant, deputy executive officer, executive officer, and in 1975, director. A skilled and resourceful administrator who understood the Indian bureaucracy, he charted the AIIS through the decades following the Government of India's decree that an Indian must be in charge of an institution operating in India.[26]

Another significant innovation in South Asian studies in the US began in 1971. Started by Professor Robert Frykenberg and his team at the University of Wisconsin, an annual South Asian conference was held in that November. It has been held annually ever since attracting about 600 attendees from the US and recently other countries as well. It was moved to October and is held on the university's Madison campus.[27]

Before the Second World War, a few teachers of Sanskrit had worked at a handful of universities, and some notable contributions, such as those by the Wisers on Indian village life, had advanced the American understanding of India. But it was in the post-war decades that the language and area centres, Ford Foundation training programme, and the AIIS stimulated an extraordinary growth of American scholarship about India. A number of Americans began to study modern Indian languages, engage in historical research, do fieldwork as anthropologists and political scientists, and contribute to the understanding of India, not only in the West, but in India as well.[28] The funds that India owed to the US for food aid—'Public Law 480 Rupees'—also proved invaluable when the US government

---

[26] Elder 1998, p. 43ff.
[27] Robert Frykenberg, 'How the Annual Conference on South Asia Began', October 2011.
[28] Elder 1998, p. 27ff.

allowed some of this vast sum to be used for educational purposes, including building up American library resources on India. About eleven American universities began to receive copies of books and periodicals published in India, and later in Pakistan as well, to place in their collections, providing rich material for research on the subcontinent which an investigator could undertake even before setting foot in India.

Alongside the Rockefeller and Ford Foundations, other private American secular and religious organizations, mostly smaller in scale, continued to operate. These included schools, colleges and medical facilities, many of which had been founded decades earlier, but which now had to operate within the new context of an Independent India. Now they were eyed more suspiciously. Were they helping the new nations in a positive way, or, as regards Christian groups, was their main goal to make converts? Who were to be the owners of the churches and other properties involved? How were different Christian denominations to relate to each other?

Christian missions were minority institutions in a predominantly Hindu nation, India; and in a heavily Muslim nation, Pakistan. As such, they were vulnerable to a variety of attacks, verbal and worse. Arun Shourie, for example, in his *Missionaries in India: Continuities, Change, Dilemmas,*[29] claimed that the Christians in India, both under the Raj and after the Raj, sought to divide the Hindu community in an effort to convert some to Christianity, targeting the tribals and the Dalits, or Untouchables, as most likely to convert.[30] At the same time, many Indians and Pakistanis greatly valued the services missionaries offered in education and medical care. The Christians themselves, both Indian and foreign, often felt that they were a besieged minority, offering a true faith in God and practical services not easily available to many Indians and Pakistanis. Since the late nineteenth century, an ecumenical movement had been underway, which was likely energized by the prospect of Independence from the British Raj. One outcome was the formation of the Church of

---

[29] Shourie 1994
[30] Ibid., p. 179ff.

South India, proclaimed on 27 September 1947. Given its British origins it was heavily Anglican, but it included Protestants from American missionary origins as well. When the Church of North India was proclaimed in 1970, it too included Protestant churches with American missionary roots, including the Presbyterians. Some denominations, including the Presbyterians, and the Vellore mission to be discussed shortly, were in the process of turning over their properties to Indian Christians.[31]

Missionary historian John C.B. Webster provides an astute account of the changes experienced in post-Independence India. In their ongoing ecumenical efforts, Christian groups were pushed closer to each other, yet they remained distinct. The Catholics seemed more prepared and more able to provide religious, social and educational services, but in schools, colleges and hospitals, both Catholics and Protestants had to deal with a declining number of Christian students and patients. Additionally, the American and British strands of missionary work became increasingly marginal, as a more international and Indian, Christian effort developed. Foreign missionaries were becoming fewer and their places were taken by Indian Christians—many from Kerala, which along with areas to the far northeast, had the largest percentage of Christians in India. Although there were still respected Christian institutions such as Ludhiana Medical Centre and St Stephen's College in Delhi, India, and some in Pakistan as well, in both countries, as new schools and medical facilities, both private and public, were built, they tended to sideline the older Christian institutions.[32]

The Vellore Medical College and hospital moved in these years to the foremost rank of Christian institutions in India. During the Second World War, Vellore began the transition to a full-fledged medical college and medical centre for men and women. Many new staff had to be hired, buildings constructed, and a new ethos

---

[31] Wikipedia, 'Church of South India'; 'Church of North India'; websites of CNI, CSI; Webster 1976, p. 292ff; MacCullouch, Diarmaid. 2010. *Christianity*. The First Three Thousand Years. NY: Penguin, p. 953ff.
[32] Webster 2007, p. 273ff.

formed. Though founded as an institution by the Reformed Church, it needed the help of many other denominations. It bought the land needed for a residential college since Dr Ida Scudder insisted that all staff be in residence.

One window into the development of the Vellore Medical College and Hospital in this period is through the exemplary career of Dr Jacob Chandy (1910–2007). A devout Kerala Christian, he was the son and grandson of Anglican priests but was attracted to medicine as a teenager, and entered the Madras Christian Medical College. Upon graduation, he wanted to join a missionary hospital, and finding no position available in India, took one in Bahrain. After three years there, he journeyed to Philadelphia, where he completed a course in neurosurgery and engaged in advanced research. He then moved to Montreal and Chicago for further training and experience. Senior officials at Vellore heard of him and recruited him, although they had no facilities and equipment for his work. He himself raised funds in the US for the equipment he needed and brought it back with him to India.

In 1949, joined by his wife and young son, Chandy moved to Vellore and within a few years set up the facilities for neurosurgery, the first such endeavour in India. Over the following two decades, he trained more than two dozen neurosurgeons and carried out thousands of operations bringing his specialty into the mainstream of Indian medical practice. He also assisted in regularizing the financial procedures at Vellore, played a key role in the Indianisation of the college and medical facilities, and served as principal of the medical college.[33] Often visited by ministers, chief ministers and prime ministers, Chandy seems to have charmed and enlightened them right until his retirement in 1970. He died in 2007 at age ninety-seven and his memory is revered at the Vellore Medical College. Jacob Chandy's son Matthew Chandy, also a neurologist, worked at Vellore from 1972–2001. As the junior Chandy pointed out when I met him in 1993, he and his father could have earned many times more in salary if they had gone to the West. As devoted Christians, they wanted to

---

[33] Chandy 1988, p. 6ff.

build a Christian institution, treating Indians of every community, but training as many Christian students as possible.

In the 1950s, Chandy and his colleagues guided the transition of the Vellore Medical College to Indian ownership. He managed, together with his allies, to shift from a system of direct funding for Vellore from abroad, to an alternate system whereby churches abroad sent their funds to Indian church affiliates which in turn funded Vellore. So although it still received foreign help, Vellore was now understood by its Indian staff members to be an Indian institution. This change, which Chandy viewed as a shift in 'power and responsibility',[34] was crucial in the following decades when Christian institutions were pressured to de-Christianize. Since they were owned and run by Indians adherents to a minority religion, and not by foreign organizations, they were better placed to defend what they saw as their mission. Although the Scudders and other foreigners had started the medical centre at the beginning of the twentieth century, Vellore was en route to becoming an Indian facility owned and run by Indian Christians and their institutions. In Chandy's words: 'The changes that were taking place promoted C.M.C. from a very small struggling medical school to a college trying to meet the bare minimum at least for recognition of the University of Madras and later into an internationally accepted Christian Medical College of excellence.'[35] The Vellore hospital treated the poor at a token cost, consistent with its Christian mission, charging the wealthy higher rates.

Among the educational institutions founded under the Raj, both of which still flourish, are two private secondary schools: the Woodstock School and Kodaikanal International School, the former in Mussoorie in the north, the latter in Kodaikanal in the south. Originally formed to educate missionary children, mainly American, they gradually opened their doors to Indians and those of other nationalities and different faiths. With the coming of Independence, they faced new challenges, and needed to find students from parts

---

[34] Chandy, Jacob. 1988. *Reminiscences and Reflections*. Kottayam: C.M.S. Press, p. 91ff.

[35] Ibid., p. 106.

of the world whose parents had the ability to pay. Furthermore, like Vellore Medical College, they had to deal with the government of India that looked askance at predominantly Christian institutions. And yet they did not want to completely lose the Christian mission that led to their founding. Leaders of both institutions learned that they had to accept non-Christian faculty members and to reach outside India for students who might or might not be Christian.

One family stands out for its distinguished connection to the Woodstock school over four generations: the Alters. Two members of the family were principals of the school: Emmet (1891–1952), from the late 1930s to early 1940s; and his son Robert, from 1968–1978. Their children, Stephen, Joseph and Andrew grew up there, and at a mission station in the plains at Etah. Their cousins were students including the actor Tom Alter, his older sister Martha, a scholar and teacher, and others into the next generation of the family. Stephen Alter's memoir *All the Way to Heaven* recalls with zest and tenderness the world of his youth at Woodstock and in Mussoorie and Etah, but he also reminds us that missionaries took home leave every five years and shuttled their families back to the US. Stephen's father, Robert, took an MA at Cornell during one such visit, and attended Columbia's Teachers' College during the next, in preparation for his principalship duties at Woodstock. Alter's memoir also tells us is that these visits made him wonder about what was 'home': was it the India he loved, or the America that he only gradually came to know, and more fully identified with later in life?

Another struggle Stephen Alter faced was losing faith in God and the Christian mission in India to which his grandparents and parents had devoted their lives. He also witnessed the divide between liberal and fundamentalist Christians. The several denominations that backed the school disagreed about what Christian teaching was to be presented in the school, not only in religion class but in science class as well. Evolution was not taught, and Stephen, an amateur naturalist of considerable skill, had to learn of it later. His father was a liberal Christian, but on occasion chose not to alienate the fundamentalists whose interpretation of the Bible was literalist.

By his senior year at Woodstock, Stephen Alter had decided that he wanted to be a writer and was already scribbling poems and stories before he left India to enter Wesleyan University in 1974. But the vivid stories he recounts in *All the Way to Heaven* demonstrate that though he was becoming more American, India was still alive within him.

The Kodaikanal International School, like Woodstock, had to cope with the loss of missionary teachers and missionary children. In the 1960s, under principal Herb Krause, Kodaikanal School was accredited by the Middle States Association of Colleges and Schools and began to recruit more international students. In 1972, its student body having grown highly diverse, the name was changed to Kodaikanal International School. A debate ensued about how Christian a school it could remain in changed circumstances and with a changing student body. Chaplain Robert Dewey, who took up his post in 1965, proposed melding the ideals of Christianity and religious freedom, outlining a revised mission in 'Project Design 1974'. The high school continued to require a course in the Bible and many faculty and students had a strong Christian commitment, but the school also incorporated an effort to understand other religions.

Forman Christian College in Lahore, Pakistan, was still flourishing during the early years of Independence. Founded as Mission College in 1864 by Charles W. Forman, an American Presbyterian missionary, it was renamed Forman Christian College in 1894. Situated first at the centre of Lahore, it was moved in 1940 to a larger campus on the outskirts of the city, where it is today. It was supported by the Presbyterians until, in 1972, with the accession of Zulfikar Ali Bhutto (1928–1979) as Prime Minister of Pakistan, it was nationalized. At the time, with about 2,500 students, a number that soon grew rapidly, it had long been known as one of the subcontinent's premier colleges, and had a host of distinguished graduates, including many political leaders, businessmen, scholars, educators and writers. Like other Christian educational institutions, it began to hire more South Asian teachers after 1947, and its Christian students were outnumbered by non-Christians. Charging only token fees, Forman has had difficulty carrying out its educational mission.

As discussed earlier, the Indian Village Service, designed by William and Charlotte Wiser to further Indian village development, was another project emerging from a Christian missionary effort. They had set out to work in an area of the United Provinces, shortly to be Uttar Pradesh, in 1945. Although Christian in origin, they worked with villagers of all persuasions, with the Indian government, and with Albert Mayer's village development project described earlier in this chapter. Mayer's and Nehru's vision was secular, that of the Wisers', Christian, but they were united in trying to build a better life for rural Indians.

In late 1945, the Wisers established their base in Lucknow, and gathered Christian workers to develop their programme. With extensive connections locally and to the Christian and development networks throughout India, they worked full steam for the next decade, attracting positive attention and visits from those from near and far. Their overall goal was 'abundant living', and under this rubric, they listed: economic efficiency, congenial human relations, balanced diet, healthful living, proficiency in agriculture and animal husbandry, industrial development, skills in communication and mutual understanding, appreciation of beauty, spiritual development and community organization—a list, surely, not only for rural Indians, but for all human beings.[36]

In 1950, Rev. J.L. Dodds, who was then based at mission central for the Presbyterian Church in the US, toured five villages in which India Village Service. His report presented his own positive impressions, and he quoted, as well, reports by other missionaries who had observed the IVS in action. One reads as follows:

A villager was asked by a Hindu official, 'Are you being pushed into Christianity by these people?' The villager's reply was, 'Oh, no. They are good Christians; they would not do that!' The I.V.S.

---

[36] Wiser, William H. 1949. *India Village Service After Four Years*. Lucknow: Lucknow Publishing House, pp. 6–7.

man was known as 'a good Christian'; his word was reliable; his advice was good, and his friendship was sincere.

Several times I have now heard the non-Christian comment, 'We cannot do it like that; we do not have the missionary spirit,' or 'We need the missionary spirit.'[37]

Dodds, like the Wisers, was keen to demonstrate to Indian officials and others that the efforts of Christian workers were to improve the lives of those they worked with, not specifically to gain converts. The Presbyterians of the IVS wanted to be living examples of Christian lives. If, consequently, some villagers wanted to become Christians, and they found their desire sincere, they would accept them into the Christian fold. In this period, around 1950, William Wiser sensed increasing anti-Americanism as all Christian missions were viewed with suspicion. So they concentrated on doing work that benefitted the villagers: getting better seeds—an example was given of superior and inferior potato plants on adjacent plots—or helping villagers raise better chickens.[38]

The Wisers were strongly supported by Dodds in New York, by Albert Mayer in many communications, and by Indian officials who came to admire their work. The Wisers hired the best Christian staff they could during the decade 1945–1955, when they thrived, before William contracted Parkinson's disease of which he died in 1961. After William's death, Charlotte continued to live in India and went back to their house in Karimpur village, where she would update their classic book, *Behind Mud Walls*, with an account of the same village thirty years later. They embodied the idea of 'service' and of living a Christian life as fully as possible, helping others, and training some of those others to lead when they themselves were no longer there.[39]

---

[37] This is an unpublished report in the Wiser papers that I was able to access. Dodds report, December 23, 1950, Wiser Papers.
[38] Wiser 1949, and reports of I.V.S., 1949–52, Wiser Papers.
[39] Wiser and Wiser 1989.

Christian missions over more than a century broadened their purpose to include not only the goals of conversion and service, especially in the areas of medicine and education, but also development. Among the institutions addressing such needs, two especially famous ones, Foreman Christian (FC) College, Lahore, and the Allahabad Agricultural Institute, were surely vital and important educational institutions in their day, but have recently deteriorated. Others thrive, although they have had to adapt over the decades as India and Pakistan moved from the Raj regime to independent nationhood. The schools, Isabella Thoburn College (Lucknow), Kinnaird College (Lahore), American College (Madurai), and the Calcutta Boys School, and hospitals in Vellore, Miraj (Maharashtra), and Ludhiana (Punjab), are managing to survive even as they have lost the backing of a government dominated by Christians under the Raj. In addition, many Indian Christians and their houses of worship and institutions have been targeted by anti-Christian groups.

The Kodaikanal International School thrives in part today by accepting the children of NRIs who want them to have at least some of their education in an Indian environment. Accepting students from abroad who can pay full fees allows both schools to give scholarships to some Indian Christians who could not afford to attend otherwise. The Woodstock School has coped by having Christian students from East Asia, especially Korea and Japan, pay their full way. Like Kodaikanal, they are then able to give scholarships to Indian Christian students. Both these schools have struggled in the last few decades in figuring out how to retain some Christian teaching when some pupils and faculty are not Christians.[40]

Newer evangelical churches have entered India to see what work for India and Christ they might do. One such is the Assembly of God, Calcutta, founded in the 1950s by Pentecostal evangelist Mark Buntain and his wife Huldah, which thrived under their leadership for decades and continues its work. Dedicated to providing food and medical care for the poor, in its heyday it had 1,500 attendees at its

---

[40] Site visits to both schools, 1999.

Sunday school and 4,000 attending church services, as well as a radio broadcast three times a week, to a considerable audience. Through its work over more than seven decades it has established many churches and schools. Mark Buntain died in 1989 and Huldah continued for years thereafter to oversee the Calcutta Mercy Ministries led by their church. (I observed their populatrity when viisting one of their meetings in 1984.) Although such Christian institutions still operate, Indian Christians and donations from abroad are increasingly under siege.[41]

Philanthropic foundations at first joined and in time superseded the efforts of Christian missions for India's development. The Ford Foundation is still one of the leading organizations working in India, but not on the same scale as earlier. Others include Indian NGOs and philanthropies that are developing apace. The Ford Foundation has encouraged them. There are NGOs in America run by those of South Asia descent actively involved in India. The gigantic American Gates Foundation, dwarfing Ford and Rockefeller, is active around the globe.

As its own presence shrank, and it became a grant-giving NGO, the foundation encouraged the development of Indian philanthropy. The Tatas and Birlas and others were at work in this line, and as the Indian economy grew over the past three decades, and Indians had more resources available, quite a few entered and did such work. The Ford Foundation was happy to have indigenous philanthropists carry on their work. Recently, Indian philanthropy by NRIs and those at home in India, has developed further, as seen at a meeting in October 2019, at Georgetown University, Washington, D.C., at which eleven Indian–American charities joined to form the India Philanthropy Alliance (IPA), whose goal was 'to advance India's humanitarian and sustainable development through increased collaboration and innovation'.[42] The organization involved included Pratham USA, The American India Foundation (AIF), Ekal USA, the Foundation

---

[41] 'Arrests, Beatings and Secret Prayers: Inside the Persecution of India's Christians', The *New York Times*, 22 December 2021; NYT, 23 and 29, 2021.
[42] 'Charity Comes of Age', *India Abroad*, 21 October 2019.

for Excellence, Dasra, CRY America, VisionSpring, Arogya World, Magic Bus USA, Akanksha Fund and Indiaspora. The founder of the last of these, M.R. Rangawami, a Silicon Valley entrepreneur, pressed for the groups to come together over the past two years. This link between NRI philanthropists and India demonstrates how powerful are their ties to their country of origin.

Another important development in the philanthropic relations between America and India is the financial support wealthy Indians are giving to American universities and organizations. The Tata Group gave $50 million to the Harvard Business School and presented funds to Cornell University (alma mater of Ratan Tata) to establish the Tata Innovation Center, while the Tata Chair for Strategic Affairs has been set up at the Carnegie Endowment for International Peace. But the Tata Group has not been alone: Chandrika and Ranjan Tandon gave $100 million to NYU; Anand Mahindra gave a large gift to Harvard to set up the Mahindra Humanities Center; and N.R. Narayana Murthy presented $5.2 million to Harvard to organize the Clay Sanskrit Library. Since many South Asians have attended top American universities and have sent their offspring there as well, their gratitude is understandable. A growing number of gifts are made to Indian institutions as well, but some have wondered why India's educational institutions should not be the primary recipients of these funds, rather than institutions in the world's wealthiest nation.[43]

Meanwhile, new missions to South Asia have taken form. One is exemplified by the Interfaith Youth Corps (IFYC) pioneered by Eboo Patel. An Ismaili Muslim whose family hailed from Gujarat, he grew up in the Chicago area. Although during his youth he had no strong faith or direction, elders and friends encountered at college, both Catholic and Jewish, inspired him. Then he made a trip to India, and understood that though his family came from there, he was an American who needed to learn more about both countries and shape his identity combining Indian roots, American education

---

[43] Alva Mishra, 'India: Charity not beginning at home for universities', *University World News*, 6 February 2011.

and experience, Islamic faith, and a need to reach out to others of different religions. Through his moving autobiographical account in *Acts of Faith* (2010), Patel shows us the path he followed in helping to shape the IFYC, an important organization seeking interfaith understanding and activity in the US and abroad.

Patel shows that the path to religious plurality and understanding involves a commitment to non-violence and service cutting across all humanly constructed barriers. Among those barriers is violence in the name of religion—violence not just in Islam, but in Judaism, Hinduism and Christianity. In presenting his case for non-violence, he aligns himself with Jesus, Gandhi, Dr King and even Mohammed. This is part of what he has to say:

> I concede that the bin Ladens of the world are not making everything up. There are indeed explicit statements about violence in the scriptures of most major religious traditions. But to think that the statements of a religious text suddenly morph into armed reality is to have a profound misunderstanding of religion. There are several layers of meaning to any religious text... Violence committed in the name of religion is really violence emanating from the heart of a particular interpreter... I believe that religious violence is the product of careful design, manipulated by human hands... The theology of the world's bin Ladens is influential because they have built powerful institutions that recruit, inspire, and train people to act in hateful and murderous ways.[44]

Patel and his co-workers have assumed a commitment to non-violence, pledging themselves to undertake activities that will help the poor and oppressed live better lives. The activists involved would learn of faiths other than their own and understand that there may be other paths to truth and what one calls 'god'.

At the same time, some of the growing population of those with South Asian ancestry have launched new kinds of missions to change the shape of America. Reshma Saujani, for example, as

---

[44] Patel, Eboo. 2010. *Acts of Faith*. Boston: Beacon Press, pp. 141–42.

Deputy Advocate for Special Initiatives at the New York City Office of the Public Advocate has worked to promote women's role in science and technology. In a 2011 TED talk on the need to train more young people in STEM (or science, technology, engineering and mathematics) subjects, she reflected on Jawaharlal Nehru's path to building India from 1947 onwards, moving from memories of his efforts towards national revival in the American forum. Then she addressed the problem of the lag suffered by girls in STEM education after a strong start in the lower school grades. In 2012, pursuing that issue, Saujani founded Girls Who Code, a non-profit organization aiming to help train and support women in computer science and other STEM subjects. It presently offers a variety of training programmes—summer immersion, afterschool sessions, clubs and the like—that has attracted considerable support from technology companies. Girls Who Code began a book programme in conjunction with Penguin Random House in 2017, the first publication of which was *Girls Who Code: Learn to Code and Change the World*. The organization has reached tens of thousands of girls, and has hopes of spreading its reach and changing the world.[45]

The New American Leaders project, organized by Sayu Bhojwani, is another complex 'mission' pioneered by a woman of South Asian background. An immigrant from Belize of Indian descent who came to America at age seventeen more than three decades ago, she served two years as New York City's head of its Office for Immigrant Affairs, then sought a wider forum. The mission statement of the NGO she has formed begins: 'New American Leaders is leading a movement for inclusive democracy by preparing first and second generation Americans to use their power and potential in elected office.' Arguing that those recently arrived citizens are grossly underrepresented in elective offices from the local to the national levels, the New American Leaders aims to help such Americans to run for office, forge coalitions, and make the political system more

---

[45] Reshma Jaujani, TED Talk, YouTube; 'Girls Who Code', organization's website; and 'Girls Who Code', Wikipedia.

inclusive.[46] Bhojwani's recent book *People Like Us: The New Wave of Candidates Knocking at Democracy's Door* (2018) describes some experiences of such new politicians, some of whom have been elected to the New York State Legislature, the New York City Council, and other similar bodies, and suggests how others, especially women, may find their voice in America's changing political system.

---

[46] Chelsey Sanchez, 'City's First immigrant Affairs Commissioner Trains Candidates to Transform Democracy', *Gotham Gazette*, 30 October 2018.

6

Gandhi in America After Gandhi

Americans did not cease dialogue with Gandhi after his death. They continued to experiment with Gandhi's teachings, blending Gandhian and Western concepts and methods of non-violent resistance. Although Gandhi was a guide to non-violence, Americans had long followed similar pathways dating back to the seventeenth century, through the anti-slavery and feminist movements of the nineteenth, and to war resistance actions during the First World War.[1] The civil rights movement flowered from the mid-1950s to the late 1960s, drawing on Gandhian teachings and on earlier American activist and non-violent tradition enshrined in several small organizations, including the War Resisters' League (WRL); the Congress for Racial Equality (CORE), which had sprouted from the Fellowship of Reconciliation (FOR); and the American Friends Service Committee (AFSC), which had grown out of the Society of Friends, or Quakers. Supporters now put into action the non-violent methods they had discussed for years working primarily for the equality of America's Black minority, but also to extend equal rights to women and to ban the bomb. A.J. Muste, Bayard Rustin, and especially Martin Luther King, Jr, were the foremost leaders of these struggles, in which many participated.

From the 1910s through the 1960s, A.J. Muste was a remarkable connecter of causes and organizations. Born in the Netherlands, Muste studied at Hope College and the New Brunswick Seminary,

---

[1] Lynd 1966, p. xvff

both associated with the Dutch Reformed Church (now the Reformed Church of America), and finished his education at Union Theological Seminary, as he moved from the Dutch Reformed to Congregationalist, to Quaker denominations. Then turning from a church career, he committed himself to war resistance and labour organizing, serving from 1921–1933 as head of a labour school in Katonah, New York. Then having met the Russian revolutionary Leon Trotsky on a trip to Europe, he plunged into Trotskyite politics before returning to Christian

A.J. Muste
Source: Wikimedia Commons

teaching blended with Gandhian activism, and devoting himself to the causes of racial justice and world peace. Tall, thin and extraordinarily energetic, Muste was a long-time executive director of the Fellowship for Reconciliation, honorary father of CORE,[2] and founder, in his later years, of the Committee for Nonviolent Action and World Peace Brigade. He was linked to two Indian activists in the Gandhian tradition, Vinoba Bhave (1895–1982) and Jayaprakash Narayan (1902–1979).

Muste had encountered Gandhian principles in Shridharani's *War without Violence*, as well as in Gregg's *Power of Nonviolence* and Bondurant's *The Conquest of Violence*. Satyagraha entered his vocabulary. In his *Of Holy Disobedience* and co-authored *Speak Truth to Power*, he lauded Gandhi's example in opposing the Raj. Of Gandhi's impact he wrote, 'The main thing Gandhi did for me was

---

[2] Muste, A.J. 1967. *The Essays of A.J. Muste*. Ed. By Nat Hentoff. NY: Clarion, p. 1ff; Hentoff, Nat. 1982. *Peace Agitator*. The Story of A.J. Muste. NY: A.J. Muste Memorial Institute, p. 25ff.

not so much in terms of teaching me special techniques—because I'd already worked out many of those—but in giving me inspiration through his successful application of nonviolent action in a large-scale political situation.'[3]

Muste was also shaped by his early Quakerism and his understanding of Christ's teaching as one of non-violent resistance. Dedicated as he was to non-violence, anti-bomb and anti-Vietnam war activities were special foci of his last eighteen years. When pressed to go beyond negative resistance to offer a positive vision for humanity, he recalled Gandhi's call to his followers, once Indian Independence was attained, to disband the Congress party and not seek positions of power, but serve the people.[4]

Muste mentored Bayard Rustin, who was from the 1940s onwards a vital African American leader in the struggle for racial equality, peace and disarmament. A charismatic and talented speaker, singer and organizer, Rustin was also bedevilled by his conspicuous homosexuality in an age when homosexuality was illegal and disparaged. Quickly rising to the top of FOR and then CORE, Rustin served a painful prison term from 1944–1946 as a conscientious objector to the Second World War. Upon his release, he helped organize the Journey of Reconciliation, a biracial bus trip through the segregated upper south.

In 1948, Rustin journeyed to India, which he toured for seven weeks, learning about the fate of Gandhism in a free India after the Mahatma's death. Although he was enthusiastic about India, he also had reservations. He suggested that non-violence in India proceeded not so much from principle as from expediency, since Indians, being unarmed, had no other means of resistance.[5] More seriously, he was concerned that India's non-violent resistance was infected by nationalism. 'We should reevaluate the Gandhian movement,' he wrote. 'We have overlooked its negative aspects. It was nonviolent in

---

[3] Hentoff 1982, p. 191.

[4] Ibid., pp. 233–34.

[5] D'Emilio, John. 2003. *Lost Prophet*. The Life and Times of Bayard Rustin. Chicago: U. of Chicago Press, p. 167.

its means, but essentially violent in its ends, which was nationalism.'
In America, Rustin implied, resisters should be guided not by
nationalist aims, but moral principle.

Upon returning from India, Rustin continued working for
the FOR, urging it to pursue an anticolonial initiative for African
colonies still held by European powers. Before this work started, he
was arrested and jailed on a charge of homosexuality, and fired by
the FOR. Released and deeply depressed, he soon became executive
secretary of another peace group, the War Resisters' League, where
he worked from 1953–1965. Dedicated to the mission of Gandhian-
inspired direct action, Rustin formed a powerful connection to
the emerging civil rights movement, especially to Martin Luther
King, Jr.[6]

The civil rights movement was a mass movement of ordinary
people seeking to combat racial inequality in American society and
to bring integration. Starting in the south, it was set off in 1955 in
Montgomery, Alabama, by the action of Rosa Parks (1913–2005),
who by defying the rule of segregated seating in public buses, spurred
a bus boycott. The organizers in Montgomery chose as their leader
Martin Luther King, Jr, a young Black minister. The resistance
organizations WRL, FOR, CORE and AFSC sent emissaries to the
south, Bayard Rustin foremost among them, who formed a strong
relationship with King that endured with sharp ups and downs until
King's murder in 1968. The first project was integration of the local
buses, but the further goals were the integration of public facilities
throughout the south.

The civil rights movement that began in Montgomery in 1955
culminated in the March on Washington in August 1963. Rustin
recruited Black policemen from the East Coast to insure that all was
orderly and the gigantic gathering went off without a hitch. Rustin
played the more important behind-the-scenes role, while King did
what he did best: he made a rousing speech, memorably intoning
over and over that 'I have a dream' of racial justice and equality.

---

[6] Ibid., p. 230ff.

Dr Martin Luther King, Jr, who had begun to read Gandhi as a graduate student, became the most important American non-violent activist. Rustin had urged King and his community to pursue their goals by following Gandhi's method of non-violent resistance, and King integrated Gandhi's teachings with the message of Christ. *In Stride toward Freedom: The Montgomery Story* (1958), an account of the Montgomery Bus Boycott, Dr King wrote:

> As the days unfolded... the inspiration of Mahatma Gandhi began to exert its influence. I had come to see early that the Christian doctrine of love operating through the Gandhian method of nonviolence was one of the most potent weapons available to the Negro in his struggle for freedom... [I]n the summer of 1957 the name of Mahatma Gandhi was well known in Montgomery. People who had never heard of the little brown saint of India were now saying his name with an air of familiarity. Nonviolent resistance had emerged as the technique of the movement...[7]

Influenced by Gandhi's teachings, Dr King wanted to visit India and had an invitation from Prime Minister Nehru in hand. On 3 February 1959, he embarked with his wife Coretta Scott King (1927–2006) and his biographer, the historian Lawrence D. Reddick (1910–1995), and spent about a month-and-a-half touring India. Dr King wrote: 'We were looked upon as brothers, with the color of our skins as something of an asset. But the strongest bond of fraternity was the common cause of minority and colonial peoples in America, Africa, and Asia struggling to throw off racism and imperialism.'[8]

King was momentarily nonplussed as he was introduced at a secondary school for the lowest of the low in the Indian caste system in Trivandrum, Kerala, when the principal said, 'Young people, I would like to present to you a fellow Untouchable from the United

---

[7] Washington, James M., ed. 1986. *A Testament of Hope.* The Essential Writings and Speeches of Martin Luther King, Jr. San Francisco: Harper, p. 447.
[8] Carson, Claybourne, ed. 1998. *The Autobiography of Martin Luther King.* NY: Warner Books, p. 123.

States of America.'[9] King understood that both India and America had caste systems, and he was to address those at the bottom rung, regardless of their personal qualities and talents.

On his tour of India, King was encouraged by what he believed was Gandhi's lasting legacy. He underestimated the resistance of Indians to the elimination of Untouchability and to significant land reform, and while he was impressed by Vinoba Bhave's work for the poor, he overestimated Bhave's impact.[10] Upon return, he often said that the India trip had reinspired him to fight for civil rights, for peace and for economic justice.

Back home, Dr King wrote the introduction to a 1959 revised edition of Gregg's 1934 work, *The Power of Nonviolence*. In 1958, Bondurant published *The Conquest of Violence*. Both were excellent guides to Gandhian concepts and methods at a time when Gandhi's teachings penetrated more deeply into American consciousness.[11] Gandhi's principal gift to America was the concept of satyagraha, or 'soul-force', which had the potential of achieving deep change even in a society addicted to violence. His connection to America inspired many selfless and courageous non-violent activists and some powerful and sensitive American writing.

Among those who King enlisted to come south and join the civil rights movement was the Methodist minister, James Lawson (1928–2024), who would become a teacher of Gandhian values. Already a member of FOR and CORE, Lawson had been imprisoned for refusing to report for the draft in 1951. Upon release he went to India for a three-year stint as a Methodist missionary, remaining until 1955. While in India he studied Gandhi's methods, which

---

[9] Ibid., p. 131.
[10] Carson, Claybourne, ed. 2005. *The Papers of Martin Luther King, Jr.* Vol. V, January 1959December 1960. Berkeley: U. of California Press, pp. 231–39.
[11] Lynd, Staughton, ed. 1966. *Nonviolence in America: A Documentary History*. Indianapolis: BobbsMerrill; Weinberg, Albert K. 1963. *Manifest Destiny*. A Study of Nationalist Expansionism in American History. Chicago: Quadrangle, 1963; Garrow, David J. 1988. *Bearing the Cross*. Martin Luther King, Jr., and the Southern Christian Leadership Conference. NY: Vintage; Weisbrot, Robert. 1991. *Freedom Bound*. A History of America's Civil Rights Movement. NY: Plume.

enabled him to become, in turn, a teacher of the techniques and principles of non-violent activism. After meeting King, Lawson studied at Vanderbilt University where he also became southern director of CORE and conducted workshops in Gandhian methods for students at many institutions through the south. These students, in turn, became leaders of the Student Nonviolent Coordinating Committee (SNCC) and other civil rights organizations. Lawson continued his training and work in the south until 1974, when he moved to Los Angeles to become pastor of a Methodist church.[12] In his memoirs, SNCC leader and later Congressman John Lewis (1940–2020) reports his understanding of Gandhi's teachings in around 1961 as transmitted to him by Lawson and through his own reading:

> One of the most fundamental principles of the Gandhian notion of satyagraha... is that is not merely a technique of achieving specific goals... It is not just a tool to achieve unity and freedom... True satyagraha... is about a fundamental shift inside our own souls. It is rooted in the achievement of inner unity, of inner freedom, of inner certainty. It is a place we find within ourselves—a calm, sure place.[13]

Through Lawson's teaching and that of those like him, Gandhi continued to speak to a variety of movements in America, although more militant activists like Malcolm X (1925–1965) and some former leaders of SNCC abandoned Gandhi's path. Malcolm X proclaimed that Blacks might need to employ 'any means necessary' to achieve their goals. There are Indian parallels: this statement echoed what Subhas Bose had told members of the Indian National Army after the setbacks of 1941: if Gandhian methods do not succeed, then violence, and the formation of a liberation army, become necessary. In India some radical communists who broke with the Communist

---

[12] Zinn 1965, 21-22; Garrow 1988, 89-90; Branch 1988, 259ff; Lawson in Wikipedia
[13] Lewis 1998, 126

Party of India, inspired by Mao rather than Gandhi, engaged in open rebellion in the countryside to try to destroy what they saw as a reactionary bourgeois state.[14]

Other activists in India kept Gandhi's teachings alive after his assassination in 1948, among them Jayaprakash Narayan and Vinoba Bhave. Narayan, educated in America in the 1920s, and a socialist through to Indian Independence, sought peaceful relations with Pakistan, and a more just political order in India. He led the JP movement against what he saw as Congress abuses of power in the 1970s and was jailed during India's Emergency. Bhave, seeking a more egalitarian society, attempted to persuade large landowners to redistribute their property by giving plots of land to those without any.[15]

Another Gandhian working in the decades after his death was the Mahatma's own physician, Sushila Nayyar (1914–2001), whose mission of better medical care for India had begun at Gandhi's Sevagram Ashram in 1939 and continued through her life.[16] In 1948, Nayyar went to America to gain medical and public health training at the Johns Hopkins School of Public Health, seeking like many others in the post-Independence era, to pursue advanced training in the US, rather than in Great Britain. After two years, she returned to India and set up a tuberculosis sanatorium outside Delhi. Then she decided to enter politics, was elected to Parliament and in the 1950s, became health minister under Prime Minister Nehru. From 1957–1971 she was elected to the Lok Sabha several times and from 1962–1967 was again health minister. After retiring from politics, she established the Mahatma Gandhi Institute of Medical Sciences.

As Nayyar travelled West to enhance her medical skills, some Americans went East to learn from Gandhians and spiritual teachers, among them, during the 1960s, the psychoanalyst Erik

---

[14] Guha 2007, 423ff

[15] Guha 2007, p. 203ff, pp. 477–96.

[16] Gandhi 2006, p. 304ff; Connelly, Matthew. 2008. *Fatal Misconception*. The Struggle to Control World Population. Cambridge: Harvard U. Press, pp. 200–230; Wikipedia, 'Sushila Nayyar', and obituaries.

Erikson (1902–1994), author of the prizewinning book, *Gandhi's Truth: On the Origins of Militant Nonviolence*.[17] Erikson made Gandhi one of his heroes, searching through the Mahatma's life and teachings for truths to revivify Western man and prepare 'tomorrow's fighters for peace'. He compared the martyrdom of the Mahatma with that of Christ and Socrates, and considered Gandhi's message a universal religious truth. In fitting Gandhi, however, into his pantheon of Western religious heroes that includes Socrates, Christ, St Paul, St Augustine, St Francis, Luther, and Kierkegaard, Erikson underestimated Gandhi's Indianness and the extent to which Gandhi was a political activist engaged in turbulent nationalist politics.

Erikson brought to India a rather rigid set of masculine and feminine categories. In dealing with a culture in which there is a different cultural configuration from the West, and in which traits that Westerners might label 'feminine', are frequently embodied by men, he employs stock phrases to describe bisexuality, the maternal culture of India and the femininity of its men. He comments with some disapproval that 'Father Time in India is a Mother'. Erikson's evaluation of Indian culture is tinged by an element of condescension and irritation, as also in the writings of many Westerners over the years. It can be argued that there may be other ways of being men and women than the standard Western one. For example, the nursing, maternal characteristics that Erikson finds in Gandhi may simply be aspects of the Indian way of being human and being a man. Similarly, Erikson's depiction of a passive India where nothing is ever 'finalized' must be queried: where could one find a set of more energetic and goal-directed men and women than Gandhi and his companions, whom Erikson met in Ahmedabad where he was based during his research?[18]

Erikson provides a few glimpses of Gandhi's powers of recruitment, where he is seen to win over loyal followers by the magic of his message. What was true for these few recruits, of

---

[17] Erikson, Erik H. 1969. *Gandhi's Truth*. On the Origins of Militant Nonviolence. NY: Norton.
[18] Ibid., p. 22ff.

course, was not necessarily true for 'the masses of India' or even for the extensive corps of lieutenants that Gandhi so expertly selected, but Erikson shows how Gandhi became a leader of men. In these sections Erikson demonstrates his extraordinary skill in dissecting a human personality. He is not as skilful, however, in dealing with a mass movement.

In the concluding part of *Gandhi's Truth*, Erikson discusses Gandhi as homo religiosus, an inherently religious being. Erikson finds that 'Gandhi was never too proud to find universal meaning in petty circumstances' and that the Mahatma was a 'politician and reformer with an honorary sainthood'. Erikson discerns the universal and contemporary message in Gandhi's life—the message powering the spread of the Mahatma's teachings worldwide.[19] The continuing presence of Gandhi's teaching was accompanied by the slow, then rapid growth of the South Asian community in America.

---

[19] Ibid., p. 371ff.

7

Immigrants
The South Asian Community in America

Changes in American law and society began during the Second World War when a very modest number, just over 100 Chinese, then a similar number of Filipinos and Indians, were allowed to become citizens by laws passed in 1943 and 1946. However, the 1924 immigration law was still in effect and it precluded any large-scale immigration from anywhere except northern and western Europe. Although more Indian students and some Indian businessmen came to the US after the Second World War and the walls of segregation were beginning to crumble in many areas of American life, the Indian community remained small for another generation.

Drawing on data compiled from census reports, demographer S. Chandrasekhar gave these figures up to 1980, and what he anticipated in 1990:[1]

---

[1] Chandrasekhar, S., ed. 1984. *From India to America.* A Brief History of Immigration. La Jolla, California, Population Review Books, pp. 139–42.

Estimated South Asian Immigrants to the US	
1820–1900	676
1901–1910	4,713
1911–1920	2,082
1921–1930	1,886
1931–1940	496
1941–1950	1,761
1951–1960	1,973
1961–1970	27,189
1980	4,00,000 (approx.)
1990	7,50,000 (approx.)

More recently Chakravorty, Kapur and Singh have given slightly different, but similar figures for the trajectory through the twentieth century.[2] Within this modest community, there were some remarkable individuals including two Nobel Prize winners, Har Gobind Khorana in Medicine/Physiology (1968) and S. Chandrasekhar in Physics (1983).

These scientists, as well as writers like Kumar Goshal and Taraknath Das and businessmen like J.J. Singh, were the forerunners of the new Indian community in the US. Singh, as leader of the India League of America, had more than any other South Asian helped open the path to American citizenship for at least, at first, a few Indians. Now it was up to others to create a new and expanded relationship between America and India—as well as Pakistan and Bangladesh—as the British Raj, formally at least, exited the stage.

The South Asian community in those years even included the first Asian Indian elected to the US Congress: Dalip Singh Saund (1899–1973). Benefitting from the 1946 immigration law, for which he had lobbied, he had become a citizen in 1949 and was elected

---

[2] Chakravorty, Kapur, Singh 2019, p. 34.

to the House of Representatives from the Imperial and Riverside Counties of California in 1956. He served on the House Committee on Foreign Relations and was re-elected in 1960.

In 1957, after his first victory for the House of Representatives, Saund undertook a wide-ranging tour of Asia. Although a fierce anti-communist, like many in his day from both parties, he nevertheless saw the shortcomings of the American approach to Vietnam and Taiwan, where he encountered anti-Americanism. At public meetings, he was faced again and again with questions about racism and segregation. He deflected these queries by saying that the better side of America was surfacing in the fight against racism. Although his meeting with Ngo Nu Diem, President of South Vietnam from 1955–1963, went smoothly, Saund argued that the military approach to involvements in Asia would simply not work. So he referred to converting 'hearts and minds' effectively to democracy and anti-communism. He believed that it was only a small coterie of communists that opposed the government of South Vietnam, and that an effective public relations effort would defeat them.

Saund was warmly greeted in India when he returned for the first time in thirty-seven years to his village in Punjab, and met with political and business leaders in Calcutta, New Delhi, Bombay and Madras. Invited to a meal with Prime Minister Nehru, he expressed his hope that 'the world's two greatest democracies' would cooperate more closely. As an Asian Indian elected to office in America, and a believer in the American dream, he was likely as effective a spokesman for the US as its government could find.[3]

Before he suffered a massive stroke in 1962 that effectively terminated his political career, Saund had completed his autobiography, *Congressman from India* (1960), writing that he saw in himself the blending of the best of India and America:

---

[3] Saund, D.S. 1960. *Congressman from India.* NY: Dutton, p. 152ff.

Kipling said, 'East is East and West is West, and never the twain shall meet.'

Clearly, he was wrong, for a Saund from the East met a Kosa from the West... My religion teaches me that love and service to fellow men are the road to early bliss and spiritual salvation.

Lincoln said once, 'Be satisfied with skim milk if you cannot get cream.' I have had to live on skim milk on occasion in life and found it both sweet and nourishing. Gandhi said, 'I love my enemies.' In my political battles I have found it impossible to malign or belittle my opponents. Yet I have won every contest against heavy odds... [I]n 1956... the citizens of my own small home town of Westmoreland, my neighbors of thirty years, voted over 80 per cent in my favor as an expression of their confidence.[4]

With India now an independent player on the world stage, a new relationship between America and India was forming. By the Immigration and Nationality Act of 1965, also known as the Hart-Celler Act, immigration quotas were changed. It provided that 20,000 persons from many countries of the world could enter the US and become citizens. Importantly, it also had a provision for family reunification, a provision meant to admit only close relations of immigrants, but since kinship systems worldwide vary widely from the American norm, it had a much broader effect. To South Asians, first cousins were frequently called 'cousin-brothers', and so might come in to the US as part of family unification. Over the following years as the act came into full operation, and thousands of relatives accompanied immigrants to the US, the immigration flows from Asia, Africa and Latin America increased greatly and reshaped the population. Instead of a European America a more global America came into being, although in the early 1970s, that new America was only barely visible.

Bruce La Brack has closely examined the experience of a community of Sikhs who entered California in the early twentieth

---

[4] Ibid., pp. v–vi.

century, an exceptional group within the larger South Asian population, and discussed earlier. Although they suffered a setback in the 1920s and 1930s, since 1947, following the 1946 Immigration Act, and still more from the 1960s, following the 1965 Immigration Act, the Sikh community underwent a remarkable revitalization. The 1965 legislation in particular, allowed a significant number of Sikhs to bring fellow Sikhs to the US, who in turn, brought thousands of others. The newcomers pressed for a shift to traditional Sikh patterns of life,[5] a reversion resisted by young Sikhs who had been educated in the US and interacted frequently with American peers, especially with regard to the custom of arranged marriages.[6]

The Sikhs in California, like their fellow South Asian immigrants elsewhere, were often the targets of racist taunts and acts, as well as legal restrictions. As a proud subgroup both in India and America, they did not meekly submit. Being called 'rag-heads', and worse, they sometimes did shave their traditional beards and heads, but they adapted and survived, even when their numbers dropped precipitately and communications with India were not easy. They persevered, as Sikhs have done in different parts of the world.

Many of the Sikhs who had settled in California were still attached to an agricultural life, and so differed significantly from the highly educated, more urban South Asian immigrants who arrived in droves from the late 1960s. Tending to settle in areas such as metropolitan New York City, including parts of New Jersey, these newcomers were doctors, scientists, engineers, as well as students and entrepreneurs. Within a generation they grew into a formidable South Asian presence in America and were helping to remake their new home.

In addition to the South Asians who became American citizens through the second half of the twentieth century, there were numerous South Asians who lived and worked in the US, but retained their Indian or Pakistani (and later Bangladeshi) citizenship. One example

---

[5] La Brack, Bruce. 1988. *The Sikhs of Northern California 1904-1975*. NY: AMS Press, p. 205ff.
[6] Ibid., p. 418ff.

is Syed Hamid Ahmed, encountered earlier as a financial officer for Tata Steel during the 1940s. Forced during the Partition years to move to Pakistan where he worked for Remington Typewriters in Lahore, Ahmed was recommended for a position at the UN in New York just as that international organization was coming to life. Although he thought he was hired for only one year, his career extended to more than two-and-a-half decades. He and his family learned to adapt to America as well as to the other foreign countries to which they moved. (Ahmed 2001, 225ff) Along with thousands of other South Asian journalists, doctors, restaurant workers, taxi drivers, and others, they contributed to the continuing internationalization of the United States during the process of decolonization that followed the Second World War.

The new South Asian American community has grown in the aftermath of the 1965 Immigration Law, which followed upon earlier legislation including the restrictive 1924 Immigration Law and the liberalizing 1946 Luce-Celler Immigration Act. The new law abolished the national origins quota system, terminated the 'barred zone' provisions of the 1917 law, set a ceiling of 1,70,000 immigrant visas for Eastern Hemisphere nations (including a ceiling of 29,000 for any one nation) exclusive of parents, spouses and children of US citizens, and set up seven selective preference categories. The latter provision favoured the entry of professional and skilled workers needed by the US.

Although changes were anticipated, few expected that within a generation and a half Asian Americans would number well over ten million with large and growing numbers now of Chinese, Japanese, Korean, Filipino, Asian Indian and Indo-Chinese Americans. In what has been called the 'brain drain', a healthy percentage of the South Asian Americans came with high educational and often professional qualifications and so helped staff American hospitals, laboratories, university faculties and corporations. Unable to find adequate employment in their countries of origin, and seeing the opportunities that they thought the US had, they made the move. In the second decade of the twenty-first century, instead, many South

Asians now come for education and work experience in the US, and then return to increasing opportunities offered in the subcontinent.

Many of the Asian Indians retain elements of their South Asian roots and culture. Thus their experience during this recent period of rapid growth has belied earlier views that these immigrants were too different in culture, religion, custom, and outlook to integrate themselves into American society. Although many Asian Indian Americans have sought to retain their heritage and instil in their children some connection to India, they have also been open and pragmatic in adapting to American society. An initial preference that children marry within the Indian community either here or in India has given way to quite a few intermarriages with those from diverse ethnic backgrounds, a practice that has helped Asian Indians blend into the greater society.

New provisions in American immigration law in 1965 changed. Earlier there had been a very modest number of those from South Asia studying, doing business and settling in the United States. They numbered perhaps 50,000 in 1965. During the heyday of empire, bright and ambitious South Asians went to Great Britain, continental Europe, and some to the United States. But by the late 1970s, a great influx into America began. Why America? It was a much bigger nation than Great Britain, more diverse, with many more opportunities. Some other destinations, like Germany, had been devastated by the war. America was a nation of immigrants, where, it was promised, anyone, from anywhere, could make good, whereas Britain was closing its doors. Some in the UK felt that too many—from the West Indies and South Asia—had entered. In 2022, those of South Asian background are about 7 per cent of the UK population, and one of those, Rishi Sunak, became prime minister. Others have succeeded in business and academia. Whether this heralds a better day for this ethnic minority there is to be seen.

For South Asia and the United States, the 'invasions' have gone both ways, though unevenly. A growing wave of South Asians into America from the 1970s has not receded. On the economic front, Indian multinationals have been developing apace since the liberalization of India's economy (from the early 1990s) and finding their place in the American and world economy. American businesses, tech firms, fast-food outlets, and such, have moved into the Indian marketplace, and are knocking on the door. In Connaught Place, New Delhi, you can buy a Big Mac from McDonalds, a burger from Burger King, chicken from KFC, a slice from Pizza Hut or Domino's, and in Khan Market, ice cream from Baskin & Robbins and a sub from Subway. These firms have learned to cope with the Indian market: no beef or pork, but lots of other choices at prices that are usually quite reasonable. With India's huge potential retail market, can Walmart and Amazon, American behemoths, be kept out? Walmart has already acquired the Indian firm Flipkart Online Services, while Amazon purchased the Indian firm, Future Retail and have developed a huge site in Hyderabad. Parts of Bangalore look like Silicon Valley, California. The arrival of American enterprises has developed gradually over half a century, and although the number of Americans in India is modest, the American presence is conspicuous.

South Asians in the US have been both unlike and similar to other ethnic groups that have entered and are entering this country. They came in considerable numbers only from the 1970s onwards. Earlier Germans, Italians, Irish, Jews, Hispanics and Chinese, as well as others, entered and made their marks earlier. Some of my Jewish ancestors congregated on the lower East Side of Manhattan in New York City. They bought and sold, entered the garment industry, played the vaudeville scene, put on Yiddish plays, and gradually made their way out of that enclave, and into wider and wider avenues of American life.

Now, South Asians have followed in the path of their predecessors. The timing of their entry has been important, as noted in the previous chapter. An aspect of their uniqueness was that many were highly educated when they came, or gained advanced education in the US. They frequently came with English-language skills that some other groups did not have at first. Initially, they were slow to enter politics and top business positions, but that has now changed. Many were in the medical line, encouraged by parents and family traditions, while quite a few bought motels, and some flocked to Silicon Valley. As India is a highly diverse country, so too the South Asians who have come to America have been quite religiously and linguistically diverse, though many have been from the upper strata of Indian society.

Since the 1970s, a vital and considerable South Asia minority has grown in America, entering almost every corner of American life. In a recent year, students from India constituted 18 per cent of the total foreign student population in America. Only China sent more. Wikipedia's list of notable men and women of South Asian background runs to more than thirty pages. Asian Americans, including those from South Asia, are said to number about twenty million, or 6 per cent of the US population, and South Asians are the fastest growing subgroup, on course to pass Chinese Americans in number.[7] The account that follows offers a few glimpses of some salient members, organizations and achievements, and problems facing this minority. The economic rise of China and India since the mid-1980s has been changing the image that non-Asian Americans have had of these heavily populated nations from laggards to developers of importance. As a university teacher about India, whose electives were occasionally cancelled because of lack of interest, today many college electives about China and India are in demand, even crowded.

Dozens of South Asians and South Asian Americans have blended into American society as students, doctors, engineers, restaurant workers, health food store operatives and motel owners. They have written dozens and dozens of books, a few of them remarkable by any standard. They have joined the mainstream media as actors and comedians, sometimes starring on network and HBO series, demonstrating that they can work in all forms of media and use their talents worldwide. New women and men enter these arenas almost daily and make their mark. Recently, they have been making their mark in American politics and public service. From the shadows, they are moving into the bright light of active participation.

---

[7] Hua Hsu, November 2, 2020 'Bloc by Bloc: Are Asian Americans the Last Undecided Voters?' The *New Yorker*. pp. 16–22, p. 17.

The Other One Percent: Indians in America by three scholars of South Asian descent, covering the period from the 1970s through 2016, provides the first, excellent social-scientific analysis of the rapid development of this community.[8] The growth of this community raises many questions. Are its members Asian Americans and linked to those from East and Southeast Asia? What links do they, or should they have to the nations they left behind in South Asia? Are they simply 'Americans', without a qualifying adjective? Or might they be South Asians in America, but not of America, not fully American? The authors of *The Other One Percent* provide statistical data and acute analysis, but do not answer these questions.

The Gujaratis, many of them named Patel, are one of the regional groups of South Asians that has thrived in America. They had been farmers in India, and traders in East Africa. Adapting to a new continent, some started hotels and motels at first in California and then in other states further east, preferring to be self-employed and utilizing all family members in their enterprises. Over time, they formed the Asian American Hotel Owners Association that now has more than 10,000 members, of whom about 70 per cent are Gujaratis, who may own, according to Pawan Dhingra, as many as 50 per cent of the motels in the United States. They have moved past ethnic stereotypes that impede business success, often employing white women as desk clerks, while challenging customers' assumptions that the brown people they encounter could not possibly be the owners. Not wanting to appear too Indian, they have prevented Indian cooking smells from permeating the front areas. They have changed their names slightly to arrive at American-sounding identifiers: Sandy Gandhi, Mike Patel and Tom Desai. Flourishing in one particular niche in which they could prosper, they have evaded marginality and climbed the economic ladder.[9]

---

[8] Chakravorty, Sanjoy, Devesh Kapur, Nirvikar Singh. 2019. *The Other One Percent: Indians in America (Modern South Asia)*. NY: Oxford U. Press.

[9] Dhingra, talk at CUNY Graduate Center, 9 February 2011; Dhingra, Pawan. 2007. *Managing Multicultural Lives*. Asian American Professionals and the Challenge of Multiple Identities. Stanford: Stanford U. Press.

A recent article, (16 September 2018), in The *New York Times* tracks the course of one successful family of Patels, whose progenitor arrived in America in 1968.[10] Jagdish Patel entered the US to study at Youngstown State University in Ohio and earned a degree in structural engineering. Gaining a good job and a Green Card upon graduation, he married in 1971, sponsoring his wife, Anita, as well as his brother and sister-in-law. 'By 1985, he had also sponsored his mother, five sisters and their husbands and children…. [H]e had American-born children… His son… [is a] a venture capitalist… his daughter… is an interior designer in Salt Lake City with 140,000 followers on Instagram.' Now seventy-two, Jagdish, the first of his family to arrive, organized a reunion of four generations of Patels in June 2018. He has celebrated America's openness to newcomers.

Many of the Asian Indians retain elements of their South Asian roots and culture. Their experience during this recent period of rapid growth has belied earlier views that these immigrants were too different in culture, religion, custom and outlook to integrate themselves into American society. Although many Asian Indian Americans have sought to retain their heritage and instil in their children some connection to India, they have also been open and pragmatic in adapting to American society. An initial preference that children marry within the Indian community either here or in India has given way to quite a few intermarriages with those from diverse ethnic backgrounds, a practice that has helped Asian Indians blend into the greater society.

Sharmila Sen's *Not Quite Not White: Losing and Finding Race in America* (2018) is one of the most penetrating works by South Asian American authors aiming to probe the inner life of an Indian immigrant. Born in Calcutta [now Kolkata] in 1970, she and her parents emigrated from India in 1982 and settled in Cambridge, Massachusetts. Possessing a keen mind and excellent memory, she rose to the top at school, then earned her BA at Harvard, her PhD in literature at Yale, then returned to teach at Harvard. As of 2018,

---

[10] 'One Face of Immigration in America Is a Family Tree Rooted in Asia', Miriam Jordan and Sabrina Tavernise, The *New York Times*, 16 September 2018.

she was executive editor-at-large at Harvard University Press. She married a Sikh, has three children, and they, along with her parents, are involved in her story.

The earlier parts of her book recount her youth in Kolkata, where she learned her place in the hierarchies of Independent India: near the top of the caste ladder, but not in a solid economic position. This precariousness led her father to move to America in search of better opportunities. Moving for economic reasons made the writer uneasy as she reflected on her family's departure from India; she wished that they had departed for reasons that to her were more compelling.

Emerging from Indian society characterized by fixed hierarchies, she entered a different society in the US, stratified in its own way: one in which she was 'not quite not white', and therefore, deemed inferior to all whites. Being rather fair, Sen might have 'passed' as white except for her name, which she would not Anglicize, and her family background. Yet wishing to become 'white', she modulated her English accent, learning everything she could about her new society's culture and manners. She learned that she could be 'accepted' by whites, but never be white. She was some kind of American, but what kind?

As she approached 'whiteness', Sen partitioned off her American and Bengali worlds, never giving up the latter in which she was most at home. Working as an interpreter in deportation cases, she interacted with potential deportees who were poor, Muslim, and Bangladeshi. She could not completely disentangle herself from them and learned anew about both South Asia and America from this work. The most transformative experience for her, however, was to become the mother of three children of South Asian descent born in America. They made English, she says, the language of her inner most feelings:

> Yet, how can I call English a stranger when it is the sole language with which I scold, soothe, and sustain my children? My three children made English the language of my emotions. For them, I had to learn to say new[11] things in English at home, things I had previously said in other languages. For them I had to learn to

---

[11] Sen, Sharmila. 2018. *Not Quite Not White*. NY: Penguin, p. 172ff.

name whiteness. My children—unable to pass as white because of their complexion, unwilling to pass as white because they belong to a more confident second generation of the immigration story— are of color… I do not want my daughter or my sons to be people of color. I want more for them. I want them to know that they are Not White… Not Whiteness dares to name whiteness. It refuses to fly the flag of color while allowing the dominant culture to retain its powerful invisibility. People of Color sings the sweet song of solidarity. It is an affirmation. Not White grunts with belligerence. It is angry.

Brought to the West by her parents at twelve, Sen has grown up to be a guide for Americans about themselves. How many South Asian immigrants share her experiences and views that only they, not a bideshi (foreigner to India) like the present author, can know?

Alongside a searching personal inquiry like Sen's stand the inquiries social scientists have made, using a variety of lenses, into the South Asian American experience. Sunaina Marr Maira in *Desis in the House* looks intensely at the second generation—those born here of South Asian parents, or brought here at a very early age.[12] Although rich with insights, Maira's book is not for the faint of heart, for she has never met a theoretical approach she did not want to use and criticize. Maira first shrewdly casts her eye on the *desi* music scene (desis are those of South Asian descent), where second-generation young men and women engage with the cool hip hop culture at mixers for their own. These young people organized clubs at many colleges, and, like other minorities, have often interacted with their own rather than mingling with others. At the same time, some of them have dated, and married, those of other communities and backgrounds. They have been forced, upon occasion, to hide these relationships from their parents.

As Maira explains, the difficulties for young women desis have been greater than for young men, for instance, with regard to dating, where some young women have found their way around the restrictions,

---

[12] Maira, Sunaina Marr. 2002. *Desis in the House*. Philadelphia: Temple U. Press.

while young men have not usually encountered them. A little older than her subjects, but in tune with their music, Maira interposes some personal reactions with her findings. She also describes the cultural shows, the trips 'home' to India, with or without parental control, and the ways in which desis are finding their ways.

The US has always been an immigrant society, as President Franklin Roosevelt recognized when he addressed the snobbish descendants of the earliest arrivals as 'my fellow immigrants'. But the immigrant population is changing dramatically as a result of the Immigration Act of 1965. About 90 per cent of the new immigrants of the 1980s were non-white or Hispanic, with the result that the percentage of white Euro-Americans in the total population is declining while the percentage of Asian and Hispanic Americans is rising rapidly. With Hispanics and Asian Americans now more than 20 per cent of America's population and continuing to grow, the shape of the country is changing. Descendants of these ethnic groups will likely constitute a majority in this century.

In this new America, immigrants from India are playing a much more significant role than ever before. Not only are their numbers vastly greater than before 1965, but many are doing well economically, socially, educationally and culturally, despite continued racism directed towards Asian Indians and other minorities. They have built a rich community life, founding thousands of organizations by profession, by region of origin, and by religion, and have started numerous publications, television programmes, and websites. They have complex relations with the land of their birth and now have offspring to whom India is but a country of the imagination.

There is a long-term shift in American immigration, permitting the mainstreaming of South Asian Americans to become American just like those Euro-Americans whose ancestors came over on the *Mayflower*. According to the US Census there were 3,71,630 South Asians in the country in 1980; 9,19,626 in 1990; and 33,61,087 in 2010.[13] In all, more than ten million immigrants from all regions of Asia

---

[13] Lee, Erika. 2015. *The Making of Asian America*. NY: Simon and Schuster, p. 295.

have become part of America,[14] many as citizens, many with Green Cards, and some here illegally. As the South Asian population of the United States has grown, with the availability of jet travel and new methods of communication, they can connect to the subcontinent ever more rapidly.

Are the Asian Indians a 'model minority', as some commentators have stated? Of the ten million immigrants of Asian origin now living in the US, Asian Indians, numbering more than one million, claim as a community a high per capita income and often achieve as individuals considerable professional success. Yet some scholars and journalists have presented persuasive data that Asian Americans and South Asian Americans, rather than constituting a minority of high-fliers, are composed of varied, unequal segments with some at the top and others at the bottom, such that for every well-compensated doctor there might be two poorly paid restaurant workers. Among the less prosperous immigrants, Chinese have run laundries and restaurants and today many Koreans are greengrocers working long, long hours and employing almost all members of their families. Similarly, some Asian Indians—but also immigrants from Pakistan and Bangladesh—work at menial restaurant jobs, drive taxis, run small shops and motels for long hours to survive, but also to ensure that the next generation in their families will have better opportunities in life.

As for the more successful newcomers, the example of Amar Bose might be considered. Amar Bose, the son of immigrant Noni Gopal Bose, who arrived in New York in 1920, gained entry to the US with the assistance of Taraknath Bose and married a Euro-American schoolteacher, went to MIT, studied electrical and acoustical engineering, and developed the Bose speakers. He ran a leading global acoustical business grossing $600 million annually. Amar Bose rose to the top financially while improving the lives of the denizens of his father's new country.

---

[14] Chan, Sucheng. 1991. *Asian Americans*. Boston: Twayne, p. 145ff; Takaki, Ronald. 1989. *Strangers from a Different Shore*. A History of Asian Americans. Boston, p. 406ff.

The authors of *The Other One Percent* conclude that the South Asian minority in America is the best-educated and best-paid of all minorities, with those from Taiwan in second place. As a sign of their prosperity and new-found rootedness, although once mostly located in a few big cities, they have spread out to certain suburbs, especially in the San Francisco area, and in New Jersey, as well as New York City, where they constitute a strong and relatively numerous section of the population.

Social scientists also demonstrate that there is considerable difference between those of South Asian birth and those of South Asian parents born in the United States. At this point of time, the highly educated and relatively high-earning South Asians fall in the first category. Their children, almost all still being schooled, fall into the second. The first group had South Asians from Punjab and Gujarat initially. But those from those regions were overwhelmed by highly educated South Asians, Tamils and Telugus, many computer specialists who came in large numbers during the past two plus decades.[15] Given such complex issues regarding the integration of Asian Indians into American society, together with the discrimination they face, it is difficult to characterize Asian Americans as a 'model minority'.[16]

According to T. P. Srinivasan, a distinguished, retired member of the Indian Foreign Service, former Prime Minister of India Jawaharlal Nehru, just after Independence, laid out India's initial approach to Indians settled abroad—one that remained in place for more than three decades. They should make their place in their new homeland, Nehru said, and not look to the Government of India as their helper and protector. Then Rajiv Gandhi, installed as prime minister in 1984, with the aid of his close adviser Sam (Satyan) Pitroda, an Indian businessman living abroad, decided on a different approach. India was to court and utilize its diaspora.[17] A wholly new

---

[15] Chakravorty, Kapur, Singh 2019, p. 29ff.

[16] See US Commission on Civil Rights, Civil Rights Issues, Report of February 1992.

[17] Srinivasan, T. P., interview, New York, 18 September 2018.

relationship, accordingly, has developed over the past three decades between the Government of India and Indians in the diaspora, or NRIs (Non Resident Indians), a group numbering some 12 million, encouraging their contributions to India's development. India has granted them PIO (Persons of Indian Origin) cards, held Overseas Indians Day in India, and sent out its top leaders—recently Prime Minister Narendra Modi—to encourage them to help build India.[18] They have offered incentives to NRIs to invest in India, maintain bank accounts in India, and gain easier entry to India upon return.

The numerous well-trained and ambitious South Asians who have come to the US as part of the post-1965 influx benefited by the preference given to those with certain skills and training—what some now call 'human capital'. Many chose to stay and become Americans, even if they retained ties to South Asia. A smaller number—almost impossible to calculate—returned to their home country. But some, while remaining based in the US, pursued ways as NRIs to help India prosper by sending funds, investing in Indian enterprises, or forming numerous organizations, including several that support political parties, religious organizations, and charities in India. Many visit India regularly.

Responding to this influx of highly-qualified immigrants, a debate begun in the 1960s concerning 'brain drain', 'brain gain', and 'brain circulation'.[19] Anjali Sahay, in a valuable study of the brain gain vs. brain drain argument, observes:

> Brain drain... is a continuing phenomenon today. It has been difficult to evaluate from the standpoints of either sending or receiving countries its causes and effects as its context can be quite diverse for different countries.
>
> Brain gain strategies such as remittances, return, and diaspora networks are hard to define, difficult to measure, multifaceted, multiform... [M]igrant remittances and savings do represent one

---

[18] Sahay, Anjali. 2009. *India Diaspora in the United States*. Brain Drain or Gain? Hyderabad: Orient BlackSwan, p. 199ff.

[19] Ibid., p. viif.

of the most direct and measurable benefits… The return of certain professionals does have some benefits for the home country with investments, usually in businesses, health, and education sectors stimulating economic growth and acting as counter-dependent on foreign capital. And diaspora networks are often able to leverage a network to raise funds, get mentorship, access distribution channels, promote the image of their country through their successes, and spawn more enterprise.[20]

Sahay employs a concept called 'asymmetrical interdependence' to characterize the recent and present relations of India and America. India sends highly trained engineers and doctors that America needs; they link the two countries; some return, but even if they do not they provide a host of benefits to India, as well as costs. Both countries do benefit, but in ways difficult to measure. As an outgrowth of the 1965 Immigration Act, many of these Indian immigrants do become citizens, and bring their family members into America as well. Another group are granted H-1B visas for three years plus a possible renewable three years to work in America. Indians overwhelmingly dominate this visa category, while American officials argue over the numbers. In 2020, President Donald Trump issued an order suspending issuing new such visas, later extending it to March 2021.

Discrimination against minority groups has a long history in the US, impacting the Irish, Italians, Jews, Catholics, African Americans and Asians. In the case of Asian immigrants, their religious diversity, and recent events have given rise to further complexities. Whatever difficulties Hindus and Sikhs have faced in the US, South Asian Muslims, especially from the late twentieth century onwards, had it worse due to a new surge in anti-Muslim feeling. Added to this, the Covid-19 pandemic, with roots in China, has given rise to renewed violence against East Asian Americans. Muslims, Sikhs, and East Asians have been subjected to wanton and unprovoked physical assaults sometimes with serious consequences.

---

[20] Ibid., p. 48.

Assaults by Muslim terrorists against American embassies, ships, and citizens abroad and, most dramatically, domestically at the World Trade Center in New York, provoked an anti-Muslim backlash. Although perhaps unprecedentedly hostile, the recent upsurge of anti-Muslim prejudice was not wholly new, as several analysts of Islamophobia have convincingly argued, since anti-Muslim feeling was likely an integral part of American life from the days of slavery. A good proportion of the slaves taken from West Africa were Muslims, and they were tarred with the brush of religious as well as racial inferiority. Blacks were considered inferior beings, and Islam an inferior religion. So Muslims who were Black were doubly 'othered', twice as inferior. After the end of slavery and the passage of the Thirteenth, Fourteenth, and Fifteenth amendments theoretically put an end to discrimination against former slaves, in practice they were denied citizenship rights until the middle of the twentieth century.[21]

Antipathy to the political and nationalist movements of the Nation of Islam or the Black Muslims was widespread in the second and third quarters of the twentieth century. But terrorist acts by militant Muslims abroad and at home triggered a broader surge of anti-Muslim acts and attitudes that has impinged on the larger Muslim community that includes many from South Asia, as, since 1965, Muslims have come to America not only from the Middle East and Africa, but also from Asia.

In the years after the 9/11 attack on the World Trade Center, anyone who looked 'Arab' or Middle Eastern, or who wore a turban or a beard, was considered, by Americans knowing little or nothing of societies outside their own, to be a potential terrorist. America has several million Muslim citizens, almost all of whom identify as Americans and have nothing to do with terrorism. Immediately after 9/11 President George Bush, to his credit, tried to separate the small group of terrorists from the great mass of law-abiding Muslims, and his successor, President Barack Obama, did the same. Nonetheless,

---

[21] Beydoun, Khaled A. 2018. *American Islamophobia*. Oakland: U. of California Press, p. 47ff.

individual incidents of violence against American Muslims took place. And unfortunately, some Americans assumed that any South Asian person with a beard and turban was a Muslim, so some of these acts of violence were perpetrated against Sikhs and Hindus as well. Meanwhile, the US government took harsher measures against terrorism that disadvantaged all Muslims, whether American citizens or resident foreigners. As political analyst Sangay Mishra has written, 'South Asians straddled the attributes of model minority and perpetual outsider that defined their position in the racial order. Based on physical features and skin color, South Asians were lumped together and perceived as "strangers", "suspicious", and "terrorists".'[22]

But these choices are not fixed. Presidential whims change and public opinion shifts, as more Americans learn that the majority of Muslims are as peaceable and law-abiding citizens as Christians, Jews and those of other faiths. But the hysterical tide of ignorance has not yet receded. While it is true that the 9/11 attack was carried out by Muslim fanatics from the Middle East, terrorist acts by white supremacists, likely Christians, in the US in recent years have killed more Americans than those by Muslim extremists. Looking across the globe, we observe ruthless and terrorist acts by those holding Buddhist beliefs in Myanmar and Sri Lanka, murders of Muslims in India by Hindus, as well as terrorism by Muslims in the Middle East, Sri Lanka and India. But in the US at present, South Asians and Middle Easterners, especially those with markers like a turban, beard or hijab, have to be cautious. South Asian Americans may be seen as 'Arabs', 'Muslims', 'Middle Easterners', one of a threatening minority.[23] More recently as the Covid-19 pandemic spread and was labelled the 'Chinese virus' by President Trump in 2020, numerous attacks on Asian Americans have taken place. This is but the latest chapter of anti-Asianism that began in the middle of the nineteenth century.

---

[22] Mishra, Sangay K. 2016. *Desis Divided*. Minneapolis: U. of Minnesota Press, p. 71.
[23] Laila Lalami, 'Made into Strangers, *New York Times Magazine*, 20 September 2020.

Although efforts to influence debate and secure beneficial legislation for the South Asian community in the United States stretch back through the twentieth century, it is only in the twenty-first that more and more of South Asian descent are standing and winning public office. But as Mishra has argued persuasively in *Desis Divided*, and as Chakravorty, Kapur, and Singh do in *The Other One Percent*,[24] they have been involved in politics in other ways for decades. A tiny group of South Asians, with others, lobbied for the right to naturalization as American citizens in the 1940s, and succeeded. And once the gates opened to much greater numbers of immigrants entering from the mid-1960s onwards, they began a rich organizational life that has flowed into the present. Along with this activity, they have contributed funds to political campaigns, and made their views known through lobbying efforts. They have been appointed to administrative posts, but few were elected to office until very recent years.

A crucial factor, as Mishra suggests, is lack of geographical concentration.[25] Although many South Asians and persons of South Asian descent live in the New York, Los Angeles and Chicago areas, and have commercial centres as in parts of Queens, New York and Edison, New Jersey, they are not sufficiently gathered together residentially, as in a Chinatown or a Koreatown, to make a strong voting bloc. Therefore, when those of South Asian background, or a mixed background (such as for example Kamala Harris), run for office, they must appeal to a mixed constituency and lack the ability to make an ethnic appeal. But some have been successful, among them two governors, Bobby Jindal and Nikki Haley, four members of the US House of Representatives, and a senator, Kamala Harris, now vice-president.

The arrival of the four Congresspersons was reported by *India Abroad* on 14 January 2019: 'Four Indian American incumbents—Representatives Ami Bera and Ro Khanna of California, Rep. Pramila Jayapal of Washington, and Rep. Raja Krishnamoorthi

---

[24] Chakravorty, Kapur, and Singh do in *The Other One Percent*, p. 148ff.
[25] Mishra 2016, p. 14.

of Illinois—were sworn into the 116th Congress on January 3 by House Speaker Nancy Pelosi for their second term in the US House of Representatives.' Quickly labelled 'the samosa caucus', they are not quiet backbenchers. They have propelled themselves into the thrust and parry of politics, policy-making, and crucial investigations. Pramila Jayapal is a key and outspoken sponsor of the bill for 'Medicare for all', and is the leader of the House Progressive Caucus. She recently wrote a personal, painful, and powerful story about 'abortion'—her own.[26] And she became the first South Asian woman to preside over the House of Representatives. Jayapal and Ro Khanna were early supporters of Senator Bernie Sanders for president in 2020, while Faiz Shakir, a Pakistani-American, was appointed his campaign manager; Krishnamoorthi was a member of the Congressional Oversight Committee that investigated the Trump administration and a member of the House Democratic leadership team. Like Jayapal, he is often interviewed about political developments in the House. Khanna as well is a House spokesperson confidently and frequently explaining issues on TV.

Two women who ran in 2019 for the Democratic nomination for president had South Asian connections of very different kinds. Kamala Harris has South Asian ancestry on one side of her family, while Tulsi Gabbard calls herself a Hindu, as does her mother. Harris dropped out of the race late in 2019. Gabbard says she is a Vaishnava, a follower of the sixteenth-century Bengali teacher of bhakti, or devotion, Chaitanya (1486–1534). Gabbard supported closer relations between the US and India, and opposed American interventions abroad. Her presidential run found little traction. In October 2022, Gabbard, who served in Congress from 2013 to 2021, resigned from the Democratic Party calling it 'an elitist cabal of warmongers'. In the 2024 elections she supported Donald Trump and has been selected by him to head U.S. national intelligence.

Kamala Harris, two decades older than Gabbard, has in contrast a considerable track record as an elected official in California, and

---

[26] 'Why I Decided to Have an Abortion', The *New York Times*, 15 June 2019.

for some years as its attorney general. Born Kamala Devi Harris, daughter of a Tamil Indian mother and a Jamaican father, she was educated in California, in Montreal, and at Howard University. Her parents divorced when she was only seven, and her mother, a breast cancer scientist, accepted positions in Montreal. Her maternal grandfather, P.V. Gopalan was an Indian diplomat, and she often visited her family in Chennai. In a 2019 interview, she is reported to have said, 'I am black and proud of it.'[27] Besides her grandfather, her south Indian Brahmin family had several highly educated and accomplished members to whom she was close. Her career and public service, and now her achievement of high office, have drawn extensive press coverage not only in the US but also in India and the UK.[28] Her ethnically-mixed heritage has also attracted support from the increasingly active South Asian American community and from African Americans as well.

After college, Harris earned a law degree from the University of California, Hastings College of Law, was admitted to the bar, and served as deputy district attorney in Alameda County, California, for eight years. She rose through the ranks of elected judicial officials, first as district attorney of San Francisco, and then as Attorney General of California, to which post she was elected in 2010. As an officer of the law in these positions, she was involved in numerous controversial issues and has received some criticism for her positions. She opposes the death penalty, supports serious gun control, and has advocated several important reform measures, including the formation of the Bureau of Children's Justice.

When Barbara Boxer retired as US senator, Harris declared her candidacy in 2015, and won the seat in 2016. As a senator, she became a member of the Committee on Homeland Security, the Judiciary Committee, and the Select Committee on Intelligence. At hearings she has become known for her sharp questioning of

---

[27] Dana Goodyear, 'First Person', *New Yorker*, 22 July 2019; 'Kamala Devi Harris', Wikipedia.
[28] *New York Times* magazine, 25 October 2020, The *Economist*, 15 August 2020, and countless others.

administration officials. She shot to renewed prominence when Democratic nominee Joe Biden selected her as his running mate. Subsequently elected, she is the first female vice-president and the first woman of colour in American history to take that post. In 2024, Harris suddenly emerged as the Democratic candidate for president when President Biden withdrew from the race. Harris was defeated decisively by Donald Trump in the November elections.

Also of South Asian descent, Nikki Haley, former governor of South Carolina, and Trump's ambassador to the UN entered the race for the Republican nomination for president in 2023. The one woman candidate, sometimes critical of her former boss, Donald Trump, she has proved herself as viable a candidate as the other non-Trump candidates. Also of South Asian descent, Bobby Jindal, a fellow southern governor of some years ago, has disappeared from sight.

One adviser to Kamala Harris in recent years has been Ajay Banga, listed above as among successful business executives of South Asian background. Banga, born in Pune in 1959 into a Sikh family, was educated in New Delhi and at an Indian Institute of Management. He joined Citigroup and rose there before becoming head of MasterCard in 2010. Although he was primarily a businessman, he also advised the US government, and in 2023, President Biden nominated him to become head of the World Bank. Upon confirmation, he took up its reins with a determination to battle climate change and empower women as well as improve its management.

In February 2023, Vivek Ramaswamy, born to South Asian parents in Cincinnati, Ohio, in 1985, boldly entered the race for the Republican nomination for president. A graduate of Harvard College and Yale Law School, he founded a pharmaceutical company and then Strive Asset Management, aided by prominent conservatives. With no prior political or public administrative experience, he appealed to right-wing Republicans and mirrored Trump's views. However, he went even further than his far-right colleagues in calling for elimination of the Department of Education, the FBI and the IRS. His programme also includes a six-week abortion ban with exceptions, and to end affirmative action. He supports a Constitutional amendment to raise the voting age to twenty-five. Ramaswamy wants to withdraw support from Ukraine and make concessions to Putin's Russia. Young, attractive and a confident fast talker whom some call a 'hustler', he ignited speculation that he might be running for vice-president on a Trump ticket. With Donald Trump's victory in the presidential race in 2024, he appointed Ramaswami to a position in the new administration. Another South Asian face in the public eye was the wife of Trump's vice president, J.D. Vance, Usha who hails from a South Asian family.

In addition to officials on the national stage, there have been and are a host of others in administrative and staff positions throughout the American political and public scene. These include Neal Katyal, former deputy attorney general and former Acting Solicitor General of the US, 2010–11; Vivek Murthy, former and present surgeon general; Vanita Gupta, assistant attorney general in the Justice Department in the Obama administration; Seema Verma, administrator during the Trump administration of the Centers for Medicare and Medicaid; Halim Dhanidivan, an Ismaili Muslim from Gujarat, a judge on the California Court of Appeals; and Ajit Pai, in 2019, chairman of the Federal Communications Commission.

Among the most prominent public servants of South Asian descent has been Preet Bharara, former US Attorney for the Southern District of New York. Born in India in 1968, Bharara was brought to New Jersey as a child by his parents, who are of Sikh and Hindu descent, while his wife's parents are Muslim and Jewish. As a result, he quipped, 'that must make his three children "Episcopalian"'.[29] Educated at Harvard and at the Columbia Law School, he worked for private law firms before becoming an Assistant US Attorney and later chief counsel to Senator Charles Schumer, a leader of the Senate Judiciary Committee, in which position he displayed his

---

[29] 'U.S. Attorney Preet Bharara on Cleaning up Wall Street and the Thin Line between Confidence and Arrogance', 12 October 2011, https://knowledge. wharton.upenn.edu/article/u-s-attorney-preet-bharara-on-cleaning-up-wall-street-and-the-thin-line-between-confidence-and-arrogance/.

investigative skills. Schumer recommended him to President Obama for US Attorney for the Southern District of New York. Bharara became known as 'The Sheriff of Wall Street', but said he was not an enemy of the business community, but simply wanted its members to approach their work 'with integrity and a dose of humility... We don't tag industries of specific types of industries. Sometimes financial institutions are our targets, other times they are themselves the victims'.[30] (Knowledge@ Wharton) His office of prosecutors has also successfully carried through cases against terrorists, arms traffickers, gamblers, etc. Bharara thought that President Trump had promised to continue his appointment, but in 2017, the new president summarily sacked him.

Another younger law enforcement officer recently in the public eye is Gurbir Grewal. A Sikh, born in 1973, and raised in New Jersey, he graduated from the Georgetown University School of Public Service and earned a JD degree from William and Mary Law School. Entering public service in his home state, he rose to become Bergen County prosecutor, and then, in 2018, was appointed Attorney General of New Jersey, and was subsequently confirmed by the state senate. He is said to be the first Sikh-American attorney general in the US. Adorned by turban and beard in the usual Sikh manner, he has been the subject of racial animosity. Undeterred, he has been an effective attorney general, in the news for his suits instituted against firms accused of polluting, for fighting discrimination based on sexual and religious bias, for working against a gambling and loansharking operation, and for opposing illegal gun-sale operations.[31]

Other persons of South Asian descent have served in other capacities as organizers and legal advisers. Bhairavi Desai is the founding member of the New York Taxi Workers Alliance, representing more than 15,000 taxi drivers in New York City, many of them of South Asian background. Born in Gujarat, she emigrated to America at the age of six with her parents, grew up in New Jersey, and graduated from Rutgers University. She has worked to support

---

[30] Ibid.
[31] 'Gurbir Grewal', Wikipedia, and numerous press articles.

victims of domestic violence, to defend the rights of Asian workers, and then with colleagues, in 1998, set up the NYTWA, and is frequently out in front fighting for them.[32]

Several persons of South Asian background have played crucial roles in campaigns for the presidency. Others have been donors or lobbyists, as Mishra notes in Desis Divided. The well-to-do of South Asian descent, the ones he calls 'elite' elements, have contributed significantly to fund raising efforts for presidential and other candidates, and lobbied on issues that touch the relationship between America and South Asia. Such efforts have been largely on India-linked issues, but Pakistani-Americans have done their own work, sometimes in opposition to Indian-Americans, on such matters as nuclear questions and arms sales. Those lower down on the economic ladder have allied with those from other ethnic backgrounds to gain their ends.

The organizational and political life of those of South Asian background has been complicated by the differentiation that is an essential feature of the community. South Asians may have multiple identifications: they may be Hindu, Sikh, Muslim or Christian; their families may come from India, Pakistan, or Bangladesh; their families may come from Gujarat, Tamil Nadu, West Bengal or Punjab. To add another layer of complexity, some have Indian and Caribbean roots, or Indian and East African, or Indian and Pacific roots: their ancestors were labourers, or traders who were pressured to emigrate or emigrated voluntarily. Those who came to America brought with them these complicated histories and identities.[33] Those with South Asian roots may decide to join one or several organizations on the basis of their region of origin, nation of origin, profession, or religious outlook. In American politics, they may be Democrats or Republicans; at the same time, they may have links to Indian political parties, especially the BJP and the Congress.

The ascendancy of the BJP in recent decades in Indian national politics has meant that their refrain of Hindutva—that India is a

---

[32] 'Bhairavi Desai', Wikipedia, and numerous press articles.
[33] Bahadur 2013, p. 163ff.

Hindu nation and others, especially Muslims, but Christians as well, are to be second-class citizens—has been echoed in the US. Although the research on the relative strength that BJP supporters have in America is only beginning, as Mishra writes, he ventures some preliminary observations:

> The growth of Hindu nationalism in the diaspora has been enabled by a strong organizational network that Hindutva groups built over a period of time. One of the earliest... Vishwa Hindu Parishad of America (VHPA), was founded by four members of the RSS in 1970... Founded as a nonprofit tax-exempt organization, VHPA, aligned closely with Hindu nationalist politics in India, claiming to be promoting Hinduism and pursuing cultural activities rather than political mobilization. Currently, the group has chapters in most states... Hindu Swayamsewak Sangh (HSS)... founded in 1989, has branches in several states... and functions through organizing weekly camps—called Shakhas—focused on imparting Hindu values, martial skills, character building, and self-discipline. Organizations like the Hindu Student Council (HSC) and Hindu American Federation (HAF) came into existence later in the 1990s, and they are seen as the second wave of Hindutva organizations... that tend to focus on second-generation Hindu Indian Americans.[34]

These organizations want to push their Hindutva ideology and their interpretation of Hinduism in American school textbooks and curricula. Muslims with South Asian roots who have settled in the US must combat the anti-Muslim prejudice presently displayed by some at the top of the American political establishment and also, at the same time, the Indian one.

Across the country, Indian Americans, as well as Pakistani-Americans, are taking office in positions from local to national, and in trade unions as well. Slow to step forward at first, a growing

---

[34] Mishra 2016, p. 194.

movement to serve is on.[35] This marks how comfortable such men and women feel as Americans. They may not want to be hyphenated Americans, but they are citizens helping run the government, locally to nationally. Not only are South Asian Americans stepping forward, but as their numbers increase they have become a minority with some voting clout. This was evident in the senatorial campaigns in Georgia in late 2020 and 2021.[36] In the words of Abraham Verghese, this is now 'their own country'.

---

[35] Reports in *India Abroad*, 14 January 2019.
[36] 'South Asians in Georgia politics', The *New York Times*, 26 November 2020.

8

American Residents in India

The architect Joseph Allen Stein (1912–2001) forged another remarkable and long-lasting Indo-American connection. Trained in the US and France and expressing regional and organic modern architectural trends through his work, Stein first worked in California, setting up his own office in the Bay Area in northern California in 1945. He wrote in 1988:

> Working initially in the Californian mountains, I have long ago decided that for myself, the principal architectural task was not the creating of innovative or striking forms, but to do my share of the necessary work of fitting more people and more institutions onto the earth without spoiling the surroundings, indeed, seeking to enhance the environment.[1]

In 1952, he took a teaching post in India, and headed the architecture department at the Bengal Engineering College, Shibpur, near Kolkata. A few years later he moved to New Delhi and started an architectural firm with an American colleague. Among his many important projects in New Delhi were the India International Centre, the Ford Foundation headquarters, the UNICEF building, and the Gandhi King Plaza, all in the Lodi Gardens, not far from the city centre. Several of these projects were aided by grants

---

[1] White, Stephen. 1998. *Building in the Garden*. The Architecture of Joseph Allen Stein in India and California. Oxford: Oxford U. Press, p. 60.

from the Rockefeller and Ford Foundations. They were fitted to their environment, modest in scale, but impressive in their tasteful beauty and functionality. Later he designed other buildings in New Delhi, including the Triveni Kala Sangam, the American Embassy School, and the Habitat Centre. Stein designed buildings in Kerala, Mumbai, Aligarh and Faridabad. Living four decades in India, Stein was honoured by the government; a lane entering the Lodi Gardens in New Delhi was named for him.

It is not altogether clear why Stein left California for India and why he formed such a powerful tie to the Indian people, landscape, traditions and possibilities, but he felt he was following the teachings and example of Gandhi. As he wrote in 1977:

Why do I continue to live and work in India? I think India offers the great possibility of beauty with simplicity. This is a rare and little understood thing in the world today; yet one sees it here in some many different ways. India is a special place because it has many highly developed people, and very intense and sharply drawn environmental problems. There is probably no possibility of solution here except along what may be called Gandhian lines, which means essentially seeking very simple and ecologically gentle solutions. And yet the whole situation is amorphous, the problems have not been really defined. In India people know they have not arrived at an acceptable or sustainable solution either to urbanism or the environment in general.[2]

Fittingly for visitors to the Lodi Gardens and happily for Stein, the Government of India, the India International Centre leaders, and the Ford Foundation all agreed to the construction of a memorial plaza adjacent to the centre and the foundation buildings dedicated to Mahatma Gandhi and Martin Luther King, Jr. Modest and moving, it features quotations from the two leaders. That from Gandhi says: 'For us today there can be no sacrifice higher than to forget the distinctions of high and low and to realize the equality of

---

[2] Ibid,, p. 35.

all men.' That from King says, 'True peace is not merely the absence of tension but it is the presence of justice and brotherhood.' Often a site of pilgrimage by civil rights leaders from America, the plaza was opened by Prime Minister Indira Gandhi and other dignitaries on 21 January 1970. Like many of Stein's designs, it fits into the world around it, it is open to nature, and it touches the heart.[3]

Besides Stein, a second American architect made great contributions to South Asian life: Louis Kahn (1901–1974). Born in Estonia, then part of Imperial Russia, he grew up in Philadelphia. Determined from the age of sixteen to become an architect, he was trained first at the University of Pennsylvania, and then on municipal projects and at architectural firms. He came to his spare, often stunning and monumental architectural style only in his fifties with the Richards Medical Research Laboratories at the University of Pennsylvania, the Salk Institute in La Jolla, California, and the First Unitarian Church in Rochester, New York. Kahn entered South Asia with the Suhrawardy Medical College and Hospital in Dhaka, and then the Indian Institute of Management, Ahmedabad. All of these fine buildings seem but a warm-up to the Jatiyo Sangshad Bhaban, or National Assembly Building, in Dhaka, Bangladesh. Started under the Government of Pakistan in 1963, work continued even as civil war broke out, and East Pakistan became the independent nation of Bangladesh. The Assembly Building, completed in 1974, sited in a large, flat open space of several hundred acres, encompasses offices, a dining hall, hostels and a mosque. While clearly modern and riveting, it also harks back to medieval castles, equipped with a moat and turrets. To many it was the culmination of Kahn's career, and remains a remarkable work set at the centre of Bangladeshi politics and life.[4]

Like the entrepreneur John Bissell and the architects Joseph Lewis Stein and Louis Kahn, the musician Lila Ray (1910–1992), born Alice Virginia Orndorff in Texas in 1910, forged strong ties to

---

[3] White 1998, pp. 170–75.
[4] Lesser 2017; documentary film, 'My Architect: A Son's Journey', 2003.

India, its culture and its people. Having studied piano in New York, she became interested in Indian music and travelled to Calcutta in 1930. In the Bengal town of Berhampore, she met Ananda Sankar Ray, a member of the Indian Civil Service and an aspiring writer. They married, he left government employ for a literary career, and they settled in Tagore's Santiniketan in 1951. They both wrote prolifically, he in Bengali and Oriya, she mainly in English, but also translating from Bengali to English. In a loving memoir of Lila, his mother, Ananda Ray writes:

> Lila fully immersed herself in Santiniketan life, and 'Lila-di' or 'Lila-mashi' became a much-loved figure. Her social network included scholars and students from abroad, for whom Lila's residence was a hub, ... Lila had become a follower of Gandhi and his eminent disciple Acharya Vinobha Bhave... She...joined Bhave's program for voluntary land distributions... She was regularly called to help women during childbirth. She organized small groups of women to teach them general hygiene, pre-natal and post-natal care, as well as the benefits of khadi and the charka... Although my mother became fully integrated into Bengali society, she never forgot her Western roots. She read voraciously, and kept herself fully informed about literary developments in English, Spanish, German and other languages: some jokingly referred to her as the 'walking encyclopedia of world literature'. She had brought her Steinway grand piano with her from El Paso...She mainly played Beethoven, Chopin and Mozart and was admired by those who appreciated Western music...[5]

I spent a weekend with the Rays in the 1960s. Warmly welcomed by them, I was also greeted by a snake in the bathtub the next morning.

Several millions of South Asian background and descent have entered American life over the past two generations. Even if they visit South Asia annually, most are based in the US, many citizens. However, only a few unusual Americans have devoted their lives to

---

[5] Ray, Anandarup, no date. 'Remembering Lila Ray, *Parabaas.com*.

India, taken permanent residence there, and contributed in diverse ways. John Bissell and Joseph Stein appeared earlier. Then we have had the late Tom Alter (1950–2017) and Sharon Lowen. In 1999, when I met Tom Alter, the son of missionaries, he was a rugged, greying, attractive, fifty-year old Indian film star, who graduated from the Woodstock School in Mussoorie and had spent his entire life in India. He had become an Indian citizen and was the first sahib to attend the Indian film institute at Poona. At his graduation, Satyajit Ray was the speaker. As he passed by Tom, sitting on the aisle, he said, 'We'll be working together soon, Tom.' Tom did not know what he was talking about. Two months later, he was contacted about *Shatranj ke Khilari* (The Chess Players). He made a tape, and Ray liked it, asking for a voice test and a snatch of hair. Then Tom went to Calcutta for two days of filming in a studio. He played the part of a translator and had to go back and forth between English and Urdu. There was hardly any direction. Tom was told: keep on doing it the way you are. In one scene, a minimal response was asked for, just head and eyes to move slightly, and Ray instructed him. Tom called him the most prepared director ever, and one who did everything, camera, direction and music. In *Sardar*, directed by Shyam Benegal, Tom played Mountbatten. Tom was made up with dark hair, and even his children did not recognize him. He had to struggle, was helped by going into television, and was not a star with recognition until he was in his forties. When I talked to Tom at the Woodstock School, he said that the school was his life and he would use what little influence he had and would do whatever he could to protect the school. He thought it should be a Christian object lesson and do Christian work, but not seek converts. He thought that he was one of the few who knew cricket and baseball equally well. He compared some cricket moments to some baseball ones to illustrate this. Tom Alter died at sixty-seven in 2017, his loss lamented by many.

Sharon Lowen is an Indian dancer, or as she says an Indian artiste, who dances in the Manipuri and Odissi styles and teaches dance in Delhi and in south India. She has lived in India for decades and when she dances, many may have trouble remembering that she is a Jewish girl from Detroit for she looks and dances like an Indian. It has not been easy for her to gain acceptance, but let me quote from something that she has written:

> So Delhi gradually became home and this city meant to me the Mandi House, the art circle, theatre, dance, art, literature, philosophy and friends…But actually being able to be an artiste, to fulfil that childhood fantasy to be a ballerina is really a great thing.
>
> That was my intention when I came to be an exponent of an Indian dance…I was a dancer, I loved to move, loved to emphathise with different movements…I never felt that things were exotic…I have lived India. I've felt India. It's a very complex country…That's what makes it so wonderful because everybody's India is a different India….
>
> The best thing about India is that its culture has survived despite the onslaught of the West. One of the fundamental things about India is the fact that it is non-communal, open-minded and receptive where people are free to practise their own beliefs….[6]

In an autobiographical essay, Sharon mentioned some hesitations about the spirit of toleration and acceptance she has long known in India.

What should we call talented individuals like Tom Alter and Sharon Lowen besides 'in-betweeners'? Friends of India? They are builders and shapers of modern India as much as many of its citizens. Are Americans, even if they live most of their lives in India, and make important contributions to India still Americans? In this period from about 1970, there are more 'in-betweeners' with complex bi-national identities they have had to work out. Each is unique.

---

[6] Narayanan, V.N. and Jyoti Sabharwal, 1997. *India at 50*. Bliss of Hope & Burden of Reality. New Delhi: Sterling, pp. 552–35.

Part IV

Cultural Explosion: South Asians in the Diaspora, 1947 to the Present

Many of us who are lucky enough to have the right papers live not in place or the other, but in a continuum of our birthplace and the place we've migrated to. Where is home for people like us? Are we Indian or American? Are we Bombayites or New Yorkers? We are both, and neither. The communities of people that move these days between two or more localities, as I do between South Bombay and Greenwich Village, might be called 'interlocals'. ... So I propose a new way of looking at migrants... as people in continuous transit between two or more places, not nation-states. Let's look at migration as not an arrow but a circle.[1]

The surge of South Asians—not only from India, but from Pakistan and Bangladesh as well—into America over the past two generations has changed the connections between these nations. South Asians are now participating in almost every sphere of American life. They are entrepreneurs carrying weight in Silicon Valley, working in hospitals and colleges, and present throughout the media. More are entering public life. Another dimension is their role in bringing their culture from South Asia and blending it into American life. Sometimes the cultural elements are quite similar to those found in India or Pakistan. Indian worshippers at the Ganesh Temple in Queens, New York, might pray similarly to believers in a temple in Bangalore or Lucknow. Oft-times South Asian cultural elements

---

[1] Mehta 2019, pp. 230–31.

have been shaped and changed into something new and arresting in the American environment. Since so many of South Asian background are flowing into business, politics, writing, acting, playing music, what follows is a very selective presentation of some of these cultural transfers and new creations. My apologies to the many talented people not mentioned here.

Sir Edwin Arnold, 1832–1904,
British translator of Indian texts

Henry David Thoreau, 1817–1862,
American writer and reader of
Indian philosophy

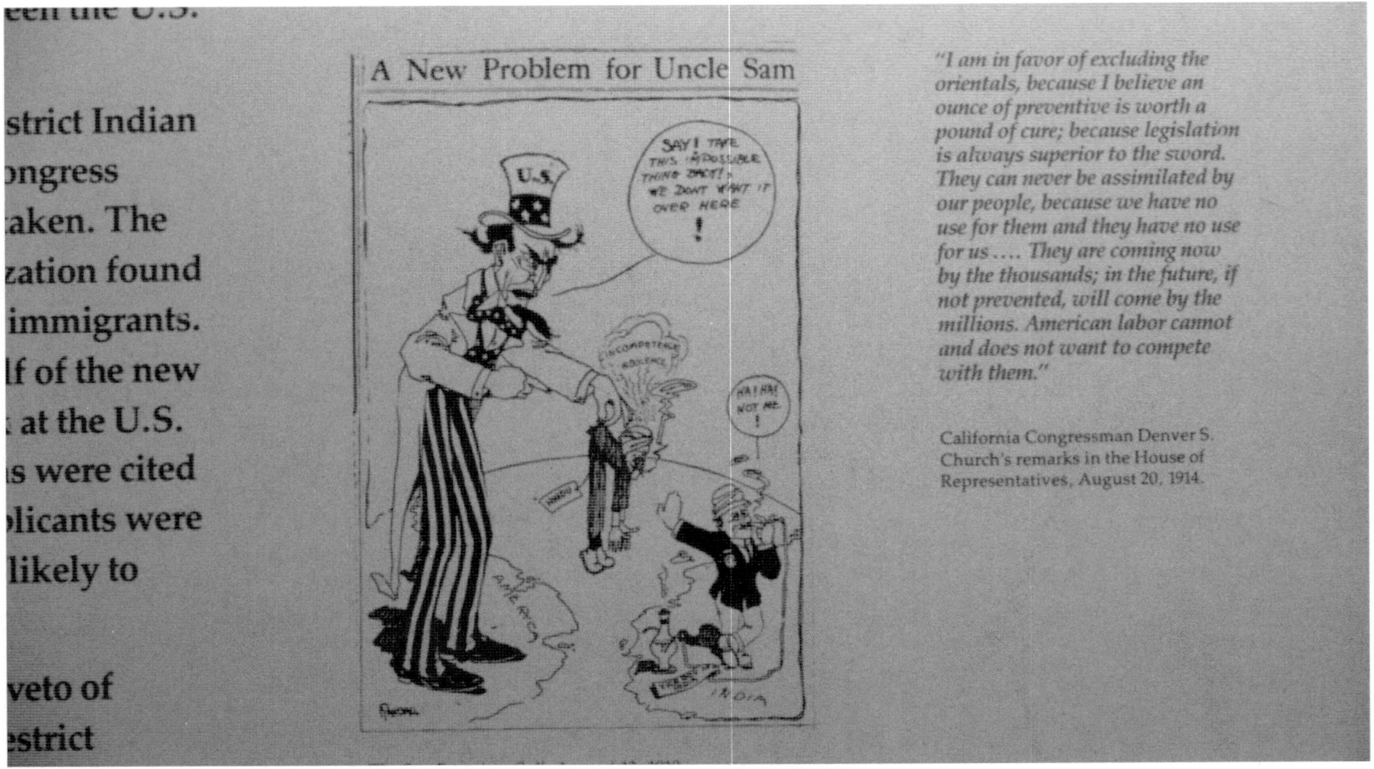

een the U.S.
strict Indian
ongress
aken. The
zation found
immigrants.
lf of the new
at the U.S.
s were cited
licants were
likely to
veto of
strict
A New Problem for Uncle Sam
U.S.
SAY! TAKE THIS IMPOSSIBLE THING BACK! WE DONT WANT IT OVER HERE !
HA! HA! NOT ME !
AMERICA
INDIA
"I am in favor of excluding the orientals, because I believe an ounce of preventive is worth a pound of cure; because legislation is always superior to the sword. They can never be assimilated by our people, because we have no use for them and they have no use for us .... They are coming now by the thousands; in the future, if not prevented, will come by the millions. American labor cannot and does not want to compete with them."
California Congressman Denver S. Church's remarks in the House of Representatives, August 20, 1914.

'Excluding Orientals', cartoon in a San Francisco newspaper, ca 1910

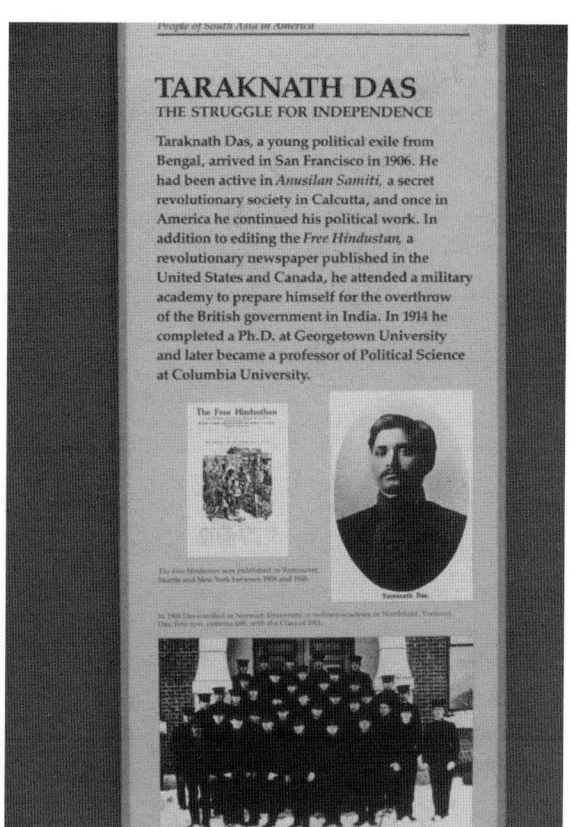

Taraknath Das, 1884–1958, Indian revolutionary, writer and teacher who lived in the US from 1905

John Kenneth Galbraith, 1908–2006, economist and American ambassador to India, 1962

Kumar Goshal,
1899–1972, centre,
Indian immigrant to
the US, translated and
put on ancient Indian
play, 1923

Har Dayal, 1884–1939,
revolutionary, founder of the
Ghadar Movement in California,
early twentieth century

William James, 1842–1910, American
philosopher, explored Indian
religious texts

The Subscription List for this issue will open on   day, the   day of
190   and will close on or before   day, the   day of   190

THE TATA IRON & STEEL COMPANY
LIMITED.
To be registered under the Indian Companies' Act, 1882.

CAPITAL - - - Rs. 2,31,75,000
DIVIDED INTO

2,00,000 Ordinary Shares of Rs. 75 each	...	...	Rs. 1,50,00,000
50,000 Cumulative 6% Preference Shares of Rs. 150 each...		,,	75,00,000
22,500 Deferred Shares of Rs. 30 each ...	...	,,	6,75,000
			Rs. 2,31,75,000

The Preference Shares will also rank in priority to the Ordinary and Deferred Shares in respect of repayment of Capital.

20,000 of the said Ordinary Shares have been agreed to be issued as fully paid up to Messrs. Tata Sons & Co. in part payment for the concessions transferred by them to the Company and they have subscribed for and will receive an allotment of 2000 Deferred Shares upon the same terms as to payment &c. as applicants for Ordinary Shares.

1,330 of the said Ordinary Shares have been agreed to be issued as fully paid up to a Syndicate of gentlemen who have rendered services in the promotion of the Company amongst whom are the Directors named below other than the two Special Directors and such gentlemen have subscribed for and will receive an allotment of 133 Deferred Shares upon the same terms as to payment &c. as applicants for Ordinary Shares.

Out of the 20,000 Ordinary Shares to be issued as fully paid up to Messrs. Tata Sons & Co. as aforesaid and the 2000 Deferred Shares subscribed for by them. Messrs. Tata Sons & Co. have agreed immediately after the issue thereof to them to transfer without payment to the said Syndicate of gentlemen in further remuneration for their services 1,330 Ordinary Shares and 133 Deferred Shares.

The Directors and their friends have applied for   Ordinary Shares   Preference Shares and Deferred Shares on the terms of this Prospectus and such Shares will be allotted to the several applicants in full at par; and   Ordinary Shares   Preference Shares and   Deferred Shares are now offered to the public for subscription on the like terms.

The profits of the Company available for distribution as dividend will in the first place be applied in paying to the holders of Preference Shares a cumulative dividend at the rate of 6 per cent per annum on the amount for the time being paid up thereon, to be calculated from the 1st April 1908; next in paying to the holders of Ordinary Shares a non-cumulative dividend at the rate of 8 per cent per annum on the amount for the time being paid up, or credited as paid up thereon respectively; and thirdly in paying to the holders of Deferred Shares a non-cumulative dividend at the rate of 25 per cent per annum on the amount paid up thereon, and the surplus will be divided as follows:—as to 50 per cent thereof by way of additional dividend on Ordinary Shares, and as to 50 per cent thereof by way of additional dividend on Deferred Shares.

Assets available on a winding-up for distribution among shareholders will be applied, first, in repayment of the amount paid up on Preference Shares, then in repayment of the amount paid up, or credited as paid up on Ordinary and Deferred Shares rateably, and the balance (if any) will be divided as to 50 per cent thereof among the holders of Ordinary Shares, and as to the balance of 60 per cent thereof, among the holders of Deferred Shares according to the amounts paid up, or credited as paid up on such Ordinary Shares and Deferred Shares respectively at the commencement of the winding up.

At the general meeting of the Company, the Members on a poll will have one vote for each share held by them whether Ordinary, Preference or Deferred.

The National Bank of India, Limited, Bombay, will receive applications for the number of Ordinary, Preference and Deferred Shares available for subscription and will receive the deposit moneys and allotment call on all the shares.

Each applicant for Ordinary Shares is entitled to apply for one Deferred Share of Rs. 30 in respect of every ten Ordinary Shares of Rs. 75 each applied for, and each applicant for Preference Shares is entitled to apply for one Deferred Share in respect of every twenty Preference Shares of Rs. 150 each applied for, and, subject to payment of application money, as hereinafter provided, the shares allotted will be allotted in these proportions.

The Shares will be payable as follows:—

ORDINARY SHARES.	PREFERENCE SHARES.	DEFERRED SHARES.
On Application, per share Rs. 5/-	On Application, per share Rs. 10/-	On Application, per share Rs. 5/-
On Allotment, per share Rs. 10/-	On Allotment, per share Rs. 20/-	On Allotment, per share Rs. 25/-

The balance of Rs 60 per share due on the Ordinary Shares will be payable by calls, each of which will not exceed Rs. 15 per share and will be at intervals of not less than 2 months.

The balance of Rs. 120 per share due on the Preference Shares will be payable by calls, each of which will not exceed Rs. 30 per share, and will be at intervals of not less than 2 months.

The calls on the Ordinary Shares will, subject as aforesaid, be in the discretion of the Directors, but if the Preference Share capital is in the opinion of the Directors sufficiently subscribed, it is the present intention to call up the Ordinary Share capital to such an extent only as will make the total called up capital of the Company approximately Rs. 1,50,00,000.

Directors.

D. J. TATA, Esq., (Messrs. Tata Sons & Co.) Special Director, *Chairman.*
Sir SASSOON DAVID, Kt. (Messrs. Sassoon J. David & Co.)
Sir J. COWASJI JEHANGIR, Kt. (Sir J. Cowasji Jehangir & Co.)
Hon. Mr. VITHALDAS DAMODHER THACKERSEY (Messrs. Thackersey Mooljee & Co.)
GORDHANDAS KHATTAU, Esq. (Messrs. Khattau Mackanji & Co.)
FAZULBHOY CURRIMBHOY EBRAHIM, Esq. (Messrs. Currimbhoy Ebrahim & Co.)
NAROTTAM MORARJEE GOCULDAS, Esq. (Messrs. Morarjee Goculdas & Co.)
A. J. BILIMORIA, Esq., (Messrs. Tata Sons & Co.) Special Director.

Bankers.
THE NATIONAL BANK OF INDIA, LIMITED.

Solicitors.
Messrs. LITTLE & Co.

Agents.
Messrs. TATA SONS & Co., Bombay.

Registered Office.
NAVSARI BUILDINGS, Hornby Road, Bombay.

Prospectus for Tata Iron and Steel, early twentieth century

Mark Twain, 1835–1910,
American writer, visited India
and wrote of his tour

Vivekananda, 1863–1902,
Indian guru and writer,
attended World Parliament of
Religions, 1893, and taught
Indian Hinduism to Americans

A QUESTION OF CONTROL.

India. "WHAT ABOUT CHANGING PLACES?"
John Bull. "WELL, YOU'RE WELCOME TO SEE WHAT YOU CAN DO AT THE WHEEL.
THINK I'D BETTER SIT BESIDE YOU—WITHIN REACH OF THE BRAKE."

John Bull cartoon from the British press, early twentieth century

Ralph Waldo Emerson, 1803–1882, American poet and philosopher, widely read in Indian texts

Dalip Singh Saund, 1899–1973, first South Asian elected to US Congress

1

Mantras, Yoga and the Beats

Ever since Swami Vivekananda came to teach in America in the 1890s, Indian religious teachers have played an increasing role in American life, their importance intensifying from the late 1950s. Some of these teachers came to the US and flourished here, others never came but exerted an influence from afar, while some were Americans who, taking an Indian name and identity, turned themselves into Indian gurus. Some gurus were based in India and were known to Americans before moving West, like Maharishi Mahesh Yogi (1918–2008). Some stayed at home

Maharishi Mahesh Yogi
Source: Wikimedia Commons

and attracted disciples in distant places, as did Sathya Sai Baba (1926–2011), whose American followers held evening meetings in an office building in New York City across the street from Macy's Department store. All attested to his ability to do miracles.

Some of the gurus emigrated and developed as spiritual teachers in the West, as did Sri Chinmoy (1931–2007) and Deepak Chopra (1946–). American natives Ram Dass and Shakti Gawain (1948–2018) transformed themselves into Indian-style gurus on their home ground. The power and influence of some gurus attracted Americans to travel to India to have *darshan* (a revelatory glimpse of a holy figure) to listen to the teachings of these gurus at first hand.

It is difficult to judge which of these gurus were or are serious spiritual teachers, which

Ram Dass
Source: Wikimedia Commons

mountebanks or frauds. British psychiatrist Anthony Storr in *Feet of Clay: A Study of Gurus* (1997) suggests that they were mostly charismatic loners when young, fiercely convinced that they were able to spread vital and prophetic truths to disciples. Some, he maintained, were truly, some were not. All of them needed disciples for affirmation of their missions, while the disciples needed a master.[1]

Why was there the 'turn East' starting in the 1950s? Jacob Needleman argues that Eastern religions and their practitioners offered understandings and 'instrumentalities'[2] that had once existed was lost in Christianity and Judaism as practiced in

---

[1] Storr, Anthony. 1997. *Feet of Clay*. A Study of Gurus, Saints, Sinners, and Madmen. NY: Free Press, pp. ix–xvii, 3ff; Gordon, James S. 1987. *The Golden Guru*. The Strange Journey of Bhagwan Shree Rajneesh. Lexington: Stephen Greene Press, p. 18; Williamson, Lola. 2010. Transcendent in America. NY: NYU Press, 2010, p. 114ff.

[2] Needleman, Jacob. 1970. *The New Religions*. Garden City: Doubleday, 1970, p. 17ff.

mid-twentieth-century America. Eastern teachings concentrated on the individual and presented techniques for reaching towards inward understandings of the divine and the inner self—if there was a self— while Western religions offered empty forms and rote practices. In *Turning East: The Promise and Peril of the New Orientalism*, Harvey Cox charted his own efforts at meditation enriched his practice of his Christian faith.[3]

In the 1970s and 1980s, the scholar and British foreign service officer John E. Mitchiner made a guru tour through India and offered details on the teachings of a dozen or so gurus, and his gloss on them. One of his strenuous objections to the teachings of most was the claim that all religions were one, and that the path offered by the guru in question subsumed within it all other religions and was the superior way. He argues that all religions were not one, all paths not the same, and that most of the gurus had little grasp of the other religions—Christianity, Islam, Judaism—that they were incorporating within their particular framework.[4] Mitchiner's survey also shows that what was demanded of disciples by different gurus varied widely. One named Ramdas, and Krishnabai, his disciple and replacement, simply asked disciples to repeat 'Ram' endlessly, and doing so would bring them to unity with the guru and the godhead. Love Ram, say his name forever, and you will be one with Ram.

Following the twentieth-century guides and organizations that first brought Indian spiritual wisdom to America—the Ramakrishna Mission, theosophists, the Self-Realization Society of Yogananda and Krishnamurti—as well as the more recent ones— the Hare Krishnas, Maharishi meditators, and followers of Ram Dass—came a new generation in recent decades.[5] The American landscape is now dotted with Indian-inspired religious institutions.

---

[3] Cox, Harvey. 1977. *Turning East*. NY: Touchstone.

[4] Mitchiner, John. 1992. *Guru*. The Search for Enlightenment. New Delhi: Viking, pp. 51, 69.

[5] Eck, Diana L. 2001. *A New Religious America*. How a 'Christian Country: Has Become the World's Most Relgiously Diverse Nation. NY: HarperCollins.

I consider a few of the gurus, South Asian or South-Asian-inspired Westerners, who have had an impact in America since 1947: Sathya Sai Baba; Maharishi Mahesh Yogi; A.C. Bhaktivedanta Swami Pradhupada (1896–1977); Ram Dass; Rajneesh; Deepak Chopra; and Sadhguru.

Sathya Sai Baba inspired the remarkable devotion of tens of thousands of followers in India and throughout the world, where his fame was said to have spread to more than 100 countries through more than 1,000 branches. Born Sathya Narayana Raju, Baba claimed he was a reincarnation of an earlier guru, Sai Baba of Shirdi, and that he was a god incarnate, or avatar, such that no one else could take his place or represent him, and that he had the power to do miracles at will. The miracles of Baba included materialization (the creation of some material object or substance out of nothing) of holy ash (*vibhuti*); appearing or seeming to appear where this could not possibly be the case; and curing the terminally ill. Disciples contributed funds allowing Baba to create wide networks of social service facilities and schools.[6] Later he established centres in Mumbai, Hyderabad and Chennai. Although he announced he would live to age 96, he died at 84, and some await his resurrection.

Although Sai Baba had taught hundreds of thousands, the Maharishi Mahesh Yogi was even more in the public eye and attracted millions of disciples and pupils of his technique of Transcendental Meditation. Although different stories are given about his background, many believe that he was born Mahesh Prasad Varma into a family of the Kayastha caste, and studied at Allahabad University, graduating in 1942. After working in a factory for some time, he became a secretary of Swami Brahmananda Saraswati and took the name Bal Brahmachari Mahesh. When his guru died in 1953, Mahesh could not be his successor because he was not a Brahmin, and therefore set out on his own to follow the path his guru had suggested: teach the masses throughout the world the method of 'transcendental meditation' (TM).

---

[6] Babb 1986, p. 159ff.

From 1955, Mahesh travelled around India starting a movement called the 'Spiritual Development Movement'. Then in 1959, he began his world tours through Southeast Asia, to Hawaii and to California, where he attracted celebrity followers, teaching them all TM and founding the International Meditation Society. His book *The Science of Being and Art of Living*[7] was later reissued as Transcendental Meditation. In 1966 he founded the Students' International Meditation Society or SIMS, with many American chapters. Although by the mid-1960s, Mahesh had become widely known as the Maharishi, or 'great sage', his fame grew to even greater heights when he became the spiritual advisor to the Beatles. In 1968, the Beatles travelled to his home base in Rishikesh, northern India, and several stayed there for a few weeks and wrote songs. Upon returning to Great Britain, they recorded the 'White Album'.

In the 1990s, he founded the Maharishi European Research University (MERU); in 2000, the Global Country of World Peace (GCWP); in 2001, the Maharishi Vedic City, Fairfield, Iowa.

Mahesh and other gurus have called their procedures and teachings 'scientific' in this case having a different meaning than what has been called 'science' in the West in recent centuries. They meant that they teach a technique which, when repeated, brings the same results, and so is 'scientific'. The Maharishi encouraged hard scientists to take measurements and run tests and to prove claims of the positive impact of meditation. Such studies confirmed that meditation could help reduce stress by lowering heart rates. The Maharishi made other claims about levitation and other feats, none of which was shown to be accurate.[8]

The disciples of A.C. Bhaktivedanta Swami Prabhupada, have long been the most conspicuous in American streets, subways and

---

[7] Mahesh Yogi, Maharishi. 1968. *Transcendental Meditation*. NY: New American Library.
[8] Goldberg, Philip. 2010. *American Veda*. NY: Harmony Books, p. 163ff.

neighbourhoods, where they appear dressed in Indian garb, in groups nearly all made up of white Americans, who sing, proselytize and spread the master's message. This guru was born Abhay Charan De in Kolkata, India. How did he come to be the swami whose words are hawked on the streets of America and elsewhere in the twenty-first century? Bhaktivedanta was raised in a modest Bengali family, and attended Scottish Church College, studying English, philosophy and economics. In accordance with his family's wishes, he had an arranged marriage when he was twenty-two and the girl eleven. Then in 1922, he met Bhaktisiddhanta Sarasvati Thakur (1874–1937), who became his guru, and encouraged him to spread the message of bhakti, or loving devotion to the godhead. In 1947, he was given the title Swami Bhaktivedanta, and in 1959, although he had been a householder with a wife, he took the path of renunciation and celibacy, dedicating himself to translating religious texts into English. In 1965, he came to the United States. Bhaktivedanta founded the International Society for Krishna Consciousness (ISKCON). He set up temples in New York and San Francisco and disciples began the street singing, chanting and proselytizing so familiar today. In the final twelve years of his life, he toured and recruited disciples in other countries. The Bhaktivedanta Book Trust established in 1972 continues to publish his translations and commentaries.

Not all the teachers of Indian spiritual paths in the past two generations have been South Asians. The American Richard Alpert, born to a well-to-do Boston family, became the spiritual guide Ram Dass. Alpert was joylessly climbing the academic ladder at Harvard University when he joined with Timothy Leary in experimenting with LSD and other psychedelic drugs, as a result of which they both were fired. In 1967, pursuing his own path as a spiritual seeker, Alpert went to India. There he encountered a young American who led him to an Indian guru, Neem Karoli Baba, whom Alpert called Maharaj-ji, who seemed to know, uncannily, everything going on in Alpert's head. So he took him as his guide on the pathway to spiritual enlightenment. The guru gave him the name Ram Dass; he dropped Richard Alpert. Upon returning to the US, Dass published *Be Here Now,9* an account of his own journeys and a guide on how to live more fully. The book, which had no page numbers and an unusual layout, became a bestseller, propelling its author to his new life course as a different kind of teacher. Was this the same man who had been my teacher in a psychology course in 1959?

Through a long career in the public eye, Ram Dass continued to be a spiritual searcher, educating himself on pathways in every spiritual tradition. He investigated Hinduism, Buddhism, Sufism, Christianity, and then went back to explore his Jewish roots with renewed comprehension. He seems to have remained firm in his views that one is always on his own spiritual journey with the aim of oneness or of 'being here now', that is, living fully in the present moment; that one should join communities of fellow-seekers; that one should love and help others. This desire to help others led Ram Dass to establish charitable institutions such as the Love Serve Remember Foundation, the Hanuman Foundation in 1974 and the Seva Foundation, with others, in 1978, and to serve on the faculty of the Metta Institute. After a stroke in 1997, he continued teaching, living in Hawaii, and understanding the prospect of death, or as he put it facing 'the music all around me' (quoted in Wikipedia) Ram Dass guided people to 'be here now,' and when he met his end in 2019, was unafraid of death.[10]

No guru was quite so flamboyant or controversial as the man who came to call himself Bhagwan Shree Rajneesh. Emphasizing expressive paths to freedom including wild dancing, group therapy, and promiscuous sex, even in public, he was called 'the love guru' by both admirers and critics. His original ashram was in Poona, western India, but in 1981, he moved to rural Oregon to set up Rajneeshpuram. He wore out the welcome mat in both places,

---

[9] Ram Dass. 1978a. *Be Here Now*. Kingsport, TN: Hanuman Foundation.
[10] 'Ram Dass is ready to die', David Marchese, *New York Times*, 2 September 2019.

and eventually returned to Poona for the final years of his life. James S. Gordon, a research psychiatrist, and Frances Fitzgerald, an experienced and insightful writer, have given searching investigative accounts complemented by the documentary film, *Wild, Wild Country*.

Ma Satya Bharti, once Jill Franklin, who joined Rajneesh in the 1970s,[11] wrote in her autobiography documenting her ambivalence towards the man and his movement:

> Bhagwan helped thousands of us awaken from the dreams and illusions of our conditioning. He helped us rediscover joy again. Then he created new dreams for us to believe in, and eager to believe in...anything, still looking for a meaning to define our lives, we bought it all, willing partners in our own deception...This book is about the dream and the deception, the love affair and the disillusionment. It's about what it means to leave the people you love most in the world to follow a dream that may turn out to be a con in the end. It's about the awesome experience of being with a spiritual Master: the risks and the beauty... [and about] how easily spiritual goals can be perverted when people suspend their critical judgement in the pursuit of lofty idealism...It's about my life with the impresario of broken dreams in a temple of total ruin.[12]

Born in 1931 into a Jain family in Madhya Pradesh, Rajneesh graduated with honours in philosophy from D.N. College in the early 1950s. After some years of teaching, he moved to Bombay, now Mumbai, and became a spiritual guide, by the 1970s attracting numerous disciples. Critical of socialism, of Gandhi, and of traditional religious teaching, he forged his own path, and took many thousands with him. Rajneesh told disciples to dissolve their egos and unshackle their attachments, but he himself seemed to have a gigantic ego—a phenomenon often encountered among gurus, but not explored or of interest to most of their disciples.

---

[11] Franklin, Satya Bharti. 1992. *The Promise of Paradise*. NY: Station Hill, p. 5ff.
[12] Ibid., pp. xvi-xvii

Although Rajneesh said, 'I am not a god', he did claim that he along with his disciples were engaged in an experiment unique in human history. He was, he claimed, 'an awakened being', while no one else appeared to be so. Thus his task was to bring others to 'awakeness', a mission echoing those in Buddhist and Hindu traditions in which a 'realized' being guides others to 'realization', or full consciousness.[13] A compilation

Rajneesh
Source: Wikimedia Commons

of his answers to disciples and the questions of potential disciples gives some idea of Rajneesh's approach. When asked on 24 May 1974, what a disciple, or a sanyasin, might tell others, he said:

> And what is sannyas?—
> It is a freedom from the mind...
> Mind is the accumulated past...
> Sannyas is getting free from the past,
> Living in the moment—
> not carrying the past in the head,
> Not being burdened by it...
> Sannyas is desirelessness,
> and desirelessness means living in the now...
> you don't desire even God... .
> Desirelessness is not the death of desire...
> It is a transformation of desire... .[14]

---

[13] 'Wild, Wild Country', *Netflix*, Episode 1.
[14] Rajneesh, Bhagwan Shree. 1979. *My Way: The Way of the White Clouds*. NY: Grove Press, pp. 567–76.

Rajneesh needed assistants for this rapidly expanding experiment. Ma Anand Sheela, born Sheela Ambalal Patel in 1949 in Baroda, replaced Laxmi, who could not cope with rising tensions with the government. Sheela had attended Montclair State College in New Jersey, and in 1972 moved back to India where, in Bombay, she fell in love with Rajneesh, and it was said, he with her.[15] Clever and capable, she ran the ashram in Poona, and served as Rajneesh's spokesperson when he retreated into silence.[16] Candidates for discipleship flocked to the ashram, more Westerners than Indians, and many were initiated.

Rajneesh organized group activities, drawing upon the great variety of possibilities within the human potential or New Age experiments in the West, mostly conducted at Esalen, as well as Indian tradition. Participants were told to shed their repressions and act out their feelings of rage and sexual desire. These cathartic sessions would prepare the ground for meditation. A few rapes and injuries transpired. Some attendees sold drugs or turned to prostitution to get the money needed to stay on. Experienced Westerners like the head of Esalen in California, offered some praise and harsh criticism.[17] Later interviews by James S. Gordon (1987) with many of the female disciples disclosed that in addition to his chosen mistress, Rajneesh also selected a pair of women each night for pleasure. They were told not to disclose details.

The operations of the ashram aroused the hostility of the Janata Party government and then of Mrs Gandhi, the prime minister, who had been friendly. This antagonism, and the press of eager would-be disciples wanting access to the ashram, led Rajneesh, with Sheela's aid, to search for an alternative location. Finding no site in India, they searched in the US. In 1981, Rajneesh went to America. Sheela

---

[15] 'Wild, Wild Country', *Netflix*.
[16] Ibid., Episode 1.
[17] Fitzgerald, Frances. 1986. *Cities on a Hill*. A Journey through Contemporary American Cultures. NY: Simon and Schuster, p. 282ff.

found a spot in Oregon and the Rajneesh organization purchased the Big Muddy Ranch, about 64,000 acres, for $5 million.

The whole ashram operation had to be resettled, and facilities built for the guru and thousands of followers. The chosen spot was remote and hilly in a sparsely settled part of a low-population state. Since he had a dark vision of what was in store for the world, he and his inner circle believed that it was best to be in the wilds where he and his disciples might survive all calamities. The disciples began an enormous building project including housing and farming facilities. Sheela was in charge: decisions came from the top down, and disciples seemed to accept their work assignments. Some told Fitzgerald that work is joy; it is religious fulfilment as guided by our master, but later she learned of negative undercurrents. Gordon and Fitzgerald recognized the transformation from wild Poona to a more organized and staid Rajneeshpuram.

Fitzgerald suggests that the Rajneesh-ism of India was transformed into a church, strictly ruled and policed from above, with dogma, specified holidays and rituals.[18] Hostesses, quaintly called 'Twinkies', accompanied investigative writers like Gordon and Fitzgerald, limiting their access to the inner workings of the ashram.[19] It seemed to be a commune of worker bees who were not to question their assignments, nor the activities of the master. He was hidden from view except for his daily drives in a Rolls Royce. He no longer offered intimate advice to disciples, nor did he deliver public lectures. Sheela was the guru's public face. [20]

After a brief period of acceptance by the local community, hostility rose into open warfare. The Rajneeshees moved to control local government, buying out whatever they could in the tiny town of Antelope, and then in Wasco county, where they brought in thousands of homeless people to vote to give them control of the county. When that plan failed, Sheela attempted to poison the locals

[18] Ibid., p. 314.
[19] Fitzgerald 1986, p. 254ff; Gordon 1987, p. 102ff.
[20] Ibid., pp. 279ff, 317ff.

in Wasco so that they would not be available to vote. This effort also failed.[21] Rajneeshpuram began to fail. The flow of funds and visitors from outside slowed. On 13 September 1985, Sheela and a few cohorts fled to Europe. Rajneesh emerged and said that Sheela was responsible for the crimes committed by members of the ashram. Rajneesh disowned the *Book of Rajneeshism* she had published and had all copies burnt.

In October 1986, Sheela was arrested in West Germany and extradited to Oregon. She pleaded guilty to immigration fraud and attempted murder and was sentenced to twenty years in jail. After serving only twenty-nine months, she was released and returned to Europe. She insisted that she had worked in close collaboration with the guru, and that he was never as uninformed as he claimed. The Immigration and Naturalization Service (INS) pursued Rajneesh and denied him an extension of his stay in America. He agreed to leave— to where, no one knew. Without him, the Oregon Rajneeshpuram collapsed, as did Rajneesh centres in Europe. After being denied entry to a number of countries, Rajneesh returned to Poona in 1987, where he died in January 1990. Yet some Rajneesh centres survived, and his movement, renamed 'Osho', lives on.

Fitzgerald suggests that the guru era may have ended with the fall of Rajneesh, but other gurus, each unique in some way, continued to ply their trade. Some gurus were survived by the movements they had initiated, which lived on at sites spread across the American landscape. Among those who flashed across the landscape was Sri Chinmoy (1931–2011), who hailed from Chittagong district, now in Bangladesh, and was based in Queens, New York, from 1964.

His own spiritual path featured bodily abstinence: avoiding drugs and alcohol and adherence to celibacy. Teaching daily meditation, he did not recommend withdrawal from the world but encouraged involvement in music, art and poetry as aids towards union with the divine. During the 1970s and early 1980s, Sri Chinmoy attracted disciples from the music world including John McLaughlin, Carlos

---

[21] Ibid., p. 348ff.

Santana and Roberta Flack, as well as the sprinter Carl Lewis. The guru founded meditation centres and gave numerous talks and concerts in New York and around the world, and was invited to lead meditation sessions at the New York headquarters of the United Nations. He painted and composed songs, holding exhibitions and giving concerts; he ran marathons and lifted weights before admiring crowds.

While some of his disciples collected his thoughts in a large volume, Jayanti Tamm, a lapsed devotee, wrote an intimate and damning account, *Cartwheels in a Sari* (2009), published shortly before his death. She explained how she joined what she called his 'cult', surrendered herself to him, abandoned any separate sense of self and had no life apart from him. She revealed that his extraordinary physical accomplishments were phony, doctored to look real, writing, 'The truth was that nothing was true. Guru Sri Chinmoy was a fabrication dreamed and designed by a young and churlish Bangladeshi intent on hypnotizing the world. He had manufactured his image as a modern swami... '[22] Tamm tore herself away from the cult and wanted to warn others against this and similar cults by writing her memoir.

Guru Sri Chinmoy
Source: Wikimedia Commons

In addition to, or alongside, Rajneesh and Sri Chinmoy, another of the

---

[22] Tamm, Jayanti. 2009. *Cartwheels in a Sari*. A Memoir of Growing Up Cult. NY: Harmony, pp. 270–71.

remarkably popular gurus was Yogi Bhajan, a Sikh, born in 1926 who emigrated to the U.S. in 1968. Although without a religious background, he persuaded thousands of Americans that his kundalini yoga was the pathway to lifelong and spiritual fulfilment. He blended in elements of the Sikh religion as well and started a camp in New Mexico and constructed a formidable structure of his religion called Sikh Dharma International. He incorporated it in 1973 to secure tax breaks. It stressed energetic stretching, vegetarianism, and long periods of sexual abstinence. His inner circle was composed solely of women and he set up centres for his kundalini yoga brand across the U.S. and in many foreign countries. He met with world religious leaders persuading them that he was a bona fide religious teacher. Yogi Bhajan died in 2004.

An ambitious American woman, the former Katie Griggs, renamed herself Guru Jagat and took over his operation. At first, she successfully expanded his establishments to include many businesses in tea, food and health related products. Some disciples saw her as charismatic, but she moved ahead to share a variety of wild conspiracy theories and then died suddenly in 2021 after an operation at the age of forty-one. In the aftermath of the death of Yogi Bhavan and Guru Jagat, details were revealed of widespread sexual abuse of women, and the manipulation of thousands with thin, sometimes absurd religious and social teachings not followed by the leaders of this cult. A revelatory television series, *Breath of Life*, was released on HBO in late 2024 presenting this history.

In contrast to the cults presented above, the two brothers Deepak and Sanjiv Chopra were medical doctors, emigrating to the US in the 1970s and moving briskly along in their careers: Deepak as an endocrinologist, Sanjiv as a liver specialist. Sanjiv, in time, joined the Harvard Medical School. With two colleagues, he authored *Live Better, Live Longer: The New Studies That Reveal What's Really Good—and Bad—for Your Health* (2012), a guide for the general public in assessing claims made about foods, medical test and treatments, and alternative medicine. In the tradition of Western medicine, Chopra and his co-authors demand scientific evidence in the evaluation of recommended remedies. The book begins with an explanation of how studies need to be organized and executed to reach his high standards of proof. He does not reject other medical traditions, including Indian and Chinese, but he insists on fact-based demonstration. Feeling that he has benefited from acupuncture and meditating, he says, if you feel it helps and it is not harmful, he says, 'Do it'; so also for prayer. We do not yet understand the mind-body connection that has so much to do with help, but perhaps, down the road, we will.

In the fascinating book co-authored by the Chopras, *Brotherhood: Dharma, Destiny, and the American Dream* (2013), they trace in alternating chapters, their development over time. Deepak has followed a different course from his brother Sanjiv, becoming both a successful physician, but more importantly, a spiritual guide. As he relates in *Brotherhood* and other books, he 'fell in with' or became attached to the Maharishi Mahesh Yogi, an attachment that changed his life. Leaving his strictly Western medical profession, he joined forces with the Maharishi, and helped to bring ayurvedic medicine into America, pursuing an initiative first taken by another South Asian healer, Dr Vasant Lad, of whom more will be said later. But the Maharishi, according to Deepak, wanted to subsume him completely into his fold, and Deepak resisted, going his own way as a guru, or rishi ('enlightened person'). Over the past quarter-century, Deepak Chopra has become a phenomenon, setting up clinics, touring the country, preaching his message, turning out books and tapes at an astounding rate, and profiting, no doubt, immensely.

Thoroughly trained in Western medical traditions, Chopra has melded that mode of thinking with ancient Indian religious teachings to construct a revised set of values for contemporary America. In his touching and concrete account of his first four decades, Chopra points to the presence of ayurvedic medicine in his life, relating how his thoroughly 'scientific' father, also a trained physician, adopted his grandmother's ayurvedic treatments for difficult patients, and how a holy man survived underground for six days. Nonetheless, he practised Western medicine for a decade and a half before opening himself up fully, under the prodding of the Maharishi, to the tenets of Ayurveda.[23] Then he changed direction: he resigned his medical position and became an advocate of Ayurveda, without abandoning some aspects of Western medicine. One of his primary guides was the sage, Ralph Waldo Emerson, who in the nineteenth century had tuned in to Indian teachings, and whose words continued to resonate with Chopra: 'Whenever I read him, I feel the sun radiating from a soul.'[24]

Whereas Western-trained doctors, Chopra came to think, generally look at the body as a machine that, if defective, must be repaired. Chopra, in contrast, believes that the mind, and not the physical brain, is crucial in understanding and treating human beings, and can effect changes and cures for ills that have defied mechanistic treatments.[25] He cites instances of 'spontaneous healing', at the same time admitting that these are few and far between and need more systematic study. He has taught that every person can find their way to perfect health and live longer—if not forever—by adopting the programme he advocates. The context is Chopra's belief in a single intelligence that underlies and connects all things. As the Maharishi explained to Chopra at their first meeting in the 1980s: 'Against everything in the relative world is a background of the absolute. Ayurveda says… that behind mortality is the aspect of immortality. The goal of Ayurveda is to restore this multiplicity to that absolute, to unity.'[26] Such teaching might be expected from an Indian guru, but is unusual as practical guidance, such as Chopra offers, for contemporary Americans seeking total health and a longer life.

Besides the teachings of the Maharishi, Chopra presents the views of his other teacher, Dr Brihaspati Dev Triguna, whom he

[23] Chopra, Deepak. 1991. *Return of the Rishi*. Boston: Houghton Mifflin, p. 121ff.
[24] Ibid., pp. 82–3.
[25] Chopra, Deepak. 2015. *Quantum Healing*. Exploring the Frontiers of Mind/Body Medicine. NY: Bantam, p. 22ff.
[26] Chopra 1991, p. 141.

called, in the 1980s, 'the preeminent living Ayurvedic physician':[27] 'Dr. Triguna... considers the whole man and tries to elevate him, first to normalcy, then beyond. Ayurveda takes the vista of man to be infinite. The universe is the macrocosm, man is the microcosm. But Ayurveda speaks delicately, so delicately that you see Western medicine as clumsy.'[28] In his presentation of the virtues and achievements of Ayurvedic medicine accompanied by meditation, Chopra came to believe that in some cases terminal cancer patients could be cured by the joint meditation of doctor and patient, that meditators could learn to levitate, and that joint meditation by 1 per cent of the world's population would bring world peace.

Another path Chopra took after his break with the Maharishi was the exploration of quantum theory, a concept used in modern science, as a complement to Ayurveda, an exploration described in his 1989 book *Quantum Healing: Exploring the Frontiers of Mind-Body Medicine*. Chopra advocates for what he called holistic medicine, at the centre of which is the outlook and teachings of Ayurveda. Critics have frequently challenged Chopra about his use of the term 'quantum', and about his broad claims, which many find simplistic, about the path to perfection.

Chopra's message is most concisely presented in *The Seven Spiritual Laws of Success: A Practical Guide to the Fulfillment of Your Dreams* (1994). If you follow his 'laws', he asserts, you will attain anything you desire, including material wealth, happiness and peace. Among the 'laws' are instructions to exert the 'least effort' and maintain a posture of 'detachment' (from passions and stress), concepts found in Christian and Hindu traditions. Chopra's promise of fulfilment seems to be out of touch with the real world in which we live.

Some scientific studies have proven that by mental processes, a trained and experienced individual can slow their heart and breathing rates, lower their body temperature, and survive in conditions under which no normal and untrained human being would. Many believe that regular meditation can reduce stress. Beyond these important

---

[27] Ibid., p. 105.
[28] Chopra 1991, p. 113.

phenomena, the claims of curing diseases, levitation and bringing world peace must be viewed sceptically, at least by those who want theories to be supported by evidence. But those tempted by tales of terminating cancer by meditation will embrace this guru or that, and hope for the best. On an earthly level, Chopra has offered advice on how to remain calm during the pandemic.[29] Entering another realm, he has founded 'Chopra Capital',[30] which offers financial advice in tough times. Surely, he is America's all-around guru.

While Deepak Chopra has continued to thrive, other spiritual teachers from the next generation have arrived. Among them is Jaggi Vasudev, called Sadhguru (meaning 'true guru'), born in Mysore in 1957, who says he found his calling with a profound spiritual experience on Chamundi Hill, Mysore. In 1993, he established the Isha Foundation and Isha Yoga Center. His teaching, which he calls 'inner engineering', centres on this notion: that each of us is one with the total environment, natural and human, around us, and that therefore, we have a responsibility to care for all of it as we care for ourselves, because it is ourself.

In India, Sadhguru spread his message to throngs of businessmen, UN agencies, prisoners in Tamil Nadu jails and ordinary people. Later, he decided to reach out to the West, and chose McMinnville, Tennessee, as the site to construct the Isha Institute of Inner-sciences. Begun in 2005, it includes a gigantic Mahima Hall for meditation and a Linga Bhairavi, a representation, his centre says, of the feminine aspects of the divine. In addressing American audiences, which include many of South Asian background, he avoids foreign or complex terms at first, providing guidance about diet and stress reduction; he slowly introduces Indian terms and concepts, reaching the schemata for the *chakras* and the process of yog, understood in his own way. Going beyond the three paths to moksha (liberation) in the Bhagavad Gita, Sadhguru preaches that the path of kriya can take one beyond these to the innermost core of selflessness and oneness. One must detach the body and

---

[29] 'Deepak Chopra's Advice', The *New York Times*, 4 October 2020.
[30] Advertisement in *The Economist*, 19 December 2020.

mind and observe these as if from some other vantage point. He instructs us: 'When you have the ability to perform action with the non-physical aspect of your energy, then it is termed a "kriya" . . . if you are inducted by someone who has mastery over the realms of energy will it become possible for you to practice kriya'.[31] Praised by Deepak Chopra, who commented on Sadhguru's *Inner Engineering*: (2016): 'If you are ready, it is a tool to help awaken your own inner intelligence, the ultimate and supreme genius that mirrors the wisdom of the cosmos.'[32]

With the turn East, Americans increasingly took up the practice of yoga. Sometimes that practice accompanied a spiritual quest; sometimes it was pursued for physical wellbeing. From the 1950s, the number of teachers and practitioners grew exponentially. Two of the best known were B.K.S. Iyengar (1918–2014) and Indra Devi (1899–2002), the first an Indian, the second a Latvian, who took an Indian name. They were both teachers of the renowned violinist Yehudi Menuhin (1916–1999) and he helped them, in turn, to spread their teaching methods.

Though an American by birth, Menuhin was a world citizen and was honoured for his generous contributions to music and human wellbeing worldwide. A violin prodigy, he came to yoga in his thirties, almost by chance. Picking up a book about yoga in 1951, he was intrigued and began to teach himself. On a visit to India that year, he was challenged by another yoga exponent, Jawaharlal Nehru, to demonstrate his mastery. Menuhin described the scene:

> I stood on my head in a somewhat rickety and unsatisfactory fashion, under the critical gaze of his daughter Indira, his sister 'Nan' Pandit, and a few members of the government. 'Oh, that's no good!' said Nehru in his sharp way. 'I'll show you.' He took off his little Gandhi hat and very elegantly—although not more

---

[31] Sadguru. 2016. *Inner Engineering*. A Yogi's Guide to Joy. Gurgaon: Penguin, p. 221.
[32] Ibid., Back cover.

elegantly than I can manage it now—upended himself on the drawing room carpet. Dutifully I did my best to emulate my first guru, and we were both on our heads when the… butler threw open the door to announce that dinner was served.[33]

A little later, Menuhin observed a sage in a loincloth teaching yoga in a forest clearing and decided to learn all he could about it. He made contact with Iyengar, a yoga teacher in Bombay previously unknown to him—while Iyengar had never heard of Menuhin. Iyengar became the violinist's chief guide in yoga, and Menuhin brought Iyengar to the West. In 1966, Iyengar published his *Light on Yoga*, with a forward by Menuhin. It sold millions of copies worldwide and in the next decades Iyengar Yoga Schools opened in many countries.

Beset with poor health as a child, Iyengar regained his health in adolescence after working with a yoga teacher, then became a yoga teacher in his own right. He thrived and gained many pupils including Krishnamurti, Jayaprakash Narayan, and later Aldous Huxley. In 1954, Menuhin invited Iyengar to Switzerland, and in 1956, Iyengar came to the US, where he became the best-known of Indian yoga teachers in the West.[34]

Not confining himself to only one yoga teacher, Menuhin also made contact in the 1950s with the Latvian-born Eugenie Peterson, who called herself 'Indra Devi'. In 1917, when the Bolshevik Revolution broke out in Russia, she left her homeland to work as an actress and dancer in Western Europe, and started learning about yoga. In 1927 she journeyed to India where she studied yoga and became a yoga teacher. Her husband, a diplomat, was transferred to China, and in the 1930s she began to teach yoga there. In 1947, after her husband's death, she migrated to the US and opened a

---

[33] Menuhin, Yehudi. 1976. *Unfinished Journey*. NY: Knopf, p. 246.

[34] Iyengar, B.K.S. 1966. *Light on Yoga*. London: George Allen and Unwin, p. 15ff; Menuhin 1997, pp. 247, 251; Stern, Eddie. 2019. *One Simple Thing*. A New Look at the Science of Yoga and How It Can Transform Your Life. NY: North Point Press, p. 244; 'Iyengar', in Wikipedia

yoga studio in Hollywood. She used Gloria Swanson and other pupils in yoga poses in *Yoga for Americans* (1959). Through her books and teachings, like Iyengar, she helped to popularize yoga in America.[35]

Teachers and their pupils alike have tried to explain precisely how yoga benefits mind, body, and spirit. Iyengar's overview says: 'Yoga is a timeless pragmatic science... dealing with the physical, moral, mental and spiritual well-being of man as a whole.'[36] He then he quotes the Bhagavad Gita:

> A lamp does not flicker in a place where no winds blow; so it is with a yogi, who controls his mind, intellect and self, being absorbed in the spirit within him. When the restlessness of the mind, intellect and self is stilled through the practice of Yoga, the yogi by the grace of the Spirit within himself finds fulfillment. Then he knows the joy eternal which is beyond the pale of the senses which he reason cannot grasp... He has found the treasure above all others. There is nothing higher than this.[37]

Explaining the benefits of yoga, Menuhin is more pragmatic than religious:

> For me yoga is primarily a yardstick of inner peace: if one is afflicted by despondency or envy... or any of a hundred other human miseries and temptations... one cannot breathe deeply, evenly and quietly, as yoga teaches. It begins with a certain peaceful concentration, and when the breathing is quiet and the body pliable, it is time to start the asanas, rejoicing in the balance, flexibility, consciousness of oneself, awareness of one's potential

---

[35] Indra Devi. 1959. *Yoga for Americans*. Englewood, Cliffs: Prentice-Hall, p. ixff; Stern 2019, pp. 244–45; 'Indra Devi', Wikipedia.
[36] Iyengar 1966, p. 15.
[37] Ibid., p. 21.

that they bestow. In my life yoga is an aid to well-being, permitting me to do more and to do better.[38]

Deploring the state of health of Americans, Indra Devi proposed that 'yoga can help solve the problems of any receptive individual, whether these problems be of a physical, mental, or spiritual nature and... also help solve the problems of a group, society, and even a nation.'[39] These claims by yoga gurus and disciples were not sufficient for social scientists. They wanted concrete evidence, at least for some of the physically demonstrable effects.

In 1968, responding to this need, the Menninger Clinic in Topeka, Kansas, brought in Swami Rama (1925–1996), a leading Indian yoga teacher, to see what they could learn. Their investigations are recounted in detail by Swami's assistant Doug Boyd in the latter's *Swami: Encounters with Modern Mystics*.[40] Over several months they carried out every physiological procedure in their repertoire. They concluded that by his inner processes, or meditation, he could change his heart rate and the temperature of parts of his body. He also, according to Boyd, through his intense mental concentration, was able to move an object at a distance from himself—at which moment, Boyd reported, he felt an electrical current pass through him. After his stay at the Menninger Clinic, Swami Rama founded in 1966 in Honesdale, Pennsylvania, the Himalayan International Institute of Yoga, Science and Philosophy, which spread to other branches. Boyd thought that the East was coming West and East and West were forming a new synthesis. [41]The spread of yoga and of training and meditation centres throughout the US by Indian as well as Western gurus adds weight to his suggestion.

While gurus and a number of Indian religious temples and centres continue to thrive, yoga, in various forms, has spread wider

---

[38] Menuhin, Yehudi. 1977. *Unfinished Journey*. NY: Knopf, p. 248.
[39] Indra Devi 1959, p. xi.
[40] Boyd, Doug. 1976. *Swami*. NY: Random House.
[41] Ibid., p. xiii.

and deeper into American life. Almost every city and town has a yoga centre where one can learn exercises, breathing techniques and meditation. A recent report in *Time*, 8 November 2018, by Jamie Ducharme, has given some statistics about the spread:

> Yoga and meditation aren't so alternative anymore. About 14% of adults and a growing number of kids now practice yoga and meditation, according to new data from the Centers for Disease Control and Prevention's National Center for Health Statistics. Between 2012 and 2017, the percentage of kids and adults who said they had done yoga or meditated in the last year rose significantly. About 14% of adults reported practicing both yoga and meditation in 2017, up from about 9.5% and 4%, respectively, in 2012. Meanwhile, the percentage of kids ages 4 to 17 who had done yoga in the last year increased from about 3% to 8%, and the percentage of kids who had practiced meditation rose from 0.6% to 5.4%.

Yoga teachers can be South Asian, of South Asian descent, or Western. They can stress yoga's connection to spirituality or not and present it in highly heated environments or not. But yoga has spread through the US and across the globe in recent decades by such instructors as Maty Ezraty, the co-founder of YogaWorks.[42] By one account, the number of Americans practicing yoga grew from eighteen to 55 million during the decade from 2008 to 2018. Eddie Stern, a prominent yoga teacher in New York puts the number at 36 million. In either case, it appears that more than 10 per cent of Americans are doing yoga.[43] It is not only the practice of yoga that is striking, whether for health or as a spiritual aid, but also the widespread utilization of meditation techniques. These are viewed as helpful to reduce stress and to increase efficiency

---

[42] 'Maty Ezraty', Obituary, *New York Times*, 18 July 2019.
[43] 'Here's How Popular Yoga and Meditation Really Are', Jamie Ducharme, https://time.com/5447850/yoga-meditation-more-popular/, 8 November 2018; Stern 2019, p. 9.

in meeting daily challenges, while many teachers believe they also offer remarkable gains in health.[44]

Dr Vasant Lad is arguably the person most responsible for bringing to the US the practice of Ayurvedic medicine, which includes meditation among its tools for improved health. In 1978, Lad moved from Pune, India, to Albuquerque, New Mexico, where he set up an institute for the practice of Ayurvedic medicine. The Maharishi, who had hoped to incorporate Lad's operation into his own, turned instead to Deepak Chopra to bring Ayurveda into his work. Lad's medical practice is linked to Indian spirituality, as documented in a 2018 film, *The Doctor from India*. Crucial to that practice is getting information from taking a patient's pulse.[45]

Meditation has been used in almost every sphere of American life, a remarkable instance of the integration into our culture of an element of Indian tradition. Few talk about its origins, but rather about its utility. As with our number system and chess, which originated in India, the Indian roots of our way of life are either not known or discounted. What matters is that such practices and outlooks can be utilized to the benefit of the users.

Among Western seekers of spiritual truth and exercises were the authors Christopher Isherwood, Aldous Huxley and Gerald Heard. After the Second World War, the scholars Huston Smith (1919–2016) and Joseph Campbell (1904–1987), two important popularizers of Eastern religion, contributed, respectively, the bestselling books *The Religions of Man* (1958) and *The Hero with a Thousand Faces* (1949). These friends divided the spiritual universe between myth and the importance of transcendent experience, with Campbell covering the first, Smith the second. Skilled writers, they boosted the idea of many pathways, through a variety of religions, to the ultimate.[46]

---

[44] Benson, Herbert. 1975. *The Relaxation Response*. NY: Avon; Ornish, Dean. 1995. *Dr. Dean Ornish's Program to Reverse Heart Disease*. NY: Ivy Books.

[45] Lad, Vasant. Ayurveda. 1985. *The Science of Self-Healing*. Twin Lakes, WI: Lotus Press, pp. 52–59.

[46] Goldberg, Philip. 2010. *American Veda*. NY: Harmony Books, p. 87ff.

Some American thinkers and poets, experimenting with drugs, became gurus as well. Harvard psychology professor Richard Alpert (1931–2019) and Timothy Leary (1920–1996), also a psychologist, preached to young people to drop out, take mind-altering drugs like LSD, and 'tune in'. Some spiritual seekers had already been experimenting with mescaline and other products, natural and artificial, to induce extraordinary experiences. Among them was the British writer Aldous Huxley who took mescaline in

Christopher Isherwood
Source: Wikimedia Commons

the 1950s and described what happened in *The Doors of Perception* (2009). Huxley believed that he saw with an intensity he had never felt before. Through this 'trip', he knew the unity of the human and non-human worlds. Then he had doubts and questions as he came down from his high.[47]

Also pointing East were those who came to be called 'the Beats'. Allen Ginsberg (1926–1997) and Jack Kerouac (1922–1969) had met at Columbia University years earlier and connected with others in the formation of the Beat Generation, a set of poets who constructed an anti-establishment world, which included the slightly older William Burroughs (1914–1997), Kenneth Rexroth (1905–1982), and their contemporaries, among them Gary Snyder (1930–) and Joanne Kyger (1934–2017). Ginsberg and his companion Peter Orlovsky (1933–2010) caught up with Snyder and Kyger in India, and the

---

[47] Huxley, Aldous. 2009. *The Doors of Perceptions & Heaven and Hell*. NY: Harper Perennial, 2009, p. 9ff.

four travelled to Hindu holy places together in 1962.[48] Snyder a poet and scholar, published *Passage through India*. One of Snyder's poems, entitled [After Ramprasad Sen] demonstrates how he blended into its culture:

> Arms shielding my face
> Knees drawn up
> Falling through flicker
> Of womb after womb,
> through worlds,
> Only begging, Mother,
> Must I be born again?

> . . . you bear me, nurse me
> I meet you, always love you,
> You dance
> On my chest and thigh
> Forever born again.[49]

An example of an American approach to Calcutta was Ginsberg's visit during 1962. He acquired a new identity characterized by plain living, the use of drugs to induce insightful 'highs', antipathy to the rich and to all forms of authority. Ginsberg could thus fit right in with the relatively poor of Calcutta; rather than what Western missionaries called the den of Satan, Kalighat was for him a frequent scene of pleasure and new experience. During the Hindu festival of Durga Puja celebrated that year, Ginsberg visited Kalighat and recorded in his journal:

> With Asoke Fakir a 37-year-old saffron robed long black hair negro who looks like my mother walked into my room a stranger one day—went to smoke ganja in his favorite haunt...

---

[48] Morgan 2006, p. 302ff
[49] Snyder, Gary. 1968. *The Back Country*. New Directions, p. 94.

To Kalighat—we lay on a marble floor in nearby Temple-arcade in park, smoked cigarettes & he talked while I lay back—Then passed to the Kali Mandir inner sanctum & kneeled & saluted the black three-eyed stone—Then to the burning ghats, I watched the bust & head of a lawyer turned over in flame—and two minutes stared in saddhu's eye.[50]

In the extended cultural dialogue between the West and India, Ginsberg started a new chapter: he did his own learning, and he also began a foreign section of the 'beat' movement in Calcutta. He induced some young Bengalis to form a poets' circle; of these the most accomplished was Sunil Gangopadhyay (1934–2012), who described Ginsberg as 'a vortex of activity'. After Ginsberg left, some of these Bengalis were arrested for obscenity, but most were soon released as their American guide eased off to recruit elsewhere.

Ginsberg also came back to sing and chant 'Hare Krishna, Hare Rama…,' and carry this message to the West.[51] In his *A Social History of the Hippies*, Warren Hinckle described an episode in Golden Gate Park's Polo Field after Ginsberg's return to America when a founder of the Beats became a cheerleader for the hippies.

Allen Ginsberg asked ten thousand people to turn towards the sea and chant with him. They did just that, and then picked up… the miscellaneous droppings on the turf… and went contentedly home. This was the end of the first Human Be-In, a gargantuan hippy happening held only for the joy of it in mid-January. The hippie tribes gathered under clear skies with rock bands, incense, chimes, flutes, feathers, candles, banners, and drums.[52]

---

[50] Ginsberg, Allen. 1970. *Indian Journals*. City Light Books: San Francisco, p. 58; Miles, Barry. 1990. *Ginsberg: A Biography*. New York: Harper Perennial, 1990, p. 308.
[51] Morgan, Bill. 2006. *I Celebrate Myself. The Somewhat Private Life of Allen Ginsberg*. NY: Penguin, p. 377, 379.
[52] Miles, p. 377ff.

So through his fierce spirit and talents, Ginsberg had an impact on India and on the West. In the following decades, he continued his chanting, becoming what Hinckle called 'father goddam to two generations of the underground', and held to his belief that there was much to learn from India and wider Asia. From the late 1960s, Ginsberg formed a close relationship with A.C. Bhaktivedanta Swami Prabhupada (1896–1977), and helped to establish ISKCON in America. Some years later, in the 1970s, Ginsberg acquired a Buddhist guide, Trungpa Rinpoche (1939–1987), took initiation as a Buddhist, but still did his free form poetry and Hare Krishna chanting. Ginsberg helped Trungpa and poet Anne Waldman (1945–) in founding the Kerouac School of Disembodied Poetics at Naropa University, Boulder, Colorado, and spent the better part of five years there.[53] A fighter for freer sexuality, expressive and unchained poetic forms, and an antagonist of American imperialism, he continued his work. This work included opposition to the Vietnam War and to American support of Pakistan in the Bangladesh war. Decades later, Ginsberg was at it—poetry, chanting, Asian religious teaching—initiated as a Buddhist, still reaching,

> Élan that lifts me above the clouds
> Into pure space, timeless, yea eternal
> Breath transmitted into words…
> of cadenced breathing—beyond time, clocks, empire, bodies, cars…
> Buddha's help, promises ordinary mind no nirvana—
> Coffee, alcohol, cocaine, mushrooms, marijuana, laughing gas?
> Nope, too heavy for this lightness lifts the brain into blue sky
> At May dawn when birds start singing on East 12th street—
> Where does it come from, where does it go forever?[54]

---

[53] Wikipedia, 'Allen Ginsberg'.
[54] 'Five A.M.', May 1996, Ginsberg 2006, p. 1100.

2

Music, Films, Theatre, Comedy and Media

Just as religious teachings, meditation, and yoga forged a link between East and West, so too did music—a connection between Indian and Western culture in which Yehudi Menuhin as well as jazz musicians played a part. Menuhin was invited to India to play concerts of Western classical music, but he encountered Indian music as he travelled through the subcontinent. In so doing, in 1951, he came to know India's foremost sitar player, Ravi Shankar (1920–2012). The latter was no stranger to the West, for as a teenager in the 1930s he had toured in Europe with his brother's troupe of dancers. But Ravi Shankar thrived more as a musician than as a dancer. Through Shankar, Menuhin came to appreciate Indian music, which he recognized as being, although very different, as sophisticated and complex as the music he had first begun to learn at three.[1] In the first of his autobiographies, Shankar writes of his first meeting with Menuhin whom a mutual friend had invited to a concert of Indian music in a private home:

> I had never before seen a Western classical musician respond so emotionally to our music, not just show interest in its technical aspects. This reaction of Yehudi's to our music and my own reaction to his personality were the beginning of a beautiful friendship between us... I have performed on the same stage many times, though not with him, there was the UNESCO celebration

---

[1] Menuhin 1977, p. 259ff

in 1958 and the Commonwealth Festival in 1966. And then at the Bath Festival in 1966... we played our first duet... in a celebration of Human Rights day, December 10, 1967, he really grasped the spirit of our music... I compose the music spontaneously and he writes it down; and then, while we are practicing, it is a joy to see this superb musician shedding all his pride and awareness of self and accepting like a child or like a devoted student my teaching and my music... Since my childhood, he was my idol and hero, and now he calls me his guru.[2]

Elsewhere Shankar wrote, 'I always had a dream to bring our (Indian) music to the west and to make Westerners appreciate it... That is how I started my mission in 1956.'[3] Menuhin facilitated this goal for Shankar. Later the two combined for numerous concerts and producing an award-winning album, 'West Meets East'.[4]

With Menuhin, Ravi Shankar was just beginning his relations with Western musicians. He also forged a tie with George Harrison (1943–2001) of the Beatles, a skilled guitarist, who was very taken with the sitar and asked Shankar to take him on as a pupil. Harrison studied with Shankar, but decided in the end, that he could not become as skilled at the sitar as he was at the guitar. Although he returned to the guitar, he did his best to blend in Indian music in some late Beatles' songs and then many that he wrote and performed on his own.

Appearing in concerts with many popular musicians, as well as in classical ones with Menuhin, Shankar and his colleague Ali Akbar Khan (1922–2009), who played the sarod, were more responsible for bringing Indian music to the West than any other musician from the subcontinent.[5] At the same time, according to Peter Lazzevoli, Menuhin was the Western musician most responsible for the links

---

[2] Shankar, Ravi. 1968. *My Music, My Life*. NY: Simon and Schuster, pp. 85–86.
[3] Lavezzoli, Peter. 2006. *The Dawn of Indian Music in the West*. NY: Continuum, foreword.
[4] Lazzevoli 2006, p. 1ff.
[5] Ibid., p. 171ff; Wikipedia on Harrison.

formed between Indian and Western musical traditions. In 1955, he introduced the first long-playing record of classical Indian music featuring Ali Akbar Khan, and then introduced him in several live concerts. Within a few years, Ali Akbar Khan settled in the San Francisco Bay Area and opened his own music school. Then in 1967, Ravi Shankar on the sitar and Ustad Alla Rakha (1919–2000) on the tabla (Indian drums), played at the Monterey Pop Festival, an event that encouraged Western musicians of jazz, classical and popular styles to experiment further in fusing Western and Indian music. Among the most noted products of this experimentation was the Beatles' 1967 album 'Sgt. Pepper's Lonely Hearts Club Band', and a subsequent solo album of Harrison's. Before his all-too-early demise, as well, the saxophonist John Coltrane (1926–1967) made his own blend of Western and Indian music after lessons with Ravi Shankar.

Ranging beyond stereotypes, Indian music—classical, Bollywood, jazz, folk—has entered the American scene, and changed and been changed by it. Classical musicians have worked with Western classical players and made new kinds of syntheses. Several musicians of South Asian background have risen to prominence, notably Zubin Mehta (1936–), who became music director of the New York Philharmonic and the Israeli Philharmonic Orchestra. Anoushka Shankar, daughter of Ravi Shankar, was trained as an Indian classical musician, but she, like her father, has been branching out, collaborating across different musical genres, traditions, and with a variety of musicians. Vijay Iyer and Rudresh Mahanthappa are accepted as leading jazz musicians. There are schools for Indian classical music in the US, such as Ali Akbar Khan's institute in Los Angeles.

Perhaps even more important for the generation now in their twenties and thirties is the spread of rap music, spanning America, Canada, the UK and India. South Asian rappers may come from Indian, Pakistani, and Bangladeshi backgrounds, they may or may not feel an intimate link to the subcontinent, they may rap in English, Hindi, Bengali, Hinglish or Banglish, but they exude a diversity and energy that has attracted millions of fans and views to their music. Bhangra, popular music from the Punjab, has become popular in the UK—fused with other musical genres—as well as America. Sandhya Shukla has described the ascent of Apache Indian in the UK.[6] Riz Ahmed and the Swet Shop Boys as well as Nish rose in UK, Raja Kumari in Canada, Anik Khan and Habib in the US, but via the Internet they have crossed seas and continents as part of a global culture, blending their own with the musical genres they draw upon from Africa, the Caribbean and Black America. Red Baraat is a popular music fusion effort, based in Brooklyn, New York, but touring the nation and world year after year,

The Punjabi 'exuberance of life', fused with other musical forms, has made its way through Brooklyn into the wider world and is a mark of the new times of India in America. Red Baraat is both one of the creators of world music and a part of this global cultural movement. At a concert performed in Symphony Space, New York City, on 10 March 2020, an exuberant crowd was encouraged to stand, wave and dance in the aisles, while a few joined the band on stage. Red Baraat played the final number prancing through the theatre aisles, mingling with the audience, blending players and listeners into one. Indian music in America may have had one important precipitating moment with the tours in the 1950s of Ravi Shankar and Ali Akbar Khan, but it has widened with the entry of the band Red Baraat. In San Francisco, Manpreet Toor has spread interest in bhangra through her exuberant videos and dedicated teaching of its dances.

Another musical connection has come through jazz. African American jazz musicians began to play at the Taj Mahal Hotel in Bombay in 1936. They came to feel at home with their mixed clientele and Indian cuisine, and brought New Orleans music to Indian audiences.[7] Some of the Indian musicians learned skills from these jazz players, and found freedom in their improvisational methods, relating them to the ways in which Indian ragas were played, finding similarities between Indian classical music and American jazz.

---

[6] Shukla, Sandhya. 2003. *India Abroad*. Princeton: Princeton U. Press, p. 218ff.
[7] Fernandes 2016, p. 10ff.

In recent decades some jazz musicians of South Asian background have come to the fore, especially Vijay Iyer (1971–) and Rudresh Mahanthappa (1971–). Born to Tamil parents in Albany, New York, and raised in Fairport, New York, Iyer trained as a Western classical musician on the violin and the piano. Studying mathematics and physics at Yale, he moved to the University of California, Berkeley, for graduate work in physics, where he shifted directions, submitting a PhD dissertation focusing on music cognition. During his years of study, he continued to work in the musical world in trio ensembles that performed worldwide. Later, as a composer of concert music, Iyer has explored music from Western classical as well as Indian roots. For years a faculty member at the Manhattan School of Music, in 2014, he joined the Department of Music at Harvard University. Completing his MacArthur 'genius' grant, Iyer became a tenured professor and encouraged the department to move away from its Eurocentric curriculum and embrace a greater variety of musical traditions.[8]

Among Iyer's talented collaborators has been the jazz saxophonist Rudresh Mahanthappa with whom he released a number of albums including 'Architextures' (1998) and 'Blood Sutra' (2003). Born in Trieste, Italy, to Indian emigrants, Mahanthappa grew up in Boulder, Colorado, and later attended the Berklee College of Music in Boston, and received an MA in jazz composition from DePaul University in Chicago. He found a unique way to explore his Indian roots in his album, 'Mother Tongue', as he explains:

> In response to having been repeatedly asked 'Do You Speak Indian?' or 'Do You Speak Hindu?' throughout my life as a son of immigrants, my goal was to somehow musically convey the fact there is no single Indian language. I did this by creating compositions that are directly based on melodic transcriptions of Indian-Americans responding to such questions in their native Indian tongues... I hope to at least engage all of the Indian languages that are spoken in the US.[9]

---

[8] *New York Times*, 12 December 2019; 'Vijay Iyer', Wikipedia.
[9] notes to 'Mother Tongue' album

Although exasperated by America's ignorance of Indian cultures, through his recordings and performances, Mahanthappa has assisted his new compatriots in understanding their diversity.

Starting from his Parsi roots, Zubin Mehta became one of the most cosmopolitan of musicians, trained in Western classical music, but reaching out to Indian classical music as well. He has also tried to bridge different cultural divides through performances in places as varied as Harlem, the largely African American neighbourhood in New York City, and Lebanon, in the Middle East, as well as in India and multiple classical music venues in the West.

Mehta's friend Ravi Shankar was even more important as a pathfinder across international and musical boundaries. Shankar met Yehudi Menuhin and began touring the US in the mid-1950s. He and Menuhin played together in the album 'West Meets East', and Shankar continued working with Western musicians and composers such as Philip Glass, as well as playing Indian classical music. Shankar left the world two musician daughters, now known across continents for their accomplishments: Anoushka Shankar and Norah Jones. Anoushka, a sitarist, followed more directly in her father's footsteps, and often played with him as he became older. When his 'Symphony' had its premiere in London in 2010, she played the sitar part, partnering with the London Philharmonic Orchestra conducted by David Murphy. Although each of the four movements is based on an Indian raga, the piece almost seamlessly integrates Western and Indian music.

Philip Glass (1937–), one of the leading American composers in a variety of genres over the last half-century and more, and influenced by Indian music, met Shankar in 1965 when Glass was chosen to assist Shankar on the soundtrack of the film *Chappaqua*. He later noted that 'Indian music pushed me towards a whole new way of thinking about music, in which the rhythmic structure became the controlling function.' On another occasion he said, speaking of Shankar: 'It may be hard to imagine that one person through the force of his talent, energy and musical personality could have almost singe-handedly altered the course of contemporary music...that is actually and simply what happened.' (notes for 'Symphony,' by David Murphy)

After his meeting with Shankar, Glass travelled to India in 1966, and met the Dalai Lama, to whose cause of Tibetan independence and culture he became devoted. His interests in Indian culture flowered in an opera about Mahatma Gandhi, 'Satyagraha' (1978–1979), and later, in a choral work, 'The Passion of Ramakrishna' (2006). He continued his contact with Shankar as well, and the two collaborated on 'Passages' (1990), a remarkable set of compositions in which each composer developed the other's themes, and Indian and Western musicians combined to perform. As he became more deeply aware about non-Western music, Glass commented, 'It was possible to graduate from a major Western conservatory, in my case Juilliard… without exposure to music from outside the Western tradition. World music was a completely unknown in the mid-60's.' (notes to 'Passages') With the educational work of Shankar and other pioneers, it has become impossible in America and Europe to ignore music from India and other non-Western traditions.

Born in 1981, Anoushka Shankar has continued her father's efforts to blend with other music and work with a wide variety of musicians, to see what is possible. One of the most felicitous of these collaborations was 'Traveller' (2011), on which she worked with flamenco guitarist Javier Limón. Along with an Indian and a Spanish singer, an Indian tabla player, and a Spanish percussion player, they fused music from Spain and India. Shankar commented, 'I find in flamenco something very close to what I cherish in Indian classical music: uninhibited musicality in expression.' (recording notes, 2011) A few years later she produced 'Land of Gold' (2016) another joint effort bringing together Indian and Western musicians, as well as poetry and song. She says it is her response 'to the humanitarian trauma of displaced people'. (jacket notes) Her connections continue in ways that her father started in the 1950s: bringing Indian classical music into the wider world, demonstrating its compatibility with many forms of music.

Norah Jones (1979–), born Geethali Norah Jones Shankar, is Anouskha Shankar's half-sister, whose life course has been very different. Jones is the daughter of Ravi Shankar and Sue Jones, an American concert producer. After her parents separated, she grew up in Grapevine, Texas, living with her mother. From her youth, she displayed singing talent, and moved to New York while in her early twenties. Her first album, 'Come Away with Me' (2001), reached the top of the Billboard 200. It was praised for combining 'acoustic pop with soul and jazz'. ('Norah Jones,' Wikipedia). She was said to have been estranged from her father, but they reconciled just before his death in 2012, when she met him in New Delhi, and held concerts in India. Jones was singing mainly melodies from 'The Fall', soulful songs about the ending of a love affair. Ravi Shankar's two daughters, from very different directions, are appreciated worldwide. After his death, in 2013 they joined together in the music video 'Traces of You', a beautiful, soulful song with brief lyrics, Jones singing, and Anoushka Shankar playing the sitar. Scenes of New York, and likely Kolkata, provide a backdrop for the blended music of the sisters.

The unique potpourri of Indian and Western music created by Falu poses a contrast to Norah Jones's blend of popular Western musical forms. Born Falguni Shah in Mumbai, perhaps in the late 1970s, and called by some the 'Devi Diva', Falu was rigorously trained in Indian classical music for many years by Ustad Sultan Khan, and did not perform in public until she was eighteen. She emigrated to the United States in 2000, and became the vocalist for the Indo-American band Karyshma. Then she began performing with her own band. Her musicians in one concert might be South Asians or Americans, using guitars, piano, drums and harmonium, or they might be more emphatically Indian, playing violin in the Indian manner, and Indian drums. In 'Rabba', the lyrics are all in Hindi, playing with a strong beat. She moves back and forth between English and Hindi. Once her son was born, and she thought of him as South Asian American, and she taught him about his dual heritage through music. This culminated in 'Falu's Bazaar', (2018), which was nominated for a Grammy as best children's album. As the only South Asian at the 2019 Grammy's, she said she felt accepted as an American, and was as at home here as she had earlier been in India.

Like music, but perhaps with even larger audiences, films set in India—with and without Indian or Western music—had been made for decades, but the number gradually swelled, and connections between Hollywood and Bollywood had begun taking centre stage. Well into the 1950s, Rudyard Kipling's writings about India still strongly shaped American images of India, as Harold Isaacs' *Scratches on Our Minds: American Images of China and India* (1958) makes clear. Not only were Kipling's stories and novels still read, but several were made into films. Two post-war films are Rudyard Kipling's *Kim* (1950), based on Kipling's novel, and *Soldiers Three* (1951). *Kim* starred Errol Flynn as an Afghan horse trader, Paul Lukas as a Buddhist lama and Dean Stockwell as Kim. Although Westerners played the Indian roles, several of the Indian characters are portrayed sensitively and sympathetically, whereas the villains of the piece are Russian spies crossing India's northwest frontier and threatening the empire. The main character Kim brings to his Western education in school subjects plus spycraft, a remarkable knowledge of Indian society.

Soldiers Three, starring Stewart Granger, David Niven and Walter Pigeon, is based on Kipling stories about British soldiers in the Indian army as they confront Manik-Rao, yet another threat from the northwest. The three ordinary soldiers drink, brawl and carouse, while Brunswick, their commanding officer, does his best to separate and save them. When a British command post is overrun by rebels, the three soldiers save the day, and Brunswick is promoted to general. As usual, the main Indian parts were played by Westerners. *The Man Who Would Be King* (1975), directed by John Houston is also based on a Kipling story.

Films about India not derived from Kipling include, *Stranglers of Bombay*, about the relatively distant past, and *Song of India* and *Bhowani Junction*. *Stranglers of Bombay* (1960), set in the early nineteenth century, is based on the adventures of Colonel Sleeman (detailed in his memoirs) as he pursues a 'cult of stranglers' dedicated to the goddess Kali called Thugs. Lewis, the Sleeman character, uncovers the work of the Thugs in attacking, robbing and killing caravans of traders. The main Indian parts are played by Westerners in this film from Columbia Pictures directed by Terence Fisher, with Guy Rolfe as Lewis. One of the few Western films set in the pre-Raj period is *The Diamond Queen* (1953), a far-fetched story of seventeenth-century South Asia with French adventurer Tavernier promising to the future French king Louis XIV a remarkable jewel from the sub-continent. In Nepal, Queen Maya (Arlene Dahl) gives them the *Eye of the Goddess*, intended for her wedding, to take back to the king. Westerners play the important South Asian roles, and the queen, portrayed by a made-up American actress, triumphs alongside the French interlopers.

Song of India (1949) is a vehicle for South Asian native actor Sabu, who had started his screen career in Britain in the 1930s. The Sabu character lives in and protects a 'forbidden jungle' where the killing of animals is prohibited and Indian villagers and the animals live in peaceful harmony. Gopal (Tahran Bey), the heir to a princely state that includes the forest, goes to hunt there with his prospective bride, Tara, an American-educated woman (Gail Russell). Several dangerous animals are captured, but Sabu releases them and is captured in turn. Freed upon promising not to release more animals, Sabu, in turn, kidnaps Tara, who is persuaded of the Indian wisdom of non-violence. Pursued by Gopal, Sabu and Tara flee to a mountaintop where a tiger, wounded by Gopal's men, kills the young prince. In yet another twist, we learn that Sabu is the heir to a lost lineage that had been dethroned. Sabu is returned to the throne of the state and wins the girl as well. Most Indian parts are played by Westerners.

Bhowani Junction (1956), a serious film about the Partition period, is based on John Masters' novel of that name. Victoria Jones, played by Ava Gardner, an Anglo-Indian woman, has three suitors: a man from her own community who has long loved her, a young Sikh man, and a British officer, played by Stewart Granger. She is tempted by the young Sikh, whom she almost marries, and the British officer, Colonel Savage, who offers her a comfortable life in an England she has never seen. The story is interwoven with a terrorist plot against the British and the hopes for a peaceful transfer of power. In the end, she decides to stay in India within her Anglo-Indian community and marry her long-time suitor.

A somewhat different take on India in this period is *The Man-Eater of Kumaon* (1948), borrowing the title, but not the content, of Jim Corbett's book about dangerous beasts, *Man-Eaters of Kumaon* (1944). The central figure is an unhappy American doctor, John Collins (Wendell Corey), taking it out on the wildlife of India. He wounds a tiger, and the tiger pursues him attacking villagers. Collins is persuaded that he must stay with them and hunt the tiger. The village headman is played by Morris Carnovsky, his daughter-in-law, Lali, by Joy Page, and his son, Narain, by Sabu. The narrator explains that the villagers' customs have not changed for generations. When a tiger attack renders Lali unable to bear a child, she is going to leave her beloved husband, Narain, because to succeed to the position of village headman, he must have a son. Fortunately, a homeless child Collins has brought to the village is accepted by the villagers as a son for Narain and Lali, so she does not have to leave.

While these Western films about India were still rolling out in the post-Partition period, some serious Indian films were also beginning to be shown in the West, including in the US. The most notable of these films were those of the Bengali director Satyajit Ray (1921–1992), starting with the Apu trilogy, *Pather Panchali*, *Aparajito* and *Apur Sansar*. Ray had long admired many American filmmakers as well as those from France and Great Britain. An avid film buff as a teenager, he was a keen student of Hollywood films, including crime films and Westerns, especially admiring director John Ford.[10]

After the war, during which American films were often shown in India to entertain the young GIs, Ray helped found a film society and slowly moved towards becoming a film director himself. Employed as a graphic artist in an advertising company, he wrote his first scripts while still at his day job. Then in the early 1950s, he made the plunge. A grant from the West Bengal government allowed him to finish *Pather Panchali*, after which he completed the trilogy, which, in time, brought him world renown. As his career progressed, Ray gained ever more confidence as director, but also as composer, orchestra conductor, script writer, and, occasionally, cameraman. Wanting to demonstrate that Indians could make movies just as well as Americans, Italians, Frenchmen, the British and the Japanese, he proved his case. Although Ray eventually made more than thirty feature films and documentaries, it is the first trilogy that has best endured, and continues to be shown in Western art houses.[11]

While he was making his own films, Ray encouraged and assisted the team of James Ivory (1928–) and Ismail Merchant (1936–2005) to produce their own. In 1963, Ray cut and edited *The Householder* for them, and several of his own crew helped them make the film. In 1965, the pair released *Shakespearewallah*, the story of a touring drama group in India, starring Shashi Kapoor, Madhur Jaffrey and Jennifer Kendal. Kapoor was one of the first Indian actors to appear in Hollywood films. (India Abroad, 15 Dec 2017) Merchant and Ivory and screenwriter Ruth Prawer Jhabwala (1927–2013) went on to make many movies, some set in India with Indian and Western actors, many to considerable acclaim. They constituted a unique team of an American director (Ivory), an Indian producer (Merchant), and a European-American screenwriter married to an Indian (Jhabwala).[12]

---

[10] Ray, Satyajit. 1976. *Our Films, Their Films*. New Delhi: Orient Longman, p. 4.
[11] Ray 1976, p. 3ff.
[12] Pym 1983, p. 13ff.

As films and television have linked South Asia, America and the UK, in recent decades, producers and directors may draw on a pool of actors from across the globe, speaking English in a variety of accents. A film might be a documentary, might focus on South Asian characters in America, or its characters might move back and forth across continents, working out romances between South Asian and Euro-American characters. *The Guru* (2002), *Bride and Prejudice* (2004), *Growing Up Smith* (2015), and *Meet the Patels* (2014) exemplify such themes.

Meet the Patels is an unusual film combining documentary and animation presentation, which involves a romance between a South Asian man in America and an American woman. In it, at the behest of his parents, Ravi Patel undertakes a quest for a South Asian mate. He had been seriously dating an American woman, Audrey, but could not commit to her, and broke off the relationship in deference to his parents' wishes. He tours America meeting potential South Asian candidates, many of them Patels, but cannot undo his heartfelt tie to Audrey. In the end, he returns to her. His parents finally give her a chance, and she wins their affection. Directed by Geeta and Ravi Patel, presented at film festivals where it won audience awards, it is charmingly constructed with animated drawings alternating with scenes of the Patel family. It comes closer to the actual experiences of South Asian Americans than fictional accounts and raises questions about cultural mixing and the evolving life of the community. Ravi Patel has continued acting, appearing in the film, *The Long Shot* (2019).

Turning to a different set of themes, the blockbuster films *Gandhi* (1982) and *Slumdog Millionaire* (2008), both set in India and directed by westerners, have won the Oscar for Best Picture and have been shown worldwide. The first is a historical film about the most famous Indian of modern times, while the second is a fantasy tale about a young, impoverished Indian from Mumbai who entered a grand quiz show. The first made Ben Kingsley an international star for his remarkable turn as Gandhi. The second moved Dev Patel up the ladder of bright young talents. *Gandhi* had long been a project of Richard Attenborough, who pulled the pieces together for this formidable film. Casting Kingsley, who is British but part Indian— his father was Gujarati and his birth name was Krishna Bhanji— proved a stroke of genius.

Gandhi follows the life of the Mahatma from his South African period through to Indian Independence and his assassination in 1948. It utilizes stars from the UK, the US, South Asia and South Africa, including such well-known figures as John Gielgud, John Mills, Geraldine James and Candice Bergen. It is wholly sympathetic to Gandhi, presenting several important figures of the Raj as stiff-backed and rigid. Jinnah, the father of Pakistan, is portrayed as diabolical, as were the British imperialists. The film won positive reviews and earned eight Oscars, including best picture, best director, best actor, best screenplay and best costume design.

Although Kingsley is masterful, and Gandhi's teachings are well-presented, much of the film is an historical jumble, with many glaring historical errors. While Gandhi is idealized, Jinnah is misrepresented and placed in scenes from the 1920s and 1930s when he had long left the main nationalist movement. Then he suddenly reappears in 1947, driving India to Partition. The first viceroy portrayed in the film is slotted in simply to show the recalcitrance of the Raj. Gandhi—in one of the major historical fallacies of the film—is shown as calling for Indian Independence in 1919, when he was only pushed to this position in 1928 by the young Turks of the nationalist movement. The film brought Gandhi's life course and his teachings about non-violent resistance once more to the attention of a world audience years after his death.

Danny Boyle, director of *Slumdog*, cast Dev Patel, who had acted on television, in his first film role, which launched his international career. Boyle says he was inspired by Indian cinema, and the film follows Bollywood traditions by including song-and-dance numbers, alongside its semi-serious story line. Dev Patel, from the Mumbai slums, emerges to become a contestant on a quiz show, and although his expertise is called into question, he demonstrates that he is the knowledgeable person capable of the answers he has given. His romance with Latika, played by Freida Pinto, runs through the story, and the two are united at a final moment, celebrated with a Bollywood musical number. Like *Gandhi*, *Slumdog Millionaire* won a generous handful of Oscars, including Best Picture, Best Director, Best Adapted Screenplay, Best Editing, Best Cinematography, Best Score and Best Song. The latter two were awarded to A.R. Rahman, a composer and performer as popular as any film star. Rahman, trained in both Indian and Western classical music, played with rock bands, succeeded as India's leading composer for films, and is a leading figure on Indian and world cultural stages.

Dev Patel followed his successful turn in *Slumdog* with roles in *Marigold Hotel* (2011) and recently *Hotel Mumbai* (2019) in which he played a main role as a waiter skilfully helping patrons avoid the Muslim terrorists attacking the Taj Hotel.

A further step for Patel was evident in 2020 with the release of *David Copperfield*, with Patel as the title character, a young nineteenth-century Englishman finding his way. Cross-casting or blind casting is now front-and-centre in the UK, in Hollywood and on Broadway. Actors of every hue and nationality can perform in *Hamilton*, and Dev Patel can play Dickens's favorite protagonist. On a lesser, but still important note, Patel's co-star in *Slumdog*, Freida Pinto, has also moved onto international screens playing a small but vital role in *Hillbilly Elegy*, (2020) as a Yale law student and romantic partner of the lead character.

Another film set in India and nominated for an Academy Award as Best Foreign film is *Lagaan* (2001), set in nineteenth-century rural India. It pits local officials of the British Raj against impoverished villagers in a wholly improbable cricket match. A wholly different kind of film, a short documentary, *Period. End of Sentence*, was nominated for the Academy Award for Best Documentary (Short Subject), in 2018, and won. It follows a group of Indian women who learn to make sanitary napkins employing several small, but ingenious machines. Then they take to the road to market their product, and, along the way, teach rural Indians about menstruation, cleanliness and better health. It was inspired by the life of Arunchalam Muruganantham, a Tamil Nadu social activist.

A very different kind of film which features Indian Muslims at the core of its story is *Gully Boy* (2018), its executive producer the famed American rapper Nas (Nasir bin Olu Dara Jones). Ranveer Singh plays Murad, a young Muslim, who lives in a Mumbai slum, like the main character in *Slumdog*, but who fights his way to prominence by discovering his talent for hip-hop singing. His tempestuous romantic partner, Safeen (Alia Bhatt), encourages him to chase his dream. Her parents try to arrange her marriage to some other Muslim man, but fail. Although Murad is a Muslim, he works with those of other communities, and once he has brought his talent to life, is appreciated by all. He defies his father, gives up his white-collar job, and enters a competition to open a show by Nas in Mumbai and wins 1 million rupees. Of course, after setbacks, taking the rapper name 'Gully Boy', Murad prevails, gets back his girl, and presumably opens for Nas. He is also encouraged by and hooks up with 'Sky', an American record producer (Kalki Koechlin) who tells him that she comes from the Berkley School of Music in the United States. The acting is skilled, and some older Bollywood touches are there, especially in the song-and-dance numbers.

In addition to the actors of note, two directors of South Asian background have made a mark in American cinema. The first is M. Night Shyamalan, who was born in south India, brought to the US at six weeks of age by his doctor parents, and grew up outside Philadelphia. Interested from an early age in making films, he learned his craft at the Tisch School of the Arts at New York University. After two earlier movies, *The Sixth Sense*, (1999) was widely successful and earned six Academy Award nominations, including one for him as director. Attracted to supernatural tales, he claims that his interest is spiritual. Through the ups and downs of a productive career, he has remained based outside Philadelphia, and has flirted with big-name projects while continuing to make his own films and acting in some of them.

The second, and, arguably, more talented artist, is Mira Nair. Born in Odisha, educated in Delhi and Shimla, and then at Harvard, she turned from acting to a career in film-making. She started with documentaries, branched out into feature films, achieving a rich, varied and remarkably productive career, reaping enthusiastic reviews, numerous award nominations, and the backing of major studios. From her bases in New York and New Delhi, and with another in East Africa, she has bridged worlds and cultures with seeming ease.

Some of Nair's films, *Mississippi Masala,* (1991), *The Perez Family,* (1995), and *My Own Country,* (1998) are set in the US, while *Salaam Bombay,* (1988), *The Kamasutra,* (1996), and *Monsoon Wedding,* (2001) are set in India. *Monsoon Wedding* is set in New Delhi, and the cast is largely Indian. Although there are a few comic moments, and several rousing song-and-dance numbers, it is a serious work which touches on important issues in contemporary India. The arranged marriage with its wedding ceremonies is at the centre but is beset with troubles because the bride-to-be has been having an affair with a married man from whom she has difficulty breaking. She feels she must confess to this relationship before the wedding, because otherwise she would be living a lie. The groom, an IIT-trained computer engineer based in Houston, Texas, accepts this situation and agrees to push ahead to the ceremony. An old incidence of paedophilia is revealed and causes yet another crisis just before the wedding. The father of the groom is severely troubled upon learning what happened decades ago, but confronts it head-on, relieving his niece (the abused party) of the shame and pain she felt and feels. Crosscutting the main pairing is another, between the marriage equipment manager and a servant, in the bride's household. This culminates at the finale of wedding in a dance number in which young and old, lower class and upper middle class all join. This extremely unlikely event ends the film and demonstrates that, though it touches several meaningful issues, it is a romance—but a beautiful one—at its core. More recently, Nair and her team have transformed the film story into a stage musical which has played to appreciative audiences in several countries and lately in New York City. She wrote in the show programme that she has returned to the theatre, a first love, and done it with aplomb. The groom says at one point, 'In America I am an Indian; in India I am an American. I am at home nowhere.' Nair, however, is at home everywhere.

Nair and her screenwriter colleague, Sooni Taraporevala, worked with a fine, international cast to make a first-rate movie, released in 2006, based on Jhumpa Lahiri's novel, *The Namesake* (2003), discussed earlier. It follows the marriage of Gogol's parents in Calcutta, then moves to Queens, New York (instead of Boston), and traces Gogol's life. Tabu plays his mother, Irrfan Khan his father, with Jacinda Barrett as his American girlfriend, Zuleikha Robinson as his wife, and starring Kal Penn as the title character. Robinson, of Burmese Indian-Malaysian and English parents, looks the Bengali Moushumi Mazoomdar she plays. Both Lahiri's novel and the film, track similar but slightly different paths, and each is successful in its own genre.

Nair has continued to make films that cross national boundaries, utilize actors from three continents, and undertake complex, interesting projects. One, the most demanding—difficult to finance and make, she has said—is *The Reluctant Fundamentalist* (2012), adapted from the novel of that name by Mohsin Hamid, discussed earlier. For this film set in Lahore, Istanbul and America, with Riz Ahmed, a British rapper and actor of Pakistani descent, playing the lead role, Nair recruited a talented international cast including Liev Schreiber, Kate Hudson, Om Puri, Kiefer Sutherland and Shabana Azmi. Educated in London and at Oxford, Ahmed had frequently succeeded in rapper competitions, and had previously played the lead in a powerful television series, *The Night of . . .* , for which he won a leading actor Emmy, the first male Muslim South Asian to do so. In the 2019 film, *Sound of Metal*, directed and co-written by Darius Marder, Ahmed played a metal music drummer who goes deaf. Learning to cope with this, Ruben, played by Ahmed, joins a deaf community, learns sign language and then gets cochlear implants. These are not successful, and Ruben returns to his deaf world. For this role, Ahmed learned both sign language and drumming. He earned an Academy Award nomination as best actor and a host of fine reviews. It demonstrated again his range of talents. As a political activist, Ahmed has objected to negative and narrow stereotypes of Muslims. Like Nair, Ahmed bridges continents in his life and his work.[13]

As seen in the preceding overview of films whose themes cut across regional boundaries, many South Asian actors and actresses based in India or the UK have become 'crossover stars' who are known on American screens, among them Archie Panjabi in *The Good Wife*. Panjabi is an experienced and talented actress from UK, who has gone back and forth across the Atlantic proving her talent in movies and on television for years. One of Bollywood's brightest stars, Deepika Padukone, starred in a 2017 action film *XXX: Return of Xander Cage*, and more recently did a remarkable turn as an acid-burned woman in the Indian film *Chhapaak*, that has been shown widely in India and in limited release in the US. ('A Bollywood Star Takes on a Global Stigma', *New York Times*, 23 January 2020) On a different but parallel path from Priyanka Chopra, Padukone is making a global mark through films, endorsements, and sitting on The Cannes Film Festival jury.[14]

The most successful of crossover stars to date in the South Asia-America entertainment world has been Priyanka Chopra. A former Miss World as a teen, then a Bollywood star, she took a step into American network television as a lead actor in *Quantico*. She drew upon her undoubted gifts: beauty, acting and singing talent, as well as hard work. There was as well an unusual circumstance: she had attended high school for several years in the United States. Her youthful movements with her doctor parents made her more cosmopolitan and adaptable.

With approval from her parents, Chopra entered the Miss India contest, and, upon winning, was a contestant for Miss World.

---

[13] Television interview with Stephen Colbert, 2016.
[14] 'Beyond Bollywood', *Time*, May 22/29, 2023.

Then she had a crucial choice to make: what next? Following the path of some other beauty contest winners, she went to Mumbai and started a film career. The path was twisted at first as she played small roles, achieved some successes, and appeared in some bad films. But dedicated to her craft, she gradually became a skilled actor in a variety of roles and with a variety of Indian accents, including Tamil and Marathi films, although most were in Hindi, most native to her. She also began to develop as a singer. A few of the films had Western settings, but according to biographer Aseem Chhabra, it was not until Anjali Acharya entered, that Priyanka seriously began to enter the American media scene.

Then came *Quantico*, a network FBI/CIA crime drama series, in which Chopra gained a starring role. To become Miss World, she had to try to lose her American accent; to become Alex Parrish, an intelligence agent in *Quantico*, she had to regain it. The series was nominated for four People's Choice Awards, with Chopra winning two: Favorite Actress in a New TV Series in 2016—making her the first South Asian to win a People's Choice Award—and Favorite Dramatic TV Actress in 2017. Her success has now allowed Chopra the flexibility in her career to choose Bollywood or Hollywood, films or TV.

A controversy arose, however, over the last season of *Quantico*, and Chopra's crucial role in an episode involving South Asian terrorists at work in America was at the heart of it. In the 1 June 2018 episode, a group of terrorists in New York City, posing as Pakistanis, turn out to be Indians. Indian viewers in the United States and at home were outraged. She apologized, and the network insisted that she had no control over the script. This blow-up did not cause a serious setback for Chopra's career. Priyanka is still a Bollywood star and appears as well in Western films and on TV. In 2018, Chopra married Nick Jonas, a rock singer a decade her junior, in widely publicized Western and Hindu wedding ceremonies that were featured in *People* magazine (17 December 2018). A few months later she sang with the Jonas Brothers in a new single song, 'Sucker', celebrating a reunion of the band after six years, with their spouses.[15] Marriage has not slowed Priyanka down: she has starred in two *Matrix* films, in *Text for You*, a romantic comedy, and in a spy series, *Citadel*. She is now able to get star billing in a Hollywood film, and then in a Bollywood film months later. With more than sixty film credits in addition to TV work, she has written a memoir, *Unfinished*, and she surely is that.[16] Chopra has become an international ambassador for UNICEF, assisting the agency in its mission to the world's children. Arrived as a media star, she is giving back as, what she calls herself, a cosmopolitan citizen of the world.[17]

The South Asian presence in films and on stage has been expanding apace. In 1993 the elephant-headed Indian God Ganesh visited Broadway, courtesy of Terrence McNally, one of America's leading playwrights. Filled with humour and insight, *A Perfect Ganesh*, was written after McNally visited India and made connections he never anticipated. An eastward traveller, like many before him, perhaps a searcher for peace and enlightenment, he found Ganesh 'humble' and a 'believer in great things', perhaps the guide he needed at the moment.[18]

An author who turned from the novel to dramatist and has won much notice is Ayad Akhtar (1970–). Born in New York City to Pakistani-American parents, he was educated in Milwaukee schools, Brown University and the Columbia University School of the Arts. In 2012, he published the well-received novel *American Dervish*, a coming-of-age story of a boy born about 1970, like the author, who grows up in Milwaukee, and is tossed this way and that by the different Islams of which he learns—fundamentalist, Sufi, liberal—as well the atheism of his father. Soon after, turning to theatre, Akhtar's play *Disgraced*, staged in Chicago, New York and London, was awarded the Pulitzer Prize for Drama in 2013. Other plays followed: *The Who and the What, The Invisible Hand*, and *Junk: The Golden Age of Debt*, the last of these brilliantly staged at Lincoln Center in 2017. Later that year, he received the Steinberg

---

[15] *Hindu*, 2 March 2019.
[16] *Vanity Fair*, February 2022.
[17] Chhabra 2018, p. 115ff.
[18] Terrence McNally, interview on American Masters, PBS.

Playwright Award and accepting the award said: 'The theatre is an art form scaled to the human . . . It only happens when and where is happens . . . A living actor before a living audience. The situation of all theater, a situation that can awaken in us a recollection of something more primordial . . .'[19]

Most recently, during the coronavirus pandemic of 2020 to 2021 when there was no live theatre, Akhtar published *Homeland Elegies*—a fiction, not an autobiography, although it draws on his own life. In it, the author plays upon the meanings of 'home' and 'homeland', and the elegies are tinged with sharp rebukes of corrupt Pakistan and Trump's mercenary America, a land of the dollar that he critiques savagely. Akhtar straddles two homelands, and he remains troubled with by the hostility to immigrants and non-whites by some white Americans.

Over the past generation, a bevy of South Asians have come to the fore not only on the screen, but on the comedy front, often making use of their cultural background in their work. One among them, Aasif Mandvi (1966–), born in Mumbai and raised in the UK and the southern US, wrote and then played in *Sakina's Restaurant* (1998), an off-Broadway, one-man show, in which he played a range of South Asian characters. Playing a young Muslim man in a Gujarati village who is 'invited' to America by an older acquaintance and restaurant owner, Hakim Agzi, Mandvi announces as he embarks from his village , 'I like hamburger, baseball and Mr Bob Dylan.' Mandvi then embodies in turn each member of Hakim's family, plus the daughter's fiancé, joking and dancing as he goes, while delving into their dreams and fears. Mandvi received an Obie Award for the production of this touching and funny show. Mandvi later moved on to other stage and television ventures, but in 2018, at age fifty-two, he revived *Sakina's Restaurant*, which a writer for the *New York Times* tells us was still fresh and relevant.[20]

---

[19] Speech published in the New York Times, selections in 'Ayad Akhtar', Wikipedia.
[20] Robin Pogrebin, 'A Play's the Same. It's the World That's Different', 9 October 2018.

Mindy Kaling (1979–), another talented comedian and performer, was born Vera Mindy Chokalingam to a Tamil-Bengali couple who met in Nigeria and emigrated to the US, where she was raised. Later attending Dartmouth College, she started majoring in classics, but switched to theatre, starring in and writing numerous college productions. After college, according to *Is Everyone Hanging out Without Me?* (2011), her autobiographical account of her first thirty years or so, she lived and worked in the New York area while trying to break into show business. A break came when she and her friend Brenda wrote a script for *Matt and Ben,* and had the chance to stage it in a small theatre. It took off and launched Mindy into her very successful career.

Kaling has used her looks and her immigrant background in her writings and the character portrayals she has had in the television series, *The Office*, and *The Mindy Project*. Beginning as a member of the writers' group for the first of these, she rose to a larger role in both writing and performing, then moved on to the second, her own network show, every aspect of which she had a hand in crafting. She has also acted in a number of movies.

In her speech on the Harvard Law School Class Day of 2014, Kaling combined the pompous and the insightful, and the funny and the serious. She is obviously proud of her achievements as the daughter of immigrants originally from India, who has lived out the American dream and climbed to the top of the entertainment ladder. But as a Dartmouth graduate who studied Latin, she could point the way to others, and tell them that the choices ahead— absurd ones, as she phrased them—were theirs: fight for justice and the public good, or evil; fight for corrupt corporations, or publics that have been harmed; try to make America better and wiser through the law, or not. She remains irreverent and funny, writing in *Hanging Out*:

In 2011, *People* magazine named me one of the Most Beautiful English-Speaking Persons in North America, in a country where I just fucking destroyed. But I don't need to remind you of this;

you probably have the page torn out and stuck on your fridge as inspiration… it was an amazing surprise, and I was very flattered and excited. I would even say it was an honor to be singled out for my looks… In case you thought the photo shoot that produced that image in People went seamlessly… here's what happened… A charismatic… French stylist took me to a trailer filled with gowns… And they were all a size zero… The only thing that came close to my size was a shapeless navy shift… Was my problem that I was this food monster destined to only wear navy shifts? Lots of stupid people were skinny, and yet I couldn't do this incredibly simple thing they could do with seeming ease. [21]

In another step forward in her career, Kaling played Molly Patel, co-starring with Emma Thompson, in the feature film *Late Night* (2019). But she does not just act: she wrote the script, and is co-producer, of this funny but serious look into the production of late night shows. As Molly shoulders her way into the writing room for Katherine Newbury's programme, she shows other women and people of colour how to break through the all-white male barrier that holds them back. At the same time, she teaches Newbury how to be a human being along with others of her species, breaking through her tough façade to find a depressed and vulnerable person who is capable of change. Throughout Molly never forgets that she comes from Indian roots, and that she is a person of colour—like Kaling herself.

Kaling with Lang Fisher created the hit series, *Never Have I Ever*, which played for four seasons on Netflix, ending in June 2023. It centres around Devi, a South Asian American girl forging her way through high school in Sherman Oaks, California. Her father dies suddenly as the series opens, and Devi, her widowed mother Nalini, a dermatologist, and her cousin Kamala each deal with serious issues of growing up and working through relationships with the opposite sex. Though Devi is only fifteen in Season One,

---

[21] Kaling, Mindy. 2012. *Is Everyone Hanging Out Without Me?* NY: Three Rivers, pp. 194–95.

she is eager to lose her virginity, and her experiences with Paxton, Ben and Ethan chart her fumblings with one or the other. She is also part of a trio of close friends, Fabiola, a Latina, and Eleanor, a Chinese American girl. The dozens of plot twists through forty episodes cannot be recounted here, but the show has helped bring the adventures and difficulties of a South Asian American family to 40 million viewers around the world, was the number one show in fifty countries, and earned excellent reviews. It is funny, serious, charming, disarming and a treat to watch and guess around what corner it will turn next. Devi is played by Maitreyi Ramakrishnan, Nalini by Poorna Jagannathan and Kamala by Richa Moorjani. The narration of John McEnroe adds to the fun. Kaling said that it follows the spirit not the details of her own youth in the Boston area. That spirit blossomed beautifully.

Hasan Minhaj (1985–) had his comedy breakthrough in 2014 as a member of the cast of *The Daily Show*, and he calls Jon Stewart, its then host, his 'comedy dad'. Minhaj was born in Davis, California, to an Indian-Muslim family, his parents having emigrated there from Uttar Pradesh. His father is a chemist, his mother a doctor, and his younger sister an attorney. Minhaj has said that his father was willing to pay 'the immigrant tax'—that is, to roll with American racism and the US habit of invading foreign countries so long as he and his family could thrive in America. But his son Hasan retorted that he was unwilling to do so: he would not pay that tax and insisted on equality with other Americans.

After college at the University of California, Davis, Minhaj tried stand-up comedy, and began acting in a variety of movie and television roles, beginning with four years at *The Daily Show*. In 2016, he was called to host the Radio and Television Correspondents Dinner, an annual event held in Washington, D.C. He climbed one step higher in 2017, when he was the main speaker at the White House Correspondents' Dinner. In his remarks, he urged the journalists in his audience to oppose then President Trump: 'We are here to talk about the truth. It is 2017, and we are living in the golden age of lying. Now's the time to be a liar, and Donald Trump is liar in chief . . . remember, you guys are public enemy no. 1. You are his biggest enemy . . . That's why you gotta keep your foot on the gas.'[22]

Later, Minhaj presented his own one-man show about the immigrant experience as a second-generation Muslim in America, and from late 2018 has had his own weekly show, *Patriot Act with Hasan Minhaj.* [23]

Born to a Tamil Muslim family, his parents both doctors, Aziz Ansari (1983–) was raised in South Carolina and earned a degree from NYU's Stern School of Business. In 2005, he joined an improvisation troupe, Human Giants, which created several short films. In 2008, he joined the cast of the NBC comedy series, *Parks and Recreation*, which ran from 2009 for seven seasons. In 2015, with Alan Young, he created the show *Master of None*, in which he starred and occasionally directed episodes, earning several Golden Globe nominations and winning an Emmy and Peabody Award. In 2018, he won a Golden Globe for acting in a TV comedy series, reportedly the first Asian-American actor to do so.

With sociologist Eric Klinenberg, Ansari wrote *Modern Romance: An Investigation* (2015), a serious and personal book about the complexities of dating. Ironically, in 2018, Ansari had to face a charge of sexual misconduct, but despite facing attacks in the media, he has emerged without significant harm to his career. Recently, however, as noted in a recent critique in the *New York Times*, (20 December 2018), Ansari has shifted gears in his stand-up routine. Previously hailing political correctness or 'woking', he has now become hyper-critical.

Kumail Nanjiani (1978–), another multi-talented South Asian finding his way to the top on the small and large screens, was raised in Karachi, Pakistan, in a Shia Muslim family. Coming to the US, he graduated from Grinnell College in Iowa in 2001, having studied computer science and philosophy. Pressed by classmates to try stand-up comedy, he overcame his shyness and developed his voice, in time finding a niche as a main cast member of the HBO series

---

[22] ' Wikipedia, 'Hasan Minhaj'.

[23] PBS, *Moment*, 27 October 2018; article on him, *India Abroad*, 29 October 2018.

Silicon Valley. Playing a talented nerd who strikes out with women, he has continued in this role for several seasons. He has played and voiced a great variety of roles on TV and in films as well as putting together a special for Comedy Central. In 2007, Nanjiani married Emily Gordon, comedy producer and psychotherapist. Together they wrote the script for the romantic comedy film, *The Big Sick*, a 2017 charming and moving film exploring the choices and dilemmas of a South Asian immigrant son (played by Nanjiani) finding his way to marriage to a non-South Asian woman. It was nominated for an Academy Award for best original screenplay and was the third highest grossing independent film for that year. [24]

As a Muslim South Asian American, Nanjiani has had to deal with the repercussions of 9/11, and he has learned not to deny who he is and to respond appropriately to taunts. And most recently, a 'totally ripped' Nanjiani has gained renewed fame and awe after a course to make him fit and muscled preparing for the role of Kingo in the Marvel Cinematic Universe film *Eternals*. He appears across multimedia bare-chested and looking ready to compete for the title of Mr Universe.[25] Branching out more widely, Nanjiani and his wife have created a series for Apple TV entitled, *Little America*, exploring diverse immigrant journeys to America. [26]

Bursting upon the comedy scene of late in the 2020s is Zarna Garg, born in India, trained as a lawyer, but a stay-at-home mom for sixteen years. Searching for a career path in her forties as her children grew older, her daughter Zoya encouraged her to try stand-up comedy. Almost effortlessly, she began to make an enormous hit in comedy clubs and attracted an immense number of viewers on Tik Tok. Unafraid to criticize her family, her culture, herself, Garg now has a comedy special, *One in a Billion* on Prime Video, a feature film,

---

[24] 'The Big Sick', and 'Kumail Nanjiani', Wikipedia; Andrew Marantz, 'The Best Medicine', *New Yorker*, 8 May 2017; E. Alex Jung, 'Kumail Nanjiani's Feelings', *New York*, 11–24 October 2021.

[25] 'More Bicep Anxiety', *New York Times*, 22 December 2019.

[26] 'Immigrant Stories Still Carry Power', *New York Times*, 26 January 2020.

and a prospective series. Calling herself 'a funny brown mom', Garg is unique and always hilarious.

While films with connections to South Asia were produced more frequently and South Asian comedians were appearing in clubs and on TV, more and more journalists from South Asian roots spread across the American landscape. In 1994, a small group of writers founded SAJA, the South Asian Journalists Association. Their aim was to help those entering the profession to make contacts and develop their skills, as well as to reward them for their successes and, in time, to dispense modest scholarships. This small party of about four grew into more than 1,500 holding national meetings and seminars, and organizing related events in New York and Washington and other places. Over the past quarter-century, SAJA has brought together some of the best with some of the youngest in this field. Members make vital contributions to newspapers and magazines, provide coverage on air to national networks and cable networks, and are active on all forms of social media.

Sree Sreenivasan, journalist, teacher, Tech Guru, and extraordinary networker, a key SAJA founder, has been dean of students at the Columbia University Graduate School of Journalism, digital officer for the Metropolitan Museum and New York City, and now roves the globe as a consultant on computer matters. He continues to run workshops for journalists on the advanced use of the Internet and multimedia reporting and remains a driving force for SAJA's work. His generosity is almost legendary.

One of the most successful and versatile journalists of South Asian origin, Fareed Zakaria, does both print media and television journalism. He writes a foreign affairs column for the *Washington Post*, has held senior posts at *Time* and *Newsweek*; and he also hosts the weekly GPS, or *Global Public Square* programme on CNN, on which he features analysts from around the world on foreign and domestic affairs. A superb interrogator, Zakaria displays a wide-ranging curiosity about many contemporary issues, drawing attention to issues concerning the possible shape of our shared future and giving his own viewpoint at the top of the show. Born into a Muslim family in Mumbai, Zakaria earned his BA at Yale University and his PhD in political science at Harvard. He hews to the middle of the political spectrum, although he did visibly back Barack Obama for President and was highly critical of Donald Trump. He can be critical of all sides, and is intent, above all, on enlightening the public. He is one of the most successful journalists of South Asian origin.

3

Writing
Fiction and Non-Fiction

Although the medium of film was perhaps the most effective route by which Westerners came to understand India, the written word remained a prime mode of communication. Among the popular writers presenting India to America was the now forgotten, but once prominent, Santha Rama Rau (1923–2009). Daughter of an Indian diplomat, graduate of Wellesley and resident of New York City, she published a string of books from the mid-1940s about her travels in India and worldwide. These included *Home to India* (1945), *East of Home* (1950), *This Is India* (1954), and *Gifts of Passage* (1961). Rama Rau's life and writing, as explicated by Antoinette Burton in *The Postcolonial Careers of Santha Rama Rau* (2007), was both an expert portrayal of India combatting facile Orientalism and a cosmopolitan positioning of herself in an increasingly complex world.[1] Raised mostly outside India in Great Britain and South Africa, just as World War II broke out in 1939, Rama Rau, her sister and their mother returned to visit India and renew connections to their family. Her father's family were south Indian Brahmins, her mother's Kashmiri Brahmins. Members of the Indian elite, Rama Rau, though only sixteen, dined with the viceroy, Lord Linlithgow, chatted with Jawaharlal Nehru and viewed India from a top seat.

She began to write when still a teenager, and positioned between India and the Anglo-American world, she tried to explain India to

---

[1] Burton, Antoinette. 2007. *The Postcolonial Careers of Santha Rama Rau*. Durham: Duke U. Press.

Americans. Rama Rau went off to Wellesley College in the US, since she felt that an American, rather than a British, higher education would better suit her for the new age dawning in India. At Wellesley she expanded her teenage notes into her first book, *Home to India*. In later years, as an experienced travel writer, she told of her adventures in Russia, Cambodia, Spain, China, Bali, Ceylon and the Philippines, while returning from time to time to India. Even as a writer for The *New Yorker*, she identified, into her thirties, more with India than with America. India needed more explaining, and as a skilled explicator, she connected the worlds of America and India.

Following people such as Rama Rau, South Asians in America, as journalists, novelists, scientists, and scholars, have taken up their pens and written on a myriad of themes. Writing about their experience as individuals and as a community, about the human condition, about healing and enlightenment, about foreign affairs and history, they have contributed richly to the culture of their adopted home while never forgetting the Indian heritage in which they were nurtured.

Over the past two generations, writers of South Asian background have produced a near flood of fiction, winning prizes and a place on bestseller lists for memorable works widely appreciated by American critics and readers. The flow started in the period following the Second World War and accelerated from the 1960s. The discussion here is limited to those writing fiction in English and is a selective sampling since the flow of novels and story collections has grown tremendously in recent years, and many deserving works cannot be detailed or even listed here. Those included are V.S. Naipaul, Bharati Mukherjee and Salman Rushdie, and continues with some of their younger successors Chitra Banjeree Divakaruni, Amitav Ghosh, Arundhati Roy, Jhumpa Lahiri, Akhil Sharma, Hari Kunzru, Mohsin Hamid, Fatima Farheen Mirza, Ayad Akhtar and Megha Majumdar.

During the last half-century in which these authors have written, the dividing line between those based in the West and those based in India has dissolved. American readers don't ask themselves where V.S. Naipaul or Arundhati Roy live, but rather whether she or he has written a novel they want to read. Many of the writers described here move freely between South Asia, the US, the UK, as easy travel and Internet connection allow. Another feature of this era is that readers in the West have bought, perused, and learned from fictions set completely in South Asia, often without any Western characters. As the world has become more interconnected, readers are no longer reluctant to approach South Asian society, religions and cultural patterns.

Indian and Pakistani writers of recent decades have offered different assessments of the Raj than those emerging from the novels of British authors Paul Scott and John Masters. V.S. Naipaul (1932–2018), born in Trinidad in 1932, moved to Oxford at age eighteen to forge a career in the UK exploring in novels and non-fiction works what he knew best and felt sharply: his family's Indian background and his roots in Trinidad and the Caribbean. Naipaul published three books about India and other former colonies, but was based at the former heart of empire. Widely read in the US as well as the UK, he settled in the UK, and won the Nobel Prize in literature.

Bharati Mukherjee (1940–2017) emerged in the 1960s from her South Asian background. Educated at Loreto House, Calcutta, and then at the University of Iowa, she married an American-Canadian, Clark Blaise, moved to Canada, had two sons, and began her career as a writer. Although she had a successful academic career in Canada, she became increasingly exasperated at the denigration she felt as a brown-skinned woman in that country. In 1981, she wrote the essay, 'An Invisible Woman', for *Saturday Night*. Then she pressed her husband to leave Canada. They moved to the US and became American citizens.

In the years that followed, Mukherjee's writing took a somewhat different direction, moving from *The Tiger's Daughter*, to *Wife*, to *Darkness* (stories), to *The Middleman* (stories), and to *Jasmine*. Frequently, her characters had South Asian roots, but some, as well, had many other kinds of American backgrounds. The stories were often set in the US as the characters explored, failed, succeeded and searched from amongst the possibilities here. Bharati Mukherjee retained familial connections to India, and held on to her love of

Mughal miniature painting. Later she wrote an historical novel about India in the time of the seventeenth-century Mughal emperor Aurangzeb—*The Holder of the World* (1993)—with European, American and Indian characters. A friend and admirer, Sandip Roy, wrote in his remembrance of her:

> She did say, 'I am American, not Asian-American. My rejection of hyphenation has been called race treachery, but it is really a demand that America deliver the promises of its dream to all its citizens equally.' But her rejection of the hyphen was not a rejection of her roots at all. She loved going to Durga Puja celebrations. She wrote about the complexities of hyphenated lives. She just did not want to be in a special section of the bookshelf. She feared a 'Balkanisation of ethnicity—minority groups pitted against each other for very small portions of the pie'.[2]

Though proud to be an American writer and adherent of American values, she never shed or denied her Indian roots and culture and continued to explore them through her life. An appropriate comparison is to Saul Bellow, Philip Roth and Bernard Malamud. Once they were categorized as Jewish American writers. Later they became American writers, after Bellow was awarded the Nobel Prize in Literature in 1976, and all of America proudly claimed him. Mukherjee, as well, just wanted to be an American writer. In a pointed and pithy essay published in the *New York Times*, 22 September 1996, Mukherjee compared her way of embracing America with that of her sister Mira's, live-here-and-stay-Indian. She wrote:

> In one family, from two sisters alike as peas in a pod, there could not be a wider divergence of immigrant experience. America spoke

---

[2] Sandip Roy: 'Remembering Bharati Mukherjee', KALW Public Media, 8 February 2017, https://www.kalw.org/show/sandip-roys-dispatches-from-kolkata/2017-02-08/sandip-roy-remembering-bharati-mukherjee.

to me—I married it—I embraced the demotion from expatriate aristocrat to immigrant nobody, surrendering those thousands of years of 'pure culture', the saris, the delightfully accented English. She retained them all...

Mira's voice, I realize, is the voice not just of the immigrant South Asian community of the millions who have stayed rooted in one job, one city, one house, one ancestral culture, one cuisine, for the entirety of their productive years. She speaks for greater numbers than I possibly can. Only the fluency of her English and the anger, rather than fear, born of confidence from her education, differentiate her from the seamstresses, the domestics, the technicians, the shop owners, the millions of hard-working by effectively silenced documented immigrants as well as their less fortunate 'illegal' brothers and sisters. [3]

Mukherjee was awarded the National Book Critics Circle award for fiction for her collection of stories, *The Middleman and Other Stories* (1988). One story that has been often praised is *The Management of Grief*,[4] tracing a woman's responses to the death of her husband and two sons, along with hundreds of other Indians abroad. It is a story which grabs the heart, as we voyage with her from Canada to Ireland to India. In the last of these places, a dreamy manifestation of her husband floats to her, saying, 'You must finish alone, what we started together.' She tries to move forward in this way, and tells a white official of the Canadian government, 'We must all grieve in our own way.' Mukherjee and Clark Blaise wrote a non-fiction account of this incident, *The Sorrow and the Terror* (1987), and *Days and Nights in Calcutta* (1977). The latter is a penetrating look into Indian life by an outsider and an insider. Winner of a National Book Critics Circle Award in 1988, Mukherjee wrote until her death in 2017, aged seventy-six.

---

[3] Kumar, Amitava, ed. 2003. *Away*. NY: Penguin, pp. 273–74.
[4] Blaise, Clark, and Bharati Mukherjee. 1988. *The Sorrow and the Terror*. NY: Penguin, p. 173ff.

In the 1980s, Americans heard of the Indian, Salman Rushdie (1947–), a writer based in the UK. Born in 1947 of Kashmiri-Muslim descent weeks before Indian Independence, raised in Bombay, schooled in the UK at Rugby and King's College, Cambridge, he was forced to live underground in response to death threats prompted by what was perceived as an attack on Islam. In 2000, he came to New York and made it his new home.[5]

Rushdie had forged connections to the United States before his move here in 2000, where he visited when he was working as a copywriter before his literary career took off, and returned for the publication of his second novel, *Midnight's Children* (1981) by Knopf, which won the Booker Prize. It focuses on the first post-Independence generation in India, exploring one part of Rushdie's heritage. He wrote that 'beneath the surface... there lurked... a fellow with an unusually adventurous heart, possessed of enough gumption to take a leap in the dark... wherever in the world his wanderings might take him... to follow the dream of 'away'... He took the westward road and ceased to be who he might have been if he had stayed at home. [6]

With *The Satanic Verses* (1989), Rushdie delved into the Islamic elements in his background. Following his father, Rushdie was a determined atheist, and no matter how he dealt with Islam, it was likely he would spark some controversy, but his mocking of the Prophet as a calculating Mahound, and his dubiousness about the One and only Truth, if not calculated to offend, did. However, given his previous track record of assailing all religious truths, the worldwide explosion that detonated in 1989 was unexpected. Not only did the Iranian Ayatollah Khomeini issue a fatwa calling for his death, but the controversy brought deaths to demonstrators in India—the first country to ban the book—and serious threats and assaults on all those connected to the book's publication. It necessitated Rushdie's living an underground existence for the next decade, protected in the UK by Britain's Special Branch. It also brought into the open arguments about literature and religion,

---

[5] Rushdie, Salman. 2012. *Joseph Anton*. NY: Random House, p. 262ff.
[6] Ibid., p. 28.

the state and blasphemy laws, and free speech and censorship. The author had a host of defenders and attackers in countries around the world. Calls for his death were sometimes linked to slogans condemning American imperialism. From his underground lair, he made several trips to America in the early 1990s, and American senators greeted him openly—the opposite of what British politicians were willing to do—and he believed their reception helped him greatly. He began summering in Bridgehampton, New York, where he could move around openly for the first time in years. In his memoir of the *fatwa* era, he wrote, '… he felt, as he always felt in America, the slow rebirth of his true self'.[7] And again, '… here in New York his life was in his own hands; he could decide for himself what was sensible and what was dangerous. He could recapture his freedom in America…'[8] Not as safe as he hoped, he was viciously attacked and wounded giving a talk in 2022.

Rushdie retained his attachment to India, the land of his birth and youth, to the UK, the land of his formal education and literary efflorescence as well as his first three marriages, and then eventually to America, the chosen land of his mature years where he felt most free and at ease. His autobiographical *Joseph Anton: A Memoir* (2012), which recounts his experience of exile, is a moving and powerful tale of resilience, survival, loss and gain. Supported by many friends, Rushdie emerges as an invaluable spokesman for the rational pursuit of truth, freedom of opinion, tolerance and cosmopolitanism. Though based in New York, he is a citizen of the world.

In *Fury* (2001), Rushdie gave us a galloping novel, set largely in New York, but with backward glances at London and Bombay. Malik, 'Solly' Solanka, the central character, follows a Rushdie-like course in some broad respects: he was born and raised in Bombay just as India achieved Independence, he moved on to London, had several wives, one of them taller than the balding author and stunningly beautiful (resembling Padma Lakshmi to whom the book is dedicated), then settled in New York. The novel charts the course

---

[7] Ibid., p. 492.
[8] Ibid., p. 557.

of Solly as he dissolves a marriage when the 'furies' temporarily take control of him, and moves to New York where he works through complicated relationships to Mila Milo and then Neela Mahendra. But furies are within him, and in the culture and society around him. Early on Rushdie writes:

> Life is fury, he'd thought. Fury—sexual, Oedipal, political, magical, brutal—drives us to our finest heights and coarsest depths. Out of *furia* comes creation, inspiration, originality, passion, but also violence, pain, pure unafraid destruction, the giving and receiving of blows from which we never recover. The Furies pursue us; Shiva dances his furious dance to create and also to destroy. But never mind about the gods!… This is what we are, what we civilize ourselves to disguise—the terrifying human animal in us, the exalted, transcendent, self-destructive, untrimmed lord of creation. We raise each other to the heights of joy. We tear each other limb from fucking limb.[9]

The furies come and go through Solly's wild rides into and out of marriages, friendships and near-fatal disasters. The furies, modelled on a trio in ancient Greek mythology, are also part of the zeitgeist of late-twentieth century and early-twenty-first century America, if not the world.

Rushdie continued with his fiction and non-fiction writing as one of the world's leading authors, but suddenly on 12 August 2022, he was brutally attacked at a writing festival in upstate New York. The knifer was intent on carrying out Ayatollah Khomeini's fatwa. Although Rushdie was not killed, he lost sight in one eye and sustained other serious injuries. He recuperated in private for some months and then reappeared in 2023 at some public events and published his latest novel, *Victory City*. From the New York of *Fury*, Rushdie returned to early modern South Asia. Pampa Kampana's tale unfolds over three centuries in the area of an historical kingdom, Vijayanagar, which existed through these years. She gains magical

---

[9] Rushdie, Salman. 2001. *Fury*. London: Vintage, pp. 30–31.

powers, marries three kings, and watches the rise and fall of kingdoms and dynasties. It is full of fun and disaster, endless twists about, and the mingling of India's religious traditions, teasing all, adhering to none, and poking at notions of gods and God. The women characters are more sympathetic than the men, and in its call for the equality of the sexes in every sphere of life, including athletics and warfare, Rushdie seems to have found one of his own beliefs. Inclusion and tolerance more widely are blessed as well. It is written with Rushdie's flare with magic realism the coin of the realm. With false modesty, the author tells us he is simply retelling what has been written in a recently discovered manuscript. Luckily it was found.

Among the accomplished writers from South Asia based in the United States, Chitra Banerjee Divakaruni (1956–) is one of the most prolific and versatile. Her shelf includes novels, children's books and poetry. Some of her novels are Earth-based and realistic, while some involve magic realism and fantasy. Born Chitralekha Banerjee in 1956 in Kolkata, educated there and in the US, she earned a PhD at the University of California, Berkeley, and is settled in Texas, attached to the University of Houston. In most of her earlier works, her rich, evocative style, frequently brings to life characters whose lives span India and the US. Her book of poetry, *Leaving Yuba City* (1997), perhaps autobiographical, is painful to read

Among Divakaruni's later achievements is her re-imagination of the two great Indian epics, the Mahabharata and the Ramayana, largely from a woman's perspective: the Mahabharata from Draupadi's, or Panchali's, viewpoint in *The Palace of Illusions: A Novel* (2008), and the Ramayana from Sita's viewpoint in *The Forest of Enchantments* (2019). These women protagonists are moved from the edge to the centre of the stage. Divakaruni writes with verve and a gifted storyteller's sense of pace and suspense. In her god-infested world, humans struggle against their destinies, while boons and curses are given by any and all. There is often foreshadowing, yet even so, we are not sure from moment to moment just how the drama will play out. Is all 'destiny', or karma, predetermined by actions in previous lives? Or, can one's efforts now, change the shape of things? Compellingly written, her Mahabharata is not easy for a non-Indian, or non-expert to read, with numerous characters, South Asian terms and concepts.

As Divakaruni explains of these retellings, she grew up with these tales and myths as a child, read and re-read many versions of them as an adult to re-gift them to readers of a new and different age and sensibility. These recreations reflect the condition of women now in India and in America, to which Divakaruni contributes in her own unique way.

One of the most talented of the South Asian writers based in America is Amitav Ghosh (1956—), an anthropologist turned creative writer, who has skilfully combined ethnographic and historical research with storytelling. *In an Antique Land* (1992), for example, which tells the story of the connection between the Middle East and India in the thirteenth century, is a history, but it reads like a novel. Since its publication, Ghosh has written mostly fiction along with cultural and literary criticism. His novel *The Hungry Tide* (2005) is set in the Sunderbans, the mouth of the Ganges as it enters the Bay of Bengal, where hundreds of islands appear and disappear as the waters move. Thousands of poor Bengalis, both in India and Bangladesh, try to eke out a living from the soil and from the sea, while avoiding tigers and alligators and coping with fearsome natural disasters. Ghosh had a family connection to this area, and did his field research in Southeast Asia and the Sunderbans so as to make his novel as realistic as possible. He produces a powerful work that draws on his past training, family history and desire to write a novel set in this unique region of the world. He has followed up his concern with environmental issues with a non-fiction book and other novels. This stamps him as a writer of the first rank, all in on an issue of global importance.

In the works of the prominent writers who have been discussed to this point, along with the themes of intermarriage, intergenerational conflict, and the difficulties of adapting to American life, another striking one is encountered: the return to India. As mature writers, all three went back to India and produced India-centred novels: Bharati Mukherjee returned to the Mughal Empire, Chitra Banerjee

Divakaruni to the Mahabharata and the Ramayana, and Amitav Ghosh returned to the Sunderbans, each of them reconstructing Indian worlds of their personal past or of Indian civilization. To reconstruct these Indian worlds satisfactorily required intensive research. The fruits have been rich in this diverse set of quests by writers based in the West, for whom complex Indian cultural worlds are never far from their minds.

Jhumpa Lahiri (1967—), born in England to Bengali parents, raised in Providence, Rhode Island, and later attended Barnard College, attained great success at a young age when her first book, *The Interpreter of Maladies* (1999), a collection of stories, won the Pulitzer Prize. She has explored the lives of Indians, usually Bengalis, as they ventured abroad, usually to the US, who as they became entwined with the lives of Americans, became Americans, and so linked the two countries. Like Bharati Mukherjee, whom she has called a role model, Lahiri considers herself an American. Following her first book of stories, she published the novels *The Namesake* (2003), *Unaccustomed Earth* (2008) and *The Lowland* (2013).

In *The Namesake*, Lahiri draws upon her Bengali family roots and her knowledge of Calcutta, New England and New York. These experiences are distilled into a touching, exquisitely detailed and elegantly written novel, at the centre of which is Gogol Ganguli, born to an educated Bengali Brahmin family, whose experience growing up in America and finding his way forward has some broad resemblances to Lahiri's own. Though he is the centre, his parents, girlfriend Maxine and wife Moushumi all come to life. Surrounding them are the two overlapping but very different cultural worlds of the main protagonists: Calcutta Bengali plus Bengalis in America, and the thriving life of educated Americans of different backgrounds.

Lahiri continued to track Indians abroad in *Unaccustomed Earth*, then introduced another dimension in *The Lowland*—the political. This third novel traces the lives of the Bengali brothers, Subhash and Udayan, and their family over seventy years, as they move between Calcutta, Providence, Rhode Island and California. Udayan became a Naxalite, member of the extreme left communist group that caused havoc and violence, and then retribution by the state in the late 1960s and 1970s. When he died young in a clash with paramilitaries, Subhash, who had emigrated to America, returned to Calcutta and married his brother's widow. The story then follows the separate lives of these figures, their offspring, and their later connections. It is a well-constructed and affecting novel, with careful delineation of settings Lahiri knows well.

Shortly after *The Lowland*, Lahiri changed directions—some would say abruptly. She discovered she had an affinity for, an almost mysterious attraction to Italy and the Italian language. She and her family moved to Rome, as she perfected her command of Italian. Seeking to go beyond simply translating from Italian, she has written *In Other Words* (2016) an account of her effort to become a writer in Italian. This collection of stories, her first book in Italian, is autobiographical, and concerns her move from her 'dominant language', English, in which she has achieved such success. English and Bengali remain within her, but she has moved on to reading and writing almost totally in Italian.[10] She describes her linguistic triangle, the relations and meaning of Bengali, English and Italian in her life:

> My very first language was Bengali, handed down to me by my parents . . . few years later, however, Bengali took a step backward... English arrived, a stepmother... I couldn't identify with either... Bengali represented the part of me that belonged to my parents, that didn't belong to America... I was ashamed to have to speak Bengali in front of my American friends... I had to joust between those two languages until, at around the age of twenty-five, I discovered Italian. There was no need to learn that language... No necessity.[11]

In the two story/dream pieces in this collection, she also heads towards a new kind of writing, more abstract and Kafka-esque.

---

[10] Lahiri, Jhumpa. 2016. *In Other Words*. NY: Knopf, pp. 173, 207, 221.
[11] Ibid., pp. 147–53.

She says that she learned long ago from Ovid's *Metamorphoses* that life is change. So Lahiri's life, as well, has changed direction. In 2021, she published a novel—not an unusual feat for her—but she had originally written it in Italian, and then translated it herself into English. This short novel, *Whereabouts*[12]is unusual: a woman (presumed to be Italian), a scholar, writer, and teacher in her mid-forties, unmarried, living alone, in a city, where she has friends and former lovers. The narrator traces her experiences of flirtation, travel, friendship through the round of a year. As the novel ends, she is invited to a scholarly retreat for a year, and the usual routine, possibly of decades, is about to be changed as she embarks on this new adventure. India is not here; Italy has conquered.

Although the majority of the renowned novelists of South Asia America have been Hindus or of Hindu background, several have been Muslims. Although often residing in Lahore and London, Mohsin Hamid (1971–) has also spent time in the US, and important parts of his novels take place here, where they are also widely read, positively reviewed and appreciated. In *The Reluctant Fundamentalist* (2007), the hero Changez, a Pakistani graduate of Princeton, meets and courts Erica, and lands a job with Underwood-Samson, a firm that evaluates companies before takeovers. Smoothly fitting into New York life at first, he later experiences difficulties, and returns eventually to his hometown, Lahore. His more recent *Exit West* (2017) is a strange novel about our contemporary world. Starting in an unnamed Muslim country beset by militants, Hamid traces the relationship of Saeed and Nadia from attraction to love and intimacy, and then to untangling. Their tie evolves in a series of settings, first in their homeland, then on the island of Mykonos, next in London, and finally in Marin county, California. They move from setting to setting via 'doors', and the physical journeys are not described. Hamid captures the evil, destructiveness, craziness and uprooting going on for millions today.

---

[12] Lahiri, Jhumpa. 2021. *Whereabouts*. NY: Knopf.

Besides the remarkable crew of novelists, storywriters, and playwrights of South Asian background surveyed in this section, some poets of note should be mentioned. The novelists Chitra Banerjee Divakaruni and Vikram Seth also published poetry, while Vijay Seshadri is an award-winning poet; Meena Alexander has written prose and poetry for decades; Agha Shahid Ali is an accomplished poet; and Rupi Kaur, in her twenties, born in India and domiciled in Canada, but hugely popular in America and elsewhere, has recently burst upon the scene.

This cast of writers listed above, along with others now on the scene, have stimulated the gathering of short pieces and extracts from longer works into several valuable anthologies of South Asian writing, two of which are mostly from writers based in South Asia— Meena Alexander, and Salman Rushdie and Elizabeth West—and two others by South Asian writers based in the West, by Sunaina Maira and Rajini Srikanth, and Amitava Kumar. All four of these demonstrate the continuing richness of this writing over a century and more. Although a few selections are translations from Indian languages, most are in English. An occupation by the British of almost 200 years, and the spread of the conqueror's languages through the educational system, made English one of India's many languages.

It is notable that, by 2020, works of fiction written in English but grounded in South Asian events and culture that may not be familiar to American readers, are given wide publicity and garner numerous prominent reviews. Today these works have come to the fore and are awarded the acclaim that they deserve. South Asian connected writers may also be placed in other contexts: with other Asian American writers, with immigrant writers from Latin America and Africa, and with writers, immigrant or not, in the span of American literature. However, as an historian and not a literary critic, what has been presented here is but a sampling. Works of other Asian Americans like Maxine Kingston Hong or Amy Tan or Viet Thanh Nguyen are not considered here, since they are not from South Asian roots, but the latter's novel, *The Sympathizer*, is to me one of the premier works of contemporary fiction.

In addition to these fiction writers, a slew of talented writers of
South Asian descent and birth have published notable works of non-
fiction aimed at a broad audience. In India throughout the twentieth
century and since, numerous authors composed in English, a
language used and taught widely by Indians as well as Europeans.
Some of them, for example, published with the Writers' Workshop of
Calcutta, founded in the 1950s by P. Lal, which published hundreds
of splendid volumes, all in English. A poet and 'transcreator' himself,
Lal brought most of these volumes out from his own house, and each
is marked by his superb calligraphy. Given this strong tradition of
English-language publication, it is no surprise that for over a century,
first-class writers from South Asia living in the United States have
produced many excellent works of investigative journalism, and
popular non-fiction. Some have written autobiographical accounts,
few as charming and penetrating as Krishnalal Shridharani's
My India, My America (1941).

Only a very few of these South Asian non-fiction writers are
mentioned here, with apologies extended to the dozens not included.
Anita Raghavan's *The Billionaire's Apprentice*, an investigation of the
career of Rajat Gupta, has already been noted. Among the important
books are Anand Gopal, *No Good Man among the Living*; Suketu
Mehta, *India Calling*, and *This Land is Our Land*; Vijay Prashad,
The Karma of Brown Folks, 2000, and *Uncle Swami*, 2012; Amitava
Kumar, *Husband of a Fanatic*, 2005, and *Lunch with a Bigot* (2015);
Anand Giridharadas, *India Calling: An Intimate Portrait of a Nation's
Remaking* (2011), *The True American: Murder and Mercy in Texas*
(2014), and *Winners Take All: The Elite Charade of Changing the World*
(2018); and Siddhartha Deb, *The Beautiful and the Damned: Life in
the New India* (2011).

Not by accident, many of these works touch on America and
the world, on South Asians in the US, on America's adventures
overseas, or on life in India today. They deal with the complexities
and intricacies of the relations among Americans of different
backgrounds interacting with a variety of foreigners, and often find
Americans out of their depth when dealing with other cultures.

They confront criminality and violence, mutual misunderstanding and understanding. Like Suketu Mehta in *Maximum City*, an exploration of Mumbai, and Somini Sengupta in *The End of Karma*, some America-based writers have returned to India to report on what they could see.

Another trend runs in the opposite direction. Several of these writers cast a critical eye on life in America, with little reference to their South Asian roots. Mehta's *This Land is Our Land* (2019) and Giridharadas' *Winners Take All* (2018) are examples. Having begun their book-writing careers as South Asian American writers, they are now simply American writers producing at the highest level of non-fiction output available in this country. Complicating any facile generalizations is Vijay Prashad, who has moved from a South Asian American view to a global perspective, while writing a bi-weekly column for the Indian magazine, *Frontline*, which is highly critical of America.

Do the South Asian backgrounds of these writers aid them in their paths to exploring their chosen topics? Yes. Quite a few want to come to terms with and make some kind of assessment of 'the new India', the country they never left behind, or never knew directly growing up. In order to do this, they have to visit and revisit, and determine how to portray an immense society that is moving and changing. Take, for example, Anand Gopal's remarkable account of the wars in Afghanistan, *No Good Men among the Living: America, the Taliban, and the War through Afghan Eyes* (2014), mentioned above. With his South Asian appearance and skills, he transformed himself, temporarily, into an Afghan, so he could approach those on the several sides of the conflict, especially Taliban fighters. Thus prepared, he gained the confidence of some of these Taliban, to give a unique account of their motivations, ambivalences and hostility to America. It is surely one of the most depressing and incisive books about America's adventures abroad that any American will ever read.

Some writers of South Asian background are responding to the diatribes directed towards immigrants. Suketu Mehta (1963–), for example, brought to the US by his parents in 1977, is ensconced here and is a citizen. Recently, based on his personal experiences and on interviews, he has explored the world of migrants and immigrants in *This Land is Our Land*. It is a set of gripping, emotional tales, an argument for acceptance and inclusion, and a plea for recognition of what is going on as people move in ever greater numbers from poor countries to others less poor ones or much richer. Presenting a pithy account of the conquest of the world by a few Western countries, argues that the Westerners took the wealth of those colonial areas, and now former colonials are moving to the West to recover a fraction of what was taken away from their native lands. His account is blunt: first the Western powers divided up most of Asia, Africa, the Middle East and Latin America; and after they gave up direct control, their multinational corporations entered to continue the exploitation.

Like several of the economists already discussed, Mehta is also concerned with the inequality existing within and between nations. He points out that the rise of India and China has created a larger middle class within each, and the richest in these countries are now as rich as their high-earning compatriots in the West. At the same time, inequality within almost every nation is increasing, as is happening in America, and happening, as well, in India.

In the latter part of the book, Mehta focused on networks, sometimes regional, like that formed from his native Gujarat, or professional. Engaged in networks, individuals usually do not emigrate alone, but link into networks that can cross borders, or form within borders, as voyagers survive and thrive in their chosen settings. He uses vivid examples from his own life and that of immigrants in New York and New Jersey. Then he tells us about the meanings of 'home':

> Many of us who are lucky enough to have the right papers live not in place or the other, but in a continuum of our birthplace and the place we've migrated to. Where is home for people like us? Are we Indian or American? Are we Bombayites or New Yorkers? We are both, and neither. The communities of people that move these days between two or more localities, as I do between South

Bombay and Greenwich Village, might be called 'interlocals.' ... So I propose a new way of looking at migrants: not as people who go in one direction and stay there, but as people in continuous transit between two or more places, not nation-states. Let's look at migration as not an arrow but a circle.[13]

Mehta finishes his book with penetrating insights like this one. Speaking at the twenty-fifth anniversary banquet of the South Asian Journalists' Association, SAJA, on 5 October 2019, Mehta was more blunt about the meaning of 'home'. We all have the same home, he said, and it is the earth. He forces us to relook at the processes of migrants moving and connecting these to the history of imperialism, capitalism, racism, war, climate change and inequality.

The prolific and acute scholar, journalist, and editor Vijay Prashad (1967–) is also, like Mehta, on the left. Born in Kolkata, he attended the Doon School in India, Pomona College in California, and in 1994, earned a PhD at the University of Chicago. On one track, Prashad has followed an academic career based at Trinity College, but at the same time, he has flourished as a Marxist writer, organizer, and journalist, turning out articles and books with amazing speed, while networking far and wide. His books range from scholarly works, such as *The Karma of Brown Folk* (2000), a study of the place of South Asians in American society, to broader works for a general audience, such as *The Darker Nations: A People's History of the Third World* (2007). Initially focused on South Asia and South Asians in the US, Prashad has widened his gaze to the wide world, particularly the Arab world. He has, like Mehta, not for a moment forgotten the global reach of American economic and military power, and it is a frequent subject of his bi-weekly reports for *Frontline*, a foremost news magazine of India.

Amitava Kumar (1963–), roughly in the same cohort as Mehta and Prashad, has described himself as a boundary crosser, who skips back and forth across national frontiers, disciplinary hedges and literary forms. Engaging at first with postcolonial writers who

---

[13] Mehta 2019, pp. 230–31.

write for an academic audience, and later discussing other writers in *Bombay London New York* (2002), he has written also in a more direct and powerful way in *Husband of a Fanatic* (2004) and *A Foreigner Carrying in the Crook of His Arm a Tiny Bomb* (2010). One of the most talented writers from South Asia, he identifies both as an expatriate but also as a South Asian, who will never leave his roots behind.

Kumar's *Husband of a Fanatic* is an emotionally draining and revealing discussion about Hindus and Muslims in South Asia. A Hindu, Kumar married a Muslim, a marriage that moved him not only to understand Hindu–Muslim relations, but also to see what he could do to defuse tensions, by urging each group to appreciate the other's point of view. He undertook a reporter's trip to India's border with Pakistan, and then, now having new relations in Karachi, he went to Pakistan. Hoping to shrink differences and animosities, he went to schools in both countries and had then youngsters write letters to those in the other nation.

Kumar went to Gujarat in 2002, just after the terrible slaughter there of Muslims, where he explored the psyche and experiences of the victims and the perpetrators. He then continued his journey through India to explore Hindu–Muslim relations from the inside of a divide or 'border', seeking to know what 'borders' mean for people everywhere. Another quest was to meet the widows of those killed in conflicts between the two nations. He reports on an interview the lived experiences, avoiding simplistic generalizations. Much of what he tells us, documenting the lack of any empathy between Hindus and Muslims, Indians and Pakistanis, is deeply disheartening.

Elsewhere in his journeys, Kumar speaks of 'the need to listen'.[14] He finds that Hindus and Muslims in Bihar, Bombay, South Africa, and the US listen very little to those perceived as enemies. As he interviews men blinded by the police in Bhagalpur, a city near to where he grew up, he recognizes that the blindness is not merely corporal, but psychological or spiritual: it is a blindness that causes conflict, the 'blindness that is the cause of religious violence'[15] infecting millions around the globe. He comes to understand that religious identities are not fixed, but can be mixed

---

[14] Kumar 2004, p. 231.
[15] Ibid., p. 274.

and complicated. Perhaps, he suggests, we are all converts, and all migrants, as Mohsin Hamid has proposed. As he moves beyond the Hinduism of his youth into cosmopolitan worlds, Kumar questions his own basic cultural concepts.

Anand Giridharadas (1981–), born in Cleveland, Ohio, attended the University of Michigan, Oxford, and Harvard, before plunging into journalism, writing for the *New York Times* from Washington and Mumbai. While continuing to publish in the *Times* and a variety of magazines, he has crafted four important books, the first of which, *India Calling: An Intimate Portrait of a Nation's Remaking* (2011), charted his paths into India. Giridharadas, the grandson of Anglophiles, who were part of the upper strata of Indians under the Raj and in the earlier years of Independence, visited his relatives in India when young, and then decided to explore India for himself when he was in his twenties. It was in India that he moved from a job at the McKinsey consulting firm to a successful career as a journalist, and now a thriving freelancer.

In the new India that he arrived at in his early twenties, Giridharadas learned that the India of his grandparents, of his youthful visits, and of his imagination now lay in the past. He was 'called' to a present-day, changing India to comprehend which required all his gifts and senses.

> I had seen a country frozen in my youth, and then returned to
> see it bursting with energy. I had seen the new cult of the self
> and new faith in self-making. I had seen, alongside this flowering
> of self-confidence, a new cultural confidence in the ascent of
> the uncolonized India... there are moment of special upheaval,
> when empires depart, when ideologies rotate, when the streets
> swell in irrepressible anger, when the laws of nature are rather
> abruptly written afresh. India was in the midst of such a moment.
> The meanings of destiny, family, love, class—of what it means
> to be Indian—were being defined a new by millions of people,
> all at once.[16]

---

[16] Giridharadas 2011, pp. 121–22.

Giridharadas is especially successful at exploring India's new balance sheet: what has been gained, what has been lost, what is connected to a social and cultural India that pre-dated the Raj and continues, but is changing. He enters convincingly into the psyches of his chosen subjects, which he views in the context of more general trends at work in today's India. His 'new India' includes extended portraits of a young man, Ravindra, on the rise in a provincial town; the Ambanis, India's wealthiest family, ensconced in Mumbai at the head of Reliance; Maoists in Hyderabad; women seeking justice in a divorce court; and the Dubey family in Ludhiana. He links his insights to his account of his parents and grandparents, and concludes, ' . . . so I sensed when returning to India that I was not undoing my parents' journey, but in some way fulfilling it. Like them, I was chasing the frontier of the future. Which just happened, in my case, to be the frontier of my own past'.[17]

Caught in a web between America and India, Giridharadas writes:

> I came of age in the interstices of two civilizations, with the inevitable confusion of identity. On the more difficult days, it was possible to feel that I didn't quite belong anywhere and that the burden of winning a place was heavier for me than for the other American kids. And even though I did not love India, suppose that I extracted a certain comfort from the knowledge that I belonged to this rooted, rarified Indian breed. My parents had education bearing class. They spokes in sparklingly enunciated English...[18]

Giridharadas's second book, *The True American: Murder and Mercy in Texas* (2014), is a meticulously detailed and moving account of the lives of the two protagonists, a Bangladeshi immigrant, and a troubled, impulsive white Texan. The two came together after 9/11, when Stroman, the Texan, declared war on men he thought looked like Arabs. Believing, perhaps, that a 'true American' like himself should seek revenge on such men, he murdered two of them and

---

[17] Ibid., p. 254.
[18] Ibid., p. 80.

grievously wounded a third. Sitting on death row, Stroman said, 'I guess I'm that dumb Texan redneck where everybody from the Middle East is an Arab to me.'[19] For, the two men he had killed, Hasan and Patel, were not Arabs but South Asians, as was also the third, Rais Bhuiyan, whom he had terribly wounded.

Giridharadas's account forces us to ask who is the 'true American': the white Texan Stroman who attacks recent immigrants, or Rais, the young man from Dhaka, who seeks to make his way upward into American society. He is concerned with the fate of these two as well as the nature of America. The author summarizes Rais's views on his adopted country:

> Rais had come to a country that nearly took his life and then generously gave him the means of retrieval—a country that seemed to him to contain the cures to its own ailments. But it was a country whose own people seemed to Rais to have lost their life force, ceased to see their potential, ceased to value the connection to other lives, ceased to look into the future and see the truth that made people like Rais come here… Rais wanted to wake them up. It was part of his idea of service. He wanted to tell them that if he, then they: if a foreign-born, half-blind ex-gas station clerk could make it here, they could too… it was a doubly complicated stance for Rais: a devout Muslim telling the Americans to become more like some supposed previous version of themselves, which also happened to mean their becoming more like him.[20]

As Giridharadas follows the Stroman family, impeded by their poverty, drug and alcohol use, and lack of education, the contrast becomes increasingly sharp with the educated, ambitious Rais. The latter embodies the willingness of the devout Muslim immigrant to do any job, to save, and to re-educate himself, so as to make a better life. Rais is unique, moreover, in his response to the tragedy. He fights to save the life of his attacker, then organizes 'World Without Hate',

---

[19] Giridharadas 2014, p. 152.
[20] Ibid., p. 259.

an NGO devoted to increasing mutual understanding in America and beyond. Giridharadas has done his own service in bringing to life his protagonists, and allowing Rais to present another version of Islam than that professed by the 9/11 terrorists.

In *Winners Take All* (2018), Giridharadas looks at the American scene to investigate what he calls Market-World and those rich Americans who say they can do good at the same time they are making pots of money. It is a trenchant exploration from another angle of the ramifications of growing inequality in America. Through attending meetings of our grandest philanthropists, a fellowship at the Aspen Institute, and numerous interviews, he has tried to understand the rationales for the 'win-win' outlook of these give-givers. They have come to believe, he shows, that the private sector is the best vehicle for societal improvement, rather than through public channels. Giridharadas argues that this approach fosters an arrogant paternalism that denigrates democracy and the public sphere. In turn, this method of doing good has led to a reaction by those supposedly 'improved' by the private philanthropists' work. One hero is Darren Walker, president of the Ford Foundation, who is trying to deal with them in a way that does not threaten the gift-givers but helps them to understand the dilemmas that must be confronted.

In his most recent effort, *The Persuaders*, Giridharadas delves into another issue he sees as fundamental in contemporary America: the split between those of opposing views and whether the persuaders—almost all left-liberals like himself—can reach those who oppose them or simply capitulate in any effort to bring them closer. The book has several heroes and heroines, but Alexandria Ocasio-Cortez and Anat Shenker-Osorio stand out and occupy about half the book. Giridharadas' investigation of how to persuade requires more subtlety than any of his previous efforts, but, I believe, is worth his efforts. He does want to persuade his gentle readers that Ocasio-Cortez is not a hard-core socialist, but rather a skilled player of the political game in the US, within the halls of Congress and outside. Shenker-Osorio as well as Diane Benscoter, Cesar Torres and John Cook employ long conversational methods to sway thousands in the undecided middle to explore, and, hopefully, change their views. The values they press forward are more inclusive and empirical rather than exclusivist and narrow. Their enemies are Q-Anon and Trumpist lies, but they want to persuade rather and condemn and alienate those whom they engage.

Although many South Asian writers, both in America and in India, are of the left, one bends well to the right and has gained considerable notoriety on that account. Dinesh D'Souza (1961–), born in Goa, India, into a Roman Catholic family, came to the US as a teenager, and earned his BA at Dartmouth College. Thereafter, as a self-proclaimed conservative, he has written twenty books and numerous articles presenting his views and produced several films as well. Over time, D'Souza has pursued his mission by attacking liberal and multicultural trends in American society and the Democratic Party, propounding views that many observers find to be ever more extreme.

Among D'Souza's books, *The End of Racism* (1995) is a lengthy explication of his ideas on race in America. Widely reviewed, it made him a public intellectual propounding a controversial agenda, including eliminating affirmative action. D'Souza insisted that African Americans have remained at the bottom of American society mainly because of pathologies in their own group culture that have impeded their path to success.[21] As a cure, he suggests that they learn to 'act white', that is, to conform to general and majoritarian expectations of behaviour.

Many of D'Souza's films have garnered a large audience, among them *2016: Obama's America* (2012), which explores the life, campaign, and administration of the 44th President, Barack Obama, claiming to reveal an unrecognized truth about his inner beliefs and aims. Addressing the history of colonialism in South Asia (where D'Souza was born) and Kenya (where Obama's father was born), D'Souza explores parallels between his own life and Obama's: both were born in the same year, both married in the same year, and both had anti-colonialist elements in their backgrounds. Obama, D'Souza believes, shared the anti-colonialist and far-left, if not communist, sympathies

---

[21] D'Souza 1995, p. 477ff.

of his father. Then D'Souza presents his principal message: that no one knew Obama's real character, and he was one who masked his true agenda.

An enthusiastic audience of right-wing viewers approved of D'Souza's critique of Obama in his 2012 film. D'Souza's later films also enthralled many viewers; these include *America: Imagine the World Without Her* (2014); *Hillary's America: The Secret History of the Democratic Party* (2016); *and Death of a Nation: Can We Save America a Second Time?* (2018). President Trump, who is compared to Abraham Lincoln, was a devoted fan. In 2014, D'Souza was charged with making illegal campaign contributions valued at $20,000 to the New York Senate campaign of the Republican attorney Wendy Long. Though contending that the charges were politically motivated, D'Souza pled guilty to a felony and was sentenced to five years' probation, eight months in a halfway house, and a $30,000 fine. In 2018, President Trump pardoned D'Souza.

4

Doctor-Writers
Stories, Science and Prescriptions

There are many physicians with a South Asian background, born in South Asia or the US, and based in America, and are part of a professional organization—the large and powerful American Association of Physicians of Indian Origin (AAPIO). In 2018, it was said to have a membership of more than 100,000, and India is also reported to be the 'single largest source of émigré physicians in the world'.[22] Physicians from India constitute at least 8 per cent of the doctors in this country.[23] Pakistani physicians and healthcare workers also have an organization, the Association of Physicians of Pakistani Descent of North America, incorporated in 1977, with more than 17,000 members.

At their thirty-sixth annual meeting in 2018, the Indian physicians gathered in Columbus, Ohio, and blended the latest medical science with a more traditional Indian practice: meditation. They invited spiritual teacher Sri Sri Ravi Shankar to address their executive committee luncheon where he called for them to work for a stress-free, violence-free life:

> The secret of meditation is in letting go… Stress arises when we have too much to do, and not enough energy or time to do it. We can neither change time nor the number of things we need

---

[22] 'American Association of Physicians of Indian Origin', Wikipedia, https://en.wikipedia.org/wiki/American_Association_of_Physicians_of_Indian_Origin.
[23] Mehta 2019, p. 206ff.

to do. So, the only option is to increase energy levels. And this can be accomplished through yoga, breathing techniques and meditation... Meditation is that space where thought has subsided and the mind is in complete rest. Meditation is the journey from movement to stillness, from sound to silence... The wise wake up and see, the unwise take a longer time.[24]

He then led a twenty-minute meditation session for the invitees.

A career in medicine is one greatly favoured by South Asian parents for their offspring and one often finds 'Dr... the son or daughter of Dr and Dr...'. There are, of course, physicians from many other foreign countries practising in the US, but the focus on medical careers is powerful for South Asians. One additional path that a few of these physicians have taken, however, is to become writers. They have sought to understand medical issues or basic human physiology. They have been critical of medical care in the United States and given incisive suggestions for improvement. They have contributed to the history of medicine, to medical science and to treatment worldwide in their numerous outstanding and recognized books.

The talented doctor-writers of South Asian descent include Abraham Verghese, Paul Kalanithi, Atul Gawande, Sandeep Jauhar, Siddhartha Mukherjee, Sanjay Gupta and Vivek Murthy. Venki Ramakrishnan, author of *The Gene Machine*, educated in America, shifted to Cambridge, England, is not discussed here, and I have analysed the Chopra brothers, Sanjiv and Deepak earlier.

Dr Abraham Verghese is a distinguished physician/writer and a pioneer among South Asian doctor-writers. He has offered us a penetrating account of his life in 'The Cowpath to America', published in the *New Yorker*, 23 and 30 June 1997.[25] Born in Ethiopia to Indian immigrant parents, his family came to the US and he worked in hospitals in the US before completing his medical education in Madras. Returning to the US, he did his internship and residency in Johnson Hill, Tennessee. Explaining his choice of America, he

---

[24] India West, 11 July 2018.
[25] Kumar 2003, pp. 280–97.

wrote, 'Our preference for America was also a form of rebellion against the British fixation of our elders. England seemed… a dead-end place, particularly for a young medical student.'[26] America had cultural attractions and what seemed like freedom and opportunity for all comers. He later tempered these judgments.

Verghese attended the Iowa Writers' Workshop and was encouraged to turn his Johnson City experiences into a book. *My Own Country: A Doctor's Story*, was published in 1994 and was immediately acclaimed for its New Yorker exquisite writing as well as the sensitivity and passion it expressed about treating AIDS in small-town, southern America. The book was made into an excellent feature film by Mira Nair. Verghese has since written the novels *The Tennis Partner* (1999) and *Cutting for Stone* (2009), as well as numerous articles. Continuing to work as a physician, he moved to El Paso, Texas, where he was the Director of the Center for Humanities and Ethics and also a Professor of Medicine at the University of Texas Health Sciences Center in San Antonio. Then he moved to Stanford University.

At an award ceremony in New York held by the Taraknath Das Foundation in 2002, Dr June Osborn, former head of the NIH taskforce on AIDS told the audience how knowledge of AIDS among rural southerners was hardly discussed before Dr Verghese. He gave a human face to AIDS sufferers and their families. Clark Blaise, Dr Verghese's writing teacher, gave him a tough report card. He said that Dr Verghese deserved a 'D' for his acute diagnoses, and a 'C' for writing a classic work, *The Tennis Partner*. Dr Sandeep Jauhar, a younger doctor-writer, explained that Dr Verghese was a role model for numerous doctor-writers. However, Verghese has gone a step farther: starting as a non-fiction writer, he has emerged as a novelist of the first rank with *Cutting for Stone* (2009) followed by *The Covenant of Water* (2023). The first is set in Ethiopia and the US, the nations of his youth, and then medical career. The second unfolds in Kerala and Madras, south India, the land of his ancestors and his medical training as well as briefly in Scotland. Each novel involves complicated medical issues allowing him to explore the

---

[26] Verghese, Abraham. 'The Cowpath to America', *New Yorker*, 23 and 30 June 1997.

worlds of human relations and intricate, life-saving procedures of medicine. Verghese's talent is such that he moves towards the plane of his fiction-writing heroes: Henry Fielding, Herman Melville and Charles Dickens.

The Covenant of Water tracks a large cast of characters including a few Britons, Indians of many castes and Anglo-Indians, those of mixed race, slotted in between the whites and the Indians, during the first three quarters of the twentieth century. Verghese moves between Parambil, a rising village, and a roaring metropolis, Madras, as well as rural parts of Kerala and Madras. As he goes, he builds in the general course of Indian history from nationalist challenges to the Raj into Independence and then involves us briefly with the Naxalites. At the centre of the many twists and turns of this novel are Big Ammachi, a village girl who grows into a loving mother, her son Philipose, his wife Elise, and her daughter, Mariamma. Parallel to the parts of the story set in Parambil, is the life course of a Scotsman, Digby Kilgour, doctor, artist, tea planter, and the biological father of Mariamma. Eventually the lives of Digby, Elise and Mariamma come together. The long and complex novel explores joy, love, sex, family, community, caste, and disease with insight and tenderness expressed through luminous prose. The book tracks through a lot of pain and death, and he writes, 'Families living their lives, no one spared the pain.'[27] In presenting the interactions of caste Hindus and pulayans, or Untouchables, Verghese with his words shocks us physically to feel their pain and anger at being dehumanized.[28] Many of the characters are Indian Christians, but several blend their faith with the Hindu concept of the One that is all pervasive. Near the end, he tells us, 'This is the covenant of war: that they're all linked inescapably by their acts of commission and omission, and no one stands alone.' The 'burbling mantra, the chant that never ceases... that all is one'.[29] Water surrounds and flows through the book, giving life, taking it away. 'The Condition' that many Kerala Christians share is, for some of them an aversion to water. But Mariamma, doctor-

---

[27] Verghese, Abraham. 2023. *The Covenant of Water*. NY: Grove Press, p. 418.
[28] Ibid., p. 487.
[29] Ibid., p. 706.

scientist, comes through all the upheavals moving towards solving the puzzle of just what this haunting malady is. Verghese has circled back from his life in the US to the India of his earlier life in Madras, summers in Kerala, and visits to the Vellore Medical Centre. The most important creator of the institutions at Vellore, Ida Scudder, has been discussed, as well as E. Stanley Jones, another American missionary who did fine work in and for India.

Verghese's role as a debuting doctor-writer is evident also in the tribute that Verghese wrote as the foreword to the posthumous book by neurosurgeon Paul Sudhir Kalanithi (1977–2015), *When Breath Becomes Air* (2016). As Verghese notes, Kalanithi's book is remarkable. The cadence: the story he tells of his life, as it was cut all too short, is told in clear, unforgettable prose that often has a stately movement as he writes determinedly in his last days, wanting to leave this memoir for each of us as we face death. He kept at it until he could not write any more. The middle of three sons of India-born parents, his father, a Christian and a doctor, his mother, a Hindu, he grew up in Westchester, New York, and Kingman, Arizona, to which rural setting his father had moved the family where he could earn enough to send his boys to college. A brilliant student from an educationally backward part of America, Kalanithi went to Stanford and Cambridge Universities, and then to Yale Medical School. Torn between literature and medicine, he chose the latter because he wanted to experience life more directly, and to understand the connections between the brain and the mind. Choosing neurosurgery, as well as medical research, as his calling, he searched for meaning:

> All of medicine, not just cadaver dissection, trespasses into sacred sphere. Doctors invade the body in every way imaginable. They see people at their most vulnerable, their most scared, their most private. They escort them into the world, and then back out. Seeing the body as matter and mechanism is the flip side to easing the most profound human suffering... I was pursuing medicine to bear witness to the twinned mysteries of death, its experiential and biological manifestations: at once deeply person[al] and utterly impersonal... I had started in this career, in part, to pursue

death: to grasp it, uncloak it, and see it eye-to-eye, unblinking. Neurosurgery attracted me as much for its intertwining of brain and consciousness as for its intertwining of life and death.[30]

Kalanithi was a rising star when, with a sudden bang, he was hit by Stage 4 lung cancer. Some advanced treatments and chemotherapy seemed to help. He returned to neurosurgery, but only temporarily. The cancer returned. His doctor-father, and even his oncologist, one of the top in the field, believed he would beat it, that he would have much more time. But some eight months after his baby daughter, Cady, was born, he succumbed. He recounts his path into medicine, and then the uneven, shockingly painful course towards death. His account is suffused with references to his wide reading, addresses questions about meaning that had always haunted him, and charts his course in his last two years from doctor-patient, to just patient. In his last two years, he said he saw that science in itself was insufficient for understanding his questions. He returned to the teachings of the Christianity with which he had grown up but abandoned. Amid the tragedy, he speaks throughout of his immense happiness with his wife and baby that he wrested from his shortened life.

Among the most successful of the South Asian doctor-writers, the surgeon Atul Gawande (1965–), a clinician and professor at the Harvard Medical School, is the son of two doctors who had emigrated from India and settled in Ohio. Reared in America, he has maintained his ties to India, detailing in his book *Better: A Surgeon's Notes on Performance* (2007), his return to India and his attempts there to understand the difficulties of medical care there. He returned to his father's home state of Maharashtra, and travelled from hospital to hospital for months, coming to understand how they coped with shortages of equipment and supplies. Part of his story is concerned with efforts to eradicate polio in India by the Rockefeller Foundation, and by the WHO.

Gawande's three other books are *Complications: A Surgeon's Notes on an Imperfect Science* (2002); *The Checklist Manifesto: How to Get*

---

[30] Kalanithi 2017, pp. 49, 53, 81.

Things Right (2009); and *Being Mortal: Medicine and What Matters in the End* (2014). The first deals with the life and challenges of a surgeon. *The Checklist Manifesto*, as its subtitle indicates, deals with the errors that Gawande believes were often made in carrying out many procedures in American hospitals, and his list of what must be done to help eliminate them. In the same book, he describes growing up in Athens, Ohio, as the son of two doctors, and how becoming a doctor was the preferred path for him as for some other Indian immigrant offspring. In *Being Mortal*, Dr Gawande confronts the issue of dealing with death in his own family and for everyone. In a 2014 radio interview, Gawande noted that we don't talk about death, and don't have adequate care for the dying, or doctors adequately trained to deal with those nearing the end.

With *Intern: A Doctor's Initiation* (2008), Sandeep Jauhar provided a vivid account of his family, his choices, and his career as a doctor-writer. Growing up in New Delhi till the age of eight, he came from a family of doctors and scientists. He recounts that his father told him, 'Non-science is nonsense.' At first he studied physics, getting a PhD, then shifted course and went to medical school. His older brother Rajiv also chose medicine, and helped Sandeep find his way. There was family pressure to choose medicine as a career: his father wanted a doctor trained at Stanford and believed that 'would be the pinnacle of professional attainment', while his mother 'wanted her children to become doctors so people would stand when we walked into a room'.[31] Once Sandeep had finished his second year, he gained confidence in his choice, supplementing medicine with writing. He chose cardiology as his specialty, and continued his medical career alongside his writing, in both short and long form. He met and married Sonia Sharma, a doctor and from a family of doctors, based in Edison, New Jersey.

A few years into his medical career, Jauhar tackles a subject both personal and professional in *Doctored: The Disillusionment of an American Physician* (2015): why had the medical profession declined in idealism, professional status and wages in the post-Medicare era? Has medicine become just another profession among several,

---

[31] Jauhar 2015, pp. 20–21.

in no way special? Jauhar points to a series of problems: excessive paperwork: the decline of hands-on doctoring skills; the reliance on expensive testing; the fear of lawsuits leading to arguments with patients over procedures; and lower salaries resulting from Medicare rules for reimbursement. He writes,

> The rising commercialism has obvious consequences for the public: ballooning costs, harm to patients, and fraying of the traditional doctor-patient bond. What is not so obvious… is the harmful effects on doctors themselves. We are trained to think like caregivers, not businesspeople. The constant intrusion of the marketplace has created serious and deepening anxiety in our profession…. We physicians deceive our patients, too. We don't always reveal when we make mistakes. We order unnecessary tests… And we deceive ourselves, too. We espouse the patriotic (but deeply misguided) notion that the American medical system is the best in the world. We deny the sickness in our system and the role we as a profession have played in creating that sickness. We obsessively push ourselves to do more and more, for reasons, both knightly and knavish, that we often hide from ourselves…. I am not immune to this sort of masquerade… I have lied to myself and to my patients in the service of a larger goal.[32]

What makes this questioning vivid is Jauhar's autobiographical account of his signing on to extra work at private clinics, much of which consisted of reading unnecessary test results and cutting corners in every direction in order to earn the extra money he needed to support his family. This outside work brought him to despair and marital crisis. He did emerge from the basement of his life back into the ground floor of renewed commitment to his primary work at the hospital, a family move from Manhattan to Long Island, and a revived marriage.

Jauhar's recent book, *Heart: A History* (2018), uses his family history to advantage as an entry point into a fascinating history

---

[32] Jauhar 2015, pp. 169, 209.

of the centrality of the heart in the cultural and medical history of humankind. A grandfather he had never met died suddenly. He had been bitten by a snake, but his demise was due to a sudden, fatal heart attack the same day. This death and those of other family members from heart failure set Jauhar on a course into medicine and cardiology. Overcoming fears of inadequate hand skills, he plunged ahead, learning the necessary tasks to become a heart specialist. His account interweaves his family history, case histories of patients, and a history of how we have come to understand the working of the heart. Jauhar delves into the development of treatments and the new technologies—stents, implantable defibrillators, angioplasty balloons, artificial hearts—that have been constructed by daring doctor-engineers. By focusing on one, perhaps the most important, organ of the body, he elucidates the history of how human beings have come to understand the working of their bodies.

In passing, Jauhar notes the famous Framingham study showing that South Asian males have a four times higher rate of heart disease than Americans, although they have lower rates of hypertension and smoking, and many have a vegetarian diet. Jauhar suggests that there is likely some genetic factor contributing to this problem for South Asians and that an analytical study is necessary to identify the root cause. Since his own family has had several deaths from heart disease and he himself feels that he is endangered, he has an added reason to call for an investigation without delay.[33]

Jauhar links the emotional and the biological connotations of the heart, and ends with a plea for all concerned to understand this relationship. Although he had started from a more mechanical, or he might have said 'scientific' understanding of the heart, his life experiences convinced him of the powerful connection between the emotions that throb within and the bodily organ. He also began to see more value in meditation, yoga, and a network of social connections, as well as diet and exercise, as factors affecting the health of the heart.

---

[33] Jauhar 2018, pp. 122–23, 234; *New York Times*, 19 February 2019.

Siddhartha Mukherjee (1970–) burst on the cultural and medical scene with *The Emperor of All Maladies: A Biography of Cancer* (2010), a brilliantly written, learned and lengthy book—later followed by a public television series based upon it—for which he was awarded the Pulitzer Prize. A student of medical history, a scholar of texts, as well as a practising doctor, except in the acknowledgments, Mukherjee barely hints at his bicultural background. Utilizing case histories of cancer patients and interviews with cancer doctors across the country who have devised workable therapies, the book traces the hopes, and then despair, when a possible treatment works initially and then fails. It is popular science and medicine at its best.

Born into a Bengali family resident in New Delhi, Mukherjee attended school there, then attended Stanford University. Awarded a Rhodes Scholarship to support his continued biomedical research, he earned a DPhil at Oxford University and graduated from Harvard Medical School in 2000. He then worked in Boston laboratories and hospitals until 2009 when he moved to Columbia Medical School. In *The Gene: An Intimate History* (2016), Mukherjee has written another elegant and extensively researched work. It begins with an account of the psychological and physical maladies of a cousin and two uncles. Was it a specific gene, Mukherjee wonders, that he and his father might also possess? Might he have it and have passed it on to his daughters? He then explores the history and our present understanding of inheritance, the gene, and the genome, taking us to the Galápagos Islands with Charles Darwin and into Gregor Mendel's garden, through debates on eugenics, and the disputes and achievements of Watson, Crick, Wilkins and Franklin, as they moved towards unveiling the double helix that is DNA. Recently he has continued his explorations with *The Song of the Cell: An Exploration of Medicine and the New Human*. As a full-fledged historian of science, a scientist, and a cancer doctor, Mukherjee is a superb storyteller who leads us deeper into genes and the genome. Mukherjee has continued to write an occasional column on medicine for the *New Yorker*. He argued in his article 'The Algorithm Will See You Now' (3 April 2017), that although machines can help doctors with diagnoses, they likely will not, and should not, remove the doctor's subtle talents from the equation that leads to healing.

Besides these four doctor-writers who have mainly expressed themselves through the written word, the neurosurgeon Sanjay Gupta (1969–) has gained fame as CNN's chief medical correspondent. His frequent appearances on a widely viewed news channel, together with his documentaries, have made him a household name. He has also written books on medical subjects, including *Chasing Life: New Discoveries in the Search for Immortality to Help You Age Less Today* (2007) and *Cheating Death: The Doctors and Medical Miracles that Are Saving Lives Against All Odds* (2009), as well as a novel. Writing in a clear style for his popular audience, the man called, 'America's doctor', has, like the other doctors described above, made a serious contribution to understanding vital health issues. He has also been frequently criticized for over-simplifying issues and relying on industry sources in his reports. Despite these criticisms, Gupta undoubtedly has called attention to vital physical and mental health issues.

In a follow-up and expansion of the issues raised in *Chasing Life*, Gupta presented in 2019, a series of television films tracking the efforts at improving health and extending life across the globe. One of these is set in India. At the outset Gupta says, 'India is in my blood…' He had visited India before, but his recent trip took him to Kerala, a new site for him, where he wanted to understand traditions of martial arts and Ayurvedic medicine. What might they contribute to his quest? He tried the exercises of the martial arts trainees, he had his own health assessed by an Ayurvedic physician, and he learned more about Indian spices and Ayurvedic cuisine. Although his parents had taught him about yoga and Ayurvedic medicine, this documentary marked his return to these traditions as an adult doctor. He came away firmly believing that they might contribute to better health, longer life, and the conquest of diseases. His adventures in India, Japan, and other countries showed his eagerness to learn from non-Western traditions in his quest for enhanced health. In Japan, for instance, where stress levels were high, he discovered methods used there to combat stress, including a forest bath, acupuncture, hot springs and karate. The quest continued as he journeyed to Colombia and Norway. He is still en route.

In the early months of 2020, as the world entered the Covid-19 pandemic crisis, several of the above doctors, and others of South Asian background, stepped forward. On television, Sanjay Gupta was omnipresent, giving Americans vital information. Atul Gawande wrote incisive articles for The *New Yorker* on the crisis. Ashish Jha, former director of the Global Health Initiative at the Harvard Medical School, and now Dean of the School of Public Health at Brown University, in mid-2020, was the government's lead Covid spokesman; Ali S. Khan, dean of the College of Public Health of Nebraska Medical Center, and Dr Susan Varma, a psychiatrist at NYU Medical School have also presented their perspectives on television. Inder Singh developed a thermometer program to track the spread of the virus across the country with his web-based Thermometer Company. They are just a few of the many South Asian physicians who have provided information and responses during the pandemic.

On the social and psychological side, many recommended the 2020 book by surgeon-general Vivek Murthy—who served in that role from 2014 to 2017 and has assumed that role again in 2021—on combatting isolation. Entitled *Together: The Healing Power of Connection in a Sometimes Lonely World*, it argues the vital need for social connection to live a healthy, fulfilled life, and to combat the increasing number of suicides and the growing opioid epidemic. Murthy was born in the UK to south Indian parents, grew up in Canada and Miami, Florida, and attended Harvard College and the Yale Medical School. After his term as surgeon general, he founded Doctors for America and continues to comment on health issues. It is striking that just as Murthy has focused on loneliness and the need for social connections, the ongoing pandemic has forced us to isolate in our small family units, and to wear masks and practice social distancing when we venture outside. In *Together*, Murthy makes moving use of his personal experiences as a bullied youngster and as a relative who lost beloved family members, including an uncle who had failed to adapt to life as an immigrant in America and committed suicide.[34] Near the end of his exploration of the cures for loneliness, he tells how the medical team in a Washington hospital rallied around his very young, seriously ill daughter, and saved her life. The moral of his tale is that when crisis strikes, each of us needs, not only close friends and acquaintances, but a larger, loving community.

Thousands of other doctors from a South Asian background are conspicuous among those medical professionals working assiduously during the present crisis, first at home in America. It is a mark of the connection between South Asia and America in the medical field that so many are intimately involved in confronting this pandemic and explaining it to us. This had become even more vital as the pandemic spread across India with a ferocity hardly seen elsewhere. It had been the product of believing too soon that the crisis was past, of pitiful public health facilities starved of resources for three generations and of the willingness of the ruling party to put politics above public safety by allowing huge gatherings of the mostly unmasked. Health professionals in India had striven yeomanly to fight the virus, aided by many others abroad.

---

[34] Murthy 2020, pp. 39, 120–25, 178–82, 273ff.

5

Scholars, Teachers, Class and Caste

During the last half-century, a big shift has taken place in teaching and scholarship about South Asia. In the 1970s there were a modest number of teachers and researchers about India and most were American-born men. Since then, there has been an influx of South Asians into American colleges and universities, and quite a few are surely among the best the world has to offer. From Harvard to Yale, to Stanford, to Duke, as well into dozens of less famous institutions, South Asians have taken positions and contributed to a richer and wider understanding of South Asia. They have come from India and Pakistan, from the UK and France, and have been joined by Americans of South Asian descent, in their sum, changing the face of Americans' knowledge and views of the South Asia world. They have joined faculties in the humanities and social sciences, and in the sciences, engineering, law, and medicine. They have enriched South Asia studies and their disciplines, and American intellectual life. Many raised in South Asia grew up with the English language as well as an Indian regional language, giving them an advantage over others for whom English was a second or third language, as well as over those whose native language was English and, to study South Asia, had to acquire one or more foreign languages.

Of course, there are still many 'anglo' scholars studying South Asia in the US, but as Ramchandra Guha points out in a perceptive essay in the 2003 collection edited by Jackie Assayag and Veronique Bénéïï, *At Home in Diaspora: South Asian Scholars and the West*,[35]

---

[35] Assayag and Bénéïï 203, p. 163ff.

they are no longer seen as important as outstanding scholars from South Asia now based here. Guha himself, based in Bangalore, but now of international repute and often travelling westward to make presentations, is part of a set of South Asian scholars who have connected to the international web of scholarship, studying not only their own societies but contributing to a variety of theoretical discussions.[36] Rajni Kothari and Ashis Nandy of the Centre for the Study of Developing Societies in New Delhi are examples of writers known as well in Berkeley and Madison, as in Kolkata and Mumbai.

The contribution of such South Asian scholars to our understanding not only of their culture, but of all of our cultures, is nowhere so prominent as in the startlingly new and suddenly successful field known as 'subaltern studies', a field that has gained international recognition.

In the early 1980s, Ranajit Guha (1923–2023) was a fine, but not widely known scholar of eighteenth-century Indian and imperial history. He had been an active communist and went underground in 1948 during the extreme left period of party work. After he surfaced, he turned full-time to scholarship and published *A Rule of Property for Bengal* (1963). In the 1960s, he gathered a group of excellent young scholars around him at the University of Sussex in the UK, where he edited a series of anthologies of essays called *Subaltern Studies*. Although the term 'subaltern' had generally been used to designate junior officers in the British military, Guha and his group, following the Italian communist theorist Antonio Gramsci, used the term to refer to the lowest, and neglected, ranked groups in society— in India, where the caste system prevailed, the stratification was especially clear. Calling for a radical reinterpretation of the received histories of nationalism in South Asia, these scholars highlighted the role of 'subaltern' classes of peasants and other non-elite groups, in contrast to elite leaders, such as those of the Indian National Congress, Muslim League, or Hindu nationalists. The subalterns, these scholars argued, existed in an autonomous domain that neither originated from, nor depended upon, elite politics.

---

[36] Kothari 2002.

Explication of the concepts of caste, class, and race have had a long history, discussed by South Asians and South Asian Americans as well as social scientists. India has been synonymous with the caste system. The term 'caste' derives from the Portuguese word *casta*, which their explorers applied to the society they found in India at the end of the fifteenth century. English usage of the term dates from the early seventeenth century.[37] A linkage of America and India, explicitly or implicitly, through investigating their systems of social stratification and discrimination against groups was well underway by the mid-nineteenth century, and has matured through the attention of social scientists, creative writers, and protagonists defending, attacking, and exploring, and occasionally comparing their socio-cultural systems. As knowledge of India filtered into America in the eighteenth and nineteenth centuries, and American traders linked to India, terms drawn from Indian culture—such as 'caste', 'Brahmins', 'yoga', 'mantra', 'karma', and such—became common. The members of the old, white, upper-class Protestant families who constituted the Boston elite, drawing on this terminology, were called 'Brahmins'. Though at the top of the social ladder, however, these Brahmins—as arrogant and inbred as they might have been—were not members of a stratum as rigidly bounded by birth and associated with a particular occupation as an Indian caste would have been. Americans, however, was characterized by a rigid form of stratification based on race that, unfortunately, was not destroyed by the Civil War, or the Thirteenth, Fourteenth, and Fifteenth amendments to the Constitution, or brief advances towards equality of the races just after that war. The African American scholar W.E.B. Dubois, and later scholars following him including the American historian C. Van Woodward (1908–1999) charted developments in the US in the post-1865 decades, but references to India were not part of the discussion. When he resided briefly in the US during the First World War, Indian nationalist Lala Lajpat Rai saw connections in his 1916 book, *The United States*

---

[37] 'Caste', Wikipedia; OED, and numerous scholarly works on caste.

of America: A Hindu's Impression. (1916) He found the position of African Americans comparable to Untouchables in India.

Noted social scientists made serious forays into the comparative arena explicitly using the idea of a caste system as well as a class system during the 1930s and 1940s. Chief among them was Gunnar Myrdal's searching and monumental *An American Dilemma* (1944), John Dollard's *Caste and Class in a Southern Town* (1937), and Hortense Powdermaker's *After Freedom: A Cultural Study in the Deep South* (1939). Published later than the studies by Dollard and Powdermaker, *Deep South* (1941) by Allison Davis, Burleigh B. Gardner, and Mary R. Gardner was based on more extensive and intensive field work, guided by the work of social anthropologist W. Lloyd Warner. They sought to uncover all the complexities of the social system of Natchez, Mississippi, for Blacks and whites, poor and rich. They found that there was class stratification on both sides of the racial divide, and, although there were no marital crossings, there were sexual ones, sometimes resulting in mixed race children, who had to live as Black. As in many caste systems, some few 'passed': they joined temporarily or for a lifetime, the majority caste.[38] The same issue was addressed by James Weldon Johnson in his novel *The Autobiography of an Ex-Colored Man* (1912); by Martha A. Sandweiss in her *Passing Strange: A Gilded Age Tale of Love and Deception Across the Color Line* (2009); and by Harold R. Isaacs in *India's Ex-Untouchables* (1965), in which he describes parallel instances in urban India. Many of these authors and others try to explicate the complex connections between social stratification based on wealth, education, race and occupation.

American social scientists rarely referred to caste in other societies. One of the few who attempted a comparative analysis was Oliver Cromwell Cox in his *Caste, Class, and Race*. (1948) While Myrdal wrote of the ongoing 'caste struggle' in the 1940s and placed American race relations in a changing world context, even he did not compare America's caste system to those existing elsewhere.

---

[38] Myrdal 1962, pp. 129–30, 683–88; Wilkinson 2010, pp. 201, 218.

Cox, in contrast, offered an extensive treatment of the Indian caste system, but one based on ancient texts and second-hand knowledge. He underestimated the amount of fluidity in the system, as well as the strength of colour prejudice in India. Absent from his account of caste India are all the anti-caste and anti-Brahmin movements through India's history. Most lacking is any mention of Dr B.R. Ambedkar, leader of the Untouchables, now called Dalits in India through the 1930s and 1940s when Cox was putting together his analysis. The latter seems to believe that the lower castes and Untouchables throughout Indian history simply accepted their place in the social order assigned to them by God or by the Brahmins who decided caste ranking. This is inadequate. After his incursion into India, he confronted the so-called 'caste school' of American social scientists, plus Myrdal, and found them wrong throughout. To call America a caste system rather than a class system, he argued, was 'mysticism'.[39] As a critical Marxist, he saw American socio-economy as a class system—part of world capitalism—with a white 'aristocracy' exploiting poor whites as well as Blacks. Race prejudice he found to be secondary, a rationalization, not primary to understanding the American political and economic system. He found the caste system and the capitalist system to be two different and distinctive social arrangements. His arguments went largely unnoticed within American social science. Some of those remembering him and his work commented that he was neglected in the Caribbean of his birth, and marginalized in the America in which he worked.[40]

In 1964, E. Digby Baltzell approached caste from another angle in *The Protestant Establishment: Aristocracy and Caste in America*, distinguishing the terms establishment, elite, aristocracy and caste. He argued that the elite was the ruling group of any society, while aristocracy, literally, meant those rising by merit, not birth. One grouping existed within American society, he argued, that of the old-school, early-arriving Anglo-Saxon Protestants, which aimed to keep control through birth, not merit—and if they succeeded,

---

[39] Cox 1948, p. 489ff.
[40] Allahar and Lewis 2014, p. 339; Robinson 1990–91, p. 5ff.

the result would be a serious decline in American life in the second half of the twentieth century. In Baltzell's view, they constituted an establishment that came to fore in the late nineteenth century, possessing both social and political power, connected by their passage through Harvard, Princeton, or Yale University, by their club memberships, and by their anti-Semitism. In contrast to that establishment was an aristocracy of the talented, who had been assimilated into American society regardless of background. Given the continuation of caste exclusivism through American history, the American elite remained a complex mix of these different groups. He compared those at the top to other elite groups including the senatorial class of Republican Rome, pre-revolutionary aristocrats and clergy in France, and the Whigs in eighteenth-century England. Baltzell was writing just before the change in America's immigration law which led, subsequently to an influx of Asians. Ending his analysis in the early 1960s, he makes no reference to caste in India, and sees American casteism as characteristically based on race, although his concern throughout his book is the casteism of anti-Semitism.

Recently, a writer who has compared caste systems in the US and India is Isabel Wilkerson, whose 2020 book *Caste: The Origins of Our Discontents* deals with 'caste' while neglecting 'class', and the complex interactions of caste, class and race. She deserves credit for this comparative effort, but it does not measure up to her earlier superb, *The Warmth of Other Suns: The Epic Story of America's Great Migration* (2010). Wilkerson argues persuasively that the rigid stratification between a dominant caste and a minority caste has characterized both America and India over centuries—and Nazi Germany as well—identifying what she calls the eight pillars of caste: endogamy, heritability connected to occupations, purity versus pollution, dehumanization, terroristic enforcement, and belief in inherent superiority vs. inherent inferiority. The pillars are appropriate, but she offers little about the genesis and history of the caste systems, only alluding briefly to Biblical rationales and the ancient Hindu, Laws of Manu, but says much about the suffering of the exploited castes. Her slotting of all the jatis (caste-on-the-ground) into the four varnas in India is a great simplification.[41]

A talented writer who uses anecdotes and parables to make her point, Wilkerson jumps back and forth in time. Yes, slavery, Jim Crow, and lynching were horrendous, but things do change over time, sometimes for the better. Going from a contemporary murder or bad incident on a recent flight, back to slavery and death camps, does not account for the fact that today there are protests by Black and white, Christian and Jew, upper, as well as, lower-caste members when serious crimes occur. To present scenes of evil from centuries, or decades ago, interspersed with contemporary events weakens her case. Now is not 1880 or 1950. Things are bad today, but were worse yesterday, and there are more fighters for positive change these days, and, hopefully, many more tomorrow.

Wilkerson, finally, does not bring South Asian Americans into her discussion. For those of South Asian background in America—the bridge between two caste nations—the questions are: Where do I fit? Where do I identify? Am I in the dominant or minority caste, especially if I am in a high prestige occupation and earn a considerable salary? How do I cope with American racism, how might I fight for the end of discrimination against anyone who is not seen as belonging to the dominant white community? South Asians in the US have long been subjected to American racism and Islamophobia including Kamala Harris, vice president, 2021–25, who is not only Black, but also South Asian.

---

[41] Wilkerson 2020, p. 76ff.

6

Curry and Spelling

In the first half of the twentieth century, only one lonely Indian restaurant existed in America to serve a few South Asians and some adventurous Americans. In 1973, the actress-turned-chef Madhur Jaffrey (1933–), who had starred in a number of Merchant-Ivory films, wrote about the dismal Indian restaurants then, in the introduction to her first book about Indian cooking:

> [T]hese establishments invariably underestimate both the curiosity and the palate of contemporary Americans. Instead of specializing in food from a particular state or district, they serve a generalized Indian food from no specific area whatsoever... There are several reasons for this. One is timidity—the fear that diners' unfamiliarity with regional specialties will make certain dishes unpopular. Another is the caliber of the cooks: most are former seamen who left their ships with the hope of making a living, somehow or other, in America, and as cooking seemed to require no unusual skills, a great many became restaurateurs, copying the standardized menus of other Indian restaurants and refusing to experiment with dishes from their own villages... The result of all this is that the sauces in such eating places inevitably have the same color, taste, and consistency... Naturally, it is difficult to recommend such a restaurant. The only alternative is to invite the people in question home for dinner. I did this for several years, justifying... the effort by telling myself that someone had to let Americans know what authentic Indian food was like...[1]

---

[1] Jaffrey 1973, p. 3.

From cooking at home for friends, she launched on her second career. Through writing cookbooks and with a successful television show that aired in both America and Great Britain, she helped to spread knowledge about Indian food and its preparation. Then, as more South Asians arrived from the late 1960s, as Madhur Jaffrey pioneered with her books and cooking show, many more Indian restaurants opened, and now scarcely a city of any size does not have one. Some present the food of a particular region of India, some are vegetarian, and some, more experimental, have blended Indian and Western dishes to make something new altogether. We can see at least two, perhaps contradictory trends at work: on the one hand, an effort to produce 'authentic' Indian cuisine, just like one's family served in Chennai, Delhi, Amritsar or Kolkata; on the other hand, experimental efforts to blend in elements of other cuisines with South Asian dishes. As food experts have noted, the same ingredients available in South Asia may not be offered for purchase in America, so there needs to be some adaptation and change. Meanwhile, in our more cosmopolitan world, the scholarly investigation of food, its production, its preparation, and its crucial part in the transnational movement of people and their cultures has proceeded apace, as attested to in such works as *Curried Cultures: Globalization, Food, and South Asia* (2012).

Most prominent in the public eye has been Padma Lakshmi (Padma Lakshmi Vaidyanathan, 1970–), a well-known advocate for Indian food, having charted a path from acting and modelling into media, product development, and advocacy for women's causes. Beautiful and ambitious, she wanted her own identity and accomplishments separate from those of her former husband, Salman Rushdie, and achieved that goal. Born in Chennai and raised in New York and California, after having graduated from Clark University she pursued a modelling career in Europe, acted in films in Italy, Hollywood, Bollywood, and appeared on numerous television shows. In 2006, she joined 'Top Chef' as a judge on this reality competition TV programme and has continued with the show for more than a decade. In 'Taste the Nation', a new show launched on Hulu in June 2020, she highlighted among others, unheralded cooks, and she has written several cookbooks as well. In an interview with *Time*, she discussed her advocacy for Indian, especially vegetarian food, the cuisine, she says, hasn't yet pervaded the US food scene as it has in the UK:

> 'Indian culture does have small moments in weird places. Like, Madonna is into yoga, so we all get into yoga,' Lakshmi says. 'And I see on Instagram that everyone is using turmeric [in their recipes] now? Stuff like that makes me laugh. My bullsh-t meter goes off.' Lakshmi predicts Indian food will become increasingly popular across the globe as we all inch closer to vegetarianism to stay healthy and limit our environmental impact. When she's not judging on Top Chef, she consumes a mostly vegan diet.[2]

Divorced from Rushdie in 2007, Lakshmi revealed in a 2018 op-ed piece for the *New York Times* that she had been sexually abused at age seven, and raped at age sixteen: 'It took me decades to talk about this with intimate partners and a therapist. Now, 32 years after my rape, I am stating publicly what happened. I am speaking now because I want us all to fight so that our daughters never know this fear and shame and our sons know that girls' bodies do not exist for their pleasure...'[3]

A beautiful woman frequently pictured at public events, by discussing a painful event in her life Lakshmi has contributed to public discourse on sexual assaults. Her long-time battle with endometriosis, and her philanthropic work to combat that disorder, led to an invitation to give the keynote address at the opening of the MIT Center for Gynepathology Research. In addition to serving as an ambassador for the UN Development Program, she has assisted other Indian chefs, including Fatima Ali, a friend who died at the age of thirty, and Priya Krishna, supplying a foreword to the latter's book *Indian-ish: Recipes and Antics from a Modern American Family* (2019):

---

[2] Dockterman, Eliana. 'Cooking in Quarantine', *Time*, 18 May 2020.
[3] 'I was raped at 16 and I kept silent', Sept. 25, 2018.

My family was like Priya's: Her mom, Ritu, working full time while also raising Priya and her sister... with their heritage somewhat intact, acclimated in the way that most immigrants do... What has sprung forth... is a new cuisine that allows for all the wacky things like using olive oil... making pizza with rotis, and baking eggless cakes that accommodate their Hindu vegetarianism... [I]t still exemplifies the flavor principles of Indian food, making it accessible for today's American cook... This cuisine is indeed authentic, and while it may not be traditional Indian food or what we think of as American food... it's actually both.[4]

Krishna, a Dallas native with south Indian roots, has appeared on national television to spread the message of *Indian-ish* and is now a food critic for the *New York Times*. She learned to cook from her mother, Ritu Krishna, who is the secondary author. Wanting to fit in, Krishna asked her mother to send her to school with peanut butter and jelly sandwiches rather than Indian fare. She says that 'Indian-ish', suggests her situated in two worlds, but not completely at home in neither. The subtitle of the book, 'Recipes and Antics from a Modern American Family', suggests how she and her family have adapted to their new home. She began to write about Indian food and its preparation. Her Indian-ish dishes bend slightly from their roots and blend with other cooking styles to make them easier to prepare, and refreshingly new as well. A note in the *New York Times* puts it this way:

In a 2019 cookbook, *Indian-ish: Recipes and Antics from a Modern American Family*, Priya and Ritu Krishna present recipes for 'Indian-American mash-ups like roti pizza, saag paneer made with feta, and Indian ribollita. Tomato rice with cripy Cheddar or 'pizza rice'... is a pleasantly addictive rice-cheese-tomato casserole that gets a little kick from Indian green chile. Garlic-ginger-cilantro-mint chicken is a riot of flavors and colors.[5]

---

[4] Lakshmi, foreword to Krishna 2019, pp. viii-ix.
[5] *New York Times*, 10 April 2019.

The geographic spread and ever-expanding efforts at new and tasty combinations are endless. Another innovator in providing Indian food in America, Meherwan Irani, who was born in the UK, returned to small-town India before emigrating to America. She held a variety of jobs in San Francisco before opening Chai Pani, a now-renowned Indian restaurant in Ashville, North Carolina. Calling herself a 'culinary mutt', she has adapted Indian street food plus a variety of dishes from around India, including Parsi elements, winning a James Beard award for her cuisine. She now has more than five restaurants, including one in Atlanta.

It is not just New York, or Dallas, or Atlanta that have hosted unusual combinations and experiments. In Panguitch, Utah, a mostly white, Mormon town of 1,500 in the rural south of the state, Ripple Desai—who proudly says, 'I'm Indian, my parents are both from India… And I love tacos'—founded the Tandoori Taqueria about five years ago. As Kirk Siegler of NPR reported: 'Her menu is a fusion of traditional Indian dishes with that dish beloved by him, the Mexican staple . . . tacos. She uses naan bread as the tortilla.' Mixtures, hybrids, wholly new food breeds: they are all part of the South Asian entry into every aspect of American life.

In addition to food, another port of entry for South Asians has been into spelling bees. Youngsters of South Asian background have found a niche in local and national competitions for those their age, especially in spelling bees. Their near monopoly of the top spots was visible in the Scripps National Spelling Bee in 2017. The AP reported the victory of Ananya Vinay over another pre-teen of South Asian descent, Rohan Rajeev:

Ananya is the 13th consecutive Indian-American to win the bee and the 18th of the past 22 winners with Indian heritage, a run that began in 1999 with Nupur Lala's victory, which was featured in the documentary 'Spellbound'. Like most of her predecessors, she honed her craft in highly competitive national bees that are limited to Indian-Americans, the North South Foundation and the South Asian Spelling Bee, although she did not win either.[6]

For more than two decades, the spelling competitions have been a particular focus of South Asian youngsters' energies and of their families' community life. Nearly all competitors have family helpers to log hundreds of hours of preparation with them. That preparation requires intense concentration, learning of the roots of words in dozens of languages, memorizing the precise spelling of unusual words, and the ability to compete in tense circumstances. Pawan Dhingra has written of the South Asian spelling phenomena:

> ....bees affirm a model minority body in contrast to the gendered rules of traditional sports, sports proved to be a governing logic to them.... It lets the hyper-model minority connect to the popular sports logic but without having the youth fail on the field.... The bees... mimic sports events with their confetti, trophies, suspense, coaching preparation, single winner, celebrity adoration, production, and more... the bees validate the diasporic community's sense of themselves with their place in the United States.[7]

Young South Asians are now playing more traditional American sports as well, including basketball, football, golf and baseball. Notable is golfer Sahith Theegala, thrice a collegiate champion, who has joined the PGA tour.[8] However, in the 2020s they continue to strive for competence, victory, and notoriety in 'brain sports'. In May 2019, South Asian dominance in spelling competition was on display. Until this date, there had been two-way ties, but this time there was an eight-way tie. The organizers ran out of words. Not stumping the remaining spellers, six of South Asian background, they declared a tie among all competitors, and decided to award each

---

[6] Nuckols, Ben. 'An Unflappable Sixth-Grader Has Won the Scripps National Spelling Bee,' AP, 1 June 2017.
[7] Dhingra 2016, pp. 139, 147.
[8] *NY Times*, 4 March 2022.

one the full first-place prize of $50,000, plus a trophy.[9] In 2021, a talented African American speller ended the run of South Asians on the winner's stand, but they remain formidable.

On 1 June 2023, starting from 11 million spellers in the US, seven of the eight finalists in the national spelling bee were of South Asian backgrounds, and the winner, Dev Shah, fourteen, according to his mother, had worked diligently at his preparation for four years, including ten hours a day in the final year. The final rounds included more obscure words than ever before. You may try your hand at defining, if not spelling: leguleian, querken, chthonic, katuka, crenel, pataca, pharetrone, and Dev Shah's winning word: psammophile. Are these remarkable young people wearing out the unabridged dictionary? Are they the best English-language spellers anywhere? Besides the spelling bees, students from South Asian backgrounds have done well in geography and history competitions, but not as well as in spelling.

In 2023, South Asian Americans celebrated India's Independence Day on 20 August in New York City for the forty-first time with thousands lining Madison Avenue. This year's event differed slightly from past years with floats touting living a full and healthy life, eating oats, meditating and practicing yoga as well as combating climate change. There were the usual floats for banks, TV networks, food companies, gurus and temples in the New York metropolitan area, but the change in emphasis could not be missed. Leading the parade was a contingent of South Asian New York police people representing the Desi Society of the force, demonstrating that South Asians have entered every sphere of American life.

---

[9] Shankar 2019.

Conclusion
The Changing Arc of Power, Culture and Influence

In concluding, I want to return to the theme of globalization. There have been connections spanning the globe for centuries, but the relationships varied, sometimes thick, often thin, not rich and vital, to the countries involved. Americans shipped out to India in the late eighteenth century, but thousands of South Asians did not settle in the new nation in North America. The trade continued in fits and starts. Then American Protestant missionaries took it as their mission to convert heathens in South Asia to the one true faith. Several thousand of such missionaries settled in British India through the nineteenth and twentieth centuries. A modest number were converted, schools and colleges were established, and hospitals erected. Some of these have endured, teaching and healing. Some have faded. Closer to the present, the Christian mission is still advocated by a small number of evangelicals, and some of those older institutions endure with their Christianity preached in a subdued tone. They are also subject to the anti-Christian message that is proclaimed by messengers of Hindutva. There remain millions of Christians in India, believing that it is an Indian religion, and most of their churches are run by Indian Christians.

The idea of 'mission' itself has been secularized by many including South Asians at home and abroad. The Rockefeller Foundation early on, linked to Christian institutions, but then backed secular missions and institutions. The Ford Foundation in India has also been in the secular mission camp. Most, but not all, funders from abroad, either of South Asian descent or birth, press for secular rather than religious missions. These missions must always be scrutinized to see what their explicit and implicit goals and means are.

Through the late nineteenth century and earlier twentieth century, Indian nationalism grew with the demand for a greater say in running their country, and then for self-rule and Independence. A remarkable leader, Mahatma Gandhi, came to the fore after the First World War, and had an impact not only in South Asia, but through the Western world including America as well. A modest number of his followers worked to influence American public opinion for Indian self-rule and found allies in the United States. Two world wars took their toll on the strength and resilience of the British Empire. The hold of the Raj was significantly weakened by the end of the Second World War, and the Labour Party came to power pledged to grant India its Independence. However, the British left and India divided: independent India and Pakistan.

Gandhi's teachings were still alive, even after his assassination in 1948, and in America it was spelled out most clearly in the words and actions of Dr Martin Luther King, Jr. He always made the link to Gandhi explicit and travelled to India to pay homage to Gandhi and also to see what was living in India of the Mahatma's work. Other Americans such as Cesar Chavez and John Lewis took up the Gandhian legacy as well, and even after the assassination of King. Many in India and abroad have been willing to wear the mantle of Gandhism, but what it actually meant and means to them has to be investigated.

With the departure of the British, the Americans rising to their powerful role worldwide, stepped in to make ties to both new nations. It was a difficult and triangular game. Although aid was given to both nations, the Republican administrations of Eisenhower and later Nixon favoured Muslim Pakistan, believing its talk of supporting America in the Cold War. However disingenuous these claims were, Americans usually swallowed them, and over more than half a century, with ups and downs, have given considerable military plus economic aid to Pakistan. Recently, this aid has been cut back drastically and American leaders have tried, yet again, to call Pakistan to account for explicit or implicit support of terrorist organizations on its frontier or even within its borders.

The ups and downs of relations between the United States and South Asian nations will likely continue. A rougher relationship with Pakistan and more cooperation with India are the order of the day now. But nation's leaders and priorities change over time. So though India and America are forging closer ties now, no one can know what the case will be a year, or two, or five, or ten years from now. The large and growing South Asian community in the United States has linked these two widely separated parts of the globe and that marks a new era. Nonetheless, separate national priorities will continue, and nuclear, trade and other issues are viewed differently. America and India have been moving closer as political, even military, cooperation. When economic issues arise that divide them, each will fight for its own priorities. This is not dissimilar from the United States and the United Kingdom, the United States and Germany, or the United States and Canada.

India rising, India moving, India becoming, China rising, thunder out of China, the titles keep tumbling out over the past two or three decades. And with good reason. Old troubled, sick, backward Asia has risen economically and is speaking ever loudly politically as well. China and India as well as smaller Asian nations have come more fully onto the world stage as challengers to—equals of?—the so-called 'advanced' nations. This has only burst into full view since the mid-1980s for China, perhaps the mid-1990s or later for India. What was called 'the American century', is over. America's assertion of itself as the world power with the collapse of the Soviet Union in the early 1990s was a moment in time. As we move onwards in the twenty-first century, new issues, new crises abound, from Covid-19, to climate catastrophes, to war in the Ukraine. India and China demonstrated their importance by global analysts probing their moves with respect to the war in Ukraine. When India's prime minister Modi pressed his view that this should not be an age for war—directly to Russia's President Putin—the world took note. However, on the UN resolutions condemning Russia's invasion, India has abstained. Russia is still quite important to India for weapons, and presently for cheap oil. On Ukraine, India wants to sit on the fence.

Through this period India has become much more important as a foreign partner as its economy has more fully awakened. In some respects it is an ally for the United States. In a 2022 visit to India, US Treasury Secretary Janet Yellen made it clear that the US wanted closer political and economic ties to India, and said, 'The United States is pursuing an approach called "friend-shoring" to diversify away from countries that present geopolitical and security risks to our supply chain. To do so, we are proactively deepening economic integration with trusted trading partners like India.'[1] A short generation ago, an American cabinet member advancing such views would have been thought ill-informed, even crazy. As Russia and China, at present are rivals of America, as well as potential, if not real, enemies, India has put forward a more friendly handshake. At the same time, Pakistan has become an exceedingly unreliable resource to fight terrorism. Pakistan cannot control terrorism within its own borders and its ISI may not be sure how to deal with the Taliban government in Kabul. The relationships between the United States and others have changed over time; they can change again.

The upsurge of the Indian economy since the early 1990s, if not slightly earlier, has vaulted India forward on the international stage. As has been described above, from the late eighteenth century onwards, India was almost throughout, a very minor economic player vis-à-vis the United States. Big, but backward—some trade, later some aid, but relatively insignificant. This has changed over time. With big technological developments, and with India vitally involved in them, the connections to America have grown apace. With the spread of outsourcing, which rapid advances in technology have allowed, Americans often hear an Indian-accented voice on the phone, pressing them to pay a bill, or make some purchase. At the same time, some Indian companies have become multinationals

---

[1] 'Yellen in India, Hopes Its Big Economy Can Limit Reliance on China and Russia', *NYT*, 12 November 2022.

and moved with alacrity into Western markets including the United States. Tata Consultancy Services, Wipro, Infosys are among them. This has marked a new era in economic relations between the more developed economies of the West and Asia over the past sixty years. India is now in the game.

In this new era for Indian entrepreneurs and players with technical expertise and business foresight, there are a few other issues about the two countries. One is increasing economic inequality taking place almost everywhere—a few making billions, while millions of the poor are left even further behind. Another issue is that of exclusivity and intolerance. Globalization in which players come from more diverse origins than ever, should foster inclusivity and tolerance. But there are signs of the opposites as well. I want to recall that three founders of modern India diverged on some issues. Mahatma Gandhi, Subhas Chandra Bose and Jawaharlal Nehru did agree that India should be inclusive and tolerant of diversity. Although this is a fitting lesson for India and for America, it will take serious education for Muslims in the two countries and in Europe to be accepted as equal citizens. And there are difficulties for Christians and Jews as well.

Surge of Immigrants Changes America

The surge of South Asians—not only from India, but from Pakistan and Bangladesh as well—into America over the past two generations has changed the connections between these nations remarkably. South Asians, a very small minority until the late 1960s and even a little later, are now an expanding, vital minority participating in almost every sphere of American life. They are entrepreneurs carrying weight in Silicon Valley; they are to be found on the airwaves and on every media channel, in almost every hospital, in public life, in the press, producing invaluable books on diverse subjects, and in every spelling bee. Advocates of meditation and yoga have spread these throughout America. Some notables of South Asian background have been delineated in the last part.

Another issue that the interchanges of the past few decades raise is: just who is an Indian, who identifies as an Asian-American or South Asian American, who is an American. With so many South Asians becoming American citizens and retaining familial links to India, they can travel back and forth and keep strong ties to their homeland of origin. As the exploration of many talented writers of South Asian backgrounds above has amply demonstrated, they retain ties, investigate connections, and build upon the societies they have left behind, while contributing to America and South Asian understanding of our new world in flux. New or improved methods of transportation and communication have facilitated these ties. One can fly straight through from New York to Mumbai or New Delhi; one can Skype with friends and relatives around the globe, or e-mail an intimate on the other side of the world at any moment of the day or night. You never have to be out of touch. With hundreds of millions of South Asians with cell, even smartphones, those in remote regions are not as far away as they once might have been. It is a changed world of connections.

Some become American citizens, some have Green Cards, and even these have different significance for each. How much does citizenship mean? One must pay taxes, and follow the laws of the land one lives in, but how powerful is the new tie? It varies greatly, with some strongly identifying as Americans, some others not so firmly. And as the rate of intermarriage between South Asians and other groups in America is rising, the fusing and mixing will be greater than ever as the years pass. This is yet another aspect of globalization and changing nations.

I am just making a simple, and I believe uncontroversial point: America has been built by people of many nations and thrives on the contributions of its recent immigrants. Our hospitals and scientific institutions would be in grave danger without our citizens and Green Card holders of Asian background. There have been lots of mixed marriages and harmonizing in post-war America, I think more than ever before in our history because our population draws on more diverse sources. Some of the South Asians in America have Euro-

American spouses and/or parents, though they may have a South Asian name like Amar Bose or Anita Desai. They may remain distinctive in certain respects and want to preserve cultural ties to their ancestral base, but many are now mainstream Americans.

By the second generation, the children of immigrants become Americans of descent from Italy or Russia or India, but they have become Americans just like those whose ancestors came on the 'Mayflower'. The idea of what is 'home', or one's 'homeland' may change over time with planting roots in America. Each new generation is likely to have looser connection to the place of family origin. But as several authors, including Anand Giridharadas, Amitava Kumar, Somini Sengupta and others, as explained above, have returned to India to explore their relation to those places of origin. One may have more than one place where one feels at home.

There are, of course, dissident voices saying only so-called Aryan white men are creators of culture and that Asians, Jews, Blacks and Hispanics have mongrelized, infected, degraded the population. This was said of the Irish and Italians in the nineteenth century. Most think these Aryan fanatics are a small fringe. They and others are opposed to the flow of immigrants, but the influx continues, and will continue. It brings diversity and vitality to America. Those from Asia, from Pakistan to Japan, now numbering more than 10 million, have been vital in the past two generations in making a richer, more diverse, more vibrant America. A talented Vietnamese refugee can win a Pulitzer Prize, as well as an immigrant from India. A nation built by immigrants, continues to be reinvented by new waves of people from other continents.

Closer to the present, the hostility against all Muslims was stoked by Presidential candidate, and, shortly, President Donald Trump. Building upon anti-Muslim sentiment after the terrorist acts in New York in 1993 and 2001, and elsewhere, he generalized about Muslims worldwide. He said all Muslims should be barred from entering the United States and attempted to put through a ban on entry of Muslims from a set of Muslim-majority countries.

Earlier, he had maintained that President Obama was born in Kenya, not the United States, and implied that he was a Muslim. A certain number of his followers, during the 2008 campaign had believed this, though the then Republican candidate John McCain had denied it. During the Trump campaign and subsequently, anti-Muslim sentiment was heated up. This distrust and antipathy to Muslims as well as against all immigrants has had impacts on the United States. The number of legal immigrants entering has dropped, the number of foreign students applying to American colleges and universities has gone down, and even steps to de-naturalize some citizens of their citizenship have been suggested. This is a different America from the one into which millions of Asians and others, some Muslim, flocked to from 1965 into this century. Thousands still press upon America's border with Mexico, and some thousands have been admitted from Afghanistan, and now the Ukraine, but resistance to large numbers being allowed entry has grown in recent years.

One theme of this book has been the slow growth of the South Asian community in the United States into the late 1960s, and then its extraordinary expansion. Like all Americans, I am the descendant of immigrants. All my grandparents were born in imperial Russia, then in the Russian Pale of Settlement where Jews were allowed to live. After the pogrom of Kishinev in 1903, twenty family members were helped to emigrate from Russia to Brooklyn, New York, in 1906, by one relative who earlier had started a successful lighting fixture business. They were among many Russian Jews who fled then.[2] The family included my mother and my favourite aunt, Regina Berman. In time, she spoke Russian, Polish, Yiddish, French, Spanish, Italian and some German. In time a high school French and Spanish teacher to thousands of New Yorkers in public high schools, she is remembered as a wonderful teacher. Although to those near to her, Regina Berman was an unusual and talented person, she was in fact one of millions of immigrants who made America through their

---

[2] Vital, People Apart, p. 509ff.

daily, ordinary, work. Her life reminds us that the US is a nation built by immigrants. In the last two generations into the present, South Asians have been among the resolute and talented makers of a US ever changing.

As I glance around at my doctors at Mount Sinai Hospital, I count two South Asian Americans, two Iranian Americans, a Korean American, and a Jewish American among their number. My podiatrist is a Chinese/African/South Asian/Portuguese American. The assistant to my heart doctor is from the Ukraine. I have a periodontist from South Asia, and a chiropractor of South Asian origin. The United States is and will remain a remarkable gathering of talented and hard-working people from around the world, immigrants and the children of immigrants. We are a nation of immigrants. Some came earlier, some later, but as President Franklin Roosevelt said, we are all immigrants or the descendants of immigrants. Some came from Asia in the nineteenth century, worked hard, and wanted to be full citizens, but they were abused and blocked. Their number by the early twentieth century included a few thousand from South Asia, more from China and Japan. There was not a significant change until after the passage of the 1965 immigration law revamping the quota system established in 1924. In the aftermath of the 1965 changes, the number of South Asians in the population grew from some thousands to more than four million over the next half century plus. Many from other parts of Asia as well as regions of Africa and Latin America called 'the third world' came as well. A more diverse America emerged from this swirling mix. It is, I think, more talented, more rich culturally, and more connected to the rest of the world. America is not simply Black and white, or these plus red and yellow, but embraces those of a great variety of hues who cannot be easily classified. Any rigid set of classifications will become ever harder to apply as intermarriages proceed apace, and will, eventually, I believe, be discarded. Some want to seal the borders, though they, too, are immigrants, or the children of immigrants. It is unlikely that these wall builders will be successful. Frontiers are too porous, the desire to come and work in America too powerful. This nation is, as it has long been, on the move. A good deal of the past has been terrible, some of it positive. This is likely the course of the future as well. Our children and grandchildren have the opportunity to make it as beneficial and successful for the human race as they can. It is up to them.

Acknowledgements

My friend Margaret King has done a yeoman job of helping me shorten and reorganize the manuscript. Arun Shourie brought the manuscript to the attention of Karthik Venkatesh at Penguin India, and he has zestfully and carefully taken the job of editing it. As the author, I am responsible for what remains.

Close friends and colleagues have supported my endeavours for many years including: Sugata Bose; Ananda Lal; Nina Rao; Sharon Lowen; Dennis Dalton; Rachel McDermott; Philip Oldenburg; David Lelyveld; Alan Rosling; Lauri Edelman; Clark Blaise and Sree Sreenivasan.

When a project has taken what seems like forever, there is a large list of family members and friends who have passed on. I have missed my parents and aunt Regina Berman for many years. Friends who were always supportive include P. Lal; Krishna and Sisir Bose; Nikhil Chakravartty; Jamini Roy; Bishnu Day; Satyajit Ray; Edward Dimock; Bernard Cohn; Bharati Mukherjee; Razi Wasti; Ainslie Embree; Suneet Chopra; M.K. and Sue Haldar; Ramesh Jain and Hari Dev Sharma.

I visited numerous missions, including hospitals, colleges and schools. I thank my gracious hosts at Isabella Thoburn College; Vellore Medical College and Hospital; Wanless Medical Centre, Miraj; FC College; Thoburn Memorial Church; Calcutta Boys School; American College, Madurai; Woodstock International School; Kodaikanal International School; the School of Tropical Medicine, Kolkata; Indian Institute of Management, Diamond Harbour; Tata Archives, Jamshedpur, and Tata Central Archives,

Pune; Kinnaird College; Literacy House, Kanpur; Indian Institute of Management, Kanpur and Ludhiana Christian Medical Centre.

The staff of the India Office Library and Records, at the British Library, London; the Bodleian Library, Oxford University; Nehru Memorial Museum and Library, New Delhi; the National Archives of India, New Delhi; the National Library of India, Kolkata; New York Public Library; Columbia University Library; Library of Congress, Washington, D.C.; Ford Foundation Archives; Rockefeller Foundation Archives; and the University of Chicago Library, were always helpful.

Over many years I have received support from the American Institute of Indian Studies, and the Research Foundation of the City University of New York; the late Pradeep R. Mehendiratta, the late Tarun Mitra and Subir Sarkar of the American Institute of Indian Studies, in particular, were helpful at every turn.

My wife has spied out films and articles about India with her usual keen eye, and been patient about a project that never seemed to end. My stepdaughter, April, her husband Steve Stackle, as well as their irrepressible and much-loved boys, Evan and Wyatt, have always been supportive of my work. My brother Jim has helped in innumerable ways.

Bibliography

Primary Sources
Government Archives and Government reports

National Archives, Government of India
Government of India, Home Department and External
Department, Files, 1905–1947.
National Archives of India, New Delhi.
Government of India, Information Department, India Office
Library, British Library, London.
Government of India, Indian Cinematograph Committee,
Evidence, 5 vols. 1928.
British Government: Public Record Office, Foreign Office files
Hindu Conspiracy Case, F.O. 371, 372

National Archives of the US
Hindu Conspiracy Trial, 1917; Record of Hindu Conspiracy
Case, 1917: US vs. Franz Bopp, et al, 75v, Criminal Docket
5852-6352, Case 6133, Record of Trial, District Court of US
for Southern Division of Northern District of California

United States Commission on Civil Rights, *Civil Rights Issues Facing
Asian Americans in the 1990s*. Report of February 1992.

Institutions and Organization Archives

American Board of Commissioners of Foreign Missions. Annual
Reports, from 1812.
Rockefeller Foundation (RFA)

Woman's American Baptist Foreign Mission Society 1919–29,
    Jubilee Fund, Rockefeller
Family Archives
Paul Russell Reports, 1934–41; W.S. Carter Survey of Medical
    Education
School of Hygiene and Public Health, Calcutta (1997); medical
    fellowships records
Population Council Annual Reports

Ford Foundation
    Grant files: CMPO; Council for Cultural Freedom
    Douglas Ensminger Oral History
    Annual Reports
    Gaither, Report of the Study for the Ford Foundation on Policy
        and Programs & 1949 Mission Statement
    Kathleen McCarthy, 'Population Programs,' 1986
    Pamphlets, 2002, review of India programs

Foreign Area Fellowship Program (now part of Social Science
    Research Council)
Nehru Memorial Museum & Library, New Delhi
    AICC Papers
    J.T. Sunderland Papers, NMLM, From U. of Michigan and U.
        of Chicago
    Jawaharlal Nehru Papers, NMLM
    B.K. Nehru Papers, NMLM
    J.J. Singh Papers, NMLM
    Vijaya Lakshmi Pandit Papers, NMLM
    Oral Histories:
    Alexander, Horace
    Bowles, Chester
    Chattopadhyay, Kamaladevi
    Dutt, Rajani Palme
    Gauba, K.L.
    Hardikar, N.S.
    Muzumdar, Haridas T.
    Sahgal, Nayantara
    Singh, J.J.

Sykes, Marjorie
Dartington Hall Records
   Leonard and Dorothy Elmhirst Papers, Dartington Hall, UK
Society of Friends, London
Friends of Vellore Medical College and Hospital, UK and USA.,
   India Office Library
Tata Central Archives, Pune
Tata Iron and Steel Company Archives, Jamshedpur

Private Papers

Frederick Bohn Fisher, Papers, Boston University
Welthy Fisher Papers, Boston University
Oswald Garrison Villard, Harvard
John R. Mott Papers, Yale Divinity School
Sherwood Eddy Papers, Yale Divinity School
William and Charlotte Wiser Papers, Yale Divinity School
Horace Alexander Papers, Friends House, London
Ida Scudder Papers, Radcliffe Library
Edward J. Thompson Papers, Bodleian Library, Oxford University
Prafulla Mukherji, author's collection

Interviews

Arise, Seiko, Tokyo, 4 August 1979
Alter, Tom, Mussoorie, February 1999
Ambler, John. New Delhi, 28 April 1995
Arnold, David. New Delhi, 1993.
Banerjee, Nirmala, Calcutta, 19 January 1995
Barkat, Anwar, F.C. College, Lahore, 1995
Beteille, Andre, New Delhi, anthropologist, 31 January 1995
Bhambri, F.C., New Delhi, 8 October 1993
Bissell, Bimala, New Delhi, 1 February1995
Bresnan, John, FF, New York, 2 February 1996
Brown, Miss Helen, Kanpur, 14 Jan 1997 Hudson Girls School
Chatterjee, Dr. P., Public Health Section, AISH & PH, 17 Jan 1997
Chen, Lincoln, NY, Rockefeller Foundation, 23 April 1997
Choudhury, Kamala, New Delhi, 11 January 1995
Chowdhury, Dr. Subir, IIM, Calcutta, 17 January 1997
Das, Somen, Calcutta, 6 August 1993

Datta, Abhijit, New Delhi, 14 January 1995
De, Barun, Calcutta, 21 January 1997
Foreman, Charles, New Haven
Geithner, Peter, FF, New York, 27 December 1994
Germain, Adrienne, FF, NY, 1997
Goheen, Robert, New York, 10 December 1998
Gupta, Partha S., New Delhi, 7 January 1995
Haldar, M.K., New Delhi, 1 June 1995
Jain, L.C., New Delhi, 1997, telephone
Lal, R.B., 1995, AAI
Lall, Arthur, New York, 12 Feb 1995
Lee, Karuna, Calcutta, 4 August 1993
Leventhal, Harold, NY, 1997
Mandal, S.C., Calcutta, 7 August 1993
Nandy, Ashish, 1995
Ojha, David, Allahabad, 27 January 1995
Phallbos, Meera, Lahore, 1995
Robinson, Margaret, Lahore, 1995
Roy, Pradipto, sociologist, AAI, 1995
Roy, S. K., Calcutta, 21 January 1997, Calcutta
Soknick, Stephen, New Delhi, 30 January 2009
Srinivasan, T. P., New York, 18 Sept 2018
Staples, Eugene, Washington, D.C., 8 August 1996
Sudarsan, Dr. 8 January 1997, New Delhi
Sutton, Francis X., Dobbs Ferry, NY, 27 December 1994; 5 August 1996
Thorner, Alice, New Delhi, 8 January 1995
Venkataraman, R., New Delhi, 8 October 1993
Ward, F. Champion, New Haven, CT

Site Visits

1. Colleges, schools, hospitals with American founders or significant aid

   Allahabad Agricultural Institute, Allahabad (1995)
   American College, Madurai (1999)
   Brown Medical College & Hospital, Ludhiana, February 2004

Calcutta Boys School, Baptists (1995)

F.C. College, Lahore (1995); nationalized, 1970s; back to church, 2004

Isabella Thoburn College, Lucknow (1997); Lucknow insane asylum

Kinnaird College, Lahore (1995)

Kodaikanal International School (1999)

Literacy House, Kanpur (1997)

Thoburn Memorial Church, Calcutta, (1995)

United Theological College Library, Bangalore, (1993)

Vellore Medical College (1993)

Wanless Medical College and Hospital, Miraj (January 2004)

Woodstock International School (1999)

2. US-aided institutions

Indian Institute of Management, Diamond Harbour, Calcutta, (1997)

Indian Institute of Technology, Kanpur (US AID) (1997)

School of Tropical Medicine, Calcutta, (2000, Rock F funds founded)

3. Other institutions and NGOs

Christian Medical Association, New Delhi (1993)

Union Theological College, Bangalore (1993)

Literacy House, Lucknow (1997)

Secondary Sources
Periodicals and Newspapers

Asia
Amerasia
The Birth Control Review
Brooklyn Daily Eagle
The Guardian
Harijan
India Today
India Abroad

The Modern Review
New Theater
New World Review
New York Post
Public Culture
The Journal of Asian Studies
Pacific Affairs
Diaspora
Young India, 1918–20
Calcutta Municipal Gazette. 1924–1939
Seminar. New Delhi. [#112, December 1968, 'Academic
    Colonialism']
Unity

Reference Works

Sen, S.P. ed. 1974. *Dictionary of National Biography.* 4v. Calcutta:
    Institute of Historical Studies.

Books and Articles

Abhedananda, Swami. 1970. *Epistles.* Calcutta: Ramakrishna
    Vedanta Math.
Abhedananda, Swami. 2007. *Leaves from My Diary.* Calcutta:
    Ramakrishna Vedanta Math.
Abhedananda, Swami. 1993. *The Works of Swami Abhedananda.* 2v.
    Calcutta: Ramakrishna Vedanta Math.
Acheson, Dean. 1969. *Present at the Creation. My Years in the State
    Department.* NY: Norton.
Adams, Henry. 1973. *The Education of Henry Adams.* Ed. Ernest
    Samuels. Boston: Houghton Mifflin.
Adams. John. 2011. *Revolutionary Writings 1755–1775.* Ed. Gordon
    Wood. NY: Library of America.
Adams, John Quincy. 2017. *Diaries 1779–1821.* NY: Library
    of America.
Ahlstrom, Sydney E. 1972. *A Religious History of the American People.*
    New Haven: Yale U. Press.

Ahmed, Akbar. 2010. *Journey into America. The Challenge of Islam.* Washington: Brookings Institution Press.

Ahmed, Syed Habib. 2001. *From South Asia to North America. An Autobiography 1915–2000.* Oxford: Oxford U. Press.

Akhtar, Ayad. 2012. *American Dervish.* NY: Back Bay Books.

Akhtar, Ayad. 2020. *Homeland Elegies.* NY: Little, Brown.

Alba, Richard and Victor Nee. 2003. *Remaking the American Mainstream. Assimilation and Contemporary Immigration.* Cambridge: Harvard U. Press.

Aldrich, Richard J. 2002. *The Hidden Hand. Britain, America, and Cold War Secret Intelligence.* NY; Overlook Press.

Aldrich, Richard J. 2000. *Intelligence and the War against Japan. Britain, America and the Politics of Secret Service.* Cambridge: Cambridge U. Press.

Alexander, Horace. 1969. *Gandhi through Western Eyes.* Philadelphia: New Society Publishers.

Alexander, Meena, ed. 2018. *Name Me a Word. Indian Writers Reflect on Writing.* New Haven: Yale U. Press.

Ali, Agha Shahid. 1991. *A Nostalgist's Map of America.* NY: Norton.

Ali, Chaudhri Muhammad. 1967. *The Emergence of Pakistan.* NY: Columbia U. Press.

Ali, Tariq. 1985. *The Nehrus and the Gandhis. An Indian Dynasty.* London: Picador.

Allahar, Anton L. and Linden F. Lewis. 2014. 'Situating Oliver Cromwell Cox'. *Canadian Journal of Latin American and Caribbean Studies.* V. 39, No.3. 339–344.

Allen, H.C. 1955. *Great Britain and the United States. A History of Anglo-American Relations (1783-1952).* NY: St. Martin's.

Allen, James Paul & Eugene James Turner. 1988. *We the People. An Atlas of America's Ethnic Diversity.* NY: Macmillan.

Alter, James P. Rev. by John Alter. 1986. *In the Doab and Rohilkhand. North Indian Christianity 1815-1915.* Delhi: P.S.P.C.K.

Alter, James P. and Herbert Jai Singh. 1961. *The Church in Delhi.* Lucknow: National Christian Council of India.

Alter, Stephen G. 2005. *William Dwight Whitney and the Science of Language.* Baltimore: Johns Hopkins U. Press.

Alter, Stephen. 1998. *All the Way to Heaven. An American Boyhood in the Himalayas.* NY: Henry Holt.

Anand, Mulk Raj. 1939. *Across the Black Waters.* Bombay: Kutub Popular.

Anand, Mulk Raj. 1935. *Untouchable.* Bombay: Kutub Popular.

Anderson, Rufus. 1874. *History of the Missions of the American Board of Commissioners of Foreign Missions.* Boston: Congregationalist Publication Society.

Andrew, Christopher. 2009. *Defend the Realm. The Authorized History of MI5.* NY: Vintage.

Andrew, Christopher. 1995. *For the President's Eyes Only. Secret Intelligence and the American Presidency from Washington to Bush.* NY: HarperPerennial.

Andrew, Christopher. 1986. *Secret Service. The Making the British Intelligence Community.* London: Sceptre.

Andrew, Christopher and Vasili Mitrokhin. *The World was Going Our Way. The KGB and the Battle for the Third World.* 2005. NY: Basic Books.

Anspprenger, Franz. 1989. *The Dissolution of the Colonial Empires.* London, Routledge.

Appadurai, Arjun. 1996. *Modernity at Large. Cultural Dimensions of Globalization.* Minneapolis: University of Minnesota Press.

Aristotle. 1941. *Politics,* in *The Basic Works of Aristotle,* ed. Richard McKeon. NY: Random House.

Armitage, David. 2000. *The Ideological Origins of the British Empire.* Cambridge: Cambridge U. Press.

Armitage, David and Sanjay Subrahmanyam, eds. 2010. *The Age of Revolutions in Global Context, c. 1760–1840.* NY: Palgrave Macmillan.

Arnold, Edwin. 1890. *The Light of Asia.* Boston: Roberts Brothers.

Arora, Ashish and Alfonso Gambardella, eds. 2005. *From Underdogs to Tigers. The Rise and Growth of the Software Industry in Brazil, China, India, Ireland, and Israel.* NY: Oxford U. Press.

Assayag, Jackie and Veronique Bénéïï, eds. 2003. *At Home in Diaspora. South Asian Scholars and the West.* New Delhi: Permanent Black.

Babb, Lawrence A. 1986. *Redemptive Encounters. Three Modern Styles in the Hindu Tradition.* Berkeley: U. of California Press.

Badley, B.H., Rev. 1886. *Indian Missionary Directory and Memorial Volume.* 3rd ed. Calcutta: Methodist Publishing House.

Bagchi, Amiya Kumar. 1972. *Private Investment in India 1900-1939.* Cambridge: Cambridge U. Press.

Bagchi, Amiya. 1982. *The Political Economy of Underdevelopment.* NY: Cambridge U. Press.

Bahadur, Gaiutra. 2014. *Coolie Woman.* Chicago: U. of Chicago Press.

Bahl, Vinay. 1995. *The Making of the Indian Working Class. The Case of the Tata Iron and Steel Co., 1880–1946.* New Delhi: Sage.

Bailyn, Bernard. 1988. *Voyagers to the West.* NY: Vintage.

Baillyn, Bernard. 2017. *The Ideological Origins of the American Revolution.* Cambridge: Harvard U. Press.

Baker, Deborah. 2008. *A Blue Hand. The Beats in India.* NY: Penguin.

Baker, Deborah. 2018. *The Last Englishmen. Love, War, and the End of Empire.* Minneapolis: Greywolf Press.

Balachandran, G., ed. 2003. *India and the World Economy 1850-1950.* New Delhi: Oxford U. Press.

Bald, Vivek. 2013. *Bengali Harlem and the Lost Histories of South Asian America.* Cambridge: Harvard U. Press.

Bald, Vivek, Miabi Chatterji, Sujani Reddy, Manu Vimalassery, eds. 2013. *The Sun Never Sets.* NY: NYU Press.

Baltzell, E. Digby. 1964. *The Protestant Establishment. Aristocracy and Caste in America.* NY: Vintage.

Banerjee, Arun Kumar. 1978. *India and Britain, 1947–68.* Calcutta: Minerva.

Banerji, Debaban. 1985. *Health and Family Planning Services in India.* Delhi: Lok Paksh.

Barnds, William J. 1972. *India, Pakistan, and the Great Powers.* NY: Praeger.

Barrett, Robert N. 1890. *The Child of the Ganges. A Tale of the Judson Mission.* NY: F. Revell.

Barrows, John Henry. Ed. 1893. *The World's Parliament of Religions. The Columbian Exposition of 1893.* 2v. Chicago: Parliament Publishing.

Bass, Gary J. 2013. *The Blood Telegram. Nixon, Kissinger, and a Forgotten Genocide.* NY: Vintage.

Bass, Gary J. 2002. *Stay the Hand of Vengeance. The Politics of War Crimes Tribunals*. Princeton: Princeton University Press.

Basu, Kaushik. Ed. 2004. *India's Emerging Economy. Performance and Prospects in the 1990s and Beyond*. New Delhi: Oxford U. Press.

Basu, Shrabani. 2016. *For King and Another Country*. Delhi: Bloomsbury India.

Basu, Shrabani. 2007. *Spy Princess. The Life of Noor Inayat Khan*. New Lebanon, NY: Omega. Bayly, C.A. 2004. *The Birth of the Modern World 1780–1914*. Oxford: Blackwell.

Bayly, C.A. 1999. *Empire and Information. Intelligence Gathering and Social Communication in India, 1780–1870*. Cambridge: Cambridge U. Press.

Bayly, C.A. 1989. *Imperial Meridian. The British Empire and the World 1780–1830*. NY: Longman.

Bayly, C.A. 2012. *Recovering Liberties. Indian Thought in the Age of Liberalism and Empire*. Cambridge: Cambridge U. Press.

Bayly, C.A. 2018. *Remaking the Modern World 1900-2015*. Hoboken, N.J.: Wiley Blackwell.

Bayly, Christopher and Tim Harper. 2005. *Forgotten Armies. The Fall of British Asia, 1941–1945*. Cambridge: Belknap Press.

Bayly, Christopher and Tim Harper. 2007. *Forgotten Wars. The End of Britain's Asian Empire*. London: Allen Lane.

Bayly, Susan. 1989. *Saints Goddesses and Kings. Muslims and Christians in South Indian Society, 1700–1900*. Cambridge: Cambridge U. Press.

Beale, Howard K. 1962. *Theodore Roosevelt and the Rise of America to World Power*. NY: Collier.

Bean, Susan S. 2001. *Yankee India. American Commercial and Cultural Encounters with India in the Age of Sail 1784–1860*. Salem, MA: Peabody Essex Museum.

Bedford, Sybille. 1974. *Aldous Huxley. A Biography*. Chicago: Ivan R. Dee.

Beisner, Robert L. 1968. *Twelve against Empire. The Anti-Imperialists 1898–1900*. NY: McGraw-Hill.

Bender, Thomas. 2006. *A Nation among Nations. America's Place in World History*. NY: Hill and Wang.

Bennett, Scott H. 2003. *Radical Pacifism. The War Resisters League and Gandhian Nonviolence in America, 1915–1963*. Syracuse: Syracuse U. Press.

Benson, Herbert. 1975. *The Relaxation Response*. NY: Avon.

Berg, A. Scott, ed. 2017. *World War I and America*. NY: Library of America.

Bernier, Francois. 1914. *Travels in the Mogul Empire A.D. 1656–1668*. London: Oxford U. Press.

Berry, Wendell. 2019. *Essays 1993–2017*. NY: Library of America.

Beydoun, Khaled A. 2018. *American Islamophobia*. Oakland: U. of California Press.

Bhagat, G. 1970. *Americans in India 1784–1860*. NY: NYU Press.

Bhagavan, Manu. 2013. *The Peacemakers: India and the Quest for One World*. NY: Palgrave Macmillan.

Bhagwan Shree Rajneesh. 1988. *The Greatest Challenge: The Golden Future*. Cologne, Germany: Rebel Publishing.

Bharara, Preet. 2019. *Doing Justice*. NY: Knopf.

Bhardhwaj, Atul. 2019. *India-America Relations (1942–62)*. London: Routledge.

Bhat, Harish. 2012. *Tata Log*. Gurgaon: Penguin.

Bhattacharya, Piyali, ed. 2016. *Good Girls Marry Doctors*. San Francisco: Aunt Lute Books.

Bhutto, Benazir. 2008. *Reconciliation. Islam, Democracy, and the West*. NY: Harper.

Bird, Kai. 1992. *The Chairman. John J. McCloy, The Making of the American Establishment*. New York: Simon & Schuster.

Bird, Kai. 2000. *The Color of Truth. McGeorge Bundy and William Bundy: Brothers in Arms*. NY: Touchstone.

Blackwill Robert D. and Ashley J. Tellis, Sept-Oct. 2019. 'The India Dividend', *Foreign Affairs*. 173–83.

Blaise, Clark, and Bharati Mukherjee. 1988. *The Sorrow and the Terror*. NY: Penguin.

Bondurant, Joan V. 1965. *The Conquest of Violence*. Berkeley: University of California Press.

Boquérat, Gilles. 2003. *No Strings Attached? India's Policies and Foreign Aid 1947–1966*. New Delhi: Manohar.

Borg, Dorothy and Shumpei Okamoto, eds. 1973. *Pearl Harbor as History, Japanese-American Relations 1931–1941*. NY: Columbia U. Press.

Borstelmann, Thomas. 2001. *The Cold War and the Color Line*. Cambridge: Harvard U. Press.

Bose, A.C. 1971. *Indian Revolutionaries Abroad*. Patna: Bharati Bhawan.

Bose, Nemai Sadhan. 1974. *Ramananda Chatterjee*. New Delhi: Government of India, 1974.

Bose, Sudhindra. 1920. *Fifteen Years in America*. Calcutta: Kar, Majumdar.

Bose, Sudhindra. 1925. *Glimpses of America*. Calcutta.

Bose, Sudhindra. 1934. *Mother America. Realities of American Life as Seen by an Indian*. Baroda: M.S. Bhatt.

Bose, Sugata. ed. 1990. *South Asia and World Capitalism*. Delhi: Oxford U. Press.

Bose, Sugata. 2006. *A Hundred Horizons. The Indian Ocean in the Age of Global Empire*. Cambridge: Harvard U. Press.

Bose, Sugata and Ayesha Jalal. 2004. *Modern South Asia*. NY: Routledge. 2nd ed.

Bourke-White, Margaret. 1950. *Interview with India*. London: Phoenix House.

Bourke-White, Margaret. 1963. *Portrait of Myself*. NY: Simon and Schuster.

Bowers, John Z. 1972. *Western Medicine in a Chinese Palace*. Peking Union Medical College, 1917–1951. Philadelphia: Josiah Macy, Jr. Foundation.

Bowles, Chester. 1955. *Ambassador's Report*. London: Victor Gollancz.

Bowles, Chester. 1971. *Promises to Keep. My Years in Public Life 1941–1969*. NY: Harper & Row.

Bowles, Cynthia. 1956. *At Home in India*. NY: Harcourt, Brace.

Boyd, Doug. 1976. *Swami*. NY: Random House.

Boyd, Nancy. 1986. *Emissaries. The Overseas Work of the American YWCA 1895–1970*. NY: Woman's Press.

Brady, Joan. 2017. *Alger Hiss: Framed*. NY: Arcade.

Braggiotti, Mary. 1 August 1944. 'Close-Up of Kumar Goshal', *New York Post*.

Branch, Taylor. 1988. *The Parting of the Waters. America in the King Years 1954–63*. NY: Simon and Schuster.

Brands, H.W. 1990. *India and the United States. The Cold Peace*. Boston: Twayne.

Braudel, Fernand. 1979. *The Perspective of the World*. NY: Harper and Row.

Brecher, Michael. 1968. *India and World Politics. Krishna Menon's View of the World*. NY: Praeger.

Brecher, Michael. 1959. *Nehru*. A Political Biography. London: Oxford U. Press.

Bremner, Robert. 1988. *American Philanthropy*. Chicago: U. of Chicago Press. 2nd ed.

Brent, Peter. 1972. *Godmen of India*. NY: Quandrangle.

Brittain, Vera. 1965. *Envoy Extraordinary. A Study of Vijaya Lakshmi Pandit and Her Contribution to Modern India*. London: George Allen & Unwin.

Brock, Peter. 1968. *Pacifism in the United States: From the Colonial Era to the First World War*. Princeton: Princeton U. Press.

Brodkin, Karen. 1994. *How Jews Became White Folks and What that Says about Race in America*. New Brunswick: Rutgers U. Press.

Bromfield, Louis. 1937. *The Rains Came*. NY: Harper.

Brown, Arthur Judson. 1936. *One Hundred Years. A History of the Foreign Missionary Work of the Presbyterian Church in the USA, with Some Account of Countries, Peoples and the Policies and Problems of Modern Missions*. NY: Fleming H. Revell Co.

Brown, Dorris D. 1971. *Agricultural Development in India's Districts*. Cambridge: Harvard U. Press.

Brown, Emily C. 1975. *Har Dayal. Hindu Revolutionary and Rationalist*. Tucson: U. of Arizona Press.

Brown, Michael Barratt. 1963. *After Imperialism*. London: Heinemann.

Brown, Rebecca M. 2009. *Art for a Modern India, 1947–1980*. Durham: Duke U. Press.

Bryan,William Jennings. 1913. 'British Rule in India', reprint of July 20, 1906 article in 'India' as a pamphlet by the British Committee of the Indian National Congress.

Buchannan, D.H. 1966. *The Development of Capitalistic Enterprise in India*. London: Frank Cass.

Bullock, Mary Brown. 1980. *An American Transplant: The Rockefeller Foundation and Peking Union Medical College*. Berkeley: U. of California Press.

Burke, Marie Louise. 1966. *Swami Vivekananda in America New Discoveries*. Calcutta: Advaita Ashrama, rev. ed.

Burns, James MacGregor. 1970. *Roosevelt, Soldier of Freedom*. NY: Harcourt Brace Jovanovich.

Burns, James MacGregor. 1985. *The Workshop of Democracy*. NY: Knopf.

Burton, Antoinette. 1998. *At the Heart of Empire*. Berkeley: U. of California Press.

Burton, Antoinette. 2007. *The Postcolonial Careers of Santha Rama Rau*. Durham: Duke U. Press.

Butler, Clementina. 1922. *Pandita Ramabai Sarasvati*. NY: F. Revell.

Butler, Jon.1990. *Awash in a Sea of Faith: Christianizing the American People*. Cambridge: Harvard U. Press.

Butler, William. 1885. *From Boston to Bareilly and Back*.

Butow, Richard. 1961. *Tojo and the Coming of the War*. Princeton: Princeton U. Press.

Butow, Richard. 1954. *Japan's Decision to Surrender*. Stanford: Stanford U. Press.

Buttinger, Joseph. 1968. *Vietnam: A Political History*. NY: Praeger.

Byres, Terence J. ed. 1998. *The Indian Economy. Major Debates since Independence*. New Delhi: Oxford U. Press.

'The Calcutta Key', 1945. Information and Education Branch United States Army Forces in India-Burma.

Caldwell, Jon and Pat Caldwell. 1986. *Limiting Population Growth and the Ford Foundation Contribution*. London: Frances Pinter.

Campbell, Joseph. 1949. *Hero with a Thousand Faces*. NY: Pantheon.

Canny, Nicholas, ed. 1998. *The Origins of Empire. The Oxford History of the British Empire*. NY: Oxford U. Press.

Carnegie, Andrew. 1884. *Round the World*. NY: Doubleday.

Carp, Benjamin L. 2011. *Defiance of the Patriots*. New Haven: Yale U. Press.

Carson, Claybourne, ed. 1998. *The Autobiography of Martin Luther King*. NY: Warner Books.

Carson, Claybourne, ed. 2005. *The Papers of Martin Luther King, Jr.* Vol. V, January 1959–December 1960. Berkeley: U. of California Press.

Caute, David. 1979. *The Great Fear. The Anti-Commuist Purge under Truman and Eisenhower*. NY: Touchstone.

Chagla, M.C. 1990. *Roses in December. An Autobiography*. Bombay: Bharatiya Vidya Bhavan.

Chakrabarty, Bidyut. 2013. *Confluence of Thought. Mahatma Gandhi and Martin Luther King, Jr.* NY: Oxford U. Press.

Chakrabarty, Dipesh. 1989. *Rethinking Working-Class History. Bengal 1890–1940*. Princeton: Princeton U. Press.

Chakravarty, Subash. 1991. *The Raj Syndrome*. New Delhi: Penguin.

Chakravarty, Subhash, convener. 1968. 'US Facts Speak about Aid & Education'. Delhi: Front against US-Imperialist Penetration.

Chakravorty, Sanjoy, Devesh Kapur, Nirvikar Singh. 2019. *The Other One Percent: Indians in America (Modern South Asia)*. NY: Oxford U. Press.

Chalou, George C., ed. 1992. *The Secrets War. The Office of Strategic Services in World War II*. Washington: National Archives and Records Administration.

Chan, Sucheng. 1991. *Asian Americans*. Boston: Twayne.

Chand, Feroz. 1978. *Lajpat Rai. Life and Work*. New Delhi: Publications Division, Government of India.

Chandra, Vikram. 2014. *Geek Sublime*. Minneapolis: Graywolf.

Chandra, Vikram. 1997. *Love and Longing in Bombay*. Stories. Boston: Little, Brown.

Chandra, Vikram. 1995. *Red Earth and Pouring Rain*. London: Faber and Faber.

Chandra, Vikram. 2006. *Sacred Games*. New Delhi: Penguin.

Chandrasekaran, Rajiv. 2006. *Imperial Life in the Emerald City*. Inside Iraq's Green Zone. NY: Vintage.

Chandrasekhar, S. 1965. *American Aid and India's Economic Development*. NY: Praeger.

Chandrasekhar, S., ed. 1984. *From India to America. A Brief History of Immigration*. La Jolla, California, Population Review Books.

Chandy, Jacob. 1988. *Reminiscences and Reflections*. Kottayam: C.M.S. Press.

Chappell, Jennie. 1938. *Pandita Ramabai*. London: Pickering and Inglis.

Chatfield, Charles. 1976. *The Americanization of Gandhi*. Images of the Mahatma. N.Y: Garland Publishing.

Chatterjee, Meera. 1988. *Implementing Health Policy*. New Delhi: Manohar.

Chatterjee, Margaret. 1983. *Gandhi's Religious Thought*. London: Macmillan.

Chatterjee, Saral Kumar. 1984. *Bipin Chandra Pal*. New Delhi: Publications Division, Government of India.

Chatterji, Basudev. 1992. *Trade, Tariffs and Empire*. Lancashire and British Policy in India 1919–1939. Delhi: Oxford U. Press.

Chattopadhyay, Kamaladevi. 1946. *America the Land of Superlatives*. Bombay, Phoenix.

Chattopadhyay, Kamaladevi. 1986. *Inner Recess, Outer Spaces. Memoirs*. New Delhi: Navrang.

Chaturvedi, Benarsidas and Marjorie Sykes. 1971. *Charles Freer Andrews*. New Delhi: Publications Division, Government of India, 1971.

Chaudhri, Sandhya. 1984. *Gandhi and the Partition of India*. New Delhi: Sterling.

Chaudhuri, Asim. 2000. *Swami Vivekananda in Chicago*. Calcutta: Advaita Ashrama.

Chaudhuri, K.N. 1982. 'Foreign Trade and Balance of Payments,' in Kumar, Dharma Kumar, ed. *The Cambridge Economic History of India*. Vol. 2: c. 1757–1970. Cambridge.

Chaudhuri, Nirad C. 1974. *Scholar Extraordinary. The Life of Professor Friedrich Max Müller*. London: Chatto & Windus.

Chesler, Ellen. 1993. *Woman of Valor. Margaret Sanger and the Birth Control Movement in America*. NY: Anchor Books Doubleday.

Chhabra, Aseem. 2018. *Priyanka Chopra*. New Delhi: Rupa.

Chithelen, Ignatius. 2018. *Passage from India to America*. NY: Bryant Park.

Chomsky, Noam. 2008. *The Essential Chomsky*. Ed. Anthony Arnove. NY: New Press.

Chopra, Deepak. 1998. *Ageless Body, Timeless Mind*. NY: Three Rivers Press, 1998.

Chopra, Deepak. 2015. *Quantum Healing. Exploring the Frontiers of Mind/Body Medicine*. NY: Bantam.

Chopra, Deepak. 1991. *Return of the Rishi*. Boston: Houghton Mifflin.

Chopra, Deepak. 1994. *The Seven Spiritual Laws of Success*. San Rafael, CA: Amber-Allen.

Chopra, Deepak and Sanjiv. 2013. *Brotherhood. Dharma, Destiny, and the American Dream*. NY: New Harvest.

Chopra, Sanjiv and Alan Lotvin. 2010. *Live Better, Live Longer*. NY: St. Martin's.

Chopra, V.D. 1985. *Pentagon Shadow over India*. New Delhi: Patriot Publishers.

Chouhan, T.R. and others. 1994. *Bhopal: the Inside Story*. NY: Apex Press.

Christian Medical Association of India, Handbook of. 1932. *The Ministry of Healing in India*. Mysore: Wesleyan Mission Press.

Churchill, Winston. 1968. *Churchill: Four Faces and the Man*. Baltimore: Penguin.

Churchill, Winston. 1953. *The Second World War*. 6v. Cambridge: Houghton Mifflin.

Clymer, Kenton J. 1995. *Quest for Freedom. The United States and India's Independence*. NY: Columbia U. Press.

Cohen, Warren. 1978. *The Chinese Connection*. NY: Columbia U. Press.

Cohen, Warren. 1971. *America's Response to China*. NY: John Wiley.

Coleman, Peter. 1989. *The Liberal Conspiracy. The Congress for Cultural Freedom and the Struggle for the Mind of Postwar Europe*. New York: The Free Press.

Coll, Steve. 2018. *Directorate S*. NY: Penguin.

Coll, Steve. 2004. *Ghost Wars*. NY: Penguin.

Collet, Sophia Dobson. 1962. *The Life and Letters of Raja Rammohun Roy*. 3rd ed. Calcutta: Sadharan Brahmo Samaj.

Colley, Linda. 2006. *Britons. Forging the Nation 1707–1837*. London: Vintage.

Collier, Peter and David Horowitz. 1976. *The Rockefellers. An American Dynasty*. NY: Holt, Rinehart and Winston.

Collins, Larry and Dominique Lapierre. 1975. *Freedom at Midnight*. NY: Simon and Schuster.

Collins, Larry and Dominique Lapierre, eds. 1985. *Mountbatten and Independent India*. Delhi: Vikas.

Collins, Larry and Dominique Lapierre, eds. 1983. *Mountbattan and the Partition of India*. Delhi: Vikas.

Commager, Henry Steele and Richard B. Morris,eds. 1958. *The Spirit of 'Seventy-Six*. NY: Harper and Row.

Conn, Peter. 1996. *Pearl S. Buck. A Cultural Biography*. Cambridge: Cambridge U. Press.

Connelly, Matthew. 2008. *Fatal Misconception. The Struggle to Control World Population*.
Cambridge: Harvard U. Press.

Cook, Blanche Wiesen. 2016. *Eleanor Roosevelt*. V.3. NY: Viking.

Cook, Gareth. August 2019. 'Raj Chetty's American Dream,' *The Atlantic*.

Coomaraswamy, Ananda K. 1957. *The Dance of Shiva*. Revised ed. NY: Noonday.

Coomaraswamy, Ananda K. 1956. *The Transformation of Nature in Art*. NY: Dover.

Cooney, Robert and Helen Michalowski, eds. 1977. *The Power of the People. Active Nonviolence in the United States*. Culver City, CA: Peace Press.

Cooper, Diana. 1985. *Autobiography*. NY: Carroll and Graf.

Corbett, Jim. 1946. *The Man Eaters of Kumaon*. NY: Oxford University Press.

Corbridge, Stuart and John Harriss. 2000. *Reinventing India*. Oxford: Polity, Blackwell's.

Corrigan, John and Winthrop Hudson. 2018. *Religion in America*. NY: Routledge.

Cortright, David. 2006. *Gandhi and Beyond. Nonviolence for an Age of Terrorism*. Boulder: Paradigm.

Cottrell, Robert. 2001. *Roger Nash Baldwin and the ACLU*. Berkeley: U. of California Press.

Cox, Harvey. 1977. *Turning East*. NY: Touchstone.

Cox, Jeffrey. 1992. *Imperial Fault Lines. Christianity and Colonial Power in India, 1818–1940*. Stanford: Stanford U. Press.

Cox, Oliver Cromwell. 1948. *Caste, Class, and Race. A Study in Social Dynamics*. Garden City, NY: Doubleday.

Crabtree, James. 2018. *The Billionaire Raj*. NY: Tim Duggan Books.

Christy, Arthur. 1978. *The Orient in American Transcendentalism*. NY: Octagon.

Cueto, Marcos, ed. 1994. *Missionaries of Science. The Rockefeller Foundation and Latin America*. Bloomington: Indiana U. Press.

Cuninggim, Merrimon. 1972. *Private Money and Public Service*. NY: McGraw Hill.

Curle, Adam. 1966. *Planning for Education in Pakistan*. Cambridge, MA: Harvard U. Press.

Curti, Merle and Roderick Nash. 1965. *Philanthropy in the Shaping of American Higher Education*. New Burnswick: Rutgers U. Press.

Curti, Merle. 1987. *American Philanthropy Abroad*. New Brunswick: Transaction.

Dadashi, Hamid. 2011. *Brown Skin, White Masks*. NY: Pluto Press.

Dalal, Ardeshir. 1980. *A Memoir*. Bombay: The Dalal Family.

Dallek, Robert. 1981. *Franklin D. Roosevelt and American Foreign Policy, 1932–1945*. NY: Oxford U. Press.

Dalton, Dennis. 1993. *Mahatma Gandhi. Nonviolent Power in Action*. NY: Columbia U. Press.

Dalvi, J.P. no date. *Himalayan Blunder*. Delhi: Orient.

Damodaran, Harish. 2008. *India's New Capitalists*. Ranikhet: Permanent Black.

Dana, Richard Henry, Jr. 2005. *Two Years before the Mast and Other Voyages*. NY: Library of America.

Daniels, Roger. 1989. *History of Indian Immigration to the United States*. NY: The Asia Society.

Dart, Martha. 1993. *Marjorie Sykes*. Quaker-Gandhian. York: Sessions Book Trust.

Das, Manmath Nath. 1982. *Partition and Independence of India*. New Delhi: Vision Books.

Das, Sisir Kumar. 1974. *The Shadow of the Cross. Christianity and Hinduism in a Colonial Situation*. Delhi: Munshiram Manoharlal.

Das Gupta, Ashin. 2001. *The World of the Indian Ocean Merchant 1500–1800: Collected Essays of Ashin Das Gupta*. New Delhi: Oxford U. Press.

Das Gupta, Uma, ed. 2003. *A Difficult Friendship. Letters of Edward Thompson and Rabindranath Tagore 1913–1940*. New Delhi: Oxford U. Press.

Dass, Ishuree. 1851. *A Brief Account of a Voyage to England and America*. Allahabad: Presbyterian Mission Press.

David, Immanuel. 1986. *Reformed Church in America Missionaries in South India, 1839–1938*. Bangalore: Phoenix.

Davies, John Paton, Jr. 2012. *China Hand. An Autobiography*. Philadelphia: U. of Pennsylvania Press.

Davis, Allison, Burleigh B. Gardner, and Mary R. Gardner. 1941. *Deep South. A Social Anthropological Study of Caste and Class*. Chicago: U. of Chicago Press.

Deb, Sandipan. 2004. *The IITians*. New Delhi: Penguin Books India.

Deb, Siddhartha. 2011. *The Beautiful and the Damned. A Portrait of the New India*. NY: Faber and Faber.

Deb, Siddhartha. 2023. *The Light at the End of the World*. NY: Soho Press.

Deb, Siddhartha. 2002. *The Point of No Return*. NY: Ecco.

Deb, Sopan. 2020. *Missed Translations. Meeting the Immigrant Parents Who Raised Me*. NY: Dey Street.

Dellinger, Dave. 1971. *Revolutionary Nonviolence*. Garden City, NY: Anchor, 1971.

Dellinger, Dave. 1993. *From Yale to Jail. The Life Story of a Moral Dissenter*. NY: Pantheon.

D'Emilio, John. 2003. *Lost Prophet. The Life and Times of Bayard Rustin*. Chicago: U. of Chicago Press.

Dennett, Tyler, 1922. *Americans in Eastern Asia*. NY: Macmillan.

Deol, G.S. 1969. *The Role of the Ghadar Party in the National Movement*. Delhi: Sterling.

Desai, Kiran. 1998. *Hullabaloo in the Guava Orchard*. London: Faber and Faber.

Desai, Kiran. 2006. *The Inheritance of Loss*. NY: Atlantic Monthly Press.

Dey, S.K. 1969. *Power to the People*. Delhi: Orient Longmans.

Dhingra, Pawan, 2016. 'Indian Americans and the 'Brain Sport' of Spelling Bees,' in Stanley I. Thangaraj, Constancio R. Arnaldo, Jr., and Christina B. Chin. *Asian American Sporting Cultures*. NY: NYU Press.

Dhingra, Pawan. 2007. *Managing Multicultural Lives. Asian American Professionals and the Challenge of Multiple Identities*. Stanford: Stanford U. Press.

Dhume, Sadanand. 2002. 'From Bangalore to Silicon Valley and Back: How the Indian Diaspora in the US is Changing India', in *India Briefing*, ed. Alyssa Ayres and Philip Oldenburg. Armonk, NY: M.E. Sharpe & the Asia Society.

Dignan, Don. 1983. *The Indian Revolutionary Problem in British Diplomacy 1914–1919*. New Delhi: Allied.

Divakaruni, Chitra Banerjee. 2019. *The Forest of Enchantments*. Noida: HarperCollins.

Divakaruni, Chitra Banerjee. 1997. *Leaving Yuba City*. NY: Anchor Books.

Divakaruni, Chitra Banerjee. 2009. *The Palace of Illusions*. London: Picador.

Dixie, Quinton H. and Peter Eisenstadt. 2011. *Visions of a Better World. Howard Thurman's Pilgrimage to India and the Origins of African American Nonviolence*. Boston: Beacon.

Dixit, J.N. 2003. *India's Foreign Policy 1947–2003*. New Delhi: Picus.

Doke, Joseph J. 1967. *M.K. Gandhi, An Indian Patriot*. Delhi: PDMIB.

Dollard, John. 1937. *Caste and Class in a Southern Town*. New Haven: Yale U. Press.

Doniger, Wendy. 2009. *The Hindus. An Alternative History*. NY: Penguin.

Dossani, Rafiq. 2008. *India Arriving. How this Economic Powerhouse is Redefining Global Business*. NY: Amacom.

Dower, John W. 1986. *War Without Mercy*. NY: Pantheon.

Down, Goldie. 1959. *Missionary to Calcutta*. Washington: Review and Herald.

Downton, James V., Jr. 1979. *Sacred Journeys. The Conversion of Young Americans to Divine Light Mission*. NY: Columbia U. Press.

Dreiser, Theodore. 2018. *The Stoic*. NY: Rosetta Books.

Drèze, Jean and Amartya Sen. 2013. *An Uncertain Glory. India and Its Contradictions*. Princeton: Princeton U. Press.

D'Souza, Dinesh. 1995. *The End of Racism*. NY: Free Press.

D'Souza, Dinesh. 1991. *Illiberal Education*. NY: Vintage.

Duberman, Martin Bauml. 1989. *Paul Robeson*. A Biography. NY: Ballantine.

Du Bois, W.E.B. 1986. *Writings*. NY: Library of America.

Dulles, John W. 1855. *Life in India*. Philadelphia: American Sunday-School Union.

Dunbar-Ortiz, Roxanne. 2014. *An Indigenous Peoples' History of the United States*. Boston: Beacon Press.

Durant, Will. 1930. *The Case for India*. NY: Simon and Schuster.

Dutta, Krishna and Andrew Robinson. 1995. *Rabindranath Tagore. The Myriad-Minded Man*. London: Bloomsbury.

Dutta, Krishna and Andrew Robinson, eds. 1997. *Selected Letters of Rabindranath Tagore*. Cambridge: Cambridge U. Press.

Dyer, Helen S. 1900. *Pandita Ramabai*. NY: Fleming H. Revell. London: Pickering and Inglis.

Dyer, Thomas G. 1992. *Theodore Roosevelt and the Idea of Race*. Baton Rouge: Louisiana State U. Press.

Eck, Diana L. 2001. *A New Religious America. How a 'Christian Country: Has Become the World's Most Religously Diverse Nation*. NY: HarperCollins.

Eddy, Sherwood. 1955. *Eighty Adventurous Years. An Autobiography*. NY: Harper, 1955.

Edwardes, Thomas. 1880. 'Christian Effort in India', *Calcutta Review*.

Elder, Joseph W., Edward C. Dimock, Jr., Ainslie T. Embree, eds. 1998. *India's Worlds and US Scholars 1947–1997*. New Delhi: Manohar.

Elder, Joseph W. and Maureen L.P. Patterson. 1998. *History of the American Institute of Indian Studies*. Printed Manuscript, Madison: University of Wisconsin.

Elkins, Caroline. 2022. *Legacy of Violence. A History of the British Empire*. NY: Alfred A. Knopf.

Ellis, Markman, Richard Coulton, Matthew Maugger. 2016. *Empire of Tea*. New Delhi: Speaking Tiger.

Elmhirst, Leonard K. 1975. *The Straight and Its Origin*. Ithaca: Cornell U. Alumni Association.

Embree, Ainslie T. 1962. *Charles Grant and British Rule in India*. NY: Columbia U. Press.

Emerson, Gertrude. 1930. *Voiceless India*. Garden City: Doubleday.

Emerson, Ralph Waldo. 1983. *Essays & Lectures*. NY: Library of America.

Emerson. Ralph Waldo. 2010. *Selected Journals 1841–1877*. Ed. Lawrence Rosenwald. NY: Library of America.

Engerman, David C. 2018. *The Price of Aid: The Economic Cold War in India*. Cambridge: Harvard U. Press.

Ensminger, Douglas. 1972. *Rural India in Transition*. New Delhi: All-India Panchayat Parishad.

Erikson, Erik H. 1969. *Gandhi's Truth. On the Origins of Militant Nonviolence*. NY: Norton.

Everest, Larry. 1995. *Behind the Poison Cloud. Union Carbide's Bhopal Massacre*. Chicago: Banner Press.

Fair, C. Christine. 2014. *Fighting to the End: The Pakistan Army's Way of War*. NY: Oxford U. Press.

Farmer, James. 1985. *Lay Bare the Heart: An Autobiography of the Civil Rights Movement*. NY: Plume.

Fast, Howard. 1998. *The Pledge*. NY: Dell.

Fee, Elizabeth. 1987. *Disease and Discovery. A History of the Johns Hopkins School of Hygiene and Public Health 1916–1939*. Baltimore: Johns Hopkins U. Press, 1987.

Fernandes, Naresh. 2016. *Taj Mahal Foxtrot. The Story of Bombay's Jazz Age*. New Delhi: Roli.

Fernández-Armesto, Felipe. 2006. *Pathfinders. A Global History of Exploration*. NY: Norton.

Fichter, James R. 2010. *So Great a Proffit. How the East Indies Trade Transformed Anglo-American Capitalism*. Cambridge: Harvard U. Press.

Field, Frederick Vanderbilt. 1983. *From Right to Left. An Autobiography*. Westport: Lawrence Hill.

Field, Henry M. 1877. *From Egypt to Japan*. NY: Scribner's.

Fischer, Fritz. 1998. *Making Them Like Us. Peace Corps Volunteers in the 1960s*. Washington: Smithsonian.

Fischer, Louis. 1942. *A Week with Gandhi*. NY: Duell, Sloan, and Pearce.

Fischer, Louis. 1962. *The Life of Mahatma Gandhi*. NY: Collier.

Fisher, Frederick B. 1932. *That Strange Little Brown Man Gandhi*. NY: Ray Long & Richard R. Smith.

Fisher, Galen M. 1952. *John R. Mott. Architect of Co-operation and Unity*. NY: Associated Press (YMCA).

Fisher, T. 1915. 'Some American Opinions on the Indian Empire'. London: Unwin.

Fisher, Welthy Honsinger. 1944. *Frederick Bohn Fisher*. World Citizen. NY: Macmillan.

Fisher, Maxine P. 1980. *The Indians of New York City. A Study of Immigrants from India*. New Delhi: Heritage.

Fitzgerald, Frances. 1986. *Cities on a Hill. A Journey through Contemporary American Cultures*. NY: Simon and Schuster.

Flexner, Abraham. 1940. *I Remember*. Autobiography. NY: Simon and Schuster.

Foner, Nancy. 2005. *In a New Land. A Comparative View of Immigration*. NY: NYU Press.

Foner, Nancy. 2022. *One Quarter of the Nation. Immigration and the Transformation of America*. Princeton: Princeton University Press.

Forem, Jack. 2012. *Transcendental Meditation*. NY: Hay House.

Forster, E.M. 1952. *A Passage to India*. NY: Harcourt, Brace.

Fortun, Kim. 2001. *Advocacy after Bhopal*. Chicago: U. of Chicago Press.

Fosdick, Raymond B. 1952. *The Story of the Rockefeller Foundation*. NY: Harper.

Frankel, Francine R. 2005. *India's Political Economy, 1947–2004*. NY: Oxford U. Press.

Frankel, Francine R. 1971. *India's Green Revolution. Economic Gains and Poilitical Costs*. Princeton: Princeton U. Press.

Franklin, Satya Bharti. 1992. *The Promise of Paradise*. NY: Station Hill.

Fraser, George MacDonald. 1988. *The Hollywood History of the World*. NY: Beech Tree Books.

Fraser, Lovat. 1919. *Iron and Steel in India*. Bombay: no publisher.

Fraser, T.G. 1984. *Partition in Ireland, India and Palestine. Theory and Practice*. NY: St. Martin's.

Friedman, Thomas L. 2005. *The World Is Flat.* NY: Farrar, Straus and Giroux.

Frykenberg, Robert Eric. 2008. *Christianity in India.* Oxford: Oxford U. Press.

Fussell, Paul. 1989. *Wartime. Understanding and Behavior in the Second World War.* NY: Oxford U. Press.

Gaddis, John Lewis. 1997. *We Now Know. Rethinking Cold War History.* NY: Oxford U. Press.

Galbraith, John K. 1969. *Ambassador's Journal.* NY: NAL.

Galbraith, John K. 1994. *A Journey Through Economic Time.* Boston: Houghton Mifflin.

Gandhi, M.K. 1941. *Christian Missions.* Ahmedabad: Navajivan.

Gandhi, Mohandas K. 1958–1995. *Collected Works.* 100v. Delhi: Government of India, Publications Division.

Gandhi, Mohandas K. 1957. *An Autobiography. The Story of My Experiments with Truth.* Boston: Beacon Press.

Gandhi, Rajmohan. 2006. *Mohandas.* New Delhi: Penguin.

Garrow, David J. 1988. *Bearing the Cross. Martin Luther King, Jr., and the Southern Christian Leadership Conference.* NY: Vintage.

Gauba, K.L. 1929. *Uncle Sham.* NY: C. Kendall.

Gautam, Vinayshil. 1972. *Aspects of Indian Society and Economy.* Delhi: Motilal Baransidass.

Gawande, Atul. 2014. *Being Mortal.* NY: Penguin.

Gawande, Atul. 2007. *Better. A Surgeon's Notes on Performance.* NY: Picador.

Gawande, Atul. 2009. *The Checklist Manifesto. How to Get Things Right.* NY: Picador.

Gawande, Atul. 2002. *Complications.* NY: Picador.

Georgia, Jennifer. 1994. *Legacy and Challenge. The Story of Dr. Ida B. Scudder. Saline,* Michigan: McNaughton & Gunn.

Ghose, Aurobindo (Sri Aurobindo). 1959. *Essays on the Gita.* Pondicherry: Sri Aurobindo Ashram.

Ghosh, Amitav. 2005. *The Hungry Tide.* Boston: Houghton Mifflin.

Ghosh, K.K. 1969. *The Indian National Army: Second Front of the Indian Independence Movement.* Meerut: Meenakshi Prakashan.

Gilbert, Martin. 1991. *Churchill. A Life.* NY: Henry Holt.

Ginsberg, Allen. 2006. *Collected Poems 1947–1997*. NY: HarperPerennial.

Ginsberg, Allen. 1970. *Indian Journals*. City Light Books: San Francisco.

Giridharadas, Anand. 2011. *India Calling*. NY: Henry Holt.

Giridharadas, Anand. 2022. *The Persuaders. At the Front Lines of the Fight for Hearts, Minds, and Democracy*. NY: Alfred A. Knopf.

Giridharadas, Anand. 2011. *The True American. Murder and Mercy in Texas*. NY: Norton.

Giridharadas, Anand. 2018. *Winners Take All*. NY: Vintage.

Gitlin, Todd. 1987. *The Sixties. Years of Hope, Days of Rage*. NY: Bantam.

Glazer, Nathan and Sulochana Raghavan Glazer, eds. 1990. *Conflicting Images*. India and the United States. Glenn Dale, Maryland: Riverdale.

Goldberg, Philip. 2010. *American Veda*. NY: Harmony Books.

Goldsmith, Arthur A. 1990. *Building Agricultural Institutions. Transferring the Land-Grant Model to India and Nigeria*. Boulder: Westview.

Goodall, Norman. 1954. *A History of the London Missionary Society, 1895–1945*. Oxford: Oxford U. Press.

Goodyear, Dana. July 22, 2019. 'First Person,' (Profile of Kamala Harris) *New Yorker*.

Gopal, Anand. 2014. *No Good Men among the Living*. NY: Picador.

Gopal, Sarvepalli. 1976. *Jawaharlal Nehru. A Biography*. V. One 1889–1947. Cambridge: Harvard U. Press.

Gordon, James S. 1987. *The Golden Guru. The Strange Journey of Bhagwan Shree Rajneesh*. Lexington: Stephen Greene Press.

Gordon, Leonard A. 1997a. 'Asia in Enlightenment and Early British Imperial Views', in Ainslie T. Embree and Carol Gluck. *Asia in Western and World History*. Armonk, NY: M.E. Sharpe.

Gordon, Leonard A. December 1989. 'Bridging India and America: The Art and Politics of Kumar Goshal', *Amerasia Journal*. Los Angeles.

Gordon, Leonard A. 1990. *Brothers against the Raj. A Biography of Indian Nationalists Sarat and Subhas Bose*. NY: Columbia U. Press.

Gordon, Leonard A. July 1978. 'Divided Bengal: Problems of Nationalism and Identity in the 1947 Partition', *Journal of Commonwealth and Comparative Politics*, XVI, No. 2.

Gordon, Leonard A. Summer–Fall 1975. 'Indian Nationalist Ideas about Palestine and Israel', *Jewish Social Studies*, XXXVII, Nos. 3-4. pp. 221–34.

Gordon, Leonard A., January 26, 2002. 'Mahatma Gandhi's Dialogues with Americans.' *Economic and Political Weekly*, Bombay.

Gordon, Leonard A. 1999. 'John Avery,' *American National Biography*.

Gordon, Leonard A. Summer 2017. 'The Red Fort Trial: Justice by a Dying Colonialism', *IIC Quarterly*.

Gordon, Leonard A. November 1997b. 'Wealth Equals Freedom? The Rockefeller and Ford Foundations in India', *The Annals*. Philadelphia: U. of Pennsylvania.

Gordon, Robert C. 2007. *Emerson and the Light of India*. New Delhi: National Book Trust.

Goshal, Kumar. 1948. *People in Colonies*, New York: Sheridan House.

Goshal, Kumar. 1944. *The People of India*. NY: Sheridan House.

Gould, Harold A. 2006. *Sikhs, Swamis, Students, and Spies. The India Lobby in the United States, 1900–1946*. New Delhi: Sage.

Gould, Harold and Sumit Ganguly, ed. 1992. *The Hope and the Reality. US-Indian Relations from Roosevelt to Reagan*. Boulder: Westview.

Gracey, (Mrs.) J.T. 1881. *Medical Work of the Woman's Foreign Missionary Society*. Methodist Episcopal Church. Dansville, NY: A.O. Bunnell.

Grant, Charles. 'Observations on the State of Society among the Asiatic Subjects of Great Britain, particularly with respect to Morals, and on the means of Improving It. Written chiefly in the Year 1792.' *Parliamentary Papers*. 1812–13, X, Paper 282.

Grant, John Webster. 1959. *God's People in India*. Toronto: Ryerson Press.

'Granthakur'. August 21, 1971. 'US Foundations and Their Activities', *Mainstream*.

Graubard, Stephen, ed. Winter 1987. 'Philanthropy, Patronage, Politics', *Daedalus*.

Gray, George W. 1941. *Education on an International Scale. A History of the International Education Board 1923–1938*. NY: Harcourt, Brace.

Greenberg, Hayim. 1953. *The Inner Eye*. V. I. NY: Jewish Frontier Association.

Greenleaf, William. 1958. *The Ford Foundation: The Formative Years*. Unpublished manuscript. Ford Foundation archives.

Greenough, Paul R. 1982. *Prosperity and Misery in Modern Bengal: The Famine of 1943–44*. NY: Oxford U. Press.

Gregg, Richard B. 1959. *The Power of Nonviolence*. Nyack, N.Y.: Fellowship Publications.

Grover, Verinder and Ranjana Arora, eds. 1993. *Sarojini Naidu. Great Women of Modern India*. Vol. 2. New Delhi: Deep and Deep.

Guha, Ramchandra. 2018. *Gandhi. The Years that Changed the World 1914–1948*. NY: Vintage.

Guha, Ramchandra. 2007. *India after Gandhi*. NY: HarperCollins.

Guha, Ranajit. 1981. 'On Some Aspects of the Historiography of Colonial India,' in *Subaltern Studies I: Writings on South Asian History and Society*. New Delhi: Oxford University Press.

Guha, Ranajit. April 1983. 'Orientalist Strains in Indian Historiography'. *ASAA Review*. V. 6, No. 3. Australia.

Guha, Ranajit and Gayatri Chakravorty Spivak. 1988. *Selected Subaltern Studies*. NY: Oxford U. Press.

Gunther, John. 1939. *Inside Asia*. NY: Harper.

Gunther, Frances. 1944. *Revolution in India*. NY: Island Press.

Gupta, Akhil. 1998. *Postcolonial Development. Agriculture in the Making of Modern India*. Durham: Duke U. Press.

Gupta, Partha Sarathi. 1975. *Imperialism and the British Labour Movement, 1914–1964*. London: Macmillan.

Gupta, Sanjay. 2007. *Chasing Life*. NY: Warner Wellness.

Gupta, Sanjay. 2009. *Cheating Death*. NY: Wellness Central.

Halberstam, David. 1972. *The Best and the Brightest*. NY: Random House.

Halbfass, Wilhelm. 1988. *India and Europe*. Albany: State University of New York Press.

Hamm, Steve. 2007. *Bangalore Tiger. How Indian Tech Upstart Wipro is Rewriting the rules of Global Competition*. Mumbai: Tata McGraw Hill.

Hammer, Ellen J. 1966. *The Struggle for Indochina 1940–1955.* Stanford: Stanford U. Press.

Hanna, Bridget, Ward Morehouse, Satinath Sarangi. eds. 2004. *The Bhopal Reader.* NY: Apex Press.

Haqqani, Husain. 2013. *Magnificent Delusions.* NY: Public Affairs.

Hariharan, Githa. 2014. *Almost Home.* Brooklyn: Restless Books.

The HarperCollins Study Bible. 1989. NY: HarperCollins.

Harr, John E. and Peter J. Johnson. 1988. *The Rockefeller Century.* NY: Charles Scriber's Sons.

Harr, John E. and Peter J. Johnson. 1991. *The Rockefeller Conscience.* NY: Charles Scribner's Sons.

Harris, Frank. 1958. *Jamsetji Nusserwanji Tata.* London: Blackie.

Harrison, Selig. 1978. *The Widening Gulf. Asian Nationalism and American Policy.* NY: Free Press.

Hart, H. Liddell. 1972. *History of the Second World War.* 2v. NY: Capricorn Books.

Hasan, K. Sarwar, ed. 1966. *The Transfer of Power. Documents on the Foreign Relations of Pakistan.* Karachi: Pakistan Institute of International Affairs.

Hasan, Mushirul, ed. 1993. *India's Partition. Process, Strategy and Mobilization.* Delhi: Oxford U. Press.

Hatch, Nathan. 1989. *The Democratization of American Christianity.* New Haven: Yale U. Press.

Hauner, Milan. 1981. *India in Axis Strategy: Germany, Japan, and Indian Nationalists in the Second World War.* Stuttgart: Klett-Cotta.

Hazaria, Sanjoy. 1987. *Bhopal. The Lessons of a Tragedy.* New Delhi: Penguin.

Heer, Jeet. 'Desi Divides', *The Nation*, New York, February 2024

Heimsath, Charles H. and Surjit Mansingh. 1971. *A Diplomatic History of Modern India.* Bombay: Allied.

Helweg, Arthur W. and Usha M. Helweg. 1990. *An Immigrant Success Story. East Indians in America.* Philadelphia: U. of Pennsylvania Press.

Hentoff, Nat. 1982. *Peace Agitator. The Story of A.J. Muste.* NY: A.J. Muste Memorial Institute.

Herring, George C. 2008. *From Colony to Superpower. US Foreign Relations since 1776.* NY: Oxford U. Press.

Hess, Gary R. 1967. *Sam Higginbottom of Allahabad.* Charlottesville: University of Virginia Press.

Hess, Gary R. 1971. *American Encounters India 1941-1947.* Baltimore: Johns Hopkins Press.

Higginbottom, Sam. 1949. *Sam Higginbottom: Farmer. An Autobiography.* NY: Charles Scribner's.

Higham, Charles and Moseley, Roy. 1983. *Princess Merle. The Romantic Life of Merle Oberon.* NY: Pocket Books.

Higham, John. 1974. *Strangers in the Land. Patterns of American Nativism 1860–1925.* NY: Atheneum.

Hitchens. Christopher. 1991. *Blood, Class and Nostalgia. Anglo-American Ironies.* London: Vintage.

Hobsbawm, E.J. 1969. *Industry and Empire.* NY: Penguin.

Hocking, William. 1932. *Re-thinking Missions.* NY: Harper.

Hodson, H.V. 1969. *The Great Divide. Britain-India-Pakistan.* London: Hutchinson.

Hoffman, Ross J.S. and Paul Levack, eds. 1959. *Burke's Politics.* NY: Knopf.

Hoffmann, Steven. 1990. *India and the China Crisis.* Berkeley: U. of California Press.

Hofstadter, Richard. 1956. *The American Political Tradition.* NY: Vintage.

Hofstadter, Richard. 1960. *The Age of Reform.* NY: Vintage.

Hofstadter, Richard. 1966. *Anti-Intellectualism in American Life.* NY: Vintage.

Hofstadter, Richard. 1982. *Great Issues in American History.* V. III. From Reconstruction to the Present Day, 1864–1981. NY: Vintage.

Hofstadter, Richard. 1959. *Social Darwinism in American Thought.* NY: George Braziller.

Hollinger, David A. 2017. *Protestants Abroad: How Missionaries Tried to Change the World but Changed America.* Princeton: Princeton U. Press.

Holmes, John Haynes. 1959. *I Speak for Myself.* NY: Harper.

Holmes, John Haynes. 1954. *My Gandhi.* London: Allen & Unwin.

Hope, Guy. 1968. *America, India, and Swaraj*. Bombay: Vora.

Hopkins, C. Howard. 1979. *John R. Mott. 1865–1955. A Biography*. NY: Eerdmans.

Horsman, Reginald. 1981. *Race and Manifest Destiny*. Cambridge: Harvard U. Press.

Hoskins, Mrs Robert. Clara A. Swain, M.D., n.d. *First Medical Missionary to the Women of the Orient. Women's Foreign Missionary Society*. Boston: no publisher.

Hossain, Syud. 1937. *Gandhi, The Saint as Statesman*. N.Y.: Suttonhouse.

Howe, Irving. ed. 1982. *The Portable Kipling*. NY: Penguin.

Howley, Kerry. June 10–23, 2019 'Tulsi Gabbard Had a Very Strange Childhood', *New York*er

Hoyland, John S. 1931. *The Cross Moves East. A Study of the Significance of Gandhi's 'Satyagraha'*. London: Allen & Unwin.

Hua Hsu, November 2, 2020 'Bloc by Bloc: Are Asian Americans the Last Undecided Voters?' *New Yorker*. Pp.16–22.

Hughes, H. Stuart. 1990. *Gentleman Rebel. The Memoirs of H. Stuart Hughes*. NY: Ticknor & Fields.

Hume, Edward H. 1950. *Doctors Courageous*. NY: Harper.

Hunt, James D. 1986. *Gandhi and the Nonconformists. Encounters in South Africa*. New Delhi: Promilla.

Hunt, James D. 1978. *Gandhi in London*. New Delhi: Promilla.

Hurst, John F. 1891. *Indika the Country and the People of India and Ceylon*. New York: Harper and Brothers.

Neill Hutheesing, Krishna Nehru. 1967. *We Nehrus*. With Alden Hatch. NY; Holt, Rinehard and Winston.

Huxley, Aldous. 2009. *The Doors of Perceptions & Heaven and Hell*. NY: Harper Perennial, 2009.

Huxley, Aldous. 1928. *Jesting Pilate. The Diary of a Journey*. London: Chatto & Windus.

Ienaga, Saburo. 1978. *The Pacific War, World War II and the Japanese, 1931–1945*. NY: Pantheon.

Ignatiev, Noel. 1995. *How the Irish Became White*. Cambridge: Harvard U. Press.

Inden, Ronald B. 1990. *Imagining India*. Oxford: Basil Blackwell

Inden, Ronald B. 1986. 'Orientalist Constructions of India', *Modern Asian Studies*. Pp. 20, 3, 402.

Indra Devi. 1959. *Yoga for Americans*. Englewood, Cliffs: Prentice-Hall.

Ingram, Catherine. 1990. *In the Footsteps of Gandhi. Conversations with Spiritual Social Activists*. Berkeley: Parallax.

Iriye, Akira. 1981. *Power and Culture, The Japanese-American War 1941–1945*. Cambridge: Harvard U. Press.

Isherwood, Bayly. 1980. *My Guru and His Disciple*. NY: Farrar Straus Giroux.

Isherwood, Christopher. 1965. *Ramakrishna and His Disciples*. NY: Simon and Schuster.

Isherwood, Christopher. Ed. 1960. *Vedanta for the Western World*. NY: Viking, 1960.

Islam, Sirajul. June 1994. 'The Cargo and Culture of the New Englanders' Voyages to Calcutta 1785-c. 1850', V. 39, No. 1. *Journal of the Asiatic Society of Bangladesh*. Dhaka.

Isphahani, M.A.H. 1967. *Qaid-e-Azam Jinnah As I Knew Him*. Karachi: Forward.

Israel, Milton. 1994. *Communications and Power. Propaganda and the Press in the Indian Nationalist Struggle, 1920–1947*. Cambridge: Cambridge U. Press.

Issacs, Harold R. 1965. *India's Ex-Untouchables*. NY: John Day.

Issacs, Harold. 1980. *Scratches on Our Minds. American Views of China and India*. White Plains: M.E. Sharpe, 1980.

Iyengar, B.K.S. 1966. *Light on Yoga*. London: George Allen and Unwin.

Jack, Homer A.1996. *Homer's Odyssey. My Quest for Peace and Justice*. Becket, MA: One Peaceful World Press.

Jackson, Carl T. 1981. *The Oriental Religions and American Thought. Nineteen-Century Explorations*. Westport: Greenwood, 1981.

Jackson, Carl T. 1994. *Vedanta for the West. The Ramakrishna Movement in the United States*. Bloomington: Indiana U. Press.

Jacobson, Matthew Frye. 2000. *Barbarian Virtues. The United States Encounters Foreign Peoples at Home and Abroad, 1876–1917*. NY: Hill and Wang.

Jaffrey, Madhur. 1973. *An Invitation to Indian Cooking*. NY: Vintage.

Jain, L.C. with B.V. Krishnamurthy and P.M. Tripathi. 1985. *Grass without Roots: Rural Development under Government Auspices*. New Delhi: Sage.

Jain, B.M. 1987. *India and the United States 1961–1963*. New Delhi: Radiant.

Jalal, Ayesha. 1985. *The Sole Spokesman: Jinnah, the Muslim League and the Demand for Pakistan*. Cambridge: Cambridge U. Press.

Jalan, Bimal. 1991. *India's Economic Crisis. The Way Ahead*. Delhi: Oxford U. Press.

James, William. 1992. 'What Makes a Life Significant', *Writings 1878–1899*. NY: Library of America.

James, Willliam. 1987. *Writings 1902–1910*. NY: Library of America.

Jauhar, Sandeep. 2015. *Doctored: The Disillusionment of an American Physician*. NY: Farrar, Straus and Giroux.

Jauhar, Sandeep. 2018. *Heart. A History*. NY: Farrar, Straus and Giroux.

Jauhdar, Sandeep. 2008. *Intern. A Doctor's Initiation*. NY: Farrar, Straus and Giroux.

Jauhri, R.C. 1970. *American Diplomacy and Independence for India*. Bombay: Vora.

Jayakar, Pupul. 1986. *J. Krishnamurti*. New Delhi: Penguin.

Jefferson, Thomas. 1984. *Writings*. NY: Library of America.

Jeffrey, Keith. 2010. *The Secret History of MI6*. New York: Penguin Press.

Jeffrey, Pauline. 1970. *Ida S. Scudder of Vellore*. Mysore: Wesley Press.

Jensen, Joan M. 1988. *Passage from India. Asian Indian Immigrants in North America*. New Haven: Yale U. Press.

Jha, Manoranjan. 1973. *Civil Disobedience and After. The American Reactions to Political Developments in India during 1930–35*. Meerut: Meenakshi Prakashan.

Jha, Manoranjan. 1971. *Katherine Mayo and India*. New Delhi: People's Publishing House.

Jog, N.G.1944. *Churchill's Blind-Spot: India*. Bombay: New Book Company.

Johnson, Chalmers. 2004. *The Sorrows of Empire*. NY: Metropolitan Books.

Johnson, James Weldon. 1995. *The Autobiography of an Ex-Colored Man*. Mineola: Dover.

Johnson, W.A. 1966. *The Steel Industry of India*. Cambridge: Harvard U. Press.

Jones, Dorothy B. 1955. *The Portrayal of China and India on the American Screen, 1896–1955*. Cambridge: Center for International Studies, MIT.

Jones, E. Stanley. 1958. *Mahatma Gandhi. An Interpretation*. N.Y.: Abingdon-Cokesbury Press.

Jones, E. Stanley. 1925. *The Christ of the Indian Road*. London: Hodder and Stoughton.

Jordan, Miriam and Sabrina Tavernise. September 18, 2018. 'One Face of Immigration in America Is a Family Tree Rooted in Asia', *New York Times*.

Josephson, Matthew. 1934. *The Robber Barons. The Great American Capitalists 1861–1901*. NY: Harcourt, Brace.

Josh, Sohan Singh. 1977. *Hindustan Gadar Party. A Short History*. New Delhi: People's Publishing House.

Josh, Sohan Singh. 1978. *Hindustan Gadar Party*. V. Two. New Delhi: People's Publishing House.

Joshi, Vijaya Chandra, ed. 1966. *Lala Lajpat Rai Writings and Speeches*. V. One 1888–1919. Delhi: University Publishers.

Kahin, George McT. 1986. *Intervention. How American became involved in Vietnam*. NY: Knopf.

Kahn, E.J. 1976. *The China Hands*. NY: Penguin Books.

Kalanithi, Paul. 2017. *When Breath Becomes Air*. London: Vintage.

Kaling, Mindy. 2012. *Is Everyone Hanging Out Without Me?* NY: Three Rivers.

Kaling, Mindy. 2015. *Why Not Me?* NY: Three Rivers.

Kamat, Sangeeta and Biju Mathew. 2003. 'Mapping Political Violence in a Globalized World: The Case of Hindu Nationalism', *Social Justice*. Vol. 30, No. 3, pp. 4–16.

Kamath, P.M., ed. 1987. *Indo–US Relations. Dynamics of Change*. New Delhi: South Asian Publishers.

Kamath, M.V. 1998. *The United States and India 1776-1996. The Bridge over the River Time*. New Delhi: Indian Council for Cultural Relations.

Kamdar, Mira. 2007. *Planet India. How the Fastest Growing Democracy is Transforming the World*. NY: Scribner.

Kaplan, David A. 2000. *The Silicon Boys*. NY: Perennial.

Kapur, Devesh and John McHale. 2005. *Give Us Your Best and Brightest. The Global Hunt for Talent and its Impact on the Developing World*. Washington: Center for Global Development.

Kapur, Sudarshan. 1992. *Raising Up a Prophet. The African-American Encounter with Gandhi*. Boston: Beacon Press.

Karaka, D.F. 1946. *New York with Its Pants Down*, Thacker, Bombay.

Keenan, John L. 1943. *A Steel Man in India*. NY: Duell, Sloan and Pearce.

Keer, Dhananjay. 1954. *Dr. Ambedkar. Life and Mission*. Bombay: Popular Prakashan.

Kendall, Patricia. 1940. *Come with Me to India*. NY: Charles Scribner's.

Kennedy, David M. 1999. *Freedom from Fear. The American People in Depression and War, 1929–1945*. NY: Oxford U. Press.

Kennedy, Paul. 1989. *The Rise and Fall of the Great Powers*. NY: Vintage.

Ker, James Campbell. 1973. [1917]. *Political Trouble in India 1907–1917*. Delhi: Oriental.

Khaliquzzaman, Choudhry. 1961. *Pathway to Pakistan*. Lahore: Longmans.

Khan, Yasmin. 2008. *The Great Partition*. New Haven: Yale U. Press.

Khan, Yasmin. 2015. *India at War*. New York: Oxford U. Press.

Kidron, Michael. 1965. *Foreign Investments in India*. London: Oxford U. Press.

King, Jr., Martin Luther. 1964. *Stride towards Freedom*. NY: Perennial, 1964.

Kinzer, Stephen. 2013. *The Brothers. John Foster Dulles, Allen Dulles, and Their Secret World War*. NY: St. Martin's.

Kipling, Rudyard. 1988. *Kim*. NY: Penguin.

Kipling, Rudyard. 1937. 'The City of Dreadful Night', in *Selected Prose and Poetry of Rudyard Kipling*. Garden City, New York: Garden City Publishing.

Kipling, Rudyard and Wolcott Balestier. 1892. *The Naulahka, A Story of West and East*. London: William Heinemann.

Kissinger, Henry. 1979. *White House Years*. Boston: Little, Brown.

Klehr, Harvey and Ronald Radosh. 1996. *The Amerasia Spy Case*. Chapel Hill: U. of North Carolina Press.

Kling, Blair. Spring 1998. 'Paternalism in Indian Labor: The Tata Iron and Steel Company of Jamshedpur'. *International Labor and Working-Class History Journal*. No. 53, pp. 69–87.

Kohler, Robert E. 1991. *Partners in Science. Foundations and Natural Scientists 1900–45*. Chicago: U. of Chicago Press.

Kolko, Gabriel. 1968. *The Politics of War. The World and US Foreign Policy, 1943–45*. NY: Random House.

Kopf, David. May 1980. 'Hermeneutics versus History'. *Journal of Asian Studies*, XXXIX, no. 3, pp. 495–506.

Kosambi, Meera, ed. 2003. *Pandita Ramabai's American Encounter*. Bloomington, Indiana: Indiana U. Press.

Kothari, Rajni. 2002. *Memoirs*. New Delhi: Rupa.

Kripalani, Krishna. 1962. *Rabindranath Tagore. A Biography*. NY: Grove.

Krishna, Priya. 2019. *Indian-ish. Recipes and Antics from a Modern American Family*. NY: Houghton Mifflin Harcourt.

Krishnan, T.V.K. 1974. *The Unfriendly Friends. America and India*. Delhi: InterCulture Associates.

Krishnamurti, Jiddu. 1910. *At the Feet of the Master*. Adyar: Theosophical Society.

Kudaisya, Medha M. 2003. *The Life and Times of G.D. Birla*. New Delhi: Oxford U. Press.

Kumar, Amitava, ed. 2003. *Away*. NY: Penguin.

Kumar, Amitava. 2002. *Bombay London New York*. NY: Routledge.

Kumar, Amitava. 2010. *A Foreigner Carrying in the Crook of His Arm a Tiny Bomb*. Durham: Duke U. Press.

Kumar, Amitava. 2005. *Husband of a Fanatic*. NY: New Press.

Kumar, Amitava. 2019. *Immigrant, Montana*. NY: Vintage.

Kumar, Amitava. 2015. *Lunch with a Bigot*. Durham: Duke U. Press.

Kumar, Amitava. 2000. *Passport Photos*. Berkeley: U. of California Press.

Kumar, Anoop. 2017. *Michelangelo's Medicine. How Redefining the Human Body Will Transform Health and Healthcare*. n.p. Anoop Kumar.

Kumar, Anoop. 2018. *Is This a Dream? Reflections on the Awakening Mind.* Washington: Mantra Books.

Kumar, Dharma, ed. 1982. *The Cambridge Economic History of India.* Vol. 2: c. 1757–1970. Cambridge: Cambridge U. Press.

Kumar, Prakash. 2019. "Modernization' and Agrarian Development in India, 1912–52', *Journal of Asian Studies'.* Pp. 1–26.

Kumar, Ravindra, ed. 1992. *Selected Documents of Lala Lajpat Rai 1906-1928.* V. 2. Delhi: Anmol.

Kumar, Satish. 1981. *CIA and the Third World. A Study in Crypto-Diplomacy.* New Delhi: Vikas.

Kunzru, Hari. 2011. *Gods without Men.* NY: Vintage Books.

Kunzru, Hari. 2002. *The Impressionist.* NY: Plume.

Kunzru, Hari. 2009. *My Revolutions.* NY: Plume.

Kunzru, Hari. 2020. *Red Pill.* NY: Knopf.

Kurzman, Dan. 1987. *A Killing Wind. Inside Union Carbide and the Bhopal Catastrophe.* NY: McGraw Hill.

Kust, Matthew J. 1964. *Foreign Enterprise in India.* Laws and Policies. Chapel Hill: U. of North Carolina Press.

Kutty, V.K. Madhavan. 1988. *V.K. Krishna Menon.* New Delhi: Publications Division, Government of India.

Kutz, Myer.1974. *Rockefeller Power.* NY: Simon & Schuster.

Kux, Dennis. 1993. *Estranged Democracies. India and the United States 1941–1991.* New Delhi: Sage.

Kux, Dennis. 2001. *The United States and Pakistan 1947–2000. Disenchanted Allies.* Washington: Woodrow Wilson Center.

Labaree, Benjamin Woods. 1979. *The Boston Tea Party.* Boston: Northeastern U. Press.

La Brack, Bruce. 1988. *The Sikhs of Northern California 1904–1975.* NY: AMS Press.

Lach, Donald F. 1965, 1977. *Asia in the Making of Europe.* V. I, Books One and Two [1965], V. II, Books One, Two and Three [1977] Chicago: U. of Chicago Press.

Lad, Vasant. Ayurveda. 1985. *The Science of Self-Healing.* Twin Lakes, WI: Lotus Press.

LaFeber, Walter. 1972. *America, Russia, and the Cold War, 1945–1971.* NY: John Wiley.

LaFeber, Walter. 1993. *The Cambridge History of American Foreign Relations*. II. The American Search for Opportunity, 1865–1913. NY: Cambridge U. Press.

Lagemann, Ellen C. 1983. *Private Power for the Public Good. A History of the Carnegie Foundation for the Advancement of Teachers*. Middletown: Wesleyan U. Press.

Lagemann, Ellen C. 1989. *The Politics of Knowledge. The Carnegie Corporation, Philanthropy, and Public Policy*. Middletown: Wesleyan U. Press.

Lago, Mary. 2001. *'India's Prisoner'. A Biography of Edward John Thompson 1886–1946*. Columbia: University of Missouri Press.

Lahiri, Jhumpa. 2016. *In Other Words*. NY: Knopf.

Lahiri, Jhumpa. 1999. *Interpreter of Maladies*. NY: Houghton Mifflin.

Lahiri, Jhumpa. 2013. *The Lowland*. NY: Vintage.

Lahiri, Jhumpa. 2003. *The Namesake*. NY: Houghton Mifflin.

Lahiri, Jhumpa. 2008. *Unaccustomed Earth*. NY: Knopf.

Lahiri, Jhumpa. 2021. *Whereabouts*. NY: Knopf.

Laird, M.A. 1972. *Missionaries and Education in Bengal 1793–1837*. Oxford: Clarendon Press.

Lajpat Rai, Lala. 1916. *The United States of America. A Hindu's Impressions and a Study*. Calcutta: R. Chatterjee.

Lal, Vinay. 2008. *The Other Indians: A Political and Cultural History of South Asians in America*. Los Angeles: University of California Press.

Lala, R.M. 2003. *Beyond the Blue Mountain. A Life of J.R.D. Tata (1904–1993)*. New Delhi: Penguin.

Lala, R.M. 2004a. *The Creation of Wealth. The Tatas from the 19th to the 21st Century*. New Delhi: Penguin.

Lala, R.M. 2004b. *For the Love of India. The Life and Times of Jamsetji Tata*. New Delhi: Penguin.

Lalami, Laila, 20 September 2020. 'Made into Strangers,' *New York Times*.

Lancaster, Carol. 2006. *Foreign Aid*. Chicago: U. of Chicago Press.

Landes, David S. 2006. *Dynasties*. NY: Viking.

Landes, David S. 1970. *The Unbound Prometheus*. Cambridge: Cambridge U. Press.

Lapierre, Dominique and Javier Moro. 2002. *Five Past Midnight in Bhopal*. NY: Warner Books.

Lapp, John Allen. 1972. *The Mennonite Church in India*. 1897-1962. Scottdale, Pa.: Herald Press.

Larson, Erik. 2003. *The Devil in the White City*. NY: Vintage.

Latham, Earl. 1966. *The Communist Controversy in Washington. From the New Deal to McCarthy*. Cambridge: Harvard U. Press.

Latourette, Kenneth Scott. 1970. *The Great Century. A History of the Expansion of Christianity*. VI. NY: Harper.

Lattimore, Owen. 1950. *Ordeal by Slander*. Boston: Little, Brown.

Lavan, Spencer. 1991. *Unitarians and India*. Chicago: Exploration Press.

Lavezzoli, Peter. 2006. *The Dawn of Indian Music in the West*. NY: Continuum.

Lears, Jackson. 2009. *Rebirth of a Nation. The Making of Modern America, 1877–1920*. NY: Harper.

Lebra, Joyce, ed. 1975. *Japan's Greater East Asia Co-Prosperity Sphere in World War II*. Kuala Lumpur: Oxford U. Press.

Lee, Erika. 2019. *America for Americans. A History of Xenophobia in the United States*. NY: Basic Books.

Lee, Erika. 2015. *The Making of Asian America*. NY: Simon and Schuster.

Leonard, Karen Isaksen. 1992. *Making Ethnic Choices. California's Punjabi Mexican Americans*. Philadelphia: Temple U. Press.

Leonard, Karen Isaksen. 2003. *Muslims in the United States: The State of Research*. New York: Russell Sage Foundation.

Leonard, Karen Isaksen. 1997. *South Asian Americans*. Westport Conn.: Greenwood Press.

Lesser, Wendy. 2017. *You Say to Brick: The Life of Louis Kahn*. NY Farrar Straus and Giroux.

Lessinger, Johanna. 1995. *From the Ganges to the Hudson*. Boston: Allyn and Bacon.

Lewis, David Levering, ed. 1995. *W.E.B. Du Bois. A Reader*. NY: Henry Holt.

Lewis, John, with Michael D'Orso. 1998. *Walking with the Wind*. NY: Harvest.

Lewis, John P. 1993. *Quiet Crisis in India*. Bombay: Asia Publishing.

Lind, Michael. 2013. *Land of Promise. An Economic History of the United States*. NY: Harper.

Lipsey, Roger, ed. 1977. *Coomarawamy, Selected Papers*. 2v. Princeton: Princeton U. Press.

Louie, Vivian S. 2014. *Compelled to Excel. Immigration, Education, and Opportunity among Chinese Americans*. Stanford: Stanford U. Press.

Louis, Wm Roger. 1978. *Imperialism at Bay. The US and the Decolonization of the British Empire*. NY: Oxford U. Press.

Love, Erik. 2017. *Islamophobia and Racism in America*. NY: NYU Press.

Love, Robert. 2010. *The Great OOM, The Improbable Birth Yoga in America*. NY: Viking.

Luce, Edward. 2007. *In Spite of the Gods. The Strange Rise of Modern India*. NY: Doubleday.

Luke, P.Y. and John B. Carman. 1968. *Village Christians and Hindu Culture*. London: Littleworth. Lycett, Andrew. 1999. *Rudyard Kipling*. London: Phoenix.

Lynd, Staughton, ed. 1966. *Nonviolence in America: A Documentary History*. Indianapolis: BobbsMerrill.

Macaulay, Lord Thomas. 1860. 'Warren Hastings', in *Critical, Historical, and Miscellaneous Essays*. Vol. V. Boston: Houghton, Mifflin.

MacColl, Gail and Carol McD.Wallace. 2012. *To Marry an English Lord*. NY: Workman.

MacCullouch, Diarmaid. 2010. *Christianity. The First Three Thousand Years*. NY: Penguin.

Macdonald, Dwight. 1958. *Memoirs of a Revolutionist*. NY: Meridian.

MacDonald, Dwight. 1989. *The Ford Foundation. The Men and the Millions*. New Brunswick: Transaction.

MacEwan, Arthur. 1990. *Debt and Disorder. International Economic Instability and US Imperial Decline*. NY: Monthly Review Press.

MacKenzie, Kenneth. 1961. *The Robe and the Sword: The Methodist Church and the Rise of American Imperialism*.

MacKenzie, John M. 1985. *Propaganda and Empire. The Manipulation of British Public Opinion 1880–1960*. NY: Manchester U. Press.

Magat, Richard. 1979. *The Ford Foundation at Work*. NY: Plenum.

Mahesh Yogi, Maharishi. 1968. *Transcendental Meditation*. NY: New American Library.

Maier, Pauline. 1972. *From Resistance to Revolution*. NY: Vintage.

Maira, Sunaina Marr. 2002. *Desis in the House*. Philadelphia: Temple U. Press.

Maira, Sunaina, and Rajini Sirkanth, eds. 1996. *Contours of the Heart*. NY: Asian American Writers' Workshop.

Majumdar, Megha. 2020. *A Burning*. NY: Alfred A. Knopf.

Mamdani, Mahmood. 1972. *The Myth of Population Control*. NY: Monthly Review.

Manela, Ezra. 2007. *The Wilsonian Moment*. NY: Oxford U. Press.

Mansergh, Nicholas, ed. 1970, 1971, 1976, 1979, 1980, 1981, 1983. *The Transfer of Power 1942–47*. 12 vols. London: HMSO, 1970–1983 (I, 1970; IV, 1971; VI, 1976; VIII, 1979; IX, 1980; X, 1981; XII, 1983).

Mansergh, Nicholas. 1969. *The Commonwealth Experience*. London: Weidenfeld and Nicolson.

Mansingh, Surjit.1984. *India's Search for Power. Indira Gandhi's Foreign Policy 1966–1982*. New Delhi: Sage.

Markovits, Claude. 1985. *Indian Business and Nationalist Politics 1931–39*. Cambridge: Cambridge U. Press.

Marshall, P.J., ed. 1970. *The British Discovery of Hinduism in the Eighteenth Century*. Cambridge: At the University Press.

Marshall, P.J., ed. 1998. *The Eighteenth Century. The Oxford History of the British Empire*. NY: Oxford U. Press, 1998.

Marshall, P.J. 1965. *The Impeachment of Warren Hastings*. London: Oxford U. Press.

Marshall, P.J. 2005. *The Making and Unmaking of Empires. Britain, India, and America c. 1750–1783*. NY: Oxford U. Press.

Marshall, P.J. 2012. *Remaking the British Atlantic. The United States and the British Empire after American Independence*. NY: Oxford U. Press.

Mason, Philip. 1974. *A Matter of Honour. An Account of the Indian Army*. NY: Holt, Rinehart, Winston.

Masters, John. 2000. *Bugles and a Tiger: My Life in the Gurkhas*. NY: Viking Press.

Masters, John. 1961. *The Road Past Mandalay*. London: Cassell.

Mathews, Basil. 1934. *John R. Mott*. World Citizen. NY: Harper.

Maugham, W. Somerset. 2003. *The Razor's Edge*. NY: Vintage.

Mawani, Renisa. 2018. *Across Oceans of Law. The Komagata Maru and Jurisdiction in the Time of Empire*. Durham: Duke University Press.

Maxwell, Neville. 1970. *India's China War*. London: Jonathan Cape.

Mayer, Albert, and Associates. 1958. *Pilot Project, India. The Story of Rural Development at Etawah*, Uttar Pradesh. Berkeley: U. of California Press.

Mayo, Katherine. 1927. *Mother India*. NY: Harcourt, Brace.

Mazumdar, Protap Chundrer. 1884. *Sketches of a Tour Round the World*. Calcutta; SK Lahiri.

McCarthy, Kathleen D. 1982. *Noblesse Oblige*. Chicago: U. of Chicago Press.

McCaughey, Robert A. 1984. *International Studies and Academic Enterprise*. NY: Columbia U. Press.

McCormick, Thomas, 1967. *China Market: America's Quest for Informal Empire, 1893–1901*. Chicago: Quadrangle.

McCormack, Win. 12 April 2018 'A Beautiful Place for an Ashram', *The New Republic*.

McDermott, Rachel F., Leonard A. Gordon, et al, eds. 2013. *Sources of Indian Tradition*. Vol. II, New York: Columbia U. Press.

McDougall, Walter 1997. *A. Promised Land, Crusader State. The American Encounter with the World since 1776*. Boston: Houghton Mifflin.

McIntosh, Elizabeth P. 1998. *Sisterhood of Spies: The Women of the OSS*. Annapolis: Naval Institute Press.

McLean, Bethany and Peter Elkind. 2004. *The Smartest Guys in the Room. The Amazing Rise and Scandalous Fall of Enron*. NY: Penguin.

McLoughlin, William G. 1980. *Revivals, Awakenings and Reform*. Chicago: U. of Chicago Press.

McLoughlin, William G. ed. 1976. *The American Evangelicals, 1800–1900*. An Anthology. Glouchester: Peter Smith.

McMahon, Robert J. 1994. *The Cold War on the Periphery. The United States, India, and Pakistan.* NY: Columbia U. Press.

McManner, John, ed. 1992. *The Oxford Illustrated History of Christianity.* NY: Oxford U. Press.

McNally, Terrence. 1994. *A Perfect Ganesh.* NY: Dramatists Play Service.

Mehra, Girish N. 2007. *Nearer Heaven than Earth. The Life and Times of Boshi Sen and Gertrude Emerson Sen.* New Delhi: Rupa.

Mehra, Rekha.1977. 'The Impact of American Private Philanthropy on India, 1930–1959'. PhD thesis, U. of Florida.

Mehta, Gita. 1994. *Karma Cola.* NY: Vintage.

Mehta, Suketu. 2005. *Maximum City. Bombay Lost and Found.* NY: Knopf.

Mehta, Suketu. 2019. *This Land is Our Land. An Immigrant's Manifesto.* NY: Farrar, Straus, and Giroux.

Mehta, Ved. 1977. *Mahatma Gandhi and His Apostles.* NY: Viking.

Meisner, Maurice. 1999. *Mao's China and After.* NY: Free Press, 1999.

Melendy, H. Brett. 1981. *Asians in America.* NY Hippocrene.

Mellor, John, ed. 1979. *India: A Rising Middle Power.* Boulder: Westview Press.

Melville, Herman. 1983. *Moby-Dick or The Whale.* NY: Library of America.

Menon, Shivshankar, Sept/Oct. 2020. 'League of Nationalists,' *Foreign Affairs.* 132–39.

Menon, V.P. 1957. *The Transfer of Power in India.* Bombay: Orient Longmans.

Menuhin, Yehudi. 1976. *Unfinished Journey.* NY: Knopf.

Merrill, Dennis. 1990. *Bread and the Ballot. The United States and India's Economic Development 1947–1963.* Chapel Hill: U. of North Carolina Press.

Meskill, Johanna Menzel. 1966. *Hitler and Japan: The Hollow Alliance.* NY: Atherton Press.

Middlekauff, Robert. 1982. *The Glorious Cause. The American Revolution, 1763–1789.* NY: Oxford U. Press.

Miles, Barry. 1990. *Ginsberg: A Biography.* New York: Harper Perennial, 1990.

Mill, James. 1969 [1858] *The History of British India.* Vol. I. NY: Chelsea House.

Miller, Webb. 1936. *I Found No Peace.* NY: Simon and Schuster.

Minear, Richard H. 2001. *Victors' Justice. The Tokyo War Crimes Trial*. Ann Arbor: University of Michigan.

Mirza, Fatima Farheen. 2018. *A Place for Us*. NY: SJP for Hogarth.

Mishra, Sangay K. 2016. *Desis Divided*. Minneapolis: U. of Minnesota Press.

Mitchiner, John. 1992. *Guru. The Search for Enlightenment*. New Delhi: Viking.

Mitter, Partha. 1994. *Art and Nationalism in Colonial India, 1850-1925*. Occidental Orientations. Cambridge: Cambridge U. Press.

Mitter, Partha. 2012. 'Frameworks for Considering Cultural Exchange: The Case of India and America', in *East–West Interchanges in American Art: A Long and Tumultuous Relationship*, eds. Cynthia Mills et al, Smithsonian Institution Scholarly Press, Washington D.C. pp. 20–37.

Mitter, Partha. 1992. *Much Maligned Monsters*. A History of European Reactions to Indian Art. Chicago: University of Chicago Press.

Mohan, Jag. 1979. *Ananda K. Coomaraswamy*. New Delhi: Publications Division, Government of India.

Montesquieu, Baron de. 1949. *The Spirit of the Laws*. NY: Hafner.

Moore, Joseph. 1886. *The Queen's Empire; or, Ind and Her Pearl*. Philadelphia, Lippincott.

Moore, R.J. 1974. *The Crisis of Indian Unity 1917–1940*. Oxford U. Press.

Moore, R.J. 1979. *Churchill, Cripps, and India 1939-1945*. Oxford: Clarendon Press.

Moore, R.J. 1983. *Escape from Empire. The Attlee Government and the Indian Problem*. Oxford U. Press.

Morison, Samuel Eliot. 1942. *Admiral of the Ocean Sea. A Life of Christopher Columbus*. Boston: Little, Brown.

Morris, Aldon D. 1984. *The Origins of the Civil Rights Movement*. N.Y.: Free Press.

Morris, Edmund. 2001. *The Rise of Theodore Roosevelt*. NY: Modern Library.

Morris, Morris D. 1982. 'The Growth of Large-Scale Industry', in Dharma Kumar, ed. *The Cambridge Economic History of India*. V. II, Cambridge: Cambridge U. Press.

Moynihan, Daniel. 1979. *A Dangerous Place*. Bombay: Allied.

Mozumder, Suman Guha. March 16, 2018. 'Band of Brothers', *India Abroad*. XLVII, No. 24.

Mudumbai, Srinivas C. 1980. *United States Foreign Policy towards India 1947–1954*. New Delhi: Manohar.

Mukerji, Dhan Gopal. *2002 [1923] Caste and Outcaste*. Ed.Gordon H. Chang, Purnima Mankekar, and Akhil Gupta. Stanford: Stanford U. Press.

Mukerji, Dhan Gopal. 1930. *Disillusioned India*. NY: Dutton.

Mukerji, Dhan Gopal. 1926. *The Face of Silence*. NY: Dutton.

Mukerji, Dhan Gopal. 1968. *Gay-Neck*. NY: Dutton.

Mukerji, Dhan Gopal. 1928. *Ghond the Hunter*. NY: Dutton.

Mukerji, Dhan Gopal. 1925. *My Brother's Face*. London: Thornton Butterworth.

Mukerji, Dhan Gopal. 1928. *A Son of Mother India Answers*, NY: Dutton.

Mukerji, Dhan Gopal. 1929. *Visit India with Me*. NY: Dutton.

Mukherjee, Bharati. 1989. *The Middleman and Other Stories*. NY: Fawcett Crest.

Mukherjee, Debashree. *Bombay Hustle. Making Movies in a Colonial City*. NY: Columbia U. Press, 2020.

Mukherjee, Janam. 2015. *Hungry Bengal. War, Famine, and Riots at the End of Empire*. Gurugram: HarperCollins.

Mukerjee, Madhusree. 2010. *Churchill's Secret War. The British Empire and the Ravaging of India during World War II*. NY: Basic Books 2010.

Mukherjee, Siddhartha. 2010. *The Emperor of All Maladies*. NY: Scribner.

Mukherjee, Siddhartha. 2017. *The Gene. An Intimate History*. NY: Scribner.

Mukherjee, S.N. 1968. *Sir William Jones: A Study in Eighteenth-Century British Attitudes to India*. Cambridge: At the University Press.

Mukherjee, Tapan K. 1998. *Taraknath Das. Life and Letters of a Revolutionary in Exile*. Calcutta: National Council of Education, Bengal.

Munson, Arley. No date. *Jungle Days: Being the Experiences of an American Woman Doctor in India*. D. Appleton & Co.: NY.

Murthy, Vivek H. 2020. *Together: The Healing Power of Connection in a Sometimes Lonely World*. HarperCollins.

Muste, A.J. 1967. *The Essays of A.J. Muste*. Ed. By Nat Hentoff. NY: Clarion.

Muster, Nori J. 2001. *Betrayal of the Spirit. My Life Behind the Headlines of the Hare Krishna Movement*. Chicago: U. of Illinois Press.

Muzumdar, Haridas T. 1986. *Asian Indians' Contributions to America*. Little Rock: Gandhi Institute of America.

Muzumdar, Haridas T. 1923. *Gandhi the Apostle. His Trial and His Message*. Chicago: Universal Publishing.

Muzumdar, Haridas T. 1932. *Gandhi versus the Empire*. NY: Universal.

Myers, Gustavus. 1936 [1909] *History of the Great American Fortunes*. NY: Modern Library.

Myrdal, Gunnar. 1962. *An American Dilemma. With the assistance of Richard Sterner and Arnold Rose. The Negro Problem and Modern Democracy*. NY: Harper and Row.

Myrdal, Gunnar. 1968. *Asian Drama. An Inquiry into the Poverty of Nations*. 3v. NY: Pantheon.

Nagar, Purushottam. 1977. *Lala Lajpat Rai. The Man and His Ideas*. New Delhi: Manohar.

NRSV Bible with the Apocrypha, The. Compact Edition. Oxford University. Press, Oxford, 1995.

Naipaul, V.S. 1988. *The Enigma of Arrival*. NY: Vintage Books.

Naipaul, V.S. 1964. *An Area of Darkness. An Experience of India*. London: Andre Deutsch.

Naipaul, V.S. 1977. *India: A Wounded Civilization*. NY: Knopf.

Naipaul, V.S. 1991. *India*. A Million Mutinies Now. NY: Penguin.

Nair, Kunhanandan. 1986. *Devil and His Dart. How the CIA is plotting in the Third World*. New Delhi: Sterling.

Nanda, B.R., ed. 2005–2006. *The Collected Works of Lala Lajpat Rai*. Vols. 6, 7, 8. New Delhi: Manohar.

Narayanan, V.N. and Jyoti Sabharwal, 1997. *India at 50. Bliss of Hope & Burden of Reality*. New Delhi: Sterling.

Natarajan, L. 1952. *American Shadow over India*. Bombay: People's Publishing House.

Natarajan, Priyamvada. 2016. *Mapping the Heavens*. New Haven: Yale U. Press.

Nayar, Baldev Raj. 1976. *American Geopolitics and India*. New Delhi: Manohar.

Needleman, Jacob. 1970. *The New Religions*. Garden City: Doubleday, 1970.

Nehru, B.K. 1997. *Nice Guys Finish Second. Memoirs*. New Delhi: Penguin.

Nehru, Jawaharlal. 1958. *A Bunch of Old Letters*. Bombay: Asia Publishing.

Nehru, Jawaharlal. 1961. *India's Foreign Policy*. New Delhi: Publications Division.

Nehru, Jawaharlal. 1958 [1936]. *Toward Freedom. The Autobiography of Jawaharlal Nehru*. Boston: Beacon Press.

Neill, Stephen. 1986. *A History of Christian Missions*. NY: Penguin.

Neill, Stephen. 1930. *Out of Bondage. Christ and the Indian Villager*. London: Edinburgh House Press.

Neill, Stephen. 1984, 1985. *A History of Christianity in India*. I. The Beginnings to 1707. II. 1707–1858. Cambridge: Cambridge U. Press.

Newman, Robert P. 1992. *Owen Lattimore and 'Loss' of China*. Berkeley: U. of California Press.

Nguyen, Viet Thanh. 2015. *The Sympathizer*. NY: Grove Press.

Nichols, Beverley. 1944. *Verdict on India*. London: Jonathan Cape.

Niebuhr, Reinhold. 1960. *Moral Man and Immoral Society*. NY: Scribners.

Nielsen, Waldemar A. 1972. *The Big Foundations*. NY: Columbia U. Press.

Nobili, Roberto di. 2000. *Preaching Wisdom to the Wise. Three Treatises*. Trans. and Introduced by Anand Amaladass and Francis X. Clooney. St. Louis: The Institute for Jesuit Sources.

Norman, Dorothy. 1987. *Encounters. A Memoir*. NY: Harcourt Brace Jovanovich.

NRSV Bible with the Apocrypha, The, Compact Edition. Oxford University. Press, Oxford, 1995.

Observer. 1968. 'Truth about the Peace Corps'. New Delhi: People's Publishing House.

Oddie, G.A. 1999. *Missionaries, Rebellion and Proto-Nationalism*. London: Curzon.

Oddie, G.A. 1979. *Social Protest in India. British Protestant Missionaries and Social Reforms 1850–1900*. Delhi: Manohar.

O'Dwyer, Michael. 1925. *India as I Knew It*. London: Constable.

Okihiro, Gary Y. 1994. *Margins and Mainstreams. Asians in American History and Culture*. Seattle: U. of Washington Press.

O'Malley, Alanna. 8 March 2018. 'Challenging the Liberal World Order: India, Apartheid and the New World Corder at the UN, 1946–1962'. Unpublished paper, presented at NYU.

Ornish, Dean. 1995. *Dr. Dean Ornish's Program to Reverse Heart Disease*. NY: Ivy Books.

Orwell, George. 1970. *The Collected Essays, Journalism and Letters of George Orwell*. Ed. Sonia Orwell and Ian Angus. 4v. London: Penguin, 1970.

Orwell, George. 1985. *The War Commentaries*. Ed. W.J. West. NY: Pantheon.

Overstreet Gene D. and Marshall Windmiller. 1959. *Communism in India*. Berkeley: U. of California Press.

Packenham, Robert A. 1973. *Liberal America and the Third World*. Political Development Ideas in Foreign Aid and Social Science. Princeton: Princeton U. Press.

Page, Bruce, David Leitch, Phillip Knightley. 1981. *The Philby Conspiracy*. NY: Ballantine Books.

Pal, Bipin Chandra. January 1938 'Five Months in the 'States'. *Modern Review*, Calcutta. pp.11–16.

Paine, Thomas. 1995. *Collected Writings*. NY: Library of America.

Painter, Nell Irvin. 2010. *The History of White People*. NY: Norton.

Painter, Nell Irvin. 2008. *Standing at Armageddon. The United States, 1877–1919*. NY: Norton.

Palmer, Norman D. 1966. *South Asia and United States Policy*. Boston: Houghton Mifflin.

Palmer, Norman D. 1984. *The United States and India. The Dimensions of Influence*. NY: Praeger.

Panagariya, Arvind. 2008. *India: Emerging Giant*. NY: Oxford.

Pandit, Vijaya Lakshmi. 1979. *The Scope of Happiness*. NY: Crown.

Paralkar, Vikram. 2014. *The Afflictions*. Philadelphia: Lanternfish.

Paralkar, Vikram. 2020. *Night Theater*. NY: Catapult.

Patel, Aakar. 2021. *Price of the Modi Years*. Chennai: Westland.

Patel, Eboo. 2010. *Acts of Faith*. Boston: Beacon Press.

Patel, Gordhanbhai I. 1950. *Vithalbhai Patel. Life and Times*. 2v. Bombay: Sree Laxmi Narayan Press.

Patel, H.M. 1982. *Vithalbhai Patel*. New Delhi: Publications Division, Government of India.

Patel, Neel. 2018. *If You See Me, Don't Say Hi*. NY: Flatiron.

Patel, Raj. 2007. *Stuffed and Starved. The Hidden Battle for the World Food System*. Brooklyn: Melville House.

Parakal, Pauly V. 1984. *Secret Wars of CIA*. New Delhi: Sterling.

Pathak, Sushil Madhava. 1967. *American Missionaries and Hinduism. A Study of Their Contacts from 1813–1910*. Delhi: Munshiram Manoharlal.

Patterson, James T. 1996. *Grand Expectations. The United States, 1945–1971*. NY: Oxford U. Press.

Patterson, Maureen L.P. 1997. 'The Study of South Asia in the United States: Institutional Base and Role of the American Institute of Indian Studies', December 1996. American Institute of Indian Studies, New Delhi, unpublished printed text.

Pawel, Miriam. 2014. *The Crusades of Cesar Chavez*. NY: Bloomsbury.

Payne, Anthony. 2005. *The Global Politics of Unequal Development*. NY: Palgrave Macmillan.

Pechilis, Karen, ed. 2004. *The Graceful Guru. Hindu Female Gurus in India and the United States*. NY: Oxford U. Press.

Pennybacker, Susan D. *From Scottsboro to Munich. Race and Political Culture in 1930s Britain*. 2009. Princeton: Princeton University Press.

Perkins, Bradford. 1969. *The Great Rapprochement: England and the United States 1895–1914*. London: Victor Gollancz.

Perlo, Victor and Kumar Goshal. 1964. *Bitter End in S.E. Asia*. NY: Marzani & Munsell.

Perry, Ralph Barton. 1935. *The Thought and Character of William James*. 2v. Boston: Little, Brown.

Persico, Joseph E. 2001. *Roosevelt's Secret War*. NY: Random House.

Philips, C.H. 1961. *The East India Company 1784–1834*. Manchester: Manchester U. Press.

Philips, C.H. and Mary Doreen Wainwright, eds. 1970. *The Partition of India. Policies and Perspectives 1935–1947*. London: Allen and Unwin.

Phillips, William. 1953. *Ventures in Diplomacy*. Boston: Beacon Press.

Pickett, Clarence. 1953. *For More than Bread*. Boston: Little, Brown.

Pickett, J. Weskom. 1933. *Christian Mass Movements in India*. NY: Abingdon Press.

Piketty, Thomas. 2020. *Capital and Ideology*. Cambridge: Harvard University Press.

Piramal, Gita. 1996. *Business Maharajas*. New Delhi: Penguin, 1996. 'A Pocket Guide to India', 1942. Washington, D.C.: War and Navy Departments.

Poliakov, Léon. 1977. *The Aryan Myth. A History of Racist and Nationalist Ideas in Europe*. NY: New American Library.

Polo, Marco. 1958. *The Travels*, ed. Ronald Latham. New York: Penguin Books.

Pope, Carl. 1972. *Sahib: An American Misadventure in India*. NY: Liveright.

Pope, Harrison, Jr. 1974. *The Road East. America's New Discovery of Eastern Wisdom*. Boston: Beacon Press.

Popplewell, Richard J. 1995. *Intelligence and Imperial Defence. British Intelligence and the Defence of the Indian Empire 1904–1924*. London: Frank Cass.

Poros, Maritsa V. 2011. *Modern Migrations. Gujarati Indian Networks in New York and London*. Stanford: Stanford U. Press.

Porter, Andrew. 2004. *Religion versus Empire? British Protestant Missionaries and Overseas Expansion, 1700–1914*. Manchester: Manchester U. Press.

Pradbuddhaprana, Pravrajika. 1990. *Tantine. The Life of Josephine MacLeod*. Calcutta: Sri Sarada Math.

Prasad, Bimla. 1962. *The Origins of Indian Foreign Policy*. Calcutta: Bookland.

Prashad, Vijay. 2007. *The Darker Nations*. NY: New Press.

Prashad, Vijay. 2001. *Everybody was Kung Fu Fighting*. Boston: Beacon Press.

Prashad, Vijay. 2003. *Fat Cats and Running Dogs*. Monroe, Maine: Common Courage Press.

Prashad, Vijay. 2000. *The Karma of Brown Folk*. Minneapolis: U. of Minnesota Press.

Prashad, Vijay. 2012. *Uncle Swami*. NY: New Press.

Price, Ruth. 2005. *The Lives of Agnes Smedley*. Oxford: Oxford U. Press.

Punshon, John. 1986. *Portrait in Grey. A Short History of the Quakers*. London: Quaker Home Service.

Pym, John. 1983. *The Wandering Company. Twenty-One Years of Merchant Ivory Films*. London: BFI (British Film Institute).

Qamar, Maria. 2017. *Trust No Aunty*. NY: Touchstone.

Radhakrishnan, Sarvepalli, ed. 1956. *Mahatma Gandhi*. Bombay: Jaico.

Raghavan, Anita. 2013. *The Billionaire's Apprentice: The Rise and Fall of the Indian-American Elite and the Fall of the Galleon Hedge Fund*. NY: Business Plus.

Raghavan, Srinath. 2018. *Fierce Enigmas. A History of the United States in South Asia*. NY: Basic Books.

Raghavan, Srinath. 2016. *India's War. World War II and the Making of Modern South Asia*. NY: Basic Books.

Raghavan, Srinath. 2013. *1971. A Global History of the Creation of Bangladesh*. Cambridge: Harvard U. Press.

Raghavan, Srinath. 2010. *War and Peace in Modern India*. New Delhi: Permanent Black.

Rahman, Ataur. 1982. *Pakistan and America: Dependency Relations*. New Delhi: Young Asia.

Rai, Saritha, Ari Altstedter, P.R. Sanjai, 13 August 2019. 'Amazon Nears Deal for Up to 10% of India's Second-Largest Retailer', New York: Bloomberg.

Rajagopal, Arvind. 2001. *Politics after Television. Hindu Nationalism and the Reshaping of the Public in India*. Cambridge: Cambridge U. Press.

Rajan, Raghuram G. 2010. *Fault Lines*. Princeton: Princeton U. Press.

Rajneesh, Bhagwan Shree. 1988. *The Greatest Challenge: The Golden Future*. Cologne: Rebel Publishing.

Rajneesh, Bhagwan Shree. 1979. *My Way: The Way of the White Clouds*. NY: Grove Press.

Ram, Janaki. 1997. *V.K. Krishna Menon*. New Delhi: Oxford U. Press.

Ram Dass. 1978a. *Be Here Now*. Kingsport, TN: Hanuman Foundation.

Ram Dass. 1978b. *The Only Dance There Is*. NY: Doubleday.

Rama Rau, Santha and the Editors of Time-Life Books. 1969. *The Cooking of India* (Foods of the World). NY: Time-Life.

Rama Rau, Santha. 1958. *Gifts of Passage*. NY: Harper.

Rama Rau, Santha. 1945. *Home to India*. NY: Harper.

Rama Rau, Santha. 1954. *This is India*. NY: Harper.

Ramabai Saraswati, Pundita. 1887. *The High-Caste Hindu Woman*. Philadelphia: J.B. Rogers Printing Co.

Ramadorai, S. 2013. *The TCS Story and Beyond*. Gurgaon: Penguin.

Ramakrishnan, Venki. 2018. *Gene Machine*. NY: Basic Books.

Raman, B.V.1976. *A Hindu in America*. Bangalore: Raman Publications.

Raman, Shankar. 2002. *Framing 'India'. The Colonial Imaginary in Early Modern Culture*. Stanford: Stanford U. Press.

Ramesh, Jairam. 2019. *A Chequered Brillance. The Many Lives of V.K. Krishna Menon*. Gurugram: Penguin India.

Ramnath, Maia. 2011. *Haj to Utopia*. Berkeley: U. of California Press.

Ramsdell, Daniel B. 1983. 'Asia Askew: US Best-Sellers on Asia, 1931–1980,' *Bulletin of Concerned Asian Scholars*. Boulder, Colorado. V.15, No. 4. pp. 2–25.

Ramusack, Barbara N. Fall 1989. 'Embattled Advocates: The Debate over Birth Control in India, 1920–40,' *Journal of Women's History*. V. 1, No. 2.

Rashid, Ahmed. 2009. *Descent into Chaos*. NY: Penguin.

Rath, Nilakanth and V.S. Patvardhan, no date. *Impact of Assistance under PL 480 on Indian Economy*. Bombay: Asia Publishing and Gokhale Institute.

Ray, Anandarup, no date. 'Remembering Lila Ray', *Parabaas.com*.

Ray, Krishnendu and Tulasi Srinivas, eds. 2012. *Curried Cultures*. Berkeley: U. of California Press.

Ray, Rajat K. 1979. *Industrialization in India. Growth and Conflict in the Private Corporate Sector 1914–47*. Delhi: Oxford U. Press.

Ray, Rajat K., ed. 1992. *Entrepreneurship and Industry in India 1800–1947*. Delhi: Oxford U. Press.

Ray, Satyajit. 1976. *Our Films, Their Films*. New Delhi: Orient Longman.

Raychaudhuri, Tapan. 1988. *Europe Reconsidered. Perceptions of the West in Nineteenth Century Bengal*. Delhi: Oxford U. Press.

Redding, Saunders. 1954. *An American in India*. Indianapolis: Bobbs-Merrill.

Reddy, E.S. and A.K. Damodaran, eds. 1994. *Krishna Menon at the United Nations*. New Delhi: Sanchar.

Reddy, Vanita. 2016. *Fashioning Diaspora*. Philadelphia: Temple U. Press.

Reeves, Thomas C. 1969. *Freedom and the Foundation: The Fund for the Republic in the Era of McCarthyism*. NY: Alfred Knopf.

Reeves, Thomas C., ed. 1970. *Foundations under Fire*. Ithaca: Cornell U. Press.

Remnick, David. 'Defiance'. February 13 & 20, 2023. The *New Yorker*. pp. 50–61.

Report of Friends Foreign Mission Association. 1904.

Research Group. Indian Institute of Public Administration. August 1983. *Political Dimensions of Multinational Corporations in India*. A Report under the Indo-Dutch Programme on Alternatives in Development.

Revoldt, Daryl L. 1982. 'Raymond B. Fosdick: Reform, Internationalism, and the Rockefeller Foundation', PhD thesis, U. of Akron.

Reynolds, David. 1991. *Britannia Overruled. British Policy and World Power in the 20th Century*. NY: Longman.

Reynolds, Reginald. 1952. *A Quest for Gandhi*. Garden City, N.Y.: Doubleday.

Richter, Frank-Jurgen and Parthasarathi Banerjee, eds. 2003. *The Knowledge Economy of India*. NY: Palgrave Macmillan.

Robbins, Keith. 1983. *The Eclipse of a Great Power. Modern Britain, 1870–1975*. London: Longman.

Roberts, Andrew. 1991. *The Holy Fox. A Life of Lord Halifax.* London: Papermac.

Robin, Marie-Monique. 2010. *The World According to Monsanto.* NY: New Press.

Robinson, Cedric J. Winter 1990-91. 'Oliver Cromwell Cox and the Historiography of the West', *Cultural Critique* 17. pp. 5–20.

Rockefeller, John D. 1933. *Random Reminiscences of Men and Events.* Garden City: Doubleday, Doran & Co.

Rodney, Robert M. 1993. *Mark Twain Overseas.* Washington: Three Continents Press.

Roelofs, Joan. 2003. *Foundations and Public Policy. The Mask of Pluralism.* Albany: State University of New York.

Rogers, W.J., Mr. and Mrs. 1911. *India from the Sublime to the Ridiculous.* Oakland, California.

Rolland, Romain. 1924. *Mahatma Gandhi.* London: Swarthmore Press.

Romanus, Charles F. and Riley Sunderland. 1953. *Stilwell's Mission to China.* United States Army in World War II China-Burma-India Theater. V. I. Washington, D.C.: Office of the Chief of Military History.

Romanus, Charles F. and Riley Sunderland. 1959. *Time Runs Out in CBI.* US Army in WWII China-Burma-India Theater. V. III. Washington: Office of the Chief of Military History, Department of the Army.

Roosevelt, Eleanor. 1953. *India and the Awakening East.* NY: Harper.

Roosevelt, Theodore. 2004. *Letters and Speeches.* New York: Library of America.

Rosen, George. 1985. *Western Economists and Eastern Societies. Agents of Change in South Asia, 1950–1970.* Baltimore: Johns Hopkins U. Press.

Rosenberg, Emily S. 1982. *Spreading the American Dream. American Economic and Cultural Expansion 1890–1945.* NY: Hill & Wang.

Rosenberg, Emily S., ed. *A World Connecting 1870-1945.* Cambridge: Harvard U. Press.

Rosinger, Lawrence. 1956. *India and the US* NY: Macmillan.

Rosling, Alan. 2018. *BOOM Country? The New Wave of Indian Enterprise.* Gurugram: Hachette.

Rothermund, Dietmar. 1988. *An Economic History of India.* Delhi: Manohar.

Rotter, Andrew J. 2000. *Comrades at Odds.* The United States and India, 1947–1964. Ithaca: Cornell U. Press.

Roy, Arundhati. 2014. *Capitalism: A Ghost Story.* Chicago: Haymarket.

Roy, Arundhati. 1997. *The God of Small Things.* NY: Random House.

Roy, Arundhati. 2019. *My Seditious Heart.* Chicago: Haymarket.

Roy, Binoy K. 1973. *US Infiltration in Indian Education.* New Delhi: Perspective.

Roy, M.N. 1964. *M.N. Roy's Memoirs.* Bombay: Allied.

Roy, Tirthankar. 2002. *The Economic History of India 1857–1947.* New Delhi: Oxford U. Press.

Rubiés, Joan-Pau. 2001. *Travel and Ethnology in the Renaissance. South India through European Eyes, 1250–1625.* Cambridge and New York: Cambridge University Press.

Rudolph, Lloyd I. and Susanne. 1967. *The Modernity of Tradition. Political Development in India.* Chicago: University of Chicago Press.

Rudolph, Lloyd I and Susanne Hoeber, et al. 1980. *The Regional Imperative. US Foreign Policy towards South Asian States.* New Delhi: Concept.

Rushdie, Salman. 2001. *Fury.* London: Vintage.

Rushdie, Salman. 2012. *Joseph Anton.* NY: Random House, 2012.

Rushdie, Salman and Elizabeth West, eds. 1997. *Mirrorwork. 50 Years of Indian Writing 1947–1997.* NY: Henry Holt.

Rushdie, Salman. 1989. *The Satanic Verses.* NY: Viking.

Rushdie, Salman. 2023. *Victory City.* NY: Random House.

Rydell, Robert W. 1984. *All the World's a Fair. Visions of Empire at American International Expositions, 1876–1916.* Chicago: University of Chicago Press.

Sabine, George H. 1960. *A History of Political Theory.* Rev. ed. NY: Holt, Rinehart, and Winston.

Sadhguru. 2016. *Inner Engineering. A Yogi's Guide to Joy.* Gurgaon: Penguin.

Sager, Peter. 1967. *Moscow's Hand in India. An Analysis of Soviet Propaganda*. Bombay: Lalvani.

Sahai, Jitendra. 1982. *Dollar in India. A Study of Two Decades*. New Delhi: National.

Sahay, Anjali. 2009. *India Diaspora in the United States. Brain Drain or Gain?* Hyderabad: Orient BlackSwan.

Said, Edward. 1978. *Orientalism*. NY: Pantheon.

Saini, Angela. 2012. *Geek Nation. How Indian Science is Taking over the World*. London: Hodder & Stoughton.

Saini, Angela. 2019. *Superior. The Return of Race Science*. Boston: Beacon Press.

Sandweiss, Martha A. 2009. *Passing Strange*. NY: Penguin.

Saran, Parmatma. 1985. *The Asian Indian Experience in the United States*. Cambridge, Mass.: Schenkman.

Saran, Parmatma and Edwin Eames, eds. 1980. *The New Ethnics. Asian Indians in the United States*. NY: Praeger.

Sareen,T.R. ed. 1994. *Selected Documents on the Ghadr Party*. New Delhi: Mounto.

Sarkar, Sumit. 1983. *Modern India 1885–1947*. Delhi: Macmillan.

Sathian, Sanjena. 2012. *Gold Diggers*. NY: Penguin.

Saund, Dalip Singh. 1930. *My Mother India*. Stockton: Pacific Coast Khalsa Diwan Society.

Saund, D.S. 1960. *Congressman from India*. NY: Dutton.

Saunders, Frances Stonor. 2000. *The Cultural Cold War*. NY: The New Press.

Sawhney, Savitri. 2008. *I Shall Never Ask for Pardon. A Memoir of Pandurang Khankhoje*. New Delhi: Penguin.

Saxenian, AnnaLee. 1996. *Regional Advantage. Culture and Competition in Silicon Valley and Route 128*. Cambridge: Harvard U. Press.

Saxenian, AnnaLee.1999. *Silicon Valley's New Immigrant Entrepreneurs*. Public Policy Institute of California.

Saxenian, AnnaLee, with Yasuyuki Motoyama and Xiaohong Quan. 2002. *Local and Global Networks of Immigrant Professionals in Silicon Valley*. Public Policy Institute of California.

Schaffer, Howard B. 1993. *Chester Bowles. New Dealer in the Cold War*. Cambridge, Mass: Harvard U. Press.

Scarfe, Alland Wendy. 1975. *J.P. His Biography*. New Delhi: Orient Longman.

Scalmer, Sean. 2011. *Gandhi in the West. The Mahatma and the Rise of Radical Protest*. Cambridge: Cambridge U. Press.

Schneir, Walter. 2010. *Final Verdict. What Really Happened in the Rosenberg Case*. Brooklyn: Melville House.

Schmidt, Earl R. 1955. 'American Relations with South Asia 1900–1940', PhD thesis, U. of Pennsylvania.

Schramm, Richard H. 1964. 'The Image of India in Selected American Literary Periodicals: 1870–1900', PhD thesis, Duke University.

Schwab, Raymond. 1984. *The Oriental Renaissance. Europe's Rediscovery of India and the East, 1680–1880*. NY: Columbia U. Press, 1984 .

Scott, Paul. 1973. *The Jewel in the Crown*. London: Panther; *The Day of the Scorpion*. 1973. London: Panther; *The Towers of Silence*. 1973. London: Panther; *A Division of the Spoils*. 1977. London: Panther. [*The Raj Quartet*]

Scudder, Dorothy Jealous. 1984. *A Thousand Years in Thy Sight. The Story of the Scudder Missionaries of India*. NY: Vantage Press.

Scudder, David E. 1864. *Life and Letters of David Coit Scudder, Missionary in South India*. NY: Hurd & Houghton.

Seagraves, Eleanor Roosevelt, ed. 1994. *Delano's Voyages of Commerce and Discovery*. Amasa Delano in China, the Pacific Islands, Australia, and South America, 1789–1807.

Stockbridge: Berkshire House, 1994.

Sen, Amartya. 1999. *Development as Freedom*. NY: Oxford U. Press.

Sen, Amartya. 2022. *Home in the World: A Memoir*. NY: Liveright.

Sen, B.R. 1982. *Towards a Newer World*. Dublin: Tycooly International.

Sen, Keshub Chunder. 1954. *Lectures in India*. Calcutta: Navavidhan.

Sen, Sharmila. 2018. *Not Quite Not White*. NY: Penguin.

Sen, Sunanda. 1992. *Colonies and the Empire. India 1890–1914*. Hyderabad: Orient Longman.

Sen, Sunil Kumar. 1975. *The House of Tata*. Calcutta: Progressive Publishers.

Sengupta, Somini. 2016. *The End of Karma. Hope and Fury among India's Young.* NY: Norton.

Seshachari, C. 1969. *Gandhi and the American Scene. An Intellectual History and Inquiry.* Bombay: Nachiketa Publicatons.

Seshadri, Vijay. 2004. *The Long Meadow.* Saint Paul: Graywolf.

Seth, Vikram. 1986. *The Golden Gate.* Delhi: Oxford U. Press.

Shah, Shashank. 2018. *The Tata Group.* Gurgaon: Penguin.

Shankar, Ravi. 1968. *My Music, My Life.* NY: Simon and Schuster.

Shankar, Ravi. 1999. *Raga Mala.* An Autobiography. NY: Welcome Rain.

Shankar, Shalini. 2019. *Beeline.* NY: Basic Books.

Sharma, Akhil. 2014. *Family Life.* NY: Norton.

Sharma, Akhil. 2000. *An Obedient Father.* NY: Harvest.

Sharma, Madan Lal. 1982. *Terrorism: American Style.* New Delhi: Kalamkar Prakashan.

Sharma, J.S. 1968. *Gandhi: A Descriptive Bibliography.* Delhi: S. Chand.

Sharma, Ruchir. 2013. *Breakout Nations.* NY: Norton.

Sharp, Gene. 1973. *The Politics of Nonviolent Action.* Boston: Porter Sargent.

Sharpe, Eric J. 1963. *J.N. Farquhar.* Calcutta: Y.M.C.A. Pub. House.

Shastri, Lalit. 1985. *Bhopal Disaster.* New Delhi: Criterion.

Sheean, Vincent. 1949. *Lead, Kindly Light.* NY: Random House.

Sheean, Vincent. 1969. *Personal History.* Boston: Houghton Mifflin.

Sherwood, Robert. 1948. *Roosevelt and Hopkins.* NY: Harper.

Shimoni, Gideon. 1977. *Gandhi, Satyagraha and the Jews: A Formative Factor in India's Policy towards Israel.* Jerusalem: The Hebrew University.

Shirer, William L. 1979. *Gandhi. A Memoir.* NY: Simon & Schuster Touchstone.

Shiva, Vandana. 1992. *The Violence of the Green Revolution. Third World Agriculture, Ecology and Politics.* Mapura, Goa: The Other India Press.

Shourie, Arun. 1994. *Missionaries in India.* Delhi: ASA.

Shridharani, Krishnalal. 1946. *The Mahatma and the World.* NY: Duell, Sloan and Pearce.

Shridharani, Krishnalal. 1941. *My India, My America*. NY: Duell, Sloan and Pearce.

Shridharani, Krishnalal. 1939. *War without Violence. A Study of Gandhi's Method and Its Accomplishments*. NY: Harcourt, Brace.

Shridharani, Krishnalal. 1942. *Warning to the West*. NY: Duell, Sloan and Pearce.

Shukla, Sandhya. 2003. *India Abroad*. Princeton: Princeton U. Press.

Sidhwa, Bapsi. 1994. *An American Brat*. London: Penguin.

Silk, Leonard and Mark. 1980. *The American Establishment*. NY: Basic Books.

Simeon, Dilip. 1995. *The Politics of Labour under Late Colonialism. Workers, Unions and the State in Chota Nagpur 1928–1939*. New Delhi: Manohar.

Singh, Anita Inder. 1987. *The Origins of the Partition of India*. 1936–1947. Delhi: Oxford U. Press.

Singh, Lilly. 2017. *How to Be a Bawse*. NY: Ballantine.

Singh, Mahendra. 1982. *Indo-US Relations 1961–64*. Delhi: Sidhu Ram.

Singh, Khushwant and Satindra Singh. 1966. *Ghadar 1915*. R & K Publishing.

Singh, Maina Chawla. 2000. *Gender, Religion, and 'Heathen Lands'. American Missionary Women in South Asia (1860s–1940s)*. NY: Garland.

Singh, Radika. 2010. *The Fabric of Our Lives. The Story of Fabindia*. New Delhi: Penguin.

Singleton, Mark. 2010. *Yoga Body. The Origins of Modern Posture Practice*. NY: Oxford U. Press.

Sinha, Mrinalini. 2006. *Specters of Mother India. The Global Restructuring of an Empire*. Durham: Duke U. Press.

Sitapati, Vinay. 2016. *Half Lion. How P.V. Narasimha Rao Tranformed India*. NY: Penguin.

Slate, Nico. 2012. *Colored Cosmopolitanism*. Cambridge: Harvard U. Press.

Slate, Nico. 2019. *Lord Cornwallis is Dead. The Struggle for Democracy in the United States and India*. Cambridge: Harvard U. Press.

Slim, Viscount William. 1971. *Defeat into Victory*. London: Corgi.

Smith, Huston. 1958. *The Religions of Man*. NY: Harper and Row.

Smith, Joseph B. 1976. *Portrait of a Cold Warrior*, NY: Ballantine Books.

Smith, Philip Chadwick Foster. 1984. *The Empress of China*. Philadelphia: Philadelphia Maritime Museum.

Smith, R. Harris. 1992. *OSS. The Secret History of America's First Central Intelligence Agency*. Berkeley: U. of California Press.

Snow Edgar. 27 March 1948 'India'. *Saturday Evening Post*.

Snow, Edgar. 1972. *Journey to the Beginning*. NY: Vintage.

Snow, Edgar. 1944. *People on Our Side*. NY: Random House.

Snow, Edgar. 1973. *Red Star over China*. NY: Grove Press.

Snyder, Gary. 1968. *The Back Country*. New Directions.

Snyder, Gary. 2007. *Passage through India*. Expanded Edition. Hong Kong: Shoemaker & Hoard.

Sobhan, Rehman. 1982. *The Crisis of External Dependence. The Political Economy of Foreign Aid to Bangladesh*. London: Zed Press.

Soderlund, Dorothy, ed.1973. *Directory, Foreign Area Fellows 1952–1972*. NY: Social Science Research Council, 1973.

Sohi, Seema. 2014. *Echoes of Mutiny. Race, Surveillance & Indian Anti-colonialism in North America*. NY: Oxford U. Press.

Solomon, Barbara Miller. 1984. *Ancestors and Immigrants. A Changing New England Tradition*. Boston: Northeastern U. Press.

Spector, Ronald. 1985. *Eagle against the Sun. The American War with Japan*. NY: Vintage.

Speer, Robert Elliott. 1928. *Sir James Ewing. 43 Years a Missionary in India*. NY: Fleming H. Revell.

Spence, Jonathan. 1969. *To Change China: Western Advisors in China, 1620-1960*. Boston: Little, Brown.

Sprinker, Michael, ed. 1992. *Edward Said. A Critical Reader*. Oxford: Blackwell.

Sri Chinmoy. 1988. *Beyond Within. A Philosophy for the Inner Life*. Jamaica, NY: Agni Press.

Sri Chinmoy. 1994. *The Garland of Nation-Souls*. NY: Sri Chinmoy Lighthouse.

Sri Chinmoy. 1989. *Meditation*. Jamaica, NY: Aum.

Stafford, David. 1999. *Roosevelt and Churchill. Men of Secrets*. NY: Overlook.

Staples, Eugene. 1992. *Forty Years of the Ford Foundation in India*. NY: Ford Foundation.

Staples, Eugene. 2007. *Old Gods New Nations*. NY: Universe.

Stavrianos, L.S. 1981. *Global Rift. The Third World Comes of Age*. NY: Morrow.

Stead, William Thomas. 2009 [1902]. *The Americanization of the World*. Danvers, MA: General Books.

Stern, Bernard S. 1956. 'American Views of India and Indians, 1857–1900', PhD thesis, U. of Pennsylvania.

Stern, Eddie. 2019. *One Simple Thing. A New Look at the Science of Yoga and How It Can Transform Your Life*. NY: North Point Press.

Stilwell, Joseph W. 1948. *The Stilwell Papers*. NY: William Sloane.

Stokes, Eric. 1959. *The English Utilitarians and India*. Oxford: At the Clarendon Press.

Stokes, Satyanand. 1977. *National Self-Realisation*. Delhi: Rubicon.

Storr, Anthony. 1997. *Feet of Clay. A Study of Gurus, Saints, Sinners, and Madmen*. NY: Free Press.

Stross, Randall E. 1986. *The Stubborn Earth: American Agriculturalists on Chinese Soil, 1898–1937*. Berkeley: U. of California Press.

Studdert-Kennedy, Gerald. 1991. *British Christians, Indian Nationalists and the Raj*. Delhi: Oxford U. Press.

Subrahmanyam, Sanjay. 2011. *Explorations in Connected History. From the Tagus to the Ganges*. New Delhi: Oxford U. Press.

Subrahmanyam, Sanjay. 2011. *Explorations in Connected History, Mughals and Franks*. New Delhi: Oxford U. Press.

Sufrin, Sidney C. 1985. *Bhopal. Its Setting, Responsibility and Challenge*. New Delhi: Ajanta.

Sultan, Tanvir. 1982. *Indo-US Relations*. New Delhi: Deep and Deep.

Sunderland, Jabeez T. 1929. *India in Bondage*. Calcutta: R. Chatterjee, 1929.

Sundkler, Bengt. 1954. *Church of South India: The Movement towards Union 1900–1947*. London: Lutterworth,.

Sutton, Francis X., ed. Winter 1990. *A World to Make*. Winter [1989 *Daedalus*]. Development in Perspective. New Brunswick: Transaction.

Swain, Clara. 1909. *A Glimpse of India*. First Medical Missionary to India of the Women's Foreign Missionary Society of the Methodist Episcopal Church in America. NY: J. Pott & Co.

Swami Ajaya, ed. 1978. *Living with the Himalayan Masters. Spiritual Experiences of Swami Rama*. Honesdale, PA: Himalayan International Institute.

Swanberg, W.A. 1980. *Whitney Father, Whitney Heiress*. NY: Scribner's.

Sward, Keith. 1948. *The Legend of Henry Ford*. NY: Rinehart.

Swenson, Sally. 1989. Welthy Honsinger Fisher. Signals of a Century. Stittsville, Ontario: Sally Swenson.

Sykes, Majorie. 1997. *An Indian Tapestry. Quaker Threads in the History of India, Pakistan, & Bangladesh*. York: Sessions Book Trust.

Sykes, Marjorie. 1980. *Quakers in India. A Forgotten Century*. London: George Allen & Unwin.

Syman, Stefanie. 2010. *The Subtle Body, The Story of Yoga in America*. NY: Farrar, Straus and Giroux.

Tagore, Rabindranath. 1921. *Greater India*. Madras: Ganesan.

Tagore, Rabindranath. 1917. *Nationalism*. New York: Macmillan.

Tagore, Rabindranath. 2001. *Three Plays*. New Delhi: Oxford U. Press. Translated by Ananda Lal. (quoting November 1913 'Topics of the Times: Our Case Isn't Desperate'. *New York Times*. p. 10).

Takaki, Ronald. 1989. *Strangers from a Different Shore. A History of Asian Americans*. Boston: Little, Brown.

Talbot, Phillips. 2007. *An American Witness to India's Partition*. New Delhi: Sage.

Talbot, Phillips and S.L. Poplai. 1958. *India and America. A Study of Their Relations*. NY: Harper.

Tamm, Jayanti. 2009. *Cartwheels in a Sari. A Memoir of Growing Up Cult*. NY: Harmony.

Tandon, Prakash. 1988. *Punjabi Saga 1857–1987*. Delhi: Viking.

Taylor, AJP. 1965. *English History, 1914–45*. Harmondsworth: Penguin.

Taylor, Carl C., Douglas Ensminger, Helen W. Johnson, Jean Joyce. 1965. *India's Roots of Democracy*. NY: Praeger.

Taylor, William. 1880. *Four Years Campaign in India*. New York: Phillips and Hunt.

Terkel, Studs. 1984. '*The Good War*'. NY: Ballantine.

Tewari, S.C. 1977. *Indo-US Relations 1947–1976*. New Delhi: Radiant.

Thangaraj, Stanley I. 2015. *Desi Hoop Dreams*. NY: NYU Press.

Tharoor, Shashi. 1997. *India from Midnight to Millennium*. NY: HarperPerennial.

Tharoor, Shashi. 1982. *Reasons of State. Political Development and India's Foreign Policy under Indira Gandhi 1966–1977*. New Delhi: Vikas.

Thenappan, Bala, Winter 2020–21. 'An Interview with Oncologist/Author Vikram Paralkar', Philadelphia. *Penn Political Review*.

Thernstrom, Stephan, et al, eds. 1980. *The Harvard Encyclopedia of American Ethnic Groups*. Cambridge: Harvard U. Press.

Thoburn, J.M. 1906. *The Christian Conquest of India*. NY: Eaton & Mains.

Thoburn, J.M. 1892. *India and Malaysia*. Cincinnati: Granston and Curts.

Thoburn, J.M. no date. *Life of Isabella Thoburn*. Jennings and Pye, Cincinnati.

Thoburn, J.M. 1884. *My Missionary Apprenticeship*. NY: Phillip & Hart.

Thomas, Evan. 2011. *The War Lovers*. New York: Little, Brown.

Thomas, P. 1954. *Christians and Christianity in India and Pakistan*. London: George Allen & Unwin.

Thomas, Wendell. 1930. *Hinduism Invades America*. New York: Beacon Press reprint.

Thompson, Edward J. and G.T. Garratt. 1934. *Rise and Fulfilment of British Rule in India*. London: Macmillan.

Thompson, Edward P. 1993. *Alien Homage. Edward Thompson and Rabindranath Tagore*. Delhi: Oxford U. Press.

Thompson, H.P. 1951. *Into All Lands: A History of the Society for the Propagation of the Gospel in Foreign Parts, 1701–1950*.

Thoreau, Henry David. 2004. *Walden*. Ed. Jeffrey S. Cramer. New Haven: Yale U. Press.

Thoreau, Henry David. 1985. *A Week on the Concord and Merrimack Rivers; Walden; or Life in the Woods; The Maine Woods; Cape Cod.* NY: The Library of America.

Thorne, Christopher. 1978. *Allies of a Kind. The US, Britain, and the War against Japan.* NY: Oxford U. Press.

Thorne, Christopher. 1985. *The Issue of War. States, Societies, and the Far Eastern Conflict of 1941–1945.* NY: Oxford U. Press.

Thorner, Alice. 24 January 1981. 'Nehru, Albert Mayer, and Origins of Community Projects'. *Economic and Political Weekly.* Vol. 16, No. 4. pp. 117–120.

Thorner, Daniel. 1976. *The Agrarian Prospect in India.* Bombay: Allied, 1976.

Thorner, Daniel. 1980. *The Shaping of Modern India.* Delhi: Allied.

Tinker, Hugh. 1979. *The Ordeal of Love.* C.F. Andrews and India. Delhi: Oxford U. Press.

Tilchin, William N. 1997. *Theodore Roosevelt and the British Empire. A Study in Presidential Statecraft.* NY: St. Martin's.

Tinker, Hugh. November 1976. 'The India Conciliation Group, 1931–1950: Dilemmas of the Mediator' *The Journal of Commonwealth and Comparative Politics*, London, V. XIV, No. 3. pp. 224–241.

Tinker, Hugh. 1993. *A New System of Slavery. The Export of Indian Labour Overseas, 1830-1920.* London: Hansib.

Tinker, Hugh. 1979. *The Ordeal of Love.* C.F. Andrews and India. Delhi: Oxford U. Press.

Tinker, Hugh. 1976. *Separate and Unequal. India and the Indians in the British Commonwealth 1920–1950.* Vancouver: U. of British Columbia Press.

Tobar, Héctor. July 2018. 'How Latinos Are Shaping America's Future'. *National Geographic.* pp. 86–103.

Tocqueville, Alexis de. 1956. *Democracy in America.* 2 vols. NY: Vintage, 1956.

Tomlinson, B.R. 1993. *The Economy of Modern India 1860-1970.* Delhi: NCHI, Cambridge U. Press.

Tomlinson, B.R. 1979. *The Political Economy of the Raj 1914–1947.* Macmillan.

Tourtellot, Arthur B. 1964. *Toward the Well-Being of Mankind. Fifty Years of the Rockefeller Foundation.* Garden City, NY: Doubleday.

Toye, Richard. 2011. *Churchill's Empire: The World that Made Him and the World He Made.* NY: St. Martin's.

Trautmann, Thomas R. 1997. *Aryans and British India.* Berkeley: U. of California Press.

Trotsky, Leon. 1965. *Permanent Revolution and Results and Prospects.* NY: Pioneer Publishers.

Tuchman, Barbara. 1971. *Stilwell and the American Experience in China, 1911–45.* NY: Bantam.

Tuker, Sir Francis. 1950. *While Memory Serves.* London: Cassell.

Twain, Mark. 1992. *Collected Tales, Sketches, Speeches, & Essays 1891–1910.* NY: Library of America.

Twain, Mark. 1989 [1897]. *Following the Equator. A Journey around the World.* NY: Dover.

United States Commission on Civil Rights, Civil Rights Issues Facing Asian Americans in the 1990s. Report of February 1992.

Vanaik, Achin, ed. 2004. *Globalization and South Asia.* New Delhi: Manohar.

Varma, Premdatta. 1995. *Indian Immigrants in USA.* Struggle for Equality. New Delhi: Heritage.

Vatuk, Sylvia, ed. 1978. *American Studies in the Anthropology of India.* New Delhi: Manohar.

Venkataramani, M.S. 1982. *The American Role in Pakistan, 1947–1958.* New Delhi: Radiant.

Venkataramani, M.S. and B.K. Shrivastava. 1979. *Quit India. The American Response to the 1942 Struggle.* Delhi: Vikas.

Venkataramani, M.S. 1973. *Bengal Famine of 1943. The American Response.* Delhi: Vikas.

Venkataramani, M.S. and B.K. Shrivastava. 1983. *Roosevelt Gandhi Churchill. America and the Last Phase of India's Freedom Struggle.* New Delhi: Radiant.

Venugopal, Arun, January/February 2021. 'The Making of a Model Minority'. *The Atlantic.*

Verghese, Abraham. 2023. *The Covenant of Water.* NY: Grove Press.

Verghese, Abraham. 2009. *Cutting for Stone.* NY: Vintage.

Verghese, Abraham. 1994. *My Own Country*. NY: Simon & Schuster.

Vernon, Roland. 2002. *Star of the East. Krishnamurti the Invention of a Messiah*. Boulder: Sentient.

Versluis, Arthur. 1993. *American Transcendentalism and Asian Religions*. NY: Oxford U. Press.

Vickery, Raymond E. 2011. *The Eagle and the Elephant. Strategic Aspects of US-India Economic Engagement*. Baltimore: John Hopkins U. Press.

Vinayshil, Gautam. 1972. *Aspects of Indian Society and Economy in the Nineteenth Century. A Study based on an evaluation of the American Consular Records*. New Delhi: Motilal Bararsidass.

Vital, David. 1999. *A People Apart*. NY: Oxford U. Press.

Vivekananda, Swami. 1962. *The Complete Works of Swami Vivekananda*. 8 vols. Calcutta: Advaita Ashram.

Vivekananda, Swami. 1975. *The East and the West*. Calcutta: Advaita Ashrama.

Voltaire. 1901. *The Works of Voltaire*, V. XIII. NY: St. Hubert Guild.

Voigt, Johannes H. 1987. *India in the Second World War*. New Delhi: Arnold-Heinemann.

Von Eschen, Penny M. 2004. *Satchmo Blows Up the World. Jazz Ambassadors Play the Cold War*. Cambridge: Harvard U. Press.

Wacha, D.E. 1915. *The Life and Life Work of J.N. Tata*. Madras: The Cambridge Press, 1915.

Wall, Joseph Frazier. 1970. *Andrew Carnegie*. NY: Oxford U. Press.

Wanless, William. 1932. *An American Doctor at Work in India*. NY: Fleming H. Revell.

Washington, James M., ed. 1986. *A Testament of Hope. The Essential Writings and Speeches of Martin Luther King, Jr.* San Francisco: Harper.

Washington, Peter. 1993. *Madame Blavatsky's Baboon*. NY: Schocken.

Watson, Blanche, compiler. 1923. *Gandhi and Non-Violent Resistance. Gleanings from the American Press*. Madras: Ganesh & Co.

Watson, James L. 1997. *Golden Arches East. McDonald's in East Asia.* Stanford: Stanford U. Press.

Wavell, Lord. 1973. *The Viceroy's Journal.* London: Oxford U. Press.

Weber, David R., ed. 1978. *Civil Disobedience in America. A Documentary History.* Ithaca: Cornell U. Press.

Weber, Thomas. 2007. *Gandhi as Disciple and Mentor.* Cambridge: Cambridge U. Press.

Webster, Anthony. 2009. *The Richest East India Merchant.* New Delhi: Viva.

Webster, John C B. 1976. *The Christian Community and Change in 19th Century North India.* Delhi: Macmillan.

Webster, John C.B. 2007. *A Social History of Christianity. Northwest India since 1800.* Delhi: Oxford U. Press.

Weinberg, Albert K. 1963. *Manifest Destiny. A Study of Nationalist Expansionism in American History.* Chicago: Quadrangle, 1963.

Weiner, Tim. 2008. *Legacy of Ashes. The History of the CIA.* NY: Anchor Books.

Weisbrot, Robert. 1991. *Freedom Bound. A History of America's Civil Rights Movement.* NY: Plume.

Wested, Odd Arne. 2005. *The Global Cold War.* Cambridge: Cambridge U. Press.

Whitaker, Ben. 1979. *The Foundations—An Anatomy of Philanthropic Bodies.* NY: Penguin.

White, Stephen. 1998. *Building in the Garden. The Architecture of Joseph Allen Stein in India and California.* Oxford: Oxford U. Press.

Whitman, Walt. 1982. *Complete Poetry and Collected Prose.* NY: The Library of America.

Wilkins, Mira. 1970. *The Emergence of Multinational Enterprise: American Business Abroad from the Colonial Era to 1914.* Cambridge: Harvard U. Press.

Wilkins, Mira. 1974. *The Maturing of Multinational Enterprise: American Business Abroad from 1914 to 1970.* Cambridge: Harvard U. Press.

Wilkins, Mira and Frank Ernest Hill. 1964. *American Business Abroad. Ford on Six Continents.* Detroit: Wayne State U. Press.

Wilkenson, Isabel. 2020. *Caste. The Origins of Our Discontents.* NY: Random House.

Wilkinson, Isabel. 2010. *The Warmth of Other Suns.* NY: Vintage.

Williamson, Horace. 1976 (reprint of 1935 edition). *India and Communism.* Calcutta: Editions Indian.

Williamson, Lola. 2010. *Transcendent in America.* NY: NYU Press, 2010.

Wills, Gary. 2008. *Head and Heart. A History of Christianity in America.* NY: Penguin.

Wilson, Bryan. 1985. *The Sacred and the Secular: Toward Revision in the Scientific Study of Religion.* Berkeley: University of California Press.

Wilson, Dorothy Clarke. 1959. *Dr. Ida. The Story of Dr. Ida Scudder of Vellore.* NY: McGraw-Hill.

Wilson, Dorothy Clarke. 1968. *Palace of Healing: The Story of Dr. Clara Swain.* First Woman Missionary Doctor and the Hospital she founded. NY: McGraw-Hill.

Wilson, Dorothy Clarke. 1990. *Take My Hands. The Remarkable Story of Dr. Mary Verghese of Vellore.* Madras: Evangelical Literature Service.

Wilson, Dorothy Clarke. 1983. *Ten Fingers for God. The Complete Biography of Dr. Paul Brand.* NY: Thomas Nelson.

Wilson, Jennifer. May 17–24, 2021 'A Solitary Trade,' *The Nation.* pp. 55–58.

Windmiller, Marshall, Spring 1995. 'A Tumultuous Time: OSS and Army Intelligence in India, 1942–1946', *International Journal of Intelligence and Counterintelligence.* V. 8, No. 1, 105–123.

Wiser, William H. and Charlotte Viall Wiser. 1989. *Behind Mud Walls 1930–1960.* With sequel by Susan S. Wadley: The Village in 1984. Berkeley: U. of California Press.

Wiser, William H. and Charlotte Viall Wiser. 1943. *For All of Life.* NY: Friendship Press, 1943.

Wiser, William H. and Charlotte Viall Wiser. 1936. *The Hindu Jajmani System: A SocioEconomic System Interrelating Members of a Hindu Village Community in Services.* Lucknow: Lucknow Publishing House.

Wiser, William H. 1949. *India Village Service After Four Years.* Lucknow: Lucknow Publishing House.

Wittner, Lawrence S. 1969. *Rebels against War. The American Peace Movement 1941–1960*. N.Y. Columbia University Press.

Witzel, Morgen. 2010. *Tata. The Evolution of a Corporate Brand*. New Delhi: Penguin.

Wood, Gordon S. 2009. *Empire of Liberty. A History of the Early Republic, 1789–1815*. NY: Oxford U. Press.

Wood, Gordon S. 1993. *The Radicalism of the American Revolution*. NY: Vintage.

Yadav, Leela. 1989. *US Policy in South Asia. A Case Study of Pakistan*. New Delhi: Harman.

Yajee, Sheel Bhadra. 1987. *CIA: Manipulating Arm of the US Foreign Policy*. New Delhi: Criterion.

Yogananda, Paramahansa. 1979. *Autobiography of a Yogi*. Los Angeles: Self-Realization Fellowship.

Young, Michael. 1982. *The Elmhirsts of Dartington. The Creation of an Utopian Community*. London: Routledge & Kegan Paul.

Zeer, Darin. 2000. *Office Yoga*. San Francisco: Chronicle Books.

Ziegler, Philip. 1985. *Mountbatten, A Biography*. NY: Knopf.

Ziff, Larzer. 2000. *Return Passages. Great American Travel Writing 1780-1910*. New Haven: Yale U. Press.

Zinn, Howard. 1965. *SNCC. The New Abolitionists*. Boston: Beacon Press, 1965.

Zinn, Howard. 1997. *The Zinn Reader*. NY: Seven Stories Press, 1997.

Index

(Note: Page locators in bold face denote images)

Scan QR code to access the
Penguin Random House India website